HANDBOOK OF FAMILY POLICY

Handbook of Family Policy

Edited by

Guðný Björk Eydal

Professor, Faculty of Social Work, University of Iceland, Iceland

Tine Rostgaard

Professor, Stockholm University, Sweden

Cheltenham, UK • Northampton, MA, USA

© Guðný Björk Eydal and Tine Rostgaard 2018

All rights reserved. No part of this publication may be reproduced, stored in a retrieval system or transmitted in any form or by any means, electronic, mechanical or photocopying, recording, or otherwise without the prior permission of the publisher.

Published by
Edward Elgar Publishing Limited
The Lypiatts
15 Lansdown Road
Cheltenham
Glos GL50 2JA
UK

Edward Elgar Publishing, Inc.
William Pratt House
9 Dewey Court
Northampton
Massachusetts 01060
USA

Paperback edition 2020

A catalogue record for this book
is available from the British Library

Library of Congress Control Number: 2018945834

This book is available electronically in the **Elgar**online
Social and Political Science subject collection
DOI 10.4337/9781784719340

ISBN 978 1 78471 933 3 (cased)
ISBN 978 1 78471 934 0 (eBook)
ISBN 978 1 78471 945 6 (paperback)

Typeset by Servis Filmsetting Ltd, Stockport, Cheshire

Printed and bound by CPI Group (UK) Ltd, Croydon, CR0 4YY

Contents

List of contributors viii
Acknowledgements xix

PART I INTRODUCTION

1 Introduction to the *Handbook of Family Policy* 2
   Guðný Björk Eydal and Tine Rostgaard

PART II FAMILY POLICY: HISTORY, CONCEPTS, THEORY AND METHODS

2 The history of family policy research 11
   Anne H. Gauthier and Judith C. Koops

3 The structure/culture divide in early childhood services – and how we might bridge it 24
   Peter Moss

4 Family and state obligation: the contribution to family policy studies 36
   Jane Millar

5 Comparing family policies: approaches, methods and databases 48
   Henning Lohmann and Hannah Zagel

6 Family policy changes across welfare and production regimes, 1990 to 2010 66
   Ji Young Kang and Marcia K. Meyers

PART III FAMILY POLICIES

7 Family benefit systems 84
   Jonathan Bradshaw

8 Childcare as a global policy agenda 96
   Tine Rostgaard

9 The social investment approach in the productivist welfare regime: the unfolding of social investment in South Korea and Japan 111
   Sophia Seung-yoon Lee and Seung-ho Baek

10 Leave policies for parents in a cross-national perspective: various paths along the same course? 124
    Olivier Thévenon

11 Work-family policies within the workplace 139
    Laura den Dulk, Mara A. Yerkes and Bram Peper

12 Triggers and drivers of change in framing parenting support in North-
    western Europe 152
    Trudie Knijn, Claude Martin and Ilona Ostner

PART IV FAMILY POLICY MODELS

13 Comparing persistence and change in family policies of conservative welfare
    states 168
    Birgit Pfau-Effinger

14 The UK and the US: liberal models despite family policy expansion? 182
    Dorian R. Woods

15 Family policies in the Nordic countries: aiming at equality 195
    Guðný Björk Eydal, Tine Rostgaard and Heikki Hiilamo

16 Child and family policy in Southern Europe 209
    Teresa Jurado-Guerrero and Manuela Naldini

17 Family policies and social inequalities in Central and Eastern Europe: a
    comparative analysis of Hungary, Poland and Romania between 2005 and
    2015 223
    Cristina Raţ and Dorottya Szikra

18 Not all in the same family: diverging approaches to family policy in East Asia 236
    Ito Peng and Yi-Chun Chien

19 Family life and family policy in South Africa: responding to past legacies,
    new opportunities and challenges 249
    Trudie Knijn and Leila Patel

20 Work-family policies: has Latin America moved towards more gender and
    social equity? 261
    Merike Blofield and Juliana Martínez Franzoni

21 Family policy in India: contradictions, continuities and change 274
    Rajni Palriwala and Neetha N.

22 Family policy patterns in autocratic countries 289
    Dorian R. Woods and Rolf Frankenberger

PART V OUTCOMES OF FAMILY POLICIES

23 Children, poverty and public policy: a cross-national perspective 308
    Janet C. Gornick and Emily Nell

24 Family policies and child well-being 325
    Daniel Engster and Helena Olofsdotter Stensöta

25	Effects of work-family policies on parenthood and wellbeing *Caitlyn Collins and Jennifer Glass*	337

PART VI FUTURE CHALLENGES FOR POLICY MAKING AND RESEARCH

26	Policies on family support and parenting support in a global perspective *Mary Daly*	351
27	Neglected families: developing family-supportive policies for 'natural' and (hu)man-made disasters *Lena Dominelli*	363
28	Women's voices and human rights: perspectives on sustainable family lives *Ulla Björnberg*	376

Index 389

Contributors

Seung-ho Baek is Professor of Social Welfare at the Catholic University of Korea. His research interests cover the precarious labour market, comparative social policy, welfare state theory and basic income. He is the co-author of *Dualisation of Korean Welfare State and Life-course Inequality* (2015) and *Precarious Workers in Korea* (2017). Recent articles include 'Why the social investment approach is not enough – the female labour market and family policy in the Republic of Korea' (*Social Policy & Administration*, 2014), 'Class and precarious work in Korean service economy' (*Korean Social Policy Review*, 2014) and 'Feasible paths to realizing Korean basic income' (*Korean Journal of Social Welfare*, 2017).

Ulla Björnberg is Emeritus Professor (since 2011) at the Department of Sociology and Work Science, University of Gothenburg, Sweden. Her research interests include family, family policy/welfare, work and family, gender, intergenerational relationships, refugees and migration, welfare and well-being of asylum-seeking children and families. Björnberg collaborated on a Nordic study reassessing the Nordic family policy model. She is currently doing research on the social organization of migrant women in Sweden as well as working for international advocacy associations regarding women's human rights, such as WIDE+ and Women and Development in Europe. Examples of publications include *Nordic Family Policies in a European Context* (2015); *Challenges for Future Family Policies in the Nordic Countries* (2013, co-edited with Mai Heide Ottosen); 'Ambivalent policies, uncertain identities', in *Refugee Protection and the Role of Law: Conflicting Identities* (2014, edited by Susan Kneebone, Dallal Steven and Loretta Baldassar).

Merike Blofield is Associate Professor of Political Science and Director of Women's and Gender Studies at the University of Miami, USA. Blofield's research is on gender and socio-economic inequalities, politics and policy, with a focus on Latin America. Her books include *Care Work and Class: Domestic Workers' Struggle for Equal Rights in Latin America* (2012); *The Politics of Moral Sin: Abortion and Divorce in Spain, Chile and Argentina* (2006); and the edited volume *The Great Gap: Inequality and the Politics of Redistribution in Latin America* (2011). Her articles have appeared in peer-reviewed journals such as *Comparative Politics*, *Latin American Research Review* and *Social Politics*. Blofield was also Coordinating Lead Author of the chapter on families for the International Panel on Social Progress.

Jonathan Bradshaw is Emeritus Professor of Social Policy at the University of York, UK. He was founding Director of the Social Policy Research Unit from 1973 to 1987 and served two terms as Head of Department in 1988–94 and 2003–07. Bradshaw's research has focused on social security policy, living standards, comparative social policy, child poverty and child well-being. He is currently the UK Coordinator for the European Union Social Policy Network. He is a Trustee of the Child Poverty Action Group and Chair of their Social Policy Committee. Bradshaw was appointed Academician of the Learned Societies for the Social Sciences in 1996, Commander of the British Empire (CBE) in 2005 for services to child poverty and Fellow of the British Academy in 2010.

In 2011 he was made Doctor of the University of Turku, Finland (honoris causa) and in 2015 Doctor of the University of Bath (honoris causa).

Yi-Chun Chien is a PhD Candidate of Political Science at the University of Toronto, Canada. Her research focuses on the politics of social welfare provision and transnational care migration in East Asia. Chien's work has been published in academic journals such as the *Journal of Ethnic and Migration* and *Critical Sociology*. She is co-editor of *Emotions, Community, Citizenship: Cross-disciplinary Perspectives* (2017). Chien's research has been supported by the China Times Cultural Foundation Young Scholar Award (2017), Chiang Ching-Kuo Foundation Dissertation Fellowship (2016) and Korea Foundation Fellowship for Field Research (2015), among others. She will join the School of Political Studies at the University of Ottawa as a Postdoctoral Fellow in Fall 2018.

Caitlyn Collins is Assistant Professor of Sociology at Washington University in St Louis, USA. She conducts cross-national qualitative research on gender inequality in the workplace and family life, and is broadly interested in the relationship between policy and social inequality. Collins's current research is an interview study of 135 working mothers in Germany, Sweden, Italy and the USA. Her work has been published in *Gender & Society*, *Social Science and Medicine*, *Michigan Family Review*, *Journal of Divorce and Remarriage*, and several edited books.

Mary Daly is Professor of Sociology and Social Policy at the University of Oxford. She has published on poverty, the welfare state, gender, family and the labour market. Much of her work is comparative, in a European and international context. Daly is a member of several European networks and boards concerned with topics related to the welfare state, employment, family and gender and an editor of the journal *Social Politics*. In 2015, she published *Families and Poverty – Everyday Life on a Low Income* (co-authored with Grace Kelly, 2015). Daly's research has been supported by the Economic and Social Research Council (UK), the European Union, Council of Europe, UNWomen and UNICEF.

Lena Dominelli, AcSS, PhD, is Professor of Applied Social Sciences and Co-Director of the Institute of Hazard, Resilience and Research at Durham University, UK. She is a social work researcher of world renown and has published extensively. Her most substantive book on the environment, *Green Social Work* (2012), has led a paradigm shift in eco-social work. Dominelli has held large transdisciplinary research grants, the most recent ones covering disasters such as climate change, floods, earthquakes and volcanoes; and received several accolades for her work including a Medal from the Social Affairs Committee of the French Senate 2002 and the Katherine A. Kendall Award, 2012. She was elected President of the International Association of Schools of Social Work (IASSW) from 1996 to 2004, and currently chairs IASSW's Committee on Disaster Interventions, Climate Change and Sustainability.

Laura den Dulk is Associate Professor at Erasmus University Rotterdam, Department of Public Administration and Sociology, the Netherlands. Her main area of expertise is cross-national research on work-life policies in organizations. Current research interests include the integration of work and personal life at the individual level (how people manage their work and personal/family life), the organizational level (the role of managers, workplace flexibility), and the country level (cross-national comparisons). In 2014 Dulk received the

Rosabeth Moss Kanter Award for Excellence in Work-Family Research for a paper in the *European Management Journal*. She is co-editor of *Community, Work and Family*. Recent publications focus on work-life balance experiences of the self-employed across national and cultural contexts. Currently, she is developing a long-term research project on the impact of flexible working.

Daniel Engster, PhD, is a Professor in the Hobby School of Public Affairs at the University of Houston, USA. His research focuses on care ethics, welfare policy and the family. He is the author of *The Heart of Justice: Care Ethics and Political Theory* (2007) and more recently *Justice, Care, and the Welfare State* (2015). He is co-editor (with T. Metz) of *Justice, Politics, and the Family* (2013) and (with M. Hamington) of *Care Ethics and Political Theory* (2015).

Guðný Björk Eydal is Professor at the Faculty of Social Work, University of Iceland. She obtained her doctorate at the Department of Sociology, University of Gothenburg in 2005. Her PhD was on the development of Icelandic family policy. Eydal has published widely on child and family policies with special emphasis on childcare and parenthood and in 2015 she co-edited the book *Fatherhood in the Nordic Welfare States* with Tine Rostgaard. She is currently participating in various comparative research projects on family policies and disaster research and directing a research project on the effects of the law on equal rights for both parents to three months paid parental leave in Iceland with Ingólfur V. Gíslason at the University of Iceland.

Rolf Frankenberger is Senior Lecturer and researcher at the Institute of Political Science, Eberhard Karls University Tübingen, Germany. He studied Political Science, Sociology and Psychology and currently is spokesperson of the working group on Comparative Dictatorship and Extremism Research of the German Political Science Association. His main research topics focus on the comparative systemic analysis of autocracies. He is especially interested in the analysis of persistence and legitimation of authoritarian rule, including the analysis of institutional patterns, functional requisits and interactions of the political system with economic and cultural social systems. Among his publications are *Autoritarismus Reloaded* (co-edited with Holger Albrecht) and the *Local Politics in a Comparative Perspective* (co-edited with Elena Chernenkova).

Juliana Martínez Franzoni is Full Professor at the Institute of Social Research and Center of Research and Political Studies, University of Costa Rica. Her areas of research are social policy formation and social and gender inequality in Latin America. Franzoni has been a Fulbright scholar and a visiting fellow at the Kellogg Institute for International Studies and LILLAS at the University of Austin (USA), the Free University of Berlin (Germany) and CIEPP (Argentina), among other institutions. Recent articles have been published in *ECLAC Review* (2016), *Social Politics* (2015) and *Latin American Research Review* (2014). In 2016, she co-authored with Diego Sánchez-Ancochea *The Quest for Universal Social Policy in the South: Actors, Ideas and Architectures*. Together with Fernando Filgueira and Silke Staab, she was lead author of the 2017 *Regional Report on Women's Economic Empowerment in Latin America and the Caribbean*.

Anne H. Gauthier is a senior researcher at the Netherlands Interdisciplinary Demographic Institute (NIDI) and Honorary Professor of Comparative Family Studies at the

University of Groningen, the Netherlands. She completed her doctorate at the Oxford University in 1992 and has since held academic positions in Britain, Canada, the Netherlands and the USA. Between 2001 and 2010, Gauthier held the Canada Research Chair in Comparative Family Policy at the University of Calgary. She has published widely in the area of family policies, fertility and family demography. Currently, she is the scientific coordinator of the 'Generations and Gender Programme' (GGP): a multi-country project aimed at understanding changes in family dynamics from a longitudinal and international perspective.

Jennifer Glass is the Barbara Bush Professor of Liberal Arts in the Department of Sociology and the Population Research Center of the University of Texas, Austin, USA. She is currently the Executive Director of the Council on Contemporary Families. Glass has published over 50 articles and books on work and family issues, gender stratification in the labour force, mother's employment and mental health, and religious conservatism and women's economic attainment, with funding from the National Science Foundation, the National Institutes of Health and the Alfred P. Sloan Foundation. Her most recent projects explore the wage effects of flexible work practices and how telecommuting facilitates longer work hours, whether governmental work-family policies improve parents' well-being, and why women's retention in STEM (Science, Technology, Engineering and Maths) occupations remains so abysmally low.

Janet C. Gornick, PhD, is Professor of Political Science and Sociology at the Graduate Center of the City University of New York, USA. She is also Director of the new James M. and Cathleen D. Stone Center on Socio-Economic Inequality, and Director of the US Office of LIS. Most of her research is comparative and concerns social welfare policies and their impact on gender disparities in the labour market and income inequality. Gornick has published articles on gender inequality, employment and social policy in several journals. She is co-author/co-editor of three books: *Families that Work: Policies for Reconciling Parenthood and Employment* (2003); *Gender Equality: Transforming Family Divisions of Labor* (2009); and *Income Inequality: Economic Disparities and the Middle Class in Affluent Countries* (2013).

Heikki Hiilamo, PhD, is Professor of Social Policy at the University of Helsinki, Finland. Previously, he worked as Research Professor at the Social Insurance Institution of Finland. Hiilamo has the title of Docent from the University of Tampere and the University of Eastern Finland. His research interests include family policy, poverty, inequality, welfare state research and tobacco control. His articles have appeared in leading international journals including *American Journal of Public Health* and *Social Science and Medicine*. He is writing a book on household debts to be published by Edward Elgar Publishing.

Teresa Jurado-Guerrero is Professor of Sociology at the Universidad Nacional de Educación a Distancia (UNED) in Madrid, Spain. She gained her PhD from the European University Institute (EUI). Her main areas of interests are family changes, comparative welfare state research, gender studies, work-family reconciliation issues and transition to adulthood. Among Jurado-Guerrero's recent work is the article (with Marta Domínguez-Folgueras, Carmen Botía-Morillas and Patricia Amigot-Leache) '"The house belongs to both": undoing the gendered division of housework' (*Community, Work & Family*, 2016). Currently, she directs a research project funded by MINECO: 'Working time, paternity and childhood. How can business policies promote father involvement in care and maintain gender equality?'

Ji Young Kang holds a PhD in Social Welfare and is an affiliated researcher in the West Coast Poverty Center at the University of Washington, USA. Her main research interest is work and family reconciliation policy, poverty and comparative welfare states. Kang's current research projects include a study of the effect of state paid family leave on low-income mothers' employment in the USA and a study of the impacts of market structures, labour institutions and family policies on gender employment gap among Organisation for Economic Co-operation and Development (OECD) countries. She also explores structure and continuity in institutional contexts for family policy, using a comparative cross-national design to examine the trajectories of change in family policy and their likely consequences for gender equality in OECD countries.

Trudie Knijn is Professor of Interdisciplinary Social Science at Utrecht University, the Netherlands, and visiting professor at the University of Johannesburg, South Africa. She participated as PI and member of the executive board in the FP6 Network of Excellence Reconciliation of Work and Welfare (RECWOWE) and also as PI and member of the executive board of the FP7 research programme bEUcitizen (2013–17), and currently co-ordinates the Horizon2020 ETHOS programme. Her research fields are comparative gender, family and child policy and practices, the evaluation of interventions in the context of welfare reforms, social and civil citizenship rights, and solidarity in a changing Europe. She has widely published on family policy and care from a comparative perspective such as *Work, Family Policy and the Transition to Adulthood in Europe* (2012) and (with Blanche Le Bihan and Claude Martin) *Work and Care under Pressure: Care Arrangements in Europe* (2013). She recently published (with Marit Hopman) 'Parenting support in the Dutch "participation society"' (*Social Policy & Society*) and 'The "turn to parenting": paradigm shift or work in progress?' (*International Journal of Child Care and Education Policy*).

Judith C. Koops is a PhD student at the Netherlands Interdisciplinary Demographic Institute (NIDI) and researcher for the 'Generations and Gender Programme'. Her research focuses on social disadvantage and parenthood decisions in young adulthood. Alongside family sociology, Koops is interested in topics related to migration and inter-ethnic relations. Some of her recent publications are 'The influence of parental educational attainment on the partnership context at first birth in 16 western societies' (*European Journal of Population*, 2017, with A.C. Liefbroer and A.H. Gauthier) and 'Are inter-minority contacts guided by the same mechanisms as minority-majority contacts? A comparative study of two types of inter-ethnic ties in the Netherlands' (*International Migration Review*, 2016, with B. Martinovic and J. Weesie).

Sophia Seung-yoon Lee, PhD, is Professor of Social Welfare at Ewha Womans University in Seoul, Korea. Her main research field is comparative social policy, the East Asian welfare state, the East Asian labour market and income protection, female labour market and precarious workers. She has conducted research on comparative analysis of welfare states, precarious work and income protection policy using historical comparative analysis and fuzzy-set analysis. Lee is the author of *Precarious Workers in Korea* (2017) and *Fuzzy-set Qualitative Comparative Method* (2015). Currently, she is conducting research on the youth labour market and income protection programme in South Korea and the Korean basic income scheme. Her main publications include *Institutional Legacy of State Corporatism in De-industrial Labour Markets: A Comparative Study of Japan, South Korea and Taiwan* (2016); *Examining Policy Configurations as Conditions for Long-term Unemployment and Non-standard Employment in OECD Countries Using Fuzzy-set Analysis* (2013); and *Ssangyong Motors Layoff and Dual Labour Market in Korea* (written in Korean, 2015).

Henning Lohmann is Professor of Sociology, in particular Social Research Methods, at the Faculty of Business, Economics and Social Sciences, University of Hamburg, Germany. His main area of research is poverty and social inequalities across welfare states. Lohmann recently edited (with Ive Marx) the *Handbook of In-work Poverty* (Edward Elgar Publishing, 2018). Other recent work focuses on educational inequalities and on defamilization.

Claude Martin is a sociologist and Research Professor at the CNRS (National Centre for Scientific Research), France. He is also Director of a unit of research in social science in Rennes, EHESP. His main fields of research are European welfare states and social policies, parenting support policies, child and elderly care policies in Europe. Martin is editor of *Work and Care Under Pressure: Care Arrangements Across Europe* (co-edited with T. Knijn, C. Martin and B. Le Bihan, 2013) and *'Être un bon parent': une injonction contemporaine* (2014). Articles include 'Parenting support in France: defining policy on an ideological battlefield' (*Social Policy & Society*, 2015) and '(Re)discovering parents and parenting in France. What's new?' (*ZfF Journal for Family Research*, Special Issue, 2017).

Marcia K. Meyers is the Narramore Scholar and Professor of Social Work and Public Affairs at the University of Washington, USA, and the founding Director of the West Coast Poverty Center. She earned an MPA at Harvard University and an MSW and PhD from the University of California, Berkeley. Meyers has published more than 50 books and research papers on issues of poverty and inequality, US social policy and workplace policies that support families and children. Her current research projects examine variation in the 'package' of social assistance available to low-income families in the USA and the impact of US state policy regimes on economic security and inequality, women's labour force participation and childcare arrangements. She has conducted extensive cross-national comparative research on social and family policy, and is the co-author with Janet C. Gornick of *Families that Work: Policies for Reconciling Parenthood and Employment* (2005), co-editor with Janet C. Gornick of a volume in the Real Utopia Project series, *Gender Equality: Transforming Family Divisions of Labor* (2009), and co-editor with Robert Plotnick, Jennifer Romich and Steven Rathgeb Smith of *Old Assumptions, New Realities: Economic Security for Working Families in the 21st Century* (2013).

Jane Millar, OBE, FBA, is Professor of Social Policy at the Institute for Policy Research, University of Bath, UK. She has been Head of Department, Associate Dean and Pro-Vice-Chancellor for Research at Bath. Her research interests include the design, implementation and impact of social policy, and comparative research on family policy, social security and employment policy, with particular reference to gender and changing family patterns. Millar's publications include 'Lone mothers and paid work: the "family-work project"' (*International Review of Sociology*, 2013) and *Understanding Social Security* (2018). Her research includes a longitudinal qualitative project, following lone mothers and their children over a period of about 15 years, and exploring issues of employment and income security, social relationships and quality of life.

Peter Moss is Emeritus Professor of Early Childhood Provision at the Thomas Coram Research Unit, UCL Institute of Education, University College London, UK. His main areas of research interest are early childhood education and care, democracy and education, and the relationship between employment, care and gender; much of his work has involved cross-national collaboration. Moss was Coordinator of the European Commission Childcare Network from 1986 to 1996; co-founder and joint coordinator of the International Network on Leave Policies and Research from 2004 to 2015. He co-edited the book series Contesting Early Childhood from 2005 to 2015. Recent books include *Early Childhood and Compulsory Education: Reconceptualising the Relationship* (2013); *Transformative Change and Real Utopias in Early Childhood Education* (2014); and *Loris Malaguzzi and the Schools of Reggio Emilia: A Selection of his Writings and Speeches, 1945–1993* (edited with colleagues from Reggio Emilia, 2016).

Manuela Naldini is Associate Professor of Sociology of the Family in the Department of Cultures, Politics and Society at the University of Turin, Italy and Fellow at the Collegio Carlo Alberto. She gained her PhD from the European University Institute (EUI). Her main areas of interests are family changes, comparative welfare state, gender studies, work-family reconciliation issues, childcare and elderly care policies, transition to parenthood. Among Naldini's recent work is the book *Transition to Parenthood in Italy: From Modern Couples to Traditional Family* (*La transizione alla genitorialità. Da coppie moderne a famiglie tradizionali*). She is currently coordinating a Workpackage within the FP7: 'All rights reserved? Barriers towards EUropean CITIZENship (bEU citizen)', focusing on gender and generational division in European Union citizenship, with Trudie Knijn (Utrecht University).

Neetha N. is Professor and Deputy Director at the Centre for Women's Development Studies (CWDS) in New Delhi, India. Prior to joining CWDS, she was Associate Fellow and Coordinator at the Centre for Gender and Labour, V.V. Giri National Labour Institute, NOIDA, India. Neetha's broad research interest is the labour and employment issues of women. Her current research work focuses on the changing dimensions of women's employment, gender statistics, the social, political and economic dimensions of care work (paid as well as unpaid). She has worked on a large-scale study on female migration and is currently working on a pan-Indian project on women and urban labour markets. She has several publications in reputed journals and books.

Emily Nell, MA, is a doctoral student in Sociology at the Graduate Center of the City University of New York, USA. As a demography fellow at the US-based office of the LIS Center, she studied the relationship between child poverty rates and government tax and transfer systems in middle-income countries.

Ilona Ostner is a sociologist and Professor Emerita at the Faculty of Social Sciences, Institute of Sociology, University of Göttingen, Germany. Main research fields are child and parenting support policies, and gender, employment and welfare state policies in the European Union. Publications include 'Explaining recent shifts in family policy' (with Margitta Mätzke, *Journal of European Social Policy*, 2010); 'Investing in children, monitoring parents: parenting support in the changing German welfare state' (with Carolyn Stolberg, *Social Policy & Society*, 2015); and 'Parents in the spotlight: parenting practices and support from a comparative perspective' (co-edited with Tanja Betz and Michael-Sebastian Honig, *Journal of Family Research*, Special Issue, 2017).

Rajni Palriwala is Professor of Sociology at the University of Delhi, India. She has served as Head of the Department of Sociology and as Dean, Faculty of Social Sciences. Her research falls within the broad area of gender relations, covering care and emotion, citizenship and the welfare state, kinship and marriage, dowry, women and work, women's movements and feminist politics, and cross-cultural studies. In addition to edited books on gender and kinship, marriage, family and migration, and journal articles and book chapters on these themes, Palriwala is the author of *Changing Kinship, Family, and Gender Relations in South Asia: Processes, Trends and Issues* (1994) and co-author of *Care, Culture and Citizenship: Revisiting the Politics of Welfare in the Netherlands* (2005, with Carla Risseeuw and Kamala Ganesh) and *Planning Families, Planning Gender: The Adverse Child Sex Ratio in Selected Districts* (2008, with Mary John, Ravinder Kaur, Saraswati Raju and Alpana Sagar).

Leila Patel is the South African Research Chair in Welfare and Social Development and Director of the Centre for Social Development in Africa at the University of Johannesburg, South Africa. She was previously the Director General for Social Welfare in the Mandela government and played a leading role in the development of South Africa's welfare policy. Some of Patel's notable publications include *Restructuring of Social Welfare: Options for South Africa* (1993); the *White Paper for Social Welfare* (1997); *Social Welfare and Social Development in South Africa* (2005); *Social Protection in Southern Africa: New Opportunities for Social Development* (co-editor with James Midgley and Marianne Ulriksen, 2013); and a second edition of *Social Welfare and Social Development* (2015). She has published widely in the field of social welfare and social development in the African context. Patel currently leads a range of social development research projects relating to social protection, gender and care; children and youth development innovations; developmental social work and the transformation of social welfare services in South Africa. She received the Distinguished Woman in Science (Humanities and the Social Sciences) Award in 2013.

Ito Peng is Professor of Sociology and Public Policy, Munk School of Global Affairs and Public Policy, and Canada Research Chair in Global Social Policy at the Department of Sociology, University of Toronto, Canada. She is also Director of the Centre for Global Social Policy at the University of Toronto. Peng teaches Political Sociology and Comparative Social Policy, specializing in family, gender, demographic issues and migration. She has written extensively on family, gender and social policies in East Asia. She is currently leading a large international partnership research project entitled Gender, Migration, and the Work of Care, funded by the Social Sciences and Humanities Research Council of Canada (SSHRC). The project brings together over 50 researchers and non-academic partners to investigate the global migration of care workers, and its impacts on family and gender relations, gender equality, government policies and global governance. Peng has been Associate Dean, Interdisciplinary & International Affairs at the Faculty of Arts and Science, Director of Dr. David Chu Program in Asia Pacific Studies and Director of the Centre for the Studies of Korea, at the Asian Institute. She is a distinguished fellow of the Asia Pacific Foundation of Canada, associate researcher with the United Nations Research Institute for Social Development (UNRISD) and international advisor for the International Labour Organization (ILO). She gained her PhD from the London School of Economics.

Bram Peper is a sociologist working as Lecturer at the Tilburg School of Social and Behavioural Sciences, Department of Sociology, University of Tilburg, the Netherlands. His area of expertise is cross-national research regarding work-family arrangements in organizations in different welfare state regimes. Peper's current research interests include the well-being of employees, the work-life balance, the role of managers and boundary management in relation to work-life issues.

Birgit Pfau-Effinger is Professor of Sociology at the University of Hamburg, Germany. Her main research interests include the relationship between culture and welfare states; explanation of cross-national differences in parents' work-family behaviour; historical development paths of the work-family relationship, and new forms of informal work. Pfau-Effinger has published numerous articles in high ranking academic journals. One of her articles in *Work, Employment and Society* was distinguished in 2012 as 'Favorite WES article of the last 25 years' by the British Sociological Association. Her article 'Culture and welfare states. Reflections on a complex interrelation' is among the top ten most cited articles in the *Journal of Social Policy*.

Cristina Raț, PhD, is Lecturer at the Sociology Department of the Babeș-Bolyai University Cluj-Napoca, Romania. Her research focuses on the relation between social policies and inequality in Central and Eastern Europe (CEE), in particular family policies and the situation of the Roma minority from marginalized, segregated settlements. Since 2009, she has been involved in comparative research in family policy transformations in Poland, Hungary and Romania, together with Tomasz Inglot and Dorottya Szikra. In 2016, she co-authored a chapter on welfare state changes in Romania in the context of the global financial crisis, in *Challenges to European Welfare Systems* (edited by K. Shubert, P. Villota and J. Kuhlmann).

Tine Rostgaard, PhD, is Professor in Comparative Social Policy at VIVE – the Danish Center for Social Science Research. She specializes in comparative research on social care for children and older people, and studies the policies and practices of care and care work. Recent publications within family policy include *Caring Fathers in the Nordic Welfare States – Policies and Practices of Contemporary Fatherhood* (co-edited with G. Eydal, 2014); book chapters 'Does parental leave lead to gender equality? Experiences from the Nordic countries' (co-authored with A.Z. Duvander, G.B. Eydal, B. Brandth, I.V. Gíslason and J. Lammi-Taskula, in *Parental Leave and Beyond*, edited by A. Koslowshi, 2018) and 'Fatherhood in five Nordic countries: policies and practices' (co-authored with G. Eydal, in *Contemporary Fathers Balancing Childcare and Work: Cultures, Practices and Policies in a Cross-country Perspective*, edited by R. Musumeci and A. Santero, 2018). Rostgaard is the founder of the international 'Transforming Care Conference Series' which are held every two years.

Helena Olofsdotter Stensöta, PhD, is Associate Professor in Political Science at the University of Gothenburg, Sweden. Her research focuses on gender, ethics, public policy and administration. Publications include 'Public ethics of care. A general public ethics' (*Ethics and Social Welfare*, 2015); 'A public ethics of care: bringing ethics of care into public ethics research', in *Ethics in Public Policy and Management: A Global Research Companion* (edited by Alan Lawton, Zeger Van Der Wal and Leo Huberts, 2015); 'Grades – for better or worse? The interplay of school performance and subjective well-being among boys and girls' (with Erica Nordlander, *Child Indicators Research*, 2014); 'Gender and corruption in different institutional settings: distinguishing the electoral arena from the bureaucracy' (with Lena Wängnerud, *Governance*, 2014); 'Political influence on street-level bureaucratic outcome: testing the interaction between bureaucratic ideology and local community political orientation' (*Journal of Public Administration Research and Theory*, 2012); 'Do family policies matter for children's well-being?' (*Social Politics*, 2011); 'The conditions of care' (*Public Administration Review*, 2010).

Dorottya Szikra, PhD, is Senior Researcher at the Hungarian Academy of Sciences, Centre for Social Sciences. Her main research field is family and social policy in Central and Eastern Europe. Since 2009, she has been involved in comparative research in family policy transformations in Poland, Hungary and Romania, together with Tomasz Inglot and Cristina Raț. Recent publications include 'Democracy and welfare in hard times: the social policy of the Orbán Government in Hungary between 2010 and 2014' (*Journal of European Social Policy*, 2014) and (with Ágota Scharle) 'Recent changes: moving Hungary away from the European social model', in *The European Social Model in Crisis: Is Europe Losing its Soul?* (edited by Daniel Vaughan-Whitehead, Edward Elgar Publishing and International Labour Office, 2015).

Olivier Thévenon is a social policy analyst at the Organisation for Economic Co-operation and Development (OECD) specializing in child and family policies. He is currently coordinating OECD work on child well-being and child poverty, and is involved in the development of the OECD Family Database and the Child Well-Being Data portal. Thévenon has contributed to analyses of childcare policies, work-family flexible arrangements, gender gaps in employment, the future of social protection and the living conditions of the elderly at the OECD as well as to the following OECD publications: *Babies and Bosses* (2003–05); *Doing Better for Families* (2011); *Closing the Gender Gap* (2012); and *The Pursuit of Gender Equality* (2017). Before joining the OECD, he was a researcher at the INED (French Institute for Demographic Studies), and Co-Head of the Research Unit on Economic Demography. He was actively involved in international projects such as FamiliesAndSocieties, Reproductive Behaviour in a Micro-Macro Context (REPRO), and Gender and Generation Program.

Dorian R. Woods is a Postdoctoral Researcher at the consortium and research hotspot Gender and Power in Politics and Management at Radboud University, The Netherlands. A political scientist and policy analyst by training, she is developing a theory to better understand gender equality, diversity and inclusion in governance and management. Woods was formerly a Lecturer and Research Assistant in the Gender Studies Department, Faculty of History and Sociology at the University of Konstanz, Germany. She held a substitute professorship at the same department in 2016. Her research covers comparative policy with a focus on care and justice theories. Woods has analysed family leave policy, social assistance, childcare and elderly care, tax and inclusion policies. Among her publications is the book *Family Policy in Transformation: US and UK Policies* (Palgrave, 2012). In addition to others, she has published articles in *European Political Science*, *German Policy Studies*, *Journal of Global Ethics* and *femina politica*.

Mara A. Yerkes is Associate Professor of Interdisciplinary Social Science, Department of Interdisciplinary Social Science, Utrecht University, the Netherlands. She obtained her PhD from the University of Amsterdam in 2006. Yerkes's research interests include work, care and family, gender, comparative welfare states, industrial relations, social inequality and women's employment. Her work has been published in journals such as *Community, Work and Family*; *European Journal of Industrial Relations*; *Gender, Work and Organization*; *International Journal of Doctoral Studies*; *Journal of Comparative Welfare Studies*; *Journal of Homosexuality*; *Journal of Social Policy*; *Journal of Sociology*; *PLoS One*; *Policy and Politics*; *Social Policy & Administration*; *Oxford Bibliographies in Sociology*. Yerkes is the author of *Transforming the Dutch Welfare State: Social Risks and Corporatist Reform* (2011) and co-editor (with Romke van der Veen and Peter Achterberg) of *The Transformation of Solidarity. Changing Risks and the Future of the Welfare State* (2011).

Hannah Zagel is a postdoctoral researcher at the Institute for Social Sciences at Humboldt-University Berlin, Germany. She holds a PhD in Social Policy from the University of Edinburgh, an MA (Sociology) from Freie Universität Berlin and a BA (Sociology) from the University of Hamburg. Her research interests include family complexity and change, social inequalities, comparative family policy and welfare states. In her recent work she has looked at lone parenthood as a life course phenomenon, and lone mothers' circumstances across different welfare states. A further research focus is on theory and methods of policies and regulations for families. Together with Henning Lohmann, in 2016 she published an article on the theoretical development and empirical measurement of the defamilization concept, 'Family policy in comparative perspective: the concepts and measurements of familisation and defamilisation' (*Journal of European Social Policy*).

Acknowledgements

We would like to thank all the authors who have contributed to this book; it has been a privilege working with such a qualified group and we appreciate their patience during the editing process. We would also like to thank Edward Elgar Publishing for inviting us to edit this volume – their cooperation, advice and support is gratefully acknowledged. Finally, we acknowledge the support received from the University of Iceland and VIVE – the Danish Center of Social Science during the editing process; in particular, we thank Emily Tangsgaard Christensen at VIVE for, amongst others, help with formatting the manuscript.

PART I

INTRODUCTION

1. Introduction to the *Handbook of Family Policy*
Guðný Björk Eydal and Tine Rostgaard

DEFINITION OF FAMILY AND FAMILY POLICY

The aim of this *Handbook* is to provide an account of contemporary research on family policies, aimed at families with dependent children around the globe. The study of family policy is a relatively young field of research, often said to date back to Alva Myrdal's work on 'programme for family security' in Sweden in 1939. Her work is regarded as the first study that paid special attention to family policy (Gauthier, 1996). Until the 1960s, studies on family policy were few but have been growing since the 1970s (Gauthier, 1996; Gauthier and Koops in this volume; Kamerman and Kahn, 1978), as both national and comparative studies (see an account of the development of comparative studies in Chapter 2 in this volume by Gauthier and Koops).

The root of the term 'family policy' is also of relatively recent origin and can be traced back to a 1958 article published in Germany with the title 'Familien-politik' (Wuermeling et al., 1958, in Gauthier, 1996). In 1978, Kamerman and Kahn (p. 3) defined family policy as 'everything that government does to and for the family'. Following this line, family policy can be defined as including all social and economic policies that affect families as such. Such a wide definition has nevertheless been criticised for being rather elastic since it encompasses almost anything policy related (Bogenschneider, 2000), and usually researchers construct a more narrow definition for their research purposes. In its most narrow scope, only the cash benefit of family allowances is examined (Barbier, 1995). The obvious problem with such a narrow definition is that it leaves out important policies, such as other cash benefits like childcare leave allowances, not to mention the many services provided to families with children. Furthermore, there is a family dimension in many other policies, such as policies of gender equality, housing, labour market, child health and education (to name a few). The solution to this problem is to construct a 'middle range' definition in order to avoid the shortcomings of both the wide and narrow definitionss. Such a definition takes the family as the starting point and examines policies that are aimed at families, hence emphasising how the policy defines the nexus between state and family and between family members. Another way of narrowing down the concept of family policy is to define which families the policies are aimed at, but, as pointed out by Lohmann and Zagel in this volume, the concepts of family vary widely across national contexts and cultures.

Scholars therefore generally agree to disagree on whether to apply a wide, middle range or narrow definition of family policy. The definition of family policy applied in constructing the framework for this book is more middle range. We emphasise the cash and service benefits for dependent children as well as for their parents in order to provide financial as well as care support. This includes policies of direct and indirect financial support (fiscal and cash benefits), support in the combination of work and family life (e.g., leave schemes) as well as policies that support children in their development (childcare) or support parents in the raising of their children (guidance and interventions). Hence, family law and child protection policies are usually left outside the scope of the studies presented in the volume. Furthermore, the book does not address family policies for children with special needs, for example, due to long-term illnesses or disability. Definitions of other key concepts are made by the individual author(s), for example, while some authors refer to early childhood education of care (ECEC), others may refer to childcare.

The family definition applied in the book focuses on families with dependent children, typically under the age of 18 years, and thus leaves out policies involving frail older people and persons with disabilities, who have received growing attention in the field of family policy, in particular in the literature on social care services (e.g., Daly, 2002; León, 2014; Pfau-Effinger and Rostgaard, 2011). Thus, the focus of the book is family policies and how these support parents with dependent children, even though other family members may be mentioned, such as the important role of grandparents (e.g., Millar in this volume).

FAMILY POLICY RESEARCH

There exists a wide body of literature on the development of family policies, the categorisation of such policies as well as their outcomes (e.g., Bradshaw, 2006; Ellingsæter and Leira, 2006; Esping-Andersen, 2009; Gauthier, 2002, 2007; Kamerman and Kahn, 1978, 1997; Kaufmann, 2002; Knijn et al., 2007; O'Connor et al., 1999; Pfau-Effinger, 2005; Saraceno, 1997; Saraceno et al., 2012). However, recent changes in family policies imply a re-drawing of family boundaries, with governments having a new interest in socially investing in families with children, facilitating female as well as family-friendly employment (Morel et al., 2012), in defining family obligations (see Millar in this volume) and at times re-positioning families and parenting as a public concern (see Knijn, Martin and Ostner as well as Daly in this volume). Facilitating and governing parenting is thus gaining a new significance, as is also the developmental potential and well-being of the child (see Rostgaard as well as Moss in this volume). As a consequence, there is great interest in how child and family policies structure and intervene in what families do (Gillies, 2011; Morgan, 2011). Likewise, there is interest in the evidence of whether family policies meet their stated outcomes for families, for example, the outcomes for child and parental well-being (see Engster and Stensöta as well as Collins and Glass in this volume). While family policies are usually initiated by the state there is also increasing interest in how family policies are part of the policies of individual companies as well as collective bargaining and collective agreements (see also den Dulk, Yerkes and Peper in this volume).

The economic crisis in 2008 was felt in some countries more than others. Like previous global economic downturns, it put welfare systems to the test, and welfare research is generally addressing both the policy measures taken as well as the consequences (e.g., Schubert et al., 2016; Starke et al., 2013). For families with children in particular, the obvious threat of the crisis is the declining income from employment, thus the level of social protection becomes a vital issue (Cantillon et al., 2017; see also Chapter 7 by Bradshaw and Chapter 23 by Gornick and Nell in this volume on the effects of family policy for alleviating child poverty). In a more long-term perspective, austerity measures targeting cash and service benefits for families may lead to less protection and worse outcomes for children. Increasing inequality among families with children is also a concern in many countries, including the risk of living in long-term poverty.

In the last decades the threat from natural and man-made disasters has also been on the rise. Global warming and wars have led to an increase in involuntary mass migration. In 2016 there were 22.5 millions refugees, with over half under the age of 18 (UNHCR, 2017). All these factors contribute to insecurity among families with children and their vulnerability is on the rise with even middle class families in rich countries unable to ensure their security (Cooper, 2014). The increased numbers of transnational families, migration and asylum seekers calls for new perspectives and research methods to address how family policies provide protection and support to families on the move (Baldassar and Merla, 2014; Björnberg, 2016; Williams, 2010; Williams and Graham, 2014; see also Chapter 28 by Björnberg and Chapter 27 by Dominelli in this volume).

Historically, the child and family policy literature has mainly addressed the countries in Western advanced economies (albeit with exceptions, e.g., Robila, 2013; Shehan, 2016) but political changes in recent decades, for example, in Eastern Europe, the Middle East, Asia and Africa, have resulted in new family policies creating a new interest and need for a wider geographical focus of the investigation of family policies. Even though most of the chapters addresses the development and status of family policies in the advanced economies, the aim of the book is to also give new insights to the changes in these regions (see, e.g., Chapter 19 by Knijn and Patel on South Africa; Chapter 20 by Blofield and Martínez Franzoni on Latin America; and Chapter 21 by Palriwala and Neetha on India).

THEMES (PARTS) AND CHAPTERS IN THE BOOK

The book is divided into five main thematic parts: Part II on the history, concepts, theory and methods of family policy research; Part III on family policies; Part IV on family policy models; Part V on outcomes of family policies; and Part VI on the future challenges for family policy making and research.

In Part II, the authors address overall how family policy is conceptualised, defined, researched and developed in different parts of the world. In Chapter 2, on the history of family policy research, Anne H. Gauthier and Judith C. Koops address the major developments in cross-national comparative family policy in the last century. They distinguish between four main bodies of studies: (1) the early comparative and mostly descriptive work dating from the early twentieth century which pioneered cross-national family policy research; (2) the studies on family policy regimes which aimed at developing typologies; (3) the research on the determinants of family policies from a quantitative perspective; and (4) the rapidly expanding research on the outcomes of family policies. In Chapter 3, Peter Moss discusses childcare services and asks how to bridge structures and culture. According to Moss, structures such as how childcare is organised, funded and provided have received far more attention in research than have cultural dimensions such as traditions, social constructions and images of the child, the worker, the parent and so on. As he argues, this limits our understanding of cross-country differences. In Chapter 4, Jane Millar presents the contribution of research on family obligations to family policy studies. As Millar points out, 'the balance between the obligations of individuals to provide for themselves, family members to provide for each other, and governments to replace, supplement or enforce family support is central to family policy'. Henning Lohmann and Hannah Zagel in Chapter 5 focus on variable-oriented approaches and provide a methodological discussion of central issues and recent developments in an indicator-based comparison of family policy across a number of countries. Lohmann and Zagel point out the importance of rigorous understanding of measurement, data and methodological perspectives for evaluation of family policy outcomes. The final chapter in this part, Chapter 6 by Ji Young Kang and Marcia K. Meyers, examines change in family policies over a 20-year period in 14 Organisation for Economic Co-operation and Development (OECD) countries by focusing on policies that support parents in their dual responsibilities as earners and caregivers. Kang and Meyers argue that nearly all countries have over time expanded policies that support work/life balance as well as degendering caregiving.

Part III of the book contains chapters on distinct fields and scopes of family policies, including cash transfers such as paid parental leave and child benefits, services such as childcare, and overall policies on parenting support and social investment, as well as work-family policies in the workplace. In the first chapter in this part, Chapter 7, Jonathan Bradshaw explores the function of the classical policy instrument of child benefits. Despite the clear evidence of its effectiveness in reducing child poverty, only few countries have in fact introduced such benefits. Bradshaw investigates the pros and cons of child benefits, applying his well-known family model method in European Union (EU) and OECD countries. He finds that the case for child benefit is overwhelming. While not quite as old as child benefits, childcare services are nevertheless considered a central policy means to facilitate female employment as well as strengthening children's cognitive and social capacities. In Chapter 8, Tine Rostgaard adresses the idea of childcare as a global policy agenda, advocated by supranational organisations such as the EU and the OECD and very often with reference to social investment. She investigates the foundation for this idea and whether it is visible in the development of domestic policy, arguing that we still have some way to go. Chapter 9 by Sophia Seung-yoon Lee and Seung-ho Baek further investigates the policy trend of social investment, this time from a particular Asian perspective. In a comparison of family policy trends in South Korea and Japan from 1990 onwards, they argue that these countries have adopted a liberal social investment perspective, which emphasises the role of the market and individual responsibility rather than the state, as otherwise seen in Northern Europe. In Chapter 10, Olivier Thévenon presents the development of maternity, paternity and parental leave policies for parents from a cross-national perspective among the OECD countries from 1970 and onwards. Over time, the length of leave has been extended, flexibility has increased and in most cases the policies enhance rights for fathers to leave but the cross-national variation in leave entitlements is still considerable. Parents in work rely on work-family policies and in Chapter 11, Laura den Dulk, Mara A. Yerkes and Bram Peper provide a state-of-the art review on the role of work-family policies across different European countries. As they argue, while there is some data on work-family policies at the national level, little is known about how these interact with collective agreements and company practices. In Chapter 12, Trudie Knijn, Claude Martin and Ilona Ostner explore a specific branch of family policy, namely, the growth of parenting policies intended to not only support but also discipline families and their children. They argue that such policies reinforce and prolong parental responsibilities well into adolescence. In contrast to gender-neutral

ECEC policies, however, these new policies target the mother and thus support a more traditional division of work among parents.

In Part IV, the chapters address family models – or families of nations to borrow the formulation of Castles (1993) – referring to nations that are neighbours and/or share cultural ties. Grouping countries together according to welfare models has been an important component of comparative research, the most influential that of Esping-Andersen (1991) when he distinguished three models of welfare capitalism, conservative, liberal and social democratic. The first chapter in this part, Chapter 13 by Birgit Pfau-Effinger, draws upon the work of Esping-Andersen and examines how the family policies in the conservative model of Austria, Germany and Switzerland have changed considerably since the model was first identified. Her results show changes from a housewife model to a more gender-egalitarian family policy model, apart from Switzerland where family policy has remained conservative. Dorian R. Woods is the author of Chapter 14 on the liberal models in the UK and US, and she asks to what extent the developments in family policy have followed a liberal agenda and whether policies in the two countries differ by examining historical legacies, policy instruments and power dynamics. In Chapter 15, the social democratic model – or the Nordic Model – is examined by Guðný Björk Eydal, Tine Rostgaard and Heikki Hiilamo who discuss the main characteristics of contemporary family policies in the Nordic countries, asking if family policies have reached their twofold aim here, namely, to work for equality between children and to enhance gender equality. Many scholars have pointed out the need for more than three worlds of welfare capitalism and particularly the need for Southern and Eastern Europe models (e.g., Arts and Gelissen, 2002). In Chapter 16, the Southern Europe model is visited by Teresa Jurarado-Guerrero and Manuela Naldini who provide a historical and a comparative account of family policy in Greece, Italy, Portugal and Spain. The chapter addresses the policies in three main areas – family benefits, childcare, parental leave and reconciliation policies – and they find overall a weak development of family policies in a context of continued 'unsupported familialism'. In Chapter 17, Cristina Raț and Dorottya Szikra present a comparative analysis of the family policies in the Eastern European model by looking at Hungary, Poland and Romania. A common feature is an upgrading of the state provisions but there are still differences between the countries and among families depending on their income level. In Chapter 18, Ito Peng and Yi-Chun Chien challenge the belief that East Asian countries have similar family policy models by comparing Japan, South Korea, Taiwan, China, Hong Kong and Singapore. Their results show a spectrum of family policy approaches, ranging from a liberal market approach to ones that align more closely to a regulated institutional approach. Hence, Peng and Chien point out the importance of investigating the within-regime cultural and institutional variations. In the following chapters, the book looks into regions which are not usually part of the 'modelling business' (Abrahamson, 1999). In Chapter 19, Trudie Knijn and Leila Patel provide an analysis of the South African family policy that they call 'Family life and family policy in South Africa', responding to past legacies, new opportunities and challenges. The chapter provides valuable insights into the development of family policies for countries that are dealing with the consequences of the AIDS epidemic and poverty. Here, South Africa has successfully enacted a child benefit scheme. In Chapter 20, Merike Blofield and Juliana Martínez Franzoni ask if Latin America has moved towards more gender and social equity, focusing on employment-based leaves following the birth of a child and childcare. Blofield and Martínez Franzoni conclude that while the policy changes lie far behind the major structural changes in the region, there is increasing political recognition of the need for public attention and state intervention to ensure reconciliation of work and family. In Chapter 21 Rajni Palriwala and Neetha N. address family policy in India, its contradictions, continuities and change. They point out that there are two competing ideals of families in India: while a modern and planned family is present in population and wage policies, the competing idea of the traditional Indian family continues to underscore how the family is expected to take care of children, dependent older people and other vulnerable members of the family. The last chapter in this part, Chapter 22 by Dorian R. Woods and Rolf Frankenberger, addresses a topic that has often been left out from the field of family policy research, namely, family policies in autocratic countries. The chapter examines three types of family leave policy: maternity, paternity and parental leave in 50 out of 51 country that are defined as autocratic countries. Four groups of autocracies emerge and autocratic regime types are found to have some explanatory power for the overall and paid duration of maternity leave and the duration of paternity leave, but the results show that region is also important.

Part V of the book is devoted to research on outcomes of family policies. Here, Janet C. Gornick and Emily Nell in Chapter 23 look at the child poverty reducing effects of total transfers and taxes. Using register and survey data from the Luxembourg Income Study, and also expanding their analysis to include high- as well as middle-income countries, they find substantial country variation in child poverty, often depending on parents' employment situation. It is the combination of government tax, cash benefits as well as more generalised income support that can alleviate poverty among children, but many countries fail to combat child poverty. Family policies may also affect another outcome, child well-being. In Chapter 24, Daniel Engster and Helena Olofsdotter Stensöta investigate the conceptualisation of child well-being and how both subjective and objective indicators are used to measure this. While they find that the research generally supports the relationship between family policy and child well-being, the mechanisms are less well understood. In addition, research has mainly concentrated on advanced economies. Parents' well-being and how family policy may affect this is the focus of Chapter 25 by Caitlyn Collins and Jennifer Glass. They suggest that in addition to a number of subjective indicators of well-being, a number of objective and structural indicators present themselves as innovative ways to conceptualise and measure parents' well-being. They also suggest that family policy is not a zero-sum game which only improves parental happiness; family policies also seem to improve the happiness of non-parents.

With Chapter 26 by Mary Daly, we move to the final part, Part VI on future challenges for policy making and research. Daly takes a global perspective and identifies what are the evolving family policies and to what extent concerns about the family and the role and practices of parents have been the mobilising policy agency in different parts of the world. Based on case studies of family policy development in countries from different regions of the world, amongst others, Belarus, Jamaica, Sweden and Chile, she finds a growth in traditional measures that seek to provide a range of resources to improve familial functioning but also the introduction of new measures aimed at modifying how parents rear their children, often part of a conservative reaction to what is perceived as a crisis of the family. Lena Dominelli takes us to a relatively new but (unfortunately) important new chapter in family policy research: how family policy supports families during natural and human-made disasters. She argues that disaster discources often assume availability of family resources for filling gaps left by formal providers from evacuation onwards, but with the 'one size fits all' approach family-supportive policies often ignore individual family members' differentiated resources and experiences of disasters. In the final chapter of the book, Chapter 28, Ulla Björnberg provides a perspective on sustainable family lives, focusing on women's rights within family contexts and from a global perspective. Inspired by the capability approach, she argues for a feminist family policy and illustrates how this may change subsistence for women in a global economy, migration and social mobility.

REFERENCES

Abrahamson, P. (1999), 'The welfare modelling business', *Social Policy & Administration*, **33** (4), 394–415.
Anttonen, A. and J. Sipilä (1996), 'European social care services. Is it possible to identify models?', *Journal of European Social Policy*, **6** (2), 87–100.
Arts, W. and J. Gelissen (2002), 'Three worlds of welfare capitalism or more? A state-of-the-art report', *Journal of European Social Policy*, **12** (2), 135–58.
Baldassar, L. and L. Merla (eds) (2014), *Transnational Families, Migration and the Circulation of Care: Understanding Mobility and Absence in Family Life*, New York: Routledge.
Barbier, J.C. (1995), 'Public policies with a family dimension in the European Union: an analytical framework for comparison and evolution', in L. Hantrais and M.-T. Letablier (eds), *The Family in Social Policy and Family Policy Cross-National Research Papers Fourth Series: Concepts and Contexts in International Comparisons of Family Policies in Europe*, Loughborough: The Cross-National Research Group, European Research Centre, pp. 15–32.
Björnberg, U. (2016), 'Nordic family policy in European context', *Sociology and Antropology*, **4** (6) 508–16.
Bogenschneider, K. (2000), 'Has family policy come of age? A decade review of the state of U.S. family policy in the 1990s', *Journal of Marriage and the Family*, **62** (4), 136–50.
Bradshaw, J. (2006), 'Child benefit packages in 15 countries in 2004', in J. Lewis (ed.), *Children, Changing Families and the Welfare State*, Cheltenham, UK and Northampton, MA, USA: Edward Elgar Publishing, pp. 69–89.
Cantillon, B., Y. Chzhen, S. Handa and B. Nolan (eds) (2017), *Children of Austerity Impact of Great Recession on Child Poverty in Rich Countries*, Oxford: Oxford University Press.
Castles, F.G. (ed.) (1993), *Families of Nations – Patterns of Public Policy in Western Democracies*, Aldershot: Dartmouth.
Cooper, M. (2014), *Cut Adrift, Families in Insecure Times*, Berkeley, CA: University of California Press.
Daly, M. (2002), 'Care as a good for social policy', *Journal of Social Policy*, **31** (2), 251–70.
Ellingsæter, A.L. and A. Leira (eds) (2006), *Politicising Parenthood in Scandinavia: Gender Relations in Welfare States*, Bristol: Policy Press.
Esping-Andersen, G. (1991), *Three Worlds of Welfare Capitalism*, Cambridge: Polity Press.
Esping-Andersen, G. (2009), *The Incomplete Revolution Adapting to Women's New Roles*, Cambridge: Polity Press.
Gauthier, A.H. (1996), *The State and the Family – A Comparative Analysis of Family Policies in Industrialized Countries*, Oxford: Clarendon Press.
Gauthier, A.H. (2002), 'Family policies in industrialized countries: is there convergence?', *Population*, **57** (3), 447–74.
Gauthier, A.H. (2007), 'The impact of family policies on fertility in industrialized countries: a review of the literature', *Population Research and Policy Review*, **26** (3), 323–46.
Gillies, V. (2011), 'From function to competence: engaging with the new politics of family', *Sociological Research*, **16** (4), 11. Accessed 16 August 2017 at http://www.socresonline.org.uk/16/4/11.html.
Kamerman, S.B. and A.J. Kahn (eds) (1978), *Family Policy: Government and Families in Fourteen Countries*, New York: Columbia University Press.
Kamerman, S. and A.J. Kahn (eds) (1997), *Family Change and Family Policies in Great Britain, Canada, New Zealand and the United States*, Oxford: Clarendon Press.
Kaufmann, F.-X. (2002), 'Politics and policies towards the family in Europe: a framework and an inquiry into their differences and convergences', in F.-X. Kaufmann, A. Kuijsten, H.-J. Schulze and K.P. Strohmeier (eds),

Family Life and Family Policies in Europe Volume 2: Problems and Issues in Coparative Perspective, Oxford: Oxford University Press, pp. 419–90.

Knijn, T., C. Martin and J. Millar (2007), 'Activation as a common framework for social policies towards lone parents', *Social Policy Administration*, **41** (6), 638–52.

León, M. (ed.) (2014), *Care Regimes in Transitional European Societies*, London: Palgrave Macmillan.

Morel, N., B. Palier and J. Palme (eds) (2012), *Towards a Social Investment Welfare State? Ideas, Policies and Challenges*, Bristol: Policy Press.

Morgan, D. (2011), *Rethinking Family Practices*, Basingstoke: Palgrave Macmillan.

O'Connor, J.S., A. Orloff and S. Shaver (1999), *States, Markets, Families: Gender, Liberalism and Social Policy in Australia, Canada, Great Britain and the United States*, Cambridge: Cambridge University Press.

Pfau-Effinger, B. (2005), 'Culture and welfare state policies: reflections on a complex interrelation', *Journal of Social Policy*, **34** (1), 3–20.

Pfau-Effinger, B. and T. Rostgaard (eds) (2011), *Care between Work and Welfare in European Societies*, London and Chicago, IL: Palgrave Macmillan.

Robila, M. (ed.) (2013), *Family Policies across the Globe*, New York: Springer.

Saraceno, C. (1997), 'Family change, family policies and the restructuring of welfare', in OECD (ed.), *Family, Market and Community: Equity and Efficiency in Social Policy, Social Policy Studies No. 21*, Paris: OECD, pp. 81–100.

Saraceno, C., J. Lewis and A. Leira (eds) (2012), *Families and Family Policies, Volumes 1 and 2*, Cheltenham, UK and Northampton, MA, USA: Edward Elgar Publishing.

Schubert, K., P. de Villota and J. Kuhlmann (eds) (2016), *Challenges to European Welfare Systems*, New York: Springer.

Shehan, C. (ed.) (2016), *The Encyclopedia of Family Studies*, Hoboken, NJ: Wiley-Blackwell.

Starke, P., A. Kaasch and F. van Hooren (eds) (2013), *The Welfare State as Crisis Manager – Explaining the Diversity of Policy Repsonses to Economic Crisis*, New York: Palgrave Macmillan.

UNHCR (The UN Refugee Agency) (2017), *Global Trends Forced Displacement in 2016*, Geneva: UNHCR.

Williams, C. and M. Graham (2014), '"A world on the move": migration, mobilities and social work', *British Journal of Social Work*, **44** (Suppl. 1), i1–i17.

Williams, F. (2010), 'Review article migration and care: themes, concepts and challenges', *Social Policy & Society*, **9** (3), 385–96.

PART II

FAMILY POLICY: HISTORY, CONCEPTS, THEORY AND METHODS

2. The history of family policy research
Anne H. Gauthier and Judith C. Koops*

INTRODUCTION

The term family policy encompasses a wide array of governmental programmes, schemes, and laws targeted at families and aimed at supporting them, especially in regard to their caring responsibilities. This includes financial support (taxes and transfers), support for the combination of work and family responsibilities, family laws, and the field of early childhood education and care. As such, family policy is best described as a patchwork of policies in view of its very disparate nature and the fact that it is rarely the responsibility of a single ministry or department within a government.

In the literature the term family policy can be traced back to the 1950s/1960s (e.g., Coser, 1951; Schorr, 1962) and became more routinely used from the 1970s (e.g., Kamerman and Kahn, 1978). Prior to this, it was the specific components of family policy instead (e.g., family allowances) that were the subject of study.[1] Its French language equivalent *politique familiale* had, however, been used much earlier: a reflection of the early interest in this topic in academic and political circles in Belgium and France (e.g., Bonvoisin, 1942; Vulhopp, 1928).

In this chapter we focus on the major developments in family policy research in the more industrialized countries in the past 100 years. To narrow our inquiry, we focus predominantly on cross-national comparative research as opposed to country-specific research. We distinguish four distinct bodies of literature: (1) the early comparative work dating from the early twentieth century which was mostly descriptive in nature but which pioneered cross-national family policy research; (2) the studies on family policy regimes which aimed at developing typologies; (3) the research on the determinants of family policies from a quantitative perspective; and (4) the research on the outcomes of family policies – an area of research which has expanded rapidly in recent decades.

Throughout the chapter and in each of the subsections, the aim is therefore to trace the development of different styles of family policy research with a view towards identifying the classic and foundational studies as well as the more recent and emerging ones. And although we aim at comprehensiveness, the scope of our review is limited by the available information as indexed in large databases (e.g., Google Scholar) and by language (English and French). Moreover, we restrict the scope of our review to policies for families with children and omit support for eldercare.

THE EARLY COMPARATIVE WORK

The first cross-national studies on family policy were published in the early decades of the twentieth century and aimed primarily at compiling information on the policies and legislation in place in various countries. This pioneering work came from two sources:

large international or national organizations involved in the monitoring or development of international agreements, and academics concerned about the well-being of families. We review below these two developments since they both resulted in invaluable historical data on family policy.

The Work of International and National Organizations

Three organizations took the lead in compiling cross-national information on family policies: the League of Nations, the International Labour Organization (ILO), and the US government, all with a focus on two major areas of family policy: maternity protection at work and family allowances. The impetus for this early work for the former two organizations came mostly from early international agreements in this field and the need to monitor their implementation. This includes the Berne Convention of 1906 on the prohibition of night work for women, the ILO Maternity Protection Convention of 1919 (no. 3), and the ILO Declaration of Philadelphia of 1944 which explicitly mentioned the provision for child welfare and maternity protection. The richness of the reports in terms of geographical coverage and detailed information is remarkable (e.g., ILO, 1924, 1929).

The other major source of information in the early decades of the twentieth century came from the government of the United States. Since in contemporary work, the United States is always classified as providing low support for families (see the next section), the early interest of the American government in this field may be surprising. The impetus in this case seemed to come from fierce social security advocates, some of them close to the government, who lobbied for the adoption of measures of social security protection partly based on their knowledge of measures in place in other countries (Hoskins, 2010). The adoption of the 1935 Social Security Act under President Franklin D. Roosevelt provided further impetus for the monitoring of developments in other countries. The series 'Social Security Programs throughout the World', which was first published in 1940 (under the title *An Outline of Foreign Social Insurance and Assistance Laws*), and which is still published every other year, is totally unique.

The other major development at this time took place in 1949 with the first international *Inquiry into the Cost of Social Security* by the ILO. The concept was also unique in that it aimed at compiling data on government expenditures on social security, including family allowances. The ILO published the results of its international inquiries until the 1990s and has since switched to an electronic database named the Social Security Inquiry.

The Early Academic Work

In parallel to the work of international and national organizations, important cross-national studies of family policy were published in the early decades of the twentieth century. This early work was, however, targeted at specific components of family policy, notably family allowances, and appears to be linked with advocates of greater government support for families with children. Among them, Eleanor Rathbone, a British scholar and Member of Parliament, devoted much of her career to the study of social conditions and argued for a system of family allowances paid directly to mothers (e.g., Rathbone, 1927). The academic work on family allowances in these early years moreover preceded the adoption of general schemes of family allowances in several countries in the 1930s (e.g., Dieude, 1929; Leveau, 1926) or shortly after (e.g., Bedwell, 1940; Callaghan, 1947; Hoffner, 1935). These early academic studies on family allowances were linked to the broader topic of family poverty and included studies on family budgets (e.g., Hanna, 1933), the cost of children (e.g., Henderson, 1949, 1950), and family wages (e.g., Douglas, 1925; Waggaman, 1924).[2]

Following these early academic studies, research on family policy then expanded rapidly from the 1970s but again with a focus primarily on providing comparative descriptive information on specific countries and based on the contribution of country informants. This includes studies on family policies (Kamerman and Kahn, 1978; Kaufmann et al., 1997; Palomba and Moors, 1995; Robila, 2014), maternity and gender policies (Bock and Thane, 1991), and population policies (INED, 1982; Kirk et al., 1975; Leridon et al., 1976). These comparative volumes continue to form a vast and rich source of historical and contemporary information on family policy.

THE STUDIES ON FAMILY POLICY REGIMES

If the early research on family policy was mainly descriptive in nature, the second wave of research in this field aimed instead at ranking countries and at classifying them in various clusters. This work was heavily influenced by that of Gøsta Esping-Andersen and his threefold typology of welfare states (Esping-Andersen, 1990; see also Chapter 5 by Lohmann and Zagel in this volume for an overview). The typology itself became very influential, but also received much criticism (Arts and Gelissen, 2002). Criticism from feminist scholars has mostly revolved around two issues (Orloff, 1993; Sainsbury, 1994). First, that in his early work Esping-Andersen ignored the place of the family as a source of welfare and care (since his typology only acknowledged the importance of the state and the market). Second, that while the decommodification dimension is applicable to full-employed male workers, it has little relevance in explaining the situation of women who are not participating in the labour market and are therefore not commodified.

These criticisms were the starting point for new typologies more specific to gender and family policies. They include, among others, the work of Lewis (1992) who suggested a typology that differentiates countries along the line of gender inequality in the labour market. On one side of her spectrum Lewis locates strong male-breadwinner states (such as the United States) which lack social policies that help women combine work and family life, and on the other side countries (such as Sweden) where policies instead reflect a dual-breadwinner model. Other scholars have modified this typology, for example, by incorporating the dual-earner/dual-carer model as the ultimate state (Crompton, 1999; Pfau-Effinger, 2005).

In response to these criticisms, and instead of basing a welfare state typology solely on gender issues, Esping-Andersen (1999, 2009) added a third dimension to his typology: the level of defamilization of the welfare states.[3] Defamilization has proved to be arbitrary as a concept, however, as some define it as the degree to which the family can function independently from the market, while others interpret it as the level to which women can be independent from the family (for a detailed discussion see Bambra, 2007; Saxonberg,

2013). This has led to suggestions to introduce the concept of degenderization as a substitute for defamilization in welfare state typologies (Saxonberg, 2013).

In parallel to these more theory-based typologies, many empirically based typologies have emerged which categorize countries according to their level of family policy support. These typologies are often fairly different in their approach and outcome. This diversity is illustrated in Table 2.1 which provides an overview of selected typologies. To allow comparison, we have restricted the selection to typologies focused on Organisation for Economic Co-operation and Development (OECD) countries. Part of the diversity arises as studies focus on different aspects of the welfare state, including typologies that group welfare states solely on the level of defamilization (Bambra, 2004, 2007) and others that combine it with the level of decommodification and economic/class inequality (Esping-Andersen, 1999; Hook, 2015). Moreover, studies vary considerably regarding the type of family policies they include, with some focusing either on childcare services or maternity leave (Bambra, 2004, 2007), and others on a combination of both (Korpi, 2000; Korpi et al., 2013). Finally, scholars differ in their methodological approach to construct typologies (Arts and Gelissen, 2002; Bambra, 2007). Most are index-based typologies using the approach of Esping-Andersen by ranking countries which score low, middle or high on various indicators (e.g., Bambra, 2004; Korpi, 2000), but more recent typologies increasingly use cluster analysis, often resulting in more groups of countries (Bambra, 2007; Hook, 2015).

Despite the variety of approaches, and as seen in Table 2.1, the differences in the typologies often reside in the name given to the cluster or regime rather than in the actual grouping of countries (Bambra, 2004). Some countries, such as the United States, Germany, and France, appear to be 'core countries' (Bambra, 2007) or 'ideal-types' (Esping-Andersen, 1990) as they are most distinctive from each other and often form the basis for the different groups. However, the vast majority of countries are less stable in their group membership as they join different categories in different studies. Studies examining countries' group membership over time have also come to dissimilar conclusions, with some finding that countries' group membership is rather stable over time (Gauthier, 2002), and others concluding that some countries have made considerable changes to their welfare state regimes (Morgan, 2013; see also Chapter 6 by Kang and Meyers in this volume).

THE RESEARCH ON THE DETERMINANTS OF FAMILY POLICIES

The third strand of research on family policy is that on the determinants of family policies which is dominated by cross-national quantitative studies. In itself, this is a relatively small body of literature, especially in contrast with that examining the consequences of family policies (see the next section).

The early work in this field followed parallel developments in the welfare state literature and typically focused on governmental expenditures on the family as an indicator of welfare effort (e.g., Pampel and Adams, 1992). The study by Wennemo (1992) therefore appears to have been the first to break with this tradition in having instead used non-expenditures-based indicators, namely, family benefits and tax allowances as a percentage of the industrial wage.

Table 2.1 Overview of a selection of family policy typologies based on OECD countries

Source/indicators-dimensions	Family policy or welfare state regime/cluster		
Esping-Andersen 1999 stratification decommodification defamilialization	*liberal/ non-familialist* Australia Canada Ireland New Zealand United Kingdom United States	*conservative/ familialist* Finland France Germany Japan Italy Switzerland	*social-democratic/ de-familialist* Austria Belgium Netherlands Denmark Norway Sweden
Korpi 2000 childcare maternity-paternity leave elderly care family benefits	*market-oriented* Australia Canada Japan New Zealand Switzerland United Kingdom United States	*general family support* Austria Belgium France Germany Ireland Italy Netherlands	*dual-earner* Denmark Finland Norway Sweden
Bambra 2004 female labour force participation maternity leave	*low defamilization* Australia Japan New Zealand United States	*medium defamilization* Austria Belgium Canada France Germany Ireland Italy Netherlands Norway Switzerland United Kingdom	*high defamilization* Denmark Finland Norway Sweden
Korpi, Ferrarini, and Englund 2013 family benefits childcare maternity and paternity leave	*market-oriented* Canada United States United Kingdom Australia New Zealand Ireland Japan Switzerland	*traditional family* Austria Belgium France Germany Italy Netherlands	*earner-carer* Denmark Finland Norway Sweden
Bambra 2007[a] female economic activity maternity leave	*Cluster 1* Australia United States	*Cluster 2* Austria Belgium France	*Cluster 5* Norway Sweden

Table 2.1 (continued)

Source/indicators-dimensions	Family policy or welfare state regime/cluster	
	Cluster 3 Italy Japan *Cluster 4* Canada Finland UK	*Cluster 2* (continued) Germany Netherlands New Zealand Portugal Switzerland

Note: [a] The following countries are marked as 'unclear cases': Denmark, Ireland, Greece, and Spain.

Recent developments in this field of research have been threefold. First, and following the earlier work of Wennemo (1992), there has been much research on capturing different components of family policy. This includes the analysis of public spending on the family (Bolzendahl, 2011), expenditures on family benefits (Linos, 2013), maternity leave length (Linos, 2013), maternity employment policy (Lambert, 2008), and childcare provision (Bonoli and Reber, 2010).

The second development has been in terms of theoretical frameworks. In line with the welfare state literature, research on the determinants of family policy has typically focused on three main theoretical explanations. (1) Demographic age structure and fertility: the argument being that population ageing can be expected to be associated with lower public spending on children because of the size of the older population and their self-interest as voters and policy makers, that is, in allocating resources to their own age groups. The alternative argument is that in view of population ageing, and especially in view of low fertility, governments may be more inclined to increase spending on families with children (see Pampel and Adams, 1992). (2) Economic development: the argument being that with more advanced levels of development, governments are more able to afford improvements in family support (Wennemo, 1992). (3) Political ideologies and power mobilization: the argument being that countries with stronger democratic parties, parties more committed to social solidarity, and stronger unions will be more favourable to state support for families (Bonoli and Reber, 2010).

Recent developments have expanded the range of theoretical explanations to also include the role of institutions and gender ideology. With regard to the former, there are several variants of this theoretical perspective, with some emphasizing path dependency (but also paradigm shifts, see Morgan, 2013), crowding out (i.e., existing spending on specific policies prevents spending on new programmes, see Bonoli and Reber, 2010), and international diffusion. In the latter case, the argument is that social policies tend to spread across countries as a result of the influence of international agreements (e.g., ILO Convention) and as a result of voters' knowledge of policies in place in other countries (Linos, 2013). As to gender ideologies and power, the argument used in recent work has been that with more women in politics, greater participation of women in the labour force, more support for gender equality by the general public, and stronger women's groups, governments are more likely to be supportive of family policy especially in the area of work-family reconciliation (Bolzendahl, 2011; Ferragina and Seeleib-Kaiser, 2015; Misra, 2003).

Finally, the third development in this field of research has been a methodological one with increasingly sophisticated methods used to adequately capture the panel or multi-level structure of the data (for an overview and discussion see Billiet, 2013; Luci-Greulich and Thévénon, 2013).

THE RESEARCH ON THE OUTCOMES OF FAMILY POLICIES

There has been a very rapid increase in this field of research mostly in terms of its expansion to new types of outcomes. Because this topic is covered in several chapters included in this volume, only a summary of key developments in this field are mentioned here (see also Part V on outcomes of family policies in this volume).

The Impact of Policies on Fertility and Employment

The early work in this field focused on the impact of family policies on fertility and on female labour force participation. With regard to the former, the theory was derived from New Home Economics and argued that any reduction in the direct or indirect cost of children – through family policy – can be expected to increase the demand for children (for reviews see Gauthier, 2007; Thévenon and Gauthier, 2011). The first studies typically used aggregated-level data in the form of pooled cross-national time-series data (e.g., Blanchet and Ekert-Jaffé, 1994; Gauthier and Hatzius, 1997). In recent years, the research in this field has increasingly been based on comparative individual-level cross-sectional or longitudinal data. It has moreover focused on the impact of a variety of family policy indicators including family policy expenditures (Kalwij, 2010), family support environment (Harknett et al., 2014), family support type (Billingsley and Ferrarini, 2014), maternity and parental leave (Baizán et al., 2014), and childcare (Van Bavel and Różańska-Putek, 2010).[4]

There is also a parallel body of work on the impact of family policies on women's labour market outcomes (see the review in Hegewisch and Gornick, 2011; see also Chapter 11 by den Dulk, Yerkes, and Peper in this volume). The theory is that by reducing the incompatibility between work and family responsibilities, family policies can be expected to increase female labour force participation and especially to reduce the interruption of women's work associated with childbirth or the presence of young children at home. Recent studies in this field have increasingly relied on individual-level data and have examined a variety of labour market outcomes including the impact of policies on female labour force participation (Boje and Ejrnæs, 2012; Nieuwenhuis et al., 2012), mothers' return to work after childbirth (Pronzato, 2009), motherhood penalty (Budig et al., 2012), and gender earnings inequality (Mandel and Semyonov, 2005). Very recent work has also focused on the effect of policies on the employment of specific subgroups of mothers (e.g., single mothers in Misra et al., 2012; separated women in Van Damme et al., 2009), the take-up of parental leave by mothers and fathers (e.g., Eydal and Rostgaard, 2016), as well as the question of the optimal duration and design of maternity and parental leave to maximize labour market outcomes (Akgunduz and Plantenga, 2013; Thévenon and

Solaz, 2013, 2014). In particular, there is a concern that long parental leave may have a negative impact on female labour force participation (Gupta et al., 2008).

There is also some recent work that has focused on the impact of family policies on unpaid work including the gender division of housework (Hook, 2010) and fathers' paid and unpaid work (e.g., Bünning, 2015; Schober, 2014). Most of these studies are, however, based on country-specific rather than cross-national data (for an exception see Bünning and Pollmann-Schult, 2015; Hook, 2006).

The Impact of Policies on Other Adult and Child Outcomes

In addition to labour market outcomes, other studies have focused on the impact of family policies on parents' experiences of work-family conflict (Allen et al., 2014) and work-life balance (Lunau et al., 2014). A particularly interesting development in this field has been the attempt at capturing the impact of both workplace support and governmental support (Abendroth and den Dulk, 2011; see also Chapter 11 by den Dulk, Yerkes, and Peper in this volume). Most studies in the field examine the broad impact of welfare or family policy regimes rather than the impact of specific indicators (e.g., Steiber, 2009). Moreover, most studies tend to be based on cross-sectional data and lack a more life-course (longitudinal) approach.

There has also been a recent interest in the impact of family policies on the mental and physical health of parents. This includes studies of the impact of family policy models (Palència et al., 2014) and parental leave on parents' health (Avendano et al., 2015; Chatterji and Markowitz, 2012).

Finally, there is a parallel literature on the impact of policies on child outcomes, dating back to work done in the early 2000s on the impact of parental leave on child health (Ruhm, 2000; Tanaka, 2005) and identified at the time as an overlooked area of research (Galtry, 2002). Since then the literature has increased rapidly to examine the impact of maternity and parental leave on a broad range of child health outcomes including mortality, birth weight, and premature birth, as well as breastfeeding (in itself not a child outcome per se but one closely linked to child health). More recent literature in this field has examined the impact of different components of parental leave policies on child health (Ferrarini and Norström, 2010; Ozdamar, 2015).

Other work on child outcomes include the impact of family policies on child poverty (Bäckman and Ferrarini, 2010; Engster, 2012; see also Chapter 7 by Bradshaw and Chapter 23 by Gornick and Nell in this volume) and the very recent literature on the impact of the structure and design of child benefit policies on child poverty (Van Lancker and Van Mechelen, 2015). Finally, there has been some work on the impact of family policies on children's well-being (see Chapter 24 by Engster and Stensöta in this volume) including children's educational outcomes (e.g., Engster and Stensöta, 2011; Hampden-Thompson, 2013).[5]

CONCLUSION

From a highly descriptive approach to the sophisticated use of statistical analyses, family policy research has been radically transformed during the past decades. It has moreover witnessed a major expansion of its field including the impact of family policy on various child, adult, and family outcomes. Yet, and as we reflect on these developments, there are six final observations that should be noted.

First, and despite the richness of various family policy databases, most of the available time-series data only became available in the 1980s, and at best in the 1960s. This omits earlier efforts by governments to support families especially in the early decades of the twentieth century. Moreover, some of the earliest sources of comparative data on family policy, not being in electronic format, are at high risk of eventually being lost. Effort to digitize and archive these invaluable sources is imperative.

Second, there is the continuing problem associated with the quantification of family policy indicators in these electronic databases often resulting in the omission of important components of the policies.[6] A good example is the issue of eligibility to policies, for example, in the case of maternity and parental leave, which is usually ignored and which may not only provide an erroneous picture of governmental support but may also introduce biases in the analyses (by assuming that everybody would have been eligible). Additional examples may be found in the field of early childhood education and care with cross-nationally comparable benchmarks and indicators difficult to obtain (e.g., UNICEF, 2008).

Third, the majority of studies continue to be focused on Western Europe or a subset of OECD countries. Family policy research in other parts of the world is much more limited but has seen a growing interest in recent years (see, e.g., OECD Korea Policy Centre, 2013; Robila, 2014).

Fourth, family policy research continues to be focused on the same 'traditional' domains, namely, cash benefits, maternity and parental leave, and early childhood education and care. Attempts at expanding the analyses beyond these domains are notoriously difficult in the absence of readily available comparative indicators, but would be important in order to provide a more comprehensive picture of governmental support for families (for an exception see Bradshaw and Finch, 2002).

Fifth, and in the context of increasing female labour force participation and changing social norms regarding gender equality, the literature has paid increasing attention to the dual-earner/dual-carer model, oftentimes by considering it as the desirable model. However, studies in this field have mainly approached the question from the mother's perspective while paying much less attention to the question of the extent to which family policies make it possible for fathers to take over part of the caring responsibilities (Eydal and Rostgaard, 2016).

Finally, and if the early advocates of governmental support for families might be astonished to see the developments in family policy research in the past decades, the increasing availability of data on family policy indicators should by no means restrict the field of research. Promising future avenues reside in ways of more accurately capturing the actual level and diversity of support received by different types of families including due consideration to the issues of eligibility to policies and support from the workplace. For if comparing and ranking countries' effort to support families continue to be important areas of research, the study of inequalities between family types may be one of the areas most needed, especially in view of the very large changes in the labour market and family dynamics that have created new forms of inequalities and as well as new challenges for governments.

NOTES

* Koops acknowledges support from the funding of the European Research Council under the European Union's Seventh Framework Programme (FP/2007-2013)/ERC Grant Agreement n. 324178 (Project: Contexts of Opportunity. PI: Aart C. Liefbroer).
1. An early exception was the use of the terms family security and family and population policy by A. Myrdal (1939, 1947) in her studies of Sweden.
2. Mention should also be made of early academic work on population policies which included governmental support for families (e.g., Doublet, 1946).
3. Note that this term was introduced earlier in the literature (Lister, 1994).
4. There is also a small body of literature on the impact of family policy on other demographic behaviour including single motherhood (González, 2007), union formation (Kokkonen, 2012), and divorce (González and Viitanen, 2009).
5. There is a whole literature on the long-term impact of preschool education and childcare on children's educational outcomes. This is not covered here.
6. Some of the recent developments trying to address this issue include the use of fuzzy set analysis (e.g., Ciccia and Verloo, 2012; Haas and Rostgaard, 2011) and simulation (Bartova and Emery, 2016).

REFERENCES

Abendroth, A.K. and L. den Dulk (2011), 'Support for the work-life balance in Europe: the impact of state, workplace and family support on work-life balance satisfaction', *Work, Employment and Society*, **25** (2), 234–56.
Akgunduz, Y.E. and J. Plantenga (2013), 'Labour market effects of parental leave in Europe', *Cambridge Journal of Economics*, **37** (4), 845–62.
Allen, T.D., L.M. Lapierre, P.E. Spector et al. (2014), 'The link between national paid leave policy and work–family conflict among married working parents', *Applied Psychology*, **63** (1), 5–28.
Arts, W. and J. Gelissen (2002), 'Three worlds of welfare capitalism or more? A state-of-the-art report', *Journal of European Social Policy*, **12** (2), 137–58.
Avendano, M., L.F. Berkman, A. Brugiavini, and G. Pasini (2015), 'The long-run effect of maternity leave benefits on mental health: evidence from European countries', *Social Science and Medicine*, **132**, 45–53.
Bäckman, O. and T. Ferrarini (2010), 'Combating child poverty? A multilevel assessment of family policy institutions and child poverty in 21 old and new welfare states', *Journal of Social Policy*, **39** (2), 275–96.
Baizán, P., B. Arpino, and C. Delclós (2014), 'The effect of gender policies on fertility: the moderating role of education and normative context', DemoSoc Working Paper, No. 2014-55.
Bambra, C. (2004), 'The worlds of welfare: illusory and gender blind?', *Social Policy and Society*, **3** (3), 201–11.
Bambra, C. (2007), 'Defamilisation and welfare state regimes: a cluster analysis', *International Journal of Social Welfare*, **16** (4), 326–38.
Bartova, A. and T. Emery (2016), 'Measuring policy entitlements at the micro-level: maternity and parental leave in Europe', *Community, Work and Family*, **19**, 1–20.
Bedwell, C.E.A. (1940), 'Family allowances', *Journal of Comparative Legislation and International Law*, **22** (4), 199–202.
Billiet, J. (2013), 'Quantitative methods with survey data in comparative research', in P. Kennett (ed.), *A Handbook of Comparative Social Policy*, Cheltenham, UK and Northampton, MA, USA: Edward Elgar Publishing, pp. 264–302.
Billingsley, S. and T. Ferrarini (2014), 'Family policy and fertility intentions in 21 European countries', *Journal of Marriage and Family*, **76**, 428–45.
Blanchet, D. and O. Ekert-Jaffé (1994), 'The demographic impact of family benefits: evidence from a micro-model and from macro-data', in J. Ermish and N. Ogawa (eds), *The Family, the Market and the State in Ageing Societies*, Oxford: Clarendon Press, pp. 79–105.
Bock, G. and P. Thane (eds) (1991), *Maternity and Gender Policies: Women and the Rise of the European Welfare States 1880s–1950s*, London: Routledge.
Boje, T.P. and A. Ejrnæs (2012), 'Policy and practice: the relationship between family policy regime and women's labour market participation in Europe', *International Journal of Sociology and Social Policy*, **32** (9/10), 589–605.
Bolzendahl, C. (2011), 'Beyond the big picture: gender influences on disaggregated and domain-specific measures of social spending, 1980–1999', *Politics and Gender*, **7**, 35–70.

Bonoli, G. and F. Reber (2010), 'The political economy of childcare in OECD countries: explaining cross-national variation in spending and coverage rates', *European Journal of Political Research*, **49**, 97–118.

Bonvoisin, G. (ed.) (1942), *La politique familiale du marechal*, L'Actualite sociale.

Bradshaw, J. and N. Finch (2002), *A Comparison of Child Benefit Packages in 22 Countries*, Department for Work and Pensions, Research report No. 174.

Budig, M.J., J. Misra, and I. Boeckmann (2012), 'The motherhood penalty in cross-national perspective: the importance of work–family policies and cultural attitudes', *Social Politics: International Studies in Gender, State and Society*, **19** (2), 163–93.

Bünning, M. (2015), 'What happens after the "daddy months"? Fathers' involvement in paid work, childcare, and housework after taking parental leave in Germany', *European Sociological Review*, **31** (6), 738–48.

Bünning, M. and M. Pollmann-Schult (2015), 'Family policies and fathers' working hours: cross-national differences in the paternal labour supply', *Work, Employment and Society*, **30** (2), 256–74.

Callaghan, H.C. (ed.) (1947), *The Family Allowance Procedure: An Analysis of the Family Allowance Procedure in Selected Countries*, Washington, DC: Catholic University of America Press.

Chatterji, P. and S. Markowitz (2012), 'Family leave after childbirth and the mental health of new mothers', *Journal of Mental Health Policy and Economics*, **15** (2), 61.

Ciccia, R. and M. Verloo (2012), 'Parental leave regulations and the persistence of the male breadwinner model: using fuzzy-set ideal type analysis to assess gender equality in an enlarged Europe', *Journal of European Social Policy*, **22** (5), 507–28.

Coser, L.A. (1951), 'Some aspects of Soviet family policy', *American Journal of Sociology*, **56** (5), 424–37.

Crompton, R. (ed.) (1999), *Restructuring Gender Relations and Employment: The Decline of the Male Breadwinner*, Oxford: Oxford University Press.

Dieude, C. (1929), 'Les allocations familiales: historique, état actuel en France et à l'étranger, résultats acquis, nature économique et juridique, avenir de cette institution', Dissertation, Louvain: Editions de la Société d'études morales sociales et juridiques.

Doublet, J. (1946), 'Aperçu sur les législations étrangères en matière de démographie', *Population*, **1** (2), 283–98.

Douglas, P.H. (1925), 'The family allowance system as a protector of children', *Annals of the American Academy of Political and Social Science, New Values in Child Welfare*, **121**, 16–24.

Engster, D. (2012), 'Child poverty and family policies across eighteen wealthy Western democracies', *Journal of Children and Poverty*, **18** (2), 121–39.

Engster, D. and H.O. Stensöta (2011), 'Do family policy regimes matter for children's well-being?', *Social Politics: International Studies in Gender, State and Society*, **18** (1), 82–124.

Esping-Andersen, G. (1990), *The Three Worlds of Welfare Capitalism*, Oxford: Polity Press.

Esping-Andersen, G. (ed.) (1999), *Social Foundations of Post-industrial Economies*, Oxford: Oxford University Press.

Esping-Andersen, G. (2009), *The Incomplete Revolution. Adapting to Women's New Roles*, Cambridge: Polity Press.

Eydal, G. and T. Rostgaard (eds) (2016), *Fatherhood in the Nordic Welfare States: Comparing Care Policies and Practice*, Bristol: Policy Press.

Ferragina, E. and M. Seeleib-Kaiser (2015), 'Determinants of a silent (r)evolution: understanding the expansion of family policy in rich OECD Countries', *Social Politics*, **22** (2), 133–46.

Ferrarini, T. and T. Norström (2010), 'Family policy, economic development and infant mortality: a longitudinal comparative analysis', *International Journal of Social Welfare*, **19** (1), 89–102.

Galtry, J. (2002), 'Child health: an underplayed variable in parental leave policy debates?', *Community, Work and Family*, **5** (3), 257–78.

Gauthier, A.H. (2002), 'Family policies in industrialized countries: is there convergence?', *Population*, **57** (3), 447–74.

Gauthier, A.H. (2007), 'The impact of family policies on fertility in industrialized countries: a review of the literature', *Population Research and Policy Review*, **26** (3), 323–46.

Gauthier, A.H. and J. Hatzius (1997), 'Family policy and fertility: an econometric analysis', *Population Studies*, **51**, 295–306.

González, L. (2007), 'The effect of benefits on single motherhood in Europe', *Labour Economics*, **14** (3), 393–412.

González, L. and T.K. Viitanen (2009), 'The effect of divorce laws on divorce rates in Europe', *European Economic Review*, **53** (2), 127–38.

Gupta, N.D., N. Smith, and M. Verner (2008), 'The impact of Nordic countries' family friendly policies on employment, wages, and children', *Review of Economics of the Household*, **6** (1), 65–89.

Haas, L. and T. Rostgaard (2011), 'Fathers' rights to paid parental leave in the Nordic countries: consequences for the gendered division of leave', *Community, Work and Family*, **14** (2), 177–95.

Hampden-Thompson, G. (2013), 'Family policy, family structure, and children's educational achievement', *Social Science Research*, **42** (3), 804–17.

Hanna, H.S. (1933), 'The international cost-of-living inquiry', *Annals of the American Academy of Political and Social Science*, **166**, 162–7.
Harknett, K., F.C. Billari, and C. Medalia (2014), 'Do family support environments influence fertility? Evidence from 20 European countries', *European Journal of Population*, **31** (1), 1–33.
Hegewisch, A. and J.C. Gornick (2011), 'The impact of work-family policies on women's employment: a review of research from OECD countries', *Community, Work and Family*, **14** (2), 119–38.
Henderson, A. (1949), 'The cost of children. Part I', *Population Studies: A Journal of Demography*, **3** (2), 130–50.
Henderson, A. (1950), 'The cost of children. Parts II and III', *Population Studies: A Journal of Demography*, **4** (3), 267–98.
Hoffner, C. (1935), 'Compulsory payment of family allowances in Belgium, France and Italy', *International Labour Review*, **32** (4), 463–91.
Hook, J.L. (2006), 'Care in context: men's unpaid work in 20 countries, 1965–2003', *American Sociological Review*, **71** (4), 639–60.
Hook, J.L. (2010), 'Gender inequality in the welfare state: sex segregation in housework, 1965–2003', *American Journal of Sociology*, **115** (5), 1480–523.
Hook, J.L. (2015), 'Incorporating "class" into work–family arrangements: insights from and for Three Worlds', *Journal of European Social Policy*, **25** (1), 14–31.
Hoskins, D.D. (2010), 'U.S. Social Security at 75 years: an international perspective', *Social Security Bulletin*, **70** (3).
INED (1982), *Natalité et politiques de population en France et en Europe de l'Est' Collection: Cahiers, n. 98*, Paris: INED.
ILO (International Labour Organization) (1924), *Family Allowances: The Remuneration of Labour According to Need*, ILO Studies and Reports Series No. 15, Geneva: ILO.
ILO (International Labour Organization) (1929), *The Protection of Women in Industry and Commerce Before and After Childbirth: A Comparative Study of Legislation*, 3rd edn, Geneva: ILO.
Kalwij, A. (2010), 'The impact of family policy expenditure on fertility in Western Europe', *Demography*, **47** (2), 503–19.
Kamerman, S.B. and A.J. Kahn (eds) (1978), *Family Policy: Government and Families in Fourteen Countries*, New York: Columbia University Press.
Kaufmann, F.X., A. Kuijsten, H.-J. Schulze, and K.P. Strohmeier (eds) (1997), *Family Life and Family Policies in Europe. Vol. 1: Structures and Trends in the 1980s*, Oxford: Clarendon Press.
Kirk, M., M. Livi Bacci, and E. Szabady (eds) (1975), *Law and Fertility in Europe: A Study of Legislation Directly or Indirectly Affecting Fertility in Europe*, Dolhain, Belgium: IUSSP.
Kokkonen, A. (2012), 'How family policies affect women's formation of domestic unions – and why it matters for fertility', in Pieter Vanhuysse and Achim Goerres (eds), *Aging Populations in Post-industrial Democracies*, London: Routledge, pp. 225–47.
Korpi, W. (2000), 'Faces of inequality: gender, class, and patterns of inequalities in different types of welfare states', *Social Politics: International Studies in Gender, State and Society*, **7** (2), 127–91.
Korpi, W., T. Ferrarini, and S. Englund (2013), 'Women's opportunities under different family policy constellations: gender, class, and inequality tradeoffs in western countries re-examined', *Social Politics: International Studies in Gender, State and Society*, **20** (1), 1–40.
Lambert, P.A. (2008), 'The comparative political economy of parental leave and child care: evidence from twenty OECD countries', *Social politics*, **15** (3), 315–44.
Leridon, H., A. Girard, L. Roussel et al. (eds) (1976), *Natalité et politique démographique Collection: Cahiers, n. 76*, Paris: INED.
Leveau, L. (ed.) (1926), *Les Allocations familiales dans l'industrie du bâtiment et des travaux publics en France et à l'étranger*, Paris: L. Tenin.
Lewis, J. (1992), 'Gender and the development of welfare regimes', *Journal Policy*, **2** (3), 159–73.
Linos, K. (ed.) (2013), *The Democratic Foundations of Policy Diffusion: How Health, Family and Employment Laws Spread Across Countries*, Oxford: Oxford University Press.
Lister, R. (1994), '"She has other duties" – women, citizenship and social security', in S. Baldwin and J. Falkingham (eds), *Social Security and Social Change: New Challenges to the Beveridge Model*, Hemel Hempstead: Harvester Wheatsheaf, pp. 31–44.
Luci-Greulich, A. and O. Thévenon (2013), 'The impact of family policies on fertility trends in developed countries', *European Journal of Population*, **29** (4), 387–416.
Lunau, T., C. Bambra, T.A. Eikemo, K.A. van der Wel, and N. Dragano (2014), 'A balancing act? Work–life balance, health and well-being in European welfare states', *European Journal of Public Health*, **24** (3), 422–7.
Mandel, H. and M. Semyonov (2005), 'Family policies, wage structures, and gender gaps: sources of earnings inequality in 20 countries', *American Sociological Review*, **70** (6), 949–67.
Misra, J. (2003), 'Women as agents in welfare state development: a cross-national analysis of family allowance adoption', *Socio-Economic Review*, **1** (2), 185–214.

Misra, J., S. Moller, E. Strader, and E. Wemlinger (2012), 'Family policies, employment and poverty among partnered and single mothers', *Research in Social Stratification and Mobility*, **30** (1), 113–28.

Morgan, K.J. (2013), 'Path shifting of the welfare state: electoral competition and the expansion of work-family policies in Western Europe', *World Politics*, **65**, 73–115.

Myrdal, A. (1939), 'A programme for family security in Sweden', *International Labour Review*, **39** (6), 723–63.

Myrdal, Alva (ed.) (1947), *Nation and Family: A Swedish Experiment in Democratic Family and Population Policy*, Cambridge, MA: MIT Press.

Nieuwenhuis, R., A. Need, and H. van der Kolk (2012), 'Institutional and demographic explanations of women's employment in 18 OECD countries, 1975–1999', *Journal of Marriage and Family*, **44** (3), 614–30.

OECD Korea Policy Centre (ed.) (2013), *Comparative Study of Family Policy in East Asia (Korea, China, Japan, Singapore)*, OECD Korea Policy Centre.

Orloff, A.S. (1993), 'Gender and the social rights of citizenship: a comparative analysis of gender relations and welfare states', *American Sociological Review*, **58** (3), 303–28.

Ozdamar, O. (2015), 'Does public spending on parental leave benefits promote child health? Evidence from panel data analyses of OECD countries', *International Journal of Economic Perspectives*, **9** (1), 32–49.

Palència, L., D. Malmusi, D. De Moortel, L. Artazcoz, M. Backhans, C. Vanroelen, and C. Borrell (2014), 'The influence of gender equality policies on gender inequalities in health in Europe', *Social Science & Medicine*, **117**, 25–33.

Palomba, R. and M. Hein (eds) (1995), *Population, Family and Welfare. A Comparative Survey of European Attitudes. Volume 1*, Oxford: Clarendon Press.

Pampel, F.C. and P. Adams (1992), 'The effects of demographic change and political structure on family allowance expenditures', *Social Service Review*, **66** (4), 524–46.

Pfau-Effinger, B. (2005), 'Culture and welfare state policies: reflections on a complex interrelation', *Journal of Social Policy*, **34** (1), 3–20.

Pronzato, C.D. (2009), 'Return to work after childbirth: does parental leave matter in Europe?', *Review of Economics of the Household*, **7** (4), 341–60.

Rathbone, E.F. (ed.) (1927), *The Disinherited Family: A Plea for Direct Provision for the Costs of Child Maintenance through Family Allowance*, London: Allen & Unwin.

Robila, M. (ed.) (2014), *Handbook of Family Policies Across the Globe*, New York: Springer.

Ruhm, C.J. (2000), 'Parental leave and child health', *Journal of Health Economics*, **19** (6), 931–60.

Sainsbury, D. (ed.) (1994), *Gendering Welfare States*, London: Sage.

Saxonberg, S. (2013), 'From defamilialization to degenderization: toward a new welfare typology', *Social Policy and Administration*, **47** (1), 26–49.

Schober, P.S. (2014), 'Parental leave and domestic work of mothers and fathers: a longitudinal study of two reforms in West Germany', *Journal of Social Policy*, **43** (2), 351–72.

Schorr, A.L. (1962), 'Family policy in the United States', *International Social Science Journal*, **14** (3), 452–67.

Steiber, N. (2009), 'Reported levels of time-based and strain-based conflict between work and family roles in Europe: a multilevel approach', *Social Indicators Research*, **93** (3), 469–88.

Tanaka, S. (2005), 'Parental leave and child health across OECD countries', *The Economic Journal*, **115** (501), 7–28.

Thévenon, O. and A.H. Gauthier (2011), 'Family policies in developed countries: a "fertility-booster" with side-effects', *Community, Work and Family*, **14** (2), 197–216.

Thévenon, O. and A. Solaz (2013), 'Labour market effects of parental leave policies in OECD countries', OECD Social, Employment and Migration Working Papers No. 141.

Thévenon, O. and A. Solaz (2014), 'Parental leave and labour market outcomes: lessons from 40 years of policies in OECD countries', INED Working Paper No. 199, Paris.

UNICEF (2008), *The Child Care Transition*, Innocenti Report Card 8, Florence.

Van Bavel, J. and J. Różańska-Putek (2010), 'Second birth rates across Europe: interactions between women's level of education and child care enrolment', *Vienna Yearbook of Population Research*, **8**, 107–38.

Van Damme, M., M. Kalmijn, and W. Uunk (2009), 'The employment of separated women in Europe: individual and institutional determinants', *European Sociological Review*, **25** (2), 183–97.

Van Lancker, W. and N. Van Mechelen (2015), 'Universalism under siege? Exploring the association between targeting, child benefits and child poverty across 26 countries', *Social Science Research*, **50**, 60–75.

Vulhopp, Tilla (ed.) (1928), *Une politique des familles nombreuses en Belgique*, Louvain: Éditions de la Société d'études morales, sociales et juridiques.

Waggaman, M.T. (1924), '"Family-wage" system in Germany and certain other European countries', *Monthly Labor Review*, **18** (1), 20–29.

Wennemo, I. (1992), 'The development of family policy: a comparison of family benefits and tax reductions for families in 18 OECD countries', *Acta Sociologica*, **35** (3), 201–17.

3. The structure/culture divide in early childhood services – and how we might bridge it
Peter Moss

INTRODUCTION

Recent years have seen a rapid development in comparative studies of early childhood services, a generic term I use for a range of formal provisions that go by many names, but which aim to provide education and/or care to children below compulsory school age.[1] Much of this comparative work has taken place within the confines of the European Union (EU) (e.g., European Commission Childcare Network, 1988, 1990, 1996; European Commission/EACEA/Eurydice/Eurostat, 2014; Oberhuemer et al., 2010; Plantenga and Remery, 2009), though one of the most renowned studies, the Organisation for Economic Co-operation and Development's *Starting Strong*, had a wider reach, drawing participating countries from that organization's global membership (OECD, 2001, 2006). This growth in comparative studies reflects an increased policy priority for early childhood services, both among international organizations and nation states, driven by narratives of employment, prevention and investment. In this context, early childhood services have increasingly come to be seen as the *sine qua non* for assuaging the social discontents of contemporary society and enabling countries to succeed in an increasingly competitive global race for economic survival (for a fuller discussion and critique of these narratives, see Moss, 2014).

In this chapter I consider two of the possible dimensions of comparative work on early education and care services: what I will term structure and culture (see also Chapter 8 by Rostgaard in this volume for a related discussion on the structure/culture dimension of childcare). There are of course other possible dimensions for study, most notably what might be termed performance. This 'performative' dimension plays a major role today in the comparative study of compulsory education, where there now exists what has been described as a 'plethora of cross-national tests of pupils' academic achievement, such as PISA (Programme for International Student Assessment), TIMSS (Trends in International Mathematics and Science Study), PIRLS (Progress in International Reading Literacy Study) and PIACC (Programme for the International Assessment of Adult Competencies), provided by international agencies such as the OECD and UNESCO' (Morris, 2016, p. 1). Recently, the OECD has extended such testing from older school children to those at the end of early childhood education, with its International Early Learning and Child Well-being Study, the first round of which took place in 2018 with three participating countries (http://www.oecd.org/education/school/international-early-learning-and-child-well-being-study.htm).

But such comparative exercises are already impinging on early childhood services, as countries increasingly frame their rationale in terms of improving later school performance (and hence PISA rankings). In this fretful context, these services are more and more spoken of as 'preparing' children for school, and are increasingly exposed to processes of 'schoolification', an expressive term for compulsory education 'taking over early childhood institutions in a colonising manner' (OECD, 2006, p. 62), leading to a 'school-like approach to the organisation of early childhood provision' and the adoption of 'the content and methods of the primary school' with a 'detrimental effect on young children's learning' (OECD, 2001, p. 129).

The comparative study of outcomes and performance raises important issues of rationale, method, use and consequence, but these must wait for another occasion. For here I want to concentrate on the dimensions of structure and culture. What do I mean by these terms?

By 'structure' I mean the way that early childhood services are organized and provided, accessed and used, regulated and governed, staffed and funded, in short the nuts and bolts of the system, including its extent and coverage. If structure may be thought of as the container, the outward manifestation of early childhood services, 'culture' is about what is inside, the contents of the container. It is an intricate weave of traditions and influences, theories and concepts, social constructions and images (of the child, the worker, the parent, the centre), procedures and practices, shaping understandings of what services are about and what constitutes 'good' work in them. However, as I shall argue later, we should beware of adopting a dualistic approach to structure and culture, for they are in fact interconnected.

My argument in this chapter is that structure has received far more attention, in comparative studies, than culture. The studies mentioned above are nearly all concerned with structure, only *Starting Strong* offers some recognition of culture, and even so only to a limited extent.[2] This means that while we know rather a lot about the structure of early childhood services, especially in the EU (largely because of its funding of comparative research), we know far less about culture; so we can make comparisons, but to a limited extent only. In this chapter I want to ask: Why has this happened? Does it matter? How might we undertake a comparative study of culture? And this leads to a concluding section revisiting the issue of why do comparative studies in the first place. But first, using some specific cases, I want to illustrate what I mean by culture.

CULTURE AT WORK

The Case of Denmark

From a structural point of view, Denmark has very similar early childhood services to its close neighbour Sweden. Both have a fully integrated early childhood service under the aegis of one government department; unlike most countries, neither Denmark nor Sweden have services split between welfare and education and/or between provision for children under and over 3 years (for a fuller discussion of integrated and split early childhood systems, see Kaga et al., 2010). Both also have a universal entitlement giving access to all children after well-paid parental leave ends and high levels of attendance from 12 months of age upwards; supply funding largely from general taxation, supplemented by modest parental contributions; and a well-qualified workforce, in which 50–60 per cent of the workforce are graduates. On this basis, both sets of early childhood services fit the model of a Nordic or Social Democratic welfare regime.

But look deeper, look into the culture, and there are major differences. Most important, Swedish services adopt an educational identity (more on which in the next section), while Danish services have a strongly social pedagogical identity. They are staffed by a mixture of qualified pedagogues and unqualified pedagogue assistants, and embody the traditions and understandings of social pedagogy. Indeed, social pedagogy is the predominant discipline in Denmark not only for working with pre-school children but also in a wide range of other services for older children, young people and adults.

First named as such in Germany in 1844, by Karl Mager, as the 'theory of all the personal, social and moral education in a given society, including the description of what has happened in practice' (Winkler, 1988, p. 41, as translated by Gabriel Thomas), social pedagogy retains this breadth of action and ambition today. It can be described variously as where education and care meet, as being concerned with children's upbringing, as a broadly educational approach to social problems, as education that takes place in everyday lives, in short as 'education in its broadest sense' (Cameron and Moss, 2011, p. 8). Social pedagogy, while a widespread discipline in Continental Europe and beyond (see, e.g., Kornbeck and Ucer, 2015 for social pedagogy in Latin America), takes a distinct form in each country, so the culture of Danish early childhood services might be summed up as Danish social pedagogic (Kornbeck and Jensen, 2009).

Some sense of the significance of a social pedagogic identity for Danish early childhood services can be found in results from a research study undertaken by Jytte Juul Jensen, a Danish researcher using SOPHOS, the Second Order Phenomenological Observation Scheme (Hansen and Jensen, 2004), a method inspired by Tobin et al. (1989), then developed further in an EU-funded project *Care Work in Europe: Current Understandings and Future Directions* (Cameron and Moss, 2007). In this study, focus groups of Danish pedagogues and others involved with pedagogical work were shown half-hour films of everyday life and practice in early childhood centres in Denmark, England and Hungary. The films pose an open question to the focus groups: What do you think when you see this? And through their responses to this question, what the viewers of the films talk about and discuss, what might be called 'the provocation of the film', it is possible to investigate and create a picture of their understandings, values and ideals of pedagogical practice (Jensen, 2011). The method of SOPHOS, therefore, provides one way of investigating the culture of early childhood services in particular countries.

Jensen is at pains to emphasize that the research is not a comparative study of practice in three countries but rather:

> A study into *Danish understandings* of good pedagogical work using films of practice from other countries (and also Denmark) to provoke discussion and reflection; the films could, of course, be used in the same way to study understandings of good work in any country. So it is important to bear in mind that the Danish pedagogues' understandings do not necessarily tell us something about English and Hungarian practice. Rather, *they say something about how these practices are interpreted through Danish eyes*. Through the practice of other countries and Danish practice viewed on film, as well as their professional knowledge and experiences, the pedagogues formulate and articulate how they view good practice. (Jensen, 2011, p. 143, emphasis added)

What the Danish viewers see in the films, their cultural perspective, is that the early childhood centre filmed in each country has its own peculiar logic, what the researcher characterizes, respectively, as 'childhood', 'pre-school' and 'home/family' logic. And in making the statements they do about the Danish, English and Hungarian films, the Danish viewers reflect, directly and indirectly, their national culture: the constructions, rationalities and practices that are valued in their society, their understanding from their perspective of what constitutes good work:

> They saw the Danish institutional logic as a 'childhood logic', where an underpinning idea is that children are experts in their own lives. The aim assumed by this rationality is children's acquisition of experiences and experiences gained by children on their own terms. The staff role includes the pedagogue viewing the child as a playing and participating child. The interaction between children and adults takes place by way of respectful relations with dialogic communications ('appreciative relations'). The pace, rhythm and atmosphere in day-to-day life are characterized by absorption in certain activities, unpredictability and humour. (Jensen, 2011, p. 146)

In contrast, the Danish viewers saw a 'pre-school logic' in the film of the English centre, with a school rationality in control of practice: the aims and objectives are understood as formal teaching and learning and the role of the staff is that of a pre-school teacher who views the children as learning children. While in the film of the Hungarian centre, the informants found an institutional logic characterized by the good family life/home and where an image of the good family or home shapes the practice; the role of the staff is the careful 'mother' and educator who sees before her, in part at least, a fragile child, and the pace, rhythm and atmosphere are characterized by regularity, order and calmness.

Jensen, the Danish researcher, notes that one reason for the differences that the Danish viewers see between the three nursery settings is *kropslighed*, a Danish word expressing a very important concept in Danish pedagogy, which can best be translated in English as 'the use and expression of the body'. The pedagogues find that both children and adults show few expressions of *kropslighed* in the English and Hungarian films. One informant, an academic in the field of pedagogy, put it this way:

> You can say that the children have their body in a different way in the Danish film, and the pedagogues as well. The children's bodies are much more present. The body is allowed to be there . . . Nursing of the body is a focal point in [the Hungarian film] and one way or the other the body has been reduced to a head in the English film. (Jensen, 2011, p. 150)

The Case of Sweden

As already indicated, early childhood services in Sweden differ from Denmark's in having a clear educational identity and culture. The graduate part of the workforce are 'pre-school teachers'[3] and the whole system is (since 1996) the responsibility of the national education ministry, with a curriculum introduced in 1998 and revised in 2010. The heads of pre-schools have the same title as heads of schools: *skolledare* (school leaders).

However, the educational culture in Sweden shares with Denmark's social pedagogic culture a holistic approach to early childhood services, the Swedish pre-school curriculum specifying that '[a]ctivities [in the pre-school] should be based on a holistic view of the child and his or her needs and be designed so that care, socialisation and learning together form a coherent whole' (Skolverket, 2010, p. 4). Moreover, adopting an educational identity does not mean that the Swedish pre-school is simply a junior version of compulsory school. In a paper prepared for a government commission in 1994 (Dahlberg and Lenz

Taguchi, 1994), two Swedish researchers explored the relationship between early childhood and compulsory education, identifying significant differences in what might be termed their culture. Central to this analysis is the significance of each sector's traditions, both to their current ways of working and to any prospect of changed relationships. In this respect, they pay particular attention to the social construction of the child inscribed in each tradition. For as they emphasize, 'the child is always a social construction and not the actual child'.

Developing this theme, Dahlberg and Lenz Taguchi argue that early childhood services and compulsory school have two separate and opposing constructions of the child – 'the child as nature' and 'the child as a re-producer of culture and knowledge'. The 'child as nature', or 'the scientific child', in the early childhood tradition, draws both on Enlightenment thinkers such as Rousseau and on psychological theories, in particular child development. Subsequently, Dahlberg has described this image of the child as 'an essential being of universal properties and inherent capabilities whose development is viewed as an innate "natural" process – biologically determined, following general laws . . . [in] a standard sequence of biological stages that constitute a path to full realization' (Dahlberg et al., 2007, p. 46). Inscribed with this construction, the early childhood tradition values 'a holistic view of the child; free play and creativity, giving rise to free and self-confident people; free expression of ideas and feelings; fun; and the here-and-now' (Dahlberg and Lenz Taguchi, cited in Moss, 2013, p. 22).

By contrast, the tradition in the Swedish compulsory school, despite its international reputation as relatively child-centred, is 'dominated by the reproduction of the prevailing culture and knowledge', and hence a social construction of the child as a 're-producer of culture and knowledge' (Dahlberg and Lenz Taguchi, cited in Moss, 2013, p. 22). With this construction, the child is 'understood as starting life with and from nothing – as an empty vessel or tabula rasa . . . [needing] to be filled with knowledge, skills and dominant cultural values which are already determined, socially determined and ready to administer – a process of reproduction or transmission' (Dahlberg et al., 2007, p. 44). This construction places greater emphasis on the future and economic life. The school is subject-centred, with the goal of learning through the transfer of concrete subject knowledge. Subjects are mostly decided and organized by others, and not the children, in contrast to the 'pre-school's tradition of child-centredness, where the ideal is that the child, as much as possible, should choose the contents and forms of expression' (Dahlberg and Lenz Taguchi, cited in Moss, 2013, p. 23).

It should not, however, be assumed from this analysis that pre-schools in Sweden – or in other countries for that matter – are all the same. For despite a uniform structure, there is considerable diversity in culture, due in large part to the adoption of different educational perspectives. One influencing many pre-schools is the early childhood education that has developed since the early 1960s in the Italian city of Reggio Emilia, and which 'has become an important and extensive source of inspiration for the Swedish preschool' (Korpi, 2007, p. 66).

The Case of Reggio Emilia

Italian early childhood services are split between a near universal education provision for 3- to 6-year-olds, under the national education ministry; and a less developed system of childcare services for children under 3 years, until recently under the national health ministry. While the former is free and staffed by a graduate workforce, the latter requires parental contributions and relies on less well-qualified staffing. It is a classic 'split' system, with 'education' the senior partner to 'childcare', and has much in common structurally with systems in countries such as Belgium, France and Spain.

Yet beneath the structural system lies great cultural diversity, going back to the 1960s. Then, faced by an early childhood education dominated by the Catholic Church and the state's reluctance to offer a public alternative, many local authorities (*comuni*), overwhelmingly left-wing and mostly in northern regions such as Emilia-Romagna, decided to take responsibility for the education of their young children and introduced their own services in what has been described as a 'municipal school revolution' (Catarsi, 2004, p. 8). While each *comune* had its own pedagogical identity, many shared a range of cultural features, and all provided a challenge to established Church schools and to the state-run schools that were eventually introduced after legislation in 1966. These culture conflicts were manifested in terminology. Early childhood services for children from 3 to 6 years were originally known as *scuole materne*, with a clear connotation of being welfare-oriented and substituting for mothers, with staff expected to display motherly qualities; the term fitted comfortably with the ideology of church-run schools. But *comuni* participating in the 'municipal school revolution' wanted to develop a different concept for their services, as places that were neither home-like nor motherly, but were instead clearly understood as primarily for children and places of education, a role expressed through the term *scuola dell'infanzia*. After many years of struggle, the *scuola dell'infanzia* eventually won out, being adopted by national government in their 1991 curriculum guidelines.

A leading player in the municipal revolution was the city of Reggio Emilia, whose system today numbers 47 schools for children from 0 to 6 years (most run by the *comune* itself, the remainder by co-operatives with agreements with the city), an unusual example of radical democratic or progressive education that has survived for many years. In fact, it has done more than survive, and has continued to evolve and become world-famous, visited by numerous people each year and reaching many others through Reggio Emilia's travelling exhibition, 'The Hundred Languages of Childhood'. As in Sweden, these services have come to influence the culture of many others.

A central figure in the evolution of Reggio Emilia's early childhood services was Loris Malaguzzi (1920–1994), the Director of the city's services from their inception in 1964. Malaguzzi was unusual in acknowledging and indeed insisting upon the importance of the cultural dimension of services. Most famously, he insisted that all education should be based on the social constructionist question – 'What is your image of the child?'.

> A declaration [about the image of the child] is not only a necessary act of clarity and correctness, it is the necessary premise for any pedagogical theory, and any pedagogical project ... The absurd thing is that this explicit public declaration of the identity of the child, which is the proper and unavoidable premise on which to base our theoretical foundation when starting work, is quite unusual in a world more usually unclear and dominated by praxis (or at any rate doing) without the need for prior references. (Malaguzzi, 2016a, p. 374)

Malaguzzi was very clear about his image: the 'rich child', born with a 'hundred languages', seeking to make and capable of making meaning of the world from the very beginning of life, a co-constructor of knowledge and identity and a citizen with rights:

> We [in Reggio] say all children are rich, there are no poor children. All children whatever their culture, whatever their lives are rich, better equipped, more talented, stronger, and more intelligent than we can suppose . . . The rich children are those requesting rich intelligence in others, rich curiosity in others, a very high and advanced capacity for fantasy, imagination, learning and culture in others. (Malaguzzi, 2016b, p. 397)

Working with this image (and images of the educator, parent and school), and with a bundle of articulated values, Malaguzzi and the schools of Reggio Emilia developed a distinctive body of pedagogical theory and practice, forming a distinctive culture of education that has proven appealing and inspiring to many others.

But Malaguzzi was more than a thinker and gifted practitioner. He was an administrator who built up a strong system that was able to survive his death in 1994. Above all, he understood the need for structure, as a necessary condition to support and sustain culture. The main features of Reggio's structure are set out in a 1972 document, the *Regolamento delle scuole comunali dell'infanzia* (The Rule Book for municipal schools). Based on an integrated 0–6 system situated within education, the *Regolamento* included: a support system for schools, consisting of a team of psychologists and pedagogistas; the provision in schools of *ateliers* and *atelieristas* (art workshops and educators with an arts qualification); two teachers per group to support collegial working; time and resources for regular professional development; and attention given to architecture and design of environments. Schools were to be managed by elected committees consisting of parents, teachers and local citizens, an expression of the importance attached to democracy as a fundamental value pervading all aspects of Reggio Emilia's project, an expression too of the importance of structure – but structure always serving the interests of culture.

WHY DO WE HAVE THE STRUCTURE/CULTURE DIVIDE IN THE COMPARATIVE STUDY OF EARLY CHILDHOOD SERVICES? AND DOES IT MATTER?

The structure of early childhood services has received far more attention than their culture, at least at a comparative level when it comes to looking across two or more countries to identify and explain similarities and differences. The comparative study of structures is far advanced both in quantity and in the development of methods, classificatory systems and understanding of issues, though there is always room for improvement. The comparative study of cultures is, however, in its infancy, while there are, to the best of my knowledge, no attempts made as yet to undertake comparative studies of early childhood services that pay equal attention to structure and culture and examine in depth their inter-connectedness. To pick up an earlier analogy, we seem to know a lot comparatively about the containers, but little about what is inside, and even less about how the outer forms and the inner contents of services relate to each other.

At one level this state of affairs simply reflects contemporary academic specialism and the splits that exist between disciplines. The comparative study of structures tends to be the domain of one group of researchers drawn from fields such as social policy or social welfare; while aspects of culture appeal more to groups drawn from fields such as education, pedagogy, psychology, philosophy or children's studies. Doubtless there is an element of self-selection: those whose personal proclivities attract them to the broad sweep of comparing structures are less attracted to the finer-grained study of cultural elements, and vice versa.

Perhaps there is another factor in the structure/culture divide. A focus on structure can more readily feed into prevalent discourses of 'best practice' and 'what works', and the hope that an example from abroad can be transferred and run successfully elsewhere. Structures, in short, can seem to be more tangible, describable, measurable, manageable, and therefore apparently 'policy relevant' and reproducible. The study of culture, however, tends to profound scepticism about transferability and reproducibility. Without denigrating the study of structures, there is no doubt that the study of culture is more complex, messier it might perhaps be said, as the examples above show. It insists on the contextual embeddedness of ideas and practices, is drawn to the singularity of the local, and highlights the complex interconnectedness of things. It leads into areas that are intangible, often hard to comprehend, not least because culture may well involve linguistic understandings that are not readily translated, and therefore not readily explained and certainly not measured, a point to which I return shortly. In neoliberal times, besotted by technical practice, instrumentality and economistic thinking, it is hardly surprising that the study of culture in early childhood services is not a priority for funding.

Does any of this matter? What, if anything, do we lose by the structure/culture divide in, for example, political discussions and academic enquiry? Yes and a lot I would answer. Structure matters, but by itself gives only a partial picture of early childhood services in any country and provides a very limited basis for comparisons; it may obfuscate as much as it illuminates. An exclusive focus on structure presents an unavoidably thin description, and at worst can lead to simplified classifications and groupings, overlooking some underlying similarities and some not instantly apparent dissimilarities. Thus, the centrality of social pedagogy in Denmark (and its similarity, in this respect, to a country like Germany) is at risk of being rendered invisible, just as is the recalcitrant municipal culture in Italy, and its influence (as opposed to that of Italy as a nation) on other countries such as Sweden.

So, to secure a full, thick description, to make deep and nuanced comparisons, to ensure the full visibility of differences and similarities, equal attention needs to be given to structure and culture. But that is easier said than done, and leads me to my last question.

HOW MIGHT WE MAKE COMPARATIVE STUDIES OF CULTURE IN EARLY CHILDHOOD SERVICES?

There is a case for proposing a moratorium on comparative work on the structural dimension of early childhood services. We know a lot already and this facet has got well in advance of the comparative study of culture. Perhaps one institution (a university or an international non-governmental organization or INGO) could be tasked with pulling together and maintaining a database on the structural features of early childhood services among (at the least) member states of the EU; other countries might be added as information and resources permit.

Research attention could then be concentrated on the comparative study of the cultural dimension of early childhood services and the relationship between structural and cultural dimensions. That will undoubtedly mean developing methods for delving into the complexities and hidden recesses of culture. One method with much potential has already been referred to: SOPHOS. Developed specifically as a method for the comparative study of understandings of work in services for children, young people and adults,[4] the method was used not only to compare Danish responses to early childhood services in three countries, but also to study the responses of early childhood workers in the other two countries (Hungary and England), providing an initial comparative exploration of national understandings of 'good work'. The use of film as a means to explore the implicit and taken-for-granted aspects of culture has great potential.

Film might also be used not so much as a provocation but as one form of documentation that, alongside other forms of documentation, might be subjected to various forms of analysis and interpretation, using it to explore the values, understandings and practices that constitute culture in different early childhood services. For example, policy documents subjected to Critical Discourse Analysis might provide rich insights not only into structure but also culture. While few, if any, will specifically speak of the image of the child that underlies structure and policy, most will be inscribed by a particular image, a particular social construction that might be made visible through the use of appropriate analytic tools.

Comparative work that attempts the hard task of addressing both structure and culture will need to be undertaken on a modest scale, perhaps initially working with just two or three countries – rather than the dozens that nowadays are often included in structural comparisons. Not only does much work need to be undertaken on developing methods for cultural analysis and for connecting the structural and cultural, but the exercise is, by its nature, time-consuming and complex. One further reason why this is so, and a key issue in comparative work of any kind on early childhood services, is language, an issue at once both vital and neglected.

We see, interpret and understand the world through language – it is an integral part of our positioning and the perspectives we adopt. Yet, the increasing dominance of English as a research language serves to reduce multiplicity and enhance homogeneity, making important aspects of culture increasingly invisible as researchers adopt English terms and concepts and, therefore, Anglo-American ways of understanding. Thus, to give a simple but significant example, 'social pedagogy' and 'pedagogue' have often been incorrectly translated into English as 'education' and 'teacher', so making the Other into the Same and nullifying a long-established tradition and profession. Or to take another example referred to earlier, translation into English loses the political significance of the different Italian terms for services for 3- to 6-year-olds: *scuola materna* and *scuola dell'infanzia*.

This trend towards the hegemony of the English language attracts little critical attention, not least from its main beneficiaries, native English speakers, who too often take it for granted that everything translates readily and perfectly into English. Moreover, in these hegemonic conditions, native English speakers can avoid questioning the meanings inscribed in taken-for-granted terms widely used in their own language, such as 'day care' and 'childcare'. It is rare to find anyone in the world of early childhood or other social research raising questions about the issue of language, the dominance of English and the implications of the linguistic position adopted for research purposes. So these comments from the multi-lingual Austrian scholar Walter Lorenz, commenting on the experience of participating in a cross-national European project, are not only trenchant but unusual. He argues that cross-national projects, for resource, time and other pragmatic reasons, usually end up adopting English as a common language. A major drawback of this compromise is the failure to explore different cultural understandings, expressed through language, and which often become apparent through the experience of non-comprehension that necessitates:

> Clarifying terminology so that it can be used reliably by interpreters and shared among all participants. This seems to hold up the works, those representing lesser spoken languages come to regard this as their personal problem, their personal deficit, and the whole language project is tilted and distorted. And yet, *it would be precisely the non-understanding which could give us the most valuable clues to differences in meaning*, to the need for further clarification of familiar terms and concepts, to the transformation of taken-for-granted perspectives into creative, shared knowledge. (Lorenz, 1999, pp. 20–21, emphasis added)

It seems to me that comparative work on early childhood services – not only cultural but also structural – needs to give priority to the language issue and the English problem. This means, at the very least, working with key terms in the language of the country being studied, ensuring there is 'enough time and space to explore the subtleties of discovering meaning through non-comprehension', and agreeing conventions about what types of words should not be translated into English but retained in their original form (with either a glossary provided for such words and/or an extended footnote discussing their meaning). If we are to be serious about comparative work, and especially its cultural dimension, then we have to be serious about language and meaning.

CONCLUSION

There are various rationales for the comparative study of services. For some there is a utilitarian belief that it will reveal ways to improve national performance. This has been especially true of the fixation on performativity in compulsory education, and can lead to simplistic and misleading conclusions and mistaken attempts at policy borrowing. For others, the attraction is academic knowledge, in particular mapping policies and service systems, creating and applying typologies, delving into causes and consequences, while understanding the strong contextual ties that anchor countries to particular approaches – so-called 'path dependency' – with the excitement of finding an occasional deviant example, a country that seems to turn away from its predetermined path. Yet for others, the main attraction of comparative work is that it acts as a profound provocation, a stimulus to thought and critique, helping as it can to reveal taken-for-granted assumptions and beliefs, unexamined practices and understandings, asserting that there are indeed always alternatives and so disturbing what Unger (2005) terms 'the dictatorship of no alternative'.

Structures can, of course, serve as provocations. When I place the early childhood services in Denmark or Sweden against the system in my own country, England, it triggers many questions. Why, for example, do we in England start children at school at 4 rather than 6? Why do we adopt a funding system heavily reliant on demand subsidies and parental fees, rather than on tax-based supply subsidies that treat early childhood services as public institutions similar to schools? Why do we in England think it acceptable to have a low-skilled and low-paid workforce in early childhood services, rather than one that is based on a relatively well-paid graduate worker?

But important as such structural provocations are, they are not enough. Comparative work on cultures raises a whole raft of new questions. To take just a few drawn from the examples given earlier: What is our image of the child? How do we understand good work? Why do we use the language we do to describe our services and the people who work in them, and with what consequences? Early childhood services, like all services for children and families, are complex institutions, a full understanding of which requires a bridging of the structure/culture divide based on a full recognition of their inter-connectedness and inter-dependency. We have hardly started that construction work.

NOTES

1. In fact, the border between early childhood services and compulsory schooling is becoming increasingly blurred, not only due to the 'schoolification' referred to below, but also as an increasing number of countries make it compulsory for children to attend at least one year in an early childhood service.
2. *Starting Strong* recognizes the significance of social constructions: 'social constructions of children, families and the purposes of ECEC [early childhood education and care] are reflected in how ECEC systems are envisaged and structured' (OECD, 2001, p. 43). I know of no other national or international policy documents, at least in the English language, which even refer to the social construction of childhood, let alone allot it any significance. It is also unusual in recognizing the existence and significance of social pedagogy in the early childhood services of some countries, a tradition and discipline discussed later on in this chapter.
3. The main form of provision in Sweden is a centre taking children from 12 months to 6 years and called a *Förskola* (literally 'pre-school'). By contrast, Denmark has both 'age-integrated institutions', which are in the majority, and age-specific services, either for children under 3 years (*vuggestue* or 'nursery') or for 3- to 6-year-olds (*børnehave* or 'kindergarten'). The structural analysis of the organization of services needs to be complemented by a cultural analysis of how they are named and the derivation of such terminology. I return to the significance of terminology in the section on Reggio Emilia.
4. In the project *Care Work in Europe*, SOPHOS was used in services for frail elderly people, as well as in early childhood services (Cameron and Moss, 2007).

REFERENCES

Cameron, C. and P. Moss (eds) (2007), *Care Work in Europe: Current Understandings and Future Directions*, London: Routledge.
Cameron, C. and P. Moss (2011), 'Social pedagogy: current understandings and opportunities', in C. Cameron and P. Moss (eds), *Social Pedagogy and Working with Young Children: Where Care and Education Meet*, London: Jessica Kingsley, pp. 7–32.
Catarsi, E. (2004), 'Loris Malaguzzi and the municipal school revolution', *Children in Europe*, 6, 8–9.
Dahlberg, G. and H. Lenz Taguchi (eds) (1994), *Förskola och skola – om två skilda traditioner och om visionen om en mötesplats* (Preschool and school – two different traditions and the vision of a meeting place), Stockholm: HLS Förlag.
Dahlberg, G., P. Moss, and A. Pence (eds) (2007), *Beyond Quality in Early Childhood Education and Care*, 2nd edn, London: Routledge.
European Commission Childcare Network (1988), *Childcare and Equality of Opportunity*, Unpublished report to the European Commission.
European Commission Childcare Network (1990), *Childcare in the European Communities, 1985–1990*, Brussels: European Commission Directorate-General V.
European Commission Childcare Network (1996), *A Review of Services for Young Children in the European Union 1990–95*, Brussels: European Commission Directorate-General V.
European Commission/EACEA/Eurydice/Eurostat (2014), *Key Data on Early Childhood Education and Care in Europe. 2014 Edition. Eurydice and Eurostat Report*, Luxembourg: Publications Office of the European Union.
Hansen, H.K. and J.J. Jensen (2004), *A Study of Understandings in Care and Pedagogical Practice: Experiences using the Sophos Model in Cross-national Studies*, Unpublished report from the 'Care Work in Europe' project.

Jensen, J. (2011), 'Understandings of Danish pedagogical practice', in C. Cameron and P. Moss (eds), *Social Pedagogy and Working with Children and Young People*, London: Jessica Kingsley, pp. 141–58.

Kaga, Y., J. Bennett, and P. Moss (eds) (2010), *Caring and Learning Together: A Cross-national Study on the Integration of Early Childhood Care and Education in Education*, Paris: UNESCO.

Kornbeck, J. and N.R. Jensen (eds) (2009), *The Diversity of Social Pedagogy in Europe*, Bremen: Europäisher Hochschulverlag.

Kornbeck, J. and X. Ucer (eds) (2015), *Latin American Social Pedagogy: Relaying Concepts, Values and Methods between Europe and the Americas?* Bremen: EHV Academic Press.

Korpi, B.M. (ed.) (2007), *The Politics of Preschool: Intentions and Decisions Underlying the Emergence and Growth of the Swedish Preschool*, Stockholm: Ministry of Education and Research.

Lorenz, W. (1999), 'The ECSPRESS approach: guiding the social professions between national and global perspectives', in *European Dimensions in Training and Practice of Social Professions*, Boskovice: Verlag ALBERT, pp. 13–28.

Malaguzzi, L. (2016a), 'An interview with Loris Malaguzzi, 1990', in P. Cagliari et al. (eds), *Loris Malaguzzi and the Schools of Reggio Emilia: A Selection of his Writings and Speeches, 1945–93*, London: Routledge, pp. 374–88.

Malaguzzi, L. (2016b), 'Speech by Loris Malaguzzi at international conference "Who am I then? Tell me that first". Knowledges in dialogue to guarantee citizenship to the rights and potentials of children and adults, 1990', in P. Cagliari et al. (eds), *Loris Malaguzzi and the Schools of Reggio Emilia: A Selection of his Writings and Speeches, 1945–93*, London: Routledge, pp. 388–400.

Morris, P. (2016), *Education Policy, Cross-national Tests of Pupil Achievement, and the Pursuit of World Class Schooling: A Critical Analysis*, London: UCL Institute of Education Press.

Moss, P. (2013), 'The relationship between early childhood and compulsory education: a properly political question', in P. Moss (ed.), *Early Childhood and Compulsory Education: Reconceptualising the Relationship*, London: Routledge, pp. 2–49.

Moss, P. (ed.) (2014), *Transformative Change and Real Utopias in Early Childhood Education: A Story of Democracy, Experimentation and Potentiality*, London: Routledge.

Oberhuemer, P., I. Schreyer, and M.J. Neuman (2010), *Professionals in Early Childhood Education and Care Systems*, Opladen: Barbara Budrich.

OECD (Organisation for Economic Co-operation and Development) (2001), *Starting Strong: Early Childhood Education and Care*, Paris: OECD.

OECD (Organisation for Economic Co-operation and Development) (2006), *Starting Strong II: Early Childhood Education and Care*, Paris: OECD.

Plantenga, J. and C. Remery (2009), *The Provision of Childcare Services: A Comparative Review of 30 European Countries*, Luxembourg: Publications Office of the European Union.

Skolverket (2010), *Curriculum for the Preschool Lpfö 98, Revised 2010*, accessed 11 January 2016 at http://www.skolverket.se/om-skolverket/publikationer/visa-enskild-publikation?_xurl_=http%3A%2F%2Fwww5.skolverket.se%2Fwtpub%2Fws%2Fskolbok%2Fwpubext%2Ftrycksak%2FBlob%2Fpdf2704.pdf%3Fk%3D2704.

Tobin, J., D.Y. Yu, and D.H. Davidson (1989), *Preschool in Three Cultures: China, Japan and the United States*, New Haven, CT: Yale University Press.

Unger, R.M. (ed.) (2005), *What Should the Left Propose?* London: Verso.

Winkler, M. (1988), *Eine Theorie der Sozialpädogik*, Stuttgart: Klett-Cotta.

4. Family and state obligation: the contribution to family policy studies
Jane Millar

INTRODUCTION

Family obligations can be defined and understood in different ways. First, family obligations are moral obligations, they are what we believe it is right to do in a particular situation. Second, family obligations are everyday life in practice, they are what we do in our families to support and care for each other. Third, family obligations are external requirements, they are what law and public policy define as the rights and duties of family members to each other.

Family obligations – in all three senses – reflect our underlying values and norms and our expectations and assumptions about self, family and society. As such, they are not fixed and unchanging but can be dynamic and fluid, particularly at times of rapid social and economic change. The balance between the obligations of individuals to provide for themselves, family members to provide for each other, and governments to replace, supplement or enforce family support, is central to family policy, implicitly and explicitly.

This chapter explores the concept of family obligations in the field of family policy research. The section that follows revisits the 'Family Obligations in Europe' research project, which studied these issues in the early 1990s (Millar and Warman, 1996), and explores developments since then. The next section examines the relationship between the social policy context and the everyday practices of care and support within families. The following section considers the experience of receiving family support, particularly for people in poverty, where the values of reciprocity, autonomy and privacy may come under challenge.

FAMILY OBLIGATIONS IN EUROPE: FROM THE EARLY 1990s

The 'Family Obligations in Europe' study, which ran from 1994 to 1996, was stimulated by three main issues or developments. First, there were the substantial and often quite rapid changes in family and employment apparent across many industrialised countries, including the Western European countries that were covered in the research.[1] These included patterns of later marriage, smaller families, more marital breakdown, more cohabitation, and more people living longer and living alone. These family changes were happening alongside changes in employment including higher rates of unemployment, less secure full-time work, more women in employment and in particular more mothers staying in, or returning to, work after shorter breaks for childbearing. These developments were seen to be putting strains on the existing welfare state provision in many countries and were also creating new needs and demands, particularly care demands.

The second impetus for the project, therefore, came from the emergence of more explicit 'family policy' in a number of countries. Family policy can, of course, be defined in various different ways (see also Chapter 2 by Gauthier and Koops and Chapter 5 by Lohmann and Zagel in this volume). The distinction made by Kamerman and Kahn (1978) between explicit and implicit family policy had drawn attention to the fact that, at one level, all social policy has an impact on families, whether intended or not. But, as Kamerman and Kahn discussed, there are specific policies that are aimed at supporting families, and also at changing or influencing family behaviour. These policies are interventions, in various different ways and to various different ends, in the caring and financial relationships within families, with implications across gender and generations. Family policy was developing rapidly in a number of European countries during the 1980s and 1990s and becoming more central to the welfare state endeavour (see also Chapter 2 by Gauthier and Koops in this volume).

Third, it was the work of Finch (1989) on 'family obligations and social change' and Finch and Mason (1993) on 'negotiating family responsibilities' that inspired the specific focus of the research. Their research explored the changing meaning and nature of family responsibility in the context of family change. Their empirical study of British families found a high degree of family support in practice but that this was not a consequence of feelings of absolute duty or obligation towards family members, rather it was a complex product of relationships that develop over time, involving notions of reciprocity, reputation and fairness. They noted that gender was fundamental to the patterns of family responsibility with women and men giving and receiving different types and amounts of care. However, this was not so much because of different views or values between women and men, but because of the way such responsibilities and exchanges develop through interactions over time. Thus, women were much more likely to be 'locked into the set of commiments that entail giving time and labour' (Finch and Mason, 1993, p. 169). This research highlighted the importance of exploring the meaning of family obligations in the lived experience of family members and the context in which these dynamics were taking place.

This view of family obligations as negotiated rather than fixed suggested that striking the right balance between family support and state provision would be an important challenge in the development of family policy at a time of social and economic change. Comparing this balance across countries would thus provide a way of exploring the cultural values underpinning policy, and highlight how social policy provisions both assume certain configurations of gender and generation and at the same time help to create these.

The aim of the 'Family Obligations' project was therefore to describe and compare the ways in which family obligations were being defined in policy in different countries. The focus was on cash (obligations to financially support another person) and care (obligations to look after another person) and evidence was collected from a network of research colleagues covering three key periods in the family life-course: partnering, parenting and caring for adult dependents. The aim was to explore not just the formal elements in the provisions but also the assumptions and normative expectations that underpin different approaches to policy. So, for example, the project looked at the rules defining eligibility for provisions such as social assistance benefits, survivor's benefits, elderly and childcare services, and also at the ways in which local discretion and professional judgement operated in practice. The main methods were through a detailed pro-forma for each country, combined with the use of policy vignettes intended to draw out what would happen in various scenarios, and – very importantly – several meetings of the research teams from all 16 countries, to discuss and clarify the emerging analysis.

In the report we identified three broad groupings of countries: those where obligations are minimal and provisions are mainly directed towards the individual (Denmark, Finland, Norway and Sweden); those where obligations are placed on members of the nuclear family, mainly downwards from parents to children but also upwards from adult children to elderly parents (Austria, Belgium, France, Germany, Ireland, Luxembourg, the Netherlands and the UK); and those where obligations are placed on members of the extended family (Portugal, Spain, Italy and Greece). This clustering of countries was based on the overall policy approach at the time, although it was also noted that policy in many countries seemed to be in a period of development and change. This was highlighted in three areas in particular.

First, the research pointed to a weakening of marriage as an institutional relationship recognised in policy and to the growing importance of parenthood. In most countries, especially in Southern Europe, marriage did retain something of a special status and protection in law and policy. But everywhere there was evidence of a distinct shift towards parenthood as the focus of policy. Parenthood was increasingly being defined as giving rise to unconditional obligations. These obligations were reaching beyond childhood itself into young adulthood, and sometimes even further, and were usually not dependent on the marital status of the parents.

This trend towards the importance of parenthood can be seen in family policy in the years since the Family Obligations study, with the increase in levels of childcare services and parental leave provisions (see below, and also Chapter 8 by Rostgaard on childcare policies and Chapter 10 by Thévenon on leave policies in this volume). However, the complexity of family life, and multiple family transitions, raises difficulties for policy measures which are primarily focused on parenthood. This is particularly the case in respect of the financial responsibilities of divorced or never-married parents towards their children. As Meyer and Skinner (2016) note, most countries have developed systems for defining the financial obligations of the resident and the non-resident biological parent. However, when further family transitions are involved, through subsequent partnerships being formed and breaking up, this may lead to different expectations about where financial responsibility can, and should, lie. They looked at 12 countries[2] and found only one example (Wisconsin, USA) where biology remained the absolute condition regardless of any other family transitions or residence. At the other side, in two countries (Sweden and the Netherlands) it was the residence rather than the biological relationship that was absolute. For the others biological parenthood was modified in some way to recognise transitions and residence arrangements. As Meyer and Skinner note, the level of family complexity is not lessening and this is true not just in the industrialised countries. Thus, they conclude that 'child maintenance schemes developed in periods of relative stability may need to be re-examined to see if they are still appropriate in contemporary circumstances' (Meyer and Skinner, 2016, p. 92).

Daly (2015a) and colleagues have been exploring the development of 'parenting support' as forming a more explicit element in family policy in recent years (see also Chapter 12 by Knijn, Martin and Ostner and Chapter 26 by Daly in this volume). Parenting support is defined as measures aimed at assisting parents to carry out their child-rearing roles, including programmes intended to change parenting behaviour. Examples of such policies are identified across their five-country[3] study. These policies – the education and re-education of parents – could be interpreted as meaning an increased 'intrusion by the state into private life and a more intense engagement on the part of the state with the conduct of family life' (Daly, 2015b, p. 606). The 'turn to parenting' implies a re-drawing of the boundaries between state and family, in particular in relation to the privacy and autonomy of parents. However, as Daly also points out, there is much complexity and contradiction in these developments and this is an area where ongoing research will be important to understand the direction of travel and the implications for family/state obligations.

Second, some of the significant shifts identified by the Family Obligations project were changes in practice, often at the local level, which made these harder to identify and track. This highlighted the importance of looking at both policy and implementation in understanding the implications of state provision on family relationships and family solidarity. This is also the conclusion of Kuronen et al. (2014) in their study of the relationship between women's labour market integration and three aspects of public policy (childcare services, support for care of the elderly and lifelong learning). They conclude that local variation is particularly important in relation to childcare provision, which also varies significantly according to age of children.

Third, the study noted a general trend towards the introduction of cash benefits or payments to support those carrying out caring roles. This included cash payments in respect of care of children, dependent adults with long-term health and disability, and elderly people with care needs. They can include payments that enable people to buy care in the market (for example, childcare subsidies or vouchers) as well as payments to enable family members to be full-time carers (for example, maternity and parental leave and benefits). A number of cross-national projects have charted the development of this area of family support policy and provision, and the implications for families. Saraceno (2011) provides an overview of childcare policies in European countries and discusses the implications for gender roles of different configurations or approaches. For example, in relation to parental leave, the specific measures that are available make a significant difference to gender equity outcomes. Thus, long periods of parental leave with low compensation tend to be taken by women more than men; if women take long leave it can be hard to re-enter the labour market; men will be more likely to take leave if there is no option to transfer it to their partner; and flexible and part-time provisions can support more gender-equal arrangements in families. Le Bihan and Martin (2012) examine the care arrangements for elderly parents made by working families, using in-depth interviews in four countries (the Netherland, Italy, Portugal and France), setting this within the context of national and local policy and provision. They conclude that that there is a process of diversification, with a range of policy instruments, and so some blurring between family-led and service-led approaches.

Payments to family carers put care relationships within families on a different basis, involving a different form of reciprocity within the family, as well as a different relationship between the family carer and the state. For example, Frericks et al. (2014) examine the legal and institutional frameworks for elderly care in the Netherlands, Germany and Denmark. These countries all have provisions whereby elderly people can choose a family member as a paid carer (although whether these are offered or used in practice may vary).

The extent to which these family carers themselves have social rights (as workers) varies, with much less social protection for paid family carers in Germany and the Netherlands compared with Denmark. Different forms of payments for care thus have very different implications for family relationships and in particular for gender roles.

FAMILIALISATION/DE-FAMILIALISATION

Saraceno and Keck (2008, 2010), and their colleagues in the 'Multilinks' project, provide the most comprehensive recent study of the policy framing of inter-generational family obligations across Europe and beyond. They develop a framework based on the concept of 'de-familialisation'. This was developed as a parallel to Epsing-Andersen's (1990) 'de-commodification' concept. As the latter refers to the extent to which social policy measures reduce the dependency on the market, so the concept of de-familialisation refers to the extent to which social policy measures reduce dependency on the family. This focuses attention onto the social entitlements of women, and the extent to which women's unpaid care in the family is substituted for by paid care, primarily through state but also through private care. However, Saraceno and Keck take this further than a simple dichotomy between familialisation and de-familialisation (or individualisation). They argue that it is important to distinguish between familialistic outcomes that are a result of specific measures to support family care (for example, cash benefits for family carers) and those where the outcomes are a result of lack of alternatives (no public support to replace family care). They thus identify three main models:

1. Familialism by default, or unsupported familialism, where there is no publicly provided alternatives to family care and financial support.
2. Supported familialism, where financial transfers in particular support families to provide inter-generational financial and caring responsibilities.
3. De-familialism, where the individualisation of social rights substantially reduces family responsibilities and dependencies.

They separately consider responsibilities towards children and towards adults, and show that these are not necessarily defined in the same way within the same country. In fact, within countries they find a combination of the three policy models outlined above with regard to both children and adults. A cluster analysis failed to identify clear boundaries between groups of countries, but some patterns did emerge. The Scandinavian countries and France are distinguished by a high degree of defamilisation, but with supported familialism as regards the care of young children. There is also a group of countries with a high degree of familialisation by default (Poland, Italy, Spain, Greece and Bulgaria, and in part, Latvia and Slovakia) but these countries also have elements of supported familialism. The remaining countries provide a very mixed picture. Thus, overall, Saraceno and Keck conclude that there is a convergence with regard to support for young children, with countries generally providing a mixture of supported familialism (parental leaves and child benefits) and partial de-familialisation, but that the care needs of the elderly are less recognised as a public responsibility than those of children. This focus on children can be seen as part of a general shift towards 'social investment' in welfare state provision, with potential implications for both socio-economic (Cantillon, 2011) and gender (Williams, 2010; Saraceno, 2015) divisions.

The research considered so far has concentrated on Europe. But the concepts of family solidarity and familialisation have also been considered as having resonance more widely around the world. In particular, there are links to the Confucian value systems and the concept of a specific Confucian welfare regime in East Asian countries. Chau and Yu (2013) and Yu et al. (2015) explore these ideas and compare four East Asian countries (Hong Kong, Taiwan, South Korea and Singapore) with 18 Organisation for Economic Co-operation and Development (OECD) countries. They make a useful distinction between what they term 'economic de-familisation' (women's economic freedom from the family) and 'care-focused familisation' (the family's freedom from the caring responsibilities). However, although they do recognise links with the Confucian concept of filial obligation and responsibility, and that there are familialistic measures in these countries, they do not find evidence of a specific East Asian welfare regime type of de-familialisation.

As noted above, private markets (and not just the state) can also provide a route to de-familialisation, if families have the means and desire to buy in care in order to replace their own care time. Thus, the development of private care markets, including the use of migrant labour to replace family care, is also relevant to understanding changing patterns of family obligations. For example, Da Roit and Sabatinelli (2013) discuss the case of Italy, where family care remains the dominant model and where a private care market, which is only loosely regulated by government, has developed. Bettio et al. (2006) discuss the use of female migrant labour for family care work in Southern Europe and Da Roit and van Bochove (2015) explore the rise of migrant care work in the Netherlands. Clearly, access to private care markets is only available to families with sufficient financial resources to meet costs, even if these are low-paid jobs with little employment protection. The edited collection by Carbonnier and Morel (2015) examines the emerging private markets across many European countries in both care and household services more generally, and what this means for the relationships between welfare states and labour markets.

WHAT DO FAMILIES DO?

The studies we have considered so far have focused on the way in which policy frames, and is framed by, different expectations about family obligations. What, if anything, does this mean for what families actually do in practice? Families provide all sorts of material and practical support to each other across the life-course, with the level and type of support depending in part on factors such as gender, geographical proximity, health, employment status, relationship quality and available resources (Brandt and Deindl, 2013). But what is the relationship between state and family support? Does more state support mean less family support?

Family and State Support and Care: Crowding Out or Complementing?

Two main arguments have been put forward about how the welfare state influences these family obligations and inter-generational transfers. The first suggests a 'crowding out' or substitution – that if state provision exists, and particularly if the state provides either adequate or generous support, then family members will be released from obligations and will not be active in providing either cash or care. The second suggests a 'complementarity' – that the state and the family provide different sorts of support in different ways. For elderly people in need of care, for example, this could mean that high levels of state support do not necessarily mean that family members will do less, but that they will do different things. For parents caring for children, high levels of state support could enable and complement family care.

In general, the evidence from cross-national comparative studies tends to support the complementarity view. For example, the 'Old Age and Autonomy' (OASIS) project covered five countries – England, Germany, Israel, Norway and Spain – and combined survey data with in-depth interviews with adult children and elderly parents (Lowenstein and Ogg, 2003; Daatland and Lowenstein, 2005). This research found that obligation norms were strong but the preferred model was a combination of family and welfare state. They did find some evidence of slightly lower rates of family support in countries with high service levels, but that this was associated with availability rather than different views about family obligations. Thus, they concluded that there was a complementarity between services and families, and also that this provided the most effective and acceptable support:

> Older people receive a higher overall level of help and support in high-service countries compared to low-service countries, indicating that a partnership between services *and* families meets the needs of elders better than a family dominated care system. Services do *not* seem to discourage family help, and are more likely to help families spread their resources in meeting other needs. Services may even be a stimulant for intergenerational exchanges. (Lowenstein and Ogg, 2003, p. 15, emphases in original)

Similar conclusions have been reached from analysis of the 'Survey of Health, Ageing and Retirement in Europe' (SHARE) panel, which includes 13 European countries (Brandt et al., 2009; Haberkern and Szydlik, 2010; Brandt and Deindl, 2013) with a focus on adult children and elderly parents. Brandt and Deindl (2013) examined not just the existence of transfers but also their direction and intensity. They found high correlations between family and public transfers, supporting the complementarity hypothesis. However, in the less generous welfare states, there tend to be higher levels of intensive support, including co-residential care, for some families. In more generous welfare states there is less intensive support but just as much or more low-level ongoing support, such as practical help and small gifts. They conclude that a 'generous welfare state enables older people to play an active role in family life, even when children leave home and have their own families. State transfers permit parents to support their children not only in times of need, but also to help sporadically and transfer smaller financial gifts' (Brandt and Deindl, 2013, p. 249). Thus, the state can, by type and level of support, facilitate family solidarity and help to sustain reciprocity in family obligations.

Cross-national studies of the level and use of formal and informal childcare have also explored the relationship between expectations, state provision and family care. Janta (2014) provides an overview of childcare, parental leave and flexible working arrangements in Europe. This highlights the importance of informal – usually family, most commonly grandmothers – care across all countries. She notes that there are different levels of co-residence across three generations in the different countries of Europe. Such co-residence is rare in North and West Europe, but it is not uncommon in Southern, Central and Eastern Europe. This will mean different opportunities for, and therefore patterns of, everyday care across the generations.

Glaser et al. (2013) focused specifically on grandparent care using SHARE data from 11 European countries.[4] They distinguished between three types of care: intensive grandchild care (daily care or over 30 hours per week without parents present), non-intensive grandchild care (occasional care without parents present), and no grandchild care. They concluded that there is 'a close relationship between the family and care policy context and the likelihood that grandmothers are providing intensive childcare' (Glaser et al., 2013, p. 14) and identified three clusters of countries:

1. *No assumption that grandparents will provide care*: Sweden and Denmark, and (in part) France. These countries have high levels of childcare and good maternal benefits. Fewer grandmothers provide intensive childcare.
2. *An assumption that grandparents will provide care*: Hungary, Portugal and Spain (where this assumption is explicit) and Italy and Romania (where this is more implicit). These countries have few part-time jobs, limited formal childcare and only limited in-kind family benefits. More grandmothers provide intensive childcare.
3. *Neutral or mixed*: the UK, Germany and the Netherlands. These countries have some state support but less than universal. Mothers often work part time. Grandmothers have a middling role in both intensive childcare and occasional/less intensive childcare.

However, the authors also note that the policy environment is not the only factor in determining the level and extent of grandparent care. The level of maternal employment, and how much of that is full time or part time, is also important, as are attitudes to formal care. So, for example, grandparent care is most likely to be intensive and at high levels in countries where mothers are working long hours and there is very little state provision. But grandparent care is also likely to be intensive, although not at high levels, in countries where most mothers are not employed and there is a preference among mothers for family, as opposed to formal, care. Similarly, Pelikh and Tyndik (2014), in a comparison of preschool childcare use in Russia and Europe, found that the most important determinants of the use of formal childcare were women's employment, education, number and age of children. They also conclude that 'informal childcare complements the formal provision, but does not substitute for it' (Pelikh and Tyndik, 2014, p. 481).

These studies tend to confirm the importance of the distinction between different policy environments and their impact, alongside other factors, on what families do in relation to realising obligations in practice. The most individualist state policy models value and enable choice but do not crowd out ongoing, if less intensive, family solidarity in practice. The most familialistic state policy models, by design or default, reduce choice, which can mean heavy levels of extensive support and care falling on families. In general, for both adult care and childcare, there is a complex mix of public and family provision, with equally complex implications for family relationships and informal caring within families. There is no simple crowding out of family by state, but at the same time the nature, level and targeting of state provision do clearly have implications for what families do, and for how much choice they have. In practice, this often means how much choice women have, in particular in the most familialistic models, where gender role divisions tend to remain strong. All the empirical research shows that women are more likely to provide assistance and help than men, an ongoing reflection of how gender is an important element in shaping the lived practice of family obligations.

When making care decisions, the value that people attach to choice and autonomy is apparent, both in relation to care of the elderly (Simoni and Trifiletti, 2004) and in parental preferences for formal or informal care for their children (Janta, 2014). People like to be able to make choices, and do not like to be forced into dependent relationships. However, as we have seen, choice may be limited in practice and, even in the more generous welfare states, is arguably becoming more so, as political choices are made about how to respond and adapt to economic recession. Thus, a process of 're-familialisation' – whereby more obligations are transferred back to the family – may become more apparent. In the final section, we therefore turn to the issue of family obligations in the context of family poverty.

RECEIVING CARE AND SUPPORT: AUTONOMY, DEPENDENCY AND PRIVACY

The state of being in poverty is defined by a lack of material resources that are sufficient to meet needs. The experience of being in poverty includes that material hardship but also the feelings of failure, stigma and exclusion. Family and family obligations enter the frame in two main ways. First, as discussed above, the family is characterised by bonds of care and support including economic, social and domestic. In this sense, the family is the lived 'unit' of poverty, as it is the family that 'governs relationships and resource exchanges among people of different generations and genders' (Daly and Kelly, 2015, p. 2). But the family is not unitary: within the family people have different obligations, responsibilities and experiences of poverty, and possibly different routes to escape poverty. Thus, there has been increasing research interest in how people in families manage poverty in their everyday lives and how they define and manage family obligations under conditions of limited material resources.

Second, the wider family can be an important source of resources, support and help for people in poverty. The family, including the extended family, is the 'first line of defence' against the impact of poverty and indeed in some contexts, the only line of defence if there is limited or lacking state support and a weak or inaccessible charitable sector. So the extent to which people can call upon their families for help, and under what conditions, is an important aspect of the condition and experience of poverty. This approach focuses attention on understanding the nature of family solidarity and the obligations of families under circumstances of poverty (Martin, 2004).

There is no doubt that family care and support is a preference and a choice in many cases, whether it is young parents seeking help with childcare, or husbands and wives caring for their dependent partners, or elderly people relying on their adult children, not just for care but also for company. But, as we have seen, caring obligations are not unconditional but are embedded in social relationships. Whether people choose or not to give care (or cash or other forms of support) is one side of the equation. But on the other side is the question of whether people choose to receive such support and what it means for their family relationships. Here issues of reciprocity, autonomy, dependency and privacy come into the frame.

The experience of receiving family support can be difficult and uncomfortable for families living in poverty. Walker (2014) explores how part of 'the shame of poverty' is the feeling of failure to be able to meet family obligations and to reciprocate. This research includes rich and poor countries but, as Walker notes:

> The capabilities to which people aspire are remarkably similar across different cultures . . . Individuals desire resources sufficient to enable them to be good husbands, wives, partners, and parents, and reliable relatives, neighbours, citizens and workers . . . There is profound shame in being unable to provide for self and family, to reciprocate where needed, and to socialize and participate in community events. (Walker, 2014, p. 185)

Daly and Kelly (2015, p. 127), in their qualitative research on everyday family life in poverty in Northern Ireland, highlight the importance of 'family networks' in which 'a large volume of practical, emotional and small-scale financial support passes between members'. But they note that these networks are quite specific and limited – not all family members play a role, or are asked to play a role. People seek to choose, if they can, who to call upon, for what and when, and this is important for maintaining their dignity and autonomy.

Poor families also have to protect themselves against calls upon their resources that they cannot meet. Offer (2012) argues that what she calls the 'burden of reciprocity' may lead people living in poverty both to withdraw themselves from possible networks of support and to exclude others who are too much of a burden from their networks. Thus, a resistance to families being expected to do more to support each other in times of economic insecurity may come as much, or more, from the receiving as the giving side of the equation. The implications of expecting families with limited resources to provide for family members who might otherwise be expected to be (and themselves expect to be) financially independent may put heavy strain on family relationships and lead to less, not more, family solidarity. The 'austerity' policy agenda being pursued in some countries is thus likely to widen, rather than reduce, social divisions between and within families. Some of the effects will no doubt be hidden within families, as people continue to try and manage and cope without having to compromise their privacy and dignity.

CONCLUSION

In this chapter we have explored family obligations as framed by policy and in the everyday lives of families. This shows a complex picture of these relationships, with much cross-national variation. But a common thread is the enduring value attached to family solidarity, even in more individualised societies. The values of autonomy and independence are not necessarily incompatible with the values of care and support, and in everyday life are bridged by the value attached to reciprocity. Thus, as Simoni and Trifiletti (2004) conclude:

> People do not move between obligation and freedom, between taking a free ride and a completely altruistic attitude; rather, they need to make sense, personally, of responsibilities they decide to

take on by redefining 'normal' family obligations on the basis of their personal experience. The task of support services should be that of eliciting and facilitating specific social practices which make sense for those involved and safeguard their relationships and connectedness. (p. 701)

Designing social policy with an explicit recognition of the way in which policy can impact on family obligations may thus be the best way to promote family solidarity and support, as well as providing a means to reduce the social divisions between families and gender divisions within families.

NOTES

1. Sixteen countries, comprising the Eueopean Union membership at the time plus Norway, Austria, Belgium, Denmark, Finland, France, Germany, Greece, Ireland, Italy, Luxembourg, Netherlands, Norway, Portugal, Spain, Sweden and the UK.
2. Australia, Austria, Canada, Denmark, Finland, Germany, the Netherlands, New Zealand, Norway, Sweden, the UK and the United States.
3. England, France, Germany, the Netherlands and the UK.
4. Austria, Belgium, Denmark, France, Germany, Greece, Italy, the Netherlands, Spain, Sweden and Switzerland.

REFERENCES

Bettio, F., A. Simonazzi, and P. Villa (2006), 'Change in care regimes and female migration: the "care drain" in the Mediterranean', *Journal of European Social Policy*, **16** (3), 271–85.
Brandt, M. and C. Deindl (2013), 'Intergenerational transfers to adult children in Europe: do social policies matter?', *Journal of Marriage and Family*, **75** (1), 235–51.
Brandt, M., K. Haberkern, and M. Szydlik (2009), 'Intergenerational help and care in Europe', *European Sociological Review*, **25** (5), 585–601.
Cantillon, B. (2011), 'The paradox of the social investment state: growth, employment and poverty in the Lisbon era', *Journal of European Social Policy*, **21** (5), 432–49.
Carbonnier, C. and N. Morel (eds) (2015), *The Political Economy of Household Services in Europe*, Houndmills, Basingstoke and New York: Palgrave Macmillan.
Chau, R.C.M. and S.W.K. Yu (2013), 'Defamilisation of twenty-two countries: its implications for the study of East Asian welfare regime', *Social Policy and Society*, **12**, 355–67.
Da Roit, B. and S. Sabatinelli (2013), 'Nothing on the move or just going private? Understanding the freeze on child- and eldercare policies and the development of care markets in Italy', *Social Politics*, **20** (3), 430–53.
Da Roit, B. and M. van Bochove (2015), 'Migrant care work going Dutch? The emergence of a live-in migrant care market and the restructuring of the Dutch long-term care system', *Social Policy and Administration*, **50** (1), 76–94.
Daatland, S.O. and A. Lowenstein (2005), 'Intergenerational solidarity and the family–welfare state balance', *European Journal of Ageing*, **2** (3), 174–82.
Daly, M. (2015a), 'Parenting support in European countries: a complex development in social policy – introduction', *Social Policy and Society*, **14** (4), 593–6.
Daly, M. (2015b), 'Parenting support as policy field: an analytic framework', *Social Policy and Society*, **14** (4), 597–608.
Daly, M. and G. Kelly (eds) (2015), *Families and Poverty: Everyday Life on a Low Income*, Bristol: Policy Press.
Esping-Andersen, G. (1990), *The Three Worlds of Welfare Capitalism*, Princeton, NJ: Princeton University Press.
Finch, J. (ed.) (1989), *Family Obligations and Social Change*, Cambridge: Polity.
Finch, J. and J. Mason (eds) (1993), *Negotiating Family Responsibilities*, London: Routledge.
Frericks P., P.H. Jensen, and B. Pfau-Effinger (2014), 'Social rights and employment rights related to family care: family care regimes in Europe', *Journal of Aging Studies*, **29**, 66–77.
Glaser, K., D. Price, G. Di Gessa, E. Ribe, R. Stuchbury, and A. Tinker (eds) (2013), *Grandparenting in Europe: Family Policy and Grandparents' Role in Providing Childcare*, London: Grandparents Plus.

Haberkern, K. and M. Szydlik (2010), 'State care provision, societal opinion and children's care of older parents in 11 European countries', *Ageing and Society*, **30** (2), 299–323.
Janta, B. (2014), 'Caring for children in Europe. How childcare, parental leave and flexible working arrangements interact in Europe', RAND Corporation (RR-554-EC), accessed 1 July 2016 at http://europa.eu/epic/studies-reports/docs/rr-554-dg-employment-childcare-brief-v-0-16-final.pdf.
Kamerman, S.B. and A.J. Kahn (eds) (1978), *Family Policy: Government and Families in Fourteen Countries*, New York: Columbia University Press.
Kuronen, M., T. Kröger, B. Pfau-Effinger, P. Frericks, R. Och, and N. Schwindt (eds) (2014), 'Local welfare systems supporting female employment in 11 European cities', FLOWS Working Paper, Aalborg.
Le Bihan, B. and C. Martin (2012), 'Diversification of care policy measures supporting older people: towards greater flexibility for carers?', *European Journal of Ageing*, **9** (2), 141–50.
Lowenstein, A. and J. Ogg (2003), *Old Age and Autonomy: The Role of Service Systems and Intergenerational Family Solidarity: Final Report*, Haifa: Center for Research and Study of Aging, University of Haifa, Israel.
Martin, C. (2004), 'The rediscovery of family solidarity: backgrounds and concepts', in T. Knijn and A. Komter (eds), *Solidarity between the Sexes and the Generations: Transformations in Europe*, Cheltenham, UK and Northampton, MA, USA: Edward Elgar Publishing, pp. 3–17.
Meyer, D. and C. Skinner (2016), 'Privileging biological or residential relationships: family policy on obligations to children in 12 countries', *Families, Relationships and Societies*, **5** (1), 79–95.
Millar, J. and A. Warman (eds) (1996), *Family Obligations in Europe*, York: Joseph Rowntree Foundation.
Offer, S. (2012), 'The burden of reciprocity: processes of exclusion and withdrawal from personal networks among low-income families', *Current Sociology*, **60** (6), 788–805.
Pelikh, A. and A. Tyndik (2014), 'Preschool services for children: cross-national analysis of factors affecting use', *International Social Work*, **57** (5), 470–85.
Saraceno, C. (2011), 'Childcare needs and childcare policies: a multidimensional issue', *Current Sociology*, **59** (1), 78–96.
Saraceno, C. (2015), 'A critical look to the social investment approach from a gender perspective', *Social Politics*, **22** (2), 257–69.
Saraceno, C. and W. Keck (2008), *The Institutional Framework of Intergenerational Family Obligations in Europe: A Conceptual and Methodological Overview*, Berlin: Wissenschaftszentrum Berlin für Sozialforschung.
Saraceno, C. and W. Keck (2010), 'Can we identify intergenerational policy regimes in Europe?', *European Societies*, **12** (5), 675–96.
Simoni, S. and R. Trifiletti (2004), 'Caregiving in transition in Southern Europe: neither complete altruists nor free-riders', *Social Policy and Administration*, **38** (6), 678–705.
Yu, S., C.M. Chau, and K.M. Lee (2015), 'Using defamilisation typologies to study the Confucian welfare regime', *Journal of International and Comparative Social Policy*, **31** (1), 74–93.
Walker, R. (ed.) (2014), *The Shame of Poverty*, Oxford: Oxford University Press.
Williams, F. (ed.) (2010), *Claiming and Framing in the Making of Care Policies: The Recognition and Redistribution of Care*, New York: United Nations Research Institute for Social Development.

5. Comparing family policies: approaches, methods and databases

Henning Lohmann and Hannah Zagel

INTRODUCTION

Over the last few decades, comparative family policy research has advanced not only theoretically but also as an empirical research field. There is a rich strand of comparative family policy research that follows a case-oriented approach, which contributes strongly to the understanding of family policy arrangements and its development in specific countries (e.g., Lewis et al., 2008; Leitner, 2010; Daly, 2011). This approach regards countries as historically defined cases. It is usually applied for the in-depth study and comparison of a few cases. The present chapter, however, focuses on variable-oriented approaches, which form another large and growing strand of the literature on family policy and its outcomes for families (Gauthier, 2002). The variable-centred approach regards countries as units of analysis for which values of variables are observed. It is concerned with describing overall patterns and testing theories about the relationship between selected characteristics of a larger number of countries rather than taking a holistic view on one or a few cases. Compared to the variable-oriented literature on other policy fields such as social security, employment and pension policy, research on family policy is engaged much less in methodological discussions. There is only very little systematic consideration on how to measure established theoretical concepts, such as the male breadwinner model (Lewis, 1992), defamilization (Lister, 1994; McLaughlin and Glendinning, 1994) or dual-earner support (Korpi, 2000). This seems of vital importance, however, given that the concepts are widely used in empirical research on the relationship between family policy and family well-being. Family policy may have diverse goals such as safeguarding child development, preventing child poverty, promoting maternal employment and gender equality. A rigorous understanding of measurement, data and methodological perspectives is required for evaluating whether family policy meets its aims in these varied areas. Not least, methodological advancement in this area will allow us to tackle data limitations, which has been a severe problem in this research field. In this chapter, we provide a methodological discussion of central issues and recent developments in comparing family policy using a cross-country perspective. We address conceptual issues, discuss different measurement approaches, as well as the range of existing databases, and finally look at some selected examples of family policy typologies and indices.

FAMILY CONCEPTS AND THE SCOPE OF FAMILY POLICY

Family and family policy are contested concepts. Defining family policy requires some careful consideration, not least due to the fragmented nature of this policy area. For one, family policy can be explicit, deliberately designed to achieve defined objectives for families, or implicit, including policies in other fields such as labour market or pension policies that have consequences for families (Kamerman and Kahn, 1978). Further, the focus of family policy may vary from being parent-centred, child-centred or directed at society at large (Kaufmann, 2002). Motives of a child-centred family policy may be the reduction of child poverty, or the support of child development and investment in future generations more broadly. Parent-centred family policy motives include fostering a more equal division of labour between partners and the improvement in reconciling work and family life. These latter motives may also be considered concerning society more generally if they are reformulated, for example, as the increase in gender equality and (female) employment. Less often today is fertility increase stated as an explicit aim of family policy, but demographic development is often used as political legitimization for work-family reconciliation policy aims (see den Dulk, Yerkes and Peper in Chapter 11 in this volume). Family policy can broadly be categorized as rights for time, money and services (Lewis, 2009), and includes such policies as parental leave regulations, child benefit or home care allowances, care for older people, and early childhood education and care policies. A narrower concept of family policy is used in this *Handbook*, which excludes care for older people.

Underpinning the question of what is family policy, a key issue is what conception of family is used, that is, who is considered the beneficiary of family policy measures. Concepts of family vary widely across national contexts, they are expressions of cultural traditions (Naumann, 2010), and they are intertwined with concepts of gender roles (Coltrane, 2000). Concepts of family are also the result of political processes and imply political intentions that vary across countries and within countries across time (Dienel, 1994). Changing definitions of family used by statistical offices further illustrate the fluctuation of dominant ideas of family (Dienel, 1994). In general, families may be defined on the basis of biological, legal or social relationships. The traditional concept of the family, based on the nuclear family ideal with a married heterosexual couple and their biological children, may still be the blueprint for family policies in many countries. However, other forms of family relationships are increasingly considered in law and policy frameworks across Europe, such as same-sex partnerships, step-families and single parents (Hantrais, 2004). For example, in 2005, the Federal Statistical Office in Germany changed its definition of a family from the traditional nuclear family with heterosexual married parents and their biological children to all parent-child units regardless of parents' marital status or sexual orientation (Kreyenfeld et al., 2014). Accordingly, a usefully broad conceptualization is to define family based on the existence of an intergenerational relationship between two individuals, be it biologically, legally or socially based, for investigating differences in family policies across countries. There are also good reasons for including partners in a couple without children in a categorization of family policy beneficiaries, because they are addressees of gender equality and fertility policies. However, we will focus here on the intergenerational relationship as the main defining criterion for family, hence categorizing the couple without children as a separate category.

Family policy, then, may be defined as any public and formal measure of intervention in family relationships. This conceptualization follows the logic of categorizing state activity by the kind of intervention proposed by Kaufmann (1982, 2002). He differentiates between four conceptual dimensions of intervention: economic (affecting people's income); legal (affecting the legal status of people); ecological (affecting the infrastructure in which people are embedded); and pedagogical (affecting people's capacities and agency). Analysis of intervention in family relationships should consider that the family is a welfare provider, a key insight from the feminist welfare state literature. For example, policy intervention can change people's power position within the couple by granting access to resources and relaxing family responsibilities (see, e.g., Orloff, 1993). Family policy can hence also be conceptualized by looking at the expected outcomes for families and couples. Gender and care relations are two of the most often analysed dimensions of family policy outcomes besides intergenerational relationships, fertility and child poverty. For example, the concept of defamilization was used to conceptualize family policy according to its expected effects on the economic and care dependencies between family members (e.g., Lister, 1994, McLaughlin and Glendinning, 1994; Leitner, 2003; Saraceno and Keck, 2010; Lohmann and Zagel, 2016), that is, intergenerational and gender dependencies. The concept of individualization similarly captures the different degrees to which family policies support economic and social independence for men as well as women (Daly, 2011). Single mothers are here a case in point, as their position exemplifies gendered dependencies of families and possible areas of intervention particularly well. Against the background of more recent trends in family policy, additional concepts have been formulated in the academic discussion of the defamilization concept. Among these is the concept of re-familization. It has been used to describe policy trends of fostering men's involvement in family care, for example, with leave rights reserved for fathers (Saraceno, 2008). Semi-formalization (Geissler and Pfau-Effinger, 2005) describes another trend in recent family policy and may be defined as policy which partially formalizes informal care by providing statutory pay to care givers.

MEASURING FAMILY POLICIES

How Can Family Policy be Measured?

Similar to other policy fields, family policies may be operationalized and compared in several different ways. Two common empirical perspectives may be identified as distinct approaches for comparing policies across countries: the expenditures and the social rights perspective. In addition to this, we present the outcome perspective as a additional approach.

The expenditure perspective uses data on public social spending for assessing countries' welfare efforts (see Obinger and Wagschal, 2010). Empirical studies in traditional welfare state research have often analysed expenditure data. Comparative analyses of family policy also apply this approach (see, e.g., Pampel and Adams, 1992; Guo and Gilbert, 2007). The expenditure perspective has been criticized for various reasons (see Esping-Andersen, 1990; Gauthier, 2002; Clasen et al., 2016). First, expenditure data do not reveal whether a given level of expenditure is due to the provision of low benefits to a large share of the population (broad coverage) or to the provision of high benefits to a small share of the population (narrow coverage). This also implies that qualitative variations in the family benefit system, and in how effectively it reduces income differences, are not adequately captured. Second, internationally comparable expenditure data are often provided in broad categories, summarizing different policy programmes, rather than being given for individual measures. Where such categories include, for example, expenditures on family benefits, parental leave policies and family services (see, e.g., Siaroff, 1994; Guo and Gilbert, 2007), variations in the impact of these different policies may not be evaluated. However, more recently the available expenditure data have become richer in detail. It is now increasingly possible to differentiate expenditures for different family benefits and services, making the data more useful for addressing specific research questions. A third criticism is that full comparability between countries is not always achieved due to national differences in the administration of expenditure data. In different countries similar policies are sometimes governed by different public agencies, and are hence categorized as different types of expenditure (e.g., child care or education for pre-schoolers). Despite these criticisms, the expenditure perspective has some distinct advantages: data are available for a large number of countries in standardized databases; the databases are updated on a regular basis and allow for broad cross-country comparisons; and they cover a broad range of family policy fields. For recent years not only information on expenditures on benefits and services are available but also on tax reductions, which can be considered as a third type of family expenditure.

In contrast to the expenditure perspective, the social rights perspective provides evidence as to whether and to what degree entitlements are granted (for a general discussion of social rights see Stephens, 2010). As mentioned above, in the field of family policy this includes rights for time, money and services. In the social rights perspective, countries' legal regulations are translated into comparative indicators which require detailed knowledge of national legislation and regulations as well as a process of standardization by the researcher. These processes are very resource intensive and rely on researchers or on stakeholders in the respective countries, who are often representatives of governments or administrations. As a consequence, the availability of social rights indicators is generally more limited compared to expenditure data. Longitudinal data or data for countries were – and often still are – difficult to obtain. Exceptions are the usual suspects of comparative welfare state research such as pension and unemployment benefits. However, the availability of social rights indicators and their coverage of countries have improved in recent years. The Organisation for Economic Co-operation and Development (OECD) has provided family benefit indicators for selected years from 2002 in the framework of its reporting on tax-benefit systems and further indicators in its Family Database.[1] Furthermore, recent additions to the Social Citizenship Indicator Program (SCIP)[2] are the Child Benefit Dataset, Child Care Dataset and the Parental Leave Dataset covering 18 countries in a trend perspective. We discuss these and other databases in more detail below.

Social rights indicators cover early childhood education and care (ECEC), parental leave programmes and home care allowances, as well as direct and indirect subsidies for parents. An example of the application of such indicators is the study by Gornick and Meyers (2003, p. 202) who use indicators on entitlements for children in two different age groups, distinguishing whether the family has the legal right to ECEC services. The same study also provides information on part-time and full-time entitlements to child care, but the authors do not differentiate by other characteristics such as the number of hours children are entitled to or by costs for child care.

Standard indicators of social rights for maternity, paternity and parental leave usually contain information on the entitlement, the duration and the conditions of leave, such as the level of wage replacement benefits (see also Chapter 10 by Thévenon for an account of leave schemes). In most countries, the basic features of leave entitlements do not differ by family characteristics, such as family structure, size and income, and can more readily be summarized in indicators. Some countries, however, do provide specific regulations for single parents or low income families as additional provisions. For determining replacement rates, indicators have to take variation across families into account because they differ by the prior level of earnings or family income (Koslowski et al., 2016).

In contrast, the entitlement to family benefits usually differs strongly across family types, which complicates the construction of quantifiable comparable indicators. One approach is to calculate the size of the benefit package for a range of distinct family types ('model families'), differing, for instance, in the level of earnings and the number and age of the children. In addition, most studies taking this approach differentiate between lone parent and couple families (Bradshaw, 2006; see also Chapter 7 by Bradshaw in this volume). The approach allows for the inclusion of all aspects of the tax-benefit system, such as tax reductions, family-related components of the social insurance system, family allowances, housing benefits and social assistance payments. The model family approach is illustrative because it provides information on the level of different types of benefits at the family level rather than at the country level. However, the computation of the family benefit package on a wide range of model families is demanding, as it requires detailed knowledge of a country's tax-benefit system. This often works as a restriction on the number of countries included in the analysis. A general criticism of the model family approach is that the results – if programmes differ across family types or earnings levels – cannot be generalized to the population level. Any one study can only provide information on a selected range of model families, which does not allow for generalization to families that differ from the model families in size, structure and earnings. Since the shares of these 'other' family types differ between countries, model families will represent different shares of the population in each country. They will also tend to portray more common family forms and neglect alternative and emerging ones. Likewise, depending on the choice of model families, the approach may yield different results for the same country. An additional issue that has been raised as a disadvantage of the model family approach is that the approach measures benefit levels based solely on the legal regulations; it does not reflect usage patterns or the income that families actually receive from transfers (Gauthier, 2002, p. 45). In the case of non-take-up, the social rights approach will hence overestimate the impact of family policy on problems such as child poverty. What is sometimes seen as a disadvantage of the family model approach can also, however, be regarded as an advantage. This is because the approach allows for analyses that differentiate between policy provision and family behaviour. For example, the benefit levels to which the model families are identified as being eligible can be contrasted with families' actual disposable incomes.

A third way that family policy is sometimes measured is what we here call the outcomes perspective. Researchers applying this approach measure the differential outcomes that family policies are assumed to create. Let us take as an example the percentage of children in full-time child care. This outcome is often interpreted as a measure of the policy itself. This means that if the percentage of children in early childhood education and care facilities is considered as an indicator for the provision of child care policy, the researcher makes the implicit assumption of full take-up and unlimited demand. Other examples of the outcome perspective are outcomes such as parental labour market participation rates or measures of child well-being. These indicators are often derived from comparative micro datasets, such as the Luxembourg Income Study (LIS) or the European Union (EU) Statistics on Income and Living Conditions (EU-SILC). It is obvious that these are indicators of potential outcomes of family policies and not of the policies themselves.

What Makes Up a Good Indicator?

In this subsection, we propose several quality criteria which can be used for selecting family policy indicators for country comparisons in quantitative analyses (given their availability). Besides standard criteria such as validity, reliability, availability and usability, a clear definition of whether the indicator measures structure and institutions or agency and outcomes should be defined. The criteria defined below are ideal requirements that will be difficult to satisfy fully by any measure. But they provide a framework against which the quality and potential problems of different indicators of family policies can be evaluated (for a similar discussion see Lohmann and Zagel, 2016).

a. *Reliability and validity.* The availability of indicators that describe macro-social phenomena is often much more restricted than the availability of indicators that describe individuals on the micro level. Researchers who aim at describing macro units such as countries are hence likely to be tempted to relax their standards of reliability and validity simply because they have no choice. In addition, indicators produced by different providers, in different contexts (i.e., countries) and in different periods of time are likely to suffer from measurement problems. How can these problems be addressed? One way to improve data availability for research on macro phenomena such as family policies is to invest in the development of reliable and valid indicators. A central requirement for such development is that shared concepts and joint standards of indicator construction would have to be applied, as done by international organizations or larger academic initiatives. A second option is to conduct sensitivity analyses for addressing issues of reliability and validity, if existing indicators are used in research. This requires, first of all, that the data providers document all steps of data collection and indicator construction available with the data in greater detail. Second, the researcher who uses the indicators for secondary analyses must have a good understanding of the underlying concepts (presuming that indicator construction is based on clearly defined concepts).

b. *Availability for a larger number of countries.* The aim of the collection of country-level measures is often to compile datasets that can be used for macro and multi-level analyses. Because the number of existing countries is limited and the number of those covered in databases even more so, the small-n problem is inherent to these approaches (cf. Bryan and Jenkins, 2016). The problem may be reduced by increasing the number of countries as much as possible, for example, by including countries beyond those which are well covered in standard databases. However, potential trade-offs between the measurement quality and the sample size need to be evaluated carefully.

c. *Time-variance*. Welfare states are subject to changes over time. Even if it is assumed that visible changes take place over long periods (or not at all) the stability of institutional arrangements can only be captured if measures are surveyed on a regular basis. Furthermore, repeated measurement offers additional options for causal analysis using within-unit change to identify effects. Comparative micro datasets, for example, the EU-SILC or the EU Labour Force Statistics, which are available in annual intervals, can be combined with macro data most fruitfully in multi-level analyses if these data are also measured annually. This allows for the analysis of change in macro contexts as well as in macro-micro relationships over time.

d. *Measuring institutional factors*. Although it is usually more difficult to gather information on institutional factors (e.g., policies which support mother's employment) than information on the assumed outcome of such factors (e.g., the female employment rate), the former are preferable because they do not require us to assume a high degree of covariation between policies and results. This assumption is not only problematic because it may be wrong, but also because in many cases such assumptions are similar to the hypotheses that the studies address. For example, if the research question is whether institutional factors indicated as the degree of defamilization have an impact on women's labour market participation, the female employment rate cannot be used as a proxy for institutional factors because it is part of the concept to be explained. Furthermore, this strategy restricts the options to test alternative hypotheses, for example, the influence of attitudes towards female employment. As we will see in the next section, family policy databases provide a large number of institutional as well as outcome indicators. However, availability varies across countries, years and policy areas.

FAMILY POLICY DATABASES: STRUCTURE, APPROACH, USAGE

The landscape of comparative family policy data is rather heterogeneous, and it is hard to gain a comprehensive overview. Data providers and sources vary widely, and databases differ in the areas of family policy they cover. There are two main kinds of sources of family policy data. First, a few centralized agencies, like the OECD, regularly produce data collected from member states applying harmonized standards. Second, researchers collect family policy data, often in the framework of a research project with temporary funding and based on a specific theoretical idea or research question. The latter, project-based type of collection often comes with limitations for data availability. Generally, the availability of family policy data has improved since the 1990s. This is partly due to the investment of the OECD, which resulted in the establishment of the OECD Family Database (Adema et al., 2009). But the trend also reflects an increased academic and governmental interest in this policy area, which is often explained with demographic developments, such as ageing societies or low fertility (Gauthier, 2002). In Table 5.1 we provide an overview of various family policy databases, illustrating the range of available data sources, topics and coverage in time and geographic regions. The listed databases are relatively visible in the field of quantitative comparative family policy research, cover a relatively large number of countries and at least two years (excluding historical databases). The table includes information on the specialization of the database, the time frame and countries covered, as well as the sources from which the data were retrieved and the number and types of indicators included.

The specialization of the databases varies between broad approaches, including a range of family policy areas, and deep approaches, including a range of indicators for a specific family policy area. The most common family policy areas covered in the databases are cash transfers to families (allowances/benefits), early childhood education and care (ECEC) policies and leave policies. As for the time covered, few studies go back further than the 1990s. Exceptions are the Comparative Family Policy Database, the newly established family policy modules of the SPIN database, and some parts of the OECD Family Database. As noted above, a common characteristic of project-based data sources, like the Multilinks Database and the Child Benefit Packages, is that they cover a limited number of years. As for the regions covered in the databases, few go beyond the industrialized countries in Europe and North America. Countries in Central and Eastern Europe tend to be included for the more recent years. Even if the databases often generally cover more than 30 countries, it is very common that information is missing for some countries on some of the indicators, or that the data are not available for all of the years. The list of data sources does not include the OECD's highly standardized database of social expenditure data (SOCX), because family policy is only one of the subfields it considers. However, SOCX appears among the data sources of other databases listed in Table 5.1 that include social expenditure data. Current expenditure databases offer an often fine-grained perspective on social policy. For example, policies may be differentiated by spending for in-cash or in-kind transfers, or by target group. A drawback of the comprehensive expenditure databases is that breaks in the time-series are not always fully documented.

While expenditure data are collected and distributed by governments or inter-/supranational entities, social rights data are usually gathered by the scientific community. One of the most prominent historical collections in this field is certainly the Social Citizenship Indicator Program (SCIP) initiated by Walter Korpi and colleagues more than 30 years ago. It covers 18 industrialized countries over a very long period of time (1930–2000). Initially, family policy was not within the scope of the SCIP but in the early 2000s information on child benefits, day-care services, gender-relevant taxation and other aspects of the tax-benefits system were included (Korpi, 2010). SCIP was discontinued in 2013 and its data are now available as a module of the SPIN Database. Apart from SCIP there are no other initiatives with such a broad scope that collect indicators on family policy from a social rights perspective. But there are a number of data sources that contain information on single aspects of family policy. One example is the work carried out by Bradshaw and colleagues (see, e.g., Bradshaw, 2006) on family benefits packages. Bennett (2008) provides a detailed description of early childhood education and care entitlements across countries. Koslowski et al. (2016) provide comprehensive data on parental leave policies. Other examples are the Comparative Family Policy Database (Gauthier, 2011), the Multilinks Database (Keck and Saraceno, 2012), and complementary databases to the Luxembourg Income Study assembled on the LIS website, such as Gornick et al. (1997), Gornick and Meyers (2003) and Boeckmann et al. (2012).

Table 5.1 Family policy databases

Database	Data producer/PI	Main topics (alphabetical)	Time Year min/max	No. of years min/max	Countries Regions	Countries min/max	Source	Number of indicators	Type of indicators
Comparative Family Policy Database	Anne Gauthier	Allowances, Leave policies	1960/2010	48/48 (Allowances) 50/50 (Leave)	OECD	21/21 (all) 22/22 (leave)	OECD SOCX, SSPW	19 (Allowances) /8 (Leave)	SR, EXP, OUT
LIS Family Database	Janet C. Gornick, Marcia K. Meyers and Katherine E. Ross	ECEC policies, Leave policies, Working time regulations	1986/2000	2/2	Europe + AUS, CAN, USA	12/36	Various, checked by national experts	22	SR
Multilinks Database	Chiara Saraceno and Wolfgang Keck	Allowances, ECEC policies, Leave policies	2004/2009	1/2	EU (2011) + Georgia, Norway, Russia	30	National policy experts	83	SR
OECD Family Database	OECD	ECEC policies, Leave policies, Public spending on benefits and ECEC	1960/2014	10/54	OECD + ARG, BRA, BRG, CHN, COL, CRI, HRV, CYP, IND, IDN, LVA, LTU, MLT, ROU, RUS, SAU, ZAF	29/51	MISSOC, Moss (2014)	70	EXP, SR, OUT
SPIN Database (Parental Leave Benefit (PLB) and Child Benefit Datasets (CBD))	SOFI Stockholm	Child benefits, ECEC policies, Leave policies	1950/2010 (PLB) 1960/2010 (CBD)	13/13 (PLB) 11/11 (CBD)	OECD	18	Various, including national government agencies	22 (PLB) 30 (CBD)	SR

Name	Authors	Topics	Year	Ratio	Countries	#	Source	#	Type
The Work-Family Policy Indicators	Irene Boeckmann, Michelle Budig, and Joya Misra	ECEC policies, Leave policies, Working time regulations	1992/2001	1/1	Europe, North America, AUS	22	Various, e.g., Moss and Deven (1999), ILO, SSPW, Gornick and Meyers (2003)	12	SR
MISSOC Tables: Maternity/ Paternity and Family Benefits	EU Commission DG Employment, Social Affairs and Inclusion	Allowances, Family benefits, Leave policies	2004/2014 (biannual update)	20/20	EU + EFTA countries + CHE	31/31	Representatives of EU Member State administrations	40	SR
International Network on Leave Policies and Research	Peter Moss, Alison Koslowski, Sonja Blum	Leave policies	2005/2017	10/10	EU-15, AUS, BRA, CAN, HRV, CZE, EST, HUN, ISL, ISR, JPN, LTU, MLT, MEX, NZL, NOR, POL, RUS, SVK, SVN, ZAF, CHE, USA, URY	19/35	Network members from participating countries	42	SR
Department for Work and Pensions Report: Comparison of Child Benefit Packages	Jonathan Bradshaw and Naomi Finch	Child benefit package (tax benefits, income-related and non-income-related child benefits, housing benefits, child care subsidies, health and education charges, social assistance and child support)	2001	1/1	EU-15 + AUS, CAN, ISR, JPN, NZL, NOR, USA	22	Bradshaw and Finch (2002)	14	SR

Note: SR = Social Rights; EXP = Expenditure; OUT = Outcomes; ECEC = Early Childhood Education and Care; OECD SOCX = Social Expenditure Database; SSPW = Social Security Programmes throughout the World produced by the US Social Security Administration, https://www.ssa.gov/policy/docs/progdesc/ssptw/ (accessed 26 June 2018); ILO = International Labour Organization.

AGGREGATING FAMILY POLICY INDICATORS

While detailed databases are a basic requirement for a fine-grained description and analysis of family policies, aggregation is needed to highlight general patterns and country differences. In this section, we describe three commonly used approaches of aggregating different family policy indicators for classifying countries' family policy profiles. Composite indices and typologies are two options for dealing with the complexity of family policies without getting lost in a universe of single indicators. In addition, league tables and scorecards are techniques for providing an overview of a country's position in comparison to other countries, either on the basis of single indicators or composite indices.

Composite Indices

There is widespread use of composite indices across different domains of research. The basic idea of index construction is to summarize information from different measures in a single one.

In the family policy domain, a well-known example is the Family Policy Index by Gornick et al. (1997, see also Gornick and Meyers, 2003) which we present below in more detail in comparison to other approaches. Other examples of family policy indices are the OECD (2001) composite index, Siaroff's (1994) indices of 'female work desirability' and 'family welfare orientation', Korpi's (2000) indices of 'dual-earner support' and 'general family support' and Kröger's (2011) dedomestication index. A composite index for defamilization is proposed by Bambra (2004). Bambra's defamilization index combines an institutional indicator for parental leave and two outcome indicators, female employment and the gender pay gap, using data from the years 1996/97.

Typologies

Typologies are another way of dealing with the complexity of single indicators. They are a central heuristic tool in welfare state research more generally, as well as in comparative family policy research (Bailey, 1994; Arts and Gelissen, 2002; Meulders and O'Dorchai, 2004). At the theoretical level, typologies are constructed as combinations of properties across two or more theoretically relevant dimensions. The resulting types are usually characterized by labels or names. Empirical cases, for example, countries, share properties of a type to some degree. Countries which closely match a given type represent typical cases. Countries which exhibit properties of different types are commonly categorized as hybrid cases. Ideally, a typology accentuates the commonalities of cases falling into a type and the differences between cases across types. It provides a systematic description of a large number of properties, their complex interrelations and complementarities (see, e.g., Esping-Andersen, 1990).

In family policy research, we find different approaches of how empirical cases are categorized as types. All attempts at creating a typology require an understanding of how to measure the dimensions that provide the basis for the typology. First, there are typologies based on the qualitative analysis of institutional arrangements of selected cases. For instance, Kamerman and Kahn's (1978) seminal study distinguishes between the types of explicit and comprehensive, explicit but narrow and implicit and reluctant family policy. Second, and more recently, formalized results of institutional analysis are used to construct typologies. In particular, set-theoretic approaches are increasingly applied. The construction of (fuzzy-)sets requires the coding of qualitative information into dichotomies or ordinal scales (e.g., Kvist, 1999; Saraceno and Keck, 2010). Third, in a large number of studies, countries are assigned to types based on (dichotomous) quantitative indicators or composite indices, which describe the institutional characteristics and policy outcomes in a relatively large number of countries. Often statistical methods are used, which reduce the complexity of the data and/or provide groupings of cases based on their degree of similarity (e.g., cluster analysis). As an alternative, the assignment of empirical cases to types is carried out by using simple classification or ranking techniques. We discuss Leitner's (2003) study as an example of the use of single indicators in detail below. An example of a study using composite indices is Korpi (2000). In his study, Korpi constructs composite indices to measure the underlying dimensions of his typology. He uses data on child benefits, early childhood education and care services, gender-relevant taxation and other aspects of the tax-benefits system to distinguish three different types: the dual-earner support regime; the general family support regime; and the market-oriented regime.

In addition to studies which use qualitative, set-theoretic and quantitative techniques we may add a fourth type of study although it does not strictly follow a typological approach but provides descriptive groupings of countries based on quantitative data. The study by Thévenon (2011) serves as an example of this type of approach in our discussion in the next section of this chapter.

League Tables and Scorecards

League tables and scorecards provide an overview of a country's position in comparison to other countries, either on the basis of single indicators or composite indices. Such approaches are primarily used at the level of inter- and supranational organizations such as the OECD, EU or United Nations (UN). There are scorecard approaches that retain several sub-dimensions and collapse the information into qualitative categories such as a yes/no dichotomy (UNICEF, 2008) or the three-dimensional 'traffic lights' categories (see OECD, 2007). Others merely use graphical tools to represent the information captured in a multitude of indicators in a form which is comparable across countries and indicators without providing a ranking. Examples are the recently introduced OECD country snapshots (see OECD Family Database website) or the scorecard approach proposed by Lohmann et al. (2009). Lohmann et al. (2009) use z-standardized indicators primarily from the OECD Family Database for producing scorecards that provide a comparable synthesis of the country context, policy measures and outcome indicators.

FAMILY POLICY CLASSIFICATIONS: EXAMPLES

In the field of family policy there are a number of applications of the methods discussed in the previous section. In a recent article, we provide a comparison of several indices

(Lohmann and Zagel, 2016). In the present chapter, we discuss three studies in more detail as examples of different approaches towards the classification of family policies. These are the two path-breaking studies by Gornick et al. (1997) and Leitner (2003) as well as a more recent proposal by Thévenon (2011). The study of Leitner (2003) stands in the tradition of the typological approach first applied to the field of family policy by Kamerman and Kahn (1978), but combines it with the use of single quantitative indicators. Gornick et al. (1997) provide an index measuring one distinct dimension of family policy, namely, policies supporting the employment of mothers. Thévenon (2011) uses a large number of indicators to give a two-dimensional description of family policies. We will now go through these examples one by one.

Guided by theoretical considerations, Leitner (2003) distinguishes four ideal-types of defamilialism and familialism. These types differ by the degree of defamilization and familization in family policy. Leitner defines defamilizing policies as those 'which aim at unburdening the family in its caring function' while familizing policies are defined as those 'which actively aim at strengthening the family in its caring function' (Leitner, 2003, p. 358). Dichotomizing the degree of defamilization and familization into 'weak' and 'strong', Leitner constructs a 2-by-2 matrix. She interprets the four types emerging from this matrix as explicit familialism, optional familialism, defamilialism and implicit familialism. In a second step, Leitner uses quantitative indicators from two family policy areas (early childhood education and care, long-term care for older people) to allocate countries to the four types. In the field of early childhood education and care, information on paid parental leave (yes/no) is used to measure the degree of familization, and data on the percentage of children under 3 in formal child care is used for measuring the degree of defamilization. Applying a threshold derived from a gap in the distribution of the indicator, Leitner distinguishes countries where formal child care is 'widespread' or 'poor'. Five countries fall into the type of optional familialism (with Finland as a borderline case), five into the type of explicit familialism, three into the type of implicit familialism and two into the type of defamilialism. In an analogous manner, using indicators on home-help coverage and payment for long-term care for older people, countries are classified in the field of care for older people. Because many countries fall into different types in the field of care for older people compared to the field of early childhood education and care, Leitner concludes that it is 'difficult if not impossible to subsume each welfare state under one exclusive category of familialism' (2003, p. 365), which calls for a more differentiated approach than simply assigning cases to types. The typology serves mostly as an analytical tool and does not provide a basis for an overall classification of countries. Leitner's approach is highly convincing in its conceptual clarity and its clear distinction between ideal-types and real-world cases. Still, from a methodological perspective it does not seem adequate to measure such complex dimensions as familization and defamilization by single categorical indicators, even if differentiated by different fields of family policy.

Gornick et al. (1997) do not provide an overall family policy index but focus on one dimension, namely, policies supporting the employment of mothers. Labour supply theory provides the theoretical background. It suggests that women's choice for market income instead of time spent outside the labour market is negatively affected by the presence of children in the household, but that policies may reduce the strength of this relationship. Gornick et al. (1997) argue that especially early childhood education and care and parental leave policies, but also public school schedules affect women's labour supply. For each of these three policy areas they collect several indicators. Indicators on parental leave not only measure the duration but also wage replacement rates, job protection legislation and other factors. The measurement of early childhood education and care includes indicators on coverage, tax relief on child care and legal entitlements to child care. Information on school schedules includes the age when starting school, the length of school days as well as school years and whether schools provide continuous schedules over the year. Gornick et al. (1997, pp. 51ff.) define a number of criteria for the selection of indicators, some with reference to the theoretical construct they measure, some with reference to data availability and quality. Finally, they use policy indicators from 14 countries to provide an overall index and indices by age group of the child. School schedule information is included only in the index for children aged 6 and above. To aggregate the information, they construct weighted additive indices of standardized indicators (using different techniques of standardization, i.e., percentage of the maximum level of an indicator). Gornick et al. (1997) and subsequent work by Gornick and Meyers (2003) are not only excellent examples of theoretically driven index construction in the field of family policy, they have also resulted in the creation of the LIS Family Policy Database.

The OECD Family Database provides the basis for Thévenon's (2011) descriptive comparative analysis of family policy. He focuses on leave entitlements, cash transfers and the provision of early childhood education and care services which are measured using 23 indicators (including social rights indicators as well as expenditure and outcome measures). Employing Principal Components Analysis (PCA) Thévenon identifies five underlying components in the data.[3] He uses the first two components – which together explain about 40 per cent of the variance – to compare the 28 countries of his analysis. Because in PCA the components are not defined in advance, the meaning of a component must be derived from the correlation pattern between the component and the original variables. Thévenon (2011, pp. 64ff.) interprets the first component as a measure of support for working parents with children under 3 years. The second component mostly picks up the generosity of leave entitlements. These two components provide the basis for a comparison of countries. Placed on a two-dimensional plane the countries cluster in different areas. Using this result, Thévenon distinguishes five groups of countries along geographical or cultural boundaries (Nordic, Anglo-Saxon, Southern European and Asian, Eastern European, Continental European) which share similar characteristics of family policy (e.g., 'Continuous, strong support for working parents of children under age 3' or 'Limited assistance to families').

Although Thévenon stresses the descriptive character of his study and does not allude to indexing or typological approaches, the components derived from PCA could be easily read as indexes and the five country groups as types. But in contrast to the approach of Gornick et al. (1997), the study does not start from a theoretically defined concept to be measured in an index. This is not to say that the selection of variables is not guided by general theoretical considerations. However, the identification of principal components is purely data driven. And in contrast to Leitner's (2003) study, Thévenon does not identify distinct criteria which separate types but provides an ad hoc classification based on graphically displayed data points. We highlight this point because the results of studies like Thévenon's are often misread as either typologies or indexes. Yet, even without exemplifying the former or the latter, the study provides important insights. Reducing a complex indicator base into a limited number of components allows the identification of the major commonalities and differences between countries at a descriptive level.

DISCUSSION AND OUTLOOK

Comparative family policy research has advanced not only theoretically but also in the use of data sources, the coverage of regions and family policy areas. Still, there is scope for future research.

First, compared to other fields of welfare state research data availability and discussions on the quality of indicators are still limited. The differences become most obvious when comparing the measurement of two central concepts of general welfare state research: decommodification and defamilization. Esping-Andersen's (1990) decommodification index has been critically replicated, it is regularly updated and alternative databases have been set up (Scruggs and Allan, 2006). In addition, a discussion on the quality and differences of the various databases and approaches to measuring decommodification has evolved (Wenzelburger et al., 2013). In contrast, measurement approaches of defamilization do not capture policy change over time and they are hampered by a lack of indicators (Lohmann and Zagel, 2016). A systematic discussion on data quality is yet missing in the literature. It is certainly true that defamilization is not as prominent a concept as decommodification. But the same lack of methodological discussion holds true for the measurement of other family policy concepts such as breadwinning/earner models.

Second, and partly related to the first issue, measurement approaches are not always derived from theoretical concepts in the field of family policy. In principle, the discussions on earner models, on familization, defamilization and individualization or on other concepts like dedomestification can provide fruitful starting points for the comparison of family policy, which goes beyond the use of single indicators or – in many cases – ad hoc aggregate measures. This is not to say that theory-based measurement approaches do not exist (we discussed a few in this chapter). But critical discussions on how the original concepts can be measured in a valid and reliable way rarely evolve.

Third, family policy research, like general welfare state research, sometimes uses 'types' as the explanatory variables. As explained above, typologies are powerful heuristic tools. But the use of 'types' as the explanatory variables confuses types and empirical cases. We cannot observe types empirically, but may only identify (more or less) typical empirical cases, that is, countries. As the assignment of countries to types is often based on institutional features and outcomes which we want to explain in an analysis, 'type' variables are likely to be endogenous. A more fundamental issue is that using 'type' as a variable (among other variables) is at odds with the holistic, case-oriented logic of typological approaches. Furthermore, it restricts the options for analysing the impact of single policies which may not only differ across the groups of countries that 'constitute' a type but also within these groups. In order to analyse and understand the – sometimes conflicting – impacts of different policies, indicators on single policy measures are required.

Fourth, with the development of family policy, sometimes the focus shifts from one to another area of family policy and new policy areas evolve. Examples are the semi-formalization of care work (Geissler and Pfau-Effinger, 2005), the expansion of parental leave policies and fathers' quotas (Eydal and Rostgaard, 2015) or the introduction of home-care allowances (Hiilamo and Kangas, 2009). Research on such newly introduced policy instruments usually starts with a focus on single cases or a small number of countries. The wider proliferation of new instruments requires an inclusion of respective indicators into wider comparative frameworks.

Fifth, methodological discussions on the measurement of family policy concepts will further demonstrate the need for better data, especially in the social rights perspective. Ideally, the advancement of family policy databases should consider such quality criteria as listed above.

Lastly, wider and better measurement approaches and databases offer additional potential not only for the comparative analysis of family policy but also for the analysis of outcomes of family policy (e.g., child well-being, parental employment, gender equality or intergenerational patterns of family living).

NOTES

1. http://www.oecd.org/els/family/database.htm (accessed 26 June 2018).
2. http://www.sofi.su.se/spin/ (accessed 26 June 2018).
3. PCA is a statistical technique for data reduction. It is based on the correlational patterns in the data and aims at reducing a large number of variables by identifying a smaller number of so-called principal components.

REFERENCES

Adema, W., M. del Carmen Huerta, A. Panzera, O. Thévenon, and M. Pearson (2009), 'The OECD Family Database: developing a cross-national tool for assessing family policies and outcomes', *Child Indicators Research*, **2** (4), 437–60.
Arts, W. and J. Gelissen (2002), 'Three worlds of welfare capitalism or more? A state-of-the-art report', *Journal of European Social Policy*, **12** (2), 137–58.
Bailey, K.D. (ed.) (1994), *Typologies and Taxonomies: An Introduction into Classification Techniques*, Thousand Oaks, CA: Sage.
Bambra, C. (2004), 'The worlds of welfare: illusory and gender blind?', *Social Policy and Society*, **3** (3), 201–11.
Bennett, J. (ed.) (2008), 'Early childhood services in OECD countries: review of the literature and current policy in early childhood field', Innocenti Working Paper, UNICEF, Florence.
Boeckmann, I., M.J. Budig, and J. Misra (2012), 'Work-family policy indicators', accessed 20 July 2017 at http://www.lisdatacenter.org/wp-content/uploads/resources-other-work-family-policy-indicators.pdf.
Bradshaw, J. and N. Finch (2002), *A Comparison of Child Benefit Packages in 22 Countries*, Department for Work and Pensions Research Report, No. 17, Corporate Document Services, London.
Bradshaw, J. (2006), 'Child benefit packages in 15 countries in 2004', in J. Lewis (ed.), *Children, Changing Families and Welfare States*, Cheltenham, UK and Northampton, MA, USA: Edward Elgar Publishing, pp. 69–88.
Bryan, M.L. and S.P. Jenkins (2016), 'Multilevel modelling of country effects: a cautionary tale', *European Sociological Review*, **32** (1), 3–22.
Clasen, J., D. Clegg, and A. Goerne (2016), 'Comparative social policy analysis and active labour market policy: putting quality before quantity', *Journal of Social Policy*, **45** (1), 21–38.
Coltrane, S. (2000), 'The social construction of gender and families', in S. Coltrane (ed.), *Gender and Families*, Lanham, MD: Rowman & Littlefield, pp. 1–24.
Daly, M. (2011), 'What adult worker model? A critical look at recent social policy reform in Europe from a gender and family perspective', *Social Politics*, **18** (1), 1–23.
Dienel, C. (1994), 'The history and political impact of family concepts', in L. Hantrais and M.T. Letablier (eds), *Conceptualising the Family*, Cross-National Research Papers. Loughborough: Loughborough University, pp. 11–16.
Esping-Andersen, G. (ed.) (1990), *The Three Worlds of Welfare Capitalism*, Cambridge: Polity Press.
Eydal, G.B. and T. Rostgaard (eds) (2015), *Fatherhood in the Nordic Welfare States: Comparing Care Policies and Practice*, Chicago, IL: University of Chicago Press.

Gauthier, A.H. (2002), 'The sources and methods of comparative family policy research', *Comparative Social Research*, **18**, 31–56.

Gauthier, A.H. (2011), Comparative Family Policy Database, Version 3 (computer file), Netherlands Interdisciplinary Demographic Institute and Max Planck Institute for Demographic Research (distributors), accessed 20 July 2017 at http://www.demogr.mpg.de/cgi-bin/databases/FamPolDB/index.plx.

Geissler, B. and B. Pfau-Effinger (2005), 'Change in European care arrangements', in B. Pfau-Effinger and B. Geissler (eds), *Care and Social Integration in European Societies*, Bristol: Policy Press, pp. 3–20.

Gornick, J. and M.K. Meyers (2003), *Families that Work: Policies for Reconciling Parenthood and Employment*, New York: Russell Sage Foundation.

Gornick, J., M.K. Meyers, and K.E. Ross (1997), 'Supporting the employment of mothers: policy applications across fourteen welfare states', *Journal of European Social Policy*, **7** (1), 45–70.

Guo, J. and N. Gilbert (2007), 'Welfare state regimes and family policy: a longitudinal analysis', *International Journal of Social Welfare*, **16** (4), 307–13.

Hantrais, L. (ed.) (2004), *Family Policy Matters: Responding to Family Change in Europe*, Bristol: Policy Press.

Hiilamo, H. and O. Kangas (2009), 'Trap for women or freedom to choose? The struggle over cash for child care schemes in Finland and Sweden', *Journal of Social Policy*, **38** (3), 457–75.

Kamerman, S.B. and A.J. Kahn (eds) (1978), *Family Policy: Government and Families in Fourteen Countries*, New York: Columbia University Press.

Kaufmann, F.X. (1982), 'Elemente einer soziologischen Theorie sozialpolitischer Intervention', in F.X. Kaufmann (ed.), *Staatliche Sozialpolitik und Familie*, Munich and Vienna: Oldenbourg, pp. 49–86.

Kaufmann, F.X. (2002), 'Politics and policies towards the family in Europe: a framework and an inquiry into their differences and convergences', in F.X. Kaufmann, A. Kuijsten, H.J. Schulze, and K.P. Strohmeier (eds), *Family Life and Family Policies in Europe. Volume 2: Problems and Issues in Comparative Perspective*, Oxford and New York: Oxford University Press, pp. 419–90.

Keck, W. and C. Saraceno (2012), 'Multilinks Database on intergenerational policy indicators', *Schmollers Jahrbuch*, **132**, 453–61.

Korpi, W. (2000), 'Faces of inequality: gender, class, and patterns of inequalities in different types of welfare states', *Social Politics: International Studies in Gender, State and Society*, **7** (2), 127–91.

Korpi, W. (2010), 'Class and gender inequalities in different types of welfare states: the Social Citizenship Indicator Program (SCIP)', *International Journal of Social Welfare*, **19** (S1), S14–S24.

Koslowski, A., S. Blum, and P. Moss (2016), 'International review of leave policies and research 2016', accessed 20 July 2017 at http://www.leavenetwork.org/lp_and_r_reports/.

Kreyenfeld, M., D. Konietzka, and V. Heintz-Martin (2014), 'Lebens- und Familienformen', in Y. Niephaus, M. Kreyenfeld, and R. Sackmann (eds), *Handbuch Bevölkerungssoziologie*, Wiesbaden: Springer, pp. 1–19.

Kröger, T. (2011), 'Defamilisation, dedomestication and care policy: comparing childcare service provisions of welfare states', *International Journal of Sociology and Social Policy*, **31** (7/8), 424–40.

Kvist, J. (1999), 'Welfare reform in the Nordic countries in the 1990s: using fuzzy-set theory to assess conformity to ideal types', *Journal of European Social Policy*, **9** (3), 231–52.

Leitner, S. (2003), 'Varieties of familialism. The caring function of the family in comparative perspective', *European Societies*, **5** (4), 353–75.

Leitner, S. (2010), 'Germany outpaces Austria in childcare policy. The historical contingencies of "conservative" childcare policy', *Journal of European Social Policy*, **20** (5), 456–67.

Lewis, J. (1992), 'Gender and the development of welfare regimes', *Journal of European Social Policy*, **2** (3), 159–73.

Lewis, J. (ed.) (2009), *Work-family Balance, Gender and Policy*, Cheltenham, UK and Northampton, MA, USA: Edward Elgar Publishing.

Lewis, J., T. Knijn, C. Martin, and I. Ostner (2008), 'Patterns of development in work/family reconciliation policies for parents in France, Germany, the Netherlands, and the UK in the 2000s', *Social Politics*, **15** (3), 261–86.

Lister, R. (1994), '"She has other duties" – women, citizenship and social security', in S. Baldwin and J. Faklingham (eds), *Social Security and Social Change: New Challenges to the Beveridge Model*, New York: Harvester Wheatsheaf, pp. 31–44.

Lohmann, H. and H. Zagel (2016), 'Family policy in comparative perspective: the concepts and measurement of familisation and defamilisation', *Journal of European Social Policy*, **26** (1), 48–65.

Lohmann, H., F.H. Peter, T. Rostgaard, and C.K. Spiess (2009), 'Towards a framework for assessing family policies in the EU', OECD Social, Employment and Migration Working Papers 88, Paris.

McLaughlin, E. and C. Glendinning (1994), 'Paying for care in Europe: is there a feminist approach?', in L. Hantrais and S. Mangen (eds), *Family Policy and the Welfare of Women, Cross-National Research Papers*, European Research Centre, Loughborough University of Technology, Leicestershire, pp. 52–69.

Meulders, D. and S. O'Dorchai (2004), 'The role of welfare state typologies in analysing motherhood', *TRANSFER*, **1** (4), 16–33.

Moss, P. (2014), 'International review of leave policies and research 2014', accessed 2 July 2018 at http://www.leavenetwork.org/lp_and_r_reports/.

Moss, P. and F. Deven (eds) (1999), *Parental Leave: Progress or Pitfall? Research and Policy Issues in Europe*, NIDI CBGS Publications No. 35, Brussels: Vlaamse Gemeenshap.

Naumann, I. (2010), 'When a family is not a "family": the value of confusion in cross-cultural research', in L. Jamieson, R. Simpson, and R. Lewis (eds), *Researching Families and Relationships: Reflections on Process*, Palgrave Studies in Family & Intimate Life, Houndmills, Basingstoke: Palgrave Macmillan, pp. 36–9.

Obinger, H. and U. Wagschal (2010), 'Social expenditures and revenues', in F.G. Castles, S. Leibfried, J. Lewis, H.P. Obinger, and C. Pierson (eds), *The Oxford Handbook of the Welfare State*, Oxford: Oxford University Press, pp. 333–52.

OECD (2001), *Employment Outlook*, Paris: OECD.

OECD (2007), 'Improved childcare policies needed to achieve better work/life balance, says OECD', accessed 10 September 2016 at http://www.oecd.org/employment/improvedchildcarepoliciesneededtoachievebetterworklifebalancesaysoecd.htm.

OECD (2012a), OECD Family Database, accessed 10 September 2016 at http://www.oecd.org/social/family/database.

OECD (2012b), OECD Social Expenditures Database, accessed 10 September 2016 at http://www.oecd.org/social/soc/socialexpendituredatabasesocx.htm.

Orloff, A.S. (1993), 'Gender and the social rights of citizenship: the comparative analysis of gender relations and welfare states', *American Sociological Review*, **58** (3), 303–28.

Pampel, F.C. and P. Adams (1992), 'The effects of demographic change and political structure on family allowance expenditures', *Social Service Review*, **66** (4), 525–46.

Saraceno, C. (2008), '"Care" leisten und "Care" erhalten zwischen Individualisierung und Refamilialisierung', *Berliner Journal für Soziologie*, **18** (29), 244–56.

Saraceno, C. and W. Keck (2010), 'Can we identify intergenerational policy regimes in Europe?', *European Societies*, **12** (5), 675–96.

Scruggs, L. and J. Allan (2006), 'Welfare-state decommodification in 18 OECD countries: a replication and revision', *Journal of European Social Policy*, **16** (1), 55–72.

Siaroff, A. (1994), 'Work, welfare and gender equality: a new typology', in D. Sainsbury (ed.), *Gendering Welfare States*, London: Sage, pp. 82–100.

Stephens, J.D. (2010), 'The social rights of citizenship', in F.G. Castles, S. Leibfried, J. Lewis, H. Obinger, and C. Pierson, (eds), *The Oxford Handbook of the Welfare State*, Oxford: Oxford University Press, pp. 511–25.

Thévenon, O. (2011), 'Family policies in OECD countries: a comparative analysis', *Population and Development Review*, **37** (1), 57–87.

UNICEF (2008), *The Child Care Transition. A League Table on Early Childhood Education and Care in Economically Advanced Countries. UNICEF Innocenti Research Centre, Report Card* 8, Florence: UNICEF.

Wenzelburger, G., R. Zohlnhöfer, and F. Wolf (2013), 'Implications of dataset choice in comparative welfare state research', *Journal of European Public Policy*, **20** (9), 1229–50.

6. Family policy changes across welfare and production regimes, 1990 to 2010
Ji Young Kang and Marcia K. Meyers

INTRODUCTION

Family policies have become an increasingly important issue for welfare state scholarship as women have become crucial constituents in welfare politics (Bonoli, 2005; Huber and Stephens, 2000). A number of scholars have examined recent changes in provisions for specific policies, such as childcare (Mahon et al., 2012) and maternity leave (Gable and Kamerman, 2006), and in aggregate expenditures for family policies as a whole (Gauthier, 2002). These studies suggest that family policy provisions have expanded in many of the advanced democracies, even in the context of economic recession and welfare state contraction. The use of highly aggregated measures, or focus on a single policy, may have obscured, however, tradeoffs in provisions that advance the multiple and sometimes conflicting goals of family policies.

In this chapter, we examine change in family policies over a 20-year period in 14 Organisation for Economic Co-operation and Development (OECD) countries. We focus on policies that support parents, and particularly mothers, in their dual responsibilities as earners and caregivers in the home. We begin by developing an integrated framework of welfare and production regime types that captures the interaction of markets and the state in distinctive family policy approaches. We further argue that taking market economies into account in family policy enriches our understanding of variations of family policy across countries. Second, using this proposed framework, we examine specific changes of family policies in welfare/production regime clusters as well as those for individual countries within the clusters. We explain family policy changes by investigating institutional contexts based on our framework. Third, we explore family policy changes by focusing on the multidimensionality of family policies.

INTEGRATING WELFARE REGIME AND VARIETIES OF CAPITALISM FRAMEWORKS

A number of scholars in the comparative welfare state tradition have found that family policies across advanced democracies conform broadly to three welfare state typologies with distinctive specific characteristics (Esping-Andersen, 1990; Korpi et al., 2013; Thévenon, 2011; see also Chapter 2 by Gauthier and Koops in this volume). A recent comparative approach that examines varieties of capitalism (VoC) across developed countries provides an alternative framework for comparing social protection (Estevez-Abe et al., 2001; Iversen and Soskice, 2001; Iversen and Stephens, 2008) and women's employment (Estevez-Abe, 2005).

At first glance, the VoC emphasis on market institutions and the power of employers to shape social policy may appear to contradict the assumptions of the welfare regime approach. An emerging literature, however, suggests complementarity between the welfare regime and VoC approaches in explaining social policy variations (Estevez-Abe, 2005; Iversen, 2005; Iversen and Stephens, 2008). With some exceptions, empirical studies employing the two frameworks also produce nearly identical clusters of countries (Esping-Andersen, 1990; Hall and Soskice, 2001; Huber and Stephens, 2001b; Iversen and Stephens, 2008; Rueda and Pontusson, 2000; Schroeder, 2009).

The integration of the VoC and welfare state regime approaches provides a useful framework for understanding the institutional context for family policies in advanced democracies. That is, how market economies and the state have interacted to produce distinctive social welfare policy approaches (Ebbinghaus and Manow, 2001; Huber and Stephens, 2001b). This understanding of institutional contexts allows a more nuanced interpretation of different paths of family policy change in different countries. Using an integrated framework, we explore how change in family policy has been mediated by the institutional context of both welfare state and market economies. Table 6.1 illustrates the application of the framework to identify clusters of countries at the intersections of the three welfare regime types and the two VoC production regimes.

VoC scholarship provides an important insight into how market economies contribute to the formation of social policies. Scholars propose two different models – *liberal market economies* (LMEs) and *coordinated market economies* (CMEs) – for advanced capitalist economies for the way firms coordinate with other institutions, such as in the area of industrial relations and corporate governance. Skill specification is key to understanding the implications of the organization of production processes on the configurations of social welfare policies. Workers in CMEs are prone to invest in specific skill development,

Table 6.1 Integrated typology of welfare states and production regime for family policy

Welfare state typologies Production regime (VoC)	Liberal welfare states	Conservative welfare states	Social democratic welfare states
Liberal market economies	Australia UK, USA, New Zealand and Ireland	–	–
Coordinated market economies	–	Austria, Belgium, France, the Netherlands and Germany	Denmark, Finland, Norway and Sweden

Note: Although Esping-Andersen (1990) categorized the Netherlands as a social democratic welfare state, this study considers it a conservative welfare state in accordance with the recent studies by Iversen and Stephen (2008) and Schroeder (2009).
Japan and Switzerland are not included in the present analysis due to their ambiguity in clusters. While the VoC literature classifies Japan and Switzerland as coordinated market economies, the welfare literature is not certain about their positions in the welfare regime (Esping-Andersen, 1999).

Source: Esping-Andersen (1990); Hall and Soskice (2001); Iversen and Stephens (2008); Schroeder (2009).

leaving them more vulnerable to displacement in changing economic conditions. To offset these risks, workers are more likely to demand a high level of social protection and employment protection from the welfare state (Estevez-Abe et al., 2001; Hall and Soskice, 2001; Iversen and Soskice, 2008). Employers in CMEs share interests with workers because they make a great investment in workers by training them to develop specific skills. Under this condition, the rational choices of employers are to build long-term employment contracts and demand the government to provide generous social insurance programs that relieve them of the costs of insuring workers for health, disability and retirement income.

In contrast, LMEs have developed processes organized around production with general skills, short-term labor contracts and the availability of a large pool of workers who cycle in and out of jobs. Countries with LMEs typically disperse policy authority across levels of government and rely on market mechanisms, rather than government regulations, to set wages and insure workers against the risks of sickness and disability. These labor market and political conditions give employers considerable influence on social policies (Mares, 2003).

Differences in the organization of production processes, and how they distribute risk and mobilize demands for public social protections, help explain differences in the overall generosity of the welfare state across countries with either liberal or coordinated market economies. When we examine family policies that are particularly relevant to women, however, we observe additional differences within market economy types. Most notably, differences in the family policy regimes of the Nordic and Continental European countries have interacted with the organization of specific skill production processes to produce different responses to women's increased labor market activity and the growing economic insecurity of families. In the following sections we consider variation across three clusters of countries suggested by our integrated framework: those with LMEs and liberal welfare regimes and those with CMEs coupled with either conservative or social democratic welfare regimes.

LMEs and Liberal Welfare State Regimes

In countries with LMEs and liberal welfare state approaches, the residual approach to government intervention and general skill production processes interact to fragment the power of women and limit the generosity of family benefits. Women face less discrimination because general skills are gender-neutral and portable (Estevez-Abe, 2005), reducing employers' reluctance to hire female workers. This creates favorable conditions for taking career breaks for family reasons, but also results in considerable employment insecurity in the absence of the generous welfare state benefits provided in most countries with CMEs.

The absence of public family support and centralized bargaining institutions in LME/Liberal welfare states have differing consequences for female workers by class and fragment political demands for public benefits (Korpi et al., 2013; Mandel, 2009; Mandel and Shalev, 2009). In the absence of inclusive government benefits in liberal welfare states, employers can use selective provision of private employment-based benefits to attract the highest skilled workers. In combination with limited public social benefits, this creates considerable economic risk for low-income individual workers and reduces their power to negotiate for better wages and working conditions. Low-income female workers may want protections, in particular, childcare or maternity leave, but may lack the political power or resources to advance their demands. In contrast, publicly provided family policies are likely to be less important to highly educated and skilled female workers because they benefit from the easy exit/entry job system and have private resources and benefits, including firm-provided maternity leave and childcare. These class differences weaken collective political demands and mobilization for improvement in public family policies.

The integration of the welfare state and VoC approaches also suggests ways in which labor market structures interact with family policies over time to institutionalize these policy approaches (Morgan, 2005). For example, the large low-wage sector in the liberal US labor market provides a readily available supply of low-skilled workers to provide low-cost private childcare on a 24/7 schedule (Morgan, 2005), further weakening female workers' demands for public childcare. At the same time, the US childcare system, which relies heavily on private labor, has reinforced the structure of the low-wage service sector produced by uncoordinated wage setting. Highly flexible, private childcare provided by low-wage workers frees higher skilled women with children for employment and also sustains the low-wage labor market for less skilled women.

Common Problems in CMEs

In CMEs the importance of firm-specific skills creates particular barriers for female employment (Estevez-Abe, 2005). High levels of social benefits for female workers, such as maternity leave and child allowances, promote employment continuity for women and protect them from the risk of income loss due to childbirth; they may also be seen by employers as imposing additional risks and costs for hiring women due to career interruptions and workplace absences. This structure discourages employers' investments in female workers for specialized and highly paid positions. Because they are more likely than male workers to exit employment to care for children, incurring a substantial economic penalty, female workers themselves may also be less inclined to invest in acquiring specific skills, but choose instead to invest in general skills and enter less remunerative jobs.

Even though it helps explain variations in social polices (Hall and Soskice, 2001), the VoC framework fails to capture differences in family policies within similar production regimes. Scholars have found heterogeneity in the family policies of Nordic and Continental European countries with similarly coordinated market economies (Gallie, 2007; Korpi et al., 2013; Thévenon, 2011).

CMEs and Conservative Welfare States

Conservative welfare state countries are characterized by generous family policies that perpetuate traditional gender roles. These policies reflect the interaction of coordinated production regimes, built on a tradition of industry-specific entitlement, with family policies that have been structured by traditional family and gender values that prioritize women's work in the home. Firm-specific skills are protected through generous social benefits that secure the health and well-being of the workforce. The traditional guild systems for employment, and reliance on charity by the Church, have organized interests by industrial sector to produce industry-specific rather than universal entitlements. Restrictions on entry and wage structures with industry-specific collective bargaining favor insiders, mostly male workers (Iversen, 2005; Rueda, 2005), and in turn create barriers to entry for female workers. Wage-setting agreements negotiated at the industry or sector level also produce wide pay gaps and segmented labor markets that channel female workers into part-time employment and the relatively less lucrative service sectors with weak and segmented union power (Morgan, 2005; Rubery, 2009; Visser, 2006). Barriers to entry and career advancement in the labor market interact with family policies that encourage women's domestic and caregiving work by supporting long absences from employment and limiting publicly subsidized alternative care arrangements.

Once institutionalized, the structures of labor market and welfare states have shaped the trajectory of change as CME/Conservative welfare state countries grappled with changing economic and social conditions. In particular, these countries responded to the need for an expanded workforce in the late twentieth century by increasing their reliance on immigrant workers rather than increasing the female labor supply (Huber and Stephens, 2000). Female labor force participation remains lower in CME/Conservative welfare state countries than in countries at comparable levels of development with LME/Liberal or CME/Social democratic regimes.

CMEs and Social Democratic Welfare States

CME/Social democratic welfare states have followed a different path in family policy development. The interaction of political interests with market and state institutions has produced family policies that are not only generous but also gender-egalitarian. Welfare state scholars point to large service sector economies that have provided job opportunities for female workers and generous family leave and childcare and other family policies have further stimulated the expansion of women's labor force participation by providing employment opportunities as caregivers and teachers in the public sector (Huber and Stephens, 2000).

The interaction between political climates and institutional settings explains strong left party political power as instrumental in the development of employment opportunities for women and demands for generous family policy support. National coordinated wage setting in these countries works to the advantage of female workers and helps mobilize their demands for family policy. Female workers in countries with national coordinated wage setting have more political leverage and have been able to secure higher wages for workers in the service sectors in which female workers are concentrated. Coordinated agreements about cost sharing among state, employers and employees reduce the cost of social protection benefits, such as childcare and paid maternity leave, relieving individual employers of the burden and risk associated with hiring female workers (Shalev, 2008). The interaction of coordinated market arrangements with generous and gender-egalitarian social policies has created incentives for both female workers and their employers to support family policies that allow female workers to take career breaks without severing employment attachments or interrupting specific skill development.

RESEARCH APPROACH, METHODS AND DATA

We turn now to an empirical analysis of changing family policy in 14 OECD countries during the period 1990 through 2010. We use country-level indicators of policy effort to first estimate the magnitude of change and then consider whether the trajectories of change during this period continued or substantially altered the characteristic approach to family policy described above for each of our three clusters of countries. Countries were selected on the basis of their inclusion in prior comparative welfare state research for both welfare regime and VoC literatures, similarities in levels of economic and welfare state development, and the availability of comparable data for constructing indicator measures.

To sharpen the focus on the consequences of family policy for women – in particular, mothers – we select policies that have explicit or implicit implications for three possible policy goals: (1) support for women's ability to manage dual responsibilities as earners and caregivers; (2) gender equalization in employment caregiving responsibilities; and (3) protecting the economic security of families with children. Although we are interested in change throughout this period we construct measures for three time points – 1990, 2000 and 2010 – for which we had the most complete and comparable data for each of the countries.

We address two questions:

1. Was there an overall expansion or contraction in family policies during this period? Were these changes similar or different in relation to the three possible policy goals of work/family balance, gender equality and family economic security?
2. Did the trajectory of policy change vary across the policy clusters defined by our integrated framework as LME/Liberal, CME/Conservative or CME/Social democratic welfare state regimes?

Method and Data

In order to capture both a broad range of relevant policies and variation in the goals, we develop and compare aggregated indices of policy indicators at the country level. We then compare changes over time on indices that capture the three different aspects of family policies: work/family balance, gender equality (both gendering and degendering) and family income protection. The value of each policy indicator is standardized and scaled from 0 to 1. Indicator scores are then added together and rescaled from 0 to 1 for each index, in which a greater score indicates more generous or active policy efforts relative to a specified goal.

Data for the study were obtained from multiple publicly available databases with country-specific data for the period of study, including the OECD Family Database (2014), OECD Social Expenditure data (2012), the Comparative Family Policy Database by Gauthier (2011) and the EC Network on Childcare (1996) (see Appendix for details).

Index Construction

To capture the three aspects of family policy we construct four separate indexes.

1. *Work/family balance* captures the extent to which family policies help female workers maintain their jobs and continue their career progress given their disproportionate responsibility for providing care to family members. The availability and length of job-protected leave have been found to increase women's labor force attachment and

career progress after childbirth, as have the availability and affordability of childcare (Gornick and Meyers, 2008; Kluve and Tamm, 2013; Pettit and Hook, 2005). Job-protected leave is defined in this study as parental leave available to mothers with or without wage replacement. Even though the difference between paid and unpaid leave may influence the actual take-up, we highlight the job protection dimension of parental leave because it has been shown to affect returns to the labor markets for female workers. Our index measures country effort as the additive effect of:

Work/family Balance Index: {(Total weeks of job-protected leave regardless of income support) + (public day-care expenditure)}/2

2. *Gender equality* gauges the extent to which family policies promote more equal gender roles. Because the goals and possible impact of family policies are often in tension or even contradictory within a single country, we conceptualize this as two theoretically distinct policy outcomes rather than as variation along a single linear dimension. A country may have policies that are *gendering* insofar as they create incentives for women to forego employment in favor of caregiving in the home alongside other policies that are *degendering* because they defamilize caregiving through provision of public childcare. For example, degendering policies encourage fathers to participate in care responsibilities that have traditionally been considered female responsibilities.

2. (a) We use three indicators to construct a *gendering index* of the extent to which policies reinforce the traditional expectation that mothers will reduce or leave employment to be the primary caregivers for children and fathers will continue to take the responsibilities of a breadwinner in a household. The provision of generous cash benefits, rather than services to families with children, promotes the maintenance of traditional gender roles by providing parents, overwhelmingly women, with opportunities to leave work and incentives to stay at home after childbirth (Nieuwenhuis et al., 2012).

Family and maternity leaves has been found to have mixed consequences for women's employment: the availability of job-protected maternity leave increases the likelihood that women will return to work after childbirth but very long periods of additional family leave after the end of the maternity leave, often providing only job protection or very low cash benefits, are associated with long absences from the workplace and lower subsequent rates of return (Budig et al., 2010; Pettit and Hook, 2005). In other words, a single policy influences multiple outcomes and advances different and even competing goals. Publicly subsidized childcare, in contrast, has an unambiguously positive effect on women's employment (Budig et al., 2010; Pettit and Hook, 2005). To capture the mixed and potentially interacting effects of these two policies we construct two separate indicators. To capture the negative effect of extensive leave we include an indicator for the total number of weeks of parental leave with or without wage replacement, weighted by half. The final indicator assumes a nonlinear interaction between the length of leave and availability of alternatives to full-time parental, usually maternal, care in the home: long periods of leave following maternity leave in combination with limited public childcare support will create the strongest incentives for maintaining traditional gender roles; moderate leave periods with high levels of public childcare will shift incentives toward returns to employment;

but very short leaves with limited childcare will have a 'work forcing' effect. We define the length of leave categorically as 1 for within 52 weeks; 2 for 52–104 weeks; and 3 for very long leaves of more than 104 weeks of job-protected leave after maternity leave regardless of income support. This indicator is multiplied by a categorically coded indicator for the inverse of public childcare expenditures (coded from 1 for the lowest quartile to 4 for the highest quartile) to capture the interaction of the two policies.

The index is calculated as:

Gendering Index: {[Proportion of cash benefits in total family expenditures] + [(0.5) × (total number of parental weeks)] + [(Existence of prolonged job-protected leave) × (inversed day-care expenditure)]}/2.5

2. (b) The potential for policies to be *degendering*, or actively challenging to traditional roles, is measured by an index capturing the policy incentives for fathers to assume more caregiving responsibilities along with the availability of public childcare to defamilize care by providing alternatives to full-time parental care. Designated paternity leave or 'father quotas' in family leave has been found to increase the likelihood that men will take breaks from employment following the birth of a child (Lappegard, 2008; Schober, 2014). Men are expected to be more likely to use available leave if the replacement rate for lost wages is higher. We measure these potential degendering effects as an indicator for the availability of any designated paternity leave multiplied by the full-time equivalent rate (FTE) for parental leave benefits. The benefit rate is weighted by half in order to avoid excessive reliance on paternity leave. Because only a few countries offer paternity leave for fathers and provide paid paternity leave, the *Degendering Index* may yield skewed values for the scores of indicators depending on both the existence of paternity leave and its FTE. We add this to the enrollment rate of children under age 3 in public childcare to capture the emphasis on defamilizing care responsibility and freeing women from traditional caregiving in the home, particularly in the period between the end of maternity leave and the beginning of preschool. The final index is calculated as:

Degendering Index: {[Existence of paternity leave] + [(0.5 × paternity leave) × FTE] + [public childcare enrollment rate under 3]}/2.5

3. The generosity of *family income protection* is captured by two policy indicators. First, we use family allowance in gross domestic product (GDP) adjusted by the population of children under age 18. We measure the generosity of these tax and transfer benefits for the second policy indicator with value of tax and benefit transfers of one-earner, two-parent, two-child families. The value is calculated by subtracting the disposable income (after taxes and transfers) of a one-earner, two-parent, two-child family from that of a comparable childless single earner and standardized in US dollars adjusted for purchasing power parity (PPP). Family allowances, targeted tax benefits and other cash transfers for families with children offset the additional costs of raising children and directly support families' economic well-being (Maître et al., 2005). Parenting leaves with high replacement rates help stabilize family income during periods when parents withdraw from the workplace to care for children (Ray

et al., 2010). We measure this as the wage replacement level of all leave – combining maternity, parental and childcare leaves.

The final index combines these indicators as follows:

Family Income Protection Index: {[Family allowance in family expenditure] + [Tax and benefits to families with children] + [FTE wage replacement of all leaves]}/3

OVERALL EXPANSION BUT DISTINCTIVE PATTERNS OF FAMILY POLICY CHANGES

Table 6.2 presents the family policy index scores for 14 individual countries from 1990 to 2010. Arithmetic averages of countries within each cluster are also calculated to provide comparable measures of the direction of changes over time in family policy clusters. As highly aggregated measures, the numeric values are not meaningful in the absolute sense and their magnitude cannot be compared directly across different policy areas. Instead, they represent an estimate of policy effort within each country relative to both the same country's effort in other time periods and the efforts of other countries.

We observe a pattern of family policy expansion overall. Comparing the patterns across policy dimensions, however, reveals important differences in where these changes were concentrated: 12 of the 14 countries expanded policies that support work/family balance through provision of job-protected leave and public childcare; all 14 countries expanded policies expected to have a degendering effect by increasing incentives for fathers to take parenting leave and/or by providing public care for children under 3. In many countries these changes were quite substantial relative to prior efforts.

The pattern was mixed, however, when we measured the potential gendering impact of policies that emphasize traditional gender roles through provision of generous cash benefits, very long job-protected leave and limited public childcare. We observe little or no change in nine of the countries and substantial reductions of potentially gendering policy effort in six countries (Belgium, France, the Netherlands, Norway and Finland). The direction and magnitude of change was also mixed in policies that support families' income security through the generosity of wage replacement for family leave, tax credits and family allowances. Despite calls for austerity in many welfare states, while the value of the index declined substantially only in France, the generosity of family benefits appears to have increased rather substantially in four countries (Australia, New Zealand, Ireland and Norway).

Variation in the direction and magnitude of change across policy dimensions underscores the importance of disaggregating measures of policy effort. A comparison across the country clusters provides further insight. Different patterns of policy change emerge for each of the three clusters with different production/welfare regimes. In LME/Liberal welfare states, the expansion was most pronounced in policies to support families' economic security. In the CME/Conservative cluster the most dramatic changes were expansions of policies expected to support work/family balance and encourage degendering of work and care. In the CME/Social democratic cluster changes were modest across all the policy areas.

Table 6.2 Family policy changes from 1990 to 2010

	LME/Liberal						CME/Conservative						CME/Social Democratic			
	M	AUS	NZ	UK	USA	IRE	M	BEL	AUT	FRA	DE	NL	M	NOR	SWE	DEN	FIN
Work/family Index																	
1990	0.22	0.26	0.30	0.21	0.11	0.20	0.25	0.02	0.22	0.65	0.26	0.12	0.59	0.38	0.72	0.50	0.74
2000	0.24	0.29	0.33	0.30	0.11	0.18	0.45	0.20	0.38	0.78	0.59	0.28	0.53	0.34	0.55	0.50	0.74
2010							0.51	0.27	0.48	0.80	0.68	0.33	0.63	0.45	0.67	0.61	0.77
Degendering Index																	
1990	0.16	0.11	0.19	0.16	0.21	0.15	0.27	0.66	0.55	0.13	0.00	0.00	0.42	0.17	0.59	0.73	0.18
2000	0.30	0.20	0.22	0.65	0.26	0.18	0.42	0.71	0.57	0.58	0.04	0.17	0.70	0.63	0.71	0.89	0.57
2010							0.59	0.73	0.58	0.70	0.54	0.77	0.81	0.93	0.81	0.82	0.66
Gendering Index																	
1990	0.25	0.36	0.27	0.15	0.14	0.35	0.61	0.55	0.59	0.79	0.65	0.45	0.27	0.45	0.17	0.09	0.35
2000	0.30	0.56	0.21	0.19	0.15	0.37	0.54	0.40	0.70	0.53	0.79	0.30	0.27	0.37	0.20	0.10	0.40
2010	0.24	0.44	0.23	0.12	0.15	0.27	0.45	0.32	0.62	0.41	0.58	0.30	0.15	0.17	0.13	0.11	0.20
Family Income Protection Index																	
1990	0.07	0.05	0.08	0.12	0.01	0.11	0.42	0.66	0.54	0.48	0.25	0.19	0.30	0.24	0.30	0.22	0.43
2000	0.11	0.24	0.08	0.13	0.00	0.12	0.44	0.74	0.56	0.43	0.30	0.16	0.31	0.31	0.27	0.24	0.42
2010	0.17	0.22	0.23	0.12	0.01	0.28	0.36	0.35	0.50	0.37	0.35	0.22	0.32	0.35	0.34	0.21	0.36

Note: AUS: Australia; AUT: Austria; BEL: Belgium; DE: Germany; DEN: Denmark; FIN: Finland; IRE: Ireland; NL: the Netherlands; NZ: New Zealand; SWE: Sweden; UK: United Kingdom; USA: United States. M indicates the average score of countries within each regime. All indexes are scaled from 0 to 1 with higher values indicating greater provision. The work/family and degendering index score in 1990 in LMEs/Liberal welfare states is not presented due to limitations in terms of compatibility of data and because of the issue of missing data.

Although policy change was substantial in some countries, the relative position of the country clusters remained consistent. At both the early and later time points, the LME/Liberal cluster was least generous, particularly in policies providing income support and incentives to degender work and care; the CME/Conservative countries had the highest index values for policies that reinforce traditional gender roles; and the CME/Social democratic countries made the greatest policy efforts in both supporting work/family balance and degendering. This suggests that the general policy approach of each cluster remained distinctive over time although there is some evidence of convergence, particularly in the CME countries.

Family Policy Encouraging Female Labor Participation in CME/Conservative Welfare States

Family policy changes were most dramatic during this period in the CME/Conservative welfare states. Increase in policy efforts to support work/family balance and degender caregiving work are particularly remarkable and position these countries close to levels of effort in the traditionally gender-egalitarian CME/Social democratic welfare states. Nonetheless, differences persisted between these two clusters, with CME/Conservative welfare states maintaining substantial commitments to policies that may reinforce traditional gender roles.

Our analyses suggest that despite calls for higher female labor market participation, and the expansion of degendering policy efforts, most of the CME/Conservative cluster have not substantially reduced the gendering effects of policies. Our integrated framework suggests that the organization of production and the welfare state will continue to reinforce this policy approach and recent changes are unlikely to bring about fundamental reorientation of family policies. In the face of economic pressures to increase productive employment, many Continental countries have encouraged women's employment (Lewis, 2006; Stratigaki, 2004) by promoting part-time labor participation for female workers. This approach has not only worked well with their traditional family policy approach but has also been seen by some as a solution to stagnant economic growth of these countries' market economies (Huber and Stephens, 2001a; Thelen, 2012) and the sustainability of social policies (Iversen, 2005). The structure of the production regime, with strong insider protections, gives disproportionate power to mostly male workers who benefit from both the market dualization (Thelen, 2012) and the availability of women's labor in the home. Politically, supporters of the traditional family policy approach also appeal to female constituents seeking part-time and flexible work arrangements.

Within this general pattern, however, we see some heterogeneity among CME/Conservative welfare state countries. For example, France has the highest index score for work/family balancing policies among the CME/Conservative countries, even higher than the scores for some Nordic countries. Index scores for France also suggest substantial efforts to both increase degendering policies and reduce those that reinforce traditional gender roles. Although lower by 2010, France's score on gendering policies remains higher than those of the CME/Social democratic countries. This finding is consistent with some studies that suggest that France is part of a different cluster of conservative countries (Thévenon, 2011) and those that find heterogeneity within CME countries with conservative welfare regimes (Huber and Stephens, 2001b; Rueda and Pontusson, 2000).

LME/Liberal Welfare States: Expansion in Family Income Protection

Our analyses suggest that countries in the LME/Liberal welfare state cluster continued to adhere to a market-oriented approach to family policy. Across all policy areas they had the lowest index scores, on average, at both the start and end of the period. We find little evidence of family policy expansion in most countries within the cluster, with the exception of family income protection policies which became more generous in three of the five countries.[1] Despite a more than twofold increase in the index scores in these countries from 1990 to 2010, however, generosity remained lower than in most of the countries in other clusters.

The interaction of production and welfare state institutions that shaped the family policy approach in the LME/Liberal cluster of countries appears to have reinforced rather than challenged this approach in recent decades, producing a distinctive trajectory for policy responses to new social and economic conditions. The weak collective bargaining power of labor, lack of powerful market regulatory institutions, and limited redistributional impact from social policy have produced the highest level of income inequality among advanced capitalist democracies. Given the lack of generous family policy, demographic changes that have increased single motherhood have further eroded families' economic resources and worsened child poverty in the LME/Liberal countries (Esping-Andersen, 1999; Thévenon, 2011).

In some of the LME/Liberal countries evidence of worsening economic conditions and increasing inequality may have increased demands to increase the generosity of policies to protect family income. But these demands do not appear to have challenged market or policy structures that sustain both income and gender inequalities. Thus, recent policy changes have continued the traditional policy approach of supporting social policy as an investment in children's human capital with a mostly private delivery system (Lewis and Campbell, 2007; Macleavy, 2007). For example, the UK adopted policies during this period that enable women to enter the labor market, and expanded social transfers and targeted tax benefits.

Stability in CME/Social Democratic Welfare States

Family policy stability is observed in the countries with CME/Social democratic welfare regimes. By the end of the period, countries in this cluster continued to have the highest scores for work/family and degendering and the lowest for gender policies among clusters.

Despite pressures to reduce, restructure and privatize social benefits, experienced by all of the advanced welfare states, the stability of policy efforts in the countries can be explained by the interaction between a production regime and a strong national welfare state structure that has allowed these countries to deal with new economic and social risks without significant retrenchment. Given both employment security and the power of collective bargaining provided through national labor policy and wage-setting institutions, women's power as a political constituency has maintained support for the generous and gender-egalitarian model of the CME/Social democratic cluster. While globalization and economic recession do not appear to have jeopardized family policies that enable and equalize women's employment, there is some evidence that they have resulted in a decrease in the generosity of family income protection and modest restructuring of the work/

family balance and (de)gendering aspects of family policy. These countries may reduce the generosity of family policies but do not appear likely to restructure these policies along the lines of those in CME/Conservative or LME/Liberal countries.

CONCLUSION

Our empirical analysis confirms that findings of other scholars that family policies, as a whole, expanded between 1990 and 2010. By comparing measures that capture different, and sometimes competing, policy goals and effects, however, we uncover important differences. Nearly all of the 14 countries expanded policies that support work/family balance and those that create incentives to degender caregiving. We observe much less expansion in benefits to protect family income and find evidence that many countries' reduced policy efforts are likely to reinforce traditional gender roles.

This disaggregation also highlights different patterns of family policy change across countries with distinctive combinations of market and welfare state institutions. Countries in each of the family policy regime clusters suggested by our integrated framework followed distinctive trajectories of change that reflected existing institutional and political realities. We see some evidence of convergence of CME/Conservative welfare states with the policies of CME/Social democratic countries, but the two approaches to family policy remain distinctive. Family policies do not change on a single dimension and in some cases the reduction of policy effort may advance an important policy goal such as the reduction of gendering effects. Countries with different family policy regimes may emphasize family income protection or stress work/family balance and degendering of policy incentives. Failure to capture these differences can lead to overly broad conclusions and miss important continuities in policy effort.

This study has several limitations. Our proposed framework is limited by the failure of production regime theory to fully explain social policy in European countries (Korpi, 2006) and by the lack of perfect one-to-one correspondence between production and welfare regimes (Huber and Stephens, 2001b). However, this integrative framework provides an important insight about the contexts in which family policies are situated and the power that institutions and policy feedback loops exert in policy change. This framework has particularly good merits for studying female employment cross-nationally. Given that the labor market is a critical nexus for relationships between state and market (Pierson, 2001), female employment is the outcome of the broad contexts of market economies, family policy and labor market policies. Also, because our examination relies on relative changes of family policy in relation to those in other countries, it may not be easy to claim how much differences in indicators should be considered as the net change that has taken place. Lastly, lack of comparable annual data for this period limits the precision of the empirical estimates in this study. Future studies with more years of comparison data may be able to develop more refined indexes for each of the family policy goals, in particular the more recent concern of policymakers to support work/family balance and degender caregiving roles.

NOTE

1. The degendering score increased for this cluster, but was largely driven by the UK.

REFERENCES

Bonoli, G. (2005), 'The politics of the new social policies: providing coverage against new social risks in mature welfare states', *Policy and Politics*, **33** (3), 431–49.
Budig, M., J. Misra, and I. Bockmann (2010), 'The motherhood penalty in cross-national perspective: the importance of work-family policies and cultural attitudes', LIS Working Paper Series, No. 542.
Ebbinghaus, B. and P. Manow (eds) (2001), *Comparing Welfare Capitalism*, London and New York: Routledge.
Esping-Andersen, G. (1990), *The Three Worlds of Welfare Capitalism*, Princeton, NJ: Princeton University Press.
Esping-Andersen, G. (1999), *Social Foundations of Postindustrial Economies*, New York: Oxford University Press.
European Commission Network on Childcare (1996), *A Review of Services for Young Children in the European Union 1990–1995*, Brussels: Equal Opportunities Unit, DGV, European Commission.
Estevez-Abe, M. (2005), 'Gender bias in skills and social policies: the varieties of capitalism perspective on sex segregation', *Social Politics*, **12** (2), 180–215.
Estevez-Abe, M., T. Iversen, and D. Soskice (2001), 'Social protection and the formation of skills: a reinterpretation of welfare state', in P. Hall and D. Soskice (eds), *Varieties of Capitalism*, New York: Oxford University Press, pp. 145–83.
Gable, S.G. and S.B. Kamerman (2006), 'Investing in children: public commitment in twenty-one industrialized countries', *Social Service Review*, **80** (2), 239–63.
Gallie, D. (2007), 'Production regimes and the quality of employment in Europe', *Annual Review of Sociology*, **33** (1), 85–104.
Gauthier, A.H. (2002), 'Family policies in industrialized countries: is there convergence?', *Population (English Edition)*, **57** (3), 447–74.
Goodman, W. (1995), 'Boom in day care industry the result of many social changes', *Monthly Labor Review*, **118** (3), 3–12.
Gornick, J.C. and M.K. Meyers. (2008), 'Creating gender egalitarian societies: an agenda for reform', *Politics & Society*, **36** (3), 313–49.
Hall, P. and D. Soskice (2001), 'An introduction to varieties of capitalism', in P. Hall and D. Soskice (eds), *Varieties of Capitalism*, Oxford and New York: Oxford University Press, pp. 1–68.
Huber, E. and J.D. Stephens (2000), 'Partisan governance, women's employment, and the social democratic service state', *American Sociological Review*, **65** (3), 323–42.
Huber, E. and J.D. Stephens (eds) (2001a), *Development and Crisis of the Welfare State*, Chicago, IL: University of Chicago Press.
Huber, E. and J.D. Stephens (2001b), 'Welfare state and production regimes in the era of retrenchment', in P. Pierson (ed.), *The New Politics of the Welfare State*, Oxford and New York: Oxford University Press, pp. 107–45.
Iversen, T. (ed.) (2005), *Capitalism, Democracy, and Welfare*, New York: Cambridge University Press.
Iversen, T. and D. Soskice (2001), 'An asset theory of social policy preferences', *American Political Science Review*, **95** (4), 875–93.
Iversen, T. and J.D. Stephens (2008), 'Partisan politics, the welfare state, and three worlds of human capital formation', *Comparative Political Studies*, **41** (4–5), 600–63.
Kluve, J. and M. Tamm (2013), 'Parental leave regulations, mothers' labor force attachment and fathers' childcare involvement: evidence from a natural experiment', *Journal of Population Economics*, **26** (3), 983–1005.
Korpi, W. (2006), 'Power resources and employer-centered approaches in explanations of welfare states and varieties of capitalism – protagonists, consenters, and antagonists', *World Politics*, **58** (2), 167–206.
Korpi, W., T. Ferrarini, and S. Englund (2013), 'Women's opportunities under different family policy constellations: gender, class, and inequality tradeoffs in western countries re-examined', *Social Politics*, **20** (1), 1–40.
Lappegard, T. (2008), 'Changing the gender balance in caring: fatherhood and the division of parental leave in Norway', *Population Research and Policy Review*, **27** (2), 139–59.
Lewis, J. (2006), 'Work/family reconciliation, equal opportunities and social policies: the interpretation of policy trajectories at the EU level and the meaning of gender equality', *Journal of European Public Policy*, **13** (3), 420–37.

Lewis, J. and M. Campbell (2007), 'Work/family balance policies in the UK since 1997: a new departure?', *Journal of Social Policy*, **36**, 365–81.

Macleavy, J. (2007), 'Engendering New Labour's workfarist regime: exploring the intersection of welfare state restructuring and labour market policies in the UK', *Gender Place and Culture*, **14** (6), 721–43.

Mahon, R., A. Anttonen, C. Bergqvist, D. Brennan, and B. Hobson (2012), 'Convergent care regimes? Childcare arrangements in Australia, Canada, Finland and Sweden', *Journal of European Social Policy*, **22** (4), 419–31.

Maître, B., B. Norland, and C. Whelan (2005), 'Welfare regimes and household income packaging in the European Union', *Journal of European Social Policy*, **15** (2), 157–71.

Mandel, H. (2009), 'Configurations of gender inequality: the consequences of ideology and public policy', *British Journal of Sociology*, **60** (4), 693–719.

Mandel, H. and M. Shalev (2009), 'How welfare states shape the gender pay gap: a theoretical and comparative analysis', *Social Forces*, **87** (4), 1873–912.

Mares, I. (2003), 'Firms and welfare state: when, why, and how does the social policy matter to employers?', in P. Hall and D. Soskice (eds), *Varieties of Capitalism*, Oxford and New York: Oxford University Press, pp. 184–212.

Morgan, K.J. (2005), 'The "production" of child care: how labor markets shape social policy and vice versa', *Social Politics*, **12** (2), 243–63.

Nieuwenhuis, R., A. Need, and H. Van Der Kolk (2012), 'Institutional and demographic explanations of women's employment in 18 OECD countries, 1975–1999', *Journal of Marriage and Family*, **74** (3), 614–30.

Pettit, B. and J. Hook (2005), 'The structure of women's employment in comparative perspective', *Social Forces*, **84** (2), 779–801.

Pierson, P. (2001), 'Investigating the welfare state at century's end', in P. Pierson (ed.), *The New Politics of the Welfare State*, Oxford and New York: Oxford University Press, pp. 1–14.

Ray, R., J.C. Gornick, and J. Schmitt (2010), 'Who cares? Assessing generosity and gender equality in parental leave policy designs in 21 countries', *Journal of European Social Policy*, **20** (3), 196–216.

Rubery, J. (2009), 'How gendering the varieties of capitalism requires a wider lens', *Social Politics: International Studies in Gender, State & Society*, **16** (2), 192–203.

Rueda, D. (2005), 'Insider-outsider politics in industrialized democracies: the challenge to social democratic parties', *American Political Science Review*, **99** (1), 61–74.

Rueda, D. and J. Pontusson (2000), 'Wage inequality and varieties of capitalism', *World Politics*, **52** (3), 350–83.

Schober, P.S. (2014), 'Parental leave and domestic work of mothers and fathers: a longitudinal study of two reforms in West Germany', *Journal of Social Policy*, **43** (2), 351–72.

Schroeder, M. (2009), 'Integrating welfare and production typologies: how refinements of the varieties of capitalism approach call for a combination of welfare typologies', *Journal of Social Policy*, **38** (1), 19–43.

Shalev, M. (2008), 'Class divisions among women', *Politics & Society*, **36** (3), 421–44.

Stratigaki, M. (2004), 'The cooptation of gender concepts in EU policies: the case of "reconciliation of work and family"', *Social Politics*, **11** (1), 30–56.

Thelen, K. (2012), 'Varieties of capitalism: trajectories of liberalization and the new politics of social solidarity', *Annual Review of Political Science*, **15** (1), 137–59.

Thévenon, O. (2011), 'Family policies in OECD countries: a comparative analysis', *Population and Development Review*, **37** (1), 57–87.

Visser, J. (2006), 'Union membership statistics in 24 countries', *Monthly Labor Review*, **129** (1), 38–49.

APPENDIX: MEASUREMENTS AND DATA

1. *Work/family Index*: {(Job-protected leave weeks) + (day-care expenditure)}/2

   - Job-protected leave weeks is defined as the period after maternity leave for which a mother can be on parental leave with her job protected. Source: OECD Family Database, 2014, OECD, Paris.
   - Day-care expenditure is defined day-care expenditure in GDP adjusted by the population of children under age 5. Source: OECD Social Expenditure, 2012, OECD, Paris; OECD StatExtracts, Demography and Population, 2012, OECD, Paris.

2. (a) *Gendering Index*: {[Proportion of cash benefits in total family expenditures] + [(0.5) × (total number of parental week)] + [(existence of prolonged job-protected leave) × (inversed day-care expenditure)]}/2.5

   - Proportion of cash benefits in total family expenditure in GDP. Source: OECD Social Expenditure, 2012, OECD, Paris; OECD StatExtracts, Demography and Population, 2012, OECD, Paris.
   - Parental leave weeks. Source: A.H. Gauthier, Comparative Family Policy Database, Version 3, 2011, Netherlands Interdisciplinary Demographic Institute and Max Planck Institute for Demographic Research.
   - Prolonged job-protected leave is coded 1 if leave weeks are less than 52 weeks; 2 if leave weeks are more than 52 and less than 104 weeks; 3 if leave weeks are longer than 104 weeks. Source: OECD Family Database, 2014, OECD, Paris.
   - Day-care expenditures for every year and every country are coded 4 for the first quartile; 3 for the second quartile; 2 for the third quartile; 1 for the fourth quartile. Source: Day-care expenditure from OECD Social Expenditure, 2012, OECD, Paris.

2. (b) *Degendering Index*: {[Existence of paternity leave] + [(0.5 × paternity leave) × FTE] + [enrollment rate under 3]}/2.5

   - If there are paid weeks reserved for the exclusive use of fathers (paternity leave, individual parental leave or father quota); coded either 0 or 1. Source: OECD Family Database, 2014, OECD, Paris.
   - FTE of paternity leave is defined as paternity leave weeks × parental leave wage replacement, Source: OECD Family Database, 2014, OECD, Paris; A.H. Gauthier, Comparative Family Policy Database, Version 3, 2011, Netherlands Interdisciplinary Demographic Institute and Max Planck Institute for Demographic Research.
   - Enrollment rate of children age under age 3 is measured as average enrollment rates for the age groups from 0 to 2 years (only for formal childcare arrangements). Source: For 1990, European Commission Network on Childcare, 1996; Goodman (1995). For 2000 and 2010, OECD Family Database, 2014, OECD, Paris. Several data are replaced due to missing data: Australia 2002 for 2000;

USA 2005 for 2000; Belgium 2002 for 2000; New Zealand 2001 for 2000, 2008 for 2010; Germany 2003 for 2000.
- Proportion of cash benefits in total family expenditure in GDP. Source: OECD Social Expenditure, 2012, OECD, Paris; OECD StatExtracts, Demography and Population, 2012, OECD, Paris.

3. *Family Income Protection Index*: {[Family allowance in family expenditure] + [Tax and benefits to families] + [FTE of all leaves]}/3

- Family allowance in GDP adjusted by the population of children under age 18. Source: OECD Social Expenditure, 2012, OECD, Paris; OECD StatExtracts, Demography and Population, 2012, OECD, Paris.
- Tax and benefits to families are measured with value of tax and benefit transfers of one-earner, two-parent, two-child families. The value was calculated by subtracting the disposable income (after taxes and transfers) of a one-earner, two-parent, two-child family from that of a comparable childless single earner and standardized in US dollars adjusted for purchasing power parity (PPP). Source: A.H. Gauthier, Comparative Family Policy Database, Version 3, 2011, Netherlands Interdisciplinary Demographic Institute and Max Planck Institute for Demographic Research.
- FTE of all leaves is calculated with {[(Replacement rate of maternity leave) × maternity leave weeks)] + [(replacement rate of parental leave) × (parental leave weeks)] + [(replacement rate of childcare leave) × (childcare leave weeks)]. Source: A.H. Gauthier, Comparative Family Policy Database, Version 3, 2011, Netherlands Interdisciplinary Demographic Institute and Max Planck Institute for Demographic Research.

PART III

FAMILY POLICIES

7. Family benefit systems
Jonathan Bradshaw

INTRODUCTION

Child benefits exist in all rich countries, in very few middle-income countries and in no poor countries. In fact, most countries in the world don't have child benefits, despite the fact that they have been advocated by most international bodies, with the notable exception of the World Bank. This chapter asks why not? It starts by reviewing the functions that child benefits serve in social security systems. It then focuses on three possible outcomes of child benefits: poverty reduction; fertility; and empowering mothers. Model family data is used to compare the level and structure of child benefit packages in the European Union and Organisation for Economic Co-operation and Development (OECD) countries, focusing on the contribution they make to reducing child poverty rates and gaps. The association between child benefits and fertility is explored. There is limited but encouraging evidence on the outcomes for children of empowering mothers. Then, some possible objections to child benefits are discussed: their cost; the case for better targeting; and the administrative demands of introducing such schemes. The conclusion is that the case for child benefits in all countries is overwhelming.

All social security systems in the European Union (EU) have child benefits (Van Mechelen and Bradshaw, 2013). They exist in the USA and Canada, New Zealand and Australia. Japan has fairly recently introduced them (Bradshaw and Tokoro, 2013) and Taiwan[1] and Mongolia have them, but they exist nowhere else in Asia. Hong Kong is in the process of introducing a family benefit. They do not exist in India. In South America, Argentina has them, but nowhere else. In Africa, South Africa has them, but nowhere else. They used to exist in the Soviet Union but now only very limited schemes exist in Russia, Belarus and the Ukraine in the whole of the non-EU, Central and Eastern Europe (CEE) and Commonwealth of Independent States (CIS) regions (Bradshaw et al., 2013). This chapter will review child benefit schemes in more detail. But first it is important to introduce a definition of child benefit. Child benefits here mean cash transfers to families with children to help parents with the costs of child rearing. They may be universal, but they are often income tested. They may be cash payments or deductions from taxes. It is important (but sometimes difficult) to distinguish between social assistance or minimum income support, which often includes a child addition and child benefits which are not necessarily concerned with minimum income, and are payable to families in employment. Many countries have targeted social assistance and some pay more if there are children. These are not child benefits or rather not under this definition, though in some countries child benefits are paid to families in work from social assistance. Child benefit is often a package of measures including universal and income tested child benefits, tax benefits and rebates, housing benefits, heating benefits, childcare subsidies, free school meals, food stamps, exemption from charges for basic health and education – and in some countries social assistance may also form part of the package. Why should a social security system have child benefits?

The chapter starts by reviewing the original objectives of child benefits from a UK perspective. Then it outlines the growing interest of international bodies in child cash grants as a means of tackling child poverty. The level and structure of child benefit schemes in rich countries is then compared using model family methods. The possible impact of child benefits on fertility rates and on mothers' purchasing power is reviewed and arguments used against child benefits are discussed, before concluding on the importance of child benefits for the future of children.

CHILD BENEFITS OVER TIME: THE UK CASE

As an initial attempt to answer why a social security system should have child benefits, let us engage in a bit of historical analysis, using the UK as an example of the changes over time and the significance of the child benefit. In the nineteenth century and before poor children died of disease, they laboured, and they were taken into the workhouse. In the first half of the twentieth century slow progress was made with child and social protection. Yet parents who could not afford to maintain their children would give them up for adoption, and many were transported to Canada and Australia (Parker, 2010). The British sociological researcher, social reformer and industrialist Seebohm Rowntree, in his first study of poverty in York published in 1901 (Rowntree, 1901), found children were the largest group in poverty. The wages paid in his father's chocolate factory were not enough to support a family with children above the primary poverty level. Influenced by this early social research, independent Member of the British Parliament Eleanor Rathbone (Rathbone, 1924) began to campaign for family allowances. She used three main arguments: first, a single wage was not enough to support two adults with children above the poverty level; second, even if it was, male breadwinners were not always sharing their wage with their wives; third, fertility had collapsed by the 1930s and people needed to be encouraged to have children. The economist and social reformer William Beveridge (Beveridge, 1942) adopted family allowances in his 1942 proposals for post-war social security. He argued that they were essential to ensure that unemployment insurance benefit did not undermine work incentives. They were the first element of his scheme to be enacted – in 1945. The then Conservative government was keen to introduce them (according to Macnicol, 1980) in order to hold down wage demands in the early post-war period. They were paid to the mother for the second and subsequent child. To cut a long story short, family allowances are now a universal child benefit[2] in the UK, paid for each child, and they are supplemented by child tax credit, childcare tax credit, free school meals, housing benefit and council tax benefit – all means-tested.

In this historical account, we observe some of the various justifications for child benefit: relief of family poverty; providing purchasing power to mothers; encouraging fertility; supplementing low wages; reducing wage demands; and maintaining work incentives. Wennemo (1992) also found these were some of the factors that motivated other welfare states to introduce child benefits. Other reasons include ensuring an income at periods of family or employment transition; and maintaining horizontal equity in the tax/benefit system (Bradshaw, 2012).

CHILD POVERTY

Perhaps the strongest case for child benefits, especially in the countries that don't have them, is the impact they would have on child poverty. Child poverty is the world's number one human problem (see also Chapter 23 by Gornick and Nell in this volume on children, poverty and public policy). If child benefit was introduced in every country in the world it would substantially reduce if not eradicate this scourge. As the literature shows (for a review see Griggs and Walker, 2008), child poverty is bad for children and bad for society – children who suffer poverty, particularly in the early years of childhood, suffer from cognitive deficit, and do not do well in school. Inadequate diets in childhood result in failure to thrive, less than optimal heights and weights and ill health in childhood and adulthood. Children are the future of all states and child poverty undermines human capital and national potential. Almost all countries in the world have signed the United Nations (UN) Convention on the Rights of the Child (CRC) – children are citizens with rights – rights under the UN Convention, especially (in Articles 26 and 27), not to be poor. But in most countries children are the largest group who are poor, they have the highest risk of poverty – so in most countries governments have failed to implement the CRC. Further, in fact, child poverty at such high levels in any country is evidence of government failure. The long-term social and economic costs are enormous (Hirsch, 2013).[3] There is growing international consensus about the value of child benefits in developing countries (Back, 2010; Department for International Development, 2005; OECD, 2009; Scott, 2009; Townsend, 2009; UNRISD, 2010). Recently, UNICEF (2014) launched its Social Protection Strategic Framework calling for child sensitive social protection with a progressive realization of universal coverage, including social transfers.

In June 2012, member countries of the International Labour Organization (ILO, 2012) adopted the Recommendation Concerning National Floors of Social Protection, which calls for ILO member states' action to build comprehensive social security systems and extend social security coverage by establishing and maintaining national social protection floors to ensure that all members of society enjoy at least a basic level of social security throughout their lives. The Recommendation stipulates that the national social protection floors comprise at least four basic social security guarantees, including basic income security for children. The Council of the European Union (2012) is now supporting the development of inclusive, nationally owned social protection policies and programmes, including social protection floors. The case for social protection was also recognised in the old African Union Social Policy Framework for Africa (2008) and in the South African Development Community (SADC, 2003) Social Policy Process/Charter of Fundamental Social Rights.

This enthusiasm for cash benefits has partly been driven by the success of these in a number of countries in South America, but especially by the experience of the Child Support Grant in South Africa. South Africa is the only country in Africa that has a cash grant for almost all poor children (see Chapter 19 by Knijn and Patel in this volume on South Africa). There are a few other countries that have cash payments for orphans and vulnerable children (OVC). Until Argentina introduced a universal family allowance in 2010 (Bertranou and Maurizio, 2011), South Africa was the only middle-income country in the world with a large, almost comprehensive child cash payment – the Child Support Grant (CSG).[4] The CSG has been subject to quite extensive evaluation. The most recent evaluation (DSD, SASSA and UNICEF, 2012) found that the CSG had improved heights. It has also improved maths ability tests and scores on reading and vocabulary for 10-year-olds. Girls' attainment at age 6 was improved by a quarter, mainly by reducing delays in entering school. The CSG has also been shown to improve health and reduce the likelihood of illness. For adolescents it has been shown to reduce school absences and the likelihood of working outside the household. It also reduces risk behaviour including sexual activity, pregnancy, alcohol use, drug use, criminal activity and gang membership. The report concluded, 'In these ways the Child Support Grant promotes human capital development, improves gender outcomes and helps to reduce the historical legacy of inequality' (DSD, SASSA and UNICEF, 2012). A country introducing a child benefit can expect it to have a profound effect on poverty and this will improve health outcomes and education outcomes but it will also increase economic activity at the local level, enhance agricultural production, enhance economic development and increase economic security.

COMPARISONS OF THE LEVEL AND STRUCTURE OF CHILD BENEFITS PACKAGES IN RICH COUNTRIES

There are a number of comparative sources on child benefits in rich countries which reveal their contribution to family incomes, though none completely up-to-date. The CSB MIPI (Minimum Income Protection Indicators) data set (Van Mechelen and Bradshaw, 2013; Van Mechelen et al., 2011) is one source and provides a picture for most EU countries and three US states (Nebraska, New Jersey and Texas) in January 2012. Figure 7.1 shows the

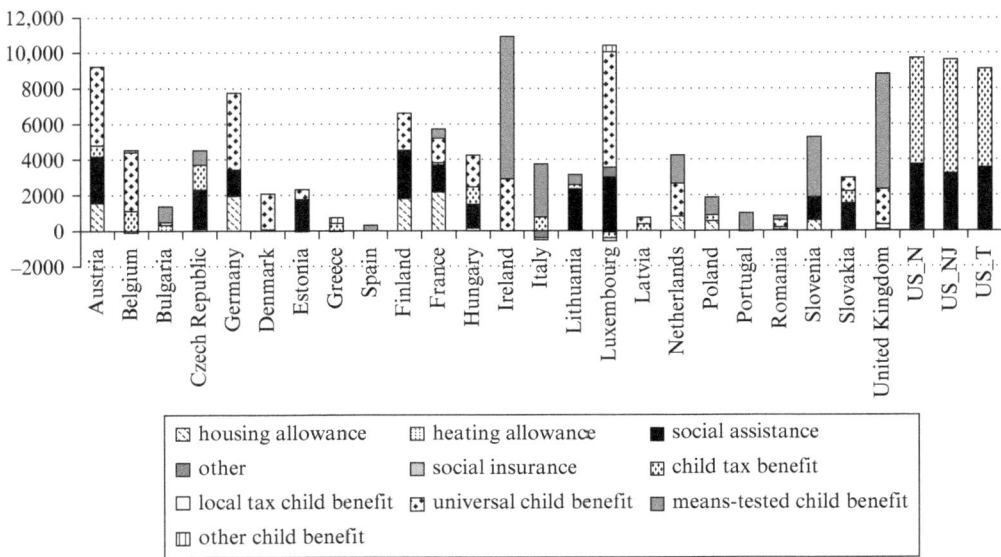

Source: CSB MIPI (US_N = Nebraska; US_NJ = New Jersey; US_T = Texas).

Figure 7.1 Child benefit package for a couple plus two children on the minimum wage in January 2012 (euros PPP per annum)

88 *Handbook of family policy*

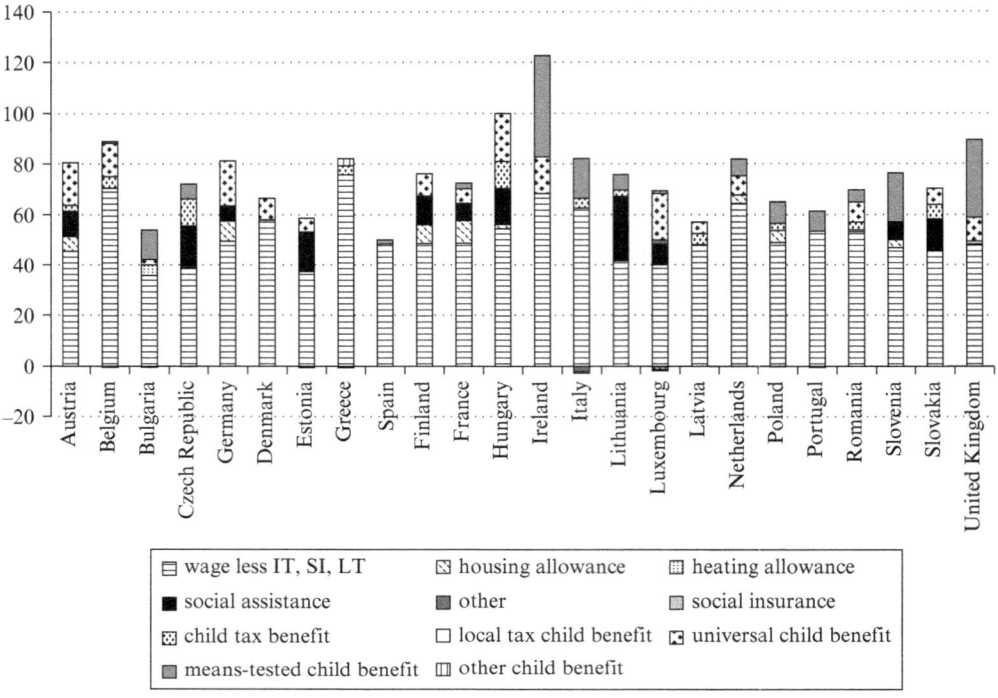

Source: CSB MIPI and Eurostat database.

Figure 7.2 Total net income for a couple plus two children on the minimum wage as a proportion of the poverty threshold in 2012

structure and level of the child benefit package per annum – this is what a couple with two children would receive in respect of their children over and above what a childless couple would receive with one earner working full time for the minimum wage (i.e., a low-paid case), assuming rent is two thirds of the median rent. Ireland has the most generous package made up of universal child benefit and a means-tested Family Income Supplement.

Figure 7.2 presents the child benefit package and the net minimum wage as a proportion of the (net income less than 60 per cent median) poverty threshold in 2013 (incomes in 2012) from the Eurostat database (http://ec.europa.eu/eurostat/data/database) for a couple and two children. Only in Ireland does the net income exceed the poverty threshold and Hungary reaches it. In all other countries a single wage earner on the minimum wage with two children would still have an income which is less than the poverty threshold. But the point is that Ireland and Hungary reach the poverty threshold thanks to the child benefit package, and in most of the other countries the poverty gap is closed substantially thanks to the child benefit package. It could be closed entirely if countries increased their child benefit package. Indeed in the UK case the child poverty gap would have been closed if child benefits had been uprated since 2010 in line with inflation instead of frozen as part of the austerity measures (Bradshaw and Judge, 2014).

Family benefit systems 89

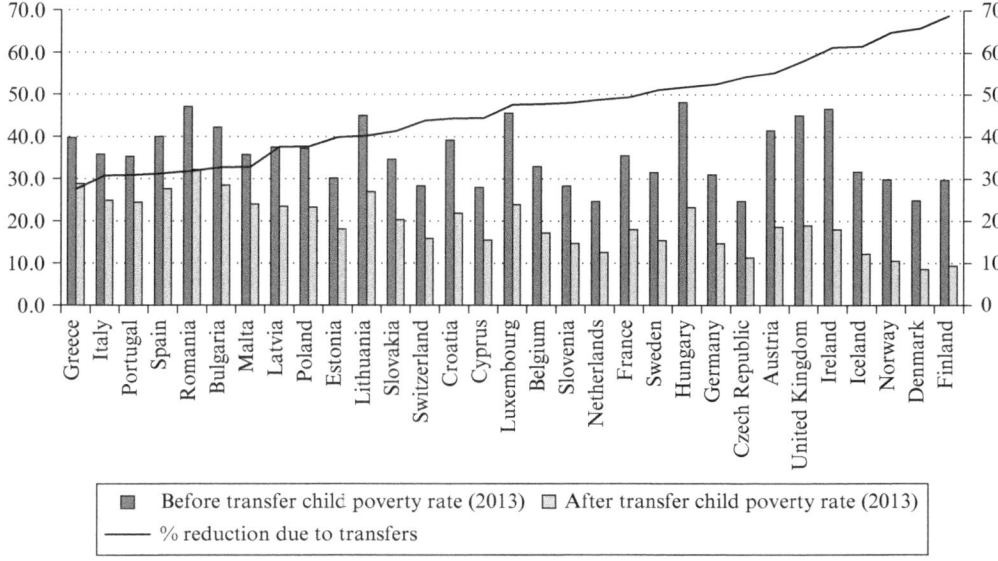

Source: http://ec.europa.eu/eurostat/data/database (accessed 8 June 2014).

Figure 7.3 Pre and post transfer child poverty rates in 2013 – pensions excluded

Another way to make the same point is to compare child poverty rates before and after transfers. This is shown in Figure 7.3 based on EU SILC data using the EU at-risk-of-poverty threshold. The figure shows what the child poverty in these countries would be if there were no public cash transfers, just market income; what the child poverty rate is after transfers; and what poverty reduction is achieved by the child benefit package. There is very considerable variation in the effectiveness of transfer systems in European countries. All countries reduce their pre-transfer poverty rates by transfers but the percentage reduction varies from 27 per cent in Greece to 78 per cent in Finland. Some countries could be doing much better if they had more generous transfers.

The other main source for comparing the structure and level of the child benefit package is the OECD Benefits and Wages Model.[5] This enables us to cover more countries, although the model is not quite as detailed as CBS/MIPI. Figure 7.4 compares the child benefit package for the half average earnings case.[6] Ireland has by far the largest child cash payment thanks mainly to the Family Income Supplement but it is offset by reduced housing benefit.[7] The UK has the highest net child benefit package at this earnings level followed by Lithuania, Ireland, Germany and the USA.

FERTILITY

Let us turn to the fertility case made for child benefits. The fact that child benefits might encourage child birth could also be an argument for why a country might not want to introduce child benefit – because their fertility rate is already too high. It is certainly the

90 *Handbook of family policy*

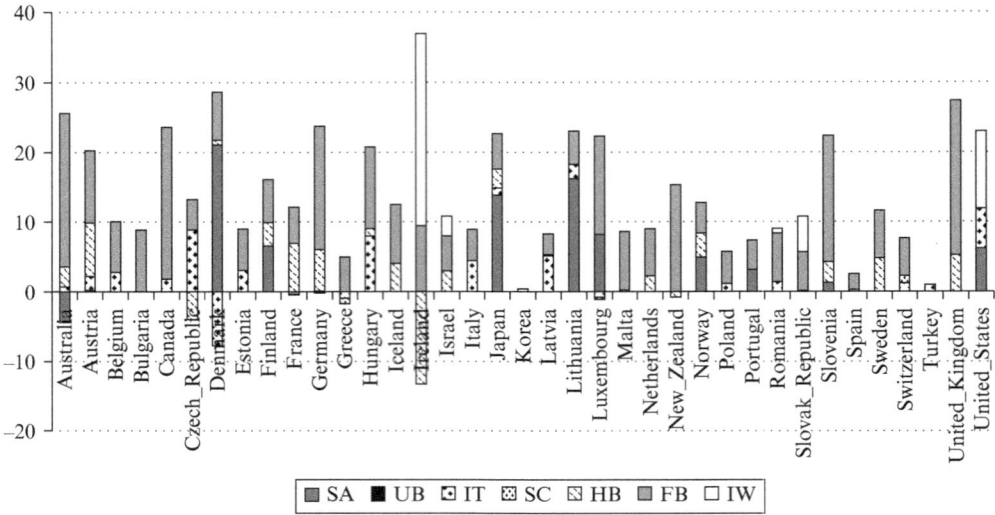

Note: SA = social assistance; UB = unemployment benefit; IT = income tax; SC = social security contributions; HB = housing benefit; FB = family benefits; IW = in-work benefits.

Source: OECD Tax-Benefit Calculator.

Figure 7.4 *Structure of the child benefit package for a couple plus two children earning the half average wage in 2013 expressed as percentage of average wage*

case that child benefit has been introduced with the objective of raising fertility.[8] It was tried in pre-transition East Germany and Romania. Russia and the Ukraine both still have fairly generous birth grants with fertility objectives in mind. The introduction of child benefit in Japan was motivated by a concern with fertility and the ageing dependency ratio. Whether or not child benefits had or have or will have any permanent effect on fertility is, however, doubtful. There are theoretical reasons why we might expect child benefits to encourage fertility – because they reduce the direct and opportunity costs of child rearing and increase maternal security (Bradshaw and Attar-Schwartz, 2009). But there is very little evidence that they actually do. The decision to have children is a highly complex one for women/couples. It is also often unplanned and unexpected. Many pregnancies do not end up as births (partly because of abortion), but in rich countries most women don't achieve the number of children they want and an increasing proportion remain unhappily childless. In the rich countries in the 1970s, countries with the most generous family benefits had the lowest fertility rates (Nordic countries). Then fertility collapsed in the Southern European countries with the least generous child benefits. Now the evidence on OECD countries in Figure 7.5 suggests that there is at best a very weak positive association between the proportion of GDP spent on family benefits and services in 2013 and fertility rates.

The fact that child benefits do not influence fertility in rich countries may not be evidence of their impact on fertility in middle-income and poorer countries. There is no evidence that fertility has been affected by the introduction of family allowances in

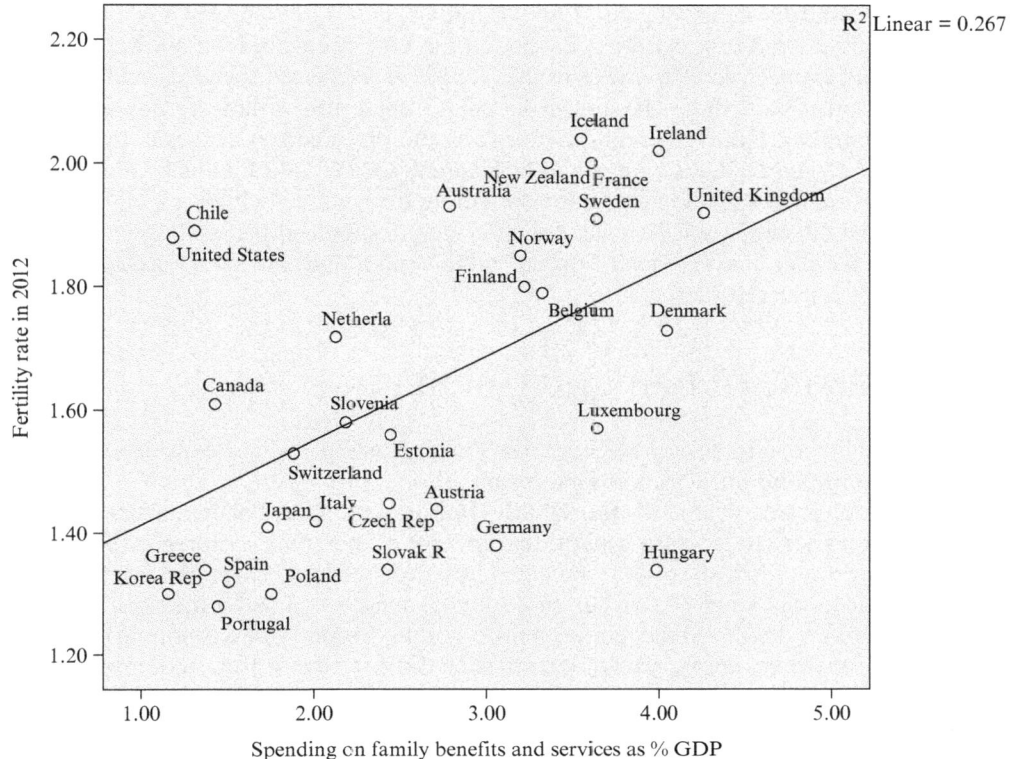

Source: OECD Family Database.

Figure 7.5 Fertility rate in 2012 and percentage of GDP spent on family benefits and services

Argentina or Child Support Grants in South Africa (in fact the opposite; see Udjo, 2014). The trajectory of fertility in developing countries is downwards, influenced by declining child mortality and rising living standards. Therefore, one might expect the introduction of child benefit in poor countries to reduce fertility because of its impact on poverty and living standards.

PURCHASING POWER OF MOTHERS

Child benefits paid to mothers or carers provide a source of income independent of the other or only earner. This is an important advantage in that it provides security where resources are not shared in the household, or where, as a result of unemployment or illness, there are no other resources available. In times of crisis in family life, such as separation, divorce, desertion or imprisonment, child benefits remain a secure and certain income for mothers. There is also evidence that mothers are more likely than fathers to spend money on children (Bradshaw and Stimson, 1997). Lundberg et al. (1997) undertook an analysis of how family expenditure patterns changed in the UK when child tax allowances were abolished and transferred to mothers in the late 1970s. Increased spending on children's clothes coincided with these changes in income distribution within the household. In research examining family spending patterns as the tax credit system was introduced in the UK in the early 2000s, Gregg and colleagues (2006) found that as income rose in low-income families, spending increased on fruit and vegetables, children's clothes, toys and books, while spending fell on alcohol and cigarettes; indeed the spending pattern of low-income families converged with that of middle- and higher-income families as their income levels converged.

ARGUMENTS AGAINST CHILD BENEFITS

Why don't child benefits exist in all countries. Three arguments will be considered: affordability; targeting; and infrastructural problems.

Without doubt a key issue is affordability. In poor countries policy makers may not think they can afford to pay cash benefits in respect of each or most children in their country. There are a number of issues to be taken into account here. Given the level of child poverty in most poor countries and given its impact and costs, a better question to ask is, can you afford not to? Until the recession most middle-income and developing countries experienced steady economic growth but children did not benefit from that growth. The GDP per capita line on the graph typically rose steadily but in contrast the child poverty line typically flat-lined. One reason was that very few countries had any mechanisms for transferring resources to children, as they did not have child benefits. They could spend their growing national resources on schools and on health, on water, sanitation and other infrastructure but they had no mechanism to tackle child poverty directly. Countries with such mechanisms in the OECD countries were spending 2.55 per cent of GDP in 2011 on family benefits (1.34 per cent on cash grants, 0.96 per cent on services – mainly childcare, and 0.25 per cent on tax breaks) (OECD, 2015). Korea was spending 1.16 per cent and Japan 1.74 per cent. Most middle- and low-income countries are spending very considerably less of their national resources on child benefits (ILO, 2015). A study for UNICEF Namibia (2013) found that Namibia was spending 0.36 per cent of GDP on its child welfare grants to orphans and vulnerable children in 2012/13. It is estimated that a universal payment at N$200 per child per month to the under 6s would costs N$615 million per year, which is 0.56 per cent of GDP in 2012/13 or if paid to all children 0–17 would costs N$2.03 billion per year, which is 1.8 per cent of GDP in 2012/13. It would reduce child poverty from 40 per cent to 12 per cent. In comparison, South Africa spends 1.3 per cent of its GDP on its very effective child grants.

Policy makers in these countries may argue that it is better to use their limited resources on basic health and education. However, health and education do not tackle poverty – at least not directly. Indeed in far too many (poor) countries they exacerbate it by imposing user charges. So policy makers may then argue why not then concentrate spending on the very poor by targeted social assistance or minimum income schemes? This is the line still being pushed by the World Bank (except for universal minimum pensions schemes which they are now advocating) (Dethier et al., 2010). Child benefits have been anathema to the World Bank. The consequences of this have been dire for children in far too many countries (Bradshaw et al., 2013).

Some countries may not have child benefits because they lack the infrastructure. For instance, in order to process child cash grants comprehensive birth certification is necessary. The right from birth to a name and nationality is part of the UN CRC. Of course, introducing child grants will itself provide an incentive for more parents to register the births, especially if the grants are paid from birth on the basis of a birth certificate.

CONCLUSION

In rich countries child benefits are now accepted as a critical mechanism for transferring resources in favour of families with children. Although international bodies acknowledge the contribution that child benefits can and do make in alleviating child poverty, the majority of middle- and low-income countries still have not introduced child benefits. Even in rich countries the level of child benefits varies considerably. Child benefits not only reduce child poverty – they provide purchasing power to mothers and a degree of security in periods without earnings. They may reduce wage demands, supplement low wages and enhance work incentives. They may increase fertility rates. There is evidence from middle-income countries that they can have a positive impact on health, educational attainment, gender relations and economic development. Given these advantages they are affordable and indeed essential. The simplest child benefit schemes are universal and require only very limited infrastructure to set up a system.

Most developing countries in the world have experienced long periods of economic growth. Yet child mortality is still killing more children each year than any war has ever done in human history. Stunting and malnutrition are epidemic. One reason for this is that children are not receiving the benefits of growth and the main reason for this is that too many countries lack the machinery to transfer resources of that growth to families with children. The targeted social assistance schemes espoused by the World Bank are not child benefit schemes but unfortunately they are attractive to some national governments because they are able to pretend that there is a safety net and one which does not cost too much. The future of children is the future of societies. Child benefits can make a critical contribution to that future.

NOTES

1. Both a generous birth grant and a child benefit worth £53.19 per month per child.
2. Actually, since 2012 they are taken back via taxation from anyone earning over £50,000 per year.
3. Estimated as 3 per cent of gross domestic product (GDP) in the UK.
4. The Child Support Grant (CSG) introduced in 1998 is a means-tested cash benefit with approximately 80 per cent of children eligible. It is paid for children aged 0–17 inclusive who live in low-income families (this includes South African citizens, permanent residents and refugees). The amount is R280 per month for the child. The means test is R33,600 per year if the primary caregiver is single. If the primary caregiver is married the means test is R67,200 per year. There is no asset test. There is no social assistance for unemployed adults in South Africa so adults without work who have children often find that they also have to rely on the CSG.
5. http://www.oecd.org/els/soc/benefitsandwagestax-benefitcalculator.htm (accessed 22 June 2018).

6. The OECD classification is not always very consistent. So, for example, SNAP (Food Stamps) are classified as social assistance, in-work benefit (IW) is Earned Income Tax Credit and child tax credits are shown in Income tax benefit. In the UK Child Tax Credit is included in child benefits. Ireland's Family Income Supplement is classified as an in-work benefit.
7. A curious result of the Irish differential rent scheme which takes Family Income Supplement into account and results in couples with children paying higher rents than childless couples.
8. Perhaps the most radical thinking on this subject was 'Romantic Singapore' – which proved ineffective.

REFERENCES

African Union Social Policy Framework for Africa (2008), accessed 20 April 2016 at http://au.int/en/dp/sa/content/social-policy-framework-africa.
Back, K. (2010), 'Social transfers: stimulating household-level growth', CPRC Policy Brief No. 14.
Bertranou, F. and R. Maurizio (eds) (2011), *Asignacio Universal por Hijo Semi-conditional Cash Transfers in the Form of Family Allowances for Children and Adolescents in the Informal Economy in Argentina*, International Labour Organization and Universidad Nacional de General Sarmiento, Argentina.
Beveridge Report (1942), *Social Insurance and Allied Services*, Cmd 6404, London: HMSO.
Bradshaw, J. (2012), 'The case for family benefits', *Children and Youth Services Review*, **34**, 590–6.
Bradshaw, J. and S. Attar-Schwartz (2009), 'Fertility and social policy', in N. Takayama and M. Werding (eds), *Fertility and Public Policy: How to Reverse the Trend to Declining Birth Rates*, Cambridge, MA and London: MIT Press, pp. 185–214.
Bradshaw, J. and L. Judge (2014), 'The non-uprating of child benefits – impact on poverty gaps', accessed 20 April 2016 at http://www.nechildpoverty.org.uk/blog/non-uprating-child-benefits-%E2%80%93-impact-poverty-gaps#1.
Bradshaw, J. and C. Stimson (eds) (1997), *Using Child Benefit in the Family Budget*, London: SPRU/The Stationery Office.
Bradshaw, J. and M. Tokoro (2013), 'Child benefit packages in the United Kingdom and Japan', *Social Policy and Society*, **13** (1), 119–28.
Bradshaw, J., E. Mayhew and G. Alexander (2013), 'Minimum social protection in the CEE/CIS countries: the failure of a model', in I. Marx and K. Nelson (eds), *Minimum Income Protection in Flux*, Houndmills, Basingstoke: Palgrave Macmillan, pp. 249–70.
Council of the European Union (2012), *Council Conclusions on Social Protection in European Union Development Cooperation*, 3191st Foreign Affairs – Development – Council meeting, Luxembourg, 15 October, para. 4.
Department for International Development (2005), *Social Transfers and Chronic Poverty: Emerging Evidence and the Challenge Ahead*, DFID Practice Paper, London.
Dethier, J.J., P. Pestieau and R. Ali (2010), 'Universal minimum old age pensions impact on poverty and fiscal cost in 18 Latin American Countries', Policy Research Working Paper 5292, World Bank.
DSD, SASSA and UNICEF (2012), *The South African Child Support Grant Impact Assessment: Evidence from a Survey of Children, Adolescents and their Households*, Pretoria: UNICEF South Africa, accessed 20 April 2016 at http://www.unicef.org/evaldatabase/files/CSG_QUANTITATIVE_STUDY_FULL_REPORT_2012.pdf.
Gregg, P., J. Waldfogel and E. Washbrook (2006), 'Family expenditures post-welfare reform in the UK: are low income families with children starting to catch up?', *Labour Economics*, **13** (6), 721–46.
Griggs, J. with R. Walker (2008), *The Costs of Child Poverty for Individuals and Society: A Literature Review*, York: Joseph Rowntree Foundation, accessed 20 April at http://www.jrf.org.uk/report/costs-child-poverty-individuals-and-societyliterature-review.
Hirsch, D. (2013), 'An estimate of the cost of child poverty in 2013', accessed 20 april 2016 at http://www.cpag.org.uk/sites/default/files/Cost%20of%20child%20poverty%20research%20update%20(2013).pdf.
ILO (International Labour Organization) (2012), *Recommendation Concerning National Floors of Social Protection*, Paper presented at the General Conference of the International Labour Organization, Geneva.
ILO (International Labour Organization) (2015), Social Protection Policy Papers, Paper 14, 'Social protection for children: key policy trends and statistics', accessed 20 April 2016 at http://www.social-protection.org/gimi/gess/RessourcePDF.action?ressource.ressourceId=51578.
Lundberg, S., R. Pollack and T. Wales (1997), 'Do husbands and wives pool their resources? Evidence from the UK Child Benefit', *Journal of Human Resources*, **32** (3), 463–80.
Macnicol, J. (ed.) (1980), *The Movement for Family Allowances 1918–1945*, London: Heinemann.
OECD (2009), DAC Policy Statement, *Making the Role of Employment and Social Protection; Making Economic Growth More Pro Poor*, Paris: OECD-DAC.
Parker, R. (ed.) (2010), *Uprooted: The Shipment of Poor Children to Canada, 1867–1917*, Bristol: Policy Press.

Rathbone, E. (ed.) (1924), *The Disinherited Family*, London: Arnold.
Rowntree, B.S. (ed.) (1901), *Poverty: A Study of Town Life*, Centennial edition, Bristol: Policy Press.
SADC (2003), Social Policy Process/Charter of Fundamental Social Rights, accessed 20 April 2016 at http://www.sadc.int/files/6613/5292/8383/Charter_of_the_Fundamental_Social_Rights_in_SADC2003.pdf.
Scott, J. (2009), 'Social transfers and growth in poor countries', in OECD (ed.), *Promoting Pro-poor Growth: Social Protection*, Paris: OECD.
Townsend, P. (ed.) (2009), *Building Decent Societies: Rethinking the Role of Social Security in Development*, Geneva: Palgrave and International Labour Office.
Udjo, E. (2014), 'The relationship between the Child Support Grant and teenage fertility in post-apartheid South Africa', *Social Policy and Society*, **13** (4), 505–19.
UNICEF (2014), Social Protection Strategic Framework, accessed 20 April 2016 at http://www.unicef.org/socialprotection/framework/.
UNICEF Namibia (2013), 'Addressing child poverty in Namibia – towards a comprehensive and integrated social protection system: an issues paper for the Ministry of Gender Equality and Child Welfare', UIVCEF, Namibia.
UNRISD (2010), *Flagship Report: Combating Poverty and Inequality*, Geneva: UNRISD.
Van Mechelen, N. and J. Bradshaw (2013), 'Child benefit packages for working families, 1992–2009', in I. Marx and K. Nelson (eds), *Minimum Income Protection in Flux*, Houndmills, Basingstoke: Palgrave Macmillan, pp. 81–107.
Van Mechelen, N., S. Marchal, T. Goedemé, I. Marx and B. Cantillon (2011), 'The CSB-Minimum Income Protection Indicators (MIPI) dataset'. CSB Working Paper No. 11/05, University of Antwerp.
Wennemo, I. (1992), 'The development of family policy: a comparison of family benefits and tax reductions for families in 18 OECD countries', *Acta Sociologica*, **35**, (3), 201–17.
World Bank (2014), *Ukraine Social Safety Nets Modernization Project (P128344)*, Report No. 84672-UA, Washington, DC: World Bank.

8. Childcare as a global policy agenda
Tine Rostgaard

INTRODUCTION

There is a growing interest in childcare[1] in advanced economies, as a research as well as a policy field. It is widely recognized that high-quality childcare benefits the child in its cognitive, emotional and social development. It is also known that childcare facilitates parental and in particular female labour force participation, thus contributing to gender equality in paid and unpaid work as well as to reducing child poverty.

The importance of childcare has been emphasized not least by supranational organizations such as the European Union (EU) and the Organisation for Economic Co-operation and Development (OECD), although with an often dual and somewhat interchanging emphasis. Since the early 1990s, the EU has been promoting childcare as part of the reconciliation of work and family life. The launching of the EU Social Investment Package in 2013 placed childcare in a central position, now as a key element in the overall strategy to strengthen children's current and future capacities as citizens and workers. Here, provision of high-quality childcare was seen as a contribution to breaking intergenerational transmission of disadvantage for children growing up in less resourceful families. Likewise, the OECD has since the late 1990s increasingly included childcare as an important component in policy advice, also shifting between seeing childcare mainly as an instrument to facilitate female labour market employment and thereby contributing to financial sustainability, to advocating the benefits for the child.

This chapter investigates what has been the foundation for the overall idea of childcare as a global agenda across advanced economies, its changing meaning as well as implementation in national policy. More specifically, it investigates how the ideational influence of seeing childcare as a global agenda has come about as a response to new contextual, scientific and policy realities in the transition to knowledge economies. Further to this, we are particularly interested in how the agenda has been adapted by the EU and the OECD as part of the identification of policy problems and legitimate policy solutions. Finally, we investigate how the agenda is translated to country-level policy actors in the EU and OECD recommendations as well as in actual national implementation of key institutional features of childcare (such as organizational structure, accessibility, quality and affordability).

We find that the current institutional approach by the OECD and the EU assumes a common interest across cultures and contexts in promoting childcare as a universal element in the life of the child and the family, from the perspective of facilitating maternal employment but increasingly also from developmental and learning perspectives. It is, however, an approach which risks losing sight of the individual child and the national contextual specificities, resulting in an instrumentalization of childcare and its outcomes. In national policy making, there is a clear implementation of the global agenda of childcare in that childcare has become more universalistic but take-up of childcare is still some way from the level advocated by, for example, the EU. We also note a worrying tendency for a trade-off between quantity and quality. The chapter is based on the research literature, policy documents and cross-national statistics.

THEORETICAL FRAMEWORK

The chapter draws on Béland's (2005, 2009) work on political agenda-setting and his claim that ideas constitute a major component in the identification and construction of social problems that enter (or do not enter) the policy agenda. The ideational process shapes the forms of assumptions that either legitimize or challenge existing institutions and policies, and thus shape the content of reform proposals as well as the understanding of the need for reforms. Béland refers here to the concept of 'rhetorical frames' in his understanding of how discursive constructions of reform imperatives often appeal to shared cultural understandings (2009, p. 706). In the chapter, we first investigate what are the overall rhetorical ideas of childcare as a global agenda by referring to three realities, the policy, contextual and scientific realities. Such rhetorical frames entail a normative dimension of the preferred direction of policy changes, identifying for supranational organizations such as the EU and the OECD, as well as national policy actors, the view of 'what is good or bad about what is, in light of what one ought to do' (Schmidt, 2008, p. 306). Ideas in this way serve as institutional blueprints for problem identification and available solutions.

The focus of the chapter is therefore the ideational process in the rhetorical framing of childcare as a global idea, especially the role of organizational actors in framing or promoting such ideas of problems and solutions, in this case the EU and the OECD. One particular aspect of Béland's work on ideational processes, which will also be applied here, is the transnational diffusion of ideas and how they are translated into the national context. We investigate this by looking at the national take-up of the global idea of childcare, as exemplified in the change in key institutional features.

CHANGING REALITIES: CHILDCARE AS A GLOBAL AGENDA IN ADVANCED ECONOMIES

Formal childcare provided outside the near family is not a recent idea. The earliest example of the contemporary childcare institution for children dates back to the kindergarten initiative by the German theorist Friedrich Froebel in 1837. These kindergartens were mainly intended for middle class children of the liberal-minded bourgeoisie. The idea that the (local) state should invest in childcare on more universal terms was first advocated in Europe by Socialists' groupings in the nineteenth century. It was followed up by the labour movement in the twentieth century, where the issue gained political attention with the need for women's labour during and after World War II (WWII). In the Scandinavian countries, the workings of the influential Myrdal couple in the post-war era managed to raise childcare as a political issue as a means to address problems of the size of the population but also to further social welfare, and resulted in a systematic expansion in formal childcare (Björnberg, 1992).

The most influential change in making publicly supported and universal childcare outside the home a global agenda issue in advanced economies has, however, come more recently. The change has come about not least due to an alignment of changes in contextual, scientific and policy realities (Kagan and Roth, 2017). Such changes in *contextual realities* include increased mobility and urbanization, declining fertility, as well as new configurations of the family, gender and post-industrial work structures, which all question traditional modes of family solidarity and the (gendered) division of family responsibility for care and work, as well as create new social risks that require political attention (e.g., Bonoli, 2005).

As for *scientific realities*, new advances in science and its application have contributed to altering our perception of childcare. Inquiry into the developing brain in neuroscience has, for instance, been influential in demonstrating how formative but also how vulnerable the brain is in the early years of the child. High-quality childcare may enhance children's cognitive and educational achievement in life and is argued to have special potential in compensating for the loss of parental resources for more disadvantaged children (Burchinal et al., 2008). Likewise, the application of evaluation and econometric science has at the same time produced measurable outcome indicators such as the PISA scores, which have helped forward the cost-effectiveness arguments for investing in childcare, most famously coined by Heckman (2008) in his 'skills begets skills' concept. His research shows that investment in early years not only improves children's opportunities in general but can be measured directly in reductions in public expenditure, including incarceration, welfare dependence, teen pregnancy, grade retention and referral to special education (Heckman, 2006). When taking account of the productivity gains from facilitating mothers' employment, the economic return from providing childcare is estimated to be up to ten times the costs of service provision (Barnett and Masse, 2007), even when also considering high-cost childcare systems as found in some European countries (Barnett and Nores, 2015). However, the compensating effect factor of childcare may be less clear-cut than often presented. While meta-studies such as Anderson et al. (2003) do find a positive short-term outcome on cognitive and non-cognitive abilities, it is often difficult to conclude on long-term effects and even more difficult to identify the causal institutional features of effective and efficient programmes. This obviously complicates policy learning across countries.

The evidence-based findings of outcomes have nevertheless contributed to the creation of a global agenda of childcare in advanced economies in relation to the success of its social-welfare function. Scientific evidence has been distilled in ways that have been easily understood by the public and policy makers, helping create a new *policy reality* where it is made legitimate that public investments in early years will yield positive outcomes for children, families and societies overall. Not least when the policy reality is also embedded in a knowledge-based economy paradigm where the overall problem is seen to be how to increase productivity. From an economic rationale, early years' education can be seen as an instrumental means to productive gains through high and long-term returns on investment and macroeconomic growth. Childcare has in this way come to the forefront of the policy discourse as a means to recalibrate developed welfare states in the post-industrial transformation to knowledge economies (León, 2017). This agenda has been brought forward not least from the perspective of social investment where children's needs are seen in terms of investments in their futures, 'preparing rather than repairing'

(Morel et al., 2012; see also Chapter 9 by Lee and Baek in this volume). While the social investment perspective has helped place the child in the centre, the criticism is nevertheless that the child has no role as an independent actor and that childhood loses value in this paradigm: it is argued that childhood has become politicized, subject to political debates and economic agendas which interpret children as a public good, seeing them mainly as citizen-workers of the future (Lister, 2003; Jenson, 2012). Children are located in terms of *becoming*, rather than *being* (Qvortrup, 1985).

THE IDEATIONAL BASIS IN THE INSTITUTIONAL RESPONSE OF THE EU AND THE OECD

Despite the criticisms, the alignment of realities has helped position childcare as a global solution in advanced economies, seemingly addressing (some of) the problems of the transition to a knowledge-based economy. This understanding of the central role of childcare is reflected but also independently brought forward by the institutional responses of supranational organizations such as OECD and the EU. Over time, the institutional identification of problem and solution has, however, shifted focus somewhat. The EU has no treaty basis for addressing family policy and can only lay down common goals but early on saw the need for a more coherent policy response in order to address new social risks. In the 1992 European Council Recommendations on Childcare, the European Commission did exactly that by emphasizing the need for policy making which took into account childcare services, as well as parental leave, labour regulations and gender equality (Council of the European Communities, 1992).

Initially, the main interest was in removing barriers to employment for parents, and mothers in particular, by increasing the *quantity* of childcare services (Campbell-Barr and Bogatić, 2017). The launch of the EU Lisbon Strategy in 2000, with the aim to 'make Europe the most competitive and dynamic knowledge-driven economy by 2010' (European Commission, 2000) consolidated this approach in visioning a 'Europe-wide Adult-Worker model' (Annesley, 2007) where childcare was a means to ensure that both men and women take up paid work. A more concrete but still 'soft policy' measure – and still mainly aimed at increasing parental employment – were the Barcelona Targets, which the European Commission introduced in 2002 as part of the European Employment Strategy. This was nevertheless also inspired by the influential evaluation by Esping-Andersen and colleagues (2002) for the EU Presidency, for the first time pinpointing the need for a child-centred (and childcare-based) social investment strategy. With the Barcelona Targets, best practice for childcare attendance was quantified in the recommendation that EU member states should achieve participation in childcare for a minimum of 33 per cent of children aged 0–2 and 90 per cent of children between 3 and school age by 2010. Quantifying these target goals ensured the possibility for monitoring the progress of jointly agreed indicators and allowed what in the Open Method of Coordination (OMC) governance literature is known as 'naming and shaming' of the member states that did not comply or deliver the expected results (Zeitlin, 2008). It also ensured bottom-up participatory governance in allowing national stakeholders to put pressure on their government (Saraceno, 2013). However, the quantification of childcare attendance also illustrated – what was later to become a recurrent criticism – a simplification based on a lack of cultural and contextual understanding of achievements of the childcare systems in the diverse countries (Urban and Swadener, 2016; see also Chapter 3 by Moss in this volume).

In later EU policy documents, it became apparent that the long-term social investment perspective had gained ground, such as the 2013 *Investing in Children: Breaking the Cycle of Disadvantage* (European Commission, 2013). Here, the European Commission emphasized childcare as the essential foundation for successful lifelong learning, social integration, personal development and – once again underlining the view of children as potential future contributors to the economy – later employability. Also noteworthy was that the new interest in the *quality* of childcare, to be achieved, amongst others, by ensuring well-integrated services that build on a joint vision of the role of childcare, effective curricular frameworks, professionalization of staff competences and integrated governance arrangements (European Commission, 2013).

The later policy work of the EU draws not least on the extensive analyses and policy recommendations brought forward by the OECD. Like the EU, the original mandate for the work of the OECD did not include family policy but the organization has over time paid increasing attention to this policy field. However, the understanding of the role of childcare has shifted over time. Most significant for the early approach were the *Starting Strong I* and *II* country studies from 2001 and 2006, including in all 20 high-income and four developing countries (OECD, 2001, 2006). Here, the OECD approach differed from that of the EU in not taking as a starting point the promotion of parental employment, but instead understanding the different systemic and cultural childcare approaches and highlighting the quality aspects. In their contextual approach, using case-study methods that were sensitive to the diversity and complexity of systems and pedagogies, the *Starting Strong* studies are generally considered landmark research in the field of comparative childcare (Urban and Swadener, 2016), as well as for asking the essential questions:

> ECEC [Early Childhood Education and Care] policy and the quality of services are deeply influenced by underlying assumptions about childhood and education: what does childhood mean in this society? How should young children be reared and educated? What are the purposes of education and care, of early childhood institutions? What are the functions of early childhood staff? (OECD, 2001, p. 63)

The OECD approach to childcare has changed since then – and perhaps more inconsistently over time than the EU – in either focusing on the gender and employment benefits or on the benefits for the child. In the 2007 report *Babies and Bosses*, the focus was thus on the availability of childcare as a general means to reconcile women's employment, leaving out the recommendations on quality and governance which were otherwise considered the centrepiece of the *Starting Strong* reports (Mahon, 2006, 2012; Moss et al., 2016). However, in 2009 with the report *Doing Better for Children*, the focus was again on the benefits for the child from public investment in childcare, especially for the most vulnerable children. Perhaps even more influential for conceptualizing childcare as standardized, measurable and assessable using evidence-based tools has been the OECD work since 2006 on indicators in the online Family Database. The database includes a collection of cross-national indicators on family structures, labour market position, family policies and child outcomes for all 30 OECD countries (Lohmann et al., 2009; see also Chapter 5 by Lohmann and Zagel in this volume). Recent work from the OECD also includes the very hands-on and instrumental approach to improve childcare services, the

Quality Toolbox for ECEC, which outlines strategy options under different policy levers (OECD, 2012).

From providing culturally sensitive analyses, such as in the *Starting Strong I* and *II* reports, the OECD has in more recent years been criticized for shifting the focus to offering policy recommendation and practical guidance on 'how to', which uncritically assumes the global application of the idea of childcare (Urban, 2017). The turn to evidence-based policy has also been criticized for using knowledge production to render 'technical' and hence depoliticize (Mahon, 2006) the issue of a global application of childcare. Most controversial has perhaps been the International Early Learning Study and Child Well-being[2] (IELS) project which intends to assess early learning outcomes from childcare among 4-year-olds (Moss and Urban, 2017; Moss et al., 2016). Critics sees this 'Baby-PISA' as a strategy that favours decontextualized measurement of standardized and predetermined outcomes (Urban and Swadener, 2016), representing a 'narrowing of early childhood education, as the IELS tail increasingly wags the early childhood dog' (Moss et al., 2016, p. 349).

KEY INSTITUTIONAL FEATURES: THE IMPLEMENTATION OF THE GLOBAL AGENDA OF CHILDCARE IN NATIONAL POLICY MAKING

The global agenda of childcare has in this way become increasingly institutionalized in the policy recommendations of both the OECD and the EU. Childcare is seen as a legitimate and multiple policy solution for both facilitating maternal employment as well as – as a more recently identified policy concern – developing children's current and future capacities.

For the sake of policy learning, the OECD and the EU have also stimulated a search for conceptualizing and measuring the effective institutional features of childcare. The identification and recommendation of such effective institutional features can be seen as a way to supply country-level policy actors with a blueprint of what is the policy problem and which solutions to apply. Whether national policy actors then decide to act on it is of course another matter which we turn to in the final section. Here, we will investigate the policy advice on key institutional features such as the role of organizational structure, accessibility, quality and affordability as well as looking into how the change in terminology reflects the changes in the application of childcare as a global agenda. We also investigate whether the global agenda of childcare is reflected in (changes in) the adaptation and implementation of these key institutional features in national policy making.

What's in a Name?

One of the apparent changes influenced in particular by the increasing focus on childcare as a developmental factor is the emphasis of the learning environment in the use of terminology by leading international organizations. Despite consistent variety in the technical umbrella terms used by different international organizations,[3] the tendency is to include 'education' in one form or another to underline the diminishing policy distinction between

102 *Handbook of family policy*

care and early learning, such as in the often used term Early Childhood Education and Care (ECEC). As Moss points out in this volume, the coining of a common English term applied in research and international policy documents has the further effect of nullifying the cultural differences in the meaning of childcare across different languages and cultures.

Organizational Structure

Another change is in the recommendations for a unitary organizational structure. The educational dimension of childcare has in many EU and OECD countries been underscored by transferring responsibility for childcare from Ministries of Social Affairs/Family Affairs to Ministries of Education. In this way, the child's childcare 'career' has become more closely linked to activities in the primary school system (see also Moss in this volume). The integration of childcare and education in a unitary system is, amongst others, favoured as a way to ensure within-country standardization of the provision of childcare services (European Commission, 2011). It may also facilitate closer cooperation between childcare centres and primary school and the introduction of a curriculum in childcare, such as learning plans. Kaga et al. (2010), however, find some variation in the depth of structural as well as conceptual integration between childcare and education across countries, even in unitary systems.

Social Expenditure

There is also consistent variation in the social expenditure investments in childcare across countries. Growth in social expenditure levels for childcare has nevertheless been quite spectacular since 2000 and has diminished the country variation somewhat. Figure 8.1

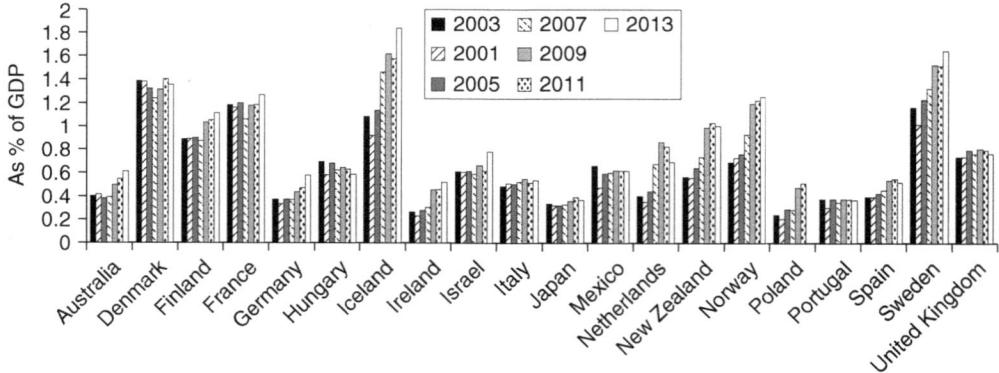

Note: Public expenditure on childcare and pre-primary education. Mexico 2011.

Source: OECD Family Database Table PF3. Available at http://www.oecd.org/els/family/database.htm (accessed 1 February 2018).

Figure 8.1 Social expenditure for childcare, percentage of GDP, 2000 and 2013 or latest year

shows that across a number of OECD countries, spending on childcare takes up an increasingly higher proportion of gross domestic product (GDP). As the figure covers the period before and after the financial crisis in 2008 when GDP generally dropped, this may be expected. If countries were to uphold a consistent investment in childcare over time, GDP investments would be expected to increase from 2008 and onwards until GDP levels stabilized again.

Investment also seems to have flattened out somewhat among a number of low-spending countries. This is the case in Southern European countries, such as Spain, Italy and Portugal, where unemployment rates soared following the financial crisis in 2008, but also in Denmark, Japan and the United Kingdom.

Neither the EU nor the OECD give concrete recommendations on minimum target goals for social investment. UNICEF sets this level at 1 per cent of GDP. Only the Nordic countries, as well as France, exceed this level. Outside these countries, spending averages 0.6 per cent of GDP.

Also noteworthy is that even if countries spend the same proportion of GDP, the redistributive effect may be quite different. For example, a comparison of Flanders and Sweden using household data illustrated that despite similar expenditure levels, childcare provision in Sweden was more equitable, ensuring a higher degree of social equality and efficiency (Lancker and van Ghysels, 2011).

Accessibility

The findings from the Flandern/Swedish study by Lancker and van Ghysels (2011) exemplify the important question of who should have access to childcare? If childcare is a means to facilitate maternal employment in the reconciliation of work and family life, it should be provided universally. If childcare is (also) seen to benefit the child in general in its social, cognitive and emotional development, it may equally well be argued that it should be a universal solution. Today, the universal approach is widely advocated by both the OECD and the EU (see, e.g., European Commission, 2011), and often with direct reference to Heckman's theory of the high economic returns from investing early in the child. The (Heckman) paradox is nevertheless that children from less resourceful families benefit disproportionally and longer lasting from high-quality childcare, compared to children who live in a more stimulating family environment (Christoffersen, 2017; Christoffersen et al., 2014). In terms of maximizing the returns from the investment in childcare, a targeted approach may therefore yield a higher societal return. Results are, however, not consistent; other research findings point to the general positive effect of high-quality childcare for all children, regardless of family circumstances (see, e.g., Van Belle, 2016).

Targeting is mainly advised with regard to those children who are considered particularly disadvantaged. Referring, amongst others, to the improved reading performance of immigrant children who have participated in childcare, the OECD recommends targeting this group of children to promote equality (OECD, 2016a). Such policy advice has been followed up, for instance, in Denmark where the political parties presently discuss making childcare mandatory for immigrant children from the age of 1 year, in order to develop their language capabilities but also to broaden their socialization environment. Needless to say, such a coercive approach is controversial. Despite the best intentions, it is based on the assumption that what is considered best for the child is adopted uniformly across the entire population regardless of ethnicity (or social class) (Rutanen et al., 2014).

What is considered best for the child may also be quite different across countries – and also supported quite differently through family policy – especially what concerns the young child under 3. For example, in Finland, a home care-oriented practice is believed to be best for the child until the age of 3, supported through extensive cash for care benefits (see also Chapter 15 by Eydal, Rostgaard and Hiilamo on the use of home care allowances in this volume), while in Brazil, non-domestic care is considered the means to overcome poverty, structural inequalities and vulnerabilities, and therefore the preferred policy option (Rutanen, 2014). Such differences in policy assumptions about what is 'best for the child' across countries can also be seen in the variation in duration of parental leave (see Chapter 10 by Thévenon in this volume), which may vary substantially even within the same care regime and create quite different policy outcomes. For instance, in Denmark 15 per cent of children under 1 year are cared for in formal childcare because the parental leave is relatively short, compared to no children in this age group in Sweden where the parental leave extends well into the second year of the child (see Eydal, Rostgaard and Hiilamo in this volume). The large cross-national differences which we find in the use of childcare is therefore partly explained by variation in policy approaches and attitudes to non-parental care, especially among children under the age of 3, reminding us that there is no 'universal yardstick by which children's best interests can be measured' (Kjørholt, 2008, p. 15).

The overall tendency is nevertheless that childcare have become more universalistic, in that access to and coverage of childcare have expanded, and in at least nine European countries, an actual right to childcare after parental leave has been introduced[4] (European Commission/EACEA/Eurydice/Eurostat, 2014; León et al., 2014a). For instance, in Germany, a right to childcare for children under 3 years was introduced in 2013, followed by a federal initiative to expand provision (Olivér and Mätzke, 2014).

As shown in Figure 8.2, enrolment rates for the 0–2-year-olds in childcare and preschool services[5] have increased since 2006 in most advanced economies, but have fallen in the United Kingdom and countries in Southern Europe (Cyprus, Portugal, Greece and Spain) (data for 2006 missing for some countries). However, the cross-country variation remains substantial, with the highest rate in Denmark (63 per cent) and the lowest in the Czech Republic (3 per cent). Across the OECD-34 on average one-third (34 per cent) of the children aged 0–2 years are in childcare and there is a similar average across EU countries (32 per cent). A number of EU countries are thus well below the Barcelona target of 33 per cent enrolment rate for this age group.

The cross-country variation is much smaller with regard to children from 3 to school age. Figure 8.3 shows children aged 3 years only but illustrates the general and historically longer tendency to provide childcare for children over 2 years, sometimes compulsory before starting primary school.[6] Enrolment rates are close to 100 per cent in most countries and have otherwise been increasing in the period 2005–14. Data for 2005 are missing for a number of countries but we see a decline over time in enrolment of the 3-year-olds in Italy, Switzerland and the Czech Republic. Again, the EU and OECD averages are close, at 80 and 74 per cent, respectively. Also shown here, the EU Barcelona target of 90 per cent coverage for this age group is not met in a number of EU countries.

However, the figures do not reveal the consistent and systematic unequal distribution of childcare resources. In most OECD countries, children's participation in childcare differs

Childcare as a global policy agenda 105

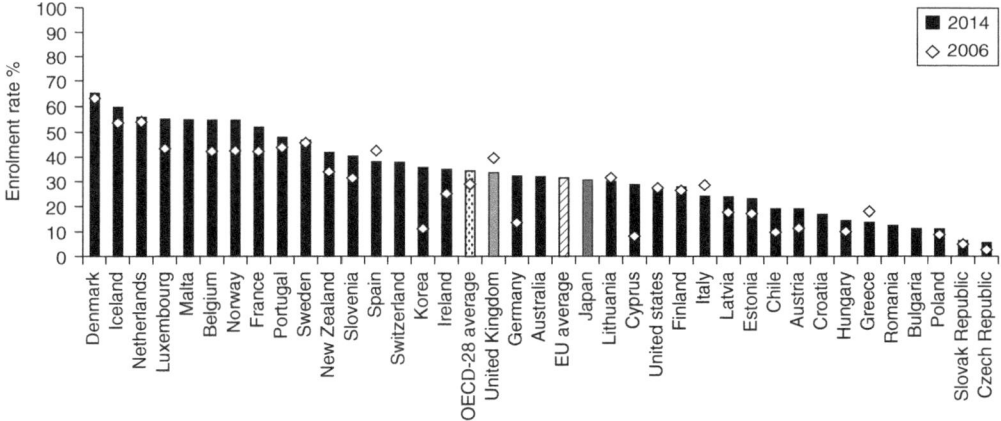

Note: Data missing for 2006 for Croatia, Malta, Australia, Switzerland, Japan, Romania, Bulgaria and EU average.

Source: OECD Family Database, PF3.2.A. Available at http://www.oecd.org/els/family/database.htm (accessed 1 February 2018).

Figure 8.2   Enrolment rates of 0–2-year-olds in formal childcare and pre-school, 2006 and 2014 or latest available year

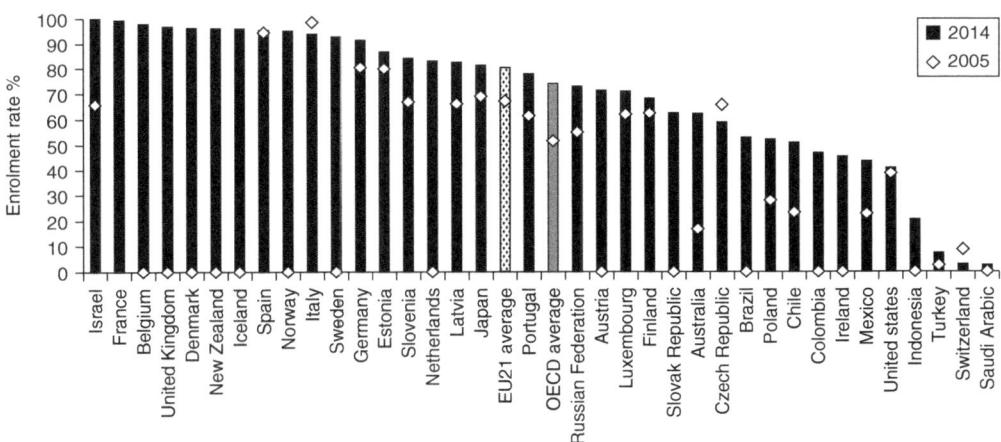

Note: 2005 data missing for Austria, Belgium, Denmark, France, Greece, Iceland, Ireland, Latvia, Netherlands, New Zealand, Norway, Slovak Republic, Sweden and the United Kingdom. Data in 2014 include early childhood educational development (ISCED 01) and pre-primary education (ISCED 02). Data in 2005 include only ISCED 02. For the sake of comparison over time, the figure shows children aged 3 only, not including the whole age group up to compulsory school age, which normally also includes 4- and 5-year-olds.

Source: OECD Education at a Glance, Indicator C2.1.

Figure 8.3   Enrolment rates for 3-year-olds in pre-primary education or primary school, 2005 and 2014 or latest available year

with parental income and/or maternal level of education, and especially for children aged 0–2. Only in the Nordic countries, such as Denmark, Iceland and Sweden, do children under 3 participate in childcare irrespective of family background. In contrast, in other countries, such as France and Ireland, children from high-income families are over four times more likely to use formal childcare than children from low-income families. In France, part of the explanation is the lack of services in disadvantaged neighbourhoods (OECD, 2016b). Given the evidence that childcare can benefit disadvantaged children in particular, this is of course not optimal.

Affordability

Part of the explanation of the large gap in participation across levels of income and education are the high parental fees. The OECD generally recommends that childcare costs are kept to an affordable level (e.g., OECD, 2016a). However, fees remain high, especially for care for the 0–2-year-olds while care for children aged 3+ may be free of charge. For instance, Irish parents in a low earning dual-earner family would need to pay 35 per cent of their disposable income for full-time centre-based care for two children aged 2 and 3. In other countries also, the out-of-pocket cost is high, for instance, 20 per cent of disposable income for a low-earner family in both the Netherlands and the United Kingdom. Across the OECD-32 countries, parents pay on average 10–15 per cent of their disposable income, depending on whether they live in a high- or low-earner two-parent family (OECD, 2016b), and costs tend to be lowest in Eastern European and Nordic countries (European Commission/EACEA/Eurydice/Eurostat, 2014).

Quality

Whereas the focus in the past was on increasing enrolment levels, in recent years in both the OECD and the EU it has also been on quality. This change reflects the shift in political focus from increasing mother's employment to ensuring that the child benefits in its social, emotional and cognitive development.

The question is how to operationalize and measure quality? Procedural indicators such as the involvement of the child or the quality of the interaction between children and staff are often difficult to measure. In addition, the contribution of the different pedagogical logics is difficult to assess. Often, it is the measurable structural indicators which are accounted for, such as adult-child ratios in the OECD Family Database. There is substantial evidence that the quality of childcare increases with a higher adult-child ratio, as this increases the adults' interaction with the child and their sensitivity to the needs of the child (for an overview see Christoffersen et al., 2014).

Adult-child ratios do, however, vary substantially across countries, but common for the countries is that the maximum number of children allowed per adult typically doubles when the child reaches 3 years of age. In Finland, for instance, the number of children per adult increases from four to seven, and in Belgium, it increases from 6/7 to 20 children (European Commission/EACEA/Eurydice/Eurostat, 2014). Also, group sizes increase with age but vary. On average across the EU the maximum group size for 5-year-olds is between 20 and 30 children. Group sizes for young children are usually smaller, but in the United Kingdom, for instance, up to 26 infants can be in a group as long at the adult-child ratio of 1/3 is maintained (European Commission/EACEA/Eurydice/Eurostat, 2014).

Regulatory frameworks that prescribe the adult-child ratios are in place in some countries, but mainly for the provisions of children aged 3 and over as this is more often part of pre-school education (OECD, 2006; León, 2017). The OECD quotes the ratio to be the 'most consistent predictor of high-quality learning environments' (OECD, n.d., p. 3). Neither the OECD nor the EU, however, gives any concrete recommendations on the adult-child ratio as this, along with other quality issues, is left to the various countries to decide.

Despite recent political focus on the quality of childcare, there seems to be a trade-off between cost containment and expansion, which compromises the quality of childcare, especially for the under-3s (León et al., 2014b). There are indications of such a trade-off in GDP investments, as shown above, which are for some countries at best stable or sometimes falling. This was the case during the financial crisis when GDP levels were lower, and despite increasing enrolment. Even in countries with relatively high investments and enrolment rates, we may note the tendency. In Denmark, in 2000 there were on average 5.2 children per adult in nursery care for the 0–2-year-olds and 9.7 children per adult in kindergartens for the 3+. By 2014, the adult-child ratio was 6.5 for nurseries and 11.8 for kindergartens (Bureau2000, various years). Blaming the low adult-child ratio, one in three employees now reports lack of time each day for solving conflicts, comforting the child and interfering in disturbing behaviour (Bureau2000, 2018). However, staff also blame the increasing time they have to set aside for documenting effective practice and monitoring the child's progress. Not having time for the child obviously puts at risk the multiple purpose of providing high-quality childcare to stimulate the development of the child and facilitating parental employment.

CONCLUSION

Over time, the idea of childcare as a global agenda has – with the alignment of contextual, scientific and policy realities – become more legitimate as a policy solution in advanced economies. Childcare has in the institutional response from supranational organizations such as the EU and the OECD served as an increasingly central policy instrument, initially to facilitate maternal employment and in recent years has shifted towards (also) considering it essential for developing children's current and future capacities as citizens and workers. From the perspective of social investment, childcare is today seen as an effective policy instrument in a knowledge-based society where the problem is considered to be how to increase productivity. Critics argue that in this change in the perspective of the function of childcare we have lost sight of the individual child and of the national contextual specificities, resulting in an instrumentalization of childcare and its outcomes.

The institutional response by the EU and the OECD reflects the change in the rhetorical framework of the increasing importance of childcare. Whereas the initial approach, such as the early investigations by the OECD in the *Starting Strong* project, acknowledged country differences in the underlying assumptions about childhood and the role of childcare, later approaches have to a greater extent assumed a common interest across cultures and contexts in promoting childcare as a universal element in the life of the child, and with specific outcomes in mind. This has included setting quantitative targets for enrolment and producing comparable indicators and outcome measurement tools that may document effective practice. This turn to evidence-based policy has been criticized for assuming the global application of a standardized idea of childcare and for depoliticizing the issue, rendering it as a mere technical issue of how to implement the institutional features that have been identified as successful.

The implementation of the global agenda of childcare in national policy making is evident in a number of ways: the move towards seeing childcare as a learning environment is reflected in the changes in organizational structure, as childcare in many countries is now placed under the auspices of the Ministry of Education. The change is also reflected in the coining of a common term for childcare in international policy documents, which positions 'education' equal to 'care'. The adaption of the global agenda of childcare in national policy making is perhaps most apparent in the increasing social expenditure investments and in the increase in the enrolment rates. Still, the social expenditure levels remain well below the minimum target goal and there is a consistent unequal distribution of childcare resources benefitting children from privileged households. Affordability also remains an issue with high parental fees. The overall tendency is nevertheless that childcare has become more universalistic, in access, coverage and also as a social right. Despite the focus on high-quality childcare for developing children's current and future capacities, the trade-off for this expansion may in some countries be at the expense of quality, with less time available for the individual child.

NOTES

1. In the chapter, we use the term childcare to cover formal provisions of care and education for pre-school children, including centre-based day care, family day care and pre-school early education programmes. For a full overview consult OECD (n.d.).
2. The original name was 'International Early Learning Study' and 'Child Well-being' was added latter (Urban and Swadener, 2016).
3. The OECD and the EU use 'ECEC' for early childhood education and care, UNICEF uses 'ECCD' for early childhood care and development, and the World Bank uses 'ECD' for early child development (Kamerman, 2007).
4. As of 2014 in Denmark, Germany, Estonia, Malta, Slovenia, Finland, Sweden and Norway. Also children are legally entitled to pre-primary education the last year or two before starting school in the Czech Republic and Liechtenstein (European Commission/EACEA/Eurydice/Eurostat, 2014).
5. Data covers centre-based services (e.g., nurseries or day care centres and pre-schools, both public and private), organized family day care, and care services provided by (paid) professional childminders. Exact definitions differ across countries.
6. In Bulgaria, Greece, Cyprus, Latvia, Luxembourg, Hungary, Austria, Poland and Switzerland the last year or two of pre-primary education is compulsory (European Commission/EACEA/Eurydice/Eurostat, 2014).

REFERENCES

Anderson, D.J., M. Binder, and K. Krause (2003), 'The motherhood wage penalty revisited: experience, heterogeneity, work effort, and work schedule flexibility', *Industrial and Labor Relations Review*, **56** (2), 273–94.

Annesley, C. (2007), 'Lisbon and social Europe: towards a European "adult worker model" welfare system', *Journal of European Policy*, **17** (3), 195–205.

Barnett, W.S. and L.N. Masse (2007), 'Early childhood programme design and economic returns: comparative benefit-cost analysis of the Abecedarian programme and policy implications', *Economics of Education Review*, **26**, 113–25.

Barnett, W.S. and M. Nores (2015), 'Investment and productivity arguments for ECCE', in P.T. Marope and Y. Kaga (eds), *Investing Against Evidence: The Global State of Early Childhood Care and Education*, Paris: UNESCO, pp. 73–90.

Béland, D. (2005), *Social Security: History and Politics from the New Deal to the Privatization Debate*, Lawrence, KS: University Press of Kansas.

Béland, D. (2009), 'Ideas, institutions, and policy', *Journal of European Public*, **16** (5), 701–18.

Björnberg, U. (1992), *European Parents in the 1990s: Contradictions and Comparisons*, London: Transaction Publishers.

Bonoli, G. (2005), 'The politics of the new social policies: providing coverage against new social risks in mature welfare states', *Policy and Politics*, **33** (3), 431–49.

Burchinal, M., N. Vandergrift, R. Pianta, and A. Mashburn (2008), 'Threshold analysis of association between child care quality and child outcomes for low-income children in pre-kindergarten programs', *Early Childhood Research Quarterly*, **25**, 166–76.

Bureau2000 (2018), *Flere børn i dagtilbud – Udviklingstendenser for dagpleje og daginstitutioner. 2018*, København: Bureau2000. Accessed 10 January 2018 at http://www.bureau2000.dk/seneste-nyt/170-flere-born-i-dagtilbud-udviklingstendenser-for-dagpleje-og-daginstitutioner-2018.

Bureau2000 (various years), *Daginstitutionens hverdag*, København: Bureau2000. Accessed 1 December 2016 at http://www.bureau2000.dk/udgivelser/born-og-unge.

Campbell-Barr, V. and K. Bogatić (2017), 'Global to local perspectives of early childhood education and care', *Early Child Development and Care*, **187** (10), 1461–70.

Christoffersen, M. (2017), 'Heckman's paradox and quality of early universal investment in human capital: a research note', Paper presented at the Statistical Symposium, University of Southern Denmark, 23–24 January.

Christoffersen, M., A.K. Højen-Sørensen, and L. Laugesen (2014), *Daginstitutionens betydning for børns udvikling – En forskningsoversigt*, SFI rapport 14:23, København: SFI.

Council of the European Communities (1992), *Council Recommendation of 31 March 1992 on Child Care*, Brussels: Council of the European Communities.

Esping-Andersen, G., D. Gallie, A. Hemerijck, and J. Myles (2002), *A New Welfare Architecture for Europe?* Report submitted to the Belgian Presidency of the European Union. Accessed 1 May 2016 at https://pdfs.semanticscholar.org/bc3f/661a6e43ef2b0220bcb4c05a5a94cbe8f3c8.pdf.

European Commission (2000), *Lisbon European Council 23 and 24 March Presidency Conclusion*, European Union Parliament Website. Accessed December 2015 at http://www.europarl.europa.eu/summits/lis1_en.htm.

European Commission (2011), *Communication from the Commission. Early Childhood Education and Care: Providing all Our Children with the Best Start for the World of Tomorrow*. Accessed 5 May 2017 at http://eur-lex.europa.eu/legal-content/EN/ALL/?uri=celex:52011DC0066.

European Commission (2013), *Recommendation on Investing in Children: Breaking the Cycle of Disadvantage*, Brussels: European Commission.

European Commission/EACEA/Eurydice/Eurostat (2014), *Key Data on Early Childhood Education and Care in Europe*. 2014 Edition. Eurydice and Eurostat Report. Luxembourg: Publications Office of the European Union.

Heckman, J.J. (2006), 'Skill formation and the economics of investing in disadvantaged children', *Science*, **312** (5782), 1900–9002.

Heckman, J. (2008), 'Schools, skills, and synapses', *Economic Inquiry*, **46** (3), 289–324.

Jenson, J. (2012), 'Redesigning citizenship regimes after neoliberalism: moving towards social investment', in N. Morel, B. Palier, and J. Palme (eds), *Towards a Social Investment Welfare State? Ideas, Policies and Challenges*, Bristol: Policy Press, pp. 61–87.

Kaga, Y., J. Bennett, and P. Moss (2010), *Caring and Learning Together: A Cross-national Study on the Integration of Early Childhood Care and Education in Education*, Paris: UNESCO.

Kagan, S.L. and J. Roth (2017), 'Transforming early childhood systems for future generations: obligations and opportunities', *International Journal of Early Childhood*, **49** (2), 137–54.

Kamerman, S. (2007), 'Strong foundations: early childhood care and education. A global history of early childhood education and care', Background paper prepared for the Education for All Global Monitoring Report 2007. Accessed 1 February 2018 at http://www.ecdgroup.com/docs/lib_003972023.pdf.

Kjørholt, A. (2008), 'Children as new citizens: in the best interests of the child?', in A. James and A. James (eds), *European Childhoods: Cultures, Politics and Childhoods in Europe*, New York: Palgrave Macmillan, pp. 15–38.

Lancker, W. and J. Van Ghysels (2011), 'Who reaps the benefits? The social distribution of public childcare in Sweden and Flanders', AIAS, GINI Discussion Paper 10, Amsterdam.

León, M. (2017), 'Social investment and childcare', in A. Hemerijck (ed.), *The Uses of Social Investment*, Oxford: Oxford University Press, pp. 118–27.

León, M., C. Ranzi, and T. Rostgaard (2014a), 'Pressures towards and within universalism: conceptualising change in care policy and discourse', in M. León (ed.), *Care Regimes in Transitional European Societies*, London: Palgrave Macmillan, pp. 11–33.

León, M., E. Pavolini, and T. Rostgaard (2014b), 'Cross-national variation in care and care as a labour market', in M. León (ed.), *Care Regimes in Transitional European Societies*, London: Palgrave Macmillan, pp. 34–61.

Lister, R. (2003), 'Investing in the citizen-workers of the future: transformations in citizenship and the state under New Labour', *Social Policy and Administration*, 37 (5), 427–43.

Lohmann, H., F.H. Peter, T. Rostgaard, and K. Spiess (2009), 'Towards a framework for assessing family policies in the EU', OECD Social, Employment and Migration Working Papers, No. 88, Paris. Accessed March 2017 at http://dx.doi.org/10.1787/223883627348.

Mahon, R. (2006), 'The OECD and the work/family reconciliation agenda', in J. Lewis (ed.), *Children, Changing Families and the Welfare State*, Cheltenham, UK and Northampton, MA, USA: Edward Elgar Publishing, pp. 173–91.

Mahon, R. (2012), 'Social investment according to the OECD/DELSA: a discourse in the making', *Global Policy*, 4 (2), 150–59.

Morel, N., B. Palier, and J. Palme (2012), *Towards a Social Investment Welfare State? Ideas, Policies and Challenges*, Bristol: Policy Press.

Moss, P. and M. Urban (2017), The Organisation for Economic Co-operation and Development's International Early Learning Study: what happened next, *Contemporary Issues in Early Childhood*, 18 (2), 250–58.

Moss, P., G. Dahlberg, S. Grieshaber et al. (2016), 'The Organisation for Economic Co-operation and Development's International Early Learning Study: opening for debate and contestation', *Contemporary Issues in Early Childhood*, 17 (3), 343–51.

OECD (2001), *Starting Strong. Early Childhood Education and Care*, Paris: OECD.

OECD (2006), *Starting Strong II. Early Childhood Education and Care*, Paris: OECD.

OECD (2012), *Starting Strong III. A Quality Toolbox for ECEC – Setting Out Quality Goals and Regulations*, Paris: OECD.

OECD (2016a), *The Pursuit of Gender Equality*, Paris: OECD.

OECD (2016b), *Who Uses Childcare? Background Brief on Inequalities in the Use of Formal Early Childhood Education and Care (ECEC) among Very Young Children*, Paris: OECD.

OECD (n.d.), 'PF4.1: typology of childcare and early education services'. Accessed January 2016 at http://www.oecd.org/els/family/PF4-1-Typology-childcare-early-education-services.pdf.

Olivér, R. and M. Mätzke (2014), 'Childcare expansion in conservative welfare states: policies, legacies and the politics of decentralized implementation in Germany and Italy', *Social Politics*, 21 (2), 161–93.

Qvortrup, J. (1985), 'Placing children in the division of labour', in P. Close and P. Collins (eds), *Family and Economy in Modern Society*, Houndmills, Basingstoke: Macmillan, pp. 129–45.

Rutanen, N., K.S. Amorim, K.M. Colus, and N. Piattoeva (2014), 'What is best for the child? Early childhood education and care for children under 3 years of age in Brazil and in Finland', *International Journal of Early Childhood*, 46, 123–41.

Saraceno, C. (2013), 'The undercutting of the European Social Dimension', Hal Science Po Papers. Accessed 1 November 2016 at https://hal-sciencespo.archives-ouvertes.fr/hal-01070426.

Schmidt, V. (2008), 'Discursive institutionalism: the explanatory power of ideas and discourse', *Annual Review of Political Science*, 11, 303–26.

Urban, M. (2017), 'We need meaningful, systematic evaluation, not a preschool PISA', *Global Education Review*, 4 (2), 18–24.

Urban, M. and B.B. Swadener (2016), 'Democratic accountability and contextualized systemic evaluation. A comment on the OECD initiative to launch an International Early Learning Study (IELS)', *International Critical Childhood Policy Studies*, 5 (1), 6–18.

Van Belle, J. (2016), *Early Childhood Education and Care (ECEC) and its Long-term Effects on Educational and Labour Market Outcomes*, Rand Report. Accessed December 2016 at https://www.rand.org/pubs/research_reports/RR1667.html.

Zeitlin, J. (2008), 'The Open Method of Coordination and the governance of the Lisbon Strategy', *Journal of Common Market Studies*, 46 (2), 436–50.

9. The social investment approach in the productivist welfare regime: the unfolding of social investment in South Korea and Japan
Sophia Seung-yoon Lee and Seung-ho Baek

INTRODUCTION

Discussions on social investment emerged in the political and research communities around the late 1990s, together with the call for a revision of welfare systems in order to adapt to the new socioeconomic context of the post-industrial era. Although there is no consensus on the definition of social investment, the concept refers to an investment in human capital and additionally, unlike social grants or benefits, the state has an explicit expectation of social returns of social investments (Perkins et al., 2004). More specifically, social investment can be regarded as an approach, perspective, policy or political strategy which involves investment in human capital with the explicit expectation of social returns such as economic development and employment growth (Morel et al., 2012, p. 2).

Depending on the stance taken in the interpretation of redistributive social expenditure, there is variation in the social investment approaches taken. The integration of the different perspectives under a single concept has caused the definitional overstretch of social investment and has led to confusion in international comparisons (Kim, 2007). In the West, two main approaches can be identified, the Northern European social democratic approach and the liberal third way approach in countries such as Canada, Great Britain and Australia. While the East Asian approach to social investment is heavily inspired by the latter, it does, however, present a unique adaptation of the idea of social investment in an East Asian welfare regime and with varied outcomes depending on which country is scrutinized. The aim of this chapter is therefore to investigate the different understandings of social investment in the East Asian welfare states, South Korea and Japan, compared to the social investment discussion in Europe.

Overall, the ideal typology of South Korea and Japan as East Asian welfare states has challenged the welfare regime typology of Esping-Andersen (1990) (see also Chapter 18 by Peng and Chien on the East Asian welfare model in this volume). The literature on Asian welfare states argues that there are limitations in explaining the development by class mobilization and class-political action structures and that an 'Asian welfare state model' must be introduced (Aspalter, 2006; Croissant, 2004; Kasza, 2006; Ku and Finer, 2007; Kwon, 2005; Kwon and Holliday, 2007; Lee and Ku, 2007). Both in South Korea and Japan, discussion on the conceptualization of a 'Japanese type welfare state' and a 'Korean type welfare state' has attracted scholars from diverse disciplines who have sought to understand and categorize developments in these two countries (Baek and Ahn, 2007; Goodman and Peng, 1996; Goodman et al., 1998; Lee, 2015; Na, 2010; Yang, 2013). Furthermore, policy makers and the general public have also become interested in the welfare program and policies, reflecting the increasing demand from citizens for the provision of welfare services since the late 1990s. The discussion on the East Asian productivist welfare state in particular highlights the subordination of social policy to economic policy. Holliday suggests common features among Japan, Korea and other East Asian states, referring to these countries as 'productivist welfare capitalism', which is defined as 'a growth-oriented state and subordination of all aspects of state policy, including social policy, to economic/industrial objectives' (Holliday, 2000, p. 709). Similar to the productivist welfare state literature, the developmental welfare state literature also elaborates the role and function of elites in the development of welfare states in South Korea and Japan, and how the emphasis on education is associated with economic development.

Since the 1990s, Japan and South Korea have faced dramatic changes in family structures, becoming aging societies with extraordinarily low fertility rates. Japanese welfare capitalism, which was institutionalized during the post-war period, faced new challenges arising from the 1990s economic downturn. Together with the aging population, these challenges caused the government to expand social protection spending both in relative and absolute terms. Nonetheless, social conflicts, poverty and inequality increased, leading to an interest in social investment related policies. In South Korea, a number of changes in welfare capitalism took place from the late 1990s when the country experienced an economic crisis, eventually leading to the idea of the 'productive welfare state'. However, social programs and social protection were insufficient to cope with labor market polarization and the rapidly aging population. Against this background, the idea of a 'social investment welfare state' was introduced, with the aim of achieving both economic development and welfare state expansion. Hence, it is unclear whether the so-called East Asian productivist welfare regime has reached a dead end. Instead of the focus on the productivist welfare regime, with ongoing changes in family structure and the fast transition to an aging society, social policies related to the idea of social investment, predominantly family policy, have been developing rapidly in these two countries. Accordingly, both countries have increased social expenditure on family and children.

This chapter focuses on the different understandings of the 'social investment approach' in the two East Asian welfare states of South Korea and Japan compared to the Western welfare states. We first review the social investment discussion in the Western context and examine how it differs from that in South Korea and Japan. Subsequently, we investigate how the social investment approach unfolded in South Korea and Japan, mainly by looking at their family policies, and discuss whether the social investment approach represents the legacy of the 'productivist welfare regime' in the two countries. We examine the policy developments and political discussion related to the social investment approach in these countries focusing on the period from the 1990s and onwards.

DIFFERENT UNDERSTANDINGS OF THE SOCIAL INVESTMENT APPROACH

The Social Investment Approach in Western Countries

The social investment approach emerged in Western countries, and particular within Europe, in the late 1990s, when modernization of the welfare system was required in order to adapt in the post-industrial era (Deeming and Smyth, 2015; Morel et al., 2012). This approach aims to address the new social risks and needs of post-industrial society, such as reconciling work and family life, single parenthood, and having low or obsolete skills (Bonoli, 2005). The key idea of this perspective is that social policies should have productive rather than redistributive potential, which is necessary for economic development and employment growth. It can be implemented in social welfare such as increasing cost-effectiveness, enhancing human capital investment, developing individual and community assets, and facilitating economic participation (Deeming and Smyth, 2015; Midgley, 1999).

The social investment perspective originated back in the 1930s and is related to the term 'productive social policy' which was developed by Gunnar Myrdal in Sweden. In the period of economic crisis caused by the Great Depression, and a severe concern about the fertility rate, a new understanding of social policy as an investment was developed by the Swedish social democrats. Policies aimed to improve the quality of life of the Swedish population were particularly targeted at children. Myrdals's argument was closely connected to economic growth and productivity (Morel et al., 2012). Thus, social policy was presented not simply as a means for redistribution, but also for the efficient organization of production (Morel et al., 2012). While the social investment approach founded in Sweden may have influenced social democratic welfare states, liberal welfare states in Europe did not accept the approach until later when they adopted the liberal social investment perspective that had been suggested, amongst others, by the British Labour Party's Third Way (Esping-Andersen, 2002, p. 5). Hence, emphasis was on the development of policies to support the formation and preservation of human capital through active labor market policies and unemployment compensation especially in terms of guaranteeing income security with a selective approach.

Meanwhile, Keynesianism came to dominate as an economic theory across the developed countries in the post-war period until the mid-1970s. Similar to Myrdals's productive social policy approach, Keynesianism also had 'a belief in the mutually reinforcing qualities of social policy and economic growth, and of equality and efficiency' (Morel et al., 2012, p. 2). Keynesianism understands slow growth and unemployment as the matter of insufficient demand and of the natural tendency towards cyclical fluctuations of uncontrolled capitalism. Government intervention policy was seen as necessary for the stability of the economy, and therefore public spending on welfare was considered a useful economic tool in periods of recession. Thus, policies to support demand, and the development of the public sector and social insurance schemes for income maintenance, such as unemployment compensation, were emphasized as a key instrument of this approach.

After the economic crisis of the 1970s, neoliberals especially in the United Kingdom and the United States led a paradigm shift from a demand-side to a supply-side approach with the perspective that social policy was a wasteful cost and as such hindered economic growth. Criticizing Keynesianism for government's inability to tackle unemployment and inflation, neoliberalism put emphasis on monetarist economic policies to solve inflation. For neoclassical economists, labor market rigidities cause high unemployment and low growth, and so they advocated deregulation of the labor market. Social policy was also addressed from a new activation and workforce approach. In other words, social policy was established in the sense that any job would be a good job, and benefit level would be reduced at the cost of working. Thus, providing incentives to return to work was more important than providing income security (Deeming and Smyth, 2015; Morel et al., 2012).

From the late 1990s in some European countries, a new social investment perspective began to emerge. This idea gave birth to a new economic rationale of social policy provision by stressing its productive factor, unlike neoliberalism (Morel et al., 2012). For productivism and social investment advocates, the emphasis in social welfare shifts from consumption and maintenance-oriented social policy to investment in people and improving their capacity to participate in the productive economy (Midgley, 1999). Jenson and Saint-Martin (2003) view the social investment state as a redesigned welfare structure of the new century, and explain social investment through the responsibility of the state for social citizenship. Thus, in this approach, the state is assigned a key role in developing human capital investment policies in order to increase competitiveness and job creation, and in providing social services and policies to support the labor market through childcare; higher education and life-long learning; active labor market policies; policies to support women's employment, and to avoid depletion of human capital by providing in-work benefits as well as support for job training and job searches (Deeming and Smyth, 2015; Morel et al., 2012).

As discussed earlier, the social investment perspective tends to integrate social investment approaches under a single umbrella term despite the possibility of divergence in approaches that range from the Northern European social democratic approach to the liberal Third Way, applied, for instance, in Great Britain, Australia and elsewhere (Deeming and Smyth, 2015; Morel et al., 2012, p. 19). The integration of the different perspectives, however, caused definitional overstretch of social investment creating confusion in international comparisons (Kim, 2007). Nonetheless, the social investment perspective is often categorized in the literature as either the liberal social investment approach or the social democratic social investment approach, depending on the stance taken in the interpretation of redistributive social expenditure, assessment of generous benefits as work incentives, and opinions on citizens' rights and duties (Esping-Andersen, 2002; Kim, 2007; Lister, 2004). The differences between the two types of social investment approaches are summarized in Table 9.1.

Because welfare capitalism could in general be characterized as having a social investment perspective, arguing whether a social investment perspective is present or not in East Asian welfare states may be pointless. Accordingly, this study focuses on which types of social investment approach have been developed and been in effect in South Korea and Japan compared with some of the Western welfare states, highlighting especially the political background. We also examine how the social investment approach has been interpreted and has unfolded in East Asian welfare states.

Understanding Social Investment in South Korea and Japan

The differences between liberal and social democratic social investment perspectives were examined above, and in this subsection we will elaborate on which type of social investment approach South Korea and Japan most closely align with by examining how social investment is understood in these two countries.

First, considering the origin of the social investment perspective, South Korea and Japan have accepted the liberal social investment perspective that was inherited from the

Table 9.1 Comparison of the two types of social investment approaches

Type	Liberal approach	Social democratic approach
Commonalities	Reinforcement of the investment features of social policies (increased investment in human capital) Consolidation of social and economic policies Expansion of citizens' employment prospects	
Origin	Third Way, United Kingdom (1990s)	Initial stage of the welfare state, Sweden (1930s)
Redistributive social expenditure	Unproductive	Synergy of redistributive and productive social expenditure
Benefit generosity	Negative work incentive	Positive work incentive
Entitlement for benefits	Targeted, means-tested benefits	Universal benefits
Citizenship	Emphasis on duty	Emphasis on rights
Equality	Equality of opportunity	Reducing inequality
Role of social policy	Investment in human capital Workfare	Capability approach Activation

Source: Based on Lister (2004) and Esping-Andersen (2002).

productivist welfare state for which investing in human capital for economic development was a major policy tool (Peng, 2015). Developmental states regard redistributive social policy to be consumptive, and therefore generally position social policy below economic policy in ranking priorities. These states also emphasize selective social policy programs that have greater affinity with the liberal social investment perspective than the social democratic social investment one.

Second, the nature of social policies in South Korea and Japan is not oriented towards 'preparing' or 'preventing', but is rather more closely oriented to 'repairing' the deficiencies of economic policies. They tend to have social policies that have been heavily deprioritized in favor of economic policies, and this is due to the countries' productivist legacies. Though welfare expenditure under Kim Dae-Jung's administration in South Korea expanded, it increased mainly within selective programs that focused on public assistance (Baek and Ahn, 2007). Additionally, when examining the details of labor market expenditure that was increased during this time, most policies that were implemented through active labor market policies were aligned towards the provision of public assistance in the form of income security for unemployed people and older people on low income, rather than extending support for upskilling the workforce (Baek and Ahn, 2007).

Third, it is debatable whether South Korea and Japan are undergoing a transition into a new phase of social investment policy that began in the 1990s. Indeed, awareness of the decreasing birth rate, increasing number of older persons and growing inequality in these contexts has led to the expansion of social policies that target support for children, families and older persons. However, these actions do not constitute sufficient indicators of a transition to a new social investment policy. South Korea has adopted a selective approach for socially vulnerable groups, such as children and older people. The policy for long-term care insurance was enacted in a selective manner, and childcare policy was primarily directed at low-income families particularly in need of child support (Lee et al., 2014) before 2013 when childcare provision was expanded to become universal. In implementing the 2013 universal childcare support policy, central government has continuously shifted responsibility for finance to local government.

The case is slightly different for Japan. While the discussion on the development of human resources came into prominence following the recession, which began in the early 1990s, the concept of social investment per se did not emerge on the political agenda. Nevertheless, expenditure for the provision of the family and long-term care for older people was exponentially increased, though this trend simply reflects awareness of the effects of low birth rates and low growth in this context. It is difficult to regard this as a policy expansion that has developed from a traditional social investment perspective, as the increase in expenditure came in the form of cash benefits.

Instead of transitioning into a new social investment perspective, the two countries have strengthened their liberal social investment approach affected by demographic factors combined with their individual developmental legacies. In summary, South Korea and Japan, given the legacy of the productivist state, have developed liberalistic social investment policies that are subordinate to economic policies, and emphasize 'repairing' and selectivism.

THE UNFOLDING OF THE SOCIAL INVESTMENT APPROACH IN SOUTH KOREA AND JAPAN

The Social Investment Approach and Policy in South Korea

In South Korea, the term for and approaches of social investment were first discussed during the time of the Kim Dae-Jung government, which emphasized the idea of 'productive welfare'. However, it was from the mid-2000s towards the later reign of Roh Moo-hyun's government when the discussion widely permeated academic circles and policy makers (Lee and Baek, 2014).

The paradigm shift in South Korea's family policy occurred from 1998 to 2003 during Kim Dae-Jung's administration (Baek, 2009; Jeon, 2015). It was based on the need to resolve the national crisis of an aging population that had resulted from a low fertility rate and poor use of women's human resources. During the Kim Dae-Jung administration there was a quantitative expansion in childcare services, and the period can be considered one of increasing publicness for childcare policy via its aggressive implementation (Jeon, 2015). Nonetheless, this did not indicate the social investment approach explicitly.

The Roh Moo-hyun's government presented 'Vision 2030 for Economic Growth and Welfare' and included a social investment approach for a 'Korean type welfare state' which could better address problems for the aging society. In parallel, a rather frantic focus on the low fertility rate was propagated by the media from mid-2000, and these issues of low fertility and an aging population became the core national agenda with the establishment of the Presidential Committee on Aging and Future Society, while childcare policy was developed into an active child-rearing support policy. In 2006, the vision to increase the publicness of childcare, such as the '1st Basic Plan for Low Fertility and Aging Society: Saeromaji Plan' was proposed, and aggressive childcare policies – a drastic increase in childcare expenditure and infrastructure and improved access to childcare services – were adopted (Baek, 2009).

This was also a period in which improvements were made to the working environment in terms of parental leave and statutory working hours (Hyun, 2014). While the first plan focused on childcare, the '2nd Basic Plan for Low fertility and Aged Society (2011–2016)' emphasized more specifically work-life balance. In other words, the discussion of social investment in South Korea focused on strategies to cope with the low fertility rate and support work-life balance. However, policy orientation was concerned with minimizing state intervention and taking a liberalistic social investment approach that relies more on the market.

The year 2009 marks the beginning of liberalization in the work-family reconciliation policy during Lee Myung-Bak's administration from 2008 to 2013. During this time, the role of the state in the supply of childcare was reduced with the reduction of public childcare centers; private service sectors were expanded, existing childcare support switched from a facility-centric to a cost-centric model with the adoption of a voucher system, and family allowances were implemented – a symbolic family policy. From these changes, the work-family reconciliation policy in South Korea became re-familialized, and familialism is seen to have become a tacit standard in the childcare policy (Jeon, 2015). It was therefore a period in which the Korean liberalistic social investment approach was reinforced. With regard to childcare services, Lee Myung-Bak's administration continued the Roh administration's policy on childcare expansion with an electronic voucher system under the guise of 'recipient-oriented childcare'. The Lee administration changed the discretionary childcare subsidy system to a universal childcare system using the electronic voucher system, rather than increasing the number of public childcare centers, and this policy is considered by some to have ultimately preserved and enlarged the private sector-oriented supply structure (Kim, 2015). Thus, the government promoted marketization of child-rearing (care services) with the implementation of a voucher system for childcare subsidies (Hyun, 2014; Jeon, 2015). Lee Myung Bak's administration can be considered the period in which reform of the liberalistic social investment approach was reinforced by paying less attention to public childcare services while at the same time emphasizing the role of the market.

Work-family reconciliation policies adopt a social investment approach with emphasis on encouraging more women to participate in the labor market. Next, we will discuss South Korea's work-family reconciliation policies on parental leave and home care allowance for childcare. Although work-family reconciliation policies only started in 1990/2000, the scope for parental leave was extended with the enactment of the Maternity Protection Act in 2001 (Jeon, 2015). Individuals were granted a fixed rate of KRW 200,000 in 2001 for parental leave, and this allowance was increased to KRW 500,000 in 2007. Later in 2011, with an objection that the real value of the previous allowance was too low, payment for parental leave changed to a 40 percent replacement rate with a payment ceiling of KRW 1,000,000 and a floor of KRW 500,000.

The home care allowance was introduced in July 2009 as a selective monthly payment of KRW 100,000 for households with infants under 2 years of age in receipt of national basic livelihood guarantees and lower income families that did not use state-funded childcare facilities (Lee et al., 2013). This was later reformed in the second Basic Plan for Low Fertility and Aging Society in 2010 to include infants under 2 years of age in the lower 70 percent income group, and the grant was increased to a possible monthly maximum of KRW 200,000. This was further expanded in 2013 to include infants up to 5 years of age in all income groups, and by 2015, this childcare subsidy program had grown in size to comprise 23 percent of the Ministry of Health and Welfare's total childcare expenditure. Taking into account the additional support for infant care in the form of vouchers, the combination of cashable childcare aid and home care allowance made up 83 per cent of the Ministry of Health and Welfare's total childcare expenditure in 2015. In tracing these transformations in the South Korean family policy, it is apparent that the spirit of the changes has moved towards 'public childcare' and 'public responsibility in childcare' from an abstract goal level (Government of the Republic of Korea, 2000).

However, despite considerable advancements in spending on childcare together with expansion of childcare services and childcare subsidies, it is difficult to attribute these changes to a strengthened sense of government responsibility or a move towards a social democratic social investment approach, as their responsibilities in managing services, finances and provisions remain ambiguous and the government is wholly dependent on the private sector for the supply of services. Others are also of the view that the state combined subsidization with existing private childcare facilities instead of revamping the system (Song, 2014). Consequently, the government is seen to be trapped in a dimension of 'cost subsidization' that is indifferent to improvements in the quality of childcare services (Song, 2014). Thus, it might be concluded that Korean childcare policies aim at a liberalistic social investment approach which utilizes the market instead of reinforcing the publicness of childcare.

The Social Investment Approach and Policy in Japan

In contrast to the heated discussions between scholars and policy makers concerning the social investment state and the related strategies in South Korea, research on social investment or even the mention of social investment in the policy-making process is almost non-existent in Japan (Kim et al., 2010). However, considering that social investment policies have appeared throughout and in response to the aforementioned socioeconomic transformations, it can be reasonably inferred that policies similar to that of social investment also exist in Japan.

There have been no political debates on social investment strategies in Japan. However, some suggest that since family policy, especially childcare policies that promote a solution to the problems of low fertility and an aging society, has recently been at the core of policy reforms, Japan can be considered to have social investment policies albeit lacking a social investment strategy (Kim et al., 2010).

In a brief examination of the development of Japanese family policy period by period, Japan maintained the 'Japanese welfare state' and strengthened its male breadwinner model to circumvent further social insecurity in the 1980s when European welfare states were faltering (Yoon, 2012). However, as the total and very low birthrate at 1.57 was recorded in 1989 due to the rapidly aging population, Japan had to fundamentally reconsider the level of gender inequality in employment, wage differences and social security coverage. This marked a period of progress in Japan as laws and policies were introduced that attempted to establish gender equality.

In the early 1990s, when economic stagnation protracted, there was a movement to switch from a male breadwinner model to a dual breadwinner model as traditional values in families and businesses weakened. Consequently, with the aim to further work-family reconciliation, childcare became increasingly socialized, that is, government expenditure on childcare increased. Starting with the enactment of the 'Parental Leave Act' in 1991, the so-called 'Angel Plan' was announced in 1994, which was the government's Basic Plan for supporting childcare. This was followed by revisions of several policy acts, including the 'Childcare Act' in 1996, and the 'Equal Employment Opportunity for Both Genders Act' in 1997, as well as the enactment of the 'Basic Act on Equal Social Participation for Both Genders' in 1999, and finally the announcement of the 'New Angel Plan' in 1999 (Yoon, 2012). There was initially no payment from the Parental Leave Act when it was implemented in 1992, but that was later changed to a 25 percent replacement rate (1,000,000 won ceiling) with the revision of the 'Employment Insurance Act' in 1995.

The Angel Plan focuses on support for the reconciliation of child-rearing and paid work through the promotion of childcare facilities in workplaces, assistance in re-employment for individuals who have left work for childcare, reduction in working hours and a cut in child-rearing costs by providing child allowance (Yoon, 2012). Moreover, in the 'Plan to Ease Regulations (Revised)' announced by the Japanese government in March 1997, there was an emphasis on enabling parents to choose a childcare facility by deregulating regulations on the childcare provider. In 1997 a revision in the Child Welfare Act regarding the childcare system was made and it became a trigger that further stimulated deregulation in the administration of childcare services in the 2000s, including the abolishment of regulations on the construction of daycare centers (Kim, 2014). In Japan, the growth in family policy has centered on cash payments as opposed to services inviting market providers into childcare provision. The economic aid policy concerning childbirth and child-rearing includes a baby bonus and parental leave payment (Hwang, 2011). As an example of one of Japan's main policy developments, a baby bonus is a cash payment made by the state to a baby's parents to subsidize the costs of rearing and educating a child, and is also known as a family allowance or a family payment. In Article 1 of the revised Child Allowance Law, it states that the purpose of this law is to foster the healthy growth of a child for the next generation and to contribute in stabilizing the livelihood of families by paying a baby bonus to those who rear the child, in the understanding that the parent or the caretaker assumes primary responsibility in child-rearing (Jeon and Choi, 2015). Regarding these baby bonuses, the campaign pledges made by the Democratic Party, which won the general election in 2009, emphasized welfare expansion without an increase in taxes, such as child allowances without income limits. However, after the party succeeded in assuming power, it realized that the budget was limited. In addition, it had to make drastic revisions to its campaign pledges on child allowances due to its failure to adequately respond to unforeseen circumstances including the 2012 Tohoku earthquake, global economic recession and the resulting increase in government deficit. Accordingly, although Japan attempted to convert to a universal welfare state, it has reverted to a discretionary welfare state due to financial problems. After a series of policy changes over two years, the 'Legislative Bill for the Partial Amendment of the Child Allowance Law' was passed in the Assembly in March 2012, which revised the original government proposal. The amendment is considered to have not only increased the amount of payment and eligibility in age, but also drastically revised eligibility requirements regarding children in Child and Family Services who were not originally subject to a grant. The recipient of child allowances is the individual caring for the 'eligible child', not the child him or herself, and child allowances were not granted if the caretaker's income exceeded the income limit over which allowance eligibility was lost (Jeon and Choi, 2015).

Moreover, in terms of the Japanese leave system, parental leave is prescribed in the 'Law Regarding the Welfare of Workers Caring for Family and Children under Parental Leave' (henceforth Parental Leave Law) and maternity leave is stipulated in Article 65 of the Labor Standards Act (Oh, 2015). The Parental Leave Law was enacted as a response to the shocking total fertility rate recorded at 1.57 in 1989, mentioned above, in order to support the continued employment of workers while encouraging both child-rearing and work. The Parental Leave Law was revised in 2005 to allow an extension in parental leave for up to one year and six months in the event that an appropriate daycare center could not be found. The Revision also includes extended eligibility for temporary workers who 'have been employed under the same employer for over 1 year' and 'have the prospect of continued employment after their child reaches 1 year of age' (Hwang, 2011, p. 514). As we examine policy development and context above, parental leave and childcare policies in Japan present strong male breadwinner model characteristics and the development of these policies was largely influenced by demographic transition and political discussion on human investment. This approach differs from the social demographic social investment approach with its universalistic rights-based approach.

Summing up, since 1990, South Korea and Japan have expanded their family policies in response to the new social problems of an aging population and low fertility rate. These policy changes, however, have not been directed towards the social democratic version of social investment, but rather the liberal version with workfare-oriented selectivism, marketization of childcare and with work-life balance policies still having male breadwinner model characteristics. The primary reason for adopting the liberal social investment approach is that in both countries social policy continues to have a subordinated position to economic policies, due to the legacy of the productivist state. As a consequence, South Korea developed market-based social benefits, such as childcare, and these social services were developed as part of the privatization of welfare state benefits rather than an expansion of social rights. Moreover, expansion in the child and family policies clearly supported children in low-income households (Lee et al., 2014). Also, despite the implementation of universal childcare services from 2013, the conservative party's efforts to transform these into selective service provision was maintained. As regards Japan, although efforts were made to introduce innovations in child and family policy such as the introduction of child allowance, the concept of social investment was not raised on the political agenda, and the developmental legacy and predominant neoliberal atmosphere prevented the success of such efforts. Furthermore, considering that the social investment approach in both countries only emphasized investment in human capital through education, instead of combining it with adequate wages and income security, both countries show a strong liberal tendency in their take on social investments.

CONCLUSION: FROM PRODUCTIVIST WELFARE STATE TO LIBERAL SOCIAL INVESTMENT WELFARE STATE?

South Korea and Japan share similarities in having a productivist welfare state and in the way they have adopted the liberal social investment perspective. One explanation of these similarities is that both countries are experiencing demographic changes such as a low fertility rate, a rapidly aging population and changes in family structure, which have triggered the need for more responsive policy measures. The two countries have increased their welfare expenditure as well as the actual number of social welfare programs, not least with regard to policies aimed at families and children. However, the approach used to expand family policies differs in both countries from the social democratic social investment approach. Both countries have expanded family policies as a response to the low fertility rate, anticipating the negative consequences of slow economic growth and demographic transition. Moreover, the way in which family policies were expanded was due more to maximizing the market function, rather than expanding the role of the state, for instance, in subsidies or providing public childcare. The policies also emphasized the personal responsibility of care rather than the realization of social rights. Thus, both South Korea and Japan can be considered to have adopted the liberalistic social investment approach.

It is noteworthy that in the social investment approach the political setting was markedly different in the two countries. South Korea, unlike Japan, has been developing policies in line with the social investment approach from the Kim Dae-Jung administration in 1998 and onwards. The explicit use of the approach may be due to the Korean center-left government having found it necessary to collaborate with the right-wing parties in order to expand welfare policies. In Japan, the conservative Liberal Democratic Party (Ja Min Dang) was in power until 2000 and although there was social consensus that the government had to deal with low fertility, expanding family policy by explicitly mentioning the social investment approach was unnecessary. Thus, although both South Korea and Japan have developed their liberalistic social investment approach within productivist traditions, they differ in how the approach was implemented given their specific political economic contexts. Despite such differences, the countries are similar in that the percentage of gross domestic product (GDP) used for family expenditure is growing steadily in each one and they have both applied the liberalistic social investment approach to deal with demographic transition.

In conclusion, it is worth highlighting that overall expenditure on family policy increased in the two countries during a period when the social investment approach was actively being discussed in South Korea, but not in Japan. Hence, it is suggested that the increase in social expenditure for family policy was a consequence of the changes in the structure of the population and the need for policy action, and this was attributed to political will to introduce and expand the social investment approach, at least in South Korea. Future studies tracking further welfare policy developments might perhaps explain whether the expansion of family policy, as witnessed in these two countries, will continue to adopt the social investment approach, with its institutional legacy of a productivist welfare regime, or not.

ACKNOWLEDGEMENT

This work was supported by the Ministry of Education of the Republic of Korea and the National Research Foundation of Korea (NRF-2017S1A5A2A01027573).

REFERENCES

Aspalter, C. (2006), 'The East Asian welfare model', *International Journal of Social Welfare*, **15** (4), 290–301.
Baek, S.H. (2009), 'Evaluation on childcare policy during 10 years of Kim, Dae-Jung & Roh, Moo-Hyun's administrations; focus on national plans', *Critical Social Policy*, **28**, 95–141.
Baek, S.H. and S.H. Ahn (2007), 'A comparative social policy study on the structure and characteristic of Korean welfare state – focused on the development of public social expenditure', *Korean Journal of Social Welfare Studies*, **35**, 337–62.
Bonoli, G. (2005), 'The politics of the new social policies: providing coverage against new social risks in mature welfare states', *Policy & Politics*, **33** (3), 431–49.
Croissant, A. (2004), 'Changing welfare regimes in East and Southeast Asia: crisis, change and challenge', *Social Policy & Administration*, **38** (5), 504–24.
Deeming, C. and P. Smyth (2015), 'Social investment after neoliberalism: policy paradigms and political platforms', *Journal of Social Policy*, **44** (2), 297–318.
Esping-Andersen, G. (1990), *The Three Worlds of Welfare Capitalism*, Princeton, NJ: Princeton University Press.
Esping-Andersen, G. (ed.) (2002), *Why We Need a New Welfare State*, New York: Oxford University Press.
Goodman, R. and I. Peng (1996), 'The East Asian welfare states: peripatetic learning, adaptive change, and nation-building', in G. Esping-Andersen (ed.), *Welfare States in Transition: National Adaptations in Global Economies*, London: Sage Publications, pp. 192–224.
Goodman, R., G. White, and H.J. Kwon (eds) (1998), *The East Asian Welfare Model: Welfare Orientalism and the State*, New York: Routledge.
Government of the Republic of Korea (2000), *Plan for Ageing Society and Population*, Sejong, Republic of Korea: Ministry of Health and Welfare (PRN: 11-1352000-000082-01).
Holliday, I. (2000), 'Productivist welfare capitalism: social policy in East Asia', *Political Studies*, **48**, 706–23.
Hwang, S.H. (2011), 'A study on the current status of family welfare policy in Japan', in *Proceedings of the Japanese Language Literature Association of Korea Conference*, Daegu: Keimyung University, pp. 512–15.
Hyun, J.E. (2014), 'The analysis on change of childcare policy and female time allocation', *Korean Public Administration Review*, **48** (1), 207–31.
Jeon, Y.J. (2015), 'Korean's work-family balance policy during 1990 and 2014 from the perspective of defamiliarization, decommodification: especially focusing on maternity leave, parental leave, and childcare policies', *Korean Women's Studies*, **31** (3), 179–218.
Jenson, J. and D. Saint-Martin (2003), 'New routes to social cohesion? Citizenship and the social investment state', *Canadian Journal of Sociology*, **28** (1), 77–102.
Jeon, I.J. and Y.J. Choi (2015), 'A study on the children's allowance law in Japan', *Journal of Law Research*, **23** (2), 179–206.
Kasza, G.J. (ed.) (2006), *One World of Welfare: Japan in Comparative Perspective*, Ithaca, NY: Cornell University Press.
Kim, J.M. (2014), 'Reorganization of the Japanese child daycare policy and familializing: a case study of Kawasaki City', *Japanese Culture Studies*, **51**, 77–101.
Kim, K.S., Y.M. Kim, Y. Choi, S.W. Kim, and B.C Kim (eds) (2010), *East Asian Social Welfare and Social Investment Strategy: Capturing a Vision and Possibility of Social Investment Strategy*, Seoul, Republic of Korea: Press of Sharing House.
Kim, S.J. (2015), 'The trilemma of child care service: Korean strategy and its consequences', *Economy and Society*, **105**, 64–93.
Kim, Y.S. (2007), 'Is the social investment state an alternative welfare model for Korea? A critical review on the recent discussion on the social investment state in Korea', *Economy and Society*, **71**, 84–113.
Ku, Y.W. and C. Jones Finer (2007), 'Developments in East Asian welfare studies', *Social Policy & Administration*, **41** (2), 115–31.
Kwon, H.J. (2005), 'Transforming the developmental welfare state in East Asia', *Development and Change*, **36** (3), 477–97.
Kwon, S. and I. Holliday (2007), 'The Korean welfare state: a paradox of expansion in an era of globalisation and economic crisis', *International Journal of Social Welfare*, **16** (3), 242–8.

Lee, M.H., H.M. Yoo, H.M. Choi, and A.R. Cho (eds) (2014), *Study on the Policy Aim after Free Provision of Child Care*, Seoul: Korean Institute of Child Care and Education.

Lee, S.S.Y. (2015), 'Japan and Korea as productivist welfare states', in M. Higo and T. Klassen (eds), *Retirement in Japan and Korea: The Past, the Present and the Future*, London: Routledge, pp. 30–47.

Lee, S.S.Y. and S.H. Baek (2014), 'Why the social investment approach is not enough – the female labour market and family policy in the Republic of Korea', *Social Policy & Administration*, **48** (6), 686–703.

Lee, S.S.Y., M.H. Kim, and J.Y. Lee (2013), 'Policy network analysis on Korean child care cash benefit expansion', *Korea Social Policy Review*, **20** (2), 195–232.

Lee, Y.J. and Y.W. Ku (2007), 'East Asian welfare regime: testing the hypothesis of the developmental welfare state', *Social Policy & Administration*, **41** (2), 197–212.

Lister, R. (2004), 'The Third Way's social investment state', in R. Surender and J. Lewis (eds), *Welfare State Change: Towards a Third Way*, Oxford: Oxford University Press, pp. 157–81.

Midgley, J. (1999), 'Growth, redistribution, and welfare: toward social investment', *Social Service Review*, **73** (1), 3–21.

Morel, N., B. Palier, and J. Palme (eds) (2012), *Towards a Social Investment Welfare State? Ideas, Policies and Challenges*, Bristol: Policy Press.

Na, B.K. (2010), 'A study on the applicability of East Asian welfare state discourse to the development of Korean welfare state (regime)', *Korean Journal of Social Welfare Studies*, **41** (3), 5–27.

Oh, M.H. (2015), 'A study on birthrates and gender equality policy in Korea and Japan', *Journal of Japanese Language and Literature*, **65**, 395–420.

Peng, I. (2015), 'The "new" social investment policies in Japan and South Korea', in R. Hasmath (ed.), *Inclusive Growth, Development and Welfare Policy: A Critical Assessment*, New York: Routledge, pp. 142–60.

Perkins, D., L. Nelms, and P. Smyth (2004), 'Beyond neo-liberalism: the social investment state?', *Just Policy: A Journal of Australian Social Policy*, **38**, 34.

Song, D.Y. (2014), 'Socialization of caring and delay of the welfare state in Korea', *Korean Women's Studies*, **30** (4), 119–52.

Yang, J.J. (2013), 'Parochial welfare politics and the small welfare state in South Korea', *Comparative Politics*, **45** (4), 457–75.

Yoon, S.H. (2012), 'Change of East Asian family policy: focused on Japan and Taiwan', *Korean Comparative Government Review*, **16** (2), 123–48.

10. Leave policies for parents in a cross-national perspective: various paths along the same course?
Olivier Thévenon

INTRODUCTION

Child-related leave entitlements provide employment protection, and often income support, to workers who take time off work to care for their children. These leave policies have developed across countries differently due to cross-national differences in goals to be achieved. The design of leave entitlements, as well as their evolution over time, is deeply shaped by societal attitudes towards the best interest for the child; the roles of mothers and fathers in raising children and in supporting child health, physical, cognitive and emotional development; parental labour market behaviour; attitudes towards gender equality; employer attitudes towards child-related leave; as well as by the economic situation which can limit countries' opportunities to extend leave rights or encourage them to use leave policies as an additional tool to regulate flows in or out of employment (Cameron and Moss, 2007; Galtry and Callister, 2005; OECD, 2011; Ray et al., 2010; Thévenon, 2014; Wall and Escobedo, 2012).

This chapter provides an overview of key cross-national differences in child-related leave entitlements and their evolution since the early 1970s in the Organisation for Economic Co-operation and Development (OECD) countries. It focuses on leave entitlements granted for a childbirth or to take care of a sick or handicapped child. The chapter first reviews the main cross-national differences regarding leave entitlements and their evolution over the past decades. It shows that most of these countries have started with the introduction of mother-specific rights to leave work around the time of childbirth and extended them with parental leave entitlements to be claimed by either of the two parents. Yet, mothers remain the main users of leave entitlements in the absence of measures that encourage or constrain fathers to take leave days. For this reason, father-specific rights have been introduced in about half of the OECD countries and these are reviewed in the chapter. These entitlements are most often limited to time periods that are incomparably shorter than those usually taken by women – and therefore they often do not dramatically modify the gender balance in leave policies. A few countries, such as Iceland especially, have been more active in promoting gender equality, however, by granting mothers and fathers the same amount of leave days to care for young childcare, which has succeeded in changing the otherwise unequal gender balance in take-up (see also Chapter 15 Eydal, Rostgaard and Hiilamo in this volume for an account of the Nordic countries). However, although all countries have expanded leave entitlements and increased the duration of paid leave, there is no significant sign of convergence in policies among countries. We observe instead a growing diversity of leave policies, with some countries making it possible for parents to choose between different options and making the use of leave entitlements more flexible, while others do not.

CROSS-NATIONAL DIFFERENCES IN LEAVE ENTITLEMENTS FOR PARENTS WITH A YOUNG CHILD

The basic right to stop work for a few weeks prior to and after the birth of a baby was in all countries first granted to working mothers to protect their health and their child's (Moss and Deven, 1999; Tanaka, 2005). This leave has been commonly called 'maternity' leave, although not legally separated from the other rights to take leave from work granted to parents in a few countries (including Australia, Canada, Iceland, New Zealand, Norway, Portugal and Sweden). Yet, the additional entitlement to leave from work to care for a (newborn) child available for both parents – 'parental' leave – has been progressively introduced after those granted to mothers. Parental leave consequently may either be shared by both parents or granted to each one separately. Its development has been especially rapid since the late 1980s, driven by some of the considerations mentioned above and in some countries supplemented by additional forms of leave (e.g., childcare leave). In an attempt to promote greater gender equality in paid and unpaid work, some countries have also introduced entitlements specifically for fathers (e.g., paternity leave – leave following the birth of the child) and/or a father's quota that is for the exclusive use of fathers and works as a use-it-or-lose-it benefit. The majority of OECD countries now offer these three types of family-related leave around and following childbirth, and in some cases they are complemented with home-care benefit on condition that parents do not use public childcare services and which can accompany a right to leave work to prtotect parental employment. Typically, the combination of these rights allows at least one parent to remain at home until the child is 2 or 3 years of age.

MATERNITY LEAVE ENTITLEMENTS

Maternity or pregnancy leave ensures women a period of rest from work before and after childbirth and a return to their previous job within a limited number of weeks after childbirth.[1] It is generally available to mothers only, but in some countries part of the leave can be transferred to fathers under certain circumstances. Because maternity leave entitlements were first introduced to protect the health of working mothers and their newborn children, they are often incorporated into social security systems, alongside health insurance and paid sick leave. In most countries the funding of maternity pay is based on insurance principles, so eligibility criteria are often linked to contributory records and/or periods of employment. In many countries the criteria stipulate a qualifying period of 6–12 months of employment or recidency. Eligibility is generally most relaxed in the Nordic countries. For instance, there is a residency requirement of 180 days in Finland, while in Denmark qualification for full maternity, paternity and adoption pay requires 120 hours of work in the 13 weeks prior to paid leave, but a range of stipulations extends eligibility to wider groups.

Maternity leave that begins and ends either side of childbirth is mandatory, although when it starts and how long it lasts vary across countries and can, in any event, be adjusted for medical reasons or by collective or workplace employer-employee agreement.

Maternity leave entitlements have extended over time, as a result of the increase in both the number of countries granting such entitlements and in the number of weeks covered.

In 1970, 24 countries granted an average of 11.3 weeks of paid leave; this average increased to 17 paid weeks in 2014, with almost all OECD countries now granting paid maternity leave. The United States is for now the only OECD country without a nationwide paid maternity leave scheme, although some employers provide paid leave benefits and some states have paid maternity/parental leave legislation (e.g., New Jersey, California) or provide income support during maternity leave through other social programmes (Adema et al., 2015). The duration of paid maternity leave thus varies considerably across the OECD, and is longest in Greece, the United Kingdom and in Eastern European countries (Figure 10.1) (see also country studies in Chapter 14 by Woods, Chapter 16 by Guerro and Naldini and Chapter 17 by Raţ and Szikra in this volume).

Parental Leave and Total Period of Paid Leave

Parental leave entitlements offer parents additional opportunities to care for a newborn child, but some systems also allow leave to be taken at a later stage, usually before the child is 8 years old. These rights were frequently introduced as supplementary rights for mothers only, but entitlements have generally been extended to fathers (for their exclusive use or not). Yet, in general, mothers rather than fathers take parental leave, and they usually take parental leave following the period of maternity leave.

In many OECD countries the entitlement to paid parental leave is family-based, which means that except for periods reserved for either the mother or the father (see next section), it is up to the parents in couple families to decide how they would like to share the paid leave entitlement. From a financial perspective, as mothers frequently get paid less than their husbands and because leave benefit is typically based on prior income, the least costly option for the household budget in the short term is for the mother to take the leave entitlement. This contributes at least in part to the predominant use of paid parental leave by mothers.

There is considerable cross-country variation in the development of parental leave entitlements. In 1970 only five countries offered such entitlements: Austria, Czechoslovakia (now the Czech and Slovak Republics), Italy, Poland and Sweden. In particular, there is a divide between most of the 'frontrunner countries' – Austria, the Czech Republic, Finland, France, Italy, Hungary, Norway, Poland, the Slovak Republic and Sweden – which first introduced parental leave entitlements in the late 1960s and early 1970s, and those which started to introduce entitlements from 1980 onwards (Thévenon, 2014). Additionally, in some countries (Finland, Norway, Portugal, Sweden and in Iceland for a limited period of time), parental leave is supplemented by a further period of leave (home care leave/childcare leave) that parents can take to care for a very young child, often up to the age of 3 (or more).

The duration of paid leave has gradually increased over time in most countries, but back-and-forth, for instance, in Austria, the Czech Republic, Denmark, Germany and Hungary. In Finland the duration of paid leave and in Sweden the payment rates decreased during the mid-1990s in response to economic upheaval following the break-up of the former Soviet Union. However, on the whole, the periods of paid leave have been increased in the vast majority of countries since 1970. In most of the frontrunner countries working parents are entitled to periods of leave (including childcare or home care leave) lasting more than one year and often between two and three years (except

Policies in a cross-national perspective 127

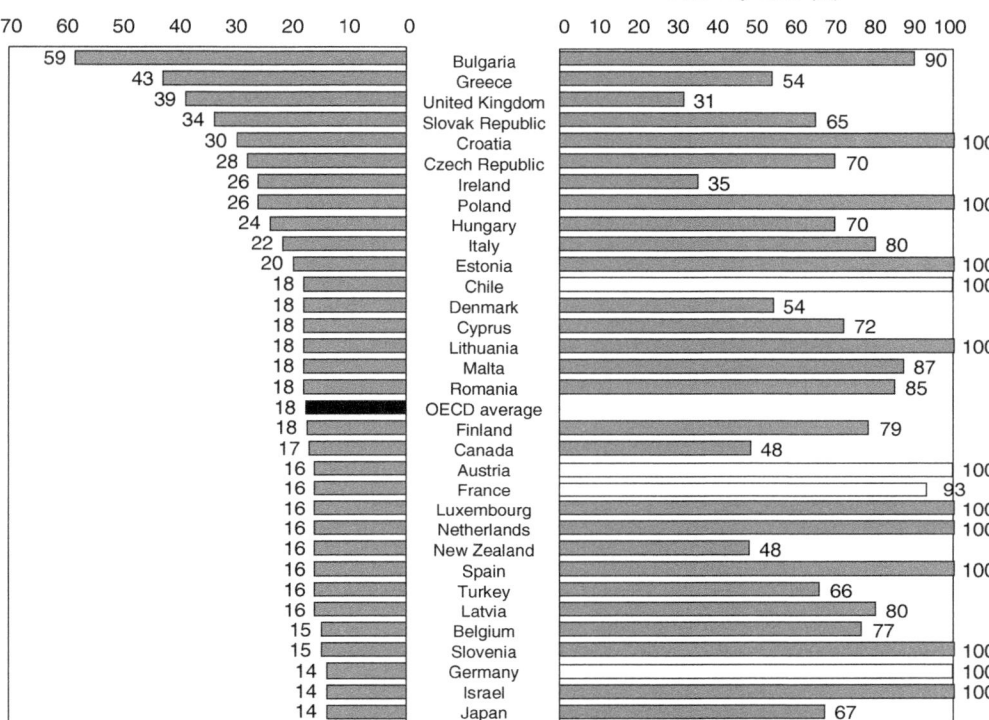

Note: The 'average payment rate' is the proportion of gross earnings replaced by the benefit over the length of the paid leave entitlement for a person on average earnings. If this covers more than one period of leave at two different payment rates, then a weighted average is calculated based on the length of each period. In some countries, a proportion of earnings is replaced up to a certain ceiling which can be lower than the average wage, in which case the actual replacement rate is lower than the rate usually advertised. Maternity benefits may be subject to taxation and may count towards the income base for social security contributions. As a result, the actual amount received by the individual on maternity leave may differ from those shown in the figure. White bars in Panel B indicates payment rates based on net earnings. See the OECD Family Database (http://www.oecd.org/els/family/database.htm) for more details. Data for Canada reflect statutory provisions at the federal level. The payment rate in Canada does not take into account the two-week unpaid waiting period that must be observed at the beginning of the leave.

Source: OECD (2016) Family Database.

Figure 10.1 Paid maternity leave, 2015

Italy), while countries that introduced parental leave after 1980 generally have shorter leave periods still in 2011 (except Germany). Sweden is an exception because entitlements to leave were gradually increased until the early 1990s.

By contrast, only a couple of countries have dramatically changed the initial scheme in a way that clearly suggests a change in policy orientation. Germany is certainly the best example of such a shift from a system bolstering the male breadwinner model to a system promoting a more gender balanced use of leave entitlements (Erler, 2009). By promoting a more equal share of childcare work between mothers and fathers, the new system, added to the sustained development of childcare services, is expected to create the conditions for a better work-life balance and to boost fertility (OECD, 2017a).

Before 2007, German parents were entitled to receive a flat-rated and means-tested 'Childrearing Benefit' (*Elterngeld*) of approximately €300 a month for 24 months if they were not employed for more than 30 hours a week. In contrast to this situation, the 2007 reform of parental leave introduced the right for parents to take leave and receive two-thirds of their earnings for 12 months, up to a ceiling of €1800 per month (and a minimum payment of €300 even for parents without prior income). A two-month bonus is also granted when each parent takes at least two months of leave. The reform thus introduces strong incentives to take leave and, for parents who can afford to pay, to use part of it for scarce and expensive childcare services upon the expiry of leave entitlements. The earlier scheme is not completely suppressed, however, since the childrearing benefit can be spread over 24 (+4) months, with a monthly benefit level that is reduced so that the overall payment is the same as for those receiving benefit for 12 months of leave. Keeping the possibility of taking longer leave is of course motivated by the relative scarcity and high cost of childcare services, and also by the strong attachment of Germans towards the role of mothers in taking care of newborn children. Also, since 2015 an additional bonus equivalent to four months of leave is granted to the spouses of a couple if each works between 25 and 30 hours per week. This additional bonus is intended to encourage equal sharing of care (OECD, 2017a; see also Chapter 13 by Pfau-Effinger on, amongst others, Germany in this volume).

An ambitious reform was also conducted in Portugal in 2009 (Escobedo and Wall, 2015) when new labour legislation introduced major changes in leave policy, and conditioned the extension of paid leave to the principle of more gender sharing of leave. Practically, parents are entitled to six months of leave (180 calendars days) paid at the full rate of their earnings instead of five months if at least one month of leave is taken by the other parent. But the most innovative aspect of the system (compared to other countries where a 'bonus' of time exists when both parents share leave) is that the payment rate is higher over the total period taken by both parents if they meet the 'gender quota'. It thus provides significant incentives for parents to meet the gender quota, above and over the non-transferable rights that exist in other countries. The Portuguese scheme is also unique in making it obligatory for fathers to take two weeks of leave.

Figure 10.2 shows that, in addition to paid maternity leave, mothers can take almost 37 weeks of paid parental leave and/or home care leave on average across the OECD. Most countries offer between 26 and 52 weeks, but 11 OECD countries offer no entitlement for paid parental or home care leave, while at the other extreme four OECD countries (Estonia, Finland, Hungary and the Slovak Republic) provide a statutory entitlement of over two-and-a-half years.

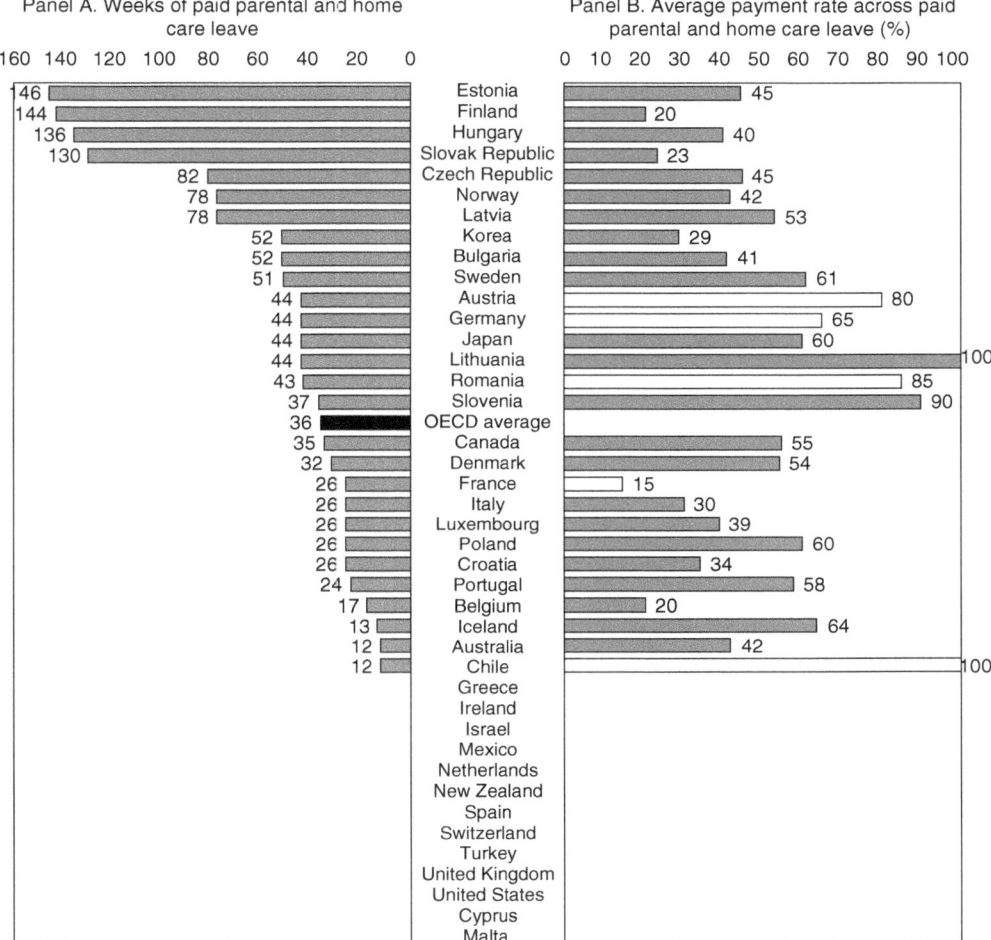

Note: The weeks of paid leave presented here are in addition to the entitlements shown in Figure 10.1. In some countries, a proportion of earnings is replaced up to a certain ceiling which can be lower than the average wage, in which case the actual replacement rate is lower than the rate usually advertised. Additional unpaid leave is available in some countries but are not accounted for in this figure which shows paid leave only. White bars indicates payment rates based on net earnings. Information on France is based on income support for mothers of a first child; income support is more generous when it concerns a mother's second or third child.

Source: OECD (2016) Family Database.

Figure 10.2 Paid parental and home care leave available to mothers, 2015

Payment rates also vary with types of leave and duration. Parental and in particular home care leave payment rates tend to be lower than those for maternity leave. Most countries provide benefits that replace somewhere between 40 to 60 per cent of previous earnings, but this varies considerably across countries. The lowest payment rates tend to be found in countries with the longest entitlements. In the Slovak Republic, for example, payments across the 130-week paid parental leave entitlement replace only 23 per cent of average gross earnings, while in Finland the payment rate falls to 20 per cent. In the latter case, this is because a substantial portion of the overall leave entitlement takes the form of an extended 'home care' leave after a period of parental leave. The objectives behind paid home care leave tend to be a little different to those behind paid parental leave – rather than providing parents with short-term compensation for earnings forgone by suspending employment, these extended benefits instead look to offer medium-term financial support to parents who wish to remain at home to care for young children, instead of using subsidized day care. As a result, these longer leaves are often paid only through low flat-rate benefits and usually replace only a small proportion of previous earnings.

In most cases, parental leave is taken by mothers upon the expiry of maternity leave, so that the durations reported in Figures 10.1 and 10.2 are 'additive'. Taken together with paid maternity leave, the average total duration of paid leave entitlements that mothers can use is just over one year across the OECD – if, for the sake of simplicity, it is assumed that mothers make full use of the right to parental leave. There are wide variations in countries' priorities to support work-life balance with important consequences on gender differences in labour market outcomes (Adema et al., 2015; Thévenon and Solaz, 2013). In practice, fathers represent from 0.5 per cent to almost 46 per cent of the recipients of parental leave benefits in Australia and Iceland, respectively, and account for a quarter or less of benefit recipients in most countries, cross-country variations being partly explained by differences in policy design to promote father's use (OECD, 2017a, PF2.2).

Only Austria, the Czech Republic, Norway, Portugal, Sweden and France (for a third child) allow parents to choose between different lengths of leave and payment rates (Table 10.1). Few other amendments have been introduced in the legislations to make the use of leave more flexible and therefore to encourage more parents (including fathers) to take leave days. For instance, most countries allow parents to take leave in one continuous block or in several shorter blocks, with the possibility or not to use all or part of the leave until the child reaches school age (Table 10.1). Parents can be on leave at the same time in the majority of countries. Most countries also offer the possibility to take leave on a part-time basis (i.e., so parents can combine part-time employment with part-time leave). By contrast, only a couple of countries (Estonia and Hungary) make it possible to transfer leave entitlements to carers who are not parents.

LEAVE DAYS TO CARE FOR A SICK RELATIVE

In addition to the aforementioned rights, many countries provide specific entitlements to care for a sick relative. The rights often vary with the identity of the person being cared for (e.g., a child, partner or parent). Leave days most often may be granted on a per episode basis, for a limited number of days. Alternatively, entitlements may concern a maximum number of care days that an employee can take within a year. The duration of leave often varies with the seriousness of the illness, but not in Sweden where there is no distinction in the duration of entitlements once a claim has been established. Most countries provide a few days leave (up to three weeks in Portugal) to employees who need to care for a relative under 'normal' circumstances.

Table 10.1   Flexibility permitted in the use of parental leave entitlements, 2012

	Possible use in separated blocks	Simultaneous use by parents	Part-time option	Short/long option	Age	Transferred to a non-parent
Australia						
Austria	✓	✓	✓	✓	✓	
Belgium	✓		✓			
Canada (Quebec)		✓			✓	
Czech Republic		✓		✓		
Germany		✓	✓	✓	✓	
Denmark	✓	✓	✓	✓	✓	
Spain	✓	✓			✓	
Estonia	✓					✓
Finland	✓	✓	✓			
France		✓	✓			
Greece	✓	✓			✓	
Hungary						✓
Iceland	✓	✓	✓		✓	
Ireland	✓	✓			✓	
Italy	✓	✓			✓	
Japan		✓				
Korea			✓			
Luxembourg			✓		✓	
Netherlands	✓	✓	✓			
Norway		✓	✓	✓	✓	
New Zealand						
Poland	✓	✓	✓		✓	
Portugal		✓	✓	✓	✓	
Slovenia	✓	✓	✓		✓	
Slovak Republic		✓				
Sweden	✓	✓	✓	✓	✓	
United Kingdom	✓				✓	

Source: Moss (2012) and OECD Family Database.

Few countries (Austria, Canada, the Czech Republic, Denmark, Estonia, Finland, France, Germany, Japan, Italy, Luxembourg, Norway, Poland, Portugal, Sweden and Switzerland) provide specific entitlements to care for a sick child. Some countries (e.g., Austria, Denmark and Hungary) allow employees to take time off for personal or exceptional reasons, and in many cases such time is used to reconcile work and family commitments.

FATHER-SPECIFIC LEAVE ENTITLEMENTS

There are different reasons for urging fathers to use parental leave, including the possibility to change gender stereotypes, foster gender equality between men and women and give children the right to be with both parents (Huerta et al., 2013). To increase the take-up of leave among fathers, many OECD countries have introduced father-specific paid leave periods. These include any period of employment-protected paternity leave which is taken in relation to birth and overlaps with maternity leave, parental leave that is reserved for the exclusive use by fathers ('fathers' quotas') or shareable parental leave that is effectively 'reserved' as it must be used by the main leave-taker's partner (often the father) in order for the family to qualify for bonus weeks. More so than paternity leave, quotas of parental leave are expected to encourage fathers to be the main carer for a certain period of time, and not just to supplement the time that mothers allocate to childcare. Sweden was the first OECD country to introduce paid parental leave in 1974, with a shareable leave period of six months (Chronholm, 2007). In 1995 a one-month leave period for the exclusive use of fathers was introduced, which was subsequently extended to two months, and extended in 2016 to three months. Over the years, the proportion of parental leave days taken by fathers has gradually increased, from 5 per cent in 1980 to 10 per cent in 1995 and 24 per cent in 2012. Similar changes in men's behaviour have been observed particularly in Iceland where only 3 per cent of parental leave days available were taken by fathers prior to the introduction in 2001 of a three-month father-specific entitlement to paid leave. Since this reform the proportion of leave days taken by fathers has increased tenfold (Eydal and Gíslason, 2014). Similarly, in Germany an overhaul of the payment scheme attached to parental leave has seen the proportion of fathers claiming parental leave allowance increase from 3.5 per cent in the last quarter of 2006 to just over 32 per cent in the third quarter of 2013 (Destatis, 2015).

Over half the OECD countries provide fathers-specific entitlements for a period that varies from 5 to 15 days to be taken immediately following childbirth (Figure 10.3). On top of this, a few countries earmark a particular period of parental leave for the exclusive use of each parent, with no possibility of transferring it to the other parent. Nordic countries (with the exception of Denmark, the only Nordic country without a father's quota), Portugal and Slovenia grant the longest father-specific leave. On average, OECD countries offer nine weeks of paid father-specific leave; nine OECD countries provide no paid father-specific leave at all; and ten countries offer two weeks or less, but these short periods are often paid in full. The period for which fathers receive the equivalent of full-rate payment is clearly longest in Norway and Portugal. However, there are a growing number of countries that provide father's leave for a longer period, and there are nine countries that reserve three months or more of paid leave for fathers. In North America, the Canadian province of Québec has introduced a five-week period of paid leave reserved for fathers in its parental leave scheme. After recent reforms in the two East Asian OECD countries – Japan and South Korea – individual paid leave entitlements last as long as 12 months. The entitlement in Japan is paid at around 58 per cent of average earnings, which is the equivalent of 30.4 weeks of leave at full pay, by far the most generous paid father-specific entitlement in the OECD (OECD, 2017b). However, less than 5 per cent of Japanese and Korean fathers use their paid leave entitlement. To some extent, this may be related to limited awareness among Japanese and Korean fathers regarding these – relatively new – entitlements. But fathers are also likely to consider that taking parental leave for a few months may have a negative effect on their career prospects. Workplace cultures are also not very well prepared to encourage male employees to take up their rights when

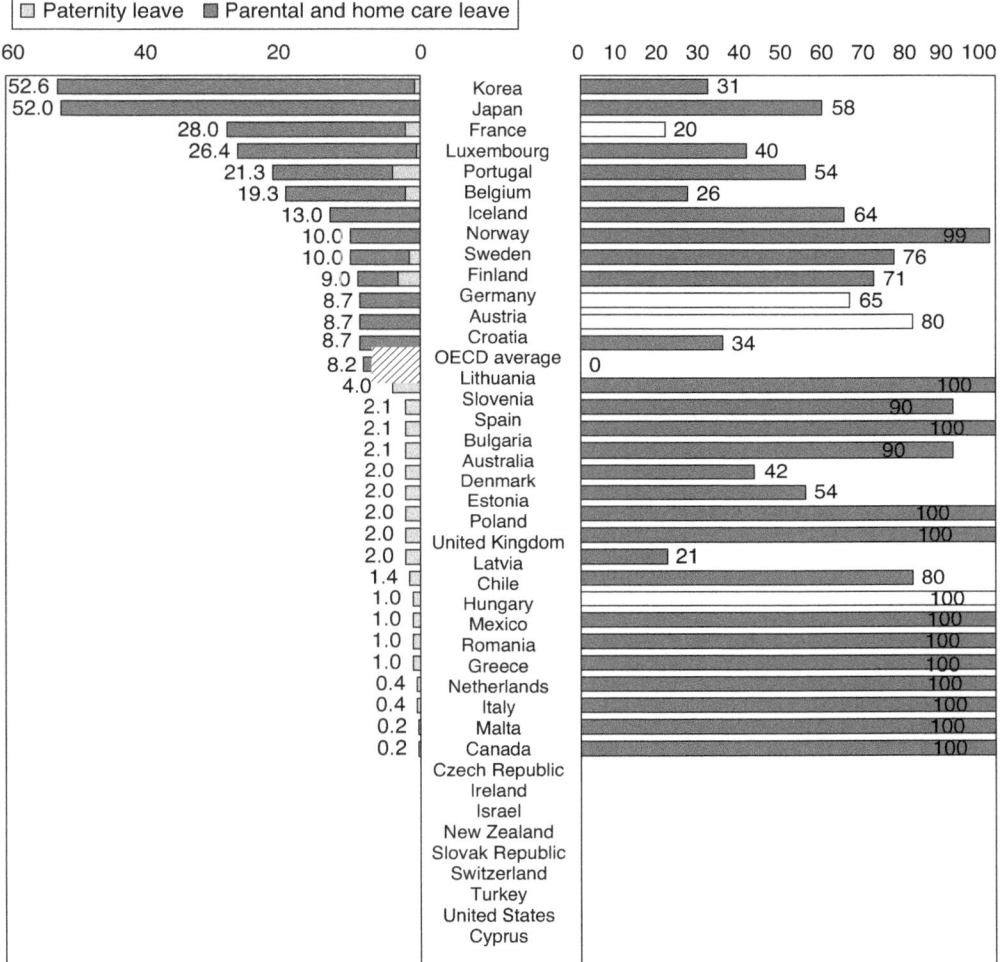

Note: The information refers to entitlements to paternity leave, 'father quotas' or periods of parental leave that can be used only by the father and cannot be transferred to the mother, and any weeks of shareable leave that must be taken by the father in order for the family to qualify for 'bonus' weeks of parental leave. Cross-hatching indicates payment rates based on net earnings. Data for Canada reflect statutory provisions at the federal level. The province of Québec has a separate parental insurance programme which includes a five-week paid leave period for exclusive use by the father.

Source: OECD (2015) Family Database.

Figure 10.3 Paid leave reserved for fathers, 2015

having a baby (Mun and Brinton, 2015; see also Chapter 11 by den Dulk, Yerks and Peper on workplace policies and cultures in this volume).

Overall, periods of leave that are father-specific and not transferable to the other parent are much shorter than the periods covered by parental leave entitlements which are usually taken by mothers in spite of the eligibility of the two parents. In addition, fathers actually take less leave days than the maximum authorized by legislation: despite the various schemes designed to encourage fathers to claim their father-specific rights, their overall take-up is 20–30 per cent short of their entitlements (Moss, 2014). The reasons for this are a mix of financial incentives and the persistence of traditional attitudes regarding care work: since men are often the main earners in families, women are likely to take most of the available leave in order to keep the loss of household income to a minimum; and this happens especially when the benefit received by parents on leave does not fully replace the income earned before the birth. Moreover, a recent study on the impact of Swedish parental leave reforms shows that the take-up of leave days is much higher among fathers with a tertiary level of education than for father with a lower degree, and significantly higher for Swedish-born than for foreign-born fathers (Duvander and Johanssen, 2015).

PUBLIC SPENDING ON LEAVE

The cost of maternity, paternity and parental leave programmes differs considerably across the OECD (Figure 10.4), largely on account of the cross-country differences in the

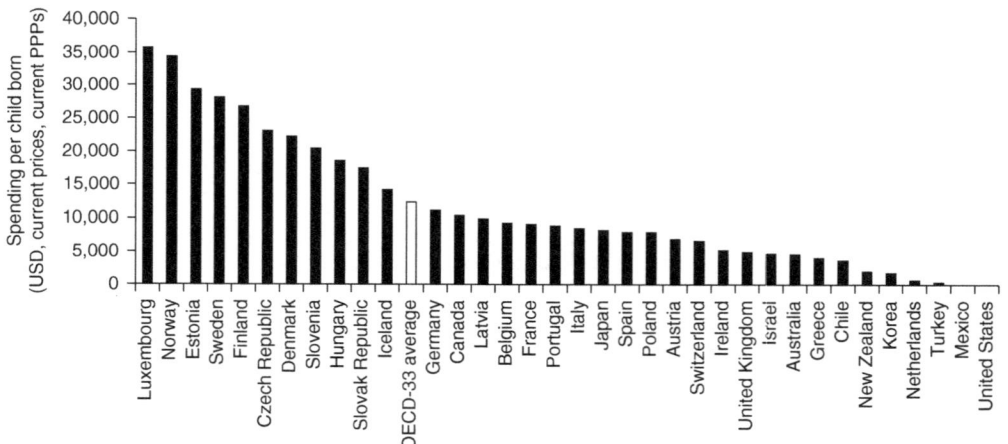

Note: Spending on maternity leave in the Netherlands is categorized as 'mandatory private' in the OECD Social Expenditure Database (it concerns payments employers are legally obliged to make for which they get reimbursed through sickness insurance legislation). As such, this is not included in the OECD average of public spending on paid leave.

Source: OECD (2016) Social Expenditure Database.

Figure 10.4 *Public expenditure on maternity and parental leave, as a percentage of GDP, 2015*

length, duration and payment rates of leave arrangements. Public spending on maternity and parental leave tends to be highest – at around or above 0.5 per cent of gross domestic product (GDP) – in the Nordic and Eastern European OECD countries. These countries offer mothers at least one year of paid leave (Figures 10.2 and 10.4), while the Nordic countries also offer generous paid leaves for fathers (Figure 10.3). Costs are generally far lower – at around or below 0.2 per cent of GDP – in those countries that provide shorter paid leaves.[2]

CONCLUSION

Overall, a wide expansion of leave entitlements has occurred over the past decades across OECD countries. Mothers and fathers have seen their entitlements to leave work to take care of newborn children expanded with the provision of rights for their exclusive use (or not), complementing the basic mother-specific 'maternity' rights which were first introduced in the vast majority of countries. A basic distinction between those countries providing short or long leaves has emerged with the introduction of parental leave entitlement, reflecting differences in the objectives and values underpinning leave policies. These initial differences have been maintained over years in most cases, suggesting the presence of constant characteristics or path dependencies in the determinants of leave policies. Hence, despite the widespread extension of leave entitlements taking place after a childbirth, the convergence of policies remains limited in this area.

Yet, all countries have extended the period for which parents with young children (and especially mothers who remain the main takers of leave) are entitled to leave work and are compensated with a benefit.

Most important are the changes in legislations that were recently made to make the use of parental leave more flexible. In this perspective, many countries have introduced the possibility for both parents to take leave at the same time, or to take it on a part-time basis in order to make it more attractive to fathers in the first case as well as to parents not willing to completely stop working. Many countries now also make it possible for parents to choose between different lengths of leave and payment rates. In most cases, the new options offer the opportunity to take leave for a shorter period than the one initially offered and to receive a higher benefit, so that leave may be more attractive to mothers and fathers of wealthy families. This greater flexibility in the use of leave rights is expected to make them less detrimental to a female career, and to better fit the specific needs and constraints of parents.

From a historical perspective, these evolutions towards more flexible use of leave entitlements are certainly a departure from the 'optional familialism' depicted by Leitner (2003) to characterize the willingness of countries to leave choice between care and work to parents (which actually means that some women – or some households – have much more 'free choice' than others (Morel, 2007). Still, the persistence of large cross-country differences shows that cultural environments matter and shape the way countries design leave entitlements and introduce reforms. For example, as pointed out by Wall and Escobedo (2012), the generosity in the form of a longer, paid parental leave may mean that policies are shifting the leave system closer to a 'mother-centred' model or, alternatively, to a flexible 'parental choice' model aiming to include varied options of leave. In this context, concerns about child well-being is prominent, but anchored in a system where the mother remains the main carer in the early years. By contrast, emphasis on gender equality, promotion of mothers' employment, support for dual-earner couples and the provision of childcare services has tended to shape a one-year leave gender equality-orientated model in which both mothers and fathers are encouraged to combine full-time work and care for very young children. While attention is paid to child well-being, there is more emphasis here on the father's role and the benefits to children of having fathers involved in childcare and education during the early years.

Leave policies are moving from their historical roots, however. The development of the father's non-transferable entitlements, added to the diversification of the options between which parents can choose, also demonstrate the willingness of a growing number of countries to encourage fathers to be more involved in childcare and to foster gender equality. Providing father-specific (e.g., non-transferable) leave seems to increase men's uptake of parental leave. In Iceland and Sweden, the 'father's quota' has led to a doubling in the number of parental leave days taken by men. It is also working in other parts of the world. In Germany too, parental benefit was taken up by 32 per cent of fathers for births in 2013 (compared to 3.5 per cent of fathers in 2006, before the new legislation). In Korea, the number of men taking leave rose more than three-fold following the introduction of a father-specific entitlement in 2007, but the take-up remains very limited with men accounting for only 4.5 per cent of leave takers in 2014, despite a quite generous system and in comparison to the rates of users achieved in other regions. This highlights the limits of what can be achieved by laws if societal values, workplace cultures and practices are not ready to encourage fathers to make use of their rights.

There are several possibilities that could help to increase fathers' take-up, however. Some governments may be willing to push legislation obliging employers and employees to take leave unless there are serious business reasons for not doing so. Granting benefit to replace loss of earnings is an important determinant of the father's use of leave rights since fathers frequently remain the main earner in the family, so that the opportunity cost of fathers taking care of a child is reduced. To increase take-up, countries could then reform the system to grant a shorter period of leave but with a higher payment rate, as done for instance in Germany with the aforementioned 2007 reform. Financial incentives could also be increased by making the payment rate higher for all the leave period taken by mothers and fathers if the father's quota is taken.

For parents who may be unwilling or unable to stop work completely, flexible or part-time leave arrangements may also provide a solution. Such arrangements can help minimize the financial impact of taking leave, while allowing employees to remain connected to their jobs and to care for children. They can also help partners to 'shift-share' part-time leave and work commitments. Employers may benefit too if they don't have to go to the expense of finding and hiring a replacement worker when the employee is on part-time leave. However, this may not provide the expected outcomes in environments where male part-time work is not well perceived (Brandth and Kvande, 2001).

There are certainly limits in the extent to which legislation can prescribe how to allocate leave days – many parents may claim that it is a matter of private life – and the variation of policies across Nordic countries shows this quite well (Eydal et al., 2015). However, countries can manipulate the incentives such that parents may have to choose one option or the other by making it more financially attractive for both parents to share parental leave according to the minimum quota, or by introducing more flexibility in how parents can use their individual rights to better meet their constraints. These measures are not revolutionary, neither do they provide a 'one fits all' solution but their main advantage is their low cost for the public budget. Moreover, they may be thought of as 'nudges' suggested by Thaler and Sunstein (2008) to influence individuals' behaviour and to promote social well-being without demonstrating strong paternalism.

NOTES

1. Details about leave entitlements can be found in the yearly reviews provided by the International Network on Leave Policies & Research, http://www.leavenetwork.org/. Detailed information is also available in the OECD Family Database (http://www.oecd.org/els/family/database.htm).
2. In Switzerland, which offers 14 weeks of paid maternity leave at an average payment rate of 56 per cent of gross earnings, plus two weeks of unpaid maternity leave, public spending amounted to only 0.13 per cent of GDP in 2011. In Australia and New Zealand – which respectively offer mothers 18 and 14 weeks of paid leave at an average payment rate of around 40–45 per cent of gross earnings, and in the case of Australia two weeks paid paternity leave – public spending on leave was just 0.09 per cent and 0.07 per cent of GDP, respectively, in 2011.

REFERENCES

Adema, W., C. Clarkem, and V. Frey (2015), 'Paid parental leave: lessons from OECD countries and selected U.S. states', OECD Social, Employment and Migration Working Papers, No. 172, Paris.
Brandth, B. and E. Kvande (2001), 'Flexible work and flexible fathers', *Work, Employment & Society*, **15** (2), 251–67.
Cameron, C. and P. Moss (eds) (2007), *Care Work in Europe: Current Understandings and Future Directions*, London: Routledge.
Chronholm, A. (2007), 'Fathers' experiences of shared parental leave in Sweden', *Recherches sociologiques et anthropologiques*, **2**, 9–25.
Destatis (2016), 'Öffentliche Sozialleistungen – Statistik zum Elterngeld, Beendete Leistungsbezüge für in den Jahren 2008 bis 2012 geborene Kinder', accessed July 2017 at https://www.destatis.de/DE/ZahlenFakten/GesellschaftStaat/Soziales/Soziales.html.
Duvander, A.Z. and M. Johansson (2015), 'For which fathers do reforms matter? A study on the impact of three Swedish parental leave reforms', Paper presented at the annual meeting of the International Network on Parental Leave Policies and Research.
Erler, D. (2009), 'Germany: taking a Nordic turn?', in S. Kamerman and P. Moss (eds), *The Politics of Parental Leave Policies: Children, Parenting, Gender and the Labour Market*, Bristol: Policy Press, pp. 119–34.
Escobedo, A. and K. Wall (2015), 'Leave policies in Souhern Europe: continuities and changes', *Community, Work & Family*, **18** (2), 218–35.
Eydal, G.B. and I.V. Gíslason (2014), 'Caring fathers and parental leave in prosperous times and times of crisis: the case of Iceland', in G.B. Eydal and T. Rostgaard (eds), *Fatherhood in the Nordic Welfare States: Comparing Care Policies and Practice*, Bristol: Policy Press, pp. 327–48.
Eydal, G.B., I.V. Gíslason, T. Rostgaard, B. Brandth, A.-Z. Duvander, and J. Lammi-Taskula (2015), 'Trends in parental leave in the Nordic countries: has the forward march of gender equality halted?', *Community, Work & Family*, **18** (2), 167–81.
Galtry, J. and P. Callister (2005), 'Assessing the optimal length of parental leave for child and parental well-being: how can research inform policy?', *Journal of Family Issues*, **26** (2), 219–46.
Huerta, M., W. Adema and J. Baxter (2013), 'Fathers' leave, fathers' involvement and child development: are they related? Evidence from four OECD countries', OECD Social, Employment and Migration Working Papers, No. 140, Paris.
Leitner, S. (2003), 'Varieties of familialism. The caring function of the family in comparative perspective', *European Societies*, **5** (4), 353–75.

Morel, N. (2007), 'From subsidiarity to "free choice": child- and elder-care policy reforms in France, Belgium, Germany and the Netherlands', *Social Policy & Administration*, **41** (6), 618–37.
Moss, P. (ed.) (2012), *International Report on Leave Policies and Research*, accessed July 2017 at http://www.leavenetwork.org/lp_and_r_reports/.
Moss, P. (ed.) (2014), 'International review of leave policies and related research 2013', accessed July 2016 at http://www.leavenetwork.org/.
Moss, P. and F. Deven (eds) (1999), *Parental Leave: Progress or Pitfall?* Brussels: Vlamme Gemeenschap, pp. xii, 366.
Mun, E. and M. Brinton (2015), 'Workplace matters: the use of parental leave policy in Japan', *Work and Occupations*, **42** (3), 335–69, http://dx.doi.org/10.1177/0730888415574781.
OECD (2011), *Doing Better for Families*, Paris: OECD Publishing, http://dx.doi.org/10.1787/9789264098732-en.
OECD (2017a), *Dare to Share: Germany's Experience Promoting Equal Partnership in Families*, Paris: OECD Publishing, http://dx.doi.org/10.1787/9789264259157-en.
OECD (2017b), OECD Family Database, accessed July 2017 at http://www.oecd.org/els/family/database.htm.
Ray, R., J. Gornick, and J. Schmitt (2010), 'Who cares? Assessing generosity and gender equality in parental leave policy designs in 21 countries', *Journal of European Social Policy*, **20** (3), 196–216.
Tanaka, S. (2005), 'Parental leave and child health across OECD countries', *Economic Journal*, **115**, F7–F28.
Thaler, R. and C.R. Sunstein (eds) (2008), *Nudge: Improving Decisions about Health, Wealth and Happiness*, New Haven, CT: Yale University Press.
Thévenon, O. (2014), 'The political economy of child-related leave policies in OECD member states: key trends and the impact of the crisis', Working Paper, No. 208, INED.
Thévenon, O. and A. Solaz (2013), 'Labour market effects of parental leave policies in OECD countries', OECD Social, Employment and Migration Working Papers, No. 141, OECD Publishing, Paris, http://dx.doi.org/10.1787/5k8xb6hw1wjf-en.
Wall, K. and A. Escobedo (2012), 'Parental leave policies, gender equity and family well-being in Europe: a comparative perspective', in A. Moreno Minguez (ed.), *Family Well-being: European Perspectives*, Netherlands: Springer, pp. 103–29.

11. Work-family policies within the workplace
Laura den Dulk, Mara A. Yerkes and Bram Peper

INTRODUCTION

Work-family researchers increasingly point out the need to broaden the scope of research in order to shed light on the interactions between public policies at the country level, collective agreements at the industry level, and workplace policies and practices at the organizational level in relation to employees' needs and work-family experiences (Ollier-Malaterre et al., 2013). Policies and practices in organizations and collective agreements at the industry and organizational level can supplement and restrict existing statutory family policies. Moreover, it is in the context of the workplace that policies play out and affect work-family experiences.

This chapter offers a state of the art review on the role of work-family policies within the workplace across different European countries. What policies and arrangements do organizations offer in the context of different family policy models and how are existing policies implemented in the workplace? We will review research on the adoption of workplace policies as well as research on the management of work-family policies in organizations. We also explore the role of collective agreements. Trade unions can pressure organizations to extend existing statutory family policies. Whether this is a factor affecting the development of support at the organizational, sector or national level is not yet clear. Powerful unions are able to influence management's decisions about employee benefits and the implementation of policies in organizations, but may also choose to raise the issue at the bargaining table at sector or national level, leading to the development of public provisions rather than specific workplace support.

In the next section, the focus is on the adoption of workplace policies and how this interacts with state policies, followed by a discussion on the role of trade unions and collective labour agreements. The following section offers an overview of research on the management of work-family policies in organizations. Specific attention will be paid to the role of top managers and supervisors on the work floor. The chapter ends with concluding remarks, accompanied by a research agenda for future research.

ADOPTION OF WORKPLACE POLICIES

There is a growing body of research on the adoption of workplace policies directed at the combination of paid work and family life. Workplace work-family policies can either extend public policies, for instance by offering enhanced leaves (longer leave or higher payment), or complement existing national policies by offering other types of policies, such as flexible working hours and teleworking (den Dulk et al., 2012). With respect to workplace work-family policies a distinction can be made between workplace childcare support and enhanced leave arrangements, which enable workers to combine their job with caring responsibilities, and flexible work arrangements, which are not restricted to employees with children or other dependent family members in need of care. In addition, employers can introduce supportive arrangements such as counselling for working parents or work-life balance management training (den Dulk, 2001). Organizations vary in the number and the nature or type of policies introduced both within and between countries. In particular, extensive within-country variation exists along the lines of organizational conditions, although the national context in which organizations operate clearly shapes the number and types of workplace policies offered (den Dulk and Groeneveld, 2013; den Dulk et al., 2010, 2012, 2013, 2014). A cluster analysis based on the *Working Time and Work-Life Balance in European Companies: Establishment Survey on Working Time 2004–2005* (European Foundation for the Improvement of Living and Working Conditions, 2006) that takes both state and workplace support into account shows, for instance, that employees working in public sector organizations, large organizations, organizations with a large proportion of female workers (up to 80 per cent), and those operating in Scandinavian countries have the most policy support (den Dulk et al., 2014). Other cross-national and single country studies confirm that, in particular, public sector and large organizations take the lead in the adoption of workplace polices (Appelbaum et al., 2005; Bond et al., 2005; den Dulk, 2001; den Dulk et al., 2010; Evans, 2001; Goodstein, 1994; Ingram and Simons, 1995; Osterman, 1995; Wood et al., 2003), and that employers operating in country contexts with generous public policies do not lag behind compared to those in more liberal policy contexts (den Dulk et al., 2013).

These findings raise relevant questions, such as why do some organizations offer more workplace support (extending legislation) than others, and how public policies at the country level interact with collective agreements and policies at the organizational level. Extant work-family research relies on a number of theoretical arguments to explain this variation in the adoption of workplace work-family policies and arrangements across organizations, including (neo) institutional theory, economic arguments (the business case), or a combination of both (Appelbaum et al., 2005; den Dulk, 2001; den Dulk et al., 2010, 2013). The (neo) institutional approach argues that coercive and normative institutional pressures influence the adoption of workplace policies because organizations wish to safeguard their social legitimacy in society. Employers not only have to meet economic considerations, but also need to respond to regulations, norms, laws and social expectations (Goodstein, 1994). Public attention towards the combination of paid work and care, the increase of public family policies, as well as a changing workforce that increasingly consists of dual-earner families leads towards norms and social expectations regarding workplace work-family support and the need for organizations to comply with laws and regulations. Hence, legislation and collective agreements designed to ease the combination of work and family life requires organizations to offer some type of support, such as parental leave. In addition, the same regulations can lead to a social climate in which organizations are increasingly expected to provide additional support, leading to workplace arrangements that complement or extend legal entitlements (den Dulk, 2001; den Dulk et al., 2013).

Next to state support, the cultural context and in particular gender ideology is expected to contribute to the degree of institutional pressure that employers experience. Lyness and Brumit Kropf (2005), for instance, examined (among others) the relationship between national gender equality and the adoption of flexible work arrangements among a sample of managers and professional workers across 20 European countries. Higher gender equality implies that women are a valuable part of the workforce and this may increase the likelihood that organizations adopt workplace work-family policies. In addition, a high level of gender equality may also contribute to a social climate in which employees experience a sense of entitlement to family support, leading to more institutional pressure on organizations (Lewis and Smithson, 2001; Poelmans and Sahibzada, 2004). Research has yet to fully confirm the expected positive relationship between national gender equality and the adoption of workplace family policies, however (den Dulk and Groeneveld, 2013; den Dulk et al., 2012, 2013). This might be related to measurement issues, that is, including gender equality outcomes rather than ideology and beliefs (Ollier-Malaterre et al., 2013) or that the cultural context is more relevant for the support of the work-family culture in organizations than for the adoption of formal work-family policies (Lyness and Brumit Kropf, 2005).

Economic or business case arguments, in contrast, emphasize the costs and benefits of workplace arrangements to the organization. Organizations will adopt workplace work-family policies and arrangements when it helps them to gain competitive advantage over other employers in the recruitment and retention of workers, when it improves the commitment and productivity of workers and when it does not entail high costs (see, e.g., Budd and Mumford, 2004; Davis and Kalleberg, 2006; Glass and Fujimoto, 1995; Wood et al., 2003). It is argued that the costs and benefits of workplace arrangements vary across organizations, depending upon organizational conditions such as size, sector and the composition of the workforce as well as macro-level factors such as labour market conditions and the economy (den Dulk et al., 2010). Moreover, it is assumed that some organizations are more sensitive to institutional pressures than others (den Dulk and Groeneveld, 2013; den Dulk et al., 2013). For example, public sector organizations are more likely to be judged according to government standards and norms (den Dulk, 2001) although their sensitivity varies depending on how close they are to politics and policymaking (i.e., the degree of publicness; Boyne, 2002) (den Dulk and Groeneveld, 2013). Private companies, in contrast, are more likely to be affected by profit-related arguments. The size of the organization is relevant since it affects economies of scale and their visibility in society. The former reduces the costs of the introduction of policies per employee and the latter makes the organization more sensitive to institutional pressure (Goodstein, 1994). In addition, a large proportion of female employees can result in more requests and demands for work-family support. Moreover, in the context of ongoing gendered assumptions about family roles, organizations with a female-dominated workforce may also benefit more from the effect of the introduction of workplace policies on productivity, absenteeism and turnover than male-dominated organizations (Budd and Mumford, 2006; Davis and Kalleberg, 2006; Goodstein, 1994; Wood et al., 2003). However, the skill level of female workers may be an important mediator here (Ingram and Simons, 1995). For organizations that depend on low-skilled, temporary workers, it makes less sense business-wise to invest in additional work-family policies with such easily replaceable employees (e.g., Whitehouse and Zetlin, 1999). However, a large proportion of women in an organization can induce employee representatives to take up this issue. Union members within organizations may also pressure employers to adopt policies to ease the combination of work and family life (Forth et al., 1997). In the next section, we will discuss the role of trade unions and collective agreements in relation to the adoption of workplace family policies in more detail.

ROLE OF TRADE UNIONS AND COLLECTIVE AGREEMENTS

A state of the art review on the role of employers in European countries would be incomplete if attention were not given to the role of collective bargaining and the role of trade unions. Trade unions can pressure organizations to adopt work-family policies. However, whether this is a factor affecting the development of support at the organizational, sectoral or national level is not yet clear. Powerful unions are able to influence management's decisions about employee benefits, but may also choose to raise the issue at the bargaining table at the sectoral or national level, leading to the development of public provisions rather than specific workplace support.

At the European level, organizations such as Business Europe (formerly the Union of Industrial and Employer Confederations Europe, UNICE) and the European Trade Union Confederation (ETUC), promote work-family reconciliation as part of a broader framework on gender equality issues (UNICE, 2005). Yet, recently, ETUC noted the difficulties in going beyond 'soft policy' instruments (e.g., recommendations, studies, reports) at the European level in relation to work-family support (Gréboval and Sechi, 2015). At the national level, the influence of trade unions is often greater. Trade unions can play a significant role in prioritizing work-family issues in both collective bargaining and the workplace (Berg et al., 2014; Budd and Mumford, 2004; Yerkes and Tijdens, 2010).

Both trade union membership and collective bargaining coverage can be important for employees' reconciliation of work and family within the organizational context. For example, as shown by Berg et al. (2004), the combined effect of high trade union membership and/or coverage, extensive collective bargaining practices and trade unions focused on working time issues was found to increase collective control over working time in Germany, Sweden and the Netherlands. But in countries where these factors are less prevalent or absent (e.g., in the US), employees are more dependent upon their own labour market position or importance to an employer for gaining control over working time. Chung (2008) finds similar effects in relation to flexible working. In countries where unions are stronger, flexi-time practices are generally more worker-friendly. In countries where unions are weaker, company-oriented options are more prevalent. Similar evidence is also found in single country studies. In the US, trade union behaviour has been found to have a significant yet varied effect on employees' access to and use of flexibility practices (Berg et al., 2014). In Spain, unions have shown a preference for managing work-family issues through collective bargaining practices, while employers continue to see work-family reconciliation as an individual human resources issue (Carrasquer et al., 2007). In Germany, in sectors where collective bargaining coverage is higher, works councils have also been found to have greater influence in achieving positive work-family outcomes for employees (Heywood and Jirjahn, 2009). It should be noted, however, that while unions clearly play an important role in work-family reconciliation at the organizational level, their power and influence has declined in recent decades, particularly through a decline in trade union density (i.e., membership; Visser, 2013).

While the issue of trade union influence on the work-family situation at the organizational level has received moderate attention in the literature (e.g., Berg et al., 2014; Budd and Mumford, 2004), research on work-family issues in collective bargaining is limited (Yerkes and Tijdens, 2010). At the European level, research suggests that collective bargaining plays only a minor role, if any, in new European Union (EU) member states. In these countries, national legislation is generally used to develop work-family provisions. Exceptions to this include Bulgaria, the Czech Republic and Slovenia, where it appears that some issues such as paid leave to care for children, the protection of pregnant women in the workplace and childcare policy have been subject to collective bargaining in some instances (European Commission, 2008). In the remaining European countries, the interaction between national-level policies and collective bargaining appears to be greater. The European Commission (2008) notes the existence of collective agreements on leave issues and career breaks at the national level in Belgium, Finland, Greece and Ireland, and at the sectoral level in Austria, Belgium, Denmark, Germany, Greece, Italy, Luxembourg, the Netherlands, Portugal and Sweden. In addition, collective bargaining agreements on these issues have been concluded at the company level in Greece, Italy and Portugal (European Commission, 2008).

At the national level, the limited evidence on work-family arrangements in collective bargaining suggests collective bargaining agreements perform at least two important functions in relation to country-level public policies. Collective agreements can complement existing policies (e.g., den Dulk, 2014; Yerkes and Tijdens, 2010), broadening the scope of policy or providing additional payment, as well as compensate for an absence of protection, although cross-country variation exists. Research from Yerkes and Tijdens (2010) on the Dutch case reveals collective agreements provided significant coverage for childcare subsidies and part-time work arrangements prior to national legislation being developed. In addition, while public sector agreements were generally found to exhibit work-family arrangements more often than private sector agreements, this was not the case for childcare subsidies and part-time work arrangements. In both of these policy areas, private sector collective agreements appeared to be more responsive to employees' work-family needs. Recent evidence from Sweden and Australia (Raven et al., 2014a) shows Swedish trade unions have succeeded in topping up parental leave benefits through collective bargaining, complementing national-level policies (Raven et al., 2014b). Compensation differs across sectors, however, with non-manual workers generally enjoying higher compensation levels than manual workers. Australian unions have been less successful than Swedish unions in developing parental leave clauses (Yerkes et al., 2014). Evidence from Whitehouse et al. (2013) suggests that employer-provided maternity leave increased from 46 per cent in 2004–05 to 55 per cent in 2009–10, although this reflects provisions in both collective agreements and company policies. Since the introduction of federal parental leave legislation in 2011 (which in essence offers paid maternity leave), unions have been less successful in topping up payment levels (Yerkes et al., 2014). The study by Raven and colleagues (2014a) further showed that in contrast to Sweden and Australia, German collective agreements neither compensate nor complement national-level parental leave policies. Evidence from Italy suggests that a minor number of collective agreements offer compensatory work-family arrangements in the face of little state support (Ponzellini, 2006). Yet the introduction of work-family measures in private company collective agreements is so low (estimated at 3.5 per cent) that the author suggests these arrangements do little to close the gap with extensive work-family policies offered through national-level policies in other countries (see also Riva, 2016).

Another way of looking at the impact of trade unions and collective agreements on the adoption of workplace work-family polices is examining the relationship between the degree of unionization and the presence of workplace work-family policies. In Europe (in contrast to the US), the (relative) level of unionization in an organization was found to be positively related to the adoption of workplace childcare and leave support, but not to the adoption of flexible work arrangements (Anxo et al., 2007; den Dulk et al., 2012). Unions might be reluctant to support flexibility in the workplace, as it can be seen as employer-led flexibility rather than supportive for employee well-being (Ravenswood and Markey, 2011). Overall, based on the limited research so far, there are strong indications that in many country contexts, unions are important partners regarding the adoption of state and workplace work-family support. In addition, unions play a role in raising employee awareness of existing policies and entitlements (Haas and Hwang, 2013; Ravenswood and Markey, 2011). We will now turn to the management of work-family policies in organizations.

MANAGEMENT OF WORK-FAMILY POLICIES IN ORGANIZATIONS

Existing research shows that there is often a gap between policy and practice, that is, workers refrain from taking advantage of existing national and/or workplace policies because they are afraid of career repercussions (Blair-Loy and Wharton, 2002; Eaton, 2003; Kossek et al., 1999; Thompson et al., 1999). Cultural assumptions within organizations, in which long hours and face time in the workplace are seen as a sign of commitment and work devotion, can co-exist with the adoption of work-family policies like flexible work hours and parental leave (Lewis, 2003). As argued by Kossek et al. (2010), both structural and cultural change is needed for organizations to become supportive. Policy alone is often not effective and needs to be accompanied by a supportive organizational culture. Managerial support is a critical aspect of organizational culture and hence critical in the use of workplace work-life policies. Organizational cultures both reflect and shape managerial attitudes and practices (den Dulk and Peper, 2007; den Dulk and de Ruijter, 2005, 2008). They can enhance or inhibit the sense of entitlement of workers to exercise rights and utilize options to combine work and family life (Kanjuo Mrčela and Černigoj Sadar, 2011). With respect to the management of policies included in legislation, collective agreements and workplace policies, different levels of management are relevant to the organizational context: the executive level or top management (managers at the highest level of the organization) and the direct supervisors to whom employees directly report. Within this section, we specifically look at the role of organizational culture given its importance in shaping how work-family policies are managed within the workplace, alongside the broader economic, cultural and policy context. As it becomes clear that the implementation of work-family policies often implies transformational change within organizations (Wells, 2016), we will end with a brief discussion of intervention research within the work-family field.

A Supportive Organizational Culture

Simply introducing work-family policies is not enough to create a supportive organization in which people feel free to use them. Work-family policies such as leave arrangements need to be integrated into an organizational culture that is aware of the responsibilities of employees outside their work. In many organizations, the idea of the ideal worker as someone who is always available and does not have any distractions outside work is still present as an organizational norm (Dumas and Sanchez-Burks, 2015; Kossek et al., 2010). Shared norms, values and assumptions form the basis for symbols and 'unwritten rules' regarding how work gets done and how people should behave within the organization. When the standards and values within the organization conflict with the utilization of work-family policies, policies are often implemented ineffectively and employees make little use of them (Allen, 2001; Dikkers et al., 2007; Thompson et al., 1999). Because values and assumptions are taken for granted and underlie the way employees behave within the organization, they are very often not talked about or discussed and it is not easy to identify and change them. It is simpler, for example, to introduce a leave policy than it is to make the transition from a culture based on workplace attendance to one that manages output.

Management of Work-family Policies

Top managers of organizations are important actors in the construction and continuation of organizational culture (Major and Litano, 2016; Schein, 2004). They are responsible for the adoption and design of formal workplace policies and are in a position to stimulate the implementation and utilization of policies throughout the organization (Major and Litano, 2016; Poelmans and Sahibzada, 2004). There are few studies that examine the role of top managers with respect to the adoption and implementation of work-family policies in organizations. A notable exception is the study of Been et al. (Been, 2015; Been et al., 2017) that investigated the views of top managers in relation to their organizational and national context in five European countries: Finland, the Netherlands, Portugal, Slovenia and the UK. The study applied a vignette design to capture the conditions under which top managers in these countries support work-family policies, namely, to what degree business case considerations and institutional pressures play a role (Been et al., 2017). The study shows that, in line with the business case argumentation, top managers in these countries are more supportive of work-family policies when they require few financial investments and contribute to employee commitment. In other words, when the top manager assumes that policies benefit the organization. European top managers in this study were inclined to stay in control of how policies are implemented by setting specific conditions on employee take-up. Top managers tend to shape policies in a way that aligns with the goals and aims of the organization by using the existing latitude within legislation (Been et al., 2016). In the UK and the Netherlands, for instance, public family policies as well as formal workplace policies often contain an element of employer discretion. For example, in both countries, managers can decline a request to reduce working hours on the basis of business needs (den Dulk et al., 2011).

However, findings also indicate that next to business case arguments, societal norms shape top managers' decision-making in relation to work-family policies. In particular, public sector top managers preferred work-family policies available to all employees rather than introducing policies targeted specifically towards employees that are costly to lose (i.e., high performers). Moreover, the types of policies that top managers supported the most were also found to be related to the national context that top managers operate in. In general, CEOs and board members in this study preferred policies that have a limited impact on the number of hours employees work, that is, flexible working hours and teleworking. They showed less support for leave policies and part-time work, although this was clearly related to the national context. For example, in countries in which part-time work is more common, like the Netherlands and the UK, top managers were more positive about the reduction of working hours, more so than in countries in which there is no tradition of part-time employment (Been et al., 2017). Moreover, in countries with extensive national family policies, top managers also framed their support for policies in terms of social responsibility and did not only apply business case arguments (Been, 2015). This finding is in line with previously discussed research on the adoption of workplace policies across countries (den Dulk et al., 2013; Ollier-Malaterre, 2009).

Supervisory Support

Another important actor in the organization affecting the everyday practices of work-family policies is the direct supervisor. The direct supervisor communicates, implements and manages formal policies (Lewis, 2003). In most work organizations, the normal procedure for an employee who wishes to use a work-family policy is to submit a request to his or her direct superior. A supervisor's negative attitude may prevent an employee from submitting a request. When an employee does submit a request to utilize a policy, his or her direct supervisor decides whether that request will be granted. In the case of a statutory right, the role of the supervisor refers to the practical arrangements for utilizing the scheme, like the duration or timing of take-up.

The manner in which managers respond to a request to utilize a policy is associated with the design of the formal policy and the organizational culture (den Dulk and de Ruijter, 2005; den Dulk et al., 2011). Supervisors assess requests in light of the prevailing standards and values within the organization, expressed for instance by the top managers in the organization. The manner in which they respond to such requests may, in turn, bring about changes in the organization's culture or in fact maintain that culture. However, the organizational culture can also contain contradictory elements (Peper et al., 2009). An organization may consider the combination of work and family life to be important but at the same time associate employee commitment with attendance and working long hours. In such cases, supervisors have to deal with contradictory signals, leaving discretionary scope for individual supervisors. Hence, factors other than organizational culture or the formal policy shape their attitude, such as practical consequences for the work that needs to be done (den Dulk and de Ruijter, 2005, 2008).

Dealing with requests to use existing policies refers to instrumental supervisory support. Hammer and colleagues (2009) developed a multidimensional measure of family supportive supervisor behaviours (FSSB) distinguishing instrumental support, emotional support, role modelling behaviours and creative work-family management. Emotional support includes feeling that your supervisor cares about you and your family life and feeling comfortable talking about family commitments. 'Role modelling behavior refers to supervisors demonstrating how to integrate work and family through modelling behaviors on the job' (Hammer et al., 2009, p. 841), for example, a supervisor who takes up parental leave, shares ideas or gives advice on how to combine work and family life. Creative work-family management refers to proactive behaviours in which supervisors look for ways to redesign work to help workers balance work and family life. This fourth dimension is based on the literature on the dual agenda (Bailyn, 2011; Rapoport et al., 2002), which emphasizes that work can be redesigned in such a way that is helpful both for workers who have family commitments outside work and the effectiveness of the organization.

Intervention Research Within the Work-family Field

Research indicates that the effects of work-family policies (state or workplace based) tend to be limited when not accompanied by a supportive organizational culture and a supportive supervisor (Allen et al., 2014; Thompson et al., 1999). Institutional theory provides an explanation for the gap between policy and practice. Work-family policies are frequently implemented for symbolic, rather than substantive reasons (Blair-Loy and Wharton, 2002). This results in policies that are not anchored in the organization, and that can conflict with organizational norms on time and career demands. In fact, in many organizations implementing work-family policies requires a fundamental cultural change, challenging existing norms and values (Dumas and Sanchez-Burks, 2015). According to Wells (2016), 'an organizational change lens is key to generating the scholarship and practice required to achieve family-friendly organizations' (p. 216). She argues that the adoption and implementation of work-family policies often requires organizational change. However, few work-family scholars draw upon a process change framework that acknowledges the complexity, disorderly and dynamic nature of the change required. So far, limited attention has been paid to how work-family policies can be successfully introduced and managed within organizational contexts. A notable exception is the work of Rapoport, Bailyn and colleagues (2002), who have argued for collaboration and participation as means to overcome resistance that occurs when existing cultural norms are challenged with the introduction of work-family policies and practices. They conducted various organizational work-family interventions, which focus on the redesign of work that contributes to gender equity, the combination of work and family life and organizational performance. They developed the Collaborative Interactive Action Research (CIAR), a form of action research that aims to engage resistance, challenges existing norms and in which collaboration and participation of workers and managers is crucial (Bailyn, 2011; Rapoport et al., 2002). There is another stream of intervention research within the work-family field focusing on evidence-based outcomes using experimental designs. Hammer and colleagues (2016) offer an overview of this new type of intervention studies that use rigorous experimental designs. Interventions studies try to determine, for instance, the causal effects of alternative work arrangements, family supportive supervisor behaviour training and work redesign to increase schedule control. They argue that sound evidence of the effectiveness of work-family interventions is necessary for the organizational adoption and implementation of work-family policies, in order to convince organizations of the added value of such policies. In fact, both types of intervention research are likely to help bring about structural and cultural organizational change to make work-family policies more effective for employees and employers.

CONCLUDING REMARKS AND RESEARCH AGENDA

Existing research on the adoption of workplace work-family policies shows large variation between organizations and increasingly provides evidence for how workplace provisions are embedded within the larger societal context. However, despite the fact that research indicates it is important to investigate the interaction between different levels of policy provisions – public policies at the national level, collective agreements at the industry level and workplace policies – cross-national data that allow such an examination are limited. Few large-scale cross-national data sets that collect data at the organizational level exist. Notable exceptions in Europe are the European Company Survey of the European Foundation and the Cranfield Network on Comparative Human Resource Management Survey (Cranet). However, they do not always pay attention to work-family issues in every round of data collection, making it difficult to track the development of workplace support over time (den Dulk et al., 2014). The lack of longitudinal data inhibits researchers from taking a more dynamic approach that takes into account policy changes that occur over time as well as rapid and sometimes dramatic changes on the labour market and in the economy (Trefalt et al., 2013). 'Policies and practices to support the reconciliation of work and family or "work-life balance" in Europe, whether stemming from government regulation or voluntary organizational initiatives, are being implemented at a time when employing organizations are undergoing massive and rapid changes in a context of global competition and efficiency drives' (Lewis et al., 2009, p. 1). In addition, the cross-sectional data preclude the ability to draw conclusions about causality. Although most research (implicitly) assumes that the national context shapes workplace policies and provisions, employers are also important actors in society influencing the design and adoption of public policies.

Multi-level analysis has shown how the national policy context interacts with workplace policies; future research should also strive to examine the role of other relevant country-level variables and in particular the role of collective agreements and trade unions in a more systematic way. However, as discussed in this chapter, research has, so far, paid only limited attention to the role of industrial relations and work-family provisions in collective agreements.

In addition, alongside the adoption of workplace work-family policies, future research should continue to pay attention to the management of work-family policies in the workplace as well as existing workplace cultures. We know that organizational culture and managerial support are crucial (Allen et al., 2014; Lewis et al., 2009). The development of sound measures of supervisory support, such as the multidimensional measure of family supportive supervisor behaviours of Hammer and colleagues (2009), and measures that examine the degree to which organizational culture is supportive to the combination of paid work and family life (e.g., Dikkers et al., 2007; Thompson et al., 1999) is an important step forward. These measures should be included in cross-national data sets in order to contribute to our understanding of how the national cultural contexts interact with norms and values in organizations, ultimately shaping the way policies play out in the workplace. The adoption of workplace work-family policies is a response to societal change and implementation often requires fundamental cultural change within organizations (Wells, 2016). Intervention studies, both based on experimental designs and action research, can be important drivers of that change and increase our understanding of the conditions under which work-family policies improve the ability to combine work and family life and the effectiveness of the organization (Bailyn, 2011; Hammer et al., 2016).

REFERENCES

Allen, T.D. (2001), 'Family supportive work environments: the role of organizational perceptions', *Journal of Vocational Behavior*, **58**, 414–35.
Allen, T.D., L.M. Lapierre, P.E. Spector et al. (2014), 'The link between national paid leave policy and work–family conflict among married working parents', *Applied Psychology*, **63**, 5–28.
Anxo, D., C. Fagan, M. Smith, M.T. Letablier, and C. Perraudin (eds) (2007), *Parental Leave in European Companies*, Dublin: European Foundation for the Improvement of Living and Working Conditions.
Appelbaum, E., T. Bailey, P. Berg, and A. Kalleberg (2005), 'Organizations and the intersection of work and family: a comparative perspective', in S. Ackroyd, R. Batt, P. Thompson, and P.S. Tolbert (eds), *The Oxford Handbook of Work and Organizations*, Oxford: Oxford University Press, pp. 52–73.
Bailyn, L. (2011), 'Redesigning work for gender equity and work-personal life integration', *Community, Work & Family*, **14** (1), 97–112.
Been, W.M. (ed.) (2015), *European Top Managers' Support for Work-Life Arrangements*, Utrecht: Utrecht University.
Been, W., L. den Dulk, and T. van der Lippe (2016), 'Dutch top managers and work-life arrangements in times of economic crisis', *Community, Work & Family*, **19** (1), 43–62.
Been, W.M., T. van der Lippe, L. den Dulk, M. Das Dores Horta Gurreiro, A. Kanjuo Mrčela, and C. Niemistö (2017), 'European top managers' support for work-life arrangements', *Social Science Research*, **65**, 60–74.
Berg, P., E. Appelbaum, T. Bailey, and A.L. Kalleberg (2004), 'Contesting time: international comparisons of employee control of working time', *Industrial & Labor Relations Review*, **57** (3), 331–49.
Berg, P., E.E. Kossek, K. Misra, and D. Belman (2014), 'Work–life flexibility policies: do unions affect employee access and use?', *Industrial & Labor Relations Review*, **67** (1), 111–37.
Blair-Loy, M. and A.S. Wharton (2002), 'Employees' use of work-family policies and the workplace social context', *Social Forces*, **80** (3), 813–45.
Bond, J.T., E. Galinsky, S.S. Kim, and E. Brownfield (eds) (2005), *The National Study of Employers*, New York: Families and Work Institute.
Boyne, G.A. (2002), 'Public and private management: what's the difference?', *Journal of Management Studies*, **39** (1), 97–122.
Budd, J.W. and K. Mumford (2004), 'Trade unions and family-friendly policies in Britain', *Industrial & Labor Relations Review*, **57** (2), 204–22.
Budd, J.W. and K. Mumford (2006), 'Family-friendly work practices in Britain: availability and perceived accessibility', *Human Resource Management*, **45** (1), 23–42.
Carrasquer, P., M. Massó, and A. Martín Artiles (2007), 'Discursos y estrategias en torno a la conciliación de la vida laboral y familiar en la negociación colectiva', *Papers Revista de Sociologia*, **83**, 13–36.
Chung, H. (2008), 'Do institutions matter? Explaining the use of working time flexibility arrangements of companies across 21 European countries using a multilevel model focusing on country level determinants', WZB Discussion Paper No. 1011-9523, Social Science Research Centre, Berlin.
Davis, A.E. and A.L. Kalleberg (2006), 'Family-friendly organizations? Work and family programs in the 1990s', *Work and Occupations*, **33** (2), 191–223.
den Dulk, L. (ed.) (2001), *Work-Family Arrangements in Organisations: A Cross-national Study in the Netherlands, Italy, the United Kingdom and Sweden*, Amsterdam: Rozenberg Publishers.
den Dulk, L. and S. Groeneveld (2013), 'Work-life balance support in the public sector in Europe', *Review of Public Personnel Administration*, **33** (4), 384–405.
den Dulk, L. and B. Peper (2007), 'Working parents' use of work-life policies', *Sociologia, Problemas e Práticas*, **53**, 51–70.
den Dulk, L. and J. de Ruijter (2005), 'Werk/privé cultuur en de houding van managers ten aanzien van werk/privé beleid in de financiële sector', *Gedrag en Organisatie*, **18** (5), 260–75.
den Dulk, L. and J. de Ruijter (2008), 'Explaining managerial attitudes towards the use of work-life policies in the United Kingdom and the Netherlands', *International Journal of Human Resource Management*, **19** (7), 1224–38.
den Dulk, L., S. Groeneveld, and B. Peper (2014), 'Workplace work-life balance support from a capabilities perspective', in B. Hobson (ed.), *Worklife Balance: The Agency and Capabilities Gap*, Oxford: Oxford University Press, pp. 153–73.
den Dulk, L., P. Peters, and E. Poutsma (2012), 'Variations in adoption of workplace work-family arrangements

in Europe: the influence of welfare-state regime and organizational characteristics', *International Journal of Human Resource Management*, **23** (13), 2785–808.

den Dulk, L., S. Groeneveld, A. Ollier-Malaterre, and M. Valcour (2013), 'National context in work-life research: a multi-level cross-national analysis of the adoption of workplace work-life arrangements in Europe', *European Management Journal*, **31** (5), 478–94.

den Dulk, L., P. Peters, E. Poutsma, and P.E.M. Ligthart (2010), 'The extended business case for childcare and leave arrangements in Western and Eastern Europe', *Baltic Journal of Management*, **4** (2), 156–84.

den Dulk, L., B. Peper, N. Cernigoj-Sadar, S. Lewis, J. Smithson, and A. Van Doorne-Huiskes (2011), 'Work, family and managerial attitudes and practices in the European workplace: comparing Dutch, British and Slovenian financial sector managers', *Social Politics*, **18** (2), 300–29.

Dikkers, J., S.A.E. Geurts, L. den Dulk, B. Peper, T.W. Taris, and M.A.J. Kompier (2007), 'Dimensions of work-home culture and their relations with the use of work-home arrangements and work-home interactions', *Work & Stress*, **21** (2), 155–72.

Dumas, T.L. and J. Sanchez-Burks (2015), 'The professional, the personal, and the ideal worker: pressures and objectives shaping the boundary between life domains', *The Academy of Management Annals*, **9** (1), 803–43.

Eaton, S.C. (2003), 'If you can use them: flexible policies, organizational commitment and perceived performance', *Industrial Relations*, **42** (2), 145–67.

European Commission (2008), *Industrial Relations in Europe*, Brussels: European Commission.

European Foundation for the Improvement of Living and Working Conditions (2006), *Working Time and Work-Life Balance in European companies. Establishment Survey on Working Time 2004–2005*, Luxembourg: European Communities.

Evans, J.M. (2001), 'Firms' contribution to the reconciliation between work and family life', *Occasional Papers*, No. 48, Paris: OECD.

Forth, J., S. Lissenburgh, C. Callender, and N. Millward (1997), *Family Friendly Working Arrangements in Britain, 1996*, Research Report No. 16, Department for Education and Employment, Policy Studies Institute, University of London.

Glass, J.L. and T. Fujimoto (1995), 'Employer characteristics and the provision of family responsive policies', *Work and Occupations*, **22** (4), 380–411.

Goodstein, J.D. (1994), 'Institutional pressures and strategic responsiveness: employer involvement in work-family issues', *The Academy of Management Journal*, **37** (2), 350–82.

Gréboval, C. and C. Sechi (eds) (2015), *ETUC 8th March Survey 2015*, 8th edn, Brussels: Confederation Syndicat European Trade Union and European Trade Union Institute.

Haas, L. and P. Hwang (2013), 'Trade union support for fathers' use of work-family benefits. Lessons from Sweden', *Community, Work & Family*, **16** (1), 46–67.

Hammer, L.B., E.E. Kossek, N.L. Yragui, T.E. Bodner, and G.C. Hanson (2009), 'Development and validation of a multidimensional measure of family supportive supervisor behaviors (FSSB)', *Journal of Management*, **35** (4), 837–56.

Hammer, L.B., C.A. Demsky, E.E. Kossek, and J.W. Bray (2016), 'Work-family intervention research', in T.D. Allen and L.T. Eby (eds), *The Oxford Handbook of Work and Family*, New York: Oxford University Press, pp. 349–61.

Heywood, J. and U. Jirjahn (2009), 'Family-friendly practices and worker representation in Germany', *Industrial Relations*, **48** (1), 121–45.

Ingram, P. and T. Simons (1995), 'Institutional and resource dependence determinants of responsiveness to work-family issues', *The Academy of Management Journal*, **38** (5), 1466–82.

Kanjuo Mrčela, A. and N. Černigoj Sadar (2011), 'Social policies related to parenthood and capabilities of Slovenian parents', *Social Politics*, **18** (2), 199–231.

Kossek, E.E., A.E. Barber, and D. Winters (1999), 'Using flexible schedules in the managerial world: the power of peers', *Human Resource Management*, **38** (1), 33–46.

Kossek, E.E., S. Lewis, and L. Hammer (2010), 'Work-life initiatives and organizational change: overcoming mixed messages to move from the margin to the mainstream', *Human Relations*, **63**, 1–17.

Lewis, S. (2003), 'Flexible working arrangements: implementation, outcomes, and management', *International Review of Industrial and Organizational Psychology*, **18**, 1–28.

Lewis, S. and J. Smithson (2001), 'Sense of entitlement to support for the reconciliation of employment and family life', *Human Relations*, **54**, 1455–81.

Lewis, S., J. Brannen, and A. Nilsen (eds) (2009), *Work, Families and Organisations in Transition. European Perspectives*, Bristol: Policy Press.

Lyness, K.S. and M. Brumit Kropf (2005), 'The relationships of national gender equality and organizational support with work-family balance: a study of European managers', *Human Relations*, **58** (1), 33–60.

Major, D.A. and M.L. Litano (2016), 'The importance of organizational leadership in managing work and family', in T.D. Allen and L.T. Eby (eds), *The Oxford Handbook of Work and Family*, New York: Oxford University Press, pp. 242–54.

Ollier-Malaterre, A. (2009), 'Organizational work-life initiatives: context matters. France compared to the UK and the US', *Community, Work & Family*, **12** (2), 159–78.
Ollier-Malaterre, A., M. Valcour, L. den Dulk, and E.E. Kossek (2013), 'Theorizing national context to develop comparative work-life research: building bricks and research agenda', *European Management Journal*, **31** (5), 433–47.
Osterman, P. (1995), 'Work-family programs and the employment relationship', *Administrative Science Quarterly*, **40**, 681–700.
Peper, B., A. van Doorne-Huiskes, and L. den Dulk (2009), 'Work-family policies in a contradictory culture: a Dutch financial sector corporation', in S. Lewis, J. Brannen, and A. Nilsen (eds), *Work, Family and Organisations in Transition: A European Perspective*, Bristol: Policy Press, pp. 113–28.
Poelmans, S.A.Y. and K. Sahibzada (2004), 'A multi-level model for studying the context and impact of work-family policies and culture in organizations', *Human Resource Management Review*, **14**, 409–31.
Ponzellini, A.M. (2006), 'Work–life balance and industrial relations in Italy', *European Societies*, **8** (2), 273–94.
Rapoport, R., L. Bailyn, J.K. Fletcher, and B.H. Pruit (eds) (2002), *Beyond Work-Family Balance: Advancing Gender Equity and Workplace Performance*, San Francisco, CA: Jossey-Bass.
Raven, J., R. van der Veen, and M.A. Yerkes (2014a), *Cao's en sociale zekerheid in vergelijkend perspectief*, Rotterdam: Stichting Instituut Gak.
Raven, J., E. Wadensjö, and A. Wennemo Lanninger (2014b), 'Sweden', in J. Raven, R. van der Veen, and M.A. Yerkes (eds), *Cao's en sociale zekerheid in vergelijkend perspectief*, Rotterdam: Stichting Instituut Gak, pp. 47–86.
Ravenswood, K. and R. Markey (2011), 'The role of unions in achieving a family-friendly workplace', *Journal of Industrial Relations*, **53** (4), 486–503.
Riva, E. (2016), 'Familalism reoriented: continuity and change in work-family policies in Italy', *Community, Work & Family*, **19** (1), 21–42.
Schein, E.H. (2004), *Organizational Culture and Leadership*, San Francisco, CA: Jossey-Bass.
Thompson, C.A., L.L. Beauvais, and K.S. Lyness (1999), 'When work-family benefits are not enough: the influence of work-family culture on benefit utilization, organizational attachment and work-family conflict', *Journal of Vocational Behavior*, **54** (3), 392–415.
Trefalt, S., M. Drnovšek, A. Svetina-Nabergoj, and R.V. Adlešič (2013), 'Work-life experiences in rapidly changing national contexts: structural misalignment, comparisons and choice overload as explanatory mechanisms', *European Management Journal*, **31**, 448–63.
UNICE (2005), *Framework of Actions on Gender Equality*, Brussels: UNICE, accessed 11 November 2015 at https://resourcecentre.etuc.org/linked_files/documents/Framework%20of%20actions%20%20on%20gender%20equality%20EN.pdf.
Visser, J. (2013), 'Wage bargaining institutions. from crisis to crisis', *European Economy Economic Papers*, No. 488.
Wells, K.J. (2016), 'Work-family initiatives from an organizational change lens', in T.D. Allen and L.T. Eby (eds), *The Oxford Handbook of Work and Family*, New York: Oxford University Press, pp. 215–28.
Whitehouse, G. and D. Zetlin (1999), '"Family friendly" policies: distribution and implementation in Australian workplaces', *Economic & Labour Relations Review*, **10** (2), 221–39.
Whitehouse, G., B. Hewitt, B. Martin, and M. Baird (2013), 'Employer-paid maternity leave in Australia: a comparison of uptake and duration in 2005 and 2010', *Australian Journal of Labour Economics*, **16** (3), 311–27.
Wood, S.J., L.M. de Menezes, and A. Lasaosa (2003), 'Family-friendly management in Great Britain: testing various perspectives', *Industrial Relations: A Journal of Economy and Society*, **42** (2), 221–50.
Yerkes, M.A. and K. Tijdens (2010), 'Social risk protection in collective agreements: evidence from the Netherlands', *European Journal of Industrial Relations*, **16** (4), 369–83.
Yerkes, M.A., J. Corrie, J. Raven, and M. Baird (2014), 'Australia', in J. Raven, R. van der Veen, and M.A. Yerkes (eds), *Cao's en sociale zekerheid in vergelijkend perspectief*, Rotterdam: Stichting Instituut Gak, pp. 133–78.

12. Triggers and drivers of change in framing parenting support in North-western Europe
Trudie Knijn, Claude Martin and Ilona Ostner

INTRODUCTION

In many European countries, family policy has been a well-established field of public policy domain for a long time, though with various nationally defined features and related to other domains of social policy. It materialized more than a century ago in countries like France, Belgium and the Netherlands, for example by the hygienic movement, early childhood healthcare and child protection policy, and in Germany, among others by the Youth Welfare Legislation of 1924. Towards the end of the nineteenth century, in reaction to high rates of child mortality and morbidity, the first programmes to guide and instruct, in particular, lower-class mothers on how to safeguard their newborn children, and how to maintain a decent family home were offered by municipalities, churches and welfare organizations, a forerunner of recent parenting support. At the end of the twentieth century some studies were published on this kind of family policy (Donzelot, 1977; Kamerman and Kahn, 1978) though the subject has hardly been the subject of family-related social policy studies in the past few decades (for an exception see Björnberg and Ottosen, 2013; see also Chapter 2 by Gauthier and Koops on the history of family policy research in this volume). Most attention recently has been devoted on either income, social security or the work-care balance from a gender-equality perspective. Hence, the specific subcategory of family policy – parenting policy – that is central to this chapter – the programmes and interventions intended to regulate the upbringing of children and related parental behaviour – is not only a rather new domain of policy analysis, but also a complex issue due to its various country-specific histories. Hence, the aim of the chapter is to analyse drives and drivers of new policies for children, their ambiguous character on the continuum of supporting and disciplining families and their children, and the variety of their manifestations in three north-western European countries, France, Germany and the Netherlands. Tensions between helping and controlling families to better meet newly defined societal demands, and social divides, which are built into a programme or may emerge in the course of its implementation, can be expected. A central question is, therefore, how do child-centred new parenting support policies redefine internal and external family relations: those between parents and children, between different categories of children and between children, parents and the wider society?

To compare welfare reforms, and, in particular reforms in parenting policies, is not only a matter of definition and boundary of what this policy sector covers in different national contexts, but also a question of understanding processes of change and reform. How can we understand changes in parenting policy? Do they represent significant turning points or merely, as Streeck and Thelen argue, 'incremental change with transformative results, rather than big changes in response to big shocks' (2005, p.9)? Another 'big question' refers to the causes and effects of the change. What are the sources and reasons for it, and what exactly is the (expected) outcome of change (Clasen and Siegel, 2007)? A final question is to what extent do these changes transform instruments and procedures of a policy, as well as its overarching purpose and logic (Hall, 1993)?

This chapter contributes to recent scholarship on institutional change in the field of parenting policy by distinguishing between triggers and drivers of change (Blau and Abramovitz, 2004 [2014]; Guiraudon and Martin, 2013). Triggers refer to the 'why?' question: Why has parenting policy been reformed in recent decades? Can reform mainly be attributed to exogenous modifications of the context, whether it concerns macro-economic, demographic, societal factors? In that sense, reforms could be understood as reactions or adaptations to external factors or (macro) trends. Blau (2004, p. 17) argues that 'change in social policy generally arises out of conflict and tension'. He suggests to study the conflicts within (and between) five main factors ('triggers'): economy, politics, ideology, social movements and history. In contrast, drivers for change refer to the 'how?' question, to the ways and strategies by which actors like governments, politicians, top bureaucrats, decision makers, experts and professionals are pursuing specific objectives and pushing reforms. As drivers of change, these actors are (re)defining the problem, developing and negotiating arguments, putting forward ideas and methods, choosing strategies, and finally making a decision between different options. So, drivers pertain to the changing process itself.

This distinction is analytical only, as triggers and drivers are continuously interacting in processes of change. One can, for example, mention the role of interest groups, lobbyists and the media as agenda-setters that are typically screening and selecting trends and problems, which contribute to (re)defining policy priorities. Sometimes, interest groups also act as quasi-decision makers when proposing a reform to a government by mobilizing different types of resources. As Kingdon (1984 [2003]) argues, suggestions for 'solutions' are necessary to get a social problem on the agenda. If such solutions are not (yet) available, a social problem will not be defined as a (to be tackled) goal of social policies. On the other hand, Kingdon suggests that even if solutions are available, the political will to put the problem on the agenda might be lacking. In that case, solutions (interventions) are waiting for the momentum to effectively be acknowledged and transformed in social policy (see also Thelen and Steinmo, 1992 on windows of opportunity and Mätzke and Ostner, 2010 on the recent German family policy reforms). Three streams – that of the problem, a solution and the political will – must come together in getting a social problem on the agenda and for using an available solution. For that reason, the role of 'policy entrepreneurs' is crucial in building acceptance of problem definition as well as proposed solutions.

Parenting support has recently emerged in a new version of the late nineteenth-/early twentieth-century policy solution for the decent upbringing of children in many European and non-European countries. The new policy solution primarily targets parents and children – mainly up to the age of 18 via parents – no longer the family as an institution, nor issues of gender equality. The novelty of the focus is mirrored in the neologism 'parenting' in English-speaking countries, which transformed a substantive into a verb, or, in French, by creating the new term: *parentalité*. Parenting support is new in the sense of a recently proposed and preferred policy solution; in reality, however, it constitutes a complex mix of old and new ways (principles and instruments) of dealing with parents in need of support; it can also be interpreted as the revival of 'policing families' (Donzelot, 1977), that is, controlling parents' practices and behaviours.

In the following we first reflect on the macro-social factors – 'triggers' – to which new family policy initiatives like parenting support are seen to respond and, second, give attention to the main actors involved, their ideas and interests ('drivers') behind those initiatives and their implementation in country-specific contexts. It is an analytical challenge to deal with three very different national configurations of family policy systems, but also with various demographic and socioeconomic trends.[1] The argument for comparing these three countries is that they differ in welfare systems as well as in family regimes, while at the same time all three envision the same tendency towards a new style of parenting support. This offers the opportunity to analyse how a more or less similar trend lands in various contexts and what the background is of these different interpretations, which at least suggests the possibility of 'travelling policy ideas' (Béland, 2007).

NEW PROBLEMS AND FAMILY POLICY FRAMING

Since their first introduction, family policies have been expanded and also reformed ('recalibrated' in Esping-Andersen's and Hemerijck's language) in many Organisation for Economic Co-operation and Development (OECD) countries. Originally oriented towards fertility, child mortality and family restoration (after World War II), then on equity and social redistribution issues (during the 1970s and 1980s), family policies were strongly reoriented towards employment issues during the 1990s and the beginning of the twenty-first century, under the heading of both labour market flexibilization and work-life balance (Lewis et al., 2008). Family policies have become more employment-friendly, designed to encourage families, and in particular women, to have and raise children – by sharing care among parents and with the help of public facilities – while being gainfully employed, and thus to increase the resources of their households (see also Chapter 11 by den Dulk, Yerkes and Peper on work-family policy in this volume). The OECD and the European Commission have set targets for the continuous extension of non-family (early) childhood education and care (ECEC) (EC, 2002; Mahon, 2006, 2009; OECD, 2001, 2009), and also for boosting female (maternal) employment ratios (see also Chapter 8 by Rostgaard on childcare in this volume). Laggard countries, like Germany, the Netherlands and the UK, have followed suit, though the last two countries, in contrast to many other European Union (EU) member states, mainly via publicly subsidized private provisions (Morgan, 2013; Knijn and Lewis, 2017).

In addition, policy-related international experts have suggested new measures to improve parenting skills in the best interests of the child, mainly by addressing the mother as the main responsible parent (Sanders, 1999; Hornby, 2000; Gershater-Molko et al., 2003). As a corollary to the shift to social investments in ECEC and new child-centred legislation, public parenting support measures – again without much attention to the emerging balance in parental responsibilities of fathers and mothers – have mushroomed (Daly, 2013) in many welfare states, while parents and their parenting practices have come under closer public scrutiny (Lee et al., 2014).

We argue that the emergence of a renewed focus on parenting could be related to parallel shifts in the labour market and in family life. The rise of the global post-industrial economy, demanding new competences and skills of future generations as well as offering less stable jobs, goes hand in hand with less stable and more diverse families (two-breadwinner households, lone parent or cohabitation-based families, older parents having fewer children, migrant families and increasing divorce rates). In such a context, the problem of caring capacities and parents' competence to properly raise their children, including the adolescent ones, could appear on the policy agenda. Nowadays, parental competence may also include parents' capacity to guide adolescents in their school careers, to minimize the risks of juvenile delinquency and further their labour market entrance. Proper upbringing of smaller children has partly become a task of professional childcare and schooling for families in many north-western European countries. Yet, adolescent delinquency, school drop-out and other deficiencies in child development (autism, obesity, attention deficit hyperactivity disorder (ADHD), dyslexia) as well as related parental responsibility have emerged as issues of growing interest. Such general developments constitute the context in which 'parenting' became an acknowledged social problem. Yet, they are insufficient per se to explain the exact mixture of national problem definitions and subsequent policy solutions.

In each of the three countries, a specific configuration of 'triggers' can explain the increased policy attention for 'raising children well', and, in consequence, why solutions implemented to solve the problem have differed. The 'turn to parenting' support and developing parental competencies is therefore only one solution, among others, to defined problems. Another option is 'social investment' (Esping-Andersen, 2002; Morel et al., 2012), which pays less attention to parents' abilities and relies more, or perhaps only, on public facilities that reduce or minimize parental responsibilities (see also Chapter 9 by Lee and Baek on social investment in this volume). The social investment approach has inspired politicians all over the world to invest on a large scale in childcare facilities and early education. This new focus and concomitant spending might come as a surprise since, on the face of it, they contradict what scholars have coined 'politics in the age of austerity' (Pierson, 2001). Pierson argued that mature welfare states' capacity to generate revenues to pay for reasonable social investments has constantly shrunk; at the same time, spending burdens have grown, mostly due to entitlements of an ageing citizenry, high rates of long-term unemployment and, in general, a decreasing number of contributions. Solutions to this squeeze are not easily at hand. Taxing the rich has become risky in the age of globalization, and taxing 'ordinary citizens' via indirect taxes and contributions is politically more costly, 'since wages have also grown more slowly, if at all' (Schäfer and Streeck, 2013, p. 2). Streeck and Mertens (2013, p. 38) therefore maintain that a trade-off between 'mandatory spending' (work-related social security, old age pensions) and 'discretionary spending' (targeted investments on, for instance, childcare, education, activating programmes) exists.

Another way of phrasing this trade-off is by opposing 'old' versus 'new' risks of welfare states (Taylor-Gooby, 2004; Bonoli, 2005). The definition of new risks for children varies and seems to be related to class, gender and ethnicity; some scholars include children's poverty risks, the risk of being working poor, especially if low skilled, working reduced hours or without a proper contract. Others focus on poorly educated parents, whether native or from a migrant background, or point to gender-related risks such as the effects of being a single parent family or living in dual earner families, hence being in need of childcare and parental leave. Several combinations of policy reactions are possible to the newly defined problem of the demand for children to be better prepared for the future labour market at a time of both highly competitive economies and fragmenting and unstable families. Social investments will require redistribution from mandatory to discretionary spending, but to a lesser degree if parents and their social networks can be held responsible for raising ('parenting') their children well. That strategy will also require public spending on professionally guided parenting programmes to guarantee, if possible, the effects.

In sum, we see a policy change towards preventing families from failing to cope with new social risks by either taking some care responsibilities from parents (by way of ECEC), which in some countries (the Nordic ones and also Germany and France) benefits all parents and in other countries (the Netherlands and the UK) mainly working middle-class parents. In addition, new parenting policies are being developed that target parenting skills and morals (by way of intervention programmes aiming to reach supposed parenting deficits of those 'at risk' though not successful per se because of middle-class bias; see Hopman and Knijn, 2017).

How to comprehend this shift in our country cases? To answer this question, a distinction is made between 'triggers' and 'drivers' of policy change. The argument is that (1) crucial macro-social and macroeconomic factors have triggered new family policy responses; (2) new family policies have been 'dualistic' in so far as they approach middle classes versus lower socioeconomic classes in different ways; (3) triggers become 'openers' of windows of opportunities for decision makers, experts and street-level professionals (drivers of change) when interpreting and implementing parenting support measures; and (4) the triggers are nearly the same in the three countries under study. In line with Kingdon (1984 [2003]), the specific configuration of problem definition and momentum providing the opportunity for policy solutions are presented as the best ways for tackling family-related social problems in France, Germany and the Netherlands. The solutions differ depending on the way the problems have been phrased.

TRIGGERS OF CHANGE FOR FAMILY POLICY TURNING POINTS

A relevant macro trigger of family policy change is the combination of demography and the pluralization and volatility of family forms. In Germany, more so than in France and the Netherlands, declining birth rates, an ageing population and shortages of skilled labour have triggered the redistribution of government budgets towards new social risks. France and the Netherlands, in contrast, have to deal with high rates of youth unemployment and precarious jobs for young adults, and have to find an answer to high levels of youth delinquency and school drop-outs, mainly among migrant youth. Pluralization and volatility of family forms or living arrangements have added to the emergence of new social risks in each of our countries and constituted probably the strongest trigger of the public turn to parenting, the focus of our concern. Since the 1970s, marriage and also parenthood have undergone a process of deinstitutionalization, substantial diversification, and hence weakening of social norms that define partners' and parents' status, and also their behaviour (Berger et al., 1974; Cherlin, 1978, 2004; Cheal, 2002).

Delayed marriage and parenthood, increasing rates of children born out of wedlock, divorce and single parent households, and increase of same-sex marriage are evidence of this process. Individualized partnerships, Giddens's 'pure relationships' (Giddens, 1992), and their volatility, parenthood by individualized choice, and growing childlessness have eroded 'life worldly' parental knowledge about how to raise and educate their children. In addition, traditional family forms of immigrant families from rural areas outside Europe do not fit the individualized family norms, and children from these families fall in between two cultures. New social norms 'concerning proper behaviour' as part of a couple or as a parent are not yet clear. In these circumstances, argues Cherlin (2004, p. 848), 'individuals can no longer rely on shared understandings of how to act. Rather, they must negotiate new ways of acting, a process that is a potential source of conflict and opportunity.' Policy answers to this trigger exist in investments in childcare facilities that substitute part of the parental responsibilities or by offering (compulsory) parenting advice and training policies – the 'scientification' of parenting by way of evidence-based programmes – as 'new risk institutions' which aim at re-institutionalizing parenthood and parenting (Hopman and Knijn, 2015).

A second trigger for parenting policies relates to democratic citizenship including children's rights. A growing body of research on the fate of democracy in times of austerity recognizes that the responsiveness of governments to voters' (that is, also parents') needs declines under the pressure of budget consolidation and lost control over taxation. In turn, citizens lose confidence that they can exert democratic control. Decreasing voter turnout and distorted (socially unequal) voter participation – disadvantaged, often new risk groups abstain from voting to a much larger extent than better off ones – are proof of this (Offe, 2013). Citizens see their governments increasingly as agents of international organizations (OECD, World Bank, International Monetary Fund, European Commission), not as *their* agents (Offe, 2013, p. 214 quoting Streeck 2011, p. 26). New family policy proposals indeed have been designed from the top down and recommended to national governments by these organizations. However, most of these policies have been recognized and accepted by national elected parliaments and implemented in path-dependent institutionalized ways, hence the variety of family policies in EU member states. For instance, in the Netherlands the issue of democratic citizenship with political support has been brought to the schools by a programme called 'citizenship education' (de Winter, 2011) in which pupils learn to deal with diversity, to debate about rights, obligations and morals and to respect minority norms. In France, family policy has been built from the bottom up with local and regional committees in which all stakeholders participate. We argue, therefore, that democratic citizenship has triggered the search for a new risk family policy response: on the one hand, facilities to balance work and care, extension of childcare facilities and early education via related subsidies, vouchers and tax allowances, and, on the other, new ways of organizing and approaching children and their families to participate in the democratic process.

A third trigger relates to the new global economic order, the related flexible labour market and how to prepare future generations of mixed descent – due to immigration – to contribute to a knowledge economy based on constant 'disruptive innovation', and hence on related higher skills. The Lisbon Treaty set the EU framework for the conditions to become the most competitive knowledge economy resulting in the Bologna agreement to streamline higher education over all the EU member states. The OECD (2001, p. 104) outlined necessary competencies of workers in the knowledge economy: 'interpersonal skills such as team-working, problem-solving and communication' must complement basic skills. Such 'soft skills' are less apparent overall among children of lower skilled parents, in particular, if these parents have a migration background (van Zenderen, 2010). Moreover, in addition to discrimination, the lack of such skills is a secondary reason for refusing apprenticeships or a job to children from this background. Children from the middle classes, too, will face more difficulties than their parents in making their way in the labour market and staying in a stable employment relationship: hence, they also need investments in their 'individualized human capital'. They can no longer expect upward social mobility, the way their parents did in the past, and parents are aware that these skills and competencies cannot be learned at school alone. Proper upbringing and social and cultural capital matter more than ever (Bourdieu, 1979). This also triggers the demand for support and advice (bottom up) by parents of all social categories.

The demographic crisis, the democratic deficit, volatile families and the requirements of the global knowledge economy are common triggers of change for the three countries under consideration, albeit they may vary in scope: responses to these triggers are country-specific, shaped by countries' policy legacies, institutional settings, rules and procedures. Hence, it is expected that there are varying portfolios of old and new parenting support policies in the comparison, and different forms of what is described as the dualization of the family policy response. Related to this, different actors, ideas and interests have driven policy change towards new family policy solutions. The next section focuses on these drivers.

DRIVERS OF CHANGE IN THREE COUNTRIES

Kingdon's (1984 [2003]) three streams – problem building (and its timing), solution and political will – are applied in this chapter to elaborate, for the French, German and Dutch cases, when and how parenting support has entered the public agenda and become a favourite policy solution for identified social problems. First, the issue of timing or turning points in policy development is considered.

Parenting support (*soutien à la parentalité*) emerged in France and the Netherlands as a policy in the second part of the 1990s. In France, two main institutional turning points can be identified (Martin, 2010, 2015). The first one corresponds to the creation in 1998 by the French government of a specific instrument to organize and develop a parenting support policy in terms of a national network to coordinate, optimize and structure diverse local initiatives: REAAP, which is a parents' counselling, support and mentoring network (*Réseau d'écoute, d'appui et d'accompagnement des parents*). This top-down framing aims at developing such networks in each *département* to regroup and coordinate a myriad of small and very local initiatives of volunteers and professionals involved in associations to support and inform parents about their role. A second turning point occurred in 2010 with the creation of the national parenting support committee (*Comité national de soutien à la parentalité*), the official current governance body for parenting policy. This new institution demonstrates a political will for supporting parents, which was confirmed with the doubling of the budget devoted to this policy in 2012 (from 75 to 150 million per year euros) (Martin, 2014).

In the Netherlands, the institutional turning point also came in the 1990s with the White Paper 'Regie in de Jeugdzorg' (Direction in Youth Care) (Ministerie van Welzijn, Volksgezondheid en Cultuur, 1994) attempting to increase central coordination by starting up the regional *Bureaus Jeugdzorg*. The Youth Care Act (*Wet op de Jeugdzorg*; Ministerie van Justitie/Ministerie van Volksgezonheid, Welzijn en Sport, 2004) in setting out the tasks and functions of these 15 *Bureaus Jeugdzorg* offered a legal framework of the support services for children and adolescents at risk and their families, and outlined whether and how the agencies had to fulfil their coordinating tasks, assessments and responsibilities for providing the proper support. A second turning point was the installation of the – first and last – Ministry for Youth and Family in 2007 that commenced to decentralize the governance of parenting support by creating local centres for children up to the age of 18 and their families (*Centra voor Jeugd en Gezin*). Its aim was to bring preventive child and youth support services closer to parents by situating existing local public child healthcare centres and organizations under one roof to offer advice and support to parents and children.

A turn to parenting materialized in the first decade of the new millennium also in Germany (see also Chapter 13 by Pfau-Effinger in this volume). However, the 1991 *German Children and Youth Support legislation* (Social Code VIII, SGB VIII), still in place, already offered a comprehensive package of universal and targeted parenting support to parents and provided routes for further extensions. The roots of the package can even be traced back to the 1920s. A novelty of the 1991 legislation, though, was its emphasis on the importance of broadly defined prevention and related preventive parenting support measures. Hence, Social Code VIII also stipulated a new targeted support for parents: the 'social pedagogical family support' (*Sozialpädagogische Familienhilfe*), typically, a home-visiting social worker. During the 1990s, some municipalities and Länder had already experimented with additional parenting support instruments, like the *Familienhebamme*, a kind of 'family-nurse partnership'. They did so to overcome still existing shortcomings of the 1991 legislation on parenting support, such as not-so-easy access for parents of lower socioeconomic strata and for migrant parents. Professionals had criticized that parenting support did not sufficiently answer to the plurality and volatility of living forms and parenting, and that it neglected very young children. Hence, they called for a larger variety of lower threshold and more preventive forms of parenting support including early intervention (for an overview see Jordan, 2005; Ostner and Stolberg, 2015). Their plea was greatly enhanced by (few though) cases of child maltreatment and subsequent child deaths in the early 2000s. These child protection cases served as catalysts for the amendments to Social Code VIII. Since 2005, an impressive series of new rules and procedures have been introduced into Private (Family) and Public (Social) Law, targeting potentially failing parents, and putting their parenting further under public auspices (Schumann, 2014). The idea of 'child protection' has been significantly extended in this process, including measures directed at parents, like parent training, but also child-directed ones, like ECEC and new forms of coordinating professional services to secure children's healthy and safe development; interestingly, measures which help parents (factually mothers, especially, single ones) to enter and stay in employment can also come under the heading of child protection. At present, a whole range of model projects, including more standardized ones, for better teaching of parents, such as those coordinated and monitored by the National Centre for Early Intervention (founded in 2006 and financed by the federal government), is being provided, mostly 'on top' of existing locally provided and financed (albeit statutory!) ones and with a special focus on children below the age of 3.

But what were the problem(s) and solution(s) to justify this explicit political will – as expressed in federal laws (Germany) or central coordination of local action (France and the Netherlands) – to invest in support for parents as close to home as possible? In France, it was the result of a clear political fight about the role of parents and their responsibility in the suspected increase of antisocial behaviour among young people. In the Netherlands, the problem has been defined in a milder way; worries about school drop-outs resulted in Operation Young (*Operatie Jong*), a government-coordinated committee with the task to improve the quality and coordination of the services offered (Ministeries van Binnenlandse Zaken, Justitie, Onderwijs en Cultuur, Huisvesting en Millieu en van Volksgezondheid, Welzijn en Sports, 2004). In contrast to France, a political fight was non-existent. In line with the older tradition, politicians and experts agreed and cooperated to facilitate support for children, youth and parents.

The very controversial issue of antisocial behaviour of young people in France played a crucial role in putting parents' responsibilities on the agenda (problem building). The first aspect of the controversy was the question of the increase itself as many experts defended the idea that the statistics on delinquency corresponded more to the recording of the police's activity than to a real increase in delinquent acts (Aubusson de Cavarlay, 2002). Nevertheless, the political agenda and successive elections put this insecurity threat and its main source, parental incompetence, on the front page. This issue was strongly politicized and led to a real fight between the French right and left-wing parties.

While it was not framed as such in the Netherlands, in both countries proposals were suggested to sanction those parents held responsible for school drop-out or a 'juvenile delinquent crime wave' by stopping payment of their family allowances. These were never really implemented in both countries, although politicians of both right- and left-wing parties tend to recognize the so-called parental responsibility deficit. The problem was clearly the result of a political concern about the ability of parents to assume their role and meet their obligations. The issue of *parentalité* in France is much more politicized than it is in the Netherlands (Martin, 2017). In France right-wing politicians stigmatized what they saw as the bad practices of parents who no longer assume their role, whether it be the result of the libertarian, individualistic and hedonistic ideology, the collapse of the institutional dimension of the family, or specific requirements for parenting (time available for this role, division of housework and childcare, pressure on the daily lives of parents and so on). In contrast, the left-wing government at the end of the 1990s and, in particular, Ségolène Royal (at the time Minister of Family and Children), but also high-ranking civil servants (in the *Délégation Interministérielle à la Famille* (DIF), created in 1998, and in the National Family Allowance Fund (CNAF), the family branch of the French social security system) defended an alternative solution to this punishing orientation: supporting and empowering parents through grassroots initiatives at the local level to inform them and give them advice on their parenting role.

To counteract the right-wing punitive orientation, which brings the parenting issue closer to the child protection issue, the CNAF set up, in the late 1990s, a committee to consider the question of responsibility and guidance of parents in their relationship with their children. Although not binding on the CNAF or the CAF (*Caisse d'Allocations Familiales*), this group clearly stated its opposition to the idea of financial penalty or added government control over family benefits, suggested by elected officials and parliamentarians: 'In the event of delinquency or antisocial behaviour of minors, the measure to take away or reduce the child benefit appears to be ineffective, and may cause adverse effects, inconsistent with the goals of the family branch' (Beaud et al., 1999, p. 27). Since then, the French parenting support policy balances between punishing and empowering, controlling and supporting parents and it leads concretely to a dualized system and instruments depending on the social belonging and characteristics of the households. This ambivalence between universal and targeted responses, control and prevention is not specific to the French configuration, but it demonstrates the persistence of this issue among family policy objectives.

A parallel problem definition that started in the Netherlands in the 1990s is related to critique on the professional youth care system as being too slow, too paternalistic and too inefficient (van Nijnatten et al., 2014). In reaction to several serious cases of child maltreatment, abuse and subsequent child deaths, the critique turned from a focus on parental and professional deficiencies into 'good parenting' as the solution. A preventive approach was introduced with the aim towards 'the empowerment of parents and to prepare parents for their parental role in order to preserve both family life and the well-being of children. The challenge was preventing children from becoming subjected to the child protection system' (van Nijnatten et al., 2014, pp. 729–30). This turn towards more preventive services implied a turn to families that might be at risk of experiencing all sorts of problems. Again, as in the French case, a double or at least ambivalent response to parenting is part of the deal. While these forms of preventive control and potential interventions are without doubt in the best interest of the child, they at the same time undermine the privacy of the family and the notion of it as a safe institution, thereby undermining parental authority and legitimacy by extension; the effectiveness of this response in improving child development has not yet been proven though (Furedi, 2008). The consequence is that all Dutch parents are now included in the range of risks that can endanger the healthy development of children. This has resulted in a package of alternative solutions for addressing parents through a preventive approach and supporting them in developing their parenting skills. Included is the introduction of evidence-based interventions, strongly advocated and supported by the Netherlands Youth Institute, which is subsidized by the Dutch government. Its databank contains lots of interventions, methods and best practices (Hopman and Knijn, 2015). Since 2007, the responsible ministry has encouraged and financed the introduction of evidence-based programmes, and plans were made to arrive at the enforced implementation of evidence-based practices (Ministerie van Jeugd en Gezin, 2007). Experts, however, are involved in a lively debate on intervention methods. Although some claim that evidence-based methods should be applied strictly in order to ensure quality of care, others emphasize participative citizenship, minor professional guidance and professional discretion based on skills and expertise. This other solution was accepted by the liberal-social-democratic coalition and is phrased the 'do-democracy' and the 'participation society', terms introduced by a number of government advisory boards. In reaction to advice from the Public Administrative Council (Raad voor Openbaar Bestuur, 2012) and the Advisory Council on Governmental Policy (Wetenschappelijke Raad voor het Regeringsbeleid, 2012), the government now proclaims that a 'do-democracy' is the best option to overcome an overly bureaucratic state apparatus that is unable to deal with a highly educated, empowered and more communicative population, and too slow to react to initiatives for societal innovation that are developed from the bottom up. Dutch parents in need of support are at the moment, on the one hand, challenged by many initiatives to help themselves via their own community and guided by professional workers and, on the other hand, too often left alone when in serious need.

In stark contrast to France and the Netherlands, 'child health', 'child protection' and 'cognitive stimulation' for children (as future workers) have been the overarching frames for new family policy initiatives in Germany. Since the late 1990s, German elites have openly worried about two issues: how to boost the birth rate via public policies, especially, birth rates of skilled middle-class women, and how to secure the safe, healthy and also stimulating upbringing of 'scarce', hence, 'precious' children once they have eventually been born (see statements by influential policy-related experts Rürup and Gruescu, 2003, Spieß et al., 2003 and Bertram et al., 2006). Boosting maternal employment and helping mothers stay employed became one path to stop and even reverse (as hoped) the negative demographic trend – a path that was, interestingly, embraced by all mainstream parties, as well as by the majority of church officials, and pushed as the preference of big business (Fleckenstein and Seeleib-Kaiser, 2011). The second worry about healthy and also 'smart' children has mostly, though not exclusively, pertained to parents of lower social strata who have been officially and regularly referred to as '*bildungsfern*' (being dull, beyond education). Here, the recommended policy solution – again by a broad all-party coalition – has been twofold: ECEC for all children (due to the preference of big business), including new 'educational partnerships' between ECEC centres, primary schools and parents (Betz, 2015) *and* parenting advice and training better targeted to potentially failing (incompetent) parents (see leading experts Bonin et al., 2013 on effectual family policies). Both solutions come under the heading of parenting support in Germany. They congenially collude with the strategic interests of business and political actors immersed in securing a healthy and qualified workforce and reducing the burdens of an ageing population.

CONCLUSION

In this chapter, a new policy targeting parents – via their children – to teach them 'appropriate parenting skills' has been presented and analysed. This 'parenting policy' deviates from ECEC in a fivefold way. First, it does not substitute parenting responsibilities – by way of childcare facilities or pre-school learning programmes as ECEC does, but instead reinforces parental responsibilities by directly approaching them on the basis of their supposed parental deficits, and offering them ways to improve their parental skills (as well as in the form of educational partnerships between professionals and parents). Second, and also in contrast to gender-neutral ECEC, parenting support matter-of-factly targets mostly mothers as the assumed main responsible parent for child upbringing. Third, parenting policies are directed to parents of all children below the age of 18, and hence also to parents of adolescents. Thereby, the expected phase of direct parental responsibility is prolonged. Fourth, parenting policies go beyond the supportive and facilitating approach of ECEC by stressing mainly the do's and don'ts of parenting, containing elements of control, surveillance and punishment in order to keep parents on the right track. Finally, parenting policies appear to be rather normative in their framing of 'new social risks for children' and the solutions/interventions offered; native-based middle-class standards are set, which, on the one hand, easily results in defining lower-class and ethnic ways of raising children as deviant, and, on the other hand, legitimizes the targeting of parents as subjects of intervention.

In order to understand how this has been implemented in three countries with different state welfare and family policy regimes, the triggers behind this turn to parenting support are assessed: changing family forms, demographic worries, and the wish of parents and governments to anticipate the global knowledge economy. These triggers are present in all three countries and have resulted in new forms of 'parenting support' there since the 1990s. Yet, there are also rather different reactions to and solutions for the problem that has been defined as the 'parental deficit' in our national studies. How to explain these different answers, policies and ideas to similar triggers? In line with Kingdon (1984 [2003]), problem definition, available solutions and political will do matter but also timing, policy legacies and institutional settings – summarized as path dependency – are of importance. All three countries had already established a comprehensive package of parenting support during the 1990s as a right of both parents and children. These packages have been amendments to and recalibrations of older ones: they mostly concern better cooperation and coordination, and also a more extensive interpretation of prevention, and they in principle target all parents, not only the ones at immediate risk. All three countries have also adopted the local/regional principle of subsidiarity in implementing parenting support and its instruments. In federalist Germany and the corporatist, once pillarized, Netherlands, subsidiarity is a long-standing constitutional principle; for France, subsidiarity refers to the balance between family obligation and public local responsibility in reaction to what is defined as the main problem, tackling youth violence at the local level. In the Netherlands, it is a reaction to the over-professionalized and bureaucratic systems of youth support in times of austerity. New communitarianism is brought forward as a means to 'empower parents' and is seen as the solution for state dependency. In Germany, worries about fertility rates and the knowledge economy prevail, but given its federalist regime, including subsidiarity, the federal level can only offer framework legislation and seed money for pilot projects in the field of social services for parents and their children.

According to our perspective which uses the triggers/drivers distinction, we suggest that the comparison is extended to more countries in order to assess more precisely the role of different institutional configurations but also the system of actors. More work is also needed to understand the impact of this new policy orientation on professional practices.

NOTE

1. See also *Social Policy & Society*, 2015, **14** (4).

REFERENCES

Aubusson de Cavarlay, B. (2002), 'Les chiffres de la délinquance: production et interprétation' (Statistics on delinquency: production and interpretation), *Cahiers français*, **308**, 26–31 (Special Issue: Etat, Société et Délinquance).

Beaud, J.-Y., F. Leprince, and F. Marinacce (eds) (1999), *La Responsabilité et l'Accompagnement des Parents dans leurs Relations avec l'Enfant* (Responsibility and support of the parents in the relations with their children), Rapport technique, Paris: CNAF.
Béland, D. (2007), 'Ideas, institutions, and policy change', *Journal of European Public Policy*, **16** (5), 701–18.
Berger, P., B. Berger, and H. Kellner (eds) (1974), *The Homeless Mind: Modernization and Consciousness*, New York: Vintage Books.
Bertram, H., H. Krüger, and K.C. Spieß (eds) (2006), *Wem gehört die Familie der Zukunft?* (Who owns the family of the future?), *Expertisen zum 7. Familienbericht der Bundesregierung*, Opladen: Verlag Barbara Budrich.
Betz, T. (ed.) (2015), *The Ideal of Educational Partnerships: A Critique of the Current Debate on Cooperation between ECEC Centers, Primary Schools and Families*, Gütersloh: Bertelsmann Stiftung.
Björnberg, U. and M.H. Ottosen (eds) (2013), *Challenges for Future Family Policies in the Nordic Countries*, Copenhagen: SFI – The Danish National Centre for Social Research.
Blau, J. and M. Abramovitz (eds) (2004), *The Dynamics of Social Welfare Policy*, Oxford: Oxford University Press, reprinted in 2014.
Bonin, H., A. Fichtl, H. Rainer, C.K. Spieß, H. Stichnoth and K. Wrohlich (2013), 'Zentrale Resultate der Gesamtevaluation familienbezogener Leistungen. Lehren für die Familienpolitik', *DIW-Wochenbericht*, **40** (October), 3–14.
Bonoli, G. (2005), 'The politics of the new social policies: providing coverage against new social risks in mature welfare states', *Policy & Politics*, **33** (3), 431–49.
Bourdieu, P. (ed.) (1979), *La Distinction*, Paris: Les Éditions de Minuit.
Cheal, D. (ed.) (2002), *Sociology of Family Life*, Houndmills, Basingstoke: Palgrave Macmillan.
Cherlin, A. (1978), 'Remarriage as an incomplete institution', *American Journal of Sociology*, **84** (3), 634–50.
Cherlin, A. (2004), 'The deinstitutionalization of American marriage', *Journal of Marriage and the Family*, **66** (November), 848–61.
Clasen, J. and N.A. Siegel (eds) (2007), *Investigating Welfare State Change: The Dependent Variable Problem in Comparative Analysis*, Cheltenham, UK and Northampton, MA, USA: Edward Elgar Publishing.
Daly, M. (2013), 'Parenting support policies in Europe', *Families, Relationships and Societies*, **2** (2), 159–74.
de Winter, M. (ed.) (2011), *Verbeter de wereld, begin bij de opvoeding. Van achter de voordeur naar democratie en verbinding* (Improve the world, start with education. From behind the front door to democracy and connection), Amsterdam: Uitgeverij SWP.
Donzelot, J. (1977), *La Police des Familles*, Paris, éditions de Minuit (Préface de Gilles Deleuze).
EC (European Council) (2002), 'Presidency Conclusion', Barcelona European Council, SN 100/1/02 REV 1, 15 and 16 March.
Esping-Andersen, G. (2002), 'A child-centred social investment strategy', in G. Esping-Andersen, D. Gallie, A. Hemerijck, and J. Myles (eds), *Why We Need a New Welfare State*, Oxford: Oxford University Press, pp. 26–67.
Fleckenstein, T.M. and M. Seeleib-Kaiser (2011), 'Business, skills and the welfare state: the political economy of employment-oriented family policy in Britain and Germany', *Journal of European Social Policy*, **21** (2), 136–49.
Furedi, F. (ed.) (2008), *Paranoid Parenting: Why Ignoring the Experts May be Best for Your Child*, London: Bloombury Academic.
Gershater-Molko, R.M., J.R. Lutzker, and D. Wesch (2003), 'Improving health, safety and parental skills in families reported for, and at-risk for child maltreatment', *Journal of Family Violence*, **18** (6), 377–86.
Giddens, A. (ed.) (1992), *The Transformation of Intimacy: Sexuality, Love and Eroticism in Modern Societies*, Cambridge: Polity Press.
Guiraudon, V. and C. Martin (2013), 'Drivers for change', in B. Greve (ed.), *The Routledge Handbook of the Welfare State*, London and New York: Routledge, pp. 283–92.
Hall, P.A. (1993), 'Policy paradigms, social learning and the state: the case of economic policymaking in Britain', *Comparative Politics*, **25** (3), 275–96.
Hopman, M. and T. Knijn (2015), 'Parenting support in the Dutch "participation society"', *Social Policy & Society*, **14** (4), 645–56.
Hopman, M. and T. Knijn (2017), 'Happy children in the Netherlands? Positive parenting and problems to solve', *Journal of Family Research/Zeitschrift für Familienforschung*, **11**, 257–72 (Special Issue: Parents under the Spotlight: Parenting Practices and Support from a Comparative Perspective, ed. T. Betz, M.S. Honig, and I. Ostner).
Hornby, G. (ed.) (2000), *Improving Parental Involvement*, London and New York: Continuum.
Jordan, E. (ed.) (2005), *Kinder- und Jugendhilfe*, Weinheim and Munich: Juventa.
Kamerman, S. and A. Kahn (1978), 'Family policy as a field and perspective', in S. Kamerman and A. Kahn (eds), *Government and Families in Fourteen Countries*, New York: Columbia University Press, pp. 476–503.
Kingdon, J.W. (1984), *Agendas, Alternatives, and Public Policies*, reprinted in 2003, New York: Longman.
Knijn, T. and J. Lewis (2017), 'ECEC: childcare markets in the Netherlands and England', in B. Unger, D. van

der Linde, and M. Getzner (eds), *Public or Private Goods? Redefining Res Publica*, Cheltenham, UK and Northampton, MA, USA: Edward Elgar Publishing, pp. 150–74.

Lee, E., J. Bristow, C. Faircloth, and J. Macvarish (eds) (2014), *Parenting Culture Studies*, Houndmills, Basingstoke: Palgrave Macmillan.

Lewis, J., T. Knijn, C. Martin, and I. Ostner (2008), 'Patterns of development in work/family reconciliation policies for parents in France, Germany, the Netherlands and the UK in the 2000s', *Social Politics*, **15** (4), 261–86.

Mahon, R. (2006), 'The OECD and the work/family reconciliation agenda: competing frames', in J. Lewis (ed.), *Children, Changing Families and Welfare States*, Cheltenham, UK and Northampton, MA, USA: Edward Elgar Publishing, pp. 173–97.

Mahon, R. (2009), 'The OECD's discourse on the reconciliation of work and family life', *Global Social Policy*, **9** (2), 183–204.

Martin, C. (2010), 'The reframing of family policy in France: actors, ideas and instruments', *Journal of European Social Policy*, **20** (5), 410–21.

Martin, C. (ed.) (2014), *'Être un bon parent': une injonction contemporaine*, Rennes: Presses de l'EHESP.

Martin, C. (2015), 'Parenting support in France: defining policy on an ideological battlefield', *Social Policy & Society*, **14** (4), 609–20.

Martin, C. (2017), '(Re)discovering parents and parenting in France. What's new?', *Journal of Family Research Zeitschrift für Familienforschung*, **11**, 283–92 (Special Issue: Parents under the Spotlight: Parenting Practices and Support from a Comparative Perspective, ed. T. Betz, M.S. Honig, and I. Ostner).

Mätzke, M. and I. Ostner (2010), 'The role of old ideas in the new German family policy agenda', *German Policy Studies*, **6** (1), 119–62.

Ministerie van Jeugd en Gezin (2007), *Alle kansen voor alle kinderen* (Every opportunity for every child), Den Haag: Ministerie van Jeugd en Gezin.

Ministeries van Binnenlandse Zaken, Justitie, Onderwijs en Cultuur, Huisvesting en Milieu en Volksgezondheid, Welzijn en Sport (2004), *Operatie Jong: sterk en resultaatgericht voor de jeugd* (Operation Young: strong and result-oriented for youth), Den Haag: Ministeries van Binnenlandse Zaken, Justitie, Onderwijs en Cultuur, Huisvesting en Milieu en Volksgezondheid, Welzijn en Sport.

Ministerie van Justitie/Ministerie van Volksgezondheid, Welzijn en Sport (2004), *Wet op de jeugdzorg* (Youth Care Act), Den Haag: Staatsblad 2004 306.

Ministerie van Welzijn, Volksgezondheid en Cultuur (1994), *Regie in de jeugdzorg, standpunt van de Ministers van Welzijn, Volksgezondheid en Cultuur en Justitie* (Direction in Youth Care, Vision of the Ministries of Well-being, Public Health and Culture, and Law), Den Haag.

Morel, N., B. Palier, and J. Palme (eds) (2012), *Towards a Social Investment Welfare State*, Bristol: Policy Press.

Morgan, K.J. (2013), 'Path shifting of the welfare state. Electoral competition and the expansion of work–family policies in Western Europe', *World Politics*, **65**, 73–115.

Offe, C. (2013), 'Participatory inequality in the austerity state: a supply-side approach', in A. Schäfer and W. Streeck (eds), *Politics in the Age of Austerity*, Cambridge: Polity Press, pp. 196–218.

OECD (2001), *Starting Strong*, Paris: OECD.

OECD (2009), *Doing Better For Children*, Paris: OECD.

Ostner, I. and C. Stolberg (2015), 'Investing in children, monitoring parents: parenting support in the changing German welfare state', *Social Policy & Society*, **14** (4), 621–32.

Pierson, P. (2001), 'Post-industrial pressures on the mature welfare states', in P. Pierson (ed.), *The New Politics of the Welfare State*, Oxford: Oxford University Press, pp. 80–104.

Raad voor Openbaar Bestuur (2012), *Loslaten in vertrouwen* (Letting go in faith), Den Haag: Raad voor Openbaar Bestuur.

Rürup, B. and S. Gruescu (2003), *Familienpolitik im Interesse einer aktiven Bevölkerungsentwicklung* (Family policy for positive population growth), Gutachten/Report, Berlin: BMfFSFJ.

Sanders, M. (1999), 'Triple P-Positive Parenting Program: towards an empirical validated multilevel parenting and family support strategy for the prevention of behavior and emotional problems in children', *Clinical Child and Family Psychology Review*, **2** (2), 71–90.

Schäfer, A. and W. Streeck (2013), 'Introduction: politics in the age of austerity', in A. Schäfer and W. Streeck (eds), *Politics in the Age of Austerity*, Cambridge: Polity Press, pp. 1–25.

Schumann, E. (2014), 'Edukatorisches Staatshandeln am Beispiel der Etablierung eines neuen Familienleitbildes' (Educative state action – how legal policy has contributed to the rise of a new family model), in *Das Erziehende Gesetz. 16. Symposium der Kommission 'Die Funktion des Gesetzes in Geschichte und Gegenwart'*, Abhandlungen der Akademie der Wissenschaften zu Göttingen, Berlin and New York: De Gruyter, pp. 1–58.

Spieß, K., J. Schupp, M. Grabka et al. (eds) (2003), *Abschätzung der Brutto-Einnahmeneffekte öffentlicher Haushalte und der Sozialversicherungsträger bei einem Ausbau von Kindertageseinrichtungen* (Estimated effects of an extension of public childcare on gross public revenues), Gutachten/Report, Berlin: BMfFSFJ.

Streeck, W. (2011), 'The crisis of democratic capitalism', *New Left Review*, **71**, 5–29.

Streeck, W. and K. Thelen (2005), 'Introduction: institutional change in advanced political economies', in

W. Streeck and K. Thelen (eds), *Beyond Continuity: Institutional Change in Advanced Political Economies*, Oxford: Oxford University Press, pp. 3–39.

Streeck, W. and D. Mertens (2013), 'Public finance and the decline of state capacity in democratic capitalism', in A. Schäfer and W. Streeck (eds), *Politics in the Age of Austerity*, Cambridge: Polity Press, pp. 26–58.

Taylor-Gooby, P. (ed.) (2004), *New Risks, New Welfare: The Transformation of the European Welfare State*, Oxford: Oxford University Press.

Thelen, K. and S. Steinmo (1992), 'Historical institutionalism in comparative politics', in S. Steinmo, K. Thelen, and F. Longstreth (eds), *Structuring Politics: Historical Institutionalism in Comparative Analysis*, Cambridge: Cambridge University Press, pp. 1–32.

van Nijnatten, C., T. Knijn, and M. Hopman (2014), 'Child protection victims and the "evil institutions"', *Social Science*, 3, 726–74.

van Zenderen, K. (2010), 'Young migrants' transition from school to work. Obstacles and opportunities', Doctoral Thesis, Utrecht University.

Wetenschappelijke Raad voor het Regeringsbeleid (2012), *Vertrouwen in Burgers* (Confidence in citizens), Den Haag: Wetenschappelijke Raad voor het Regeringsbeleid.

PART IV

FAMILY POLICY MODELS

13. Comparing persistence and change in family policies of conservative welfare states
Birgit Pfau-Effinger

INTRODUCTION

The chapter aims to explore how family policies have developed since the early 1990s in welfare states classified as conservative types of welfare regime by Esping-Andersen (1990). The empirical study compares the welfare states of Austria, Germany and Switzerland which have been classified as a conservative welfare regime types (Esping-Andersen, 1990), Switzerland was sometimes also regarded as a mixture of a conservative and a liberal type of welfare regime (Carigiet and Opielka, 2006; Bonoli and Häusermann, 2011). In family policy research, there was for a long time general agreement with Esping-Andersen's classification of these three welfare states, on the premise that these countries strongly supported the housewife model of the male-breadwinner family (Daly and Lewis, 2000; Kreimer and Schiffbänker, 2005; Lewis and Ostner, 1994; Nadai and Nollert, 2015).

The chapter shows that strong changes have subsequently taken place in the institutions of family policies in Austria and Germany towards a more gender-egalitarian family policy, while the family policy of the Swiss welfare state has remained conservative. The main question investigated in the chapter is how it is possible to explain this difference regarding persistence and change in the institutions of family policies. There have been relatively few attempts to explain cross-national differences in the development of family policies in conservative welfare states.

In its theoretical framework, the chapter uses the theoretical approach of the 'work-family arrangement'. According to this approach, cross-national differences in the development of family policies can be explained in the complex context of cultural, institutional and socio-economic factors and the ways in which these interact. The empirical study analyzes the role of cultural ideas related to the work-family relationship, welfare culture, institutional factors and women's employment rate for the explanation of persistence and change in family policies in the time period between 1990 and 2015 in Germany, Austria and Switzerland. It uses document analysis, analysis of statistical data and surveys, and secondary analysis of historical studies.

The chapter then analyzes the change in family policies of the welfare states of Austria, Germany and Switzerland from 1990 until 2015. This is followed by an analysis of the factors that explain the differences in the development of family policies between the three countries on the basis of the theoretical framework. The chapter ends with a summary and conclusion.

OVERVIEW OF THE STATE OF RESEARCH

An important impetus for international comparative analysis of welfare state policies was given by works of the Danish author Esping-Andersen (1990). His analysis focuses on how varying types of welfare state policy result in different forms of social inequality, and on that basis he distinguished between the social democratic, the conservative and the liberal types of welfare regime. These differences, Esping-Andersen argues, go hand in hand with specific differences in the way in which the state intervenes in the labor market and in the family, and also, especially, with respect to the extent to which it promotes the formalization of care. Thus, in the social democratic welfare regime women tend to be fully integrated into employed activity, on the basis of a strongly developed state social service sector and comprehensive formalization of informal care. With regard to the ways in which they frame women's labor market integration, conservative welfare states, according to Esping-Andersen, are characterized by a family-centred approach to social services and a low degree of support for women's employment. Liberal welfare states tend to produce high levels of women's employment, made possible by childcare services offered on the market and realistically only accessible to the middle classes. Esping-Andersen argues that the welfare state institutions are relatively stable, and that change is path dependent (see also Pierson, 2000). Therefore, one might assume that conservative family policies, once established, tend to remain conservative in the long run. However, the assumption that welfare states tend to develop in a path dependent manner is a contested issue. It has been shown that welfare state institutions and policies can experience relatively fundament change in their main features (Eydal and Rostgaard, 2011; Saxonberg, 2014).

Feminists in part have criticized Esping-Andersen's approach, since empirical studies have shown that care policies do not vary systematically with the type of welfare regime. In feminist social policy analyses, various approaches have been developed which have classified welfare states according to their care policies. What should be particularly mentioned here is the distinction between weak, moderate and strong male breadwinner states made by Lewis (1992) and Lewis and Ostner (1994).

Some authors have analyzed historical change in family policies in a cross-national perspective (Daly and Lewis, 2000; Eydal and Rostgaard, 2011; Ferragina and Seeleib-Kaiser, 2015; Javornik, 2014; Pfau-Effinger, 2004; Saxonberg, 2014). It is common to explain the differences with politics and the role of political parties. Some authors also stress the role of cultural ideas for the explanation (Ferragina and Seeleib-Kaiser, 2015; Fleckenstein, 2011; Pfau-Effinger, 2005a). However, rarely analyzed and explained is why conservative family policies have remained conservative in some countries and have changed towards a more gender-egalitarian approach in others.

THE THEORETICAL FRAMEWORK: EXPLAINING THE DEVELOPMENT OF FAMILY POLICY IN THE CONTEXT OF 'WORK-FAMILY ARRANGEMENTS'

The theoretical framework of the empirical study in this chapter is based on the theoretical approach of the 'work-family arrangement' of the author Pfau-Effinger (1998, 2004) which is here briefly sketched as follows. The specific work-family arrangement of a society is based on the interaction between cultural ideas, institutions, social factors and economic factors that frame childcare and the work-family relationship at the macro level. 'Culture' is defined here as a potentially contradictory and dynamic system of collective ideas relating to the 'good' society and the 'ideal' way of living and (morally) 'good' behavior. Culture comprises cultural values, cultural models or 'ideals', and world views, in brief, *cultural ideas at the macro level of society*. Culture can be coherent or contradictory, fragmented and contested. The work-family arrangement in every modern society is based on cultural values and models related to the 'ideal' ways to organize gender overall, childcare and the work-family relationship within the family, and with regard to the different types of family members ('gender culture'; Pfau-Effinger, 1998) (see also Chapter 4 by Millar on family obligations in this volume). With time it is either reproduced or changed by the relevant social actors through the process of ongoing conflict, discourse, negotiation and compromise. Such cultural ideas at the macro level offer action orientation to the individuals at the macro level, but they do not determine their behavior.

The institutional setting of family policies is influenced by the respective 'gender culture' in a society and by the dominant 'welfare culture' in a society as well. The 'welfare culture' is based on cultural ideas related to the role of the welfare state vis-à-vis the family, the market, the state and the third sector for the provision of welfare in a society (Pfau-Effinger, 2005b).

The cultural basis of family policies can be firmly established and coherent in the long term, but it can also be incoherent or even contradictory. It can also happen that it changes relatively independently from change in the family policy institutions. It should be considered that cultural ideas mainly only influence the institution when it is established or when it experiences a fundamental change. Therefore, it is possible that the institution remains relatively stable while substantial cultural change takes place outside this institution. If change of the cultural basis of family policy institutions has taken place, this can also lead to change in the family policy institutions, under specific circumstances. Social actors may use discourses about values and notions in relation to the welfare state to exert influence on welfare state policy. The power relations and how they change during these processes are relevant for the success of new ideas. Therefore, cross-national differences in the development of the gender culture and its interplay with the welfare culture can contribute to the explanation for why conservative family policies may shift towards more gender-egalitarian policies in some countries and remain stable in other countries.

Other factors may also contribute. These include socio-economic change that may increase the pressure on the relevant policy actors to change the family policy. In the case of family policy, a strong increase in women's employment may lead to such an increase of the pressure on political actors. Also, political factors may contribute to the explanation of differences, like the degree of centralization/decentralization of politics and the role of the European Union (EU).[1]

THE DEVELOPMENT OF FAMILY POLICIES IN CONSERVATIVE WELFARE STATES SINCE THE EARLY 1990S

This section analyzes the development of family policies in Austria, Germany and Switzerland for the time period from 1990 until 2015 (see also Chapter 2 by Gauthier and Koops on the history of family policy research in this volume). It uses the following indicators: the generosity of family policy related to public childcare; the generosity of family policy towards pay for parental leave; and the degree of support for parental childcare by fathers.

The Conservative Family Policies in the Early 1990s

In the early 1990s, Austria, Germany and Switzerland mainly supported women's caring role at home and offered little support for their labor market integration. Public childcare was only provided for a rather small group of children from poor families. In Germany and Austria parental leave programs with job protection for three years, after a period of 14 weeks of full paid maternity leave, were introduced in the 1980s (see also Chapter 10 by Thévenon on parental leave in this volume). The pay was based on a fixed and means-tested amount which was clearly below the poverty level.[2] The aim was to offer women a return to their job after three years of maternal childcare at home, and to offer men the option to participate in the childcare at home (Kreimer and Schiffbänker, 2005; Pfau-Effinger, 2005a). It was also possible to combine the pay with part-time employment.

The Swiss welfare state did not offer support for parental leave; there was not even a maternity leave scheme for employed women before 2005. The state instead relied on the parents for family care and the market for the provision of extra familial childcare (Kreimer, 2009). The main focus of family policies in the Swiss welfare state is traditionally some degree of financial support for low-income families.

Change in Family Policies since the Mid-1990s

In the time period between the early 1990s and 2015, the welfare states of Germany and Austria strongly changed their family policies and started to support women's employment and gender equality (Behning and Leitner, 1998; Mätzke and Ostner, 2010). In contrast, there was little change in the family policies of the Swiss welfare state. Prevention of poverty for families with children is still at the centre of family policies in all countries, though the issue of whether policies should react in some way or other to the change in the gender culture in the population has been a contested issue in the last decade (Nadai and Nollert, 2015).

Public childcare for children under school age

In Germany and Austria, in the 1990s, comprehensive support for public childcare for children aged 3 to 6 years was introduced (see also Chapter 8 by Rostgaard on childcare in this volume). In Germany, in 1996, an individual right of children aged 3 to 6 years to daily and affordable public childcare on a part-time basis (at least half days) was established. Both countries had nearly full coverage of public childcare for children aged between 3 and 6 in the mid-1990s. However, there was only little support for extra familial care for children under 3 in both countries; and demand for it exceeded to some extent public supply (Esch and Stöber-Blossey, 2002; Kreimer and Schiffbänker, 2005).

Around a decade later, in the mid-2000s, the German government decided on a path-breaking reform of family policy (Ferragina and Seeleib-Kaiser, 2015; Mätzke and Ostner, 2010). The aim was that family policy should offer generous support for public childcare for all children under school age. The municipalities were obliged with the task to extend public childcare so that it fitted with demand. Since 2013, each child aged 1–6 has an individual right to (full-time) public childcare, and the municipalities are obliged to offer comprehensive publicly funded childcare to all parents who demand public childcare for their children. In addition, all parents of children under age 1 are entitled to care, if the parents are employed, in education or professional training or if the child has special needs (§24 Social Code VIII, SGB VIII). Also, the fees that parents have to pay in addition to the public finances are relatively low, and they vary with the income of the parents. Yet, regarding the quality of public childcare, Germany still faces some problems concerning the numbers of professionally skilled staff and the numerical relationship between carers and children (Aurich et al., 2018). In the same time period, the Austrian government introduced public childcare for children under 3 to help meet the demand for public care for this age group. On the basis of a contract between the government and the Federal Republics, the provision of public childcare has been strongly extended since 2009. However, the demand of parents of children under 3 for longer caring hours still considerably exceeds the supply (Schratzenstaller, 2015).

The case is different for Switzerland. The public provision of childcare of the Swiss welfare state is still rather small, and children and parents do not have social rights in relation to care. The national state has introduced a program of co-financing the establishment of new crèches and nursing homes that started 2002 and was extended twice until 2019 (EKFF, 2009a). However, the amount of financing is comparably low: the finances in the time period from 2002 until 2012 only covered the establishment of 20,000 new places for children under school age, and the program only provides subventions for building costs (EKFF, 2009b). In part the Kantons, which are regions and administrative units in Switzerland, offer more generous public childcare, at least for children from 3 to school age. This leads to a rather uneven regional distribution of the chance for parents to have the option to use public childcare (Schmid et al., 2011). Altogether, until the present, experts find that the supply of public childcare in Switzerland is far below the demand (EKFF, 2009b).

Paid parental leave
From 2007, family policy of the German welfare state has also offered generous parental leave on the basis of the Act on Childcare Allowance and Parental Leave (*Bundeselterngeld- und Elternzeitgesetz* or BEEG) (see also Chapter 10 by Thévenon on parental leave in this volume). The leave options are still based on fully paid maternity leave of 14 weeks, of which eight weeks are paid after childbirth, and a right to parental leave (*Elternzeit*) until the child is 3 years old, with job protection and the right to return to the previous job. The time period in which the leave is paid is the same as in the previous time of the *Erziehungsurlaub*; the parents can still choose between 12 months with higher pay per month and 24 months with lower monthly pay. The leave is paid for 12 months on the basis of two-thirds of the employment income; low income earners receive up to 100 percent of their employment income. If parents choose a longer leave up to two years, the monthly pay is lower. As before, the parents can share the leave. It is also possible to combine the parental leave with part-time employment.

In Austria, during the last decade, the paid parental leave program has also been transformed into generously paid parental leave (*Kinderbetreuungsgeld*). Parents can get a childcare allowance of 1000 euros per month. In addition, they can work part time and earn up to 60 percent of their previous employment income. The amount of pay that they get is lower if they take the leave for two years. The other option is for parents to get 80 percent of their employment income during 12 months of parental leave. With this generous system of childcare allowance, the Austrian government aims to support the reconciliation of childcare and employment for women and men, and to motivate fathers to participate in parental childcare at home (Schratzenstaller, 2015).

Until 2005, the Swiss did not even have paid maternity leave around the time of childbirth. In 2005, 14 weeks of paid maternity leave with 80 percent of former income was introduced, which is a first small step in catching up with the other welfare states in Western Europe, the majority of which had already introduced maternity leave schemes by the 1960s or 1970s, and a gender-neutral parental leave scheme does not exist. Therefore, the possibility of providing family care after the short period of maternity leave is for the most part restricted to persons who are financially dependent in the framework of a male-breadwinner marriage (Stutz, 2006; Wecker, 2006).

Promotion of the equal sharing of childcare
The welfare states of Germany and Austria have introduced active measures to promote the participation of fathers in family care through the introduction of special periods for fathers in the parental leave schemes. This is an active measure to support a more equal sharing of family responsibility and employment. Traditionally, in both countries mainly only women take parental leave, even if the leave is offered to both parents (Kreimer and Schiffbänker, 2005). The experiences of the Nordic welfare states show that the introduction of the 'father's quota' into the parental leave scheme can be a successful instrument for considerably increasing the rate of parental leave taken by fathers (Eydal, 2005; Eydal and Rostgaard, 2011). In Germany, after the introduction of two generously paid 'daddy months' in the parental leave program, the share of fathers who participate in parental leave is more than one-third (Reimer, 2013). The share is about half in Austria (Schratzenstaller, 2015).

The findings for Germany and Austria show that a substantial transition of family policies has taken place. Family policy no longer has the support for women's caring role at home as its main focus. Instead, there is relatively strong support for women's labor market integration and gender equality. Both the German and the Austrian welfare states offer comprehensive public childcare and the option to choose generously paid parental leave with job protection for one year. The generosity of welfare state support for children under 3 and their parents is even higher in the German welfare state since all children from 1 to 6, and working parents with children under 1 have individual social rights to affordable public childcare. Moreover, fully paid maternity leave and generously paid parental leave until the child is 1 year old give parents who want to care of their children themselves during the first year after birth the option to stay at home or work part time without being financially dependent on their partner. Family policies of the Swiss welfare state, in contrast, have remained conservative and changed only very marginally since the 1960s. Because of such reasons, Müller-Muralt (2014) characterizes Switzerland as a 'developing country' with regard to family policies.

The findings are also reflected in the Organisation for Economic Co-operation and Development (OECD) data about public spending for families. The share of public expenditure for family policies of the gross domestic product (GDP) is only 1.3 percent in Switzerland, which is clearly below the OECD average of 2.23 percent. It is 2.8 percent in Germany and 3 percent in Austria (OECD, 2015).

EXPLANATION OF THE DIFFERENCE BETWEEN PERSISTENCE AND CHANGE

The Role of Women's Employment

Since the 1990s, in Western European societies, women have changed their labor market behavior considerably. Consequently, women's employment has increased substantially, particularly the employment of mothers with dependent children. This development has placed strong pressure on the welfare states to extend the supply of public childcare and to support women's labor market integration. In this subsection, I explore whether the differences concerning the departure from a conservative family policy in Austria and Germany and the persistence of a conservative family policy in Switzerland can be explained by differences in the development of women's employment.

As shown in Table 13.1, the share of employed women was somewhat higher in Switzerland in 1995 than in the other two countries. One might conclude that the problem of pressure on family policy was even stronger in Switzerland than in Austria and Germany. Also, the increase in women's employment rate since 1995 was higher in Switzerland, at least in comparison with Austria. Altogether, the data indicate that the pressure on the welfare state that might have been caused by the increase in women's employment rates has not been stronger in Austria and Germany in comparison with Switzerland.

These three countries share a long history of low fertility, and they are currently among the countries with the lowest fertility rates (Sobotka, 2011). The low fertility rates are a concern among the political elites in all three countries. Therefore, the differences in family policies cannot be explained by differences in the demographic pressure concerning fertility.

Table 13.1 Differences in the development of women's employment rates between Austria, Germany and Switzerland (percentage)

Country	1992	1995	2000	2005	2010	2014	Increase since 1995 in percentage points
Austria	60.7*	61.2	62.3	64.0	64.5	68.5	+7.3
Germany	57.8	60.9	63.1	63.1	69.6	73.1	+12.2
Switzerland		68.9**	72.2	72.7	74.6	77.4	+8.5

Note: * for 1994; ** for 1996; employment rates for women aged 20–64.

Source: OECD *Employment Outlook* (2015).

The Role of Cultural Differences

In this subsection, I will analyze how far the development of the gender culture contributes to the explanation of the differences in the development of family policies in the three countries of the study since the mid-1990s. The time sequence is important in this respect. I analyze the development of the dominant model of the family in the population before policy change, and discourses that have developed that mediate between the new ideas related to the gender culture in the population and relevant political actors.

The gender culture of Austria, Germany and Switzerland shared common features in the middle of the twentieth century and has developed rather similarly in the three countries (Pfau-Effinger and Euler, 2014). In all three societies the 'housewife model of the male breadwinner family' (in brief, 'housewife model') was the main cultural basis of the family in the 1950s and 1960s. This model is based on the premise of a fundamental separation of the 'public' and 'private' spheres, and a corollary location for both genders: the husband's proper work is in the 'public' sphere, while the housewife is responsible for the private household and childcare; her financial security exists on the basis of his income. This model is linked with the cultural construction of 'childhood', according to which children need special care and comprehensive individual tutelage by the mother in the private household.

Since the 1970s, a fundamental cultural transformation has taken place in Austria and Germany which exhibits a relatively high dynamic. In both societies, the central cultural position of the traditional housewife model of the family has strongly eroded. This transformation began principally towards the end of the 1960s when a fundamental contradiction at the cultural level came to a head: the incongruity between the cultural construct of the autonomy and equality of members of modern industrial societies, on the one hand, and the construct of the inequality and dependence of women in the housewife-model, on the other. In addition, at this point alternative family models emerged on the level of family values, made possible by the newly forming international and national feminist movements that seized upon these contradictions (Pfau-Effinger, 2004). As a consequence, the housewife model as the dominant cultural image was increasingly replaced by the 'male-breadwinner/female part-time carer' model of the family. This image essentially rests on the vision of full integration of women and men into paid economic activity. At the same time, however, it presupposes that women as mothers may interrupt their economic activity after childbirth for a while, after which they combine employment and responsibility for childcare through part-time work, until their children are no longer considered to require particular care. The new 'male breadwinner/female part-time carer family model' in both countries is based on the idea that the mother should be employed, but also that parental childcare should still play an important role in family life (Kreimer and Schiffbänker, 2005; Nadai and Nollert, 2015; Pfau-Effinger and Euler, 2014). In this cultural context, parental care also has a new meaning. It is connected with a new type of parenthood, one based on the expectation that parents – until today this has meant mainly mothers – who are otherwise oriented towards full participation in working life, for a limited period take over informal childcare in their own family household, either full or part time (Kreimer and Schiffbänker, 2005; Pfau-Effinger, 2004).

The new cultural family model on which the new gender arrangements of Austria and Germany are based is still somewhat contradictory. The financial dependence assumed by a woman who cares for her own children stands in contrast to the high cultural esteem enjoyed by autonomous financial security. This problem might to some degree be resolved by welfare state programs that provide generously paid parental leave and offer women (and men) the option to act temporarily as a 'financially autonomous parental carer'.

It should be mentioned that Germany, with respect to family values, is clearly still split. In East Germany, the family tradition of the former GDR still influences the family values of the majority of the population in the *Neue Länder*. Different to the West, a family model that I call a 'dual-breadwinner/state care-provider model' is dominant here. It is based on the idea of full employment of both parents and full-time public childcare provision. While cultural change in the West German society was mainly based on modernization of the cultural family model of the housewife marriage towards a male breadwinner/female part-time carer model, which is still dominant today, the dual-breadwinner/state care-provider family model has survived as the dominant cultural family model in East Germany (Pfau-Effinger and Smidt, 2011).

It can be shown that in both Germany and Austria, cultural change has been ahead of change in family policies. Also, discourses were established that mediate between the different levels of cultural change. In a first step, in the 1970s and 1980s, these discourses, mainly established by the feminist movement, were directed towards the issue of a just gender division of labor and women's right to participate in the labor force. Since the late 1990s, a new type of discourse has developed that focuses on the issue of demographic change and the need to increase fertility rates. In this context, there is also a popular argument that efforts should be strengthened to motivate more well-educated middle class women to have children (Pfau-Effinger, 2004).

The persistence of the housewife model of the family might explain why the conservative family policy has practically not changed since the 1960s in the Swiss welfare state. However, such an assumption is not supported by the findings of empirical studies. These indicate instead that in the Swiss society of the last decades of the twentieth century, a similar cultural transition has taken place in the field of family values, towards a 'male-breadwinner/female part-time care-provider model', as in the other two societies (Bühler, 1996, 2001). This is demonstrated by data from International Social Survey Programme (ISSP) (2012).

In a comparative perspective of all three countries, the majority of people do not think that women's employment contradicts the well-being of their children. Most people think that a working mother can establish just as warm and secure a relationship with her children as a mother who does not work. The share is highest in the German population and lower in Austria. Only a minority of the population support a traditional division of labor in couples that is based on the housewife model of the family. The share is highest in Austria (33.5 percent) and lowest in Germany (24.9 percent). Also, the majority of people think that fathers of young children are just as competent as mothers for childcare. The share is even higher in Switzerland (88 percent) in comparison with Austria (80 percent), while the Germans are somewhat more conservative in this regard (73 percent). The share of people who think that women with children under school age should work full time is very low in Austria and Switzerland and somewhat higher in Germany (14.3 percent versus 2.0 percent and 3.7 percent, respectively). Culturally, the fact that people in East Germany have much stronger support for the full-time employment of mothers

Table 13.2 Attitudes indicating differences between Austria, Germany and Switzerland regarding gender culture

	Proportion of respondents who agree (in %)		
Item	Austria	Germany	Switzerland
Q1a A working mother can establish just as warm and secure a relationship with her children as a mother who does not work	73.1	87.3	78.4
Q2b A man's job is to earn money; a woman's job is to look after the home and family	33.5	16.8	24.9
Q48G In general fathers are as competent as mothers to care for their children*	80	73	88
Q3 Do you think that women with children under school age should work outside the home full time, part time or not at all?			
• full time	2.0	14.3	3.7
• part time	45.3	66.0	71.6
• stay at home	52.8	19.7	24.6

Source: International Social Survey Programme (ISSP) (2012); * European Value Survey (EVS) (2008).

of children under 3 may contribute to the explanation (Pfau-Effinger and Smidt, 2011). In Austria, about half of the population share a more conservative idea about women's employment since they think that mothers with children under school age should stay at home (52 percent). In Switzerland, nearly three-quarters of the population support the part-time employment of women with children under school age (71.6 percent). The share is somewhat lower in Germany (66 percent) and only 45.3 percent in Austria. Altogether, the profile of the gender cultural ideas differs mainly between Austria, on the one hand, and Germany and Switzerland, on the other, in that the Austrian people are somewhat more conservative towards gender equality and the employment of mothers of young children. Therefore, differences in the gender culture do not explain the differences between the persistence of family policy in Switzerland and the change of family policies in Austria and Germany.

Another explanation for the lack of family policy change might be that, even if considerable cultural change has taken place, the social groups who aimed to change family policies were not powerful enough to influence the decision-making process of the political elites. Such asynchrony in development between the cultural and political level might be caused, for example, in the strongly decentralized federal organization of the Swiss welfare state. In that case, one would expect considerable discrepancies between the dominant attitudes in the population and those of the political elites towards family policies. It seems that the efforts to establish a discourse on the issue of further development of family policies has not been very effective, being restricted to the debate surrounding the introduction of a few weeks of maternity leave (Grassl et al., 2005). It seems that, despite the substantial change in family values having taken place in the Swiss society, a majority of the population do not think that the contradiction between their own family values and the traditional family policies is an important issue, or that family policies should be substantially modified.

It seems that the main reason why the crucial change in family values has not resulted in further development of family policies can be found in the ambiguity of the cultural values themselves. So far, the main focus of my analysis has been on change in family values. However, besides family values, welfare values also exist in a population; these are related to the general role of the state vis-à-vis the market and the state (Pfau-Effinger, 2005b). In this respect, particular differences exist between the conservative welfare states of Germany and Austria, on the one hand, and the Swiss welfare state, on the other. Whereas in conservative welfare states like Germany and Austria – as also emphasized by Esping-Andersen (1990) – the state is given a relatively strong role in shaping social change in the attitudes of the population, this is not the case in liberal welfare states where the 'free powers of the market' are given priority. It seems that in the welfare culture of Switzerland, liberal market ideas play a substantial role. In relation to the role of the welfare state in general, to a considerable degree liberal market values are dominant. Accordingly, the state is not seen as the institution responsible for shaping change in family structures. This argument is supported by an analysis of the discourses that emerged in the context of the referendum of 2013 on Constitution Chapter 115a in Switzerland. The referendum (*Eidgenössische Volksabstimmung – Verfassungsartikel 115a über die Familienpolitik*) was based on a proposal of the Parliament and the National Council to introduce a duty for the municipalities to offer comprehensive affordable public childcare. The majority of the voters were against the proposal. What is interesting in this context is how the parties that successfully mobilized opinion against the referendum argued not against the employment of mothers but rather against the further extension of the welfare state, which was seen as a threat to the existing welfare organizations and to economic prosperity. The financing of maternity leave was seen as improper intervention of the state into the private sphere, and the term 'state owned children' was used in order to defame public childcare (Müller-Muralt, 2014).

With respect to the liberal market basis of family policies, therefore, a large part of the population seems to conform to the thinking of the policy elites who themselves characterize these policies as liberal, according to Müller-Muralt (2014). This argument is supported by attitude data of the ISSP from 2012 (Table 13.3). Even if Swiss people substantially support the employment of mothers of children under school age, which

Table 13.3 Attitudes indicating differences between Austria, Germany and Switzerland regarding welfare culture (in %)

Q13 ISSP Who do you think should primarily cover the costs of childcare?	Austria	Germany	Switzerland
The family itself	38.4	36.3	74.6
The government/public funds	59.9	61.7	23.0
The employers	1.7	2.0	2.4

Source: International Social Survey Programme (ISSP) (2012).

was shown above, most do not think that extra familial childcare should be publicly paid. Instead, they think that the family itself is responsible for paying for any kind of childcare outside the family. While in Austria and Germany, the majority of people believe that the government or public funds should cover the costs for childcare – 59.9 percent in Austria, 61.7 percent in Germany – only 23 percent of Swiss people share this attitude. In Switzerland, most people (74 percent) think that the family itself should primarily cover the costs of childcare. Only 38.4 percent of Austrian people and 36.3 percent of people in Germany share this attitude. These findings show that people in Austria and Germany believe that the state should take over responsibility for family policy and should have a strong role in this regard, while the Swiss welfare culture, as far as it is indicated by the welfare ideas in the population, has a strong liberal market orientation and does not support a strong role of the state vis-à-vis the family.

The fact that Germany and Austria are members of the EU and Switzerland is not an EU member may also to some degree contribute to the explanation as to why Germany and Austria, in contrast to Switzerland, much earlier started to modernize their family policies. However, it is not possible to explain family policy change in Germany and Austria during the last decades through EU policies. The analysis of discourses in the period of policy formation before family policy reforms in Austria and Germany shows that EU policies did not play any relevant role in this context. Instead, family policies were to a great degree a reaction to endogenous change in these countries (Aurich et al., 2018; Kreimer and Schiffbänker, 2005).

To conclude, it seems that a main reason why family policies in the Swiss welfare regime have not departed from the 1990 conservative policy, while family policies have fundamentally changed in Austria and Germany, is the strong role of liberal market values in the welfare culture, as far as it is indicated by the cultural ideas in the Swiss population. According to these cultural ideas, the welfare state is not responsible for shaping the direction of family change, or for supporting the realization of a new family model.

CONCLUSION

According to the findings of the study, fundamental change in family policies towards a new family policy that supports women's employment and father's involvement in parental childcare took place in the Austrian and German welfare state, while the family policy of the Swiss welfare state remained conservative. The analysis of cultural change shows that in all three societies, the cultural values towards gender, childcare and the work-family relationship have fundamentally changed. Today, public childcare and the employment of mothers of young children are broadly accepted in the population. Different to the other two countries, in Switzerland, family policy has not been adapted to this cultural change. Differences in the gender cultural values do not seem to explain the differences between persistence and change in family policies. Instead, differences in the welfare cultural ideas in the population about the role of the welfare state in shaping the family change towards a more gender-egalitarian family form seem to make a strong contribution to the explanation. The population in Austria and Germany support the cultural idea that the welfare state should have a strong role on the way to more gender-egalitarian family structures. On the basis of a liberal market value orientation, the majority of the population in

Switzerland do not accept that the state should support families in their reconciliation of work and family with public finances. Instead, childcare is seen as a private matter of the family, that parents must organize and finance themselves.

The findings show that cultural change in the population can be an important explanatory factor for change in welfare state policies. However, cultural change does not per se create policy change, the lack of which can, for example, be caused by ambiguity in the cultural change itself, as in the example of Swiss family policies.

NOTES

1. It should be noted that such processes can take place in specific parts of welfare state policy without taking place in other parts. Therefore, welfare states should not be treated as a coherent unity in cross-national comparison and classification when processes of change are analyzed.
2. The parental leave benefit was 300 euros per month in Germany, and somewhat higher at 436 euros per month in Austria.

REFERENCES

Aurich, P., M. Bigoteau, P. Caillaud et al. (2018), 'Women's labour market integration and local social citizenship in the German and French welfare states', in P.H. Jensen (ed.), *Women, Welfare and Employment: Local Adaptation of EU Policies*, Cheltenham, UK and Northampton, MA, USA: Edward Elgar Publishing (forthcoming).
Behning, U. and S. Leitner (1998), 'Zum Umbau der Sozialstaatssysteme Österreichs, der Bundesrepublik Deutschland und der Schweiz nach dem "care"-Modell', *WSI-Mitteilungen*, **11**, 787–99.
Bonoli, G. and S. Häusermann (2011), 'Swiss welfare reforms in a comparative European perspective: between retrenchment and activation', in C. Trampusch and A. Mach (eds), *Switzerland in Europe: Continuity and Change in the Swiss Political Economy*, London: Routledge, pp. 15-47.
Bühler, E. (ed.) (1996), *Regionale Arbeitsmärkte für Frauen und Männer: Gemeinsamkeiten und Unterschiede in der vertikalen Geschlechtersegregation*, Bern: Bundesamt für Statistik.
Bühler, E. (2001), 'Zum Verhältnis von kulturellen Werten und gesellschaftlichen Strukturen in der Schweiz – Das Beispiel regionaler Gemeinsamkeiten und Differenzen der Geschlechterungleichheit', *Swiss Journal of Geography*, **2**, 77–89.
Carigiet, E. and O. Michael (2006), 'Deutsche Arbeitnehmer – Schweizer Bürger? Zum deutsch-schweizerischen Vergleich sozialpolitischer Dynamiken', in E. Carigiet, M. Opielka, and F. Schulz-Nieswand (eds), *Wohlstand durch Gerechtigkeit Deutschland und die Schweiz im sozialpolitischen Vergleich*, Basel: Rotpunktverlag, pp. 15-47.
Daly, M. and J. Lewis (2000), 'The concept of social care and the analysis of contemporary welfare states', *British Journal of Sociology*, **51** (2), 281–98.
EKFF Eidgenössische Koordinationskommission für Familienfragen (2009a), *Familien- und Schulergänzende Kinderbetreuung in der Schweiz*, Bern: EKFF.
EKFF Eidgenössische Koordinationskommission für Familienfragen (2009b), *Die Leistungen der Familien anerkennen und fördern. Strategische Leitlinien 2015*, Bern: EKFF.
Esch, K. and S. Stöber-Blossey (2002), *Kinderbetreuung: Ganztags für alle? – Differenzierte Arbeitszeiten erfordern flexible Angebote*, IAT-Report 2002-09, Gelsenkirchen: Institut für Arbeit und Technik.
Esping-Andersen, G. (1990), *The Three Worlds of Welfare Capitalism*, Cambridge: Polity Press.
Eydal, G. (2005), 'Childcare policies of the Nordic welfare states: different paths to enable parents to earn and care', in B. Pfau-Effinger and B. Geissler (eds), *Care and Social Integration in Europe*, Bristol: Policy Press, pp. 153–72.
Eydal, G. and T. Rostgaard (2011), 'Gender equality revisited – changes in Nordic Childcare policies in the 2000s', *Social Policy and Administration*, **45** (2), 161–79.
Ferragina, E. and M. Seeleib-Kaiser (2015), 'Determinants of a silent (r)evolution: understanding the expansion of family policy in rich OECD countries', *Social Politics*, **22** (1), 1–37.
Fleckenstein, T. (2011), 'The politics of ideas in welfare state transformations: Christian democracy and the reform of family policy in Germany', *Social Politics*, **18** (4), 543–71.

Grassl, H., C. Bender and M. Schaal (2007), 'Der Schweizer Arbeitsmarkt: Sonderfall unter Modernisierungsdruck', in T.S. Eberle and K. Imhof (eds), *Sonderfall Schweiz*, Zürich: Seismo Verlag, pp. 172–87.
Javornik, J. (2014), 'Measuring state de-familialism: contesting post-socialist exceptionalism', *Journal of European Social Policy*, **24** (3), 240–57.
Kreimer, M. and H. Schiffbänker (2005), 'Informal family-based care work in the Austrian care arrangement', in B. Pfau-Effinger and B. Geissler (eds), *Care and Social Integration in European Societies*, Bristol: Policy Press, pp. 173–94.
Lewis, J. (1992), 'Gender and the development of welfare regimes', *Journal of European Social Policy*, **2** (3), 159–73.
Lewis, J. and I. Ostner (eds) (1994), *Gender and the Evolution of European Social Policy*, Working Chapter 4 of the Centre for Social Policy Research, University of Bremen.
Kreimer, M. (ed.) (2009), *Ökonomie der Geschlechterdifferenz: Zur Persistenz des Gender Gap*, Wiesbaden: VS Verlag für Sozialwissenschaften.
Mätzke, M. and I. Ostner (2010), 'The role of old ideas in the new German family policy agenda', *German Policy Studies*, **6** (1), 119–61.
Müller-Muralt, J. (2014), 'Schweiz als familienpolitisches, Entwicklungsland', *Schweizer Revue*, **2**, 54–63.
Nadai, E. and M. Nollert (eds) (2015), *Geschlechterverhältnisse im Post-Wohlfahrtsstaat*, Weinheim and Basel: Beltz Juventa.
OECD (2015), *Employment Outlook*, Paris: OECD.
Pfau-Effinger, B. (1998), 'Gender cultures and the gender arrangement – a theoretical framework for cross-national comparisons on gender', *Innovation: The European Journal of Social Sciences*, **11** (2), 147–66.
Pfau-Effinger, B. (ed.) (2004), *Development of Culture, Welfare States and Women's Employment in Europe*, Aldershot: Ashgate.
Pfau-Effinger, B. (2005a), 'Culture and welfare state policies: reflections on a complex interrelation', *Journal of Social Policy*, **34** (1), 3–20.
Pfau-Effinger, B. (2005b), 'Welfare state policies and care arrangements', *European Societies*, **7** (2), 321–47.
Pfau-Effinger, B. and T. Euler (2014), 'Wandel der Einstellungen zu Kinderbetreuung und Elternschaft in Europa – Persistenz kultureller Differenzen', *Soziale Welt*, **20** (1), 175–94.
Pfau-Effinger, B. and M. Smidt (2011), 'Differences in women's employment patterns and family policies: Eastern and Western Germany', *Community, Work and Family*, **14** (2), 217–32.
Pierson, P. (2000), 'Increasing returns, path dependence, and the study of politics', *American Political Science Review*, **94** (2), 251–67.
Reimer, T. (ed.) (2013), *Elterngeld: Analyse der Wirkungen*, Wiesbaden: Springer VS.
Saxonberg, S. (2014), *Gendering Family Policies in Post-Communist Europe*, Houndmills, Basingstoke: Palgrave Macmillan.
Schmid, T., I. Kriesi, and M. Buchmann (2011), 'Wer nutzt familienergänzende Kinderbetreuung? Die Betreuungssituation 6-jähriger Kinder in der Schweiz', *Swiss Journal of Sociology*, **37** (1), 9–32.
Schratzenstaller, M. (2015), 'Familienpolitische Leistungen in Österreich im Überblick', *WIFO-Monatsberichte*, **88** (3), 185–94.
Seeleib-Kaiser, M. (2010), 'Socio-economic change, party competition and intraparty conflict: the family policy of the grand coalition', *German Politics*, **19** (3–4), 416–28.
Sobotka, T. (2011), 'Fertility in Austria, Germany and Switzerland: is there a common pattern?', *Comparative Population Studies*, **36** (2–3), 263–304.
Stutz, H. (2006), 'Familienpolitik in der Schweiz', in E. Carigiet, M. Opielka, and F. Schulz-Nieswand (eds), *Wohlstand durch Gerechtigkeit: Deutschland und die Schweiz im sozialpolitischen Vergleich*, Basel: Rotpunktverlag, pp. 135–45.
Wecker, R. (2006), 'Gender und Care: Veränderungen und Traditionen in der Sozialpolitik der Schweiz', in E. Carigiet, M. Opielka, and F. Schulz-Nieswand (eds), *Wohlstand durch Gerechtigkeit: Deutschland und die Schweiz im sozialpolitischen Vergleich*, Basel: Rotpunktverlag, pp. 227–38.

14. The UK and the US: liberal models despite family policy expansion?
Dorian R. Woods

INTRODUCTION

The UK and the US governments design their child and family policy within a liberal model of social policy. This label 'liberal' does not mean 'free and easy' or connote a political 'leftist' orientation of a person or institution. The term 'liberal', instead, characterizes liberal ideas of minimal economic regulation and social policy. The 'liberal' model of the UK and the US connotes a well-running economy will by default boost the prosperity of families. Extensive family policy is therefore superfluous in free markets that supply services for family needs. Such markets encourage individual freedom, flexibility and innovation to meet demand. Free markets and minimal social policy differ, however, and a comparison of the UK and the US is informative for understanding policy diversity among liberal cases. The UK and the US are often at the opposite spectrum of 'liberalism', with their own historical legacies, policy instruments and power dynamics. Even under similar initial intentions and policy instruments, the UK and US have differing trajectories. Readers interested in a liberal model for viable options in cost-containment or austerity measures might be surprised to learn that family policy measures have grown in the UK and US during the last two decades. They have undergone transformations, making family policy more explicit and in some ways more extensive (see Chapter 2 by Gauthier and Koops in this volume; Woods, 2012). Such growth calls for a re-examination of these liberal market-family-state dynamics.

This chapter pursues the following questions: To what extent have developments in the US and the UK followed a liberal family policy agenda and how have they been similar or different? The chapter first outlines the theoretical approach to liberal family policy and how family policy in the UK and the US has been compared. The subsequent and main sections explore British and US-American policy developments from the 1980s to the present. In particular, these sections examine the agendas, policy settings and instruments of income maintenance, early childhood education and care services (ECEC), tax credits and family leave policies. The final section of the chapter draws conclusions about UK and US similarities and differences in family policy, as well as the development of liberal ideals and approaches.

LIBERAL FAMILY POLICY

The literature on family policy has consistently labeled the UK and the US as 'liberal' because of their design and justification of policies with classical liberal ideals of minimal state intervention and reliance on the market. Kamerman and Kahn (1997) and O'Connor et al. (1999) were some of the first to explicitly compare 'liberal' family policy across countries (see also Chapter 5 by Lohmann and Zagel in this volume). Kamerman and Kahn's research emerged out of an international study of family policy from the 1970s, one of the first of its kind to systematically categorize family services and instruments. Later, O'Connor et al. explored women's equality within liberal models of Australia, Canada, the UK and the US (1999). They examined data and policy in the areas of employment, social security, ECEC, anti-discrimination, poverty and reproduction policies. A characteristic of liberal family policy, they concluded, is high inequality among women with different family types and labor force participation as well as disparities due to class, race and ethnicity. Additional authors, such as Anttonen and Sipilä (1996), characterize the UK's care system as Anglo-Saxon with an emphasis on means-testing and a focus more on elderly than ECEC services. Other authors, such as Orloff (1993a, p. 20), draw similarities between liberal policy development in minimal service intervention in Britain, Canada and the US, stating that it was politically reinforced through the combination of early targeted insurance-based policies and reactively late developments of additional social policy for the needs of a wider population. Generally, the liberal cases of the UK and the US are characterized by implicit and residual family policy with a high tolerance for inequality.

Analytically, the liberal British and US-American models have been said to have 'market defamilization': this means that the market overwhelmingly provides family services for families in place of extensive state supports (Esping-Andersen, 1999; Lohmann and Zagel, 2016). For example, the liberal model will promote inexpensive (and widely available) child care through the market. The 'minimalistic' characterization of liberal family policy in current debates originated from Esping-Andersen's (1990) category of liberal states' low 'decommodification' which also describes (minimal) state intervention, but in relation to employment regulations and benefits. Decommodification measures the extent to which the state unburdens individuals' risk in the labor market and the term became controversal in terms of its application to women and families. According to Orloff (1993b), the main problem of this analysis was that it could not account for women's inability to head households as men do: constrained by extra responsibilities in the home, women cannot directly engage in the labor market to the full extent that men can and so cannot be similarly 'decommodified' as men. Lewis and Ostner (1994) followed with an examination on the extent to which women's risk is measured, not dependent on the market but dependent on male breadwinners. Responding to these critiques and others, Esping-Andersen adopted the terms 'familialization' and 'defamilialization' from Lister (1995) and McLaughlin and Glendinning (1994). The terms are complementary to decommodification: Before decommodification can take place, 'familialization' and 'defamilialization' set the stage relative to how families care for their members and are available to work in the labor market. Extensive defamilialization, in effect, frees the family from extra care duties so that they can engage in paid employment. Once family members enter the labor market, according to this analysis, varying degrees of decommodification can follow (see more on these arguments in Woods, 2006).

However, the original intention of measuring/evaluating an individual's risk is lost in the various steps of defamilialization and this is particularly problematic for examining family policy in liberal models. First of all, the assumed time sequence of defamilialization (i.e., it must occur before commodification and decommodification) does not apply in a liberal model because adults with care responsibilities do not wait to be defamilialized before they enter the labor market. 'Market defamilialization' can only apply to some families who have the means to afford ECEC at market prices (even if these prices are relatively low). In the liberal model, often child care is privately organized among extended relatives or neighbors, or there is the phenomenon of latch-key children among low-income families. Differences in purchasing power affect the access to (quality) care and reduction of overall risk of individuals and families. Thus, 'market defamilialization' applies so unequally to individuals and families in liberal welfare state models that it is difficult to apply the term for family policy in general or to measure/evaluate individuals' or families' risk in particular. Instead, the term 'market defamilialization' seems to describe a liberal state's prevailing high tolerance for unequal access to family supports.

And yet, it is questionable to characterize liberal welfare states as having only negligible state intervention and a more nuanced exploration of liberal family policy is needed. In order to better illustrate liberal family policy in light of this ambiguity, the chapter examines the UK and the US because the literature differentiates between them as two opposites on a liberal spectrum. The US is often called the 'exceptional' welfare state because of its extremes. For example, the US has been characterized as a 'pure liberal welfare state' with high inequality (Castles and Mitchell, 1993). O'Connor et al. emphasize the US primacy of the market and its more severe public and private division compared to the UK (1999, pp. 28–9, 226–7). Many authors have pointed to a 'gender sameness' strategy in US politics for creating social policy that emphasizes women's and men's similar needs while de-emphasizing gender role differences in child bearing/care, elderly care or household responsibilities (Lewis, 2009; O'Connor et al., 1999; Baker and Tippin, 1999). On the other hand, the UK has often taken a 'difference' approach, which is apparent, for example, in how many policies were initially established and developed for mothers. While the UK follows a liberal focus of means-testing and targeting certain groups in benefits, many of these programs fall under a larger rubric of social services and this has consequences for the extent and eligibility of benefit receipt as well as for policy legitimization. For example, the UK's income assistance program supplies support for a wide range of clientele, and does not primarily target single mothers as the US does. Most notably, the UK has a history of universal health care and a larger public housing sector than the US, so that social intervention is more embedded in the UK system (Walker and Wiseman, 2003; Woods, 2012).

Differences between the UK and the US can be observed in the spending levels, poverty rates and 'generosity' of benefits. Table 14.1 illustrates that the UK spent 4.3 percent of its gross domestic product (GDP) on family benefits in 2011 compared to 1.11 percent in the US. ECEC expenditure is similarly more generous in the UK where spending was 1.1 percent compared to 0.04 percent of GDP in the US. Poverty rates in liberal countries tend to be high but the UK brought its child income poverty rate down to 10.4 percent in 2011 (lower than the average of 13 percent for Organisation for Economic Co-operation and Development, OECD, countries) while the US had a child income poverty rate of 20.9 percent. A comparison of poverty rates by household seems to indicate that the US depends on the job market to reduce poverty (Table 14.1) as households with more earners have fewer rates of poverty.

The UK and the US also illustrate variance in state intervention, for example, in family leave. Maternal paid leave in the UK is 39 weeks (with 52 weeks of protected leave

Table 14.1 Family and family policy characteristics

	UK	US	OECD[a]
Total public spending on family benefits (% of GDP) 2011[b]	4.3	1.2	2.55
Child income poverty rate (% of children 0–17) 2012[c]	10.4	20.9	13.3
Poverty rates by households with at least one child (%) 2012[c]			
One adult, jobless	27.7	84.7	62.6
One adult, one earner	7.5	33.1	20.0
Two adults, jobless	37.2	64.0	60.7
Two adults, one earner	13.1	24.8	19.6
Two adults, two earner	2.3	5.1	4.0
All households	9.8	16.0	10.3
Total public spending on ECEC (% of GDP) 2012[d]	1.1	0.4	0.8
Children in public child care by age (%) 2013[e]			
0–2 year olds	35.1	28.0	32.9
3–5 year olds (2012)	96.3	65.7	82.0[f]
Out-of-pocket child care costs (% of family net income) 2012[g]			
Dual earner (full-time earnings, 150% of average wage)	34.0	29.0	13.0
Single parent (full-time earnings, 50% of average wage)	8.0	52.0	14.0
Maternal and paternal leave length (weeks) 2015[h]			
Maternal paid	39.0	0.0	52.6
Maternal protected	70.0	12.0	n.a.
Paternal paid	2.0	0.0	9.1
Paternal protected	20.0	12.0	n.a.
Employment rates (%) 2013			
All men aged 25–54[i]	86.5	82.8	84.9
All women aged 25–54[j]	75.2	69.3	71.8[f]
Mothers (15–65) with at least one child aged 0–14[j]	66.6	65.0	66.8[f]
Fertility rate 2014[k]	1.8	1.9	1.7

Notes:
Websites last accessed 4 October 2017.
a. OECD-30 average, when not otherwise noted.
b. http://www.oecd.org/els/family/database.htm – PF1_1_Public_spending_on_family_benefits_Oct2013-1.
c. http://www.oecd.org/social/family/database.htm – CO2.2, Child poverty.
d. http://www.oecd.org/els/family/database.htm – PF3.1, Public spending on childcare and early education.
e. http://www.oecd.org/social/family/database.htm – PF3.2, Enrolment in childcare and pre-school.
f. OECD-28 average.
g. https://www.oecd.org/els/soc/PF_3_4_Childcare_support_May2014.pdf.
h. https://www.oecd.org/els/soc/PF2_1_Parental_leave_systems.pdf, Total paid leave available to mothers.
i. https://stats.oecd.org/Index.aspx?DataSetCode=LFS_SEXAGE_I_R.
j. http://www.oecd.org/els/family/database.htm – LMF1.2, Maternal employment.
k. https://data.oecd.org/pop/fertility-rates.htm.

altogether). The US is 'exceptional' in that it has no federal compensation for maternity leave but 12 weeks a year of protected unpaid leave for both mothers and fathers. There are a few states that provide paid leave, such as California, but availability of this is usually dependent on employers. Out-of-pocket ECEC costs are 52 percent of family net income for single parents in the US. In contrast, out-of-pocket ECEC costs for single parents in the UK are 8 percent because of a directed effort to reduce costs for this household type.

The labor force participation rate of mothers in the UK and in the US is similar with 66.6 percent and 65 percent, respectively (with an OECD average of 66.8 percent) and fertility rates (1.8 and 1.9 percent, respectively) are also similar to the OECD average (1.7 percent).

Varying degrees of 'targeting' and 'generosity' in family policies beg the question as to how the UK and the US, as liberal models, have grown and developed in the past couple of decades and how they have (or have not) towed a liberal line of policy. The UK experienced a series of programs as it transitioned from the austerity era of the Thatcher and Major governments to an explicit expansion in the Blair and Brown governments to the Liberal/Conservative Coalition under Cameron and the subsequent May government. In the same way, the US has developed clear family policy instruments as it progressed from the administrations of Reagan and Bush Sr into the Clinton and then Bush Jr administrations, then into the Obama and now the Trump administrations.

UK CHARACTERISTICS AND DEVELOPMENTS

The UK experienced the most dramatic changes to family policy in the late 1990s and 2000s. In the previous decades leading up to this, the Thatcher and Major governments had consistently curbed policy measures with cuts in spending and eligibility. In conjunction with 'Thatcherism', the government, for example, froze the universal child benefit in 1987 and let one-parent allowances erode in their real value over time. These policies became less central as family policies, and the means-tested programs, such as the Income Support and a new Family Credit program, grew more prominent. The eligibility criteria became more stringent for the means-tested Family Credit and Income Support so that dual-earner families dropped out of this program and the clientele became narrower, creating more stigmatizing effects for the policy. The Family Credit had an in-work allowance, but, at the same time, the Conservative government was ambivalent about work incentives for mothers. To ease poverty in low-income single-parent family households, the government, instead, focused on child support enforcement as a policy. But the policy proved unpopular and difficult to enforce. Aside from income-based policy, there was a growing public demand for ECEC. The debates around ECEC had become so present in the public sphere that John Major, in his campaign for prime minister, followed his rivals and pledged universal nursery education for 3- and 4-year-olds. In 1994 the new Major Conservative government introduced nursery vouchers and a means-tested ECEC supplement for those not receiving support through the Family Credit. Both the residual nature of these Thatcher and Major policies as well as the government's turn to market solutions for family policy can be characterized as 'liberal' family policy.

In 1997 the Blair government won a landslide victory with the New Labour 'Third Way' agenda which transformed family policy in the UK from what it had been. Labour's New Deal program was a welfare-to-work program embodying new ideas of the incoming party. It had aimed first to reduce the high unemployment rates of young people, but quickly the government expanded New Deal clientele to all those economically inactive or 'workless', including single mothers. Initial pilot studies and then a full New Deal for Lone Parents program targeted single parents with school children first, and was then extended to parents with younger children, and eventually to children under 3 years of age. Voluntary interviews and counseling evolved into mandatory requirements.

Emphasizing the responsibility to work in order to achieve independence, the government argued that it was committed to ending social exclusion through employment. Also, the government set out a national goal to halve child poverty by 2010 and eradicate it by 2020. As part of this plan, the new government set up a National Childcare Strategy, the Sure Start programs and the Childcare Tax Credit to replace the Conservative nursery voucher system and the child care supplement. Officials explicitly stated in policy papers that the scarcity and cost of good quality ECEC were recognized as indubitable reasons why women in particular, and especially lone parents, were not able to take up paid work (Wheatley, 2001, pp. 47–8). Bringing down high prices of care and improving services would encourage women's employment. ECEC support would assist parents and single mothers in low-paid work and prevent poverty: a mother's employment and earnings would be important in preventing low incomes, and these earnings could in turn also benefit the national economy by reducing the number of families relying on means-tested benefits (Brown, 1997, sec. 121). This was a high-profile issue to promote 'social inclusion instead of exclusion'. The Sure Start program was loosely based on Head Start in the US and was targeted at improving disadvantaged children's care and education. New Labour broke substantially away from previous family policy in its expanse and explicitness. At the same time, true to liberal ideals, Labour emphasized means-testing and focused on child care in mainly disadvantaged areas. In addition, couched in liberalism, the Labor government promoted 'partnerships' between the private and public sector for ECEC enlargement as a conglomerate of local initiatives with business associations.

The Labour government promoted mothers' employment as it stimulated employment in general with tax credits and incentives for low-income families. The government first replaced the Family Credit with Working Families' Tax Credit in 1999 and eventually changed it to the Working Tax Credit, phased in during 2003 and 2004. This credit was inspired by the US Earned Income Tax Credit that gives working low-income families and individuals additional payments (depending on hours worked) to boost overall income. As in the US, the credit was payable through the wage packet and administrated by the Inland Revenue (instead of the Department of Social Security). This symbolically emphasized work and not benefits. In addition, the government introduced a minimum wage. Policies shifted focus away from a breadwinner model towards policies that focused on families with children regardless of marriage status: the Children's Tax Credit was a non-refundable tax credit for two years from the period April 2001 to April 2003. It replaced the Married Couple's Allowance (MCA) from the previous Conservative government. Through the new policy, married couples without children lost a tax break, and families with children saw their tax break more than double in value, especially advantaging families with children under 1 year of age (Brewer and Gregg, 2003). Its predecessor, the Child Tax Credit, was also means-tested: the Labour government continued to uphold mothers' employment but it focused on targeted and means-tested family policy.

Another explicit turn-around from the previous Conservative government was Labour's maternity and parental leave. It became more far-reaching and more generous than any previous UK family leave. The UK had inherited a maternity pay framework from the Beveridge health insurance plan. This was later linked to maternity leave but by the time the Conservative government succeeded in 1979, its terms of eligibility and pay were complex. The 1980 and 1982 Employment Act and the Social Security Act in 1986 actually made it more complicated (Ringen, 1997, pp. 51ff.). During the 1980s, the Conservative government also restricted the Protection of Pregnant Women at Work, weakening women's right to return to their jobs after pregnancy. While the European Community was developing its social plan (including a minimal family leave) in the 1980s, the UK did not sign the Social Charter in 1989, ignored the Maastricht Treaty 1991, and refused to accept the European Council Directive EEC 92/85 on Pregnant Workers in 1992. But with pressure from Europe, the Conservative government offered alternatives in the Trade Union Reform and Employment Rights Act 1993. Maternity rights were extended to 14 weeks of maternity leave with statutory sick pay and eligibility was improved by reducing the length of service qualification to 12 months for the higher rates. Momentum grew for family leave as New Labour came to power, and following the European Council Directive (EC) 96/34 on Parental Leave, the government extended maternity leave in 1999 to 18 weeks of ordinary maternity leave, bringing it in line with the same period for entitlement to Statutory Maternity Pay. Rights for mothers were strengthened and streamlined, with a reduction of the two-year eligibility restriction to one. A right to unpaid parental leave for three months was introduced for parents with children under 5 years of age. The Welfare Reform and Pensions Act 1999 also expanded Statutory Maternity Allowance so that more low-income women were eligible (Ogus et al., 2002, p. 560). For the first time, in 2003, paid paternity leave was enacted and adoptive parents were included.

The dramatic increases in (comparatively generous) explicit UK family policy during the Labour government have not been seen since, although the Liberal/Conservative Coalition government under Cameron placed its own accents on family policy. Interestingly, family issues remained a central aspect in social policy for the government, documented by the announcement of the prime minister that all domestic policy would be subject to a 'family test' to understand its impact on families. As Knijn, Martin and Ostner explain in Chapter 12 on parental policy reform generally in this volume, the Cameron government focused on Conservative values of family, minimal government and individual responsibility. One example of this was the government's replacement of Labour's welfare-to-work Jobseeker's Allowance and Income Support with Universal Credit. Recipients of Universal Credit are required to accept and sign contracts ('claimant commitments') with their case workers ('work coaches') before receipt of benefits. Outlined are responsibilities to find work, or if recipients are already in work, they must increase their earnings. Sanctions or cuts in benefits can last up to three years. Work requirements, however, were eliminated for 'primary carers' with children under 3 years of age. Part-time work is required for primary carers when children are aged 3 to 12, and Universal Credit requires full-time work for carers when their children are aged 13 and older. The Credit is no longer paid to the individual, but rather paid in a lump sum to the household. Austerity has been an issue as well: the government has restricted migrants' access to Universal Credit and added a strong element of combating fraud. New are across-the-board caps on all out-of-work benefits except for the Working Tax Credit. Thus, Housing Benefit, Child Tax Credit, Child Benefit and Maternity Allowance, among others, are calculated together. Single adults are allowed up to £296 per week, and couples and lone parents are allowed up to £442 per week. True to liberal ideals of minimal government, the administration has also implemented a program that incentivizes personal responsibility of divorced parents to negotiate their own arrangements around child maintenance.

These current developments emphasize individual responsibility and place many family obligations of individuals back into the private sphere. Family policies have remained explicit, but more emphasis has been on austerity, sanctions and targeting – as well as on personal responsibility and individual (or city) 'contracts' with the government. For example, the Troubled Families program is designed to provide financial support to communities dealing with difficult individuals and their families. The government only pays the promised lump sum in full dependent on whether services have positive results. The community concentrates on servicing families whose members are involved in 'anti-social behavior' and crime, families that have truant children, or families that have an adult on out-of-work benefits and where a family has caused the community high costs. Targeting specific recipient groups is typical of liberal policy and instrumenting means-testing measures (often with stigmatization) is in line with liberal welfare state policy making. However, these last examples show that services explicitly bind individuals more closely to familial units. By concentrating on families and not individuals, policy is practicing a form of familialization, not defamilialization. This short historical view seems to show that defamilialization, or the unburdening of familial risk, tends to fluctuate, depending on outside pressures and who is in power. When the Labour government incorporated defamilialization in the late 1990s and early 2000s, the party bound this closely with business and market partnerships, clearly a form of market defamilialization. In all, however, the above policy-making examples from both Conservative and Labour parties show that liberal policies explicitly aim to intervene in directing family members' behavior, which is not necessarily the 'neutral' policy espoused for liberal non-intervention in families and in the market. 'Liberal' policy seems to intervene readily into families.

US CHARACTERISTICS AND DEVELOPMENTS

Just as tensions and differing interpretations of family policy arose in the UK between the Conservative and Labour governments, so too did Republicans and Democrats place distinct accents on the unfolding of US family policy. Especially in the 1990s, the policies were reinterpreted and transformed from the Reagan/Bush era to the Clinton administration. As Thatcherism boomed in the UK, the Reagan administration promoted what was to become known as 'Reaganomics', introducing large cuts in government expenditure on social policy and reducing taxes as well as embarking on decentralization. Austerity measures for social policy were conveyed with the idea of paternalism, that is, a state's encouragement through policy to promote benefit recipients' self-sufficiency. Similarly to the Thatcher and Major governments, the Reagan and Bush Sr governments were ambivalent about mothers' employment, first reducing work incentives in social assistance and then reintroducing them. The government's first 1981 budget reduced social assistance eligibility, income disregards in benefit calculations and recipients' deductions for work-related and ECEC expenditures. This caused a certain type of welfare recipient to slowly emerge, as some recipients lost eligibility because of too high earnings and others reduced their employment to stay on benefits and receive Medicaid. Seven years later, the Family Support Act reintroduced work-oriented family allowances with increased earnings disregards, transitional ECEC and Medicaid. Added was the Job Opportunities and Basic Skills Program (JOBS) that required training participation for women and workfare for Aid to Families with Dependent Children (AFDC)-recipient fathers. Implicitly, the policies became more targeted in the first stage but reached a wider recipient pool in the second round. Still, the employment of fathers was emphasized more than mothers. A significant change to social assistance under the Republican administration was the programs' elements of decentralization, as legislation allowed states to experiment. These state trials could include 'family caps' (i.e., denial of additional benefits for children born while a mother is still on welfare), work requirements, provision of cash supplements for the education of low-income workers, as well as time limits on cash benefits.

ECEC under the Reagan and Bush administrations was interpreted through distinct liberal ideals. As public pressure for improved ECEC arose, Democrats proposed the Act for Better Child Care (ABC) in 1987. This would have established federal grants for ECEC for low-income families, improved ECEC for all families and created national standards. As an alternative, the Republicans offered tax credits and vouchers, concentrating on means-tested ECEC for low-income families. As a compromise, the Child Care and Development Block Grant and the At-Risk Child Care Program were enacted as part of the Omnibus Budget Reconciliation Act of 1990. The legislation was the first of its kind to extend beyond families on social assistance and provide low-income families with ECEC. However, the Republican Party was more interested in expanding the Earned Income Tax Credit (EITC) as an alternative to publicly funded ECEC. Republicans argued that the EITC refund money would give families an individual choice to pay for ECEC or perform it themselves. These tax returns might support a traditional male breadwinner model, if families chose to compensate one parent to stay out of the workforce. The Republican administration found the EITC attractive, and considerably expanded it twice. The other expansion took place in 1986, as Congress was negotiating tax reform in the budget and the Democrats and Republicans were at loggerheads on raising the minimum wage.

Coming to power in 1993, the Clinton administration offered an alternative direction for family policy. In the election campaign, Clinton proposed 'ending welfare as we know it' with drastically changing welfare policies, ECEC and family leave. On the one hand, expansive policies were put on the table, such as universal child care and universal health care as well as more generous instruments that would 'make work pay' (such as a wider-reaching EITC). On the other hand, in the process of recreating itself in the election process, the Democratic Party publically shifted its ideology: the party of 'New Democrats' embraced the dominant discussion around fiscal and personal responsibility as well as self-sufficiency. Also, as a former governor, Clinton was not opposed to devolution of national policy to the state. These new ideas laid the foundation for a different dynamic in the negotiations over policy. For example, discussions around social assistance were focused more on single mothers and employment, and less on issues such as poverty and children (Weaver, 2000). Furthermore, Clinton adopted family leave as a major issue. In his election campaign, Clinton had promised to sign the Family and Medical Leave Act (FMLA) into law after the bill had gone through several transformations and two vetoes during the Bush Sr administration. From early on in the bill's development, policymakers had settled for an unpaid leave in their negotiations with coalition partners, considering a paid leave as too controversial for getting the necessary votes in Congress (Elving, 1995). The Clinton administration signed it unchanged as its first law in 1993, and the FMLA became the first US national family leave policy to protect employees from losing their job for missing work due to familial or medical reasons.

The beginning of Clinton's administration saw policy movements on other fronts. The 1993 Omnibus Budget Reconciliation Act increased the maximum credit rate available for the EITC and the income level at which individuals could qualify for the credit. It also allowed certain low-income taxpayers without children to receive the credit for the first time. The Republican control of Congress in 1996 with the 'Contract with America' campaign narrowed Democrats' room to negotiate family policy, however. By connecting child care to welfare (to work programs), the Clinton administration showed that it considered ECEC as a workforce issue. The Clinton administration held a readiness to 'leave it to the states' so that block grants for social assistance and ECEC became quickly uncontested. Since this legislation, individual states have the discretion to direct this funding to ECEC as they see fit or redirect it to other programs. The ensuing Child Care Development Block Grant no longer entitled single parents to ECEC and established no federal requirements for care quality. A two-year limit on welfare payments was introduced with a lifetime five-year limit that parents had to benefits. After 1996, Congress and the administration could not agree on further developments for the EITC.

There has been little family policy change on the US federal level since the transformations into more explicit US family policy during the Clinton administration. The law Temporary Assistance for Needy Families (TANF) with the child care block grants still stands from 1997. Just as the UK has continued to uphold the importance of family in its current political discussions around policy, so too have recent adminstrations emphasized family. However, the Obama administration set accents on fathers' roles in families. For example, state programs focused on preparing fathers for gainful employment, for their taking more responsibility for child care maintenance and child involvement. Policy discussions in the Obama administration placed less political intensity on single mothers' employment compared to the TANF debates during the Clinton administration. Because of the difficulty of the Obama administration and Congress's ability to pass federal budgets, temporary funding to bridge gaps increased the precariousness of policies and burdened the states' abilities to plan long term. On the other hand, momentum for family policy innovation and change can be observed at the state level for paid family leave, such as the expansion of eligibility or leave length. Paid programs were implemented in California in 2004, New Jersey in 2009, Rhode Island in 2014 and New York in 2016. Insurance programs that act similarly to parental leave are also in place in Hawaii, Washington, DC, and Puerto Rico. The proposed family policy from the Trump administration includes ECEC and paid maternity leave, but there remain some questions about how this policy will develop in Congress, because of costs, estimates of negative effects for low-income families and its targeting of only mothers, not to mention partisan politics that has made policy making difficult. In 2015 President Obama issued a presidential memorandum for federal employees to receive up to six weeks of paid leave after birth, adoption or fostering of a new child, and the Trump administration has followed suit with interest in supporting a bill introduced in Congress with this legislation. These changes all point to more US government involvement in family policy, which is not necessarily a liberal trait. However, because ECEC is targeted to the very needy and not guaranteed, the EITC is means-tested and family leave regulations are unpaid (and cover only about half of the working population), all characteristics point to liberal tendencies. Policies remain rudimentary and decentralized, so that a more detailed account of market defamilialization would need to be examined on the individual state level. Just as in the UK, however, the US has explicitly aimed to direct family behavior, and this involvement stands in contrast to liberal welfare states' minimal involvement in market regulations and family affairs.

CONCLUSION

The family policies in the UK and the US have progressed somewhat similarly. Since the 1980s the UK and the US have instrumented a series of programs that have made family policy more explicit. These developments were especially apparent in the 1990s and early 2000s. The UK and the US considerably expanded their family leave, tax credits and, at certain junctions, they broadened public ECEC to include not only social assistance recipients but also low-income families – a policy otherwise instituted only during historical war times. The UK and the US overhauled policies addressing parents' employment and streamlined welfare-to-work programs. In many cases, they appropriated ideas and policy from one another: for example, the Blair government borrowed extensively from the Clinton administration on single mothers' employability and on tax credits for low-income families. The UK and the US have both made families and parenting more of a public concern, and expanded policy, for the most part, by emphasizing 'activation' into employment.

Explicit and expanded family policy is, on first consideration, surprising and uncharacteristic of liberal states in itself. However, this might not be so surprising after observing general trends in family policy expansion across developed welfare states, as documented in other chapters of this *Handbook*. And UK and US expansion has consistently emphasized liberal ideals with minimal policy. This is apparent in the welfare states' insistence on building partnerships with business communities and in repeated exploration of market solutions for social problems, such as vouchers and business tax breaks (e.g., in ECEC). The liberal idea of personal responsibility is epitomized in the continuous contractual emphasis on benefit receipt. For example, policy has been justified on the grounds that it helps individuals 'lift themselves out of poverty' and government support should be a 'hand up' instead of a 'hand-out'. The UK and the US have followed a liberal family policy agenda in that they emphasize means-testing for the very needy and encourage the market and employment to be solutions for poverty and social risk problems. This is so much so that the market should work: for example, political discourse in the Clinton administration and the Blair government emphasized 'it must pay to work'. This has been echoed in current UK political discourse around raising the minimum wage. Liberal ideals of labor market participation, freedom and choice have been an integral and consistent part of the expansion and explicitness of family policy in the UK and the US.

While the UK and the US have experienced similar trajectories, some issues seem to stand out in having particularly influenced differing policy developments. First of all, party politics and institutional settings were extremely important in each case. The need for congressional consensus played and still plays a decisive role in the US. This has tended to promote compromises for minimal standards during policy making. The UK, on the other hand, has been held to more generous European standards that have tended to encourage more largesse. A second issue, related to the first, was the UK's high child poverty rate in the 1990s and the Labour government's commitment to eliminating it. This made it easier to justify higher benefits for needy families with children and reform across policy areas – not just in activation policies. In contrast, policymakers in the US have focused on poverty primarily as an employment issue. This encourages reform to focus less on children than on adult policy recipients. Less focus on child vulnerability encourages less generosity in coverage. A third significant difference between the UK and the US has been approaches to gender roles. The consideration of policy impact on men and women has had more of a presence in policy making in the UK than in the US. For example, the Blair, the Brown and the Cameron governments continuously addressed whether benefits should be paid to the 'purse' or the 'wallet', indicating that the choice of benefit recipient (the carer or the breadwinner) ultimately influences how family members share or redistribute their resources. US policymakers have de-emphasized gendered effects of redistribution within the household and more readily take a gender-neutral approach. Race and ethnity has been a fourth issue that has been incorporated in policy making differently in the UK and the US. For example, US social assistance policy-making debates in the 1990s characterized recipients as African-Americans, and this perception and dialog of 'otherness' might have encouraged less solidarity generally. On the other hand, the Labour Party debated social assistance reform with repect to how it impacted different community groups.

Overall, the UK and US have constantly upheld liberal ideals during an uncharacteristic expansion of explicit family policy, even if their policy has varied in generosity and eligibility, but a nuanced exploration of family policy development in these two opposite sides of the liberal spectrum exposes some issues. The UK and the US have consistently upheld the primacy of the market for solving social problems, for example, with means-testing or with private partnerships in public services, but when policy in the UK and the US remains minimal, we still know very little about what this means for family members' interdependence (familialization) or the extent of market defamilialization to unburden familial responsibilities. Indeed, differences in generosity in allowances and eligibility – as well as their gendered and racial impacts – call for a closer examination of familialization and defamilialization characteristics in liberal regimes and social risk. This chapter illustrates that the US and the UK deliberately intervene into family lives and explicitly aim to influence individual behavior. This calls into question the very nature of what 'liberal' claims, in terms of encouraging freedom and individual choice. It seems as if liberal policy has different standards for families than for the markets. This chapter chronicles policy making in the UK and the US with comparable liberal ideas, policy instruments and institutional settings for family policy developments, and provides food for thought in terms of liberal states' involvement in families' lives.

REFERENCES

Anttonen, A. and J. Sipilä (1996), 'European social care services. Is it possible to identify models?', *Journal of European Social Policy*, **6** (2), 87–100.

Baker, M. and D. Tippin (1999), *Poverty, Social Assistance, and the Employability of Mothers: Restructuring Welfare States*, Toronto: University of Toronto Press.

Brewer, M. and P. Gregg (2003), 'Eradicating child poverty in Britain: welfare reform and children since 1997', in R. Walker and M. Wiseman (eds), *The Welfare We Want? The British Challenge for American Reform*, Bristol: Polity Press, pp. 81–114.

Brown, G. (1997), *The Chancellor's 1997 Budget Speech*, HM Treasury, accessed 2 July 2003 at http://archive.treasury.gov.uk/pub/html/budget97/speech.html.

Castles, F.G. and D. Mitchell (1993), 'Worlds of welfare and families of nations', in F.G. Castles (ed.), *Families of Nations: Patterns of Public Policy in Western Democracies*, Aldershot: Dartmouth, pp. 93–128.

Elving, R.D. (1995), *Conflict and Compromise: How Congress Makes the Law*, New York: Simon and Schuster.

Esping-Andersen, G. (1990), *The Three Worlds of Welfare Capitalism*, Cambridge: Polity Press.

Esping-Andersen, G. (1999), *Social Foundations of Postindustrial Economies*, Oxford: Oxford University Press.

Kamerman, S.B. and A.J. Kahn (eds) (1997), *Family Change and Family Policies in Great Britain, Canada, New Zealand, and the United States: Family Change and Family Policies in the West*, Oxford: Clarendon Press.

Lewis, J. (2009), *Work-family Balance, Gender and Policy*, Cheltenham, UK and and Northhampton, MA, USA: Edward Elgar Publishing.

Lewis, J. and I. Ostner (1994), 'Gender and the evolution of European social policies', ZeS- Discussion paper, Bremen, pp. 1–62.

Lister, R. (1995), 'Dilemmas in engendering citizenship', *Economy and Society*, **24** (l), 1–40.

Lohmann, H. and H. Zagel (2016), 'Family policy in comparative perspective: the concepts and measurement of familization and defamilization', *Journal of European Social Policy*, **26** (1), 48–65.

McLaughlin, E. and C. Glendinning (1994), 'Paying for care in Europe: is there a feminist approach?', in L. Hantrais and S. Morgan (eds), *Concepts and Contexts in International Comparisons: Family Policy and the Welfare of Women*, Longborough: Center for European Studies, pp. 62–9.

O'Conner, J.S., A.S. Orloff, and S. Shaver (1999), *States, Markets, Families. Gender, Liberalism and Social Policy in Australia, Canada, Great Britain and the United States*, Cambridge: Cambridge University Press.

Ogus, A.I., E.M. Barendt, and N. Wikeley (eds) (2002), *The Law of Social Security*, 5th edn, London: Lexis Nexis.

Orloff, A.S. (1993a), *The Politics of Pensions: A Comparative Analysis of Britain, Canada and the United States, 1880s–1940*, Madison, WI: University of Wisconsin Press.

Orloff, A.S. (1993b), 'Gender and the social rights of citizenship: state policies and gender relations in comparative research', *American Sociological Review*, **58** (3), 303–28.

Ringen, S. (1997), 'Family change and family policies: Great Britain', in S.B. Kamerman. and A.J. Kahn (eds), *Family Change and Family Policies in Great Britain, Canada, New Zealand, and the United States: Family Change and Family Policies in the West*, Oxford: Clarendon Press, pp. 29–102.

Walker, R. and M. Wiseman (eds) (2003), *The Welfare We Want? The British Challenge for American Reform*, Bristol: Polity Press.

Weaver, R.K. (2000), *Ending Welfare as We Know It*, Washington, DC: The Brookings Institute.

Wheatley, J. (2001), *WFTC Work in Progress: CAB Clients Experiences of Working Families' Tax Credit*, London: National Association of Citizens Advice Bureau.

Woods, D. (2006), 'Focusing on care. Family policy and problems of analysis', WiP Working Paper Series, No. 30, accessed 8 July 2018 at https://www.researchgate.net/publication/228557703_Focusing_on_care_Family_policy_and_problems_of_analysis.

Woods, D. (2012), *Family Policy in Transformation: US and UK Policies*, Houndmills, Basingstoke: Palgrave Macmillan.

15. Family policies in the Nordic countries: aiming at equality
Guðný Björk Eydal, Tine Rostgaard and Heikki Hiilamo

INTRODUCTION

The Nordic countries consist of Denmark, Finland, Iceland, Norway and Sweden and their associated territories, the Faroe Islands, Greenland and Åland. They share historical and cultural heritage. The countries have established institutions of various kinds to enhance their co-operation, for example, the Nordic Council of Ministers and they have had formal and informal co-operation in the field of family and gender policies for decades (Eydal and Kröger, 2009). The Nordic welfare model, sometimes referred to as the Scandinavian or Social Democratic welfare model, is a well-known feature in the literature on comparative welfare research (Esping-Andersen, 1991; Kvist et al., 2012). According to Sainsbury (1999, p. 75), the Nordic welfare model is characterised by 'comprehensive social provision where entitlement to benefits and a wide variety of services has been based on citizenship or residence. Other characteristics have included generous benefit levels, the funding of benefits through taxation rather than contributions from insured persons, and egalitarian redistribution.' This applies also in the comparative literature on family policies that usually groups the five Nordic countries under the same model, with the exception of care policies for young children where difference in policy sometimes places the Nordic countries in separate categories (Duvander and Ellingsæter, 2016; Hiilamo, 2002, 2008; Leira, 2002, 2006; Ostner and Schmitt, 2008; Ottosen and Björnberg, 2013; Thévenon, 2011; see also Chapter 4 by Millar and Chapter 10 by Thévenon in this volume).

Despite the importance of family policy in all the countries, only Norway and Iceland have policy documents that explicitly declare the goals and measures of the policies (St. meld. nr. 29, 2002–03; Þingskjal 1230, 1996–97), hence the policies are often implicit. Furthermore, the Nordic literature is not in an agreement about the definition of family policy; usually it applies to services and benefits for families with children but it can also be much wider, for example, including care policies for other family members and the role of extended family, family law, school and services provided in school, child protection, as well as policies on gender equality, family violence and issues that pose challenges for families that have immigrated or fled to the Nordic countries (e.g., Ottosen and Björnberg, 2013). The core aims of the policies aimed at families with children in the Nordic countries are nevertheless twofold: to work for equality between children by ensuring that all children can enjoy a good and safe childhood regardless of family form and/or the social situation of their families and to enhance gender equality by enabling both parents to work and care (Brandth and Gíslason, 2011; Duvander and Ellingsæter, 2016; Eydal and Kröger, 2009; Hiilamo, 2002; Kjörholt and Qvotrup, 2011; Ottesen and Björnberg, 2013).

This chapter discusses the main characteristics of contemporary family policies in the Nordic countries and asks if the family policies have reached this twofold aim by investigating outcomes, fertility rates, labour market participation of parents as well as child poverty. The chapter takes stock of the Nordic literature on family policy and is based on policy documents and comparative statistics. First, we analyse cash benefits in the forms of paid parental leaves and cash for care benefits as well as the public provision of Early Childhood Education and Care services (ECEC). Then follows a discussion on the outcomes with regard to fertility and parental employment. We argue that while the Nordic family policies enhance both gender equality in line with the goals of the dual earner/dual carer model, there is still some way to go in equal sharing of parental leave, time spent with the child and in paid work. Second, we discuss how the Nordic countries support families to provide for children. Here, the main features of the family benefit systems are presented as well as the outcomes regarding child poverty. The family benefits and supports for the dual earner model ensure low child poverty rates but the high number of children in lone parent families at risk of poverty raises concerns about the success of the Nordic family policies.

NORDIC FAMILY POLICIES FROM MALE BREADWINNER TO DUAL EARNER/DUAL CARER MODEL

Throughout the last century the Nordic family policies gradually developed from a male breadwinner model, where the father was the main provider and the mother cared for the home and children, towards what is often referred to as the dual earner/dual carer model in the Nordic literature (Leira, 2006) or the individual model (see Chapter 4 by Millar in this volume; Sainsbury, 1999), where policies facilitate and encourage fathers' involvement in housework and care for children and mothers' employment. This change was supported, amongst others, by replacing breadwinner entitlements in social security and tax policies with individual entitlements (Sainsbury, 1999). The journey started in the early 1900s when the five countries co-operated in making new family law emphasising equality of husbands and wives and ensuring the best interests of children (Therborn, 1993). However, the journey has not been taken at the same speed nor always following the same roadmap, hence closer examination reveals differences in both the historical development and outcomes of family policies (Boje and Eirnæs, 2013; Ellingsæter and Leira, 2006; Eydal and Kröger, 2009; Hiilamo, 2002; Leira, 2002; Ottesen and Björnberg, 2013; Skevik, 2001).

The Nordic countries have all been economically efficient and politically stable democratic states and have thus been able to develop and implement far-reaching and encompassing family policies (Rostgaard, 2015). While the literature has emphasised the role of the Social Democratic parties and the strong labour movement in the making of the Nordic welfare states (Korpi, 2000), many other actors have contributed to family policy making, not least women's organisations and professional groups (Therborn, 1993; Wennemo, 1994). Nordic family policy has been regarded as successful as it has, in the combination of social and labour market policies, enhanced the dual earner/dual carer model and relatively high fertility rates. However, scholars have also pointed out that neo-liberalism followed by privatisation, deregulation and New Public Management has left its mark on Nordic family policies, for example, Björnberg (2016) points out that in the case of Sweden, provision of social and health services has been outsourced to private for-profit providers. Present family policy is also challenged by the needs of immigrants and asylum seekers in that the needs and rights of these families are not taken into consideration (Björnberg, 2016; Liversage, 2016; Skevik Grødem, 2017).

The literature shows how family policy plays an important role with regard to ensuring both parents have opportunities to work and care for their children, for example, Thévenon (2011) points out that while female employment rates in Organisation for Economic Co-operation and Development (OECD) countries are influenced by both tax rates and leave policies, it is the provision of formal childcare services for children under the age of 3 that is the main driver of mothers' labour force participation. And while the Nordic countries have enjoyed very high labour market participation among women, it should be noted that the policies in the Nordic countries have encouraged part-time work of mothers and, according to Mandel and Semyonov (2006), the resulting high level of part-time work might contribute to the relatively high degree of gendered occupational segregation and the low proportion of women in top positions in the Nordic region compared to other countries (see also Mandel, 2012; Mandel and Shalev, 2009). Furthermore, Grönlund et al. (2017) point out that according to the Varieties of Capitalism (VoC) school (e.g., Estévez-Abe, 2005, 2006; see also Chapter 6 by Kang and Meyers in this volume), the fact that Nordic labour market institutions encourage long-term employment through employment protection legislation might exacerbate gender inequalities when the family policies facilitate work interruptions.

The Nordic countries have also stood out for a number of years with respect to fertility rates, which have remained relative high compared to most other European countries and well above the EU28 overall rates. Generally, the high fertility rates in the Nordic countries have been associated with their generous family policies (Crompton et al., 2007; Jensen and Ottosen, 2013; McDonald, 2002).

Historically, the Nordic countries have been among the forerunners with regard to ensuring children receive the best possible care. Originally, legislation was aimed at child protection, but gradually legal rights to benefits and services were increased (Satka and Eydal, 2004; Therborn, 1993). The Nordic family policies ensure that parents are provided with support to care for their young children, paid parental leaves, and offered subsidised childcare and family benefits. Additionally, there are social, health and school services aimed at ensuring children have the best possible service and outcomes, and these services are either fully financed by the public sector or the parents might pay small user fees (Hiilamo, 2008; Ottosen and Björnberg, 2013).

While the Nordic countries may stand out as regards the amount of gross domestic product (GDP) devoted to some family policies, this is not the overall picture and some investments are even declining. Thévenon (2011) shows that among the OECD countries in 2005–07, the Nordic countries invested much more than the other countries in parental leave and childcare services, 53 per cent of per capita GDP for each child compared to 21 per cent on average. However, the spending on child benefits is not exceptionally high in the Nordic countries in international comparison (Eydal and Kröger, 2009; Thévenon, 2011).

If we look only at the Nordic countries and the spending on families with children in total, in 2000, Denmark had the highest expenditure with 3.9 per cent of GDP and Finland the lowest with 3.0 per cent (Table 15.1).

Table 15.1 Social expenditure on families with children as percentage of GDP in 2000 and 2015, percentage of 0–17 year olds and the expenditure ratio in Nordic countries in 2015

	% of GDP in 2000	% of GDP in 2015	0–17 year olds as % of the population in 2015	Expenditure ratio:% of GDP/% of 0–17 years in 2015
Denmark	3.9	3.5	20.7	0.17
Finland	3.0	3.2	19.7	0.16
Iceland	3.2	2.5	24.3	0.10
Norway	3.6	3.3	21.8	0.15
Sweden	3.5	3.0	20.4	0.15

Note: Expenditure ratio: own calculations.

Source: NOSOSCO (2009, 2017).

In 2015, all the Nordic countries except Finland spent a smaller proportion of their GDP compared to 2000 on families with children; Iceland, in particular, has seen a considerable decrease in expenditure. Furthermore, by examining the expenditure ratio, and hence taking into consideration the percentage of the population aged 0–17 years that is actually benefiting from the expenditure, the country difference between Iceland and the other countries becomes even clearer.

CARE POLICIES

Care policies are intended to support parents to care for their young children, thus include paid parental leave, Early Childhood Education and Care (ECEC) services as well as cash benefits for the care of young children (CFC) (Eydal and Rostgaard, 2011).[1] The general aim of the Nordic care policies is to ensure that the child receives the best possible care in accordance with age and to support both parents to take on work outside the home and the care of their children. Hence, the generous provision of ECEC services facilitates gender equality in the take-up of paid work, low child poverty as well as early investment in children's beings and becomings (Kjörholt and Qvotrup, 2012).

Paid Parental Leave

In all the Nordic countries the parents are entitled to paid leave of absence from their work after birth and the law guarantees that the parent can return to the same job after the leave (Eydal and Rostgaard, 2011). In the 1970s to 1980s the Nordic countries introduced paid parental leave schemes that opened up the possibility for fathers to take part of the leave. They also enacted the right to paternity leaves to be taken by the father with the mother during the first weeks after birth. Despite these changes, the leave participation among fathers remained low and this – and the growing recognition of the importance of paternal care – gave rise to attempts to implement new policies to encourage a more active

Table 15.2 Paid parental leave in Nordic countries, percentage of income and covered weeks of entitlements as of 1 July 2017

	DK	FI	IS	NO	SW
% of income	100	70–90	80	100/80	80
Total weeks	50–64	48	39	47–57	69
• only mother	18	18	13	10	13
• only father	0	9	13	10	13
• father with mother	2	3	0	2	2
2015: days taken by fathers as % of total days	10.7	10.5	28.8	18.8	28.2

Source: Blum et al. (2017); NOSOSCO (2017).

role of fathers. Norway was the first Nordic country in 1993 to establish a 'use it or lose it' policy, a one-month non-assignable parental leave reserved for the father with payment, the so-called father's quota (Leira, 2006). Other Nordic countries followed suit, Sweden in 1996 and Iceland in 2000 (Eydal and Rostgaard, 2011). Denmark introduced a quota for fathers in 1998 but then abolished it in 2002 but many larger labour unions have since then negotiated such rights for their members (Rostgaard and Lausten, 2016). The need for the paid parental leave schemes is not a politically debated issue in the Nordic countries but there have been some political debates regarding the length of the father's quota and in the case of Denmark about its existence (Eydal et al., 2015). As shown in Table 15.2, all the Nordic countries provide paid parental leave for 12 months or more, except Iceland that provides nine months in total. In 2017 the father's quota was three months in Iceland and Sweden, ten weeks in Norway and nine weeks in Finland. In all the countries, the parents can extend the leave over a longer period and the schemes provide some flexibility with regard to rules on take-up. If the parents have been gainfully employed they are entitled to a proportion of their previous salaries, but if not they are entitled to relatively low flat rate benefit.

As Table 15.2 shows (bottom row) the different policies have led to quite big differences in the leave take-up figures for fathers. Iceland, Norway and Sweden that have implemented extensive father's quotas have experienced an increase in fathers' take-up of parental leave while Denmark and Finland have only witnessed a very slow increase (Eydal et al., 2015). Thus, the experience of the Nordic countries shows that the higher the number of days allocated to father's quotas, the higher the number of total benefit days used by the fathers.

Early Childhood Education and Care Services

Just as the use of the leave is part of everyday life in the Nordic countries, nearly all Nordic children will at some point before they start school have experienced the early childhood and education system. All the Nordic countries, except Iceland, have in fact given children legal rights to ECEC services from a certain age. They will be cared for outside the family, either in institutional care or, for children under 2, possibly in family day care which is

Table 15.3 Children receiving ECEC services in 2015 as a percentage of respective age groups in Nordic countries

	Denmark*	Finland	Iceland	Norway	Sweden
0 years	15	1	7	4	–
1–2 years	90	41	85	81	70
3–5 years	98	75	96	97	96

Note: * 2014 rather than 2015 for Denmark.

Source: NOSOSCO (2002, 2016).

provided in a private home by authorised and in most cases trained carers. ECEC services are intended to facilitate not least female labour market participation but also ensure the child's well-being and – in more recent years – support the child in its development of social and cognitive skills or, in other words, an investment in the child's being and becoming (Kjörholt and Qvotrup, 2011). ECEC services are subsidised by the public sector and parents pay relatively modest user fees, compared to other countries. The Nordic countries have provided quite different volumes of ECEC services. During the 2000s there was a constant increase in these volumes, but Finland has lower volumes compared to the other countries, as Table 15.3 shows for 2015.

In Denmark, children usually start ECEC from the end of the parental leave and this is also the case in Sweden but due to longer parental leave they usually start between 1 and 2 years old. However, children in Norway and, in particular, Finland start ECEC at a later age due to the system of cash for care benefits, discussed further below (Duvander and Ellingsæter, 2016; Sipilä et al., 2010). In Iceland, the parents need to bridge the gap between the nine-month paid parental leave and time the children start ECEC, usually at the age of 2 (Arnalds et al., 2013). Hence, care policies provide quite different support for parents during the first two years in their children's lives: Sweden and Denmark provide the best support for the dual earner model, while Sweden, Iceland and Norway provide more support for the dual carer model due to their long father's quota (Duvander and Ellingsæter, 2016; Eydal et al., 2015).

Cash for Care

Cash for Care (CFC) are relatively low flat rate benefits paid to parents after paid parental leave. The benefits do not fully compensate for wage loss, hence they are fundamentally different to the paid parental leave payments. The first CFC was enacted in Finland, in 1985, in order to offer alternative support to families who did not take advantage of ECEC services while their youngest child was under the age of 3 (Hiilamo and Kangas, 2009). The scheme has become an important part of Finnish care policies and in the 2000s more than 50 per cent of eligible children were cared for by parents, almost exclusively by mothers, who receive CFC. Parents receive a flat rate benefit with each child but municipalities can add to the benefits if they like. The high take-up rates of the CFC scheme in Finland explains the lower take-up rates for ECEC compared to the other Nordic countries. A similar scheme was enacted in Norway in 1998 but it has been highly debated. Originally the benefits were paid for children under 3 but from 2011 the benefits have been paid only for children under 2. The take-up of CFC has gradually decreased due to an increase in ECEC volumes and in 2016 about 25 per cent of parents of 1 year olds received the benefits (Duvander and Ellingsæter, 2016). In Sweden, the idea of CFC has been highly politically debated but a CFC scheme has been enacted twice, in 1994–95 and 2008–16. The aim of the legislation from 2008 was to increase the choice for families with children, with the municipalities choosing whether or not they implemented the scheme; however, in 2016 a new government left of the centre decided to abolish the legislation (Giuliani and Duvander, 2017). In Denmark, it is by law possible to receive CFC, but it is only used by very few parents, hence, it is not an important component in the Danish care policies that emphasise ECEC services for children from the age of 1 year. In Iceland, there has not been any legislation on CFC schemes but a few municipalities have experimented with such schemes in order to support parents to bridge the gap between paid parental leave and placement in ECEC (Eydal and Rostgaard, 2011).

While both paid parental leaves and ECEC services have contributed to the dual earner/dual carer model, the policies on CFC are regarded as going against the Nordic dual earner/dual carer model and ideals of gender equality, since they are mainly used by mothers (Duvander and Ellingsæter, 2016; Eydal and Rostgaard, 2011). Furthermore, it is argued that the CFC schemes work against the idea of equal rights of all children to ECEC services and the interests of children that are in special need of ECEC services (Brandth and Gíslason, 2011; Sipilä et al., 2010).

Both Parents Able to Work and Care?

One of the key components of the Nordic welfare model is the emphasis on active labour market policies and the Nordic countries do have high labour market participation among both fathers and mothers (Ottosen and Björnberg, 2013). However, there is still a gender gap in terms of type of jobs, labour market participation, hours worked and salaries (Grönlund and Öun, 2017; Grönlund et al., 2017). The statistics on labour market participation in OECD countries show that it is more usual for mothers than fathers to take longer leaves from the labour market after birth and hence the number of mothers, particularly the mothers of young or multiple children, in work is lower compared to other women (OECD, 2013). Another indicator on how countries differ with regard to the possibility of combining work and family is the fertility rates. If parents do not consider it possible to combine work and family, this has a negative impact on the fertility rates, which are lower than in the countries that do enhance reconciliation of work and family (OECD, 2011).

As shown in Table 15.4, parents in all the Nordic countries are active in the labour market to a high extent but there are some important differences among the countries.

While the Nordic countries have been successfully enhancing the employment of both parents, there are still quite large gender differences among groups of parents, in particular, parents of children under the age of 6. The difference between fathers' and mothers' employment is biggest by far in Finland, which also has the lowest fertility rate. The lower employment rate of mothers reflects the fact that due to the Finnish CFC system, mothers have a long absence from employment. Iceland has slightly larger differences than

Table 15.4 *Nordic countries in 2016, percentage of adults aged 20–49 in employment by sex, without children, with children under 6, with one child, and fertility rates*

	DK	FI	IS	NO	SW	EU28
Men total	86.8	80.6	91.2	NA	84.6	83.1
Women total	80.2	74.7	84.6	NA	80.7	72.0
Men without children	80.3	73.7	87.0	NA	77.6	78.2
Women without children	75.3	76.4	84.0	NA	74.5	76.3
Fathers with children under of 6	93.0	89.5	96.3	NA	94.1	89.6
Mothers with children under 6	79.5	60.2	80.9	NA	82.0	62.4
Fathers with one child	91.5	88.3	93.9	NA	94.5	86.8
Mothers with one child	79.3	71.7	82.5	NA	87.3	72.2
Fathers in part-time employment*	5.6	3.6	5.3	NA	8.7	5.8
Mothers in part-time employment*	27.6	15.5	29.9	NA	34.5	36.0
Fertility rates	1.78	1.56	1.74	1.70	1.85	1.59

Note: NA = Not available. * The distinction between full-time and part-time work is made on the basis of the spontaneous answer given by the respondent (Eurostat, 2016).

Source: Fertility rates: Eurostat (n.d.a); employment rates: Eurostat (n.d.b); Figures for Iceland: Statistic Iceland (n.d).

Denmark and Sweden and that is probably explained by the gap between the nine-month paid parental leave and ECEC that is usually bridged by mothers.

The other side of the coin is whether the policies have enabled parents to share the care of their children more equally. Nordic men are known for their participation in childcare, indicating that this is an integral part of contemporary fatherhood. For instance, Danish studies on time use show that fathers in Denmark are spending more and more time playing with and caring for their small children (Bonke, 2009). A recent study by Nordenmark (2016) finds that fathers living in a Nordic dual earner/dual carer regime are more inclined to agree that men should assume an equal responsibility for family life compared to fathers living in the male breadwinner model in the South. As for childcare, 50 per cent of fathers in the dual earner/dual carer model and 36 per cent of fathers in the male breadwinner model report that they look after their children relatively often and 64 per cent of fathers in the dual earner/dual carer regime were considerably involved in housework compared to 24 per cent of fathers in the male breadwinner regime. Furthermore, despite the fact that mothers still take the majority of leave days in all the Nordic countries (see Table 15.2) the literature on the effect of the take-up of paid parental leave shows that fathers that do take leave are more involved in the care of their children after the leave (Arnalds et al., 2013; Brandth and Kvande, 2016; Duvander and Jans, 2009; Ottosen, 2014).

FAMILY CASH BENEFITS

All five Nordic countries have developed systems of family benefit packages for families with children in order to support parents and to contribute to the cost of having and raising children.² This section explores the family benefit systems and asks to what extent these benefits move families with children above the poverty line.

Historically, families with children have enjoyed special tax deductions in the Nordic countries but gradually these deductions have been replaced with benefits, Finland being the last country to do so in 1994 (Hiilamo, 2002). Earlier the joint taxation of couples, in line with the breadwinner model, was replaced in the Nordic region by the individual model, where mothers and fathers are taxed as individuals (Hakovirta et al., 2015).

The most important family cash benefit is the child benefit paid to parents, usually without consideration of the parents' income or means, thus the same benefits for all children, except in Iceland where child allowance is means tested. All the countries, except Sweden, pay additional benefits to single parents and Finland, Iceland and Sweden pay a supplement for additional children (Iisakkala, 2013).³ In addition to the child benefits, in case of partnership dissolution and single parenthood, a parent that shares the legal residence with the child often receives a child maintenance payment from the non-resident parent. The amount and the arrangement of the payment is decided during divorce proceedings or in connection with the birth of a child out of marriage, through mutual agreement or a decision from the court or local authorities. In all the Nordic countries, public authorities guarantee an advanced maintenance payment, mostly in cases where the non-resident parent for some reason fails to pay. Some countries pay additional benefits to single parents (Hakovirta and Hiilamo, 2012; Hakovirta et al., 2015; NOSOSCO, 2016).

All the Nordic countries also provide a scheme of means-tested social assistance that is regarded to be the last safety net if other types of income fail and all other income possibilities have been exhausted. These schemes do not follow the logic of the dual earner model but usually regard the family (household) to be the benefit unit and thus the income of the whole family is taken into consideration when the amount of benefit is calculated (Eydal and Kröger, 2009). This also goes for housing benefits in all the countries besides Sweden, where housing benefit is an individual entitlement and specifically aimed at families with children. In all the countries, except Finland, the social assistance is administrated by local authorities but national minimum guidelines have been set by central authorities, except in the case of Iceland. A considerable proportion of families with children receive social assistance; in 2015, 5.5 per cent of all families with children in Denmark, 9.2 per cent in Finland, 4.6 per cent in Iceland and 4.2 per cent in Norway (NOSOSCO, 2017). It is, however, far more usual for single parent families to receive social assistance than two-parent families (NOSOSCO, 2017).

The expenditure figures on cash benefits for families are an indicator of the size of the support in the Nordic countries. When measured by public spending on family benefits in purchasing power parity (PPP) per 0–17-year-old child, Norway has the highest figure and Iceland the lowest (NOSOSCO, 2016). If and how these schemes meet the needs of the families is difficult to say, but an indicator showing that the systems are to a certain extent successful in supporting families with children is the fact that the Nordic countries have relatively low at-risk-of-poverty rates for families with children (Table 15.5, see further below).

Child Poverty in the Nordic Countries

The literature on child poverty recognises the importance of parents' participation in the labour market in order to prevent families with children from falling below the poverty line, but it also shows the importance of social transfers (see Chapter 7 by Bradshaw and Chapter 23 by Gornick and Nell in this volume). The Nordic countries all participate in Eurostat's annual survey on *Income and Living Conditions*, in which those households who have incomes below 60 per cent of the median income are defined to be at risk of poverty. In Table 15.5, the percentage of households with children at risk of poverty before and after social transfers shows how children are lifted above the poverty line by social transfers.

Table 15.5 *At-risk-of-poverty (AROP), households with children under the age of 18 years with under 60 per cent of median income before and after social transfers in Nordic countries in 2015*

	AROP (60% of median income) before social transfers, excluding pensions	AROP (60% of median income) after social transfers	Absolute difference (ppt)	Relative decrease (%)
Denmark	21.6	9.4	12.2	56.5
Finland	30.6	9.3	21.3	69.6
Iceland	25.6	10.9	14.7	57.4
Norway	31.2	12.8	18.4	59.0
Sweden	35.6	18.7	16.9	47.5

Source: Eurostat, n.d.c; own calculations.

The table shows that quite large numbers of households with children would be at risk of poverty if there were no social transfers, highest in Sweden at 35.6 per cent and lowest at 21.6 per cent in Denmark. After social transfers, Sweden has still by far the highest proportion of household with children at risk of poverty, at 18.7 per cent, followed by Norway at 12.8 per cent and Iceland at 10.9 per cent while Finland and Demark have the lowest proportions, at 9.3 and 9.4 per cent, respectively. The Finish welfare system provides the most influential social transfers, taking the level of the proportion of households with children at risk of poverty down by 69.6 per cent. In Sweden, on the other hand, the social transfers have the smallest effect, taking down the proportion by 47.5 per cent. The statistics from Eurostat also show that child poverty is higher among single parent households compared to two-parent households; in 2015 it was 17 per cent in Finland and 21.1 per cent in Denmark, about 30 per cent in Norway and Iceland, and Sweden has a record high proportion of 35.1 per cent that is actually higher than the European average of 33.9 per cent (Eurostat, n.d.c).

Thus, the statistics show that the family benefit system is playing an important role in decreasing child poverty and, as both Bradshaw and Gornick and Nell show in their chapters in this volume, the Nordic countries have been performing a leading role in this respect. However, Nordic scholars have pointed out that a rise in the number of families with children having incomes below the risk of poverty line is out of character for the Nordic welfare states, whose goal has been to ensure an equal income distribution and to support parents in providing for their children regardless of their social situation (Haataja et al., 2016; O'Brien and Salonen, 2011). Furthermore, the fact that child poverty is higher among single parent families compared to two-parent families is also in contradiction with the policy aims of ensuring provision for all children regardless of their social and family situation. The fact that Denmark and Finland were able to bring down the poverty level of single parent households below 20 per cent in 2015 shows that it is definitely possible (NOSOSCO, 2016).

CONCLUSION

The Nordic countries have been forerunners in ensuring gender equality and children's well-being by supporting both parents to earn and to care. Parents are enabled to take on paid work, and active labour market policies and gender equality policies support the extensive care and family policies in this regard. All parents have the right to paid parental leave and all countries – except Denmark – emphasise through legislation the importance of care from both parents by issuing certain periods of paid parental leave as a quota for each parent. Aside from the quota, parents can decide how to share the leave. Denmark provides the most extensive ECEC services for young children, followed by Iceland, Norway and Sweden. The extensive scheme of CFC benefits in Finland results in children starting day care usually around the age of 3. This is also reflected in the employment figures for parents, with Finnish mothers having lower figures compared to the mothers in the other Nordic countries. The literature shows that while Nordic family policy supports the dual earner/dual carer model, it also contributes to gender segregation in the labour market, for example, by promoting part-time work. Furthermore, despite the strong emphasis on providing care from both parents, Nordic fathers take only a minority of the paid parental leave in all the countries and hence mothers are left with the leading care roles. Fathers have increased their participation in care as well as domestic work but they are still working longer hours and taking on a bigger role as breadwinners. Hence, ensuring child care from both parents and providing both parents with opportunities to reconcile work and family is still an ongoing mission and far from being accomplished.

Ensuring children's equality through the family benefit system has been the other main goal of the Nordic family policies in line with the emphasis on equal income distribution in the Nordic welfare model. All the countries pay universal child benefits to all parents, with the exception of Iceland where benefits are means tested to income. The countries all have advanced maintenance schemes and other types of family benefits. However, post-benefit risk of poverty rates for housholds with children vary across the countries, for example, Finland is taking down poverty by 70 per cent compared to 47 per cent in Sweden. Single parent households are generally more at risk than two-parent households, pointing to the inadequacy of the policies for children in single parent families. Statistics also show that child poverty is on the rise in Sweden, a strong contradiction to the aims of the Social Democratic welfare model. Thus, despite the relatively good outcomes of the Nordic countries in comparative research on child poverty, there are still groups of children that have not been ensured good and safe childhoods.

NOTES

1. The OECD has proposed using the term Early Childhood Education and Care (ECEC) which includes 'all care and learning arrangements for children under school age, regardless of location, funding, opening hours or content of the programme' (OECD, 2001, p. 14).
2. Additionally, health care is mostly free of charge for children, parents pay a monthly fee for pre-schools but they are also subsidised by the state and/or the municipality and the elementary schools are fully financed by the public sector (Hiilamo, 2008).
3. There are also schemes of benefits in case the child has long-term illnesses or is disabled (Eydal and Rostgaard, 2013).

REFERENCES

Arnalds, Á., G.B. Eydal, and I.V. Gíslason (2013), 'Equal rights to paid parental leave and caring fathers – the case of Iceland', *Stjórnmál og stjórnsýsla*, **9**, 323–44.

Björnberg, U. (2016), 'Nordic family policy in European context', *Sociology and Anthropology*, **4** (6), 508–16.

Blum S., A. Koslowski, and P. Moss (2017), 'International Review of Leave Policies and Research 2017', accessed 15 July 2017 at http://www.leavenetwork.org/lp_and_r_reports/.

Boje, T. and A. Ejrnæs (2013), 'Flexibility in work-family relations, allocation of time', in M.H. Ottosen and U.B. Björnberg (eds), *Challenges for Future Family Policies in the Nordic Countries – Reassessing the Nordic Welfare Model*, Copenhagen: SFI, pp. 171–206.

Bonke, J. (2009), *Forældres brug af tid og penge på deres børn*, Odense: University Press of Southern Denmark.

Brandth, B. and I.V. Gíslason (2011), 'Family policies and the best interest of children', in I.V. Gíslason and G.B. Eydal (eds), *Parental Leave, Childcare and Gender Equality in the Nordic Countries*, TemaNord 2011: 562, Copenhagen: Nordic Council of Ministers, pp. 109–45.

Brandth, B. and E. Kvande (2016), 'Parental leave and classed fathering practices in Norway', in G.B. Eydal and T. Rostgaard (eds), *Fatherhood in Nordic Welfare States: Comparing Care Policies and Practice*, Bristol: Policy Press, pp. 121–40.

Crompton, R., S. Lewis, and C. Lyonette (eds) (2007), *Women, Men, Work and Family in Europe*, Houndmills, Basingstoke: Palgrave Macmillan.

Duvander, A.-Z. and A.L. Ellingsæter (2016), 'Cash for childcare schemes in the Nordic welfare states', *European Societies*, **18** (1), 70–90.

Duvander, A. and A. Jans (2009), 'Consequences of fathers' parental leave use: evidence from Sweden', *Finnish Yearbook of Population Research 2009*, **44**, 49–62.

Ellingsæter, A.L. and A. Leira (eds) (2006), *Politicising Parenthood in Scandinavia: Gender Relations in Welfare States*, Bristol: Policy Press.

Esping-Andersen, G. (1991), *Three Worlds of Welfare Capitalism*, Cambridge: Polity Press.

Estévez-Abe, M. (2005), 'Gender bias in skills and social policies: the varieties of capitalism perspectives on sex segregation', *Social Politics*, **12**, 180–215.

Estévez-Abe, M. (2006), 'Gendering the varieties of capitalism: a study of occupational segregation by sex in advanced industrial countries', *World Politics*, **59**, 142–75.

Eurostat (2016), *EU Labour Force Survey Explanatory Note*, Luxemburg: European Commission Eurostat, accessed 2 April 2017 at http://ec.europa.eu/eurostat/documents/1978984/6037342/EU-LFS-explanatory-notes-from-2016-onwards.pdf/0fd0fa60-b533-4a94-8766-fe3d78bcccad.

Eurostat (n.d.a), *Database by Themes: Fertility Rates*, accessed 10 April 2017 at http://appsso.eurostat.ec.europa.eu/nui/show.do?dataset=demo_frate&lang=en.

Eurostat (n.d.b), *Database by Themes: Employment Rate of Adults by Sex, Age Groups, Educational Attainment Level, Number of Children and Age of Youngest Child (%)*, accessed 10 April 2017 at http://appsso.eurostat.ec.europa.eu/nui/show.do?dataset=lfst_hheredch&lang=en.

Eurostat (n.d.c), *Database by Themes: Incomes and Living Conditions*, accessed 12 April 2017 at http://ec.europa.eu/eurostat/data/database.

Eydal, G.B. and T. Kröger (2009), 'Nordic family policies: constructing contexts for social work with families', in T. Kröger and H. Forsberg (eds), *Social Work and Child Welfare Politics: Through Nordic Lenses*, Bristol: Policy Press, pp. 11–29.

Eydal, G.B. and T. Rostgaard (2011), 'Gender equality re-visited: changes in Nordic child-care policies in the 2000s', *Regional Issue, Social Policy & Administration*, **45** (2), 161–79.

Eydal, G.B. and T. Rostgaard (2013), 'Caring families: policies and practices in Nordic countries', in M.H.

Ottosen and U. Björnberg (eds), *Challenges for Future Family Policies in the Nordic Countries – Reassessing the Nordic Welfare Model*, Copenhagen: SFI, pp. 133–70.

Eydal, G.B., I.V. Gíslason, T. Rostgaard, B. Brandth, A.-Z., Duvander, and J. Lammi-Taskula (2015), 'Trends in parental leave in the Nordic countries: has the forward march of gender equality halted?', *Community, Work & Family*, **18** (2), 167–81.

Giuliani, G. and A.-Z. Duvander (2017), 'Cash-for-care policy in Sweden: an appraisal of its consequences on female employment', *International Journal of Social Welfare*, **26**, 49–62.

Grönlund, A. and I. Öun (2017), 'In search of family friendly careers? Professional strategies, work conditions and gender differences in work-family conflict', *Community, Work & Family*, **21** (1) 87–105.

Grönlund, A., K. Halldén, and C. Magnusson (2017), 'A Scandinavian success story? Women's labour market outcomes in Denmark, Finland, Norway and Sweden', *Acta Sociologica*, **60** (2), 97–119.

Haataja, A., I. Airio, M. Saarikallio-Torp, and M. Valaste (eds) (2016), *Laulu 573566 perheestä. Lapsiperheet ja perhepolitiikka 2000-luvulla*, Helsinki: Kela.

Hakovirta, M. and H. Hiilamo (2012), 'Children's rights and parents' responsibilities: child maintenance policies in Finland', *European Journal of Social Security*, **14** (4), 286–303.

Hakovirta, M., A. Haataja, G.B. Eydal, and T. Rostgaard (2015), 'Fathers' rights to family cash benefits in Nordic countries', in G.B. Eydal and T. Rostgaard (eds), *Fatherhood in the Nordic Welfare States: Comparing Care Policies and Practice*, Bristol: Policy Press, pp. 79–102.

Hiilamo, H. (2002), *The Rise and Fall of Nordic Family Policy? Historical Development and Changes During the 1990s in Sweden and Finland*, Helsinki: STAKES.

Hiilamo, H. (2008), *Promoting Children's Welfare in the Nordic Countries*, Reports of the Ministry of Social Affairs and Health 15, Helsinki: The Ministry of Social Affairs and Health.

Hiilamo, H. and O. Kangas (2009), 'Trap for women or freedom to choose? The struggle over cash for child care schemes in Finland and Sweden', *Journal of Social Policy*, **38** (3), 457–75.

Iisakkala, A. (2013). *Jämförande studie om barnpensioner och förmåner för barnets försörjning i de nordiska länderna Danmark, Finland, Island, Norge och Sverige* (Comparative study on child pension and benefits for children in the Nordic countries). Licentiatavhandling inom TOPSOS-yrkesinriktad fortbildning inom socialförsäkringssektorn Handelshögskolan vid Åbo Akademi. Åbo: Åbo Akademi.

Jensen, A.M. and M.H. Ottosen (2013), 'Diversities in family formation and family forms', in M.H. Ottosen and U. Björnberg (eds), *Challenges for Future Family Policies in the Nordic Countries – Reassessing the Nordic Welfare Model*, Copenhagen: SFI, pp. 39–72.

Kjørholt, A.T. and J. Qvotrup (eds) (2011), *The Modern Child and the Flexible Labour Market: Early Childhood Education and Care*, Houndmills, Basingstoke: Palgrave Macmillan.

Korpi, W. (2000), 'The power resources model', in C. Pierson and F.G. Castles (eds), *The Welfare State Reader*, Cambridge: Polity Press, pp. 77–89.

Kvist, J., J. Fritzell, B. Hvinden, and O. Kangas (2012), *Changing Social Equality: The Nordic Welfare Model in the 21st Century*, Bristol: Policy Press.

Leira, A. (2002), *Working Parents and the Welfare State*, Cambridge: Cambridge University Press.

Leira, A. (2006), 'Parenthood change and policy reform in Scandinavia, 1970s–2000s', in A.L. Ellingsæter and A. Leira (eds), *Politicising Parenthood in Scandinavia: Gender Relations in Welfare States*, Bristol: Policy Press, pp. 27–52.

Liversage, A. (2016), 'Minority ethnic men and fatherhood in Danish context', in G.B. Eydal and T. Rostgaard (eds), *Fatherhood in Nordic Welfare States: Comparing Care Policies and Practice*, Bristol: Policy Press, pp. 209–30.

McDonald, P. (2002), 'Sustaining fertility through public policy: the range of options', *Population*, **57** (3), 417–46.

Mandel, H. (2012), 'Winners and losers: the consequences of welfare state policies for gender wage inequality', *European Sociological Review*, **28** (2), 241–62.

Mandel, H. and M. Semyonov (2006), 'A welfare state paradox: state interventions and women's employment opportunities in 22 countries', *American Journal of Sociology*, **111** (6), 1910–49.

Mandel, H. and M. Shalev (2009), 'Gender, class, and the varieties of capitalism perspective', *Social Politics*, **16**, 161–81.

Nordenmark, M. (2016), 'Gender regime, attitudes towards childcare and actual involvement in childcare among fathers', in G.B. Eydal and T. Rostgaard (eds), *Fatherhood in the Nordic welfare States: Comparing Care Policies and Practice*, Bristol: Policy Press, pp. 163–87.

NOSOSCO (2002), *Social Protection in the Nordic Countries. Scope, Expenditure and Financing 2000*, Copenhagen: Nordic Statistical Committee, NOSOSCO.

NOSOSCO (2009), *Social Protection in the Nordic Countries. Scope, Expenditure and Financing 2007*, Copenhagen: Nordic Statistical Committee, NOSOSCO.

NOSOSCO (2016), *Social Protection in the Nordic Countries. Scope, Expenditure and Financing 2014/15*, Copenhagen: Nordic Statistical Committee, NOSOSCO.

NOSOSCO (2017), *Social Protection in the Nordic Countries. Scope, Expenditure and Financing 2015/16*, Copenhagen: Nordic Statistical Committee, NOSOSCO.
O'Brien, M. and T. Salonen (2011), 'Child poverty and child rights meet active citizenship: a New Zealand and Sweden case study', *Childhood*, **18** (2), 211–26.
OECD (2001), *Starting Strong: Early Education and Care*, Paris: OECD.
OECD (2011), *Doing Better for Families*, Paris: OECD, accessed 10 June 2016 at http://dx.doi.org/10.1787/9789264098732-en.
OECD (2013), *Labour Force Statistics 2012*, Paris: OECD, accessed 15 August 2017 at http://dx.doi.org/10.1787/oecd_lfs-2012-en.
Ostner, I. and C. Schmitt (eds) (2008), *Family Policies in the Context of Family Change: The Nordic Countries in Comparative Perspective*, Wisbaden: Verlag fur Sozialwissenschaften, pp. 37–56.
Ottosen, M.H. (2014), 'The long-term impact of early paternal involvement in childcare in Denmark', in G.B. Eydal and T. Rostgaard (eds), *Fatherhood in the Nordic Welfare State: Comparing Care Policies and Practice*, Bristol: Policy Press, pp. 251–76.
Ottosen, M.H. and U.B. Björnberg (eds) (2013), *Challenges for Future Family Policies in the Nordic Countries – Reassessing the Nordic Welfare Model*, Copenhagen: SFI, accessed 5 February 2016 at https://pure.sfi.dk/ws/files/202132/1338_Challenges_for_future_family_policies.pdf.
Rostgaard, T. (2015), 'Family policy in Scandinavia. Comparative study of family policy in Scandinavia', accessed 20 May 2016 at http://library.fes.de/pdf-files/id/11106.pdf.
Rostgaard, T. and M. Lausten (2016), 'The coming and going of father's quota in Denmark: consequences for fathers' paid leave take up', in G.B. Eydal and T. Rostgaard (eds), *Fatherhood in the Nordic Welfare States: Comparing Care Policies and Practice*, Bristol: Policy Press, pp. 79–102.
Sainsbury, D. (1999), 'Gender and Social-Democratic welfare states', in D. Sainsbury (ed.), *Gender and Welfare State Regimes*, Oxford: Oxford University Press, pp. 75–114.
Satka, M. and G.B. Eydal (2004), 'History of Nordic welfare policies for children', in H. Brembeck, B. Johansson, and J. Kampmann (eds), *Beyond the Competent Child – Exploring Contemporary Childhoods in the Nordic Welfare Societies*, Roskilde: Roskilde University Press, pp. 33–63.
Sipilä, J., K. Repo, and T. Rissanen (2010), *Cash-for-Childcare: The Consequences for Caring Mothers*, Cheltenham, UK and Northampton, MA, USA: Edward Elgar Publishing.
Skevik, A. (2001), *Family Ideology and Social Policy Policies towards Lone Parents in Norway and the UK*, Oslo: NOVA.
Skevik Grødem, A. (2017), 'Family-oriented policies in Scandinavia and the challenge of immigration', *Journal of European Social Policy*, **27** (1), 77–89.
Statistic Iceland (n.d.), Unpublished labour market statistics for parents' employment, Statistic Iceland, Reykjavík.
St.meld. nr. 29 (2002–03), *Om familien–forpliktende samliv og foreldreskap, setter kjærlighet, omsorg og forhold innad i familien i sentrum* (A parliamentary resolution: about family–family obligations in couples and parenthood, brings love, care and relations in families in centrum).
Therborn, G. (1993), 'Politics of childhood: the rights of children in modern times', in F.G. Castles (ed.), *Families of Nations – Patterns of Public Policy in Western Democracies*, Aldershot: Dartmouth Publishing, pp. 241–93.
Thévenon, O. (2011), 'Family policies in OECD Countries: a comparative analysis', *Population and Development Review*, **37** (11), 57–87.
Wennemo, I. (1994), *Sharing the Cost of Children: Studies on the Development of Family Support in the OECD Countries*, Stockholm: Stockholm University.
Þingskjal 1230 (1996–97), Þingsályktun um mótun opinberrar fjölskyldustefnu og aðgerðir til að styrkja stöðu fjölskyldunnar (Parliamentary Resolution on making of explicit family policy and measures to strengthen the position of the family), *Alþingistíðindi A-deild*, 121.

16. Child and family policy in Southern Europe
Teresa Jurado-Guerrero and Manuela Naldini

INTRODUCTION

Comparative research on welfare states has often regarded Southern countries as the more 'family-oriented' or 'familialistic' ones (e.g., Esping-Andersen, 1990, 1999). Unlike other countries belonging to Continental welfare regimes (i.e., France, Austria and Germany), or more recently to the Eastern European welfare regime (Saraceno and Keck, 2010), in Southern Europe 'familialism' has not translated into state support for families with children. In terms of the 'varieties of familialism' (Leitner, 2003), it is difficult to define the relationship between public policies and familialism in Southern Europe as *supported familialism*, such as supporting families through parental leave, cash benefits for care or tax relief. Rather, Southern countries may be described as having *familialism by default* or *unsupported familialism*, as the responsibility for providing the care is assigned mainly to the family (women) due to the comparatively low provision of care services and/or government subsidies for families (Saraceno and Keck, 2010).

In the South, the family was and remains the key provider of welfare, a factor which marks a specific way of the functioning of the welfare state (Martin, 1997; Ferrera, 2005; Naldini and Saraceno, 2008). This chapter provides a historical and comparative account of the Southern European family policy model. The chapter is divided into three main sections. We first provide a historical analysis (1980–2014) of the (under)development of family policy in Southern Europe (Greece, Italy, Portugal and Spain) in three main areas: family benefits, Early Childhood Education and Care (ECEC), parental leave and reconciliation policies. We then focus on the Italian and Spanish cases as examples of the model. We attempt to explain the underdevelopment of family policy by looking at the strength of intergenerational ties and kin solidarity, the role of religion, the authoritarian past, the strength of unions/left parties and late industrialization. Finally, we discuss what the future of family policies in the Southern countries may look like after the economic crisis.

THE SOUTHERN MODEL OF FAMILY POLICY (1980–2014)

The Underdevelopment of Family Benefits in a Comparative Perspective

From a comparative and historical perspective, family policies in Southern Europe, since the downfall of various dictatorships, have been characterized by a very fragmented array of measures that are poorly publicly funded (Bradshaw and Ditch, 1993; Gauthier, 1996; Symeonidou, 1996; Carlos and Alipranti, 2000; Pfenning and Bahle, 2000; Naldini, 2003). In addition, family policies in Southern countries have subsumed child policies, except for pre-school services (3–6), which belong to educational policies. According to

Pfenning and Bahle (2000), European family policy models can be clustered historically into five groups. First, there are the Scandinavian countries with child-oriented policies and emphasis on gender equality; second, the English-speaking countries with a liberal and non-interventionist family policy; third, the Southern countries with weak welfare states and strong kinship, fourth, the French-speaking countries as the European pioneers of family policy with a combination of traditional and progressive elements; and fifth, the German-speaking countries with less developed and more conservative family policies (see also Chapter 2 by Gauthier and Koops, Chapter 4 by Millar and Chapter 13 by Pfau-Effinger in this volume).

Southern European countries indeed had the lowest level of public funding for families with children during the 1980s (Bradshaw and Ditch, 1993). From 1990 until 2000, public expenditure on family cash benefits in Spain, Italy and Portugal remained low and without any significant change, except in Greece where a slight increase of expenditure can be observed. In 2000, cash family benefits as a proportion of gross domestic product (GDP) were: 1 per cent in Greece, 0.2 per cent in Spain and 0.5 per cent in Italy and Portugal, compared to 2.1 per cent in Germany, 2 per cent in France and an average of 1.4 per cent in the EU-15 (Eurostat, 2003). Italy, Spain and Greece were the only countries in the European Union (EU) without a 'universal' system of family allowances (MISSOC, 2002). These long-term comparisons do not include tax allowances. Fiscal policies are generally very hard to calculate and to compare. It is, however, worth mentioning that Spain introduced in 2002, for the first time, a tax benefit of €100 per month for formally employed mothers with children under 3. Since the mid-1990s, national studies for Italy show the increasing importance of tax allowances for children as a policy instrument (Guerra, 2011). The most recent data collected by the Organisation for Economic Co-operation and Development (OECD, 2016a) show that in 2011 Southern countries continued to spend less than the 33 OECD countries' average and that tax allowances do not significantly alter their international ranking position. Cash and tax family benefits in the South as a percentage of GDP are well below the 2.55 per cent OECD average: 1.2 per cent for Spain and Portugal, 1.4 per cent for Greece and 1.5 per cent for Italy. If services for families are included for 2011, then the four countries spent somewhat more: 1.5, 1.4, 1.4 and 2, respectively (OECD, 2016b). In Italy, tax measures accounted for one-quarter of the total public spending on family benefits, a relatively high share for the South.

Since the twenty-first century in Southern Europe cash benefits for households have assumed a selective nature, becoming a measure for fighting family poverty. In some countries this is stronger than in others. Eurostat figures for 2012 show that the EU-29 spent on average 13 per cent of its cash family benefits on means-tested benefits, while in Greece the proportion was 23 per cent, 20 per cent in Spain, 56 per cent in Italy and 63 per cent in Portugal (Eurostat, 2016a). However, despite the greater effort in spending on means-tested family allowances, the capacity of state transfers to reduce the risk of child poverty is comparatively small. In Southern European countries, child poverty rates remain higher than the EU average, amongst others, due to the lower incidence of public transfers (see Figure 16.2; see also Chapter 7 by Bradshaw and Chapter 23 by Gornick and Nell in this volume).

Childcare Services, Parental Leave and Reconciliation Policies

Southern European welfare states and family policies have traditionally displayed deficits especially in the provision of ECEC, such as childcare facilities for very young children and social services for the frail elderly (Flaquer, 2000). In Southern countries, the lack of childcare services for the youngest children, the inadequacy of most childcare services in terms of quality and time schedules, as well as the low number of part-time jobs make it difficult for dual-earner couples to combine family with work. Dual-earner families with small children have increased in the last decade and represent more than half of the couples with small children (Escobedo and Wall, 2015). The economic crisis has not significantly decreased employment of mothers, but on the contrary in Greece it has grown. As can be seen in Figure 16.1, the enrolment rates in childcare services for children under 3 were very limited in Southern countries in 2000, despite around half of the mothers with small children being employed. Enrolment rates were 3 per cent in Greece, 5 per cent in Spain, 6 per cent in Italy and 12 per cent in Portugal compared to a higer average of 23 per cent for the 16 European countries. Since 2000 childcare coverage for children under 3 has improved in all Southern countries. The increase for Italy and Greece has been less impressive and their current coverage rates are still among the lowest. In contrast, Spain and Portugal have made great improvements and reached levels above the European average.

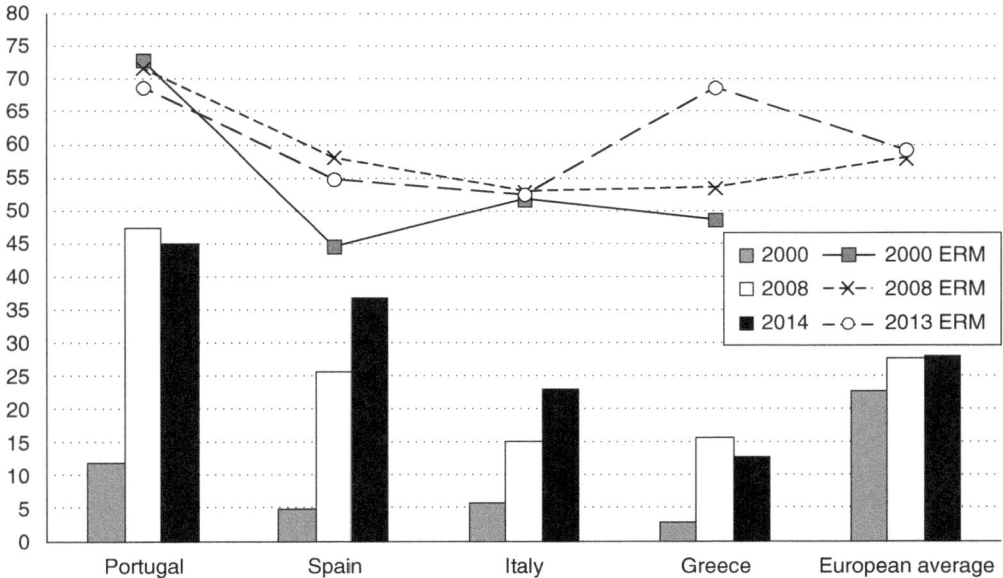

Note: ERM refers to the employment rates of mothers with children under 6.

Source: For 2000: OECD (2001, table 4.7); for 2008: OECD (2018, table PF3.2.A), except Italy and Spain (Naldini and Jurado Guerrero, 2013); for 2013 and 2014: Eurostat (2016d).

Figure 16.1 Enrolment rates in formal childcare 0–2 years and mothers' employment rates

Data reflect children in childcare centres and pre-school formal care arrangements (both public and private) and those who are cared for by liscensed childminders.

In all Southern countries, as in most other European countries, the situation has been better for children between 3/4 and 6 years old, especially where the public services are directly dependent on the Ministry of Education and are free of charge, as in Italy, Spain, Portugal and to some extent Greece (Sims-Schouten, 2000; Eurydice, 2015). In 2014, children aged 3 to 5 years were nearly all enrolled in pre-primary schools, except in Greece, where this was the case for 47 per cent of this age group (OECD, 2018).

The enrolment rates described can only partly be taken as indicators of the public effort to provide childcare, because each country may offer a wide array of different care arrangements, such as public, publicly supported and non-subsidized private services. For instance, in Spain the data for 2008 and 2014 in Figure 16.1 include public and for-profit formal childcare services. Mostly, parents also have to pay fees for public childcare facilities and may receive public subsidies to pay for private ones, depending on the region. Thus, if one wants to know how much public investment really is, enrolment rates have to be complemented with additional information. Recent data on public expenditure on ECEC for 2012 show that Southern countries invest below the EU average for children under 6: Italy and Spain spend 0.6 per cent of GDP on ECEC followed by Portugal (0.4 per cent), and Greece (0.1 per cent), while the average for the 20 European countries is 0.8 per cent (OECD, 2016b: see also Chapter 8 by Rostgaard in this volume).

Thus, in 2014, in Southern Europe most children under 3 continued to be cared for by their parents, relatives or in other informal arrangements. Formal childcare is provided for 17 to 45 per cent of these pre-school children, but public administrations only pay for some of the formal care services and parents have to complement this by paying direct fees. Only from age 3 onwards are most care costs fully funded by public administrations and enrolments reach near universality, except in Greece. In line with these administrative statistics showing a care deficit for the smallest children, different studies show that grandparents, in particular grandmothers, provide more intensive childcare in Southern Europe compared to other European countries (Albertini et al., 2007).

However, erroneous conclusions about public investment in childcare may be drawn if one does not take into account national differences in parental leave regulations. If parental leave and childcare service are taken together, then Portugal, Spain and also Italy show similar coverage rates of children under 3 through a combination of childcare and parental leave; Italy compensates for a lower offer of services with a longer paid parental leave. However, considering all childcare policies together, the Southern European countries still may be classed as belonging to an unsupported universal breadwinner model or a male breadwinner model, because the design of parental leave, the offer of childcare services and the level of public payment of these two policies do not provide effective care of children from zero to three years outside the family (Ciccia and Bleijenbergh, 2014).

Parental leave arrangements and flexible working time are crucial policies for the care of small children and their wellbeing in dual-earner families, but great variation exists with respect to duration of leaves, the transferability between parents and the wage replacement level paid during leaves (see also Chapter 11 by den Dulk, Yerkes and Peper in this volume). Southern European countries share a duality between well-paid short maternity and paternity leaves, that is, initial leaves related to childbirth and the care of a newborn, on the one hand, and relatively long but unpaid or low paid parental leaves. As a consequence, the take-up of these leaves is low and strongly gendered, as men hardly use them. In all four countries, the coverage of maternity leaves has been increased to include the self-employed and now basic schemes also cover employed women who previously did not qualify for entitlement. Maternity/initial leaves in 2015 range from three months of leave after childbirth in the Greek public sector to six months in Portugal, if the leave is shared by the father. In addition, fathers' involvement in childcare through specific leaves for fathers is also advancing as non-transferable and well-paid paternity leaves have been partly implemented. In Spain in 2007, a 15-day non-transferable paternity leave was created, which was enlarged to 30 days in 2017 (35 days in 2018), and in Portugal the existing paternity leave increased to 20 days in 2009. In Italy in 2015, a two-day paternity leave was implemented, and in Greece employers grant two days of leave to fathers (Ciccia and Verloo, 2012; Blum et al., 2017).

After these initial leaves, parental leaves to care for small children range from 10/11 months in Italy to 60 months in the Greek public sector (Blum et al., 2017). In addition, they are unpaid (Spain, Portugal and Greece) or low paid (Italy), which prevents men from taking them up. The countries producing figures on take-up rates for parental leaves show very low rates for women in Portugal (2.8 per cent) and Spain (7.8 per cent), while they are higher in Italy (54 per cent), because the leave is paid at 30 per cent of the wage level. Men's take-up rates are always well below women's, even in Italy where wage loss is somewhat compensated and a father's bonus was introduced in 2000. Thus, to take full-time parental leave beyond maternity leave is not a mainstream option. This design of well-paid initial/maternity leaves and low or unpaid parental leaves is related to the early return to work of mothers (Escobedo and Wall, 2015).

So, children are mainly cared for by the mother during the first four to six months after childbirth. In some countries, the father can also become involved in early care, but after the first four to six months most couples have to look for care elsewhere, since wage-replacement is very low for full-time parental leave. The latter developments in paternity leaves are the reasons why Southern Europe diverges with respect to the Parental Leave Equality Index (PLEI) (Castro-García and Pazos-Morán, 2016). This index measures the proportion of leave men are likely to use out of the total available in each country and thus indicates their entitlement to care in early childhood. Portugal belongs to those countries that promote co-responsibility, in Spain men are considered to be 'incidental collaborators' in childcare, while Italy and Greece reinforce the traditional gendered division of labour. This gender imbalance in the time for caring in early childhood has consequences for children's attachment to fathers. Fathers involved in care may influence children's well-being in many positive ways, such as, for instance, cognitive development (Sarkadi et al., 2008).

Finally, it should be noted that flexibility in working arrangements can have a considerable impact on reconciliation issues. For many people, especially women, part-time work or the statutory right to reduce working hours provides one important way to combine work and family life.[1] Southern Europe has been characterized by low levels of part-time work, and part-time jobs are often of low grade, poorly paid, and without long-term career prospects (OECD, 2001). During the Great Recession, from 2008 to 2014, part-time jobs for women increased in all four southern countries, although there was also an increase in the proportion of involuntary part-timers. In 2013, 33 per cent of female employment in Italy was part time, it was 23 per cent in Spain, while Greece (16 per cent) and Portugal (14 per cent) had lower levels (OECD, 2016). Jobs with flexible working hours were comparativley less common in Southern European countries (OECD, 2001, table 4.8), whereas this has improved somewhat in the last decade.

To sum up, contrary to the development of family benefits, increasing divergence can be observed in Southern Europe with respect to the development of ECEC for children under 3 and leave policies. Portugal and Spain have expanded childcare services considerably. Leave policies have improved to some extent in Portugal and Italy (length and payment), but only in Portugal and Spain do non-transferable paternity leaves paid at 100 per cent exist.

HOW CAN THE DEVELOPMENT OF FAMILY POLICIES BE EXPLAINED?

Persistence of Underdevelopment until the 1980s

There are different explanations for the development of family policies in the Southern European region in each of the decades since World War II, as shown by recent research (Ferragina and Seeleib-Kaiser, 2014), in addition to national-specific traits of polities and welfare state development in each of the countries (Ferrera, 1996). Generally, however, family policies have been underdeveloped. Although the reasons for inadequate family policies are not identical for Italy and Spain, they do have certain similarities.[2] First of all, in Italy and Spain, the underdevelopment of family policy is a legacy of the previous authoritarian regimes. The Italian fascist experience left strong and widespread opposition to any policy seeming to have pronatalist connotations, including those aimed at supporting the cost of raising children (Saraceno, 1994; Naldini, 2003). The same is true of Spain, where lawmakers avoided family policy-making for a long time after the authoritarian period (Valiente, 1995).

Second, in Italy and Spain, demands by political parties for social policy for families with children have been further constrained by ideological divisions over which family model the state should support. Left-wing parties in these countries avoided including family and social policy for children on the political agenda, framing instead requests in terms of social rights for women and individual rights (Naldini, 2000). Also, the trade unions in Southern European countries remained male-dominated and had no interest in putting family policy demands on the agenda for a long time (Andreotti et al., 2001).

Third, the generally late and qualitatively varied form of modernization in Southern Europe has affected women's accession to the labour market. Most ECEC programmes in the rest of Europe were developed in response to women's access to the labour market. In Southern Europe, protracted periods of high unemployment and a sizeable informal economy contributed to making women the main providers of informal care and the key actors in promoting intergenerational solidarity. The continuing predominance of self-employment and small family enterprises was also significant, particularly insofar as they are considerable sources of employment for women and other family members (Andreotti et al., 2001; Karamessini, 2006). These types of jobs allow women to continue to provide care at home, since the boundaries between family and work are often blurred in family businesses.

Fourth, the latecomers to democracy had to invest a lot of resources in the consolidation of social security income-support benefits (mainly pensions), and in the creation of universal health and education services. Electoral speeches by politicians across parties were typically devoted to issues such as wage increases, unemployment benefits and social security rights, rather than to family issues, despite the very low fertility rates reported from the 1980s. In contrast to countries such as France, which responded to the fertility decline by implementing explicit pronatalist policies, Southern Europe omitted the problem from the political agenda until the 1990s. In Spain, recurrent unemployment and the coming of age of the large baby-boom generation of the 1980s and 1990s prevented politicians and voters from perceiving fertility decline as a social problem (Garrido and Malo, 2005).

Fifth, in both Italy and Spain the Church exercised a strong cultural hegemony on family definition and family issues. In particular, the Catholic social doctrine played a role in shaping the welfare state in Southern Europe (Castles, 1994). The Catholic Church and the Orthodox Church in Greece have continued to emphasize, for instance, the principle of 'subsidiarity', which means that priority is given to smaller and voluntary organizations over the state, whenever possible. This had a negative influence for a long time on the development of public childcare services, kindergartens and services for the elderly. It has also shaped the way in which these two welfare states have developed poor relief schemes (Naldini, 2003).

Finally, the strength of intergenerational ties and kin solidarity was based on the enduring norms of 'rural' society and patriarchal relationships. Family solidarity has bridged the functional gap created by late and limited provision of social protection and care services by the state (Naldini, 2003). In turn, this has a reciprocal influence on social policy development, insofar as both the intra-family pooling of resources and intergenerational redistribution have probably reduced the social and electoral pressure for further expanding the welfare state. Similarly, structural unemployment among the young, and the strength of family businesses, segmented labour markets and the informal economy have contributed to the strengthening of family and kinship solidarity networks (García and Karakatsanis, 2006). A broad set of social and economic relationships are linked within a reinforcing spiral where cause and effect are interwoven.

New Family Challenges and New Policy Drivers from the 1990s Onwards

The historical reasons for the underdevelopment of family policy are, however, growing less important and some new family policies are being unfolded. In the last two decades the institutional dimension of the family has been exposed to great change in Southern Europe. The biggest challenges are the very profound demographic and social changes affecting Southern European families. Family support and especially intergenerational solidarity may not have decreased as a value system, but family help will no longer suffice to cope with the 'care deficit' these societies are experiencing. In Italy and Spain very low fertility patterns and, in particular, the very low proportions of households with three or more children are some of the results of a sharp increase in the number of highly educated women and of uninterrupted female careers. These trends have not been offset by a supportive context for combining family commitments and employment, something which Esping-Andersen (2009) labels as the incomplete revolution. Male participation in care and domestic tasks remains low, and public policies in support of the family and the reconciliation of paid and unpaid work are insufficient. Given that many more mothers in Southern Europe now carry a double burden, the limitation of the number of children is a rational individual strategy to combine work and family duties.

Marriage in Spain and (to a limited extent) in Italy has undergone a process of de-institutionalization (Cherlin, 2004). Crude marriage rates have declined all over OECD countries but this decline has been especially acute in South Europe. More generally, cohabitation as an alternative to marriage has become much more widespread especially in Portugal and Spain (Domínguez and Castro, 2013), as is the case in other Southern European countries. In general, changes for women and family, both in society and in social policies, have been much more profound in Spain than in Italy (Naldini and Jurado-Guerrero, 2013). Since the 1990s, Spain has changed in the direction of Nordic countries by increasing the share of dual-earner households, which has stagnated at lower levels in Italy in the last decade. Spain has been praised for its public commitment to gender equality, which symbolically achieved important results in April 2004 with the first gender-parity government in Spanish history. Not only have family values and the reality of family changed in Spain, but also the legal definitions of family relations and public policies have followed a slightly different trajectory to that in Italy, characterized by 'a quasi frozen landscape' (Palier and Martin, 2008; Naldini and Saraceno, 2008; León and Pavolini, 2014). Despite low family benefits, Spain has increased public childcare services steadily and rapidly, as described above. A number of scholars have attributed the different Spanish welfare expansion to being a latecomer, which turned out to be a comparative advantage compared to Italy (Guillén and León, 2011; León and Migliavacca, 2013; León and Pavolini, 2013). However, this explanation is not sufficient, because countries such as Germany, which did not need to catch up, have also introduced reforms in family/care policies.

Why then did Italy not change ECEC like Spain or achieve similar gender-parity objectives? Again, a region-specific answer might emphasize the role of the Catholic Church in Italy. One can argue that the veto power of the Vatican has always been much stronger in Italy than in Spain. In Italy, a stronger cultural hegemony exercised by the Catholic Church on family issues has for a long time hindered any suggestion of alternative definitions, and delayed reforms, for example, not acknowledging the diversity of family forms; the divorce law changed only in 2014; the family name is taken only from the father; and only a two-day paternity leave was introduced in Italy in 2012 (Musumeci et al., 2015). However, this kind of explanation does not lend itself to generalization.

In recent studies examining the political factors affecting the coverage and spending rates on childcare, some authors point to the importance of the percentage of women in the parliament (Bonoli and Reber, 2010), while studies on childcare and parental leave policies emphasize the causal importance of party competition over female votes and electorate preferences on such policies at least until the 1990s (Morgan, 2013; Ferragina and Seeleib-Kaiser, 2015). Morgan (2013) provides an attractive causal argument for explaining the expansion of work-family policies in several European countries by using the electoral competition thesis. The expansion of work-family policies in Germany and Britain is seen as a way for political parties to appeal to female voters. This has indeed also occurred in Spain, where the socialists (PSOE) and the conservatives (PP) have both targeted women, and for some time, 1989–2008, the former has attracted more female votes (Calvo and Martín, 2009). Interestingly, the electoral competition and the provisions of the 2007 equality law have also increased the number of female politicians in Spain (36 per cent of deputees in the parliament from 2008–15 and 39 per cent in 2016). By the same token, the lack of electoral competition around female voters in Italy has impeded the advancement of women in politics and the entrance on the political agenda of issues related to care and support of women's employment (Estevez-Abe and Naldini, 2016). Though, as some scholars argue, Italy's childcare landscape does not mean that there were no efforts or any legislative initiatives to expand childcare during the last two decades. On the contrary, since the 1990s there have been numerous legislative initiatives and attempts at all levels of the government – including initiatives at regional and local levels in what has been labelled as a process of 'modernization from below' (Ferrera and Maino, 2014; Léon and Pavolini, 2014; Olivier and Mätzke, 2014). However, the services enacted by regional and local authorities have not been sufficient to produce any clear shifts in favour of a general expansion of childcare services and defamilialization of care (Estevez-Abe and Naldini, 2016). In a comparative study including Italy and other non-Southern European countries the researchers concluded that since the 2000s partisanship and socio-economic factors have become less important as drivers of changes in family policies, while cultural change as indicated by preferences of urban women for gender equality and employment-oriented family policy may push political parties to new agendas. In addition, family policy expansion may also have a positive feedback effect on public opinion pushing for these sort of policies (Ferragina and Seeleib-Kaiser, 2015).

POST-ECONOMIC CRISIS SCENARIO

The Great Recession of 2008–14 hit South European countries very strongly. Male and female unemployment rates rose and, as a consequence, in Italy, Spain, Greece and Portugal the proportion of children aged 0–17 living in jobless households increased from around 4–6 per cent in 2007 to 10–14 per cent in 2013 (Eurostat, 2016b). Unemployment benefits mitigated parents' unemployment at the beginning of the crisis to a large extent, but long-term unemployment (longer than one year) later began to affect increasing proportions of the active population throughout the South, in particular in Greece (20 per cent) and Spain (13 per cent), and less so in Portugal and Italy (7 per cent). The strong impact of unemployment in Greece and Spain was alleviated by increasing female labour activity rates during the Great Recession: Greek and Spanish women aged 25 to 54 increased their activity rates from around 70 per cent in 2007 to 75 per cent and 82 per cent, respectively, in 2014, approaching the Portuguese rate (86 per cent) and leaving behind the Italian rate (66 per cent) (Eurostat, 2016c). Increasing female labour force activity and the pooling of resources within larger households mitigated income inequalities to some extent in Greece and Spain (Hellebrandt, 2014). However, these family efforts, in the absence of more generous public transfers, have not prevented the relative growth of child poverty rates in most of Southern Europe.

As can be seen in Figure 16.2, the rates of children under 18 at risk of poverty after social transfers were already higher in Southern European welfare states compared to France and Germany in 2007. The crisis increased the relative poverty rates of children in most Southern countries and social transfers are comparatively less able to mitigate them.

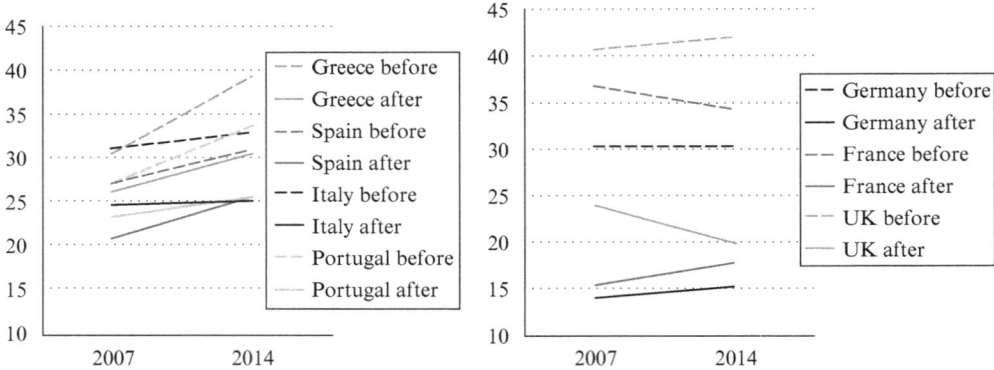

Source: Eurostat online, ilc_li10 and ilc_li02, accessed January 2016.

Figure 16.2 At-risk-of-poverty rate before and after social transfers (pensions excluded from social transfers) for children aged under 18 years (cut-off point: 60 per cent of median equivalized income after social transfers)

In 2014, poverty rates in Southern Europe after social transfers continued to be at a higher level, between 25 and 33 per cent, than in France, Germany and the UK, where they range from 15 to 20 per cent, despite the fact that in these countries the market also produces very high poverty rates. Thus, after the crisis the low capacity of the welfare states in the South to tackle child poverty persists or even worsens.

With respect to parental leave and ECEC, the crisis has not changed entitlements or enrolment rates, but has prevented enlargement of some crucial polices. In Spain, paternity leave has become a victim of the crisis, since it should have been increased from two to four weeks in January 2011, but this has been postponed for the time being for cost savings reasons. The increasing female activity rates in Spain and Greece may help to understand why enrolment rates in day care centres increased or at least remained stable throughout the Great Recession of 2008.

CONCLUSIONS

Family policy constitutes a wide domain of public intervention and includes many policy instruments (Gauthier, 1999; Pfenning and Bahle, 2000). Family policy as a field of intervention has had a multivalent character and variable outcomes and it developed during the twentieth century for reasons which vary according to country, to historical periods and to the policy field analysed (Gauthier, 1996). Most importantly, family policies have had and still have a multiplicity of purposes (to increase fertility, to reduce child poverty, to promote gender equality, to achieve horizontal redistribution and so son). In the last two decades, even during the era of austerity, family policies have expanded in most European countries to varying degrees (Morgan, 2013; Ferragina and Seeleib-Kaiser, 2015). There has been a readjustment of old welfare programmes and the expansion of programmes for 'new social risks' (Morel et al., 2012). This often meant the expansion of those family policies which aim to support maternal employment and enhance ECEC policies, even in countries characterized as a 'strong male breadwinner' type, such as Germany and the UK (Morgan, 2013).

This chapter has shown that since the 1980s family policies in Southern Europe have changed to some extent, but the overall picture remains the one featured at the beginning of this chapter: weak development of family policies in a context of important 'unsupported familialism'. Family policies in Southern Europe have changed somewhat in relation to services and time but to a lesser degree in relation to family benefits. Employment-related family policies have expanded, though differently across Southern countries, as shown by the increase of enrolment rates of small children in day care services and by a new paternity or father's bonus in parental leave in recent years. However, family allowances or tax breaks for families are still less generous than in Continental, Anglo-Saxon and Northern Europe, which to a large extent explains the higher relative poverty rates among children in the South. In addition, despite the expansion of ECEC, Southern countries still receive less public funding than in Nordic and some Continental welfare states, and in comparison to these countries well-paid parental leave is in general shorter too. Thus, altogether in Southern Europe in 2016 family policies as a policy package were still less developed and less generous than in other European welfare states. We explored in the chapter whether this is only a question of lagging behind and whether Southern countries need more time to develop generous policies for children and a stronger orientation of policies towards female employment. This is not a good explanation, however, because Spain, being a laggard compared to Italy, has achieved more changes in the last decade than the latter. Both countries share similar demographic challenges of a very low fertility rate and rapidly ageing population, but Spain has advanced more on the way to reconciling employment and family. We have interpreted these divergent paths to be caused by political party competition for female voters in Spain in contrast to Italy, by diverging female employment patterns, and the resulting pressures for more employment-oriented family policies.

Future developments in Southern Europe may depend, first, on the evolution of public opinion about how to reconcile employment and family life without compromising equal opportunities for women and men. Second, the way the fiscal crisis is to be resolved will also be essential for the future generosity of family policies and child wellbeing. Finally, all Southern countries will have to face care deficit issues in the near future, given the phenomena of women's increasing participation in the workforce, the ageing of societies and the rising age of retirement. In this respect, more childcare-oriented policies to support working parents are not only measures aiming at gender equality but are also crucial for social investment and for reducing child poverty, which is dramatically high in the Southern countries.

NOTES

1. In Portugal, Greece and Spain a statutory right to reduce working hours until a given age of the child exists (for more see Blume et al., 2017).
2. In this section we only focus on Italy and Spain.

REFERENCES

Albertini, M., M. Kohli, and C. Vogel (2007), 'Intergenerational transfers of time and money in European families: common patterns – different regimes?', *Journal of European Social Policy*, **17** (4), 319–34.
Andreotti, A., S. Marisol Garcia, A. Gomez, P. Hespanha, Y. Kazepov, and E. Mingione (2001), 'Does a Southern European model exist?', *Journal of European Area Studies*, **9** (1), 43–62.
Blum, S., A. Koslowski, and P. Moss (eds) (2017), '13th international review of leave policies and related research 2016', International Network on Leave Policies and Related Research, accessed July 2018 at http://www.leavenetwork.org/lp_and_r_reports/review_2017/.
Bonoli, G. and F. Reber (2010), 'The political economy of childcare in OECD countries: explaining cross-national variations in spending and coverage rates', *European Journal of Political Research*, **49**, 97–118.
Bradshaw, J. and J. Ditch (1993), *Support for Children. A Comparison of Arrangements in Fifteen Countries*, Research Report, 21, London: HMSO.
Calvo, K. and I. Martín (2009), 'Ungrateful citizens? Women's rights policies in Zapatero's Spain', *South European Society and Politics*, **14** (4), 487–502.
Carlos, M. and L. Maratou-Alipranti (2000), 'Family policy and new family forms: the cases of Greece and Portugal', in A. Pfenning and T. Bahle (eds), *Families and Family Policies in Europe: Comparative Perspective*, Frankfurt am Main: Peter Lang Verlag der Wissenschaften, pp. 34–49.
Castles, F.G. (1994), 'On religion and public policy: does Catholicism make a difference', *European Journal of Political Research*, **25** (1), 19–40.
Castro-García, C. and M. Pazos-Morán (2016), 'Parental leave policy and gender equality in Europe', *Feminist Economics*, **22** (3), 1–23.
Cherlin Andrew, J. (2004), 'The deinstitutionalization of American marriage', *Journal of Marriage and Family*, **66** (4), 848–61.
Ciccia, R. and I. Bleijenbergh (2014), 'After the male breadwinner model? Childcare services and the division of labor in European countries', *Social Politics: International Studies in Gender, State & Society*, **21** (1), 50–79.
Ciccia, R. and M. Verloo (2012), 'Parental leave regulations and the persistence of the male breadwinner model: using fuzzy-set ideal type analysis to assess gender equality in an enlarged Europe', *Journal of European Social Policy*, **22** (5), 507–28.
Domínguez Folgueras, M. and T. Castro Martin (2013), 'Cohabitation in Spain: no longer a marginal path to family formation', *Journal of Marriage and Family*, **75** (2), 422–37.
Escobedo, A. and K. Wall (2015), 'Leave policies in Southern Europe: continuities and changes', *Community, Work & Family*, **18** (2), 218–35.
Esping-Andersen, G. (1990), *The Three Worlds of Welfare Capitalism*, New York: Polity Press.
Esping-Andersen, G. (ed.) (1999), *Social Foundations of Postindustrial Economies*, Oxford: Oxford University Press.
Esping-Andersen, G. (2009), *Incomplete Revolution: Adapting Welfare States to Women's New Roles*, Cambridge: Polity Press.
Estevez-Abe, M. and M. Naldini (2016), 'Politics of defamilialization: a comparison of Italy, Japan, Korea and Spain', *Journal of Social Policy*, **26** (4), 327–43.
Eurostat (2003), 'Social protection: cash family benefits in Europe', *Statistics in Focus. Population and Social Conditions*, theme 3, 19, Luxembourg.
Eurostat (2016a), 'Social protection expenditure (spr_exp_ffa)', accessed October 2016 at http://ec.europa.eu/eurostat/web/social-protection/data/database.
Eurostat (2016b), 'Employment and labour market statistics (lfsi_jhh_a)', accessed June 2016 at http://ec.europa.eu/eurostat/web/lfs/data/database.
Eurostat (2016c), 'Employment and labour market statistics (lfsi_act_a)', accessed June 2016 at http://ec.europa.eu/eurostat/web/lfs/data/database.
Eurostat (2016d), 'Living conditions (ilc_caindformal)', accessed May 2016 at http://ec.europa.eu/eurostat/web/income-and-living-conditions/data/database.
Eurydice (2015), 'Greece. Organisation of programmes for children under 4 years', accessed June 2016 at https://webgate.ec.europa.eu/fpfis/mwikis/eurydice/index.php/Main_Page.
Ferragina, E. and M. Seeleib-Kaiser (2015), 'Determinants of a silent (r)evolution: understanding the expansion of family policy in rich OECD countries', *Social Politics*, **22** (1), 1–37.
Ferrera, M. (1996), 'The "Southern model" of welfare in social Europe', *Journal of European Social Policy*, **6** (1), 17–37.
Ferrera, M. (ed.) (2005), *Welfare States and Social Safety Nets in Southern Europe*, London: Routledge.
Ferrera, M. and F. Maino (2014), 'Social innovation beyond the state. Italy's second welfare in a European perspective', Working Papers Secondo Welfare, 2/2014, accessed October 2016 at http://www.secondowelfare.it/allegati/ferrera_maino_wp2_2014_2wel.pdf.

Flaquer, L. (2000), 'Is there a Southern European model of family policy?', in A. Pfenning and T. Bahle (eds), *Families and Family Policies in Europe*, Frankfurt am Main: Peter Lang Verlag der Wissenschaften, pp. 15–33.

García, M. and N. Karakatsanis (2006), 'Social policy, democracy, and citizenship in Southern Europe', in R. Gunther, P.N. Diamandouros, and D.A. Sotiropoulos (eds), *Democracy and the State in the New Southern Europe*, New York: Oxford University Press, pp. 87–137.

Garrido, L. and M.A. Malo (2005), 'Postponement of family formation and public budget: another approach to very low fertility in Spain', *Public Finance and Management*, **5** (1), 152–77.

Gauthier, A.H. (ed.) (1996), *The State and the Family: A Comparative Analysis of Family Policies in Industrialised Countries*, New York: Oxford University Press.

Gauthier, A.H. (1999), 'Family change: practices, policies and values', *The Sources and Methods of Comparative Family Research in Comparative Social Research*, **18**, 31–56.

Guerra, M.C. (ed.) (2011), 'Fisco e welfare per le famiglie, in Ascoli, U', in *Il welfare in Italia*, Bologna: Mulino, pp. 225–55.

Guillén, A.M. and M. León (2011), *The Spanish Welfare State in European Context*, Aldershot: Ashgate.

Hellebrandt, T. (2014), *Income Inequality Developments in the Great Recession*, LIS Working Paper Series, No. 604, Luxembourg Income Study.

Karamessini, M. (2006), 'Gender equality and employment policy', in M. Petmesidou and E. Mossialos (eds), *Social Policy Developments in Greece*, Aldershot: Ashgate, pp. 239–65.

Leitner, S. (2003), 'Varieties of familialism. The caring function of the family in comparative perspective', *European Societies*, **5** (4), 353–75.

León, M. and M. Migliavacca (2013), 'Italy and Spain: still the case of familistic welfare models?', *Population Review*, **52** (1), 25–42.

León, M. and E. Pavolini (2013), 'Cross national variations in care and care as a labour market', in M. León (ed.), *The Transformations of Care in European Societies*, Houndmills, Basingstoke: Palgrave Macmillan, pp. 34–61.

León, M. and E. Pavolini (2014), 'Social investment or back to familism: the impact of the economic crisis on care policies in Italy and Spain', *South European Society & Politics*, **19** (3), 353–69.

Martin, C. (1997), 'Social welfare and the family in Southern Europe: are there any specificities?', *Mire Florence Conference, Comparing Social Welfare Systems in Southern Europe*, Vol. 3, Paris: Mire, pp. 315–35.

MISSOC (2002), 'Mutual information system on social protection', *Social Protection in the EU Member States and the European Economic Area*, Situation on 1 January 2001.

Morel, N., B. Palier, and J. Palme (eds) (2012), *Towards a Social Investment Welfare State? Ideas, Policies and Challenges*, Bristol: Policy Press.

Morgan, K.J. (2013), 'Path shifting of the welfare state electoral competition and the expansion of work-family policies in Western Europe', *World Politics*, **65** (1), 73–115.

Musumeci, R., M. Naldini, and A. Santero (2015), 'First-time fathers and child care. Persistence and innovation in the Italian fatherhood regime', *Interdisciplinary Journal of Family Studies*, **1**, 1–19.

Naldini, M. (2000), 'Family allowances in Italy and Spain, long ways to reform', in A. Pfenning and T. Bahle (eds), *Families and Family Policies in Europe: Comparative Perspective*, Frankfurt am Main: Peter Lang, pp. 70–89.

Naldini, M. (ed.) (2003), *Family in the Mediterranean Welfare States*, London: Frank Cass.

Naldini, M. and C. Saraceno (2008), 'Social and family policies in Italy: not totally frozen but far from structured reforms', *Social Policy & Administration*, **42** (7), 733–53.

Naldini, M. and T. Jurado-Guerrero (2013), 'Family and welfare state reorientation in Spain and inertia in Italy', *Population Review*, **54** (1), 43–61.

OECD (2001), 'Balancing work and family life; helping parents into paid employment', *Employment Outlook*, http://www.oecd.org/social/family/2079435.pdf.

OECD (2016a), Social Expenditure Database, accessed October 2016 at http://www.oecd.org/social/expenditure.htm.

OECD (2016b), OECD Family Database, accessed October 2016 at http://www.oecd.org/els/family/database.htm.

OECD (2018), OECD Family Database, PF.3.2, Enrolement 0-2, accessed July 2018 at http://www.oecd.org/els/soc/PF3_2_Enrolment_childcare_preschool.xlsx.

Oliver, R.J. and M. Mätzke (2014), 'Childcare expansion in conservative welfare states: policy legacies and the politics of decentralized implementation in Germany and Italy', *Social Politics*, **21** (2), 167–93.

Palier, B. and C. Martin (eds) (2008), *Reforming the Bismarckian welfare systems*, Malden, MA, Oxford, UK and Carlton, Australia: Blackwell.

Pfenning, A. and T. Bahle (eds) (2000), *Families and Family Policies in Europe*, Frankfurt am Main: Peter Lang.

Saraceno, C. (1994), 'The ambivalent familism of the Italian welfare state', *Social Politics*, **1** (Spring), 60–82.

Saraceno, C. and W. Keck (2010), 'Can we identify intergenerational policy regimes in Europe?', *European Societies*, **12** (5), 675–96.

Sarkadi, A., R. Kristiansson, F. Oberklaid, and S. Bremberg (2008), 'Fathers' involvement and children's developmental outcomes: a systematic review of longitudinal studies', *Acta paediatrica*, **97** (2), 153–8.

Sims-Schouten, W. (2000), 'Child care services and parents' attitudes in England, Finland and Greece', in A. Pfenning and T. Bahle (eds), *Families and Family Policies in Europe: Comparative Perspectives*, Frankfurt and New York: Peter Lang International Academic Publishers, pp. 270–89.

Symeonidou, H. (1996), 'Social protection in contemporary Greece', *South European Society & Politics*, **1** (3), 67–86.

Valiente, C. (1995), 'Children first: central government child care policies in post-authoritarian Spain (1975–1994)', in J. Brannen and M. O'Brien (eds), *Childhood and Parenthood*, London: Institute of Education, University of London, pp. 249–66.

17. Family policies and social inequalities in Central and Eastern Europe: a comparative analysis of Hungary, Poland and Romania between 2005 and 2015
*Cristina Raț and Dorottya Szikra**

INTRODUCTION

State interventions generally placed under the header of 'family policies' have an uneven impact across class lines and this plainly appears in Central and Eastern European (CEE) societies, which experienced growing inequalities after the fall of communism. This chapter explores family policy developments in Hungary, Poland and Romania, three countries with different, yet comparable welfare state histories, from the perspective of their impact on inequality and child poverty. Our investigation starts at the time of accession to the European Union (EU) (Hungary and Poland in 2004, Romania in 2007), a period marked by relative economic growth and political stability, and goes through the years of the global financial crisis until 2015, when gradual economic recovery was adversely accompanied by intensified nationalist-populist discourses. We contend that in all three countries family policy changes mostly favoured the middle class, while their effects on the situation of socially deprived families with irregular or no employment differed and fluctuated more prominently over time. While nationalistic population policies have been interwoven with family policies in all the three countries, attempts to stigmatize poor families gained emphasis only in Romania and Hungary, often targeting the Roma minority.

We interpret family policies here as cash transfers, subsidies and tax credits directed towards families with dependent children, and services for children below 6 years of age, mainly nurseries and kindergartens. Although we also mention private and non-governmental organizations, our focus remains on public institutions providing support for families. Concerning the level of analysis, we refer to Kvist (2007) and emphasize the importance of investigating both policy outputs and outcomes. In doing so, we go beyond macro-statistics on spending and scrutinize changes in benefit structures, eligibility conditions and the generosity of benefit amounts.[1]

The chapter is organized as follows. First, we provide a synthesis of the state-of-art in family policy analysis related to the CEE region and explain the relevance of our case selection. Second, we analyse the patterns of family policy spending in the three countries as compared to European averages, and recent developments in the most important family policy provisions. Third, we measure the poverty reduction effects of family policies with the help of Eurostat indicators and search for explanations in the national welfare regulations. Special attention is paid to child poverty, the situation of lone parents and large families. Finally, we outline our main findings and point out continuities and recent, potentially path-shifting changes.

OVERVIEW ON CEE FAMILY POLICY RESEARCH AND OUR THREE CASES OF 'FAMILIALISM'

In comparative welfare state analysis, CEE countries have for a long time been either grouped together as 'post-communist' welfare states or clustered alongside older welfare capitalisms (Deacon, 2000). While acknowledging similarities stemming from the early years of social insurance and social assistance programmes from the late nineteenth to the early twentieth century, as well as the somewhat homogenizing effects of the communist rule, contemporary authors have tried to point out a range of differences among post-communist welfare states (Ferge, 2008; Cerami and Vanhuysse, 2009; Szikra and Tomka, 2009; Aidukaite, 2011; Romano, 2014; Kuitto, 2016) and in the more narrow field of family policies (Szelewa and Polakowski, 2008; Szikra and Szelewa, 2009; Inglot et al., 2013; Javornik, 2014; Saxonberg, 2014; Hasková and Saxonberg, 2015).

The strong embeddedness of nationalistic sentiments has roots in their history of ethno-nation state building and the powerful emphasis on the 'nation' even under state-socialism, and these have recently been on the rise especially in Hungary and Poland, with populist right-wing parties in power. Family and population policies are at the centre of the governing programmes of these conservative parties (in power in Hungary since 2010 and in Poland since 2015), endorsing pronatalist measures and rewards for large families. Similar tendencies remain marginal to mainstream politics in Romania. Instead, widespread prejudice against the Roma ethnic minority and concerns over high fertility among the poorest segments of the population (discursively associated with the 'Tsigane' stereotype) leave large families systematically disadvantaged by social policy regulations. In both Romania and Hungary, poor families in general and the Roma minority in particular are often the target of discourses blaming the 'undeserving poor', and face disciplinary conditionings and other mechanisms of 'unfavourable inclusion' (Sen, 2000, p. 28), or even exclusion from welfare rights (Szalai, 2012; Raț, 2013).

The neoliberal discourse largely discredited the idea of social solidarity and replaced it with 'the changed welfare paradigm' of individual responsibility in post-communist countries (Ferge, 1997; Popescu, 2004). This was reflected in the very low social spending on families and children in Romania and Poland until 2015. Hungarian family policy (as opposed to other fields of welfare) resisted any significant cuts, except from a short-lived austerity-package in the mid-1990s (see also Haney, 2002). The coincidence between the emergence of the Lisbon agenda and the timing of EU accession of CEE countries put pressure on governments to address the problem of poverty and social exclusion, while 'activation' (mother's employment), gender equality and work-life balance challenged the old structure of family policies. As argued elsewhere (Inglot et al., 2013), domestic responses to EU expectations were largely shaped by the legacies of well-entrenched family policies, and the different traditions of combining means-tested, universal and insurance-based benefits and services.

The gender emancipation project of state socialist regimes channelled women into paid work and widened opportunities for education and professional carrier development, often more than in some of the capitalist democracies of the time (Fodor, 2002). However, the quest to dismantle patriarchal relations within the family and to radically de-familialize care work remained far behind the communist thesis of equality and socializing the costs of labour reproduction (Pascall and Kwak, 2005). Since the fall of state socialism CEE countries have followed different paths in combining familialistic and individualistic policies (Daly, 2010) and in mixing state support with reliance on the family or the market (Glass and Fodor, 2007; Szelewa and Polakowski, 2008; Javornik, 2014). Romania and Poland embraced more eagerly the European agenda of women's employment, while Hungary remained on the conservative side of supporting mothers as domestic care providers.

Besides important similarities, family policy traditions are quite distinct in the three countries and precisely this difference makes the comparison worthwhile. Hungary pioneered child care services in the late nineteenth century (Szikra, 2011) and provided generous cash transfers and leave schemes for families from the late 1960s. Comparative statistics depict Hungary as among the highest spending countries on family policies within the EU in the past decades, and not even the financial crisis reduced the government's commitment to support families from the state budget. Triggered by political concerns for declining fertility, the Hungarian state provided financial incentives for parents (mothers) to care for their children within the family, setting forth a case of 'explicit familialism' (Lewis, 2001; Leitner, 2003; Szelewa and Polakowski, 2008; Javornik, 2014).

Poland, on the other hand, has long been a laggard in family policy spending (Inglot, 2008), yet consistently redistributes income towards families in the lowest income quintiles, and especially lone parents and large families (Balcerzak-Paradowska et al., 2003). The central state refrained from strong intervention into family life and child care arrangements, while symbolically praising the family and motherhood. Thus, Poland can be regarded as a case of 'implicit familialism', where the state retains a subsidiary role to parents' child-rearing duties (Szelewa and Polakowski, 2008; Javornik, 2014). However, a sharp decline in fertility and vast out-migration after EU integration called for better family policy programmes to be put in place. Cash transfers for families with children and public child care services picked up by 2008 and have been expanding since then, raising the question of whether we are witnessing a departure from 'implicit familialism' towards a more 'explicit' or even 'optional' approach.

Similar to Poland, Romania has been facing serious problems of child poverty, especially in rural areas. The communist regime built a relatively large-scale system of child care services, yet crèches and kindergartens remained underfunded and, after the aggressive measures of coercive pronatalism introduced in 1966, overcrowded (Kligman, 1998; Popescu, 2006). Family allowance, while rather generous for urban workers, excluded altogether the large number of agricultural cooperative members until 1977. Enforced pronatalism and the very low living standards in the 1980s increased the number of children placed in residential institutions, and their appalling situation demanded a prompt reform in child protection on the road to EU accession (Popescu, 2006). Romania thus concentrated after 1990 on overcoming the legacy of child neglect and made efforts to decrease child poverty and (in stark opposition to Hungary and Poland) to discourage families from having more than three children. Rapidly decreasing fertility and growing out-migration led to policy responses that favoured working parents and offered generous earnings-related child care leave benefits for the middle class. Public efforts to subsidize child care services increased and parents' early return to work from child care leave was rewarded with a novel monthly benefit. Thus, Romania might be regarded as a weak case of 'optional familialism', applied selectively only for parents with regular employment.

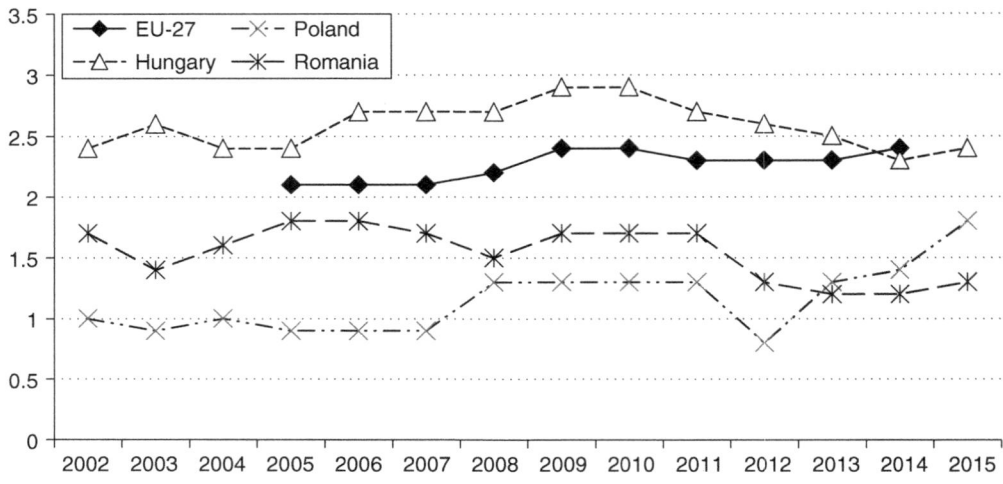

Source: Authors' graph based on data provided by Eurostat (2017).

Figure 17.1 The evolution of expenditures on family benefits as a percentage of GDP in Hungary, Poland and Romania between 2002 and 2015 (without tax credits)

PATTERNS OF PUBLIC EXPENDITURES AND RECENT DEVELOPMENTS IN FAMILY POLICY PROVISIONS

The evolution of family policy expenditures as a share of gross domestic product (GDP) (Figure 17.1), together with the structure of spending according to the countries' targeting of low-income families via means-testing, offer preliminary indicators for our analysis. Hungary has traditionally been very generous in its spending (2.4 per cent in 2005, reaching 2.9 per cent in 2009), yet this has declined since 2010 (dropping back to 2.4 per cent in 2015). Means-tested benefits aimed at tackling income inequalities between families represented only 4 per cent of total spending in 2012 (0.1 per cent of GDP). However, data on Hungary can be misleading, as they do not include the major source of increase in the disposable income, namely, the boost to family tax reliefs since 2010 that amounted to 0.67 per cent of GDP by 2013. Tax reliefs included family policy spending increases over 3 per cent of GDP. As no upper limit to the tax reliefs applies and no tax refund for those on low income exists, an important share of state support is channelled towards higher income families.

In contrast, total family policy spending has been traditionally low in Poland, and the largest share was targeted towards low-income families (66 per cent in 2005 and 55 per cent in 2012). Between 2002 and 2007, family policy spending accounted for only 1 per cent of the GDP, while between 2008 and 2011 it stagnated at around 1.3 per cent of GDP. After a sudden decrease in 2012, family policy spending increased at 1.8 per cent of GDP by 2015, fostered by Poland's relative economic prosperity unharmed by the global financial crisis. Tax credits for families were also adopted in 2007, and gradually extended later, with an upward redistribution towards wealthy families (in a similar vein to the Hungarian case), amounting to approximately 0.4 per cent of Polish GDP in 2010, contributing to 1.7 per cent spending on family policy cash transfers in this country. With the remarkable boost of family-related benefits in 2016, total family policy spending is likely to significantly increase.

Within the same period, Romanian family policy spending fluctuated, with slightly more generous time spans during the years of economic growth and EU accession, but never exceeding 1.8 per cent of GDP. Between 2011 and 2013 the overall tendency was that of a decline, with a historical low of 1.2 per cent of GDP in 2014, followed by a slight increase at 1.3 per cent of GDP in 2015. Similar to Hungary, means-tested benefits account for a small segment of total spending on family-related cash transfers – 7 per cent cf. 0.1 per cent of GDP in 2012. Tax reliefs are higher for low-wage earners and cut entirely for parents earning above the average gross income. This may decrease inequalities somewhat, but the financial gain remains modest, smaller than the value of the universal child allowance.

The evolution of spending in terms of PPS (Purchasing Power Standards) per capita portrays a similar general picture for the three countries. Whereas Poland and Romania both register low amounts of spending, Hungary reaches around 2.5 times higher values, but still remains well below the EU-15 average (Eurostat, 2017).

In order to analyse family policy outputs, it is crucial to go beyond simple statistics on spending. The actual expansion or retrenchment of family policies should be determined at the level of eligibility conditions and generosity of benefit amounts. The most significant form of cash benefits has long been *family allowance* in all the three countries. It served primarily as a tool to increase family incomes and prevent child poverty. In Hungary, family allowance has progressively increased according to the number of children even under state socialism, while the amount has been higher in the case of single parents, typically lone mothers, and also for disabled children. All these important features were kept unchanged from 1990, and the benefit was paid out to every family with children under 18 (21 in the case of university students), with the exception of a short period between 1996 and 1998, when it became means-tested. A major change took place in 2006 when the benefit was doubled, as suggested in the newly formed National Program to Combat Child Poverty (2006) under the Socialist-Liberal coalition. With this increase, means-tested family-related benefits as well as family tax reliefs were (nearly) stopped and thus effectively 'merged' into one, universally available family allowance (Darvas and Mózer, 2004). After the outbreak of the 2008 financial crisis, the minority Socialist government did not directly cut this benefit, but froze the allowance, which has not been increased since then. The Conservative coalition elected in 2010 (and re-elected in 2014) embraced a completely different understanding of family policies and has directed resources to 'working families' instead of *all* families. To this aim, spending on family tax allowance, utilized most effectively by families with average income or above, was boosted by over ten times, from 0.05 per cent to 0.67 per cent of GDP, while universal family allowance was not indexed at all. Thus, there has been a visible shift from universal cash transfers to fiscal welfare, benefiting better-off families. Since 2010, approximately 10 per cent of formerly eligible children were 'pushed out' by decreasing the age of compulsory education from 18 to 16 years and the strict conditioning of family allowance on school attendance.

Poland registered significant upgrading of the family allowance between 2005 and 2014, when it was eventually doubled. Still, the increase was not reflected in the total spending given the decline in birth rates, considerable out-migration from the country and the relatively low eligibility threshold to this historically means-tested benefit. Similarly, *becikowe*, the one-time birth grant, maintained its value, but overall spending decreased as the number of recipients dropped. In 2016, the new right-wing government led by the Law and Justice Party (PiS) made the family allowance universal for all families with two or more children, and substantially increased its amount. If sustainable, this step marks a path-shifting change in Poland.

In Romania, corresponding to the family allowance is the universal child allowance, a constitutional right granted to every child below 18 years of age (and up to 19 for those in secondary education). Even if the amounts have been modest, spending accounts for one-third of the social protection budget, and was eventually boosted 2.4 times between 2005 and 2010, as the allowance for children below the age of 2 significantly increased in 2007. This upgrading should be interpreted by taking into account the lack of widely available paid child care leave due to strict eligibility conditions related to the work record, as we explain later in this chapter. Family allowance has a means-tested top-up for low-income families (in place since 2003), with higher amounts for lone-parent families. Similar to Hungary, the benefit is strictly conditioned on school attendance, which results in low uptake among families from the most severely deprived, marginalized settlements, where access to school is difficult and child labour frequent. Birth-grants had been available between 2001 and 2010, but phased out through crisis-led austerity measures. In 2015 the amount of the universal child allowance doubled again, now reaching approximately €20 per child per month.

Regulations on *maternity leave* are similar in all three countries: high replacement rates ranging between 70 per cent and 100 per cent of previous earnings and 24 to 26 weeks of leave. Fathers' rights nonetheless differ. In Hungary, merely five days of paternity leave are provided for fathers and approximately one-quarter of fathers take it. In Romania, the same five days leave can be supplemented, since 1999 with ten more days, on the condition that fathers take a training course on infants' care. In Poland, paternity leave introduced in 2003 offers two weeks. This comparison shows that the two countries that have long been laggards in family policy are now more open to change than Hungary with a longer and more 'sticky' history of conservative family policies with more emphasis on motherly care.

Parental and child care leaves and related benefits are typically earnings-related and overwhelmingly taken by mothers in all three countries, but their length and availability for non-wage earners differ. In Hungary, the earnings-related paid child care leave, lasting until a child's second birthday, is backed by a universal, flat-rate provision of a much smaller value, granted until a child's third birthday. The latter is utilized by parents with no work record as well as by parents who have been taking earnings-related leave and want to extend leave until the third birthday of their child. Importantly, both types of child care leaves count as contributory years in terms of social insurance. Since 2015, parents returning earlier to the formal labour market have been able to fully maintain their benefits in the case of both types of leaves, until their children's second and third birthdays, respectively. The system of child care leaves also includes the symbolic construction of 'motherhood as a profession' with the possibility for mothers of three or more children to receive a 'homemaker' leave until their youngest child reaches 8 years of age.

Poland offers earnings-related paid leave only until a child's first birthday, while for the second year a means-tested, flat-rate benefit might be claimed by those with the proper work record. Since 2016, Polish parents lacking a work record have been able to apply for a flat-rate child care benefit, again a breakthrough in Polish family policy development.

In Romania, earnings-related paid child care leave lasts until a child's second birthday, but early return to work is rewarded with a generous benefit ('stimulant'), extended in 2016 until a child's third birthday. While some categories of non-wage earners qualify for the minimum value of the benefit (students, persons on sickness leave or registered unemployed still receiving insurance-based benefits), the majority of irregular workers (two out of ten women in Romania) are still not eligible.

The structuring of child care leave benefits favours higher earners in all three countries, even if their financing mechanism is not insurance based per se. The rather costly measure of lengthy job-return bonuses in Romania and more recently in Hungary shows the tension between the traditionalist idea of keeping the popular long paid child care leaves, on the one hand, and giving in to (internal and external) pressures to increase employment of mothers, on the other. Between 2005 and 2015, women's employment rate (aged 20–64 years) increased from 55 to 62.2 per cent in Hungary, from 58 to 61.4 per cent in Poland, while in Romania it stayed at around 56 per cent (Eurostat, 2017). Importantly for estimating the demand for child care services, the share of part-time employment and fixed-term contracts remained much lower than in the 'old' member states, and registered a relatively modest increase during the years of the financial crisis, in 2009–11 (KSH, 2013). Consequently, women from new member states typically have full-time jobs and work more hours than women from the EU-15. As Figure 17.2 illustrates, the employment rate of mothers with three or more children, the youngest below the age of 6, has been significantly lower in Hungary (around 20 per cent until 2010, then a rise to 28 per cent in 2015) than in Poland (50 per cent) and Romania (45 per cent). The explanation resides largely in the construction of long child care leaves keeping mothers at home. The amount

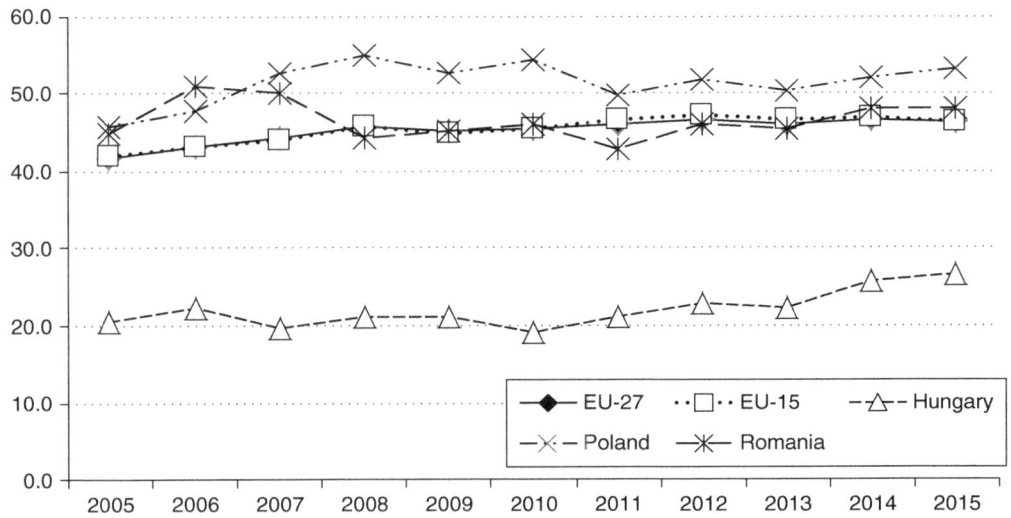

Source: Authors' graph based on data provided by Eurostat (2017).

Figure 17.2 Employment rate of mothers aged 20–49 with three or more children, youngest below 6

of flat-rate leaves is, however, set at a very low level at 90 euros per month, approximately one-quarter of the minimum wage, not indexed since 2008. Consequently, while diminishing future prospects of a return to employment, flat-rate long leaves increase mothers' economic dependence in Hungary, creating a peculiar form of 'motherhood penalty' on the labour market.

Besides cash transfers, access to subsidized *child care services* plays a major role in shaping inequalities, promoting mothers' employment and alleviating the long-term effects of deprivation in children's life trajectories (see also Chapter 8 by Rostgaard in this volume). Since 2005, all three countries have progressed in terms of coverage of child care services, paralleled by a shift of emphasis from 'care' to 'early education'. In Hungary, 15 per cent of children below the age of 3 were enrolled in nurseries (mostly in cities), and 90 per cent of children between 3 and 6 years of age attended kindergarten by 2015 (Eurostat, 2017). Albeit in Poland nurseries did not have a significant role for a long time, their number increased five times between 2005 and 2014 (GUS, 2015, p. 172), and nursery enrolment increased from 3 per cent in 2005 to 6 per cent in 2015 (UNICEF, 2016). Similar to Hungary, services diversified and demand for them increased, yet kindergarten attendance remained around 72 per cent (UNICEF, 2016). The alternative of contracting private nannies, now subsidized by the Polish state, proved to be popular for the middle class (above 8000 contracted nannies in 2014; see GUS, 2015, p. 175). Romania gradually improved its child care infrastructure with kindergartens available even in remote rural areas and attendance growing at 84 per cent in 2015 (UNICEF, 2016). The availability of nurseries remained below demand even in the larger urban centres, and enrolments registered 3.5 per cent in 2015 (UNICEF, 2016). Since 2006, employers may offer crèche vouchers. Importantly for the lowest income segments of the population, and similar to a Hungarian programme in existence until 2016, a means-tested kindergarten attendance grant of around €12 per child per month was introduced in 2015.[2]

CHILD POVERTY IN RELATION TO FAMILY POLICY OUTPUTS AND OUTCOMES

Decreasing child poverty[3] has been a common quest of the EU countries since the first national action plans for social inclusion in 2002, setting ambitious targets for 2010 (see also Chapter 7 by Bradshaw and Chapter 23 by Gornick and Nell in this volume). By now it is clear that expectations to reach these targets may fail even for 2020 (Figure 17.3). Between 2007 and 2010, Hungary was still among the leading EU countries in terms of child poverty reduction (Romano, 2014). However, between 2010 and 2014 the relative poverty reduction of welfare transfers for children below 16 years old, roughly translated as the share of children who avoid poverty due the fact that their families receive social benefits, declined from above 60 per cent to 47 per cent (Figure 17.4), with immediate negative consequences for child poverty rates. Poverty reduction improved in 2015. This progress was, however, not due to increased benefits directed to the poor (these have been halted since 2008), but a result of the extension of public works programmes that provide a higher income to long-term unemployed parents than meagre social assistance. In Poland, child poverty reduction effectiveness fell sharply in 2009 and 2013, but each time it rose again and fluctuated around 45–47 per cent.

Family policies and social inequalities in Central and Eastern Europe 231

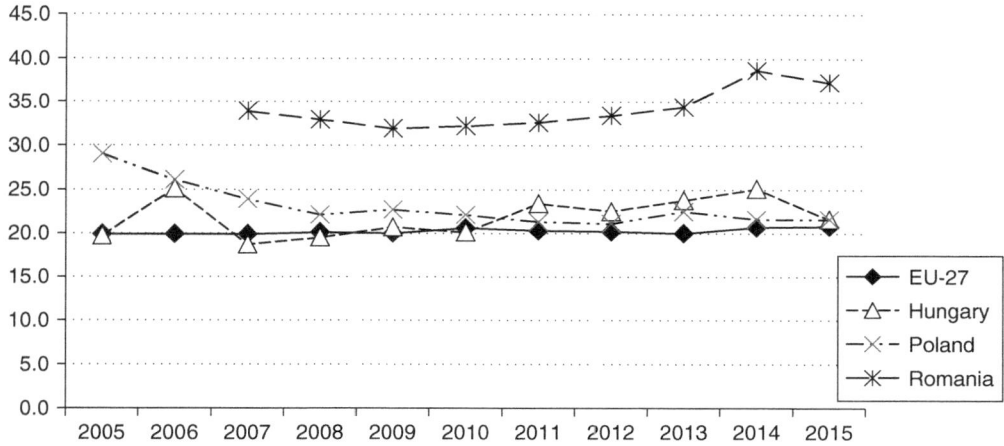

Source: Authors' graph based on data provided by Eurostat (2017).

Figure 17.3 The evolution of the at-risk-of-poverty rate for children below 6 years old

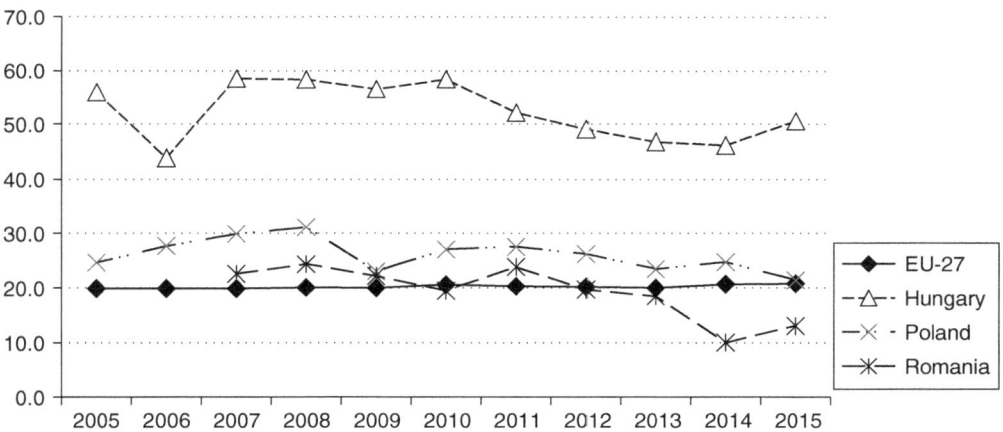

Source: Authors' graph based on data provided by Eurostat (2017).

Figure 17.4 The evolution of relative poverty reduction of social transfers (excluding pensions) for children below 6 years old

Romania was among the poorest performers, with only around 45 per cent relative child poverty reduction that decreased below 38 per cent in 2014 due to widening of the median poverty gap from 33 per cent in 2012 to 44 per cent in 2015 (see Eurostat, 2017). In comparison, Eurostat (2017) reported a 22 per cent median poverty gap for children below 16 years old in the cases of both Hungary and Poland. Similar to Hungary,

Romania improved its poverty rate reduction performance by 2015, partly by upgrading family benefits, partly by increasing wages.

In Poland, the tendency to increase and then halt the effectiveness in child poverty reduction appeared in the context of the expansion and indexation of family benefits, as discussed above. In Hungary, cuts in the means-tested benefits (Mózer et al., 2015) and a fall in the real value of universal benefits (Farkas and Ferge, 2014; Scharle and Szikra, 2015) since 2009, and continuing after the financial crisis, resulted in decline. Both in Romania and Hungary, the strict conditioning of means-tested benefits on school attendance penalizes poor families for the structural barriers they face. It also perpetuates the derogatory image that being a poor parent means being an 'irresponsible' parent, who should be foremost controlled and disciplined by the state. In this respect, Romanian regulations resemble the Hungarian Family Protection Act of 2011, which included the explicit aim to only promote 'responsible' child bearing, referring to the exclusion of families who did not comply with certain behavioural norms.

Besides analysing family policy outcomes in terms of child poverty reduction in general, it is important to scrutinize the situations of different types of vulnerable families, who face higher risks of poverty, such as one-parent and large families with three or more children. The welfare of single parent families, overwhelmingly consisting of lone mothers, can also be regarded as a 'test' of state support for independent households led by women (Orloff, 2006). Despite largely differing welfare efforts in the three countries, there is no significant difference among lone-parent families, with around one-third facing the risk of poverty as of 2014 (Eurostat, 2017). This figure is actually close to the EU average, with some convergence of poverty rates in Hungary and Romania between 2012 and 2015 due to an increase of poverty rates in Hungary and a pronounced decrease in Romania. Potential explanatory factors for the improvement in Romania may reside outside of the welfare state: mothers' higher employment rates, remittances sent home by relatives working abroad, or the better educational-professional position of lone parents (and especially mothers) that allows them to live independently.

In the case of families with three or more children we can observe a great difference between Poland and Hungary, on the one hand, with approximately 34–35 per cent of large families living at risk of poverty, and Romania, on the other hand, where the vast majority of such families lived in poverty in the first half of the current decade: 60.6 per cent in 2013, worsening to 73.1 per cent in 2014. Eurostat data also point to the failure of relative poverty reduction for large families in Romania, with less than 10 per cent safeguarded from income poverty through state transfers during recent years. Following upgrading of the family allowance and its means-tested components, this situation might slightly improve from 2016. In Hungary, despite a significant decline caused by the decrease of family allowance in real values, poverty reduction in the particular case of large families still seems significantly high, at 45 per cent in 2014. This is due especially to the positive discrimination of families with three or more children in terms of tax relief, parental leave as well as family allowance. Poland shows a reduced level of poverty reduction for large families (from 28 per cent in 2010 to 22 per cent in 2014) that might have been caused by the shift to fiscal welfare. This situation is, however, expected to change very soon, following the adoption of the generous 500+ programme in 2016.

CONCLUSIONS

During the last decade, family policies in Hungary, Poland and Romania have been on the move towards selectively upgrading state provisions, but their historically entrenched pathways are still visible. Shifts towards greater reliance on fiscal measures (through strengthening tax credits for families with children), greater gender equality (child care leaves also available for fathers), subsidies for mothers' early return to work and the diversification of child care options occurred with different emphases and timing in the three countries. One important conclusion of our chapter is that most reforms favoured middle-class families, especially in the post-crisis years, as these reforms strengthened earnings-relatedness and fiscal welfare. In Poland, the extension and increase of family allowance (500+ programme) and paid child care leave in 2016 to better-off families represented a turning away from the legacy of 'implicit familialism' to more 'explicit' support. Preference for state-subsidized private options is also characteristic of this country. In Hungary, tax reliefs as well as generous earnings-related leaves led to increased redistribution towards the better-off. Romania, after a brief interlude in the years of the global financial crisis, also increased the earnings-relatedness of leaves and upgraded the benefit for early return to work.

At the other end of the socio-economic spectrum, low-income families with irregular or no employment remained adversely included or straightforwardly excluded from some of the mainstream family policy programmes. They are not entitled to paid child care leave in Romania, and receive low flat-rate benefits in Hungary and Poland. Family allowance became stigmatizing in Hungary and Romania with newly applied behavioural controls, which often exclude the most vulnerable children from eligibility. Despite a recent increase in the values of the family allowance in Romania, they have remained much below European standards.

The analysis of the influence of state transfers on child poverty revealed that, despite maintaining its historically high spending on family policies, Hungary decreased its poverty reduction effectiveness, while Poland slightly improved it. If recent changes are maintained by the Polish government, they might have a profound positive effect on tackling child poverty. In Romania, child poverty reduction deteriorated in the years of the global financial crisis, and changes after 2015 might only bring some modest improvement. Varying support for large families depicts divergent views of pronatalism: while Romanian regulations contain disincentives for raising more than four children and hardly ameliorate the risk of poverty in the case of large families, Poland and Hungary grant more generous support, which helps them avoid impoverishment. Strict conditionings on school attendance in Hungary and Romania often fail to reach their purpose and, instead, provide discursive devices for blaming parents who face multiple deprivation, and ultimately pose barriers in combating child poverty and further deepen the inequalities in these countries.

NOTES

* We are grateful for Tomasz Inglot's generous and valuable input on the Polish case, as well as for our engaging and highly rewarding collaboration on comparative family policy research that started in 2009. The research on the Hungarian case was supported by the János Bolyai Research Scholarship of the Hungarian Academy of Sciences. All potential errors belong to us.

1. Comparative information on social policy schemes in various European countries is provided, for example, by the Mutual Information System on Social Protection (MISSOC) under the European Commission, see http://www.missoc.org (accessed March 2017). In the narrower field of family policies, the OECD Family Policy Database offers useful information on the OECD area: http://www.oecd.org/els/family/database.htm (accessed March 2017). For the present study, however, we relied on national sources, as they are more detailed and up to date.
2. The promotion of the law was preceded by the success of a similar programme implemented by the non-governmental organization Ovidiu Ro in rural areas in several counties, in villages with large shares of impoverished children, many of them ethnic Roma. The preamble of the law refers to this programme (see Law 248/2015). This can be seen as a case of scaling-up a local programme to the national level.
3. In this chapter, we measured poverty as income below the at-risk-of-poverty monetary threshold used by Eurostat and set at 60 per cent of the national median income per equivalent person. The equivalence scale applied by Eurostat follows the modified OECD scale and weights every adult (except for the first adult in the household) by 0.5 and every child below the age of 14 by 0.3. This methodology underestimates poverty in the case of families with children whenever a substantive part of the family income is spent on food and other basic non-durable goods, as it happens in CEE countries. Eurostat regularly reports poverty measures also based on the AROPE approach, which includes alongside monetary poverty material deprivation and low work intensity. For details on the construction of the AROPE indicator, see the web page of Eurostat: http://ec.europa.eu/eurostat/statistics-explained/index.php/People_at_risk_of_poverty_or_social_exclusion (accessed March 2017).

REFERENCES

Aidukaite, J. (2011), 'Welfare reforms and socio-economic trends in the 10 new EU member states of Central and Eastern Europe', *Communist and Post-Communist Studies*, **44** (3), 211–19.
Balcerzak-Paradowska, B., A. Chłoń-Domińczak, I.E. Kotowska, A. Olejniczal-Merta, I. Topińska, and I. Wóycicka (2003), 'The gender dimensions of social security reform in Poland', in E. Fultz, M. Ruck, and S. Steinhilber (eds), *The Gender Dimension of Social Security Reform in Central and Eastern Europe: Case Studies of Czech Republic, Hungary and Poland*, Budapest: International Labour Office, pp. 187–248.
GUS (Central Statistical Office of Poland) (2015), *Statistical Yearbook of the Republic of Poland 2015*, Warsaw: GUS.
Cerami, A. and P. Vanhuysse (eds) (2009), *Post-Communist Welfare Pathways: Theorizing Social Policy Transformations in Central and Eastern Europe*, Houndmills, Basingstoke and New York: Palgrave Macmillan.
Daly, M. (ed.) (2010), *Families versus State and Market: Oxford Handbook of the Welfare State*, Oxford: Oxford University Press, pp. 139–51.
Darvas, Á. and P. Mózer (2004), 'Kit támogassunk?', *Esély*, **6**, 64–99.
Deacon, B. (2000), 'Eastern European welfare states: the impact of the politics of globalisation', *Journal of European Social Policy*, **10**, 146–61.
Eurostat (2017). Population and Social Conditions Database, European Commission, Brussels.
Farkas, Zs. and Zs. Ferge (2014), 'A Nemzeti Társadalmi Felzárkózási Stratégia: Kormányzati vállalások, követésük, teljesítésük', in A. Darvas and Zs. Ferge (eds), *Civil jelentés a gyerekesélyekről, 2012–2013*, Budapest: Gyerekesély Közhasznú Egyesület, pp. 19–44.
Ferge, Zs. (1997), 'The changed welfare paradigm: the individualization of the social', *Social Policy and Administration*, **31** (1), 20–44.
Ferge, Zs. (2008), 'Is there a specific East-Central European welfare culture?', in W. van Oorschot, M. Opielka and B. Pfau-Effinger (eds), *Culture and Welfare State: Values and Social Policy in Comparative Perspective*, Cheltenham, UK and Northampton, MA, USA: Edward Elgar Publishing, pp. 141–61.
Fodor, É., C. Glass, H. Kawachi, and L. Popescu (2002), 'Family policy and gender in Hungary, Poland, and Romania', *Communist and Post-Communist Studies*, **35**, 475–90.
Glass, C. and É. Fodor (2007), 'From Public to Private Maternalism? Gender and Welfare in Poland and Hungary after 1989', *Social Politics: International Studies in Gender, State and Society*, **14** (3), 323-350.
Haney, L. (2002), *Inventing the Needy: Gender and Politics of Welfare in Hungary*, Berkeley/Los Angeles: University of California Press.
Hašková, H. and S. Saxonberg (2015), 'The revenge of history – the institutional roots of post-communist family policy in the Czech Republic, Hungary and Poland', *Social Policy and Administration*, **50** (5), 559–79.

Inglot, T. (ed.) (2008), *Welfare States in East Central Europe, 1919–2004*, New York and Cambridge: Cambridge University Press.
Inglot, T., D. Szikra, and C. Raţ (2013), 'Reforming post-communist welfare states. Family policies in Poland, Hungary and Romania since 2000', *Problems of Post-Communism*, **59** (6), 27–49.
Javornik, J. (2014), 'Measuring state de-familialism: contesting post-socialist exceptionalism', *Journal of European Social Policy*, **24** (3), 240–57.
Kligman, G. (ed.) (1998), *The Politics of Duplicity: Controlling Reproduction in Ceausescu's Romania*, Berkeley, CA: University of California Press.
KSH (Központi Statisztikai Hivatal) (2013), Stadat Database, KSH, Budapest.Kvist, J. (2007), 'Exploring diversity: measuring welfare state change with fuzzy-set methodology', in C. Jochen and N. Siegel (eds), *Investigating Welfare State Change – the 'Dependant Variable' Problem*, Cheltenham, UK and Northampton, MA, USA: Edward Elgar Publishing, pp. 198–214.
Leitner, S. (2003), 'Varieties of familialism: the caring function of the family in comparative perspective', *European Societies*, **4**, 353–75.
Lewis, J. (2001), 'The decline of the male breadwinner model: implications for work and care', *Social Politics*, **8** (2), 152–69.
Mózer P., K. Tausz, and A. Varga (2015), 'A segélyezési rendszer változásai' (Changes in the system of social assistance), *Esély*, **3**, 43–66.
National Program to Combat Child Poverty (2006), Hungarian Academy of Sciences, Budapest.
Orloff, A.S. (2006), 'From maternalism to "employment for all": state policies to promote women's employment across the affluent democracies', in J. Levy (ed.), *The State after Statism*, Cambridge, MA: Harvard University Press, pp. 230–68.
Pascall, G. and A. Kwak (2005), *Gender Regimes in Transition in Central and Eastern Europe*, Bristol: Policy Press.
Popescu, L. (2004), 'Romanian post-communist social policy. Towards the Third Way', in W. Seelisch (ed.), *Soziale Verantwortung in Europa: Analysen und Professionelles Handeln in verschiedenen Hilfesystemen*, Darmstadt: Bogen Verlag, pp. 175–86.
Popescu, L. (2006), 'Child care, family and state in post-socialist Romania', in M. Mesner and G. Wolfgruber (eds), *Politics of Reproduction at the Turn of the 21th Century; the Cases of Finland, Portugal, Romania, Russia, Austria, and the US*, Innsbruck: StudienVerlag, pp. 109–27.
Raţ, C. (2013), 'Bare peripheries: state retrenchment and population profiling in segregated Roma settlements from Romania', *Studia UBB Sociologia*, **58** (2), 155–74.
Romano, S. (ed.) (2014), *The Political and Social Construction of Poverty: Central and Eastern European Countries in Transition*, Bristol: Policy Press.
Saxonberg, S. (ed.) (2014), *Gendering Family Policies in Post-communist Europe: A Historical-Institutional Analysis*, Houndmills, Basingstoke: Palgrave Macmillan.
Scharle, Á. and D. Szikra (2015), 'Recent changes moving Hungary away from the European social model', in D. Vaughan-Whitehead (ed.), *The European Social Model in Crisis: Is Europe Losing its Soul?* Cheltenham, UK and Northampton, MA, USA: Edward Elgar Publishing, pp. 229–61.
Sen, A. (2000), 'Social exclusion: concept, application and scrutiny', *Social Development Papers*, No. 1 (June), 1–60.
Szalai, J. (2012), 'Fragmented social rights in Hungary's post-communist welfare state', in A. Evers and A.M. Guillemard (eds), *Social Policy and Citizenship: The Changing Landscape*, Oxford: Oxford University Press, pp. 283–304.
Szelewa, D. and M.P. Polakowski (2008), 'Who cares? Changing patterns of childcare in Central and Eastern Europe', *Journal of European Social Policy*, **18**, 115–31.
Szikra, D. (2011), 'Tradition matters: child care and primary school education in modern Hungary', in K. Hagemann, K. Jarausch, and C. Allemann-Ghionda (eds), *Children, Families and States*, New York and Oxford: Berghahn Books, pp. 364–85.
Szikra, D. and D. Szelewa (2009), 'Do Central and Eastern European Countries fit the Western picture? The example of family policies in Hungary and Poland', in C. Klenner and S. Leiber (eds), *Welfare States and Gender Inequality in Central and Eastern Europe: Continuity and Post-Socialist Transformation*, Brussels: European Trade Union Institute (ETUI), pp. 81–116.
Szikra, D. and B. Tomka (2009), 'Social policy in East Central Europe: major trends in the 20th century', in A. Cerami and P. Vanhuysse (eds), *Post-Communist Welfare Pathways: Theorizing Social Policy Transformations in Central and Eastern Europe*, Houndmills, Basingstoke and New York: Palgrave Macmillan, pp. 17–34. UNICEF Regional Office for CEE/CIS (2016), TransMonEE 2016 Database, accessed 21 April 2017 at http://www.transmonee.org.

18. Not all in the same family: diverging approaches to family policy in East Asia
*Ito Peng and Yi-Chun Chien**

INTRODUCTION

It is often assumed that East Asian countries have very similar familistic welfare policies. Because of their shared Confucian cultural heritage, governments in these countries have historically relied heavily on the family to provide care and welfare, and consequently offered very little public support or programmes for the family. While this may have been the case before, it is no longer so today. Most East Asian countries have experienced rapid social, economic and cultural changes over the last few decades. This, in turn, has led to noticeable changes in their family policies, and increased policy diversity across the region. In this chapter we first describe the common familistic root of East Asian family policies. We then discuss diverse new policy approaches to family and care that are being implemented across the region. Although in most East Asian countries 'family policies' include both elder care and childcare, we focus on childcare in this chapter. We compare family policies in six East Asian countries – Japan, South Korea, Taiwan, China, Hong Kong and Singapore[1] – to show a spectrum of family policy approaches ranging from those premised on what we call a *liberal market approach* to ones that align more closely to a *regulated institutional approach*. We argue that these variations arise from their different political and institutional contexts. In the last section we summarize the implications of our learning.

THE FAMILISTIC ROOT OF EAST ASIAN FAMILY POLICIES

Japan, South Korea, Taiwan, China, Hong Kong and Singapore share in common the Confucian precept that posits the family as the base of society, and filial piety as the central pillar of the family ethos. Accordingly, parents are expected to raise and educate their children, and in turn, children are obliged to be obedient and to look after their parents in old age (Chan and Tan, 2004). It is therefore not surprising that East Asian governments that subscribe to Confucian political economy have traditionally delegated welfare and care tasks to the family. Indeed, all the six East Asian welfare states have been hitherto low welfare spenders, particularly in relation to the family. Until 1990, all six countries, with the exception of Japan, had public social spending well below 10 per cent of gross domestic product (GDP) as compared to the Organisation for Economic Co-operation and Development (OECD) average of 17.5 per cent. Even for Japan, which had the highest public social spending in East Asia, the figure was only 11 per cent (OECD, 2016). However, because of social, demographic and economic changes since then, Japan's social spending has now risen to about 23 per cent while South Korea and Taiwan's spending has

Table 18.1 Demographic profiles of the East Asian countries

Countries	Percentage of the population aged 65+	Total fertility rate	Women's employment rate	Percentage of social expenditure to GDP
Year	2016	2016	2016	2016
Japan	28.0 (2018)	1.41	67.5	23.1 (2013)
South Korea	13.6	1.17	56.9	10.4
Taiwan	13.2	1.13	50.8	11.6
China	11.4	1.63	63.3	7.7 (2014)
Hong Kong	16.6	1.21	54.2	8.5 (2014)
Singapore	12.4	1.20	60.4	6.0 (2013)
OECD total	17.6	1.70	60.1	21.0

Source: UNDESA, *World Population Prospectus 2017* (https://esa.un.org/unpd/wpp/); Taiwan Ministry of Health and Welfare (https://www.mohw.gov.tw/lp-3781-2.html); *Taiwan Statistical Databook 2017* (https://www.ndc.gov.tw/en/News_Content.aspx?n=607ED34345641980&sms=B8A915763E3684AC&s=1897C8025B0899A0); OECD Social Expenditure Database (SOCX); Statistics Japan (http://www.stat.go.jp/english/data/handbook/c0117.html); Statistics Korea (http://kostat.go.kr/portal/eng/index.action); Census and Statistics Department Hong Kong (https://www.censtatd.gov.hk/home/); Department of Statistics, Singapore (https://www.singstat.gov.sg/).

reached over 10 per cent (Table 18.1) (see also Chapter 9 by Lee and Baek in this volume on recent developments in Japan and South Korea).

East Asian societies have undergone significant transformations since the 1990s. First, all the six countries have been experiencing rapid demographic ageing, so much so that they are all among the top ten fastest ageing countries in the world today (UNDESA, 2015). Whereas in 1990 only about 12 per cent of the Japanese population was over the age of 65, today the figure is 28 per cent. By 2035, the proportion of the Japanese population aged 65+ is projected to reach 32 per cent (UNDESA, 2016). Similarly, South Korea, Taiwan, Hong Kong and Singapore are projected to have over 25 per cent of their population over the age of 65 by 2035. These changes will continue to alert policymakers to the issues of old age social security, childcare and elder care. Second, the rise in women's paid employment and the concomitant decline in the co-residency of elderly parents/adult children in all the six East Asian countries have contributed to growing demands for both child and elder care (Table 18.1).[2] Third, fertility rates in these countries have dropped precipitously as a result of long working hours, economic insecurity, lack of housing space and high educational costs. Changes in the last three decades, therefore, have posed real challenges to the traditional Confucian values, such as intergenerational familial dependency, strict gender role segregation and filial piety. In all these societies, family values and relations have become more diverse, ambiguous and contradictory. Today, widespread ideals about modern love-based and democratic marriages, individualism, the nuclear family, women's higher education and aspiration for greater gender equality clash with traditional values upholding patriarchy, filial piety and gender discrimination (Canda, 2013; Chang and Song, 2010; Martin, 1990; Sechiyama, 2013; Yi, 2013). In addition to the increased distanciation between generations, young people, especially women, are less willing and/or able to provide care to their elderly parents and in-laws. These changes have compelled East Asian families to increasingly 'subcontract out filial piety' (Lan, 2002). The governments have also begun to respond to these structural and cultural shifts by developing and expanding social care programmes and/or financial support to help meet families' care and welfare needs. The result is an increased public policy focus on the family and an increased externalization of family care and welfare.

DIVERGING APPROACHES TO FAMILY POLICY IN EAST ASIA

Despite similar structural and cultural transformations, recent family policy reforms in the six East Asian countries have resulted in increased diversity in family policy models across the region. We see a spectrum of approaches ranging from what we call the *liberal market approach* (Singapore and Hong Kong) to the *regulated institutional approach* (Japan and South Korea), with Taiwan and China adopting neither liberal market nor institutional approaches, and instead, promoting family-based childcare through childcare allowances (Taiwan) or by default (China). Under the liberal market approach, governments rely heavily on the private market for care delivery, and they encourage families to use private market options by offering subsidies and tax incentives to purchase care. This has led to extensive uses of foreign domestics and nannies within private homes. In contrast, under the regulated institutional approach, governments actively promote socialization of care through expansion of publicly provided and/or subsidized early childhood education and care (ECEC). In Taiwan and China, both governments have been reticent to provide publicly funded or subsidized ECEC despite its growing popularity amongst middle-class parents. Instead, in both these countries families are encouraged to rely on private familial sources of care. For example, the Taiwanese government has extended the length of parental leaves and now offers allowances for grandparents to care for their grandchildren. Having identified these divergent approaches to family policies in East Asia, it is however important to point out, first, that this diverging pattern is nevertheless circumscribed within the East Asian context, that is, it does not take away the fact that all six countries are basically familistic in terms of their welfare state orientation. In other words, these different approaches to care should be considered variations *within* the familistic world, and not a categorical departure from the East Asian welfare regime. Second, family and care policies in these countries are also still in a process of change, and as such, they will continue to shift over time.

Liberal Market Approach

Singapore and Hong Kong represent ideal cases of liberal market approaches to family and care because of their governments' extensive reliance on and use of the private market for the provision and delivery of care. In both cases, public provisions of ECEC is either non-existent or limited only to the very poor; instead, subsidies, vouchers and tax incentives are applied to encourage families to seek private solutions, which often involve purchasing care in the private market. In both countries, the very low fertility rates (approximately 1.2 in both places) have compelled the governments to introduce a series of pronatalist family policies since the 2000s. In Hong Kong, the ten-week paid maternity leave for working mothers – legislation that had been in existence since 1968 but employers in practice rarely abided by – was reaffirmed in 2006 and reinforced with a three-day paid paternity leave for fathers in 2015 (both at 80 per cent wage replacement rate) (Council for Sustainable Development in Hong Kong, 2006). In Singapore, a three-day fully paid marriage leave for employees was introduced in 2000 to encourage marriage and childbirth (Yap, 2009). Since then, the government has steadily ratcheted up maternity and childcare leave provisions for working parents, including extension of eight-week paid maternity leave to 12 weeks, and then to 16 weeks with employment protection in 2008, introduction of four-week's paid maternity leave for child adoption, extension of paid childcare leave from two to six days per year, with an additional six days of unpaid infant care leave, and the introduction of three-day's paternity leave for men in the civil service (Sun, 2012).

Both Hong Kong and Singapore's family support policies are heavily reliant on the private market, and to some extent the community, for service delivery. The Hong Kong government established a community babysitters' register system (*Child Service Draft*) in 2005 to help parents access childcare services. Private for- and not-for-profit childcare providers can receive government subsidies to set up a childcare service business, and financial assistance to establish neighbourhood Mutual Help Child Care Centres has been available to non-governmental organizations (NGOs) since 2011. Women's and religious organizations are also encouraged to participate in the *Neighbourhood Support Child Care Project* by providing local home- and centre-based childcare. In Hong Kong the Education Commission review of 2000 resulted in the overhaul the entire education system. The new ECEC policy led to the merger of early childcare and education, resulting in expansion of kindergartens-cum-childcare centres, all of them run by private for- or not-for-profit enterprises. The Hong Kong government then implemented the *Pre-primary Education Voucher* in 2007 to help low-income families access ECEC in the private market. Subsequently, the *Kindergarten and Child Care Centre Fee Remission Scheme* has also been made available for low-income families to cover part or the whole of the childcare centre fee. A total of 37,495 children were in receipt of the scheme in 2015,[3] accounting for 21.8 per cent of all children aged 3–6. Currently, more than 90 per cent of all pre-school children aged 3–6 years are enrolled in ECEC programmes either on a part-time or full-time basis (Wong and Rao, 2015).

The Singaporean government has been offering financial incentives to vigorously promote childbirth. The *Baby Bonus Scheme*, introduced in 2001, and initially targeted towards the third and fourth child, was extended to the first and second child and to beyond the fourth child in 2004 and 2008. The scheme provides a one-time gift of S$4000 to the first two children and S$6000 for the third child and beyond. To encourage parents to save for their children's care and education the *Child Development Account* offers a dollar-for-dollar matching grant for savings contribution made by parents up to S$6000 for the first and second child, S$12,000 for the third and fourth child, and S$16,000 for the fifth child and beyond. Parents can use the funds for childcare, kindergarten, and enrichment programmes offered by approved institutions for the child or for his or her siblings. While a universal childcare subsidy is provided to all parents, it favours full-time working mothers needing full-day childcare. Whereas non-working mothers can receive S$150 per month subsidy per child if they enroll their children in full-day ECEC programmes, working mothers receive S$300 per child for a half-day programme and S$600 per child per month if they are enrolled in a full-day ECEC programme. The universal childcare subsidy was doubled in 2008, but given the high childcare costs the subsidy only partially covers the costs, even with the increase. For very low-income families, the centre-based financial assistance scheme together with the universal subsidy cover 75–95 per cent of the fees of a *non-profit* childcare centre (Choo, 2010). To encourage mothers to return to work, a *Back-to-Work scheme* offers a one-time payment to offset the initial expenses incurred in sending a child to childcare. It pays for uniforms, registration fees, deposits, the first month's fee and insurance. Like Hong Kong, completely public ECEC does not exist, as kindergartens and childcare centres in Singapore are all run by private for- or not-for-profit enterprises.

The expansions of private ECEC services in Hong Kong and Singapore are, however, relatively recent phenomena. A more common policy approach to childcare in the two places has been to encourage families to employ foreign live-in domestic workers or nannies at home by providing tax concessions and incentives. The two countries have similar colonial traditions of using domestic services, which until the 1990s were largely limited to professional or wealthy households. For example, a 1982 survey found that 21.3 per cent of professional and 11 per cent of white collar working mothers in Hong Kong were using foreign domestic workers to care for their children while middle- and working-class working mothers were not able to afford such a childcare option (Wong, 1992). However, as the two countries experienced strong economic growth, rising domestic wages, increased women's labour force participation in the 1990s, and increased availability of foreign domestic workers from neighbouring countries, hiring of foreign domestic workers became much more affordable for middle-class Hong Kong and Singaporean families. In lieu of publicly provided ECEC, the two governments actively supported middle-class families to employ foreign domestic workers by making legal procedures for private employment of such workers relatively easy. The Hong Kong government has reduced levies on family employers hiring foreign domestic workers. Similarly, the Singaporean government has created a special immigration channel for families hiring foreign domestic workers and reduced the levy on employers of foreign domestic workers. The proportion of households employing foreign domestic workers in Hong Kong increased sharply from 3.6 per cent in 1987 to 10 per cent in 2000 (Chan, 2005), while the number of registered foreign domestic workers more than quadrupled, from 38,000 in 1987 to 150,000 in 1995, and then further increased to 352,000 in 2016 (Hong Kong Census and Statistics Department, 1995; Hong Kong Legislative Council Secretariat, 2017). In Singapore the reduction of the foreign domestic worker levy led to a 144 per cent increase in the number of registered female domestic workers, from 140,000 in 2002 to 201,000 in 2010 (TWC2, 2011). Currently there are approximately 231,500 and 320,000 registered foreign live-in domestic workers working in private homes in Singapore and Hong Kong, respectively – a ratio of approximately one domestic worker to every 5 and 7.5 households, respectively (Peng, 2017). Until very recently, most of the foreign domestic workers in Hong Kong were primarily caring for young children. Since the 2000s, however, with the introduction of the *Pre-primary Education Voucher*, the increased popularity of ECEC among middle-class Hong Kong parents, and the growing elderly population, foreign domestic workers are increasingly caring for the elderly as well as children. In Singapore, most of the foreign domestic workers are providing care for the elderly and children.

Regulated Institutional Approach

Unlike Hong Kong and Singapore, Japanese and South Korean governments have adopted a more regulated institutional approach to their family policies. Rather than encouraging families to purchase care in the private market, the two governments have opted to expand publicly provided and/or publicly funded/subsidized childcare through the regulated or semi-regulated market. The Japanese government has been enhancing its family support policies in an effort to shore up the country's declining birth rate since the beginning of the 1990s (Japan Ministry of Health and Welfare, 1997). The *Child Care Leave Act* of 1992 granted one parent the option to take unpaid parental leave of up to ten months, following the 14-week maternity leave (see also Chapter 10 by Thévenon in this volume for more information on Japanese parental leave). The *Act on the Welfare of Workers Who Take Care of Children or Other Family Members Including Child Care Leave* (1995) strengthened support for parental leave by offering 40 per cent income replacement for the one-year parental leave (raised to 60 per cent in 2005), and the 1999 revision of the *Childcare and Family Care Leave Law* made the family care leave system mandatory for all workplaces (Peng, 2002). In 2005 the government redoubled its support for the family care leave system by extending the duration of the one-year parental leave to three years. In the same year the government also established a childcare system for sick or injured children, and relaxed the restrictions on the amount of leave taken by parents. Since the 2009 *Bill to Revise the Child Care and Family Care Leave Law* parents are entitled to work shorter and flexible hours to cope with their childcare needs. Employees can also take family care leave on a daily basis. Employees with one pre-school-aged child can now take up to five days of paid childcare leave per year, and up to ten days per year if they have two or more children. Fathers are also encouraged to take childcare leave, and the 2009 bill extends childcare leave to 14 months if both parents take it (Peng, 2011).

Family care leave (i.e., to care for sick family members) has also become more generous since the mid-1990s. The three-month unpaid care leave introduced in 1996 was bolstered in 1998 by the addition of 25 per cent wage replacement. The replacement rate then rose to 40 per cent in 2001, and to 50 per cent in 2007 (Japan Ministry of Health, Labour and Welfare, 2008). The Japanese government also raised the maximum eligible ages of children covered by the universal child allowance from 3 to 7 years in 2000, then to 10 years in 2004, to 12 years in 2006, and finally to 15 years in 2009. At the same time, the benefit for under 3 year olds was doubled, from ¥5000 to ¥10,000 in 2007, and then to ¥15,000 in 2010. By 2010, the child allowance system provided ¥13,000 per month to each child to the end of junior high school (i.e., age 15) (Peng, 2011).

Generous public support for working parents notwithstanding, what differentiates Japan's and South Korea's from Singapore's and Hong Kong's family policies is the former two governments' commitment to publicly supported childcare. Since the establishment of the national plan (*Angel Plan*) to expand public childcare and support for families with young children in 1994, the number and proportion of children in ECEC in Japan have risen markedly. Total childcare space increased from 1.92 million in 1995 to 2.16 million in 2010 (at a time when the number of children born was declining), and the proportion of children aged 0–2 enrolled in ECEC rose from 11.1 per cent in 1998 to 30.6 per cent in 2014, while the ECEC enrolment rates of those aged 3–5 increased from 83.9 per cent in 2002 to 91.0 per cent in 2014 (OECD, 2017). The most recent childcare policy reform, *Vision for Child and Childcare*, clearly shows the Japanese government's effort to ensure guaranteed childcare space for all families wanting childcare (Peng, 2012). Japan has a long history of institutionalized childcare dating back to the end of the World War II. In the 1960s as Japan entered its rapid economic growth period, public childcare became a national policy priority as the women's movement took up the cause (Peng, 2002). The existence of a public childcare policy, albeit one that initially targeted low-income and single mother families, established the institutional framework for a public childcare system and created a path-dependent trajectory for the government to expand the public childcare system in the 1990s. The two main childcare facilities providing care and education to pre-school children in Japan are full-day centre-based daycare available to children 0–5 years old, and half-day kindergartens that provide early child education for children 3–5 years old. Kindergartens are operated by national, public and/or private (for and not-for-profit) providers, while licensed childcare centres are usually offered by public or private not-for-profit providers. In order to receive the public funding, the licensed childcare centres are required to meet strict standards and regulations. In recent years, however, non-licensed but regulated commercial childcare centres have grown in response to the demand for more flexible care services (An, 2013).

Like Japan, the South Korean government has also adopted a regulated institutional approach to family policy, albeit with less regulation than Japan because the national public childcare system was not created until 1990. South Korea started implementing family support policies in the early 2000s in a direct response to the declining fertility. With the total fertility rate down to 1.08 in 2005, the government launched the *Basic Plans for Low Fertility and Ageing Society* in 2006, promising to improve work-family reconciliation legislation and expand childcare (Peng, 2012). The eligibility for the *National Basic Livelihood Guarantee Programme*, a basic income support for low-income households, was extended from families with incomes below 50 per cent of the average monthly income of the urban working class to 70 per cent in 2006 and to 100 per cent in 2007 (meaning that families with income less than the average monthly household income are now eligible for the basic income support). The coverage increased to cover all families with children in the bottom 70 per cent of the income distribution (An, 2013). Childcare subsidies were made available to most families with pre-school-age children. Employment reforms after 1998 ensured working parents' right to flexible working hours, care leaves, the choice of switching to part-time employment, and the guarantee of employment upon return. The *Basic Plans for Low Fertility and Ageing Society* (2006–09) further universalized and expanded paid maternity and parental leaves. The plan also expanded ECEC subsidies for families with small children and provided subsidies and incentives for private sector childcare providers. These policies proved to be extremely successful. The total number of childcare centres increased from 19,276 in 2000 to 32,149 in 2008 (KICCE, 2016), and the proportion of children aged 0–2 enrolled in ECEC rose from 3.9 per cent in 2002 to 35.7 per cent in 2014, while the figures for those aged 3–5 increased from 83.1 per cent in 2010 to 92.2 per cent in 2012 (OECD, 2017).

Like Japan, the South Korean government also introduced fully paid maternity leave (16 weeks) and one-year paid parental leave (with income replacement of 40 per cent) in 1996. Maternity and parental leave systems in South Korea are regulated by the *Labour Standard Act* and the *Equal Employment Act*. The *Labour Standard Act* ensures women a total of 90 days paid maternity leave before and after childbirth (see also Chapter 10 by

Thévenon on leaves in South Korea in this volume). Cash allowances during maternity leave are paid by employers for the first 60 days and by the government for the remaining 30 days through the employment insurance system. In addition to the 90-day maternity leave period, a leave period for child-rearing with cash allowance is also available. The *Equal Employment Act* stipulates that the employer must allow a leave of absence up to the child's first birthday if an employee requests a leave for the purpose of child-rearing. The *Maternity Protection Act* in South Korea also raised paid maternity leave to 90 days (at 100 per cent wage replacement) and made the one-year parental leave more generous and flexible, with the provision of 500,000 KRW per month flat rate income replacement and up to three years of flexible uptake period (Korea Net, 2006). In sum, a total of 90 days paid maternity leave and one-year parental leave (with cash allowance of 500,000 KRW per month) have been implemented since 2000.

Back to the Family?

Although Taiwan is considered one of the most socially progressive democracies in Asia today – for example, it has a universal health care system that is paid through general taxation and has implemented one of the most progressive gender equality laws in Asia – it has been rather reticent in terms of childcare. Overall, Taiwanese family policies have focused largely on extending time and financial support for families to provide care for their children, suggesting a strong preference for the family-based childcare option. The first *unpaid* maternity leave policy was introduced in 1989, but the coverage was limited to women working in the public sector. The extension of maternity leave to other working women only came after the enactment of the *Gender Equality in Employment Act* (GEEA) in 2002 and the revisions of the *Labour Standards Act* made in the same year granting female employees with more than six months of employment eight weeks of fully paid maternity leave, and fathers three days of fully paid paternity leave. The GEEA also granted working parents up to one year of parental leave each, with 60 per cent income replacement during the first six months.[4] The subsequent revision of the GEEA extended the parental leave period to two years, to be taken before the child reaches the age of 3 (Tsai, 2012). Partly due to the GEEA, and partly due to the changes in cultural norms vis-à-vis maternal employment, the labour market participation rate of women and mothers in Taiwan has increased since the 1980s (Yu, 2005). For example, the employment rate of women with children under the age of 6 rose from 29.1 per cent in 1982 to 58.0 per cent in 2012. Whereas 57.3 per cent of women aged 20–49 were in sole male earner households as compared to 37.5 per cent in dual earner households in 1980, by 2010 the proportions had reversed, to 31.6 per cent and 60.1 per cent, respectively (Tsai, 2014).

Ironically, the increase in maternal employment in Taiwan was achieved not by increased childcare, but rather despite the lack of public childcare. To be sure, the country's policies towards childcare have been explicitly familistic. Rather than expanding public childcare, the Taiwanese government introduced the *Community Childcare System Programme* in 2000 to recruit certified childcare providers and babysitters for private homes and launched the 'community babysitter support system' to help families access a babysitter when needed. The *Universal Infant and Childcare System Plan* was launched in 2006 to provide childcare assistance for working parents with children under 2 years old. The *Early Childhood Education and Care Act* (2011) further divided childcare into two categories: nursery childcare for children under 2 and pre-schools for 2–6 year olds. In addition, the Act has made workplace childcare facilities compulsory for companies with more than 250 employees. The *Affordable Childcare Centre Subsidy Programme* was implemented in 2012, with the government subsidizing and integrating resources from both public and private childcare systems. Local governments are also encouraged to provide unused public spaces to enable non-profit organizations to run daycare centres. Despite these attempts, nearly four-fifths (79.5 per cent) of children aged 0–3 were being cared for by their family in 2010, while another 20.6 per cent were being cared for by market-based or pubic care providers (17.8 per cent by child minders and nannies, 0.7 per cent by migrant care workers, 1.9 per cent by private childcare centres, and only 0.2 per cent by public childcare centres). These figures show little change since 1990 when 85.0 per cent of children were being cared for by their families, and 15.0 per cent by market-based or pubic care providers. What is interesting is that a large proportion of childcare is being provided by grandparents: among those children who are being cared for by their families in 2010, 81 per cent were being cared for by their grandparents as compared to 15 per cent by their own parents, a significant increase from 1990 when the figures were 60 per cent and 39 per cent, respectively (Tsai, 2014).

The high level of family-based childcare for young infants in Taiwan can be explained by the combination of extended parental leave and increased government subsides for family childcare. The *Infant Care Subsidies Policy* (implemented in 2008) offers a NT$3000 per month subsidy for each infant to families with a total annual household income less than NT$1.5 million. Given that the average cost of a child minder is about NT$15,000 per month, the subsidy is hardly enough to purchase adequate care. The subsidy also requires one (or both) of the parents to be employed. For very low-income families, the subsidy could increase to NT$5000 per month per infant if at least one parent is employed. In 2012, the government introduced the *Childcare Unemployment Allowance* to subsidize a parent to stay at home to care for the child, as well as the *Grandparents Allowance*, providing a monthly allowance of NT$2000–4000 for grandparents or relatives to take care of children under 2 years of age. In addition, various local governments have provided additional childcare allowance for families ranging from NT$2500–5000 per month. In sum, Taiwan's childcare subsidies and allowances have encouraged family-based child-rearing practices, particularly by grandparents, in the present decade (An and Peng, 2015; Tsai, 2014).

In China, basic social security for individuals and families during the Maoist era (1949–78) were negotiated by the state-work unit-citizens' tripartite system in the urban areas and the state-commune-citizens' system in rural areas. These systems ensured full employment, basic social security and welfare, including social care for children, the elderly and disabled (Du and Dong, 2013; Zhang and McLean, 2012). During this period the government adhered to the idea of men and women's equal contributions to the national economy, and vigorously promoted socialization of childcare to support women's labour force participation (Liu et al., 2009). Indeed, as recent as in 1990, Chinese women's total labour force participation rate was 73 per cent (about 90 per cent for those between the ages of 25 and 34), significantly higher than other East Asian countries (Dasgupta et al., 2015). In the urban areas, the governments and work units provided good quality childcare and kindergartens for children aged 0–6 at low cost for working parents. Women were also entitled to 56 days of maternity leave, and upon returning to work children could be admitted to childcare centres. In some cases, work units also provided other support for mothers such as free commuter buses for pregnant women and mothers and breastfeeding times during work hours (Liu et al., 2009). In the rural areas, socialization of childcare was extensive until the three-year famine of 1959–61 that left millions dead, mostly in the rural regions. After this time public childcare in rural areas receded. Because of the high multigenerational co-residency rate, most children in rural areas after 1961 were cared for by their families, mainly by mothers and grandmothers.

Chinese family policies changed from an institutional to a much more private market form after 1979. During the reform era (1979 to now) state-owned enterprises and public institutions were dissolved and/or privatized. The privatization of enterprises accompanied the discharging of employers' social welfare obligations, including childcare (Du and Dong, 2013; Liu et al., 2009; Zhang and McLean, 2012). In the 1980s a new trend in favour of ECEC also began to replace the pre-reform era idea about public childcare. Together, these factors led to state and employer divestments in public and employer supported childcare, particularly for children under the age of 3; reallocation of public resources from childcare to early child education, often in the form of kindergartens; and increased emphasis on and rapid expansion of privately run kindergartens in the market. The 1989 *Regulation for Kindergartens* decoupled public institutions' ECEC functions and terminated public subsidies for childcare programmes for 0–2 year olds (Du and Dong, 2013). This resulted in a steady decline in public and employer supported childcare centres for infants aged 0–3. Between 1997 and 2006 the number of publicly funded kindergartens fell by 65 per cent, while the share of private kindergartens increased from 13.5 per cent to 57.8 per cent (Du and Dong, 2013, pp. 135–6). By 2010, 73 per cent of kindergartens in urban China were privately run, accounting for 58 per cent of all kindergarten enrolment. At the same time, the majority of children aged 0–3 were cared for at home (Zhang and McLean, 2012). In the rural areas, the increased migration of young people to urban areas has exacerbated childcare problems. In recent decades, cross-generational childcare (by grandmothers, mothers and other female relatives) has become much more prevalent in rural areas, where family-based childcare was already dominant during the Maoist era (Liu et al., 2009).

For working women, the maternity leave period increased from 56 to 90 days in 1988, and then to 98 days through the amendment of *Provisions Concerning the Labour Protection of Female Staff and Workers* in 2012 (Guo and Xiao, 2013). There has been a re-familization of childcare in China since the economic reform. Researchers agree that the combination of the policy reforms and state and employer withdrawal of welfare support have led to increased gender inequality not only in the labour market but also within the family (Dasgupta et al., 2015; Du and Dong, 2013; Guo and Xiao, 2013; Liu et al., 2009). Since the 1980s, women's total labour force participation rate has declined, from 81.6 per cent in 1982 to 63.9 per cent in 2013, while the gender wage gap in urban areas rose from 22.5 per cent in 1990 to 32.7 per cent in 2010, and in rural areas from 21 per cent to 44 per cent (Liu et al., 2014). In conclusion, Taiwan and China are moving in quite different directions from each other, and from the other four East Asian welfare states. Whereas extended parental leave and childcare allowances for parents and grandparents in Taiwan have positively reinforced family-based, and non-market, childcare, in China family policies are moving towards both private market and family-based models as the communist government deepens its commitment to the capitalist economic system and withdraws from its state childcare obligations.

CONCLUSION

Today, East Asian societies are facing multiple challenges. Rapid population ageing and the extraordinarily low fertility rate are creating concerns about rising dependency ratios, declining labour force and growing care needs. The decline of male breadwinner households, increased economic pressures on both men and women to work, and increased distanciation between generations – the kind of socio-cultural changes that are also seen in other parts of the world – have created serious care deficits. Faced with these social, cultural and demographic transformations, East Asian families are increasingly outsourcing childcare, and their governments are also reforming family policies to enable families to care for their members while at the same time supporting adults to participate in the labour market, and to incentivize women to have more children. In this chapter we examined recent family policy changes in Japan, South Korea, Taiwan, China, Hong Kong and Singapore. Our comparative study reveals a wide range of policy responses to family and care amongst the six countries, despite their shared Confucian cultural heritage and despite their similar social and demographic contexts. Moreover, family policies in these countries appear to have diverged from one another even further since the 1980s when most of these governments (with the exception of urban China) assumed that the family would provide care and therefore provided little in the way of family support or childcare. What we see are increased state commitments to the family, even if the policy tools they use to support the family might differ from each other.

Second, our comparative study shows broadly three possible groupings along a spectrum of approaches towards family support and childcare amongst the East Asian welfare states. In Japan and South Korea, the governments have adopted what may be called a regulated institutional approach by socializing the care of children, largely through publicly or privately provided and centre-based ECEC programmes. In contrast to this, the governments of Singapore and Hong Kong have employed a more liberal market approach to childcare by offering tax and other financial incentives to help families purchase care through the private market. This has resulted in extensive use of foreign domestic workers in private homes. Unlike these two approaches, Taiwanese family policies appear to reinforce family-based childcare, particularly for young infants, by grandparents, through a combination of extended parental leave and family and grandparent carer allowances. In China, the retrenchment of state support for childcare has resulted in increased reliance on both family-based care and private ECEC.

These divergent policy trajectories amongst East Asian familistic welfare states also point to the limits of regime analytics, and the importance of paying closer attention to national-level cultural and institutional contexts and regime change over time. Hitherto, the familistic welfare regime in East Asia had been largely understood in terms of its strong state reliance on the family for welfare and care that derives from the common Confucian heritage. While this regime typology has been useful in helping researchers compare and contrast East Asian welfare states from Western and other welfare states, it can also overlook the important within-regime cultural and institutional variations and institutional change over time. This chapter shows that as these familistic East Asian welfare states face the critical juncture for policy changes. In light of new social, economic and demographic contexts, they have responded with policy reforms that leverage and build on their existing institutional frames. The diverse policy responses to family and childcare in East Asia thus suggest dynamic change processes, as institutions change and evolve over time. With this in mind, it is important to note that while we have identified three broad approaches to family and care policies within East Asia, there are nevertheless some national variations within each of these approaches. For example, between Japan and South Korea, childcare policies in the former country are more regulated than the latter, partly because Japan has a longer institutional history of providing public childcare than South Korea, and partly because the South Korean government was more willing to open the social care market to private care providers. Similarly, there was a rapid shift to the private market model for childcare in China whereas it remains less evident in Taiwan.

NOTES

* Funding for research leading to this chapter comes from a Social Science and Humanities Research Council Partnership Grant on *Gender, Migration, and the Work of Care* (File No: 895-2012-1021), Ito Peng, PI.
1. Singapore is technically a Southeast Asian country, not an East Asian country. But because of its large ethnic Chinese population and Confucian heritage, it shares similar familistic family policy roots with other East Asian countries.
2. Long-term care policy for the elderly is an important part of family policy in East Asia because of the significant demographic ageing and the cultural importance attached to the notion of filial piety. However, in this chapter we focus primarily on childcare and family leave policies.
3. http://www.wfsfaa.gov.hk/sfo/pdf/common/Form/kcfr/Briefing.pdf
4. If the period of employment is less than six months, the employee should be paid wages at least half of the regular salary during the maternity leave period.

REFERENCES

An, M.-Y. (2013), 'Childcare expansion in East Asia: changing shape of the institutional configurations in Japan and South Korea', *Asian Social Work and Policy Review*, 7 (1), 28–43.
An, M.-Y. and I. Peng (2015), 'Diverging paths? A comparative look at childcare policies in Japan, South Korea and Taiwan', *Social Policy & Administration*, 50 (5), 540–58.
Canda, E.R. (2013), 'Filial piety and care for the elders: a contested Confucian virtue reexamined', *Journal of Ethnic and Cultural Diversity in Social Work*, 22 (3/4), 213–34.
Chan, A.K.L. and S.-H. Tan (eds) (2004), *Filial Piety in Chinese Thought and History*, London: Routledge Curzon.
Chang, K.-S. and M.-Y. Song (2010), 'The stranded individualizer under compressed modernity: South Korean women in individualization without individualism', *British Journal of Sociology*, 61 (3), 539–64.
Choo, K.K. (2010), 'The shaping of childcare and preschool education in Singapore: from separatism to collaboration', *International Journal of Child Care and Education Policy*, 4 (1), 23–34.
Council for Sustainable Development in Hong Kong (2006), *Enhancing Population Potential for a Sustainable Future*, Hong Kong: Council for Sustainable Development in Hong Kong.
Dasgupta, S., M. Matsumoto, and C. Xia (2015), 'Women in the labour market in China', ILO Asia-Pacific Working Paper Series, ILO, Geneva.
Du, F. and X.-Y. Dong (2013), 'Women's employment and child care choices in urban China during the economic transition', *Economic Development and Cultural Change*, 62 (1), 131–55.
Guo, J. and S. Xiao (2013), 'Through the gender lens: a comparison of family policy in Sweden and China', *China Journal of Social Work*, 6 (3), 228–43.

Hong Kong Census and Statistics Department (1995), 'Domestic helpers', accessed July 2018 at https://www.statistics.gov.hk/pub/B79503FA1995XXXXB0100.pdf.

Hong Kong Legislative Council Secretariat (2012), 'Foreign domestic helpers and evolving care duties in Hong Kong', accessed July 2018 at https://www.legco.gov.hk/research-publications/english/1617rb04-foreign-domestic-helpers-and-evolving-care-duties-in-hong-kong-20170720-e.pdf.

Japan Ministry of Health and Welfare (1997), *Health and Welfare White Paper*, Tokyo.

Japan Ministry of Health, Labour and Welfare (2008), *White Paper on Working Women*, Tokyo.

Korea Institute of Child Care and Education (KICCE) (2016), 'Annual number of childcare centres', accessed 10 October 2016 at http://www.kicce.re.kr/eng/reference/01.jsp?mode=view&idx=4007&startPage=0&listNo=62&code=englishresc01&search_item=&search_order=&order_list=10&list_scale=10&view_level=0.

Korea Net (2006), 'Childcare leave to extend to 3 years', accessed 14 April 2008 at http://www.korea.net/News/News/NewsView.asp?serial_no=20061004019.

Lan, P.-C. (2002), 'Subcontracting filial piety: elder care in ethnic Chinese immigrant families in California', *Journal of Family Issues*, **23** (7), 812–35.

Liu, B., L. Li, and C. Yang (2014), 'Gender equality in China's economic transformation', UN Women, accessed 10 October 2016, at http://www.un.org.cn/uploads/kindeditor/file/20160311/20160311114613_1571.pdf.

Liu, B., Y. Zhang, and Y. Li (2009), 'Reconciling work and family: issues and policies in China', *ILO Conditions of Work and Employment Series No. 22*, Geneva.

Martin, L. (1990), 'Changing intergenerational family relations in East Asia', *The Annals of the American Academy of Political and Social Science*, **510** (1), 102–14.

OECD (2016), Social Expenditure Database, accessed 6 September 2016 at http://www.oecd.org/els/soc/expenditure.htm.

OECD (2017), Family Database, accessed 17 June 2017 at http://www.oecd.org/els/family/database.htm.

Peng, I. (2002), 'Social care in crisis: gender, demography and welfare state restructuring in Japan', *Social Politics*, **9** (3), 411–43.

Peng, I. (2011), 'Social investment policies in Canada, Australia, Japan and South Korea', *International Journal of Child Care and Education Policy*, **5** (11), 41–53.

Peng, I. (2012), 'Social and political economy of care in Japan and South Korea', *International Journal of Sociology and Social Policy*, **32** (11/12), 636–49.

Peng, I. (2017), 'Transnational migration of domestic and care workers in Asia Pacific', ILO, Geneva, accessed 6 September 2016 at http://www.ilo.org/wcmsp5/groups/public/---ed_protect/---protrav/---migrant/documents/publication/wcms_547228.pdf.

Sechiyama, K. (ed.) (2013), *Patriarchy in East Asia: A Comparative Sociology of Gender*, Kyoto: University of Kyoto Press.

Sun, S.H.-L. (ed.) (2012), *Population Policy and Reproduction in Singapore: Making Future Citizens*, London and New York: Routledge.

TWC2 (Transient Workers Count Too) (2011), 'Fact sheet: foreign domestic workers in Singapore (basic statistics)', accessed July 2018 at http://twc2.org.sg/2011/11/16/fact-sheet-foreign-domestic-workers-in-singapore-basic-statistics/.

Tsai, P.-Y. (2012), 'The transformation of leave policies for work-family balance in Taiwan', *Asian Women*, **28** (2), 27–54.

Tsai, P.-Y. (2014), 'Difficulties in work-family reconciliation in Taiwan', in Mika Marcus Mirvio (ed.), *Contemporary Social Issues in East Asian Societies: Examining the Spectrum of Public and Private Spheres*, Hershey, PA: IGI Globa, pp. 164–77.

UNDESA (United Nations Department of Economic and Social Affairs) (2015), *World Population Ageing, 2015*, New York, accessed 3 October 2016 at http://www.un.org/en/development/desa/population/publications/pdf/ageing/WPA2015_Report.pdf.

UNDESA (United Nations Department of Economic and Social Affairs) (2016), *2015 Revision of World Population Prospectus*, New York, accessed 3 October 2016 at https://esa.un.org/unpd/wpp/.

Wong, C.K. (1992), 'Economic growth and welfare provision: the case of child daycare in Hong Kong', *International Social Work*, **35** (4), 389–404.

Wong, J.M.S. and N. Rao (2015), 'The evolution of early childhood education policy in Hong Kong', *International Journal of Child Care and Education Policy*, **9** (1), 1–16.

Yap, M.-T. (2009), 'Ultra-low fertility in Singapore: some observations', in Gavin Jones, Paulin Tay Straughan, and Angelique Chan (eds), *Ultra-low Fertility in Pacific Asia: Trends, Causes and Policy Dilemmas*, London and New York: Routledge, pp. 160–80.

Yi, C.-C. (2013), 'Changing East Asian families: values and behaviors', *International Sociology*, **28** (3), 253–6.

Yu, W.-H. (2005), 'Changes in women's postmarital employment in Japan and Taiwan', *Demography*, **42** (4), 693–717.

Zhang, Y. (ed.) (2003), *Pacific Asia: The Politics of Development*, London and New York: Routledge.

19. Family life and family policy in South Africa: responding to past legacies, new opportunities and challenges
Trudie Knijn and Leila Patel

INTRODUCTION

Twenty years after the ending of apartheid, South Africa continues to struggle with the legacy of the impact of apartheid policies on family life. The migrant labour system reinforced by restrictions on the freedom of movement of women and children to urban areas resulted in the separation and disruption of families, the violation of their dignity and human rights. Since the establishment of a constitutional democracy in 1994, the welfare system was fundamentally overhauled and aligned to the newly adopted Constitution of the Republic of South Africa of 1996 and the Bill of Rights (Constitution of the Republic of South Africa Act No. 108, 1996). Taken together, a conceptual framework is in place for the enhancement of family and community life based on international human rights standards (see also Nussbaum, 2011). Welfare policies are now geared to achieving social justice, citizen participation in development, the achievement of a minimum standard of living, equal opportunities and equitable access to services and benefits that favour the most disadvantaged (Patel, 2015). Expanded access to basic services such as water, sanitation and electricity, housing and social security created opportunities to enhance the living conditions of families.

Although South Africa has a progressive and egalitarian constitution and one of the most encompassing social security systems and social policies in Africa, poverty and inequality, including gender inequality, remain significant challenges. Persistently high poverty and extraordinarily high unemployment rates combined with high HIV and AIDS prevalence have had further negative impacts on family composition and structure, child vulnerability and the general quality of life of families. Father absence in the lives of children continues to be a significant feature in child well-being with almost one out of two fathers not living with their children. Statistics South Africa (2011) shows that on average 39 per cent of South African households were female-headed households which were over-represented among the poor (Rogan, 2014) and among Black African (43 per cent) and Coloured families (34 per cent) (Stats SA, 2011, p. 6). The global economic crisis of 2008 impacted significantly on the living standards of people living in extreme poverty. There is also a considerable gender gap in income poverty (Rogan, 2014). It is safe to say that the country faces a dual challenge of responding simultaneously to the legacy of the past and to contemporary economic challenges including the changing social dynamics and structure of families.

To combat child poverty, the country's publicly funded social assistance policy was redesigned and the Child Support Grant (CSG) was implemented in 1998. The CSG is not fashioned on the male breadwinner model and the nuclear family and represents a progressive approach to the design of child and family interventions which is discussed further below (see also Chapter 7 by Bradshaw in this volume). However, and in contrast to this approach, South Africa's newly adopted family policy, presented in a recent White Paper on Families (WPF) in 2013, advocates marriage and the heteronormative nuclear family model (Department of Social Development, 2013; Rabe and Naidoo, 2015).

In this chapter we examine the two national policies mentioned above. These policies were adopted at different times in post-apartheid South Africa. We argue that although the policies are of a different type, they nevertheless take divergent stands on the notion of families in the society and on the direction of social interventions. This reflects the ideological shifts in policy thinking that occurred since the mid-1990s when there was greater openness to progressive policy innovation compared to the more conservative and traditional notions about families in the contemporary period. In the early years, no over-arching family policy existed. An analysis of the CSG provides insight into how families were conceptualized and how this shaped the design of the policy. We therefore commence our analysis with an examination of the CSG followed by the successive WPFs (1997, 2005 and 2013). The two approaches to families and their relevance in the local context are compared and we conclude that the CSG is a more enabling family policy and is more contextually appropriate than the family policy as presented in the WPFs. The chapter is organized as follows: the next section sets out the context of family life followed by sections offering an analysis and critique of the two policies being reviewed: the CSG and the National Family Policy (NFP) with reference to secondary sources of literature. In the concluding section, the implications of the analysis are outlined for the future direction of family policy in South Africa.

FAMILY CONTEXTS AND CHANGING SOCIAL DYNAMICS

In most North Western countries diversity of family forms is the consequence of wide-ranging changes in socio-economic and cultural processes. Factors that drive these changes are the growing trend towards individualization; greater participation of women in the labour market coupled with increased financial independence; freedom of choice to co-habit with a partner as an alternative to marriage; making choices about whether to raise children on their own (single parenthood) or seek a divorce based on mutual agreement. While some of the latter factors are often cited as pertinent in understanding changing family structures and norms in South Africa and their consequences, the dominant drivers of changes in family structure are considered to be of a structural, political and socio-economic nature such as high poverty and unemployment with negative consequences for the quality of life of families (du Preez, 2010; Richter and Morell, 2006). Income poverty and inequality coupled with gender inequality persist in post-apartheid South Africa and vary significantly according to the race and the sex of the household head. In 2011 average household annual income of Black African households (4185 euros) was still the lowest of all population groups. The annual income for households of mixed race (also known as 'Coloureds') was 7746 euros, for Indians it was 17,367 euros and for White South Africans it was 252,010 euros. Also striking is the difference between male and female-headed households, whose income was, respectively, 8862 euros and 4650 euros (Stats SA, 2011).

While poverty decreased by 13 per cent between 2004 and 2008, two-thirds of children (11.9 million) were still living below the poverty line of 515 ZAR per month (30.4 euros) (Hall and Wright, 2010). Four out of ten children live in the former homelands, a vast majority of them being Black African children. The homelands were self-governing territories that were established by the apartheid government as part of its geo-political spatial planning to separate the race groups. Child poverty is worst in rural areas and in the former homelands. This indicates continuity with past patterns of poverty distribution. Another feature of the country's poverty profile relates to the gendered nature of poverty with the extent and depth of poverty being worst among Black and Coloured women and women-headed households (Posel and Rogan, 2012). These income differences between race groups are partly due to the different labour participation rates of White and Black persons as well as the variance (16 per cent) in the participation rates of women compared to men (Stats SA, 2011). The National Census of 2011 (Stats SA, 2011) also shows that fewer women are employed than men (34 per cent versus 47 per cent, respectively). The income differences between Black and Coloured South Africans and the other population groups – Whites and Indians – are mainly related to the skewed distribution of jobs and wages between the various population groups, with the Black African and Coloured populations being over-represented in low-skilled and low-wage jobs (Stats SA, 2011). Overall, gender inequality in the labour market has increased for women relative to men. Although poverty rates have declined since 2000, women and female-headed households remain poorer with women being up to 30 per cent poorer than men (Rogan, 2014). Consequently, the quality of life of children and families is most severely impacted by persistently high rates of poverty that intersect with racial, gender and spatial dimensions. These aspects underlie the inequality gaps between advantaged and disadvantaged families.

A further challenge facing the country is the unusually high HIV and AIDS prevalence rates of 17 per cent of the total population of 50 million with 6.4 million people out of 35 million people between 15–49 years being infected in 2013. This is considered to be among the highest prevalence rates in the world (Republic of South Africa, 2013). Females between 15 and 24 years old are four times more likely to be infected (17.5 per cent) than male adolescents (5 per cent). For the 25–29-year-old cohort, the percentages are 28.5 and 17.5, respectively (Human Science Research Council, 2014). HIV infections in South Africa primarily result from heterosexual contact and mother-to-child transmission. Other drivers are intergenerational sex, multiple concurrent partners, low condom use, excessive alcohol and drug use, and low rates of male circumcision (UNAIDS, 2013). South Africa has been, due to political denial, a late responder to the epidemic (Schneider and Fassin, 2002). However, it now has one of the largest (although very costly) anti-retroviral treatment programmes globally (UNAIDS, 2015). The pandemic has placed severe pressure on extended families especially grandmothers who care for their adult children who are sick and their grandchildren. The care of those who are chronically sick and of vulnerable children is borne mainly by female family members. These burdens have resulted in increased unpaid care responsibilities which remain largely invisible and limits women's participation in the labour market or in informal livelihood activities (du Preez, 2010; Hunter, 2012). Finally, the HIV and AIDS pandemic has resulted in unusually large numbers of orphans and vulnerable children and has had significant impacts on the lives of children and families in South Africa who have been faced with the loss of breadwinners and caring parents.

There is wide agreement among scholars and policy makers that South Africa has a diversity of family and household structures (Rabe and Naidoo, 2015). This is due in part to past patterns of rural-urban migration of both men and women that continue into the present. However, changes are occurring in family structures over time due to multiple and interlocking social, economic and political factors as well as socio-cultural practices, beliefs and norms. Amoateng and Heaton (2007) identified four main family types in South Africa: extended families made up of one or two parents and children plus other relatives (57 per cent); the nuclear family type which is made up of a household head, spouse and children (35 per cent); single persons without children (5 per cent); and complex households comprising members who are not related to the household members (3 per cent). This indicates that the dominant family/household structure is the extended family. Census data between 2001 and 2011 shows that there have been noticeable changes in family composition and structure over the past decade such as a decrease in the size of households, decrease in the numbers of children in households in line with lower fertility rates, and decreasing numbers of extended family members in the households except in very poor households where there are also larger numbers of children (Amoateng and Heaton, 2007). These changes are more marked in Black African and Coloured families than in White and Indian families that have more nuclear family structures. Statistics South Africa shows that on average 40 per cent of South African households are female-headed households with major differences between population groups. Female-headed households made up 22 per cent of White, 25 per cent of Indian, 34 per cent of Coloured and 44 per cent of Black African households (Stats SA, 2011).

In addition, Ntshongwana et al. (2015) draw attention to the particular needs and challenges of the often very poor 'lone mother family' headed by either the biological or a non-biological female caregiver. Lone mothers are over-represented in the 20–29 year age group, they tend to live with other adults in their household and on average they care for 2.1 children. Their social situation requires very specific forms of social support such as material and non-material support, childcare, and access to basic and psychosocial support services. The impact of the global economic crisis on the local economy has resulted in lower economic growth rates, job losses and rising food insecurity. Social assistance in the form of cash transfers is one of the key poverty reduction interventions in post-apartheid South Africa which is discussed in the next section.

CHILD SUPPORT GRANT: SOCIAL POLICY GOALS, REACH AND EFFECTS

In an effort to deal with the social challenges facing the population at the end of apartheid, the new democratically elected government expanded social assistance for vulnerable populations. Social assistance for children, older persons and people with disabilities reached 16.5 million beneficiaries in 2016/17, of whom 11.4 million children receive the Child Support Grant (CSG) (Republic of South Africa National Treasury, 2014, p. 13). This programme is fully publicly funded, it is non-contributory and is means-tested. It is now recognized to be the post-apartheid government's largest poverty reduction programme making up 15 per cent of government spending and 3.4 per cent of gross domestic product. Social assistance goes along with free compulsory schooling, universal primary health care and free health services for pregnant mothers and children. However, many problems remain with the quality of education as well as care and access to quality health care services (Knijn and Slabbert, 2012; Sayed and Motala, 2012). These social measures support the poorest families with vulnerable groups who are cared for in the home and the community. It has been found to improve the living conditions of those individuals and their families who earn a low income or who earn low wages that fall below the qualifying thresholds for the various public assistance programmes. The most expansive of these social protection programmes is the CSG.

In contrast to many North Western industrialized countries, South Africa does not offer a universal child allowance. The country only offers the CSG which is restricted to supporting poor children only. The main aim of the CSG is to provide supplementary income support to improve food security for poor children subject to a qualifying means test which is set fairly generously. When the CSG was introduced in 1998, it was targeted at poor children under 6 years old and intended to reach 3 million children over a five-year period. As a result of the positive effects of the CSG on poverty, inequality and food security for children (Neves et al., 2009; Van der Berg et al., 2007), the government scaled up the programme to include poor children up to 18 years of age. Children not reached by the programme either come from families/households that earn more than the means test or do not have the necessary identity documents (the latter affects mostly maternal orphans). A flat-rate benefit is paid to caregivers for each child who qualifies, amounting to 330 ZAR per month per child in 2016 (20.30 euros).

The CSG was designed as a gender-neutral policy for which male and female caregivers – not per definition the biological parent – could qualify. However, it was not designed to promote gender equality and women's empowerment. Nevertheless, the CSG is likely to have unintended gender-equalizing effects. For instance, a study by Patel et al. (2015) provides evidence that the CSG contributes to the female caregivers' financial decision-making, and also, although to a lesser extent, to her decision-making about the children in her care. However, since women are by and large the primary caregivers of children, the grant indirectly ends up 'prioritizing' women caregivers as beneficiaries (e.g., the biological parent, relative or non-relatives responsible for the care of the child). Only a small percentage (between 3 and 8 per cent) of men take up the grant (Patel et al., 2017; Vorster and de Waal, 2008). Several studies on the effects of the CSG have pointed to its positive impacts on health, nutrition, school attendance of the children as well as increased engagement of caregivers in the care of children (Aguero et al., 2006; Case et al., 2005; Patel et al., 2015). The poverty reduction effects on children and their families have been empirically demonstrated and it is argued that without the CSG, these families and their households would be significantly poorer (Bhorat and Cassim, 2014; Leibbrandt et al., 2010; Patel, 2015; Van der Berg and Moses, 2012; World Bank, 2012). The value of the grant is, however, small, which limits the potential for CSG beneficiaries to escape from income poverty. The majority of female caregivers are unemployed with fewer beneficiaries being formally employed. Those who are employed are in low-wage jobs. A lack of formal public childcare and the opportunity costs of working such as high transport costs also affect their potential to pursue alternative livelihoods.

The design of the CSG did not have any behavioural conditions attached to grant receipt as is the case in some Latin American countries that require the caregivers to take children for health checks or that they participate in community-based social programmes as volunteers. Nonetheless, in 2010 the government added the requirement that children should attend school to be eligible for the grant (Republic of South Africa, 2009). Since then primary caregivers are obliged to demonstrate to the South African Social Security Agency (SASSA) that the child is regularly attending school. Although the final version of the legislation is less punitive than the draft proposed regulations of the Social Assistance Act (Act No. 13 of 2004; Lund, 2011), the system has been slow in its implementation and at this stage little is known about its effects on access to the CSG.

From a family policy perspective, the CSG is an important intervention in the lives of disadvantaged children and women. The policy approach breaks with the male breadwinner and nuclear model of families that was associated with the post-World War II British welfare state approach to social policy (Lund, 2008). The design of the CSG took into account that the nuclear family was not the norm in South Africa and extended and single parent families were dominant. A further assumption underpinning the policy was that large numbers of children were cared for apart from their parents and were in the care of kin. It was also anticipated that the burden of care could increase in light of the impact of the HIV and AIDS epidemic. The gender-neutral eligibility criteria are a significant advance in that the policy envisioned the idea that men could also be primary caregivers of children (Lund Committee on Child and Family Support, 1996).

More recent data confirms the importance of the design features of the CSG in relation to family structure. An analysis of the National Income Dynamics Survey Wave 1 (Patel et al., 2017) shows that the majority of caregivers are women (97 per cent) with only 3 per cent being males. Table 19.1 provides an indication of the family structure of CSG beneficiaries. The typical family structure of CSG children consists of a child, one single parent and relatives (34 per cent) followed by a child and his or her relatives (29 per cent), a child and both parents (15 per cent), and a child with both parents and relatives (11 per cent). Few children live with one parent only; 71 per cent of children live with one or more biological parents and 64 per cent live in households where there are relatives present. It is likely that the growing trend towards increasing numbers of relatives in poor households with children may be due to the need to pool resources and share caregiving responsibilities especially in light of the increased burden of care that arose from the HIV and AIDS epidemic and rural-urban migration of parents in search of employment (Patel, 2015). These findings do not deviate very much from the average South African family composition described above (Amoateng and Heaton, 2007) except that the latter

Table 19.1 Description of family structure of CSG beneficiaries in 2008

Family structure	Frequency (N)	Percentage
Child and one parent	326	11
Child and both parents	451	15
Child, one parent and adult relatives	1043	34
Child, both parents and adult relatives	345	11
Child and relatives	897	29
Total	3062	100

Source: Patel et al. (2017).

did not factor in relatives in the households. The data in Table 19.1 shows that a large number of children continue to live apart from their parents. In these cases, parents see their children irregularly, although some parents do support them financially.

In conclusion, these findings point to the complexity of the living arrangements of children, their family composition and structures. Delivering the CSG to the main caregiver, whether they are the biological parent or not, is therefore still appropriate in light of these social dynamics. The CSG breaks with the 'male breadwinner model' of social assistance policies in other countries in that there is the explicit recognition that the family structure in South Africa does not follow the traditional Western nuclear family norm. This policy alternative has been shown to have positive benefits for children (Patel et al., 2015). But other challenges such as father absence and how cash transfers may work together with other child and family policies need to be explored further. Structural unemployment combined with large-scale and long-term unemployment of female beneficiaries who have limited access to affordable and quality childcare services remains a significant challenge. This is a critical imperative if the country is to respond adequately to meet women's reproductive and productive roles in the family, and on the labour market.

NATIONAL FAMILY POLICY

The country's first national welfare policy after apartheid, the *White Paper for Welfare* adopted by parliament in 1997 (Department of Welfare, 1997), held that families are the basic unit of society and advocated for welfare services that are family and community-based. The overall approach to welfare policy advocates a shift from a social treatment approach to a developmental one. However, this national welfare policy has been criticized for not taking into account the gendered nature of the welfare system (Sevenhuijsen et al., 2003) in keeping with Knijn and Kremer's (1997) ideas about the right of all people to receive and give care. In 2005 the government produced its first explicit family policy, the *Draft National Policy Framework for Families*. This policy identified the need for the protection and support of families through service delivery, on the one hand, and promoting the self-reliance of families, on the other hand. The National Family Policy (NFP) also received much criticism from feminist authors. In her analysis of the 2005 version of the NFP, Hochfeld (2007, p. 89) held that the:

> Implicit notions of motherhood and fatherhood [upheld in the policy] are conservative, with mother conflated with the caring duties of women, and father referred to almost exclusively as a source of harm or in the peripheral role of (defaulting) economic provider. Hence the traditional gendered division of labour remains unchallenged.

She also pointed out that the neoliberal ideology of self-reliance of families, which is mainly out of the reach of many poor families, 'presupposes a nuclear, middle-class family structure' (p. 89). Hochfeld concludes that 'despite intentions to the contrary, conservative discourses on the family have not changed significantly since the demise of apartheid and still suffuse welfare policy' (p. 89). Similar arguments were advanced by Sewpaul (2005) in her critique of the NFP. She argued that the 2005 draft White Paper was not informed by how race, class and gender intersect to influence access to power, privilege, status and resources in contemporary South Africa, nor did it take account of the way neoliberal capitalism and market-induced inequality impacted on people's lives. Faced with much criticism, the 2005 version of the NFP was withdrawn and the current *White Paper on Families in South Africa* (Department of Social Development, 2013) was adopted following consultations on the draft policy. Its main objective is to promote and strengthen families and family life in general in South Africa (Department of Social Development, 2013).

The latest White Paper on Families (WPF) (Department of Social Development, 2013) and the 2005 White Paper are very similar in their approach. The 'new' policy framework contains an introduction that reiterates the roles and contribution of families to society and the reciprocal benefits of promoting family life for both individual and societal well-being. In this articulation it takes very much a structural functionalist approach to families that is reminiscent of Talcott Parsons's structural-functionalist model of societies that held sway in the mid-twentieth century (Parsons and Bales, 1955) and that has been critiqued by family sociologists (Cheal, 2002). The 2013 White Paper is overly concerned with 'disorganized families', individual social pathologies and a social treatment approach which is associated with clinical psychology and clinical social work. The role of the family is understood to mitigate social ills rather than with the creation of an enabling and facilitating social and economic environment that is conducive to child and family well-being (Patel, 2015). The country's developmental welfare policy attempted to address systemic challenges as well as meet individual, family and community needs; it was pro-poor and promoted the building of human capabilities among others. The implementation of the new developmental approach to social welfare has been uneven and has been hampered by funding and human resource constraints including a lack of knowledge of how the new ideas were to be implemented in practice (Patel, 2015).

Although the WPF of 2013 aimed to draw attention to the plight of family-related problems, it is striking that in its presentation of solutions the accent is placed on treatment-oriented interventions and the need for families (and their communities) to help themselves. The scale of poverty in the country especially among Black African and Coloured families demonstrates the need for social interventions that could address the structural causes of poverty and inequality in South Africa as well as meet the everyday needs of families for both material and non-material support.

Further, the WPFs advocate marriage and interventions to strengthen marital relations. This is despite the fact that there is a steady decline in the number of people who are married (civil and customary marriages) compared to previous years (Stats SA, 2010). This trend is identified in the 2013 White Paper as a pathology that should be remedied. Despite the commitment to the principles of human rights and family diversity in the social policy (CSG), the family policy expressed in the WPFs represents a clear preference for the marriage-based nuclear family model in contemporary South Africa. Data was presented in the WPFs that suggests that the nuclear family (although only representing 26 per cent of all households) is the dominant family form in South Africa. This is clearly not the case for CSG families as indicated in Table 19.1, and also not for the average South African family. Besides the nuclear family, 13 other family types are identified in the WPF of 2013 ranging from three-generation, skip generation, single parent unmarried, single parent married (absent spouse) to older persons, sibling families with or without adults and with adults and children, among others. This wide-ranging classification includes a range of approaches to classify families along the lines of generation, life stage, vulnerability and marriage versus not married individuals and couples. This may be useful to understand. For example, how many 'child families' and older person families exist and how their needs may be most appropriately met. But these expansive categories hide the real social trends in a changing society such as the fact that the majority of children live in extended families and that the nuclear family is in fact declining in its significance as outlined previously. Neither do the WPFs explore the literature on the reasons why some researchers (Posel and Rudwick, 2014) argue that declining marriage rates are due in part to the commercialization of *ilobolo* or bride price that is paid in customary Black African families. This is considered to be an important factor in young couples choosing to delay marriage because they cannot afford it. To what extent this trend is due to women's awareness of their rights in contemporary South Africa is not explored at all in the 2013 White Paper.

Contrary to the Parsonian family sociology approach that places the emphasis on the relationship between the structure and functions of families for society, Cheal (2002) stresses that family relationships are not given by nature. Instead, they are defined and redefined according to the situations and circumstances people are dealing with. From this theoretical point of view, the dynamic circumstances and reality of how families are constructed in the real world need to inform policy development. In advocating the nuclear family as a solution, the family policy as presented in the recent WPF disregards what the family 'is' in the contemporary South African context. Instead, it proclaims what an appropriate family 'ought' to be. The White Paper is also out of sync with the country's Civil Union Act of 2006 which allows for same sex marriages. Very little is said about this emerging family type and the choices that same sex couples make to marry or not.

Finally, the current family policy offers a puzzling perspective since its social treatment orientation of how to solve 'family deficiencies' is not accompanied by enabling family interventions, and how exactly a cross-cutting policy of this nature might work in practice. Prevention of becoming a 'disorganized' family, as referred to in the White Paper, pays scant attention to addressing the systemic barriers to improving the quality of family life. Instead, voluntary and charitable initiatives are promoted in combination with a call for self-reliance of families. The WPF reads like the 'Baron von Munchhausen' story; families will have to help themselves out of the swamps.

CONCLUSIONS

Two policies adopted at different times in post-apartheid South Africa are analysed in the chapter with reference to how these social policies conceptualize families and their underlying assumptions and preferences in relation to family forms, individual autonomy, gender equality and what might be appropriate social intervention approaches to enhance child and family life. Our analysis shows that there are divergent perspectives on how families are understood in contemporary South Africa. Flowing from this, divergent approaches to intervention are proposed. While the social assistance policy – the CSG – is rights-based, it adopts a more open approach to families and to social policy for children. It also acknowledges different family structures, mainly the extended family system, and the fact that large numbers of children live apart from their biological parents as well as in single parent families with relatives. This family reality acknowledged in the White Papers on Families of 2005 and 2013 is not analysed in relation to the structural unequal living conditions, high unemployment, poverty and HIV/AIDS rates and, by consequence, the lack of choice of the majority of poor families. Instead, the WPF of 2013 still continues to advocate the marriage-based nuclear family despite the existence of a variety of family forms, norms, social dynamics and practices. The social interventions that are proposed lean more to a social treatment approach, viz. individual pathology and clinical practice, rather than the more comprehensive, promotive and developmental approach off the CSG that tries to tackle the structural and systemic factors that weaken and disrupt family life as well as meet their immediate needs.

There is, therefore, a lack of policy coherence in the South African government which may be due to the fact that the social assistance policy was developed in the early years after the creation of the new democracy and the adoption of the new developmental approach to social welfare. In the early years of democracy, the political space existed to adopt bolder policies and to innovate. Over time, a major gap developed between policy ideas and implementation due to challenges relating to inadequate knowledge and understanding of the new policies, a lack of skills and implementation capacity as well as resource constraints (Patel, 2015). Negative public discourses about public assistance leading to dependency on the state and promoting teenage pregnancies are reflected in calls for moral regeneration in the society. These views have been expressed by political parties including the ruling party, the African National Congress (Patel et al., 2012; Patel et al., 2014). How these tensions will be resolved remains uncertain, but what this reflects is a growing social conservatism at this time in the ruling party and among public administrators responsible for the implementation of family policies. These political and institutional dynamics do impact on the direction and efficacy of public policies such as the National Family Policy.

Looking ahead, South African welfare policies and the National Development Plan 2030 (NPC, 2011) advocate social policies that build human capabilities and the rights of people to choose who constitutes their family and to genuinely acknowledge a diversity of family forms in the society. Family policies need to be based on the lived realities of people's lives rather than on what an ideal family ought to be. Innovative developmental family and community-centred interventions that challenge dominant perspectives and social and gender inequalities are needed. Synergies also need to be created between cash transfers, education and health care, social and care services, for example, childcare and family strengthening programmes, and infrastructure investments, for example, water, sanitation, electricity and housing. Support for the livelihood activities for families are also needed. Since these social welfare and development policies and programmes operate in isolation from one another and deliver poor quality services, child and family well-being is compromised. Finally, for social and family policies to be authentic, they need to be in sync with the changing realities, norms and social dynamics of family life in contemporary South Africa.

REFERENCES

Aguero, J.M., M.R. Carter, and I. Woolard (eds) (2006), *The Impact of Unconditional Cash Transfers on Nutrition: The South African Child Support Grant*, Cape Town: Southern Africa Labour and Development Research Unit (SALDRU), University of Cape Town.

Amoateng, A.Y. and T.B. Heaton (eds) (2007), *Families and Households in Post-apartheid South Africa: Sociodemographic Perspectives*, Cape Town: HSRC.
Bhorat, H. and A. Cassim (2014), 'South Africa's welfare success story II: poverty-reducing social grants', Brookings Africa in Focus blog, 28 January, accessed 16 June 2016 at http://www.brookings.edu/blogs/africa-in-focus/posts/2014/01/27-south-africa-welfare-poverty-bhorat.
Case, A., V. Hosegood, and F. Lund (2005), 'The reach and impact of Child Support Grants: evidence from KwaZulu-Natal', *Development Southern Africa*, **22** (4), 467–82.
Cheal, D. (ed.) (2002), *Sociology of Family Life*, Houndmills, Basingstoke: Palgrave Macmillan.
Department of Social Development (2013), *White Paper on Families*, Pretoria: Government of the Republic of South Africa.
Department of Welfare (1997), 'The White Paper for Social Welfare', *Government Gazette Notice 1108 of 1997*, Pretoria: Ministry for Welfare and Population Development.
du Preez, C.J. (ed.) (2010), 'Living and care arrangements of non-urban households in KwaZulu-Natal, South Africa, in the context of HIV and AIDS', Doctoral thesis, Wageningen University.
Hall, K. and G. Wright (2010), 'A profile of children living in South Africa in 2008', *Studies in Economics and Econometrics*, **34** (3), 45–68.
Hochfeld, T. (2007), 'Missed opportunities. Conservative discourses in the Draft National Family', *International Social Work*, **50** (1), 79–91.
Human Science Research Council (2014), *South African National HIV Prevalence, Incidence and Behaviour Survey, 2012*, Cape Town: Human Science Research Council.
Hunter, N. (2012), 'The economic and gender consequences of South Africa's home-based care policy', *Social Policy & Administration*, **46** (6), 654–762.
Knijn, T. and M. Kremer (1997), 'Gender and the caring dimension of welfare states: toward inclusive citizenship', *Social Politics: International Studies in Gender, State and Society*, **4** (3), Special Issue, 328–61.
Knijn, T. and M. Slabbert (2012), 'Transferring HIV/AIDS related healthcare from non-governmental organizations to the public healthcare system in South Africa: opportunities and challenges', *Social Policy & Administration*, **46** (6), 636–54.
Leibbrandt, M., I. Woolward, A. Finn, and J. Argent (eds) (2010), *Trends in South African Income Distribution and Poverty Since the Fall of Apartheid*, Cape Town: Southern Africa Labour and Development Research Unit, School of Economics, University of Cape Town.
Lund Committee on Child and Family Support (1996), *Report of the Lund Committee on Child and Family Support*, Pretoria, accessed July 2018 at http://www.gov.za/reports/1996/lund/lund3.htm.
Lund, L. (2008), *Changing Social Policy: The Child Support Grant in South Africa*, Cape Town: HSRC Press.
Lund, F. (2011), 'A step in the wrong direction: linking the South Africa Child Support Grant to school attendance', *Journal of Poverty and Social Justice*, **19** (1), 5–14.
Neves, D., M. Samson, I. Van Niekerk, S. Hlatshwayo, and A. Du Toit (eds) (2009), *The Use and Effectiveness of Social Grants in South Africa*, Research Report 8, Johannesburg: FinMark Trust.
NPC (National Planning Commission) (2011), *National Development Plan 2030*, Pretoria: Government Gazette.
Ntshongwana, P., G. Wright, H. Barnes, and M. Noble (2015), 'Lone motherhood in South Africa: some methodological challenges and policy imperatives', *South African Review of Sociology*, **46** (4), 80–98.
Nussbaum, M. (ed.) (2011), *Creating Capabilities*, Cambridge, MA: Harvard University Press.
Parsons, T. and R.F. Bales (eds) (1955), *Family, Socialization and Interaction Process*, Glencoe, ILL: The Free Press.
Patel, L. (ed.) (2015), *Social Welfare and Social Development* (2nd edn), Cape Town: Oxford University Press.
Patel, L., T. Hochfeld, J. Moodley, and R. Mutwali (eds) (2012), *The Gender Dynamics and Impact of the Child Support Grant in Doornkop, Soweto*, Johannesburg: Centre for Social Development in Africa, University of Johannesburg.
Patel, L., Y. Sadie, V. Graham, D. Aislinn, and K. Baldry (eds) (2014), *Voting Behaviour and the Influence of Social Protection*, Johannesburg: Centre for Social Development in Africa, University of Johannesburg.
Patel, L., T. Knijn, and F. van Wel (2015), 'Child support grants in South Africa: a pathway to women's empowerment and child well-being?', *Journal of Social Policy*, **44** (2), 377–97.
Patel, L., T. Knijn, D. Gorman-Smith et al. (2017), *Family Contexts, Child Support Gants and Child Well-being*, Johannesburg: Centre for Social Development in Africa, University of Johannesburg.
Posel, D. and M. Rogan (2012), 'Gendered trends in poverty in the post-apartheid period, 1997–2006', *Development Southern Africa*, **29** (1), 97–113.
Posel, D. and Rudwick, S. (2014), 'Contemporary functions of ilobolo (bridewealth) in urban South African society', *Journal of Contemporary African Studies*, **32** (1), 118–36.
Rabe, M. and K. Naidoo (2015), 'Families in South Africa', *South African Review of Sociology*, **46** (4), 1–4.
Republic of South Africa (2009), 'Social Assistance Act 13 of 2004 as amended', *Government Gazette*, No. R.1252, Pretoria: Republic of South Africa, pp. 3–6.

Republic of South Africa (2011), 'National Development Plan (2011)', *National Development Plan 2030*, Pretoria: Republic of South Africa.
Republic of South Africa (2013), *Global AIDS Response Progress Report*, Pretoria: Government Printer.
Republic of South Africa National Treasury (2014), *Adjusted Estimates of National Expenditure*, accessed 30 March 2016 at http://www.treasury.gov.za/documents/mtbps/214/adjustments/Voteper cent2019per cent20Social per cent20Development.pdf.
Richter, L. and R. Morell (eds) (2006), *Baba: Men and Fatherhood in South Africa*, Cape Town: HRSC Press.
Rogan, M. (2014), 'Poverty may have declined, but women and female-headed households still suffer most', accessed June 2016 atError! Hyperlink reference not valid. http://www.econ3x3.org/article/poverty-may-have-declined-women-and-female-headed-households-still-suffer-most.
Sayed, Y. and S. Motala (2012), 'Equity and "No Fee" schools in South Africa: challenges and prospects', *Social Policy & Administration*, **46** (6), 672–88.
Schneider, H. and D. Fassin (2002), 'Denial and defiance: a socio-political analysis of AIDS in South Africa', *AIDS*, **16** (4), S45–S51.
Sevenhuijsen, S., V. Bozalek, A. Gouws, and M. Minnar-McDonald (2003), 'South African social welfare policy: an analysis using the ethic of care', *Critical Social Policy*, **23** (3), 299–321.
Sewpaul, V. (2005), 'A structural social justice approach to family policy: a critique of the Draft South African Family Policy', *Social Work/Maatskaplike Werk*, **41** (4), 310–22.
Stats SA (2010), *Marriages and Divorces: 2010*, Pretoria: Statistics South Africa.
Stats SA (2011), *Census 2011 Report*, accessed 31 March 2016 at http://mobi.statssa.gov.za/census2011/HouseholdIncome.html.
UNAIDS (2013), *Global Report. UNAIDS Report on the Global Aids Epidemic 2013*, Joint United Nations Programme on HIV/AIDS, New York: UNAIDS.
UNAIDS (2015), *Access to Antiretroviral Therapy in Africa: Status Report on Progress towards the 2015 Targets*, Joint United Nations Programme on HIV/AIDS, New York; UNAIDS.
Van der Berg, S. and E. Moses (2012), 'How better targeting of social spending affects social service delivery in South Africa', *Development Southern Africa*, **29** (1), 127–40.
Van der Berg, S., M. Louw, and L. Du Toit (2007), 'Poverty trends since the transition: what we know', Stellenbosch Economic Working Papers, 19/09.
Vorster, J. and L. de Waal (2008), 'Beneficiaries of the Child Support Grant: findings from a national survey', *The Social Work Practitioner-Researcher*, **20** (2), 233–48.
World Bank (2012), *South Africa Economic Update: Focus on Inequality of Opportunity*, Washington, DC: The International Bank for Reconstruction and Development (The World Bank).

20. Work-family policies: has Latin America moved towards more gender and social equity?
*Merike Blofield and Juliana Martínez Franzoni**

POSITIVE CHANGES IN THE CONTEXT OF DEEP INEQUALITIES

The position of women in Latin America has dramatically changed over the past two decades, as women's educational levels have surpassed those of men, millions have entered the labor force, family composition has diversified and fertility has on average approached a replacement level rate (ECLAC, 2009, 2010).[1] In 1990, only 32 out of every 100 women had a paid job and by 2010 there were already more women in than outside the labor force – 53 out of every 100 women and 70 percent among women of childbearing age. Dual earner families currently surpass the number of male-breadwinning families, and female-headed families have consistently increased across countries to become close to a third of all households (UNDP and ILO, 2009).

Yet, time-use surveys on the region indicate that care work continues to be carried out mostly within the family and to fall heavily on women even when they participate in the workforce, producing the so-called 'double burden' or 'care squeeze' (CEPAL, 2009; ECLAC, 2010; UNDP and ILO, 2009). Care responsibilities pose barriers to entering formal jobs; work interruptions for child-rearing have negative effects on earnings and human capital; and access to pensions and other forms of social protections is diminished, increasing women's risk of falling into poverty compared to men (see Filgueira et al., 2011; Martínez Franzoni, 2008; Martínez Franzoni and Voorend, 2009, 2011). Indeed, women are over-represented in informal jobs across Latin American countries – both salaried and self-employed – which are unregulated and lack social protections such as maternity leave (Gerecke, 2013; ILO, 2012).

In addition, given that Latin America is the region with the highest income inequality in the world, changes in women's lives are deeply stratified along income levels. Gender inequality must therefore be addressed at its intersection with social inequality. The gap in female labor participation between the lowest and highest quintiles reaches, on average, 30 percentage points – the same as it was in 1990 (Blofield and Martínez Franzoni, 2014; ECLAC, 2012). The higher up women are in the social structure, the more they can outsource care responsibilities and diminish the effect of these responsibilities on their working lives. Domestic workers, mostly women, often migrants and indigenous people, hired by wealthy families for long hours and for low wages, make up 15 percent of the urban female labor force, making paid domestic work a dominant and unequal mode of care resolution in the region (CEPAL, 2009, 2012).[2]

In the absence of affordable institutionalized care, low-income working women rely on informal care networks (paid and unpaid, and mostly composed of extended family and neighbors); reduce their paid working hours; move from formal and socially protected jobs to informal ones; or are unable to be part of the labor force altogether (e.g., Blofield and Madalozzo, 2017; Chioda, 2011; Hallman et al., 2005). For example, while just under half (47 percent) of the total working population lacked old-age social insurance as of 2008, three-quarters of paid domestic workers did (ILO, 2010). Altogether, these strategies reduce the wages of already low-income households, and therefore such coping mechanisms tend to aggravate poverty and social inequality (ECLAC, 2009; UNDP and ILO, 2009). Last but not least, in female-headed households – which account for about 30 percent of households with children in the region – many of these trends are exacerbated, as women bear the burden of income provision and care alone.[3]

Clearly, government policies can play a huge role in maintaining, exacerbating or reducing gender and social inequalities. Recently, the work-family nexus has entered government policy agendas more forcefully than before. Below, we examine two policies that are at the intersection between work, family and care: employment-based leaves following the birth of a child and full-time early child education and care services. We thus focus on policies geared towards parents of young children, although we recognize that other forms of policies towards people in need of assistance for their daily autonomy whether or not they are care-dependent (such as the elderly and people with disabilities) are important as well. Drawing on our categorization (Blofield and Martínez Franzoni, 2015a) we examine the gender and social equity implications of policy design on both. We then present regional trends in policy in light of these implications.

POLICY REFORMS ON PARENTAL LEAVES AND CARE SERVICES AND THEIR IMPLICATIONS FOR GENDER AND SOCIAL EQUITY

Employment-based leaves allow workers time off to look after care-dependent family members, or, in the words of Durán (2004), sequence time devoted to work and time devoted to care responsibilities while maintaining care provision within the family. Early child education and care (ECEC) services, on the other hand, 'de-familialize' care responsibilities by partially shifting them from families towards states or markets (see Martínez Franzoni, 2008; Orloff, 2009; Chapter 8 by Rostgaard and Chapter 22 by Woods and Frankenberger in this volume).[4] Both are essential strategies to reconcile work and family, and both can reinforce or positively alter social and gender inequalities, depending on policy design and implementation. Drawing on Blofield and Martínez Franzoni (2015a), we categorize these measures according to whether they promote maternalism, paternal co-responsibility, state co-responsibility and/or socio-economic equity.

To define maternalist policies, we draw on Koven and Michel's (1993, p. 4) definition: state interventions that recognize the importance of caregiving and 'exalt women's capacity to mother' while making it solely or primarily women's responsibility. Such policies are different from policies that establish what we call a 'maternalist floor', which acknowledges the role of women in giving birth and breastfeeding. This is the case of a maternity leave that helps women recover physically and emotionally as well as establish routines and bonds with the newborn. Instead, generous maternity leaves (as opposed to paternity or shared parental leaves) or subsidizing unpaid care work through a wage for stay-at-home mothers can be considered maternalist. The demarcation between maternalist floors and plain maternalism changes over time – for example, between 1952 and 2000 the International Labour Organization (ILO) determined regular maternity leaves to be 12 weeks (as established in Agreement 103) but since 2000 they have been expanded to 14 weeks (Agreement 183).

Co-responsibility policies can be of two types: they can seek to involve states and/or men in caregiving, both distributing responsibility away from sole reliance on mothers. *State co-responsibility* policies defamilialize some of the care responsibilities to the government by providing public ECEC or by subsidizing private ECEC that corresponds to full-time work hours. If ECEC does not take into account a typical workday and is only part time, the state has assumed co-responsibility in providing education to children (an important goal, of course) but not in participating in work-family reconciliation. *Paternal co-responsibility* policies promote sharing of caregiving by incentivizing fathers' involvement through employment-based leaves. Such policies are sequential policies that promote the reorganization of gender roles among parents and can include shared parental leaves, paternity leaves or so-called 'fathers' quotas', making part of the leave non-transferable between parents.

In terms of *social equity*, we draw on the distinctions made regarding eligibility based on contribution, need or citizenship (Esping-Andersen, 1990). Historically, Latin American social protection reached only formal salaried workers, while the majority of the workforce, especially low-income women, worked in informal, unprotected jobs. We assess policies on whether they extend protections to a broader scope of salaried workers (e.g., temporary workers, domestic workers) and beyond salaried workers to self-employed workers. We also assess policies on whether they extend beyond the labor market altogether, on the basis of citizenship or need, which is often the case with public or subsidized care services. If any of the above is the case, we consider that work-family policies enhance social equity.[5]

EMPLOYMENT-BASED LEAVES IN LATIN AMERICA

To assess maternity leaves in Latin America, we consider the ILO standard of 14 weeks to be the maternalist floor. Leaves beyond this standard, when restricted only to the mother, we consider maternalist. Extended maternity leaves can be positive in many ways (e.g., for breastfeeding) but even on the rare occasions in which these leaves do not endanger women's labor market reintegration, they do not allow for or encourage a redistribution of caregiving between women and men. As such, these leaves do not promote and in fact deter paternal co-responsibility.

Paternity leaves are not established in international agreements and determining a cut-off point between maternalism and paternal co-responsibility is a challenge. Here, we consider paternity leaves of one to five days immediately following birth, established to allow fathers to accompany mothers as they recover from delivery, as providing a maternalist floor. Any paternity leaves beyond this we consider as promoting paternal co-responsibility. Given that most paternity leaves are currently minimal or non-existent in Latin America, this cut-off is designed to capture *initial steps* to reconceive the role of men in caregiving responsibilities.

Parental leaves follow maternity and/or paternity leaves. Any time off that is shareable

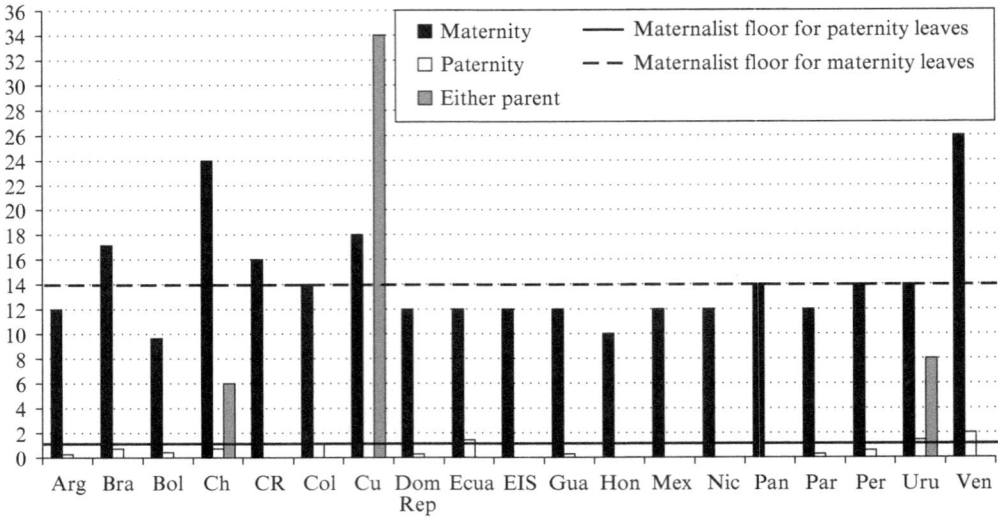

Source: Own elaboration.

Figure 20.1 Latin America: fully paid employment-based leaves for salaried workers, in weeks, 2015

between mothers and fathers we consider as promoting paternal co-responsibility – the more sharing itself is made part of the bargain, the better for co-responsibility.

Finally, all these measures may be restricted to some salaried mothers and/or fathers in the formal sector; reach all salaried workers (including paid domestic workers) and/or informal and/or temporary workers; and/or reach parents on the basis of need or as a right. The first reproduces social inequalities while the latter three promote social equity.

Cross-national comparisons of policy adoption on leaves are rather straightforward, as leaves have well-established units of measurement: weeks and days. These units also allow us to directly compare the length of maternity, paternity and parental leaves.

Figure 20.1 presents a snapshot of the length of fully paid maternity and paternity leaves across the region as of 2015. In all cases we focus on federal policies reaching the overall population and examine statutory minimums.[6] Unpaid leaves are not included, and in the case of Bolivia, where leaves are 75 percent funded, we convert the length to weeks of fully paid leave for purposes of comparison.

Maternity Leaves

As noted, Figure 20.1 outlines fully paid maternity leave, which in some countries involves caps.[7] We therefore leave out unpaid maternity leaves (like in Argentina, up to 13 weeks). As of December 2015, half of all Latin American countries are under the maternalist floor of 14 weeks: Bolivia at 9.6 weeks (equivalent to 90 days at 75 percent pay), Honduras at 10 weeks, and Argentina, Ecuador, El Salvador, Guatemala, Nicaragua, Paraguay and the Dominican Republic at 12 weeks. The large number of countries with 12 weeks (seven of them) reflects the international standard of 12 weeks up until the year 2000 (ILO Agreement 103). Four countries have 14 weeks, reflecting the maternalist floor: Colombia (since 2011), Panama (since 1971), Peru (since December 2015) and Uruguay (since 2013). Five out of 18 countries in the region exceed the ILO standard of 14 weeks: these are Venezuela (26 weeks), Chile (24 weeks), Cuba (18 weeks), Brazil (120 days, or just over 17 weeks) and Costa Rica (16 weeks). Of these countries, the oldest reforms are the shortest (Brazil and Costa Rica).

For social equity, the key dimension is eligibility through status in the labor force. Over the past decades, maternity leave reforms have in many countries sought to reach less formal, more vulnerable female workers. In Brazil, rural and domestic workers gained this legal right in 1991, and a court ruling in 2012 granted the legal right to maternity leave to temporary workers. In Argentina, a 2013 reform for the first time granted domestic workers the legal right to maternity leave. By 2014 Chile, Costa Rica, Brazil, Honduras and Mexico legally granted this right to all workers registered in social security, the self-employed included, and in Costa Rica, Brazil and Chile temporary workers as well. The latter involves particularly vulnerable women – often not only poor but also migrants – that deserve further study to grasp their actual and not just formal access to this right.

The incorporation of the self-employed under maternity leaves has often been carried over from other reforms. For example, in Costa Rica a pension reform in 2000 made insurance for the self-employed mandatory. While at first it only included pensions and healthcare services, a court ruling in 2004 interpreted that monetary transfers and therefore maternity leaves should be covered as well.

The past decade and a half has also seen improvements in actual take-up rates, following the increased formalization of the labor force in several South American countries – Brazil being the most prominent given the size of its population (Martínez Franzoni and Sánchez-Ancochea, 2014). Indeed, in Brazil, the share of all working mothers who received maternity leave went from 26 percent in 2000 to 41 percent in 2011, mostly due to an increase in access to social security rather than higher levels of employment (our database; Ministério de Prêvidencia Social, IBGE, PNAD).[8] In one survey of 700 low-income parents with young children in São Paulo, 50 percent of working mothers with small children had received maternity leave (Blofield and Madalozzo, 2017).

In addition, to assess the equity-enhancing effects of policies that reach poor women more broadly we must consider Conditional Cash Transfer programs which by 2012 had reached one in every four Latin Americans (Stampini and Tornarolli, 2012). These policies target poor mothers with children (and, increasingly, pregnant women) and provide small monthly cash transfers in return for medical check-ups and school attendance when appropriate. Access is means tested, and these transfers help provide a basic, if meager, income floor to many mothers and families with small children in the region. As such, these programs have been very positive for social equity yet heavily maternalist (Martínez Franzoni and Voorend, 2012; Molyneux, 2006; Provoste Fernández, 2012). Not only do they approach care as mothers' sole capacity and responsibility but by and large lack links to programs such as training and active labor policy measures that have women – not mothers – as primary recipients.

Paternity and Parental Leaves

As Figure 20.1 indicates, paternity leave in the region is minimal. Seven countries have no paternity leave and are thus under the floor; eight meet the floor (2–5 days); and only four countries are above the floor, granting more than five days of paternity leave: Venezuela (14 days), Ecuador and Uruguay (10 days) and Colombia (8 days). In both Venezuela and Ecuador constitutional reforms that enshrined paternal co-responsibility into the constitutions (1999 and 2008, respectively) preceded legislative reforms on paternity leave. In most cases, it is employers who pay for paternity leave.[9]

The short length of paternity leaves has been the object of reform attempts in several countries. For instance, in Costa Rica since 2001 five initiatives have sought to introduce paternity leaves between 3 and 15 days long. In Brazil, several initiatives to increase paternity leave anywhere from two to four weeks stalled in legislative committees, and in Argentina similar initiatives were also presented in Congress. As of December 2015, they had not prospered.

On shared parental leaves, ten countries in the region have ratified ILO Convention 156 on workers with family responsibilities. Nonetheless, only three countries currently have a shared parental leave: Cuba, Chile (since 2011) and Uruguay (since 2013). In Cuba, legislation establishes that once maternity leave is over (and nursing along with it), either parent can take up the rest of the leave until the child is 1 year of age (Gobierno de la República de Cuba, 2003; Hopenhayn et al., 2011).

Uruguay and Chile are the two most recent instances of maternity leave reform where paternal co-responsibility entered the policy agenda. In Chile, a 2011 reform extended maternity leave to all salaried women, temporary workers and own-account workers registered in social security. The reform also increased the post-natal leave from three to six months, and allowed the father to take up to six weeks of the last three months at the behest of the mother. Paternity leave was also enshrined at five days. While paternal co-responsibility was introduced into the debate, the main focus was on allowing mothers more time to breastfeed, and attempts to draw fathers in remained tepid.

In Uruguay, paternal co-responsibility entered the policy debate more forcefully. Maternity leave was extended to the maternalist floor of 14 weeks (from 13 weeks), paternity leave was extended to ten days, and a shared parental leave was established for workers in the private sector, allowing the mother or the father to work a half-day after the maternity leave is over, until the child is 6 months old. This part-time leave will last for up to four months or, to make comparison easier, eight weeks full time. Framing revolved around reducing labor market discrimination against women by encouraging more paternal co-responsibility. Finally, own-account workers were included in all forms of parental leave.

In sum, over the past decade the region has seen some efforts to extend maternity leaves to reach the minimum floor defined by the ILO or to extend beyond that floor, and to make them accessible to more vulnerable women (e.g., paid domestic workers and temporary rural workers). Many countries have also established paternity leave, mostly five days or less and concurrent with maternity leave, but only Chile, Uruguay and Cuba have established consecutive, shared parental leaves. Overall, though, leaves remain overwhelmingly restricted to mothers. Indeed, encouragement of breastfeeding has factored into many debates which, while important for other reasons, does not encourage paternal co-responsibility.

EARLY CHILDHOOD AND EDUCATION SERVICES IN LATIN AMERICA

During the first decade and a half of the twenty-first century, ECEC services for under 6 year olds became a more prominent focus of policy attention in the region. Much of this attention has been on the preschool age group, mainly of 4 and 5 year olds, among whom coverage rates tend to be higher, although policies show significant cross-national variation. Overall, however, services are mostly part time and much of the expansion is framed in exclusively educational terms.[10] Here we focus on children 0 to 3 years old whose care was until recently presumed to be a private family (female) responsibility. Changes in policy towards this age bracket help us measure the seriousness of government commitment to co-responsibility in work-family reconciliation.

While demand still far outweighs supply, between 2000 and 2010 access of children 0–3 years of age to care services reached a historical record (Berlinski and Schady, 2015). Policy efforts also placed an emphasis on social equity, with a focus on reaching children in low-income families. While educational concerns are central – as they should be – there is also a recognition of the changing roles of mothers, and attempts to level the playing field by providing full-time care services, therefore increasing state co-responsibility.

A comparative assessment of policy adoption on care services is more challenging. To tap into this, in Table 20.1 we use a variety of measures for what we call 'executive policy effort' on co-responsibility in childcare for the 0–3-year-old age group. First, we list whether a national-level executive action plan – in virtually all cases, a national action plan regarding infancy – specifies a commitment to increasing daily ECEC services to 0 to 3 year olds. Here, we draw on the most current available executive plan or program. Second, we list whether a national-level ECEC program with full-time hours (however minimal) exists in the country. A national-level program must come from the central government, with funding, and provide at least eight hours of daycare, on average. Third, we list the eligibility criteria for the national-level programs, which taps into the implications for social equity and maternalism. The final two indicators tap into implementation efforts. The fourth column lists the number of children served as of 2011, and the fifth column indicates whether national-level program coverage reaches over 10 or 5 percent of 1 to 2 year olds as of 2011.

As Table 20.1 indicates, almost all countries have paid lip service to the need for ECEC for 0 to 3 year olds and have some kind of a national ECEC program with full-time hours, even if minimal, recognizing that the state *should* have a role in this. The three exceptions are Bolivia, Guatemala and Paraguay.[11] In Nicaragua, a national-level program for 0 to 3 year olds exists but provides ECEC only three hours a day and thus does not meet the criteria of state co-responsibility in work-family reconciliation. In Argentina, while a national daycare program exists, both its funding level, eligibility criteria and funding mechanisms or size are unclear, thus indicating less policy effort on the part of the federal government on this issue.

In terms of the eligibility criteria, most programs target the poor, thus promoting social equity. Brazil stands out with its commitment to universal ECEC services; all others range from broad targeting – for example, the bottom three quintiles in Chile – to a focus on the extremely poor and malnourished as in several Central American countries.[12] In addition, programs in Chile, Ecuador, Guatemala, Honduras, Mexico, Panama and Peru also

Table 20.1 *Executive policy effort on co-responsibility in care of 0 to 3 year olds at the national/federal level*

Country	Executive plan/program specifies goal of increasing daily ECEC services to 0–3 year olds, 2014	National-level ECEC program with full-time hours for 0–3 year olds exists, 2014	Eligibility criteria	National program size as of 2011	Coverage estimate based on 2011 national program size
Argentina	yes	yes	N/A	N/A	< 5%
Bolivia	no	no	–	–	–
Brazil	yes	yes	universal	2.3 million	>10%
Chile	yes	yes	bottom 60%, mothers working, studying or looking for work	243 497 under 5 year olds	>10%
Colombia	yes	yes	low-income, vulnerability	1.2 million under 6 year olds	> 10%
Costa Rica	yes	yes	poor, malnourished	31 624 under 6 year olds	< 5%
Cuba		yes	universal in urban areas	1 130 centers for under 6 year olds	N/A
Dominican Republic[a]	yes	yes	low-income, vulnerability	10 275 under 6 year olds	< 5%
Ecuador	yes	yes	poor, those at social risk, working mothers	138 117 under 5 year olds	> 5%
El Salvador	yes	yes	low-income families	5 463 under 6 year olds	< 5%
Guatemala	no	yes	poverty, social risk, malnourished children, working mothers	16 143 under 6 year olds	< 5%
Honduras	yes	yes	poverty, social risk, malnourished children, working mothers	1 848 under 6 year olds	< 5%
Mexico[a]	yes	yes	mothers who work, study, are looking for work, or single fathers, and whose family income is below poverty line	266 406 under 6 year olds	< 5%
Nicaragua	yes	no	–	–	< 5%

Table 20.1 (continued)

Country	Executive plan/program specifies goal of increasing daily ECEC services to 0–3 year olds, 2014	National-level ECEC program with full-time hours for 0–3 year olds exists, 2014	Eligibility criteria	National program size as of 2011	Coverage estimate based on 2011 national program size
Panama	yes	yes	poor, working mothers	3 653 under 5 year olds	< 5%
Paraguay	no	no	–	–	< 5%
Peru	yes	yes	working mothers, socio-economic criteria		< 5%
Uruguay	yes	yes, partly[b]	vulnerability	44 282 under 5 year olds[b]	>10%
Venezuela	N/A	N/A	N/A	N/A	N/A

Notes:
a. Both Mexico and the Dominican Republic also have a childcare program via social security for mothers who are in the formal workforce (registered in social security) that covered 205,203 under 4 year olds in Mexico, and 6640 under 5 year olds in the Dominican Republic in 2011. National coverage rates remained below 5 percent with these programs included.
b. Only some of the ECEC services are full time.

Source: Blofield and Martínez Franzoni (2015b).

explicitly prioritize working mothers – yet it is unclear whether any of them may restrict services only to working mothers. While this is maternalist in its operating assumption that childcare is a mother's responsibility, in the short term it can also be recognized as an attempt to level the playing field regarding labor force participation between mothers and fathers in the context of scarce resources.

Despite the increased public statements of commitment from governments around the region, the level of prioritization and resources granted to ECEC services varies widely. Even taking into account quite small populations, the programs in El Salvador, Honduras and Panama cover 1 percent or less of children in the age group and national programs coexist with a myriad of other, even smaller efforts. Only in Brazil, Chile, Colombia and Uruguay does the national program cover more than 10 percent of 1 to 2 year olds.

Some of the national-level programs involve direct state services and others, like Mexico and Uruguay, also the subsidization of private care services for poor children. Service delivery varies as well, from public or regulated private delivery with salaried personnel, like in Chile, Brazil and Uruguay, to home-based and community services relying on volunteers (mothers) who may receive a stipend but do not have a formal labor relation with benefits, like in Mexico and Colombia.[13]

These figures do not address the important issue of unmet demand. National and comparative figures on unmet demand are lacking and, indeed, measuring this can face empirical challenges. The evidence does show that there is vast unmet demand in the region in general. As just one example, data from the Municipal Secretary of Education for the city of São Paulo in Brazil indicate that there were over 127,000 children on waiting lists for public daycare spaces for 0 to 3 year olds in 2013 (Rede Brasil Atual, 2013). In Chile, the expansion of care services between 2006 and 2009 under the Chile Crece Contigo program had a significant effect on the enrollment of children 0 to 3 years of age (Aguirre, 2012).

In addition to national programs, in several countries such as Brazil and Chile, preexisting national legislation establishes employer mandates upon large companies to fund limited care services. This legislation, while promoting some state/employer co-responsibility, does not contribute much to either social equity or paternal co-responsibility. Such services were established based on a minimum number of female workers and were restricted to working mothers to allow them to nurse. In Brazil, companies with more than 50 female employees have to enable mothers to nurse their babies until they are 6 months old. In Chile, a more substantial mandate requires employers of 20 or more women to provide care services to children up to 2 years old. In fact, the latter mandate is considered to promote labor market discrimination against women, and multiple attempts have been made, to date not successful, to reform or overturn this law. In Mexico and the Dominican Republic, social security provides some ECEC services to working mothers in the formal sector.

Last but not least, collective agreements are present with a broad range of prominence across a diverse set of countries: those with robust social policies and higher levels of unionization (like Argentina, Brazil and Uruguay); those with robust social policies and low levels of unionization (like Chile and Costa Rica); and even countries with weak social policies (like Paraguay). Here, and unlike maternalist employer mandates in Chile, Argentina and Brazil, both female and male employees are eligible, thus promoting paternal co-responsibility. They are less likely, however, to promote social equity in a region with very low unionization rates. Regrettably, we lack estimations of how many children or employees make use of employment-based services across the region.

Policy interventions that are framed as part of a broader effort to reorganize care were launched in Uruguay starting in 2009. It is the most ambitious effort in terms of dependent populations (children, the elderly and the disabled as well as workers in the care occupations) as well as measures (leaves, services and regulations). The National Care Network in Costa Rica, launched in 2010, explicitly aimed to involve the state in caregiving. Ongoing efforts at creating specific programs in Chile and El Salvador also have shown progress in the commitment of executive offices with caregiving.

CONCLUSION

Post-millennium, Latin America witnessed a period of intense statecraft as governments across the region pursued more equity-enhancing policies. This has been the case with ECEC services especially, as well as parental leaves. The novelty is that the measures taken reflect a deliberate government response to involve state institutions, and to a lesser degree men, in caregiving.

In terms of care services, we see most governments declaring service expansion as a goal. The recent wave of public or subsidized services has established eligibility through children or family income, although several programs prioritize the children of working *mothers* as well. Programs thus combine eligibility criteria focused on social equity and maternalism, although, as noted, the effects of prioritizing mothers in public services on gender relations and gender equity is an empirical question. While the framing tends to focus on children – and is part of national action plans to address early childhood – it takes place against the backdrop of extant programs which are mostly full time, in recognition of the needs of working mothers specifically. There thus tends to be an implicit if not explicit recognition that such services perform an important double function, and are thus favorable to state co-responsibility in work-family reconciliation.

In employment-based leaves, policy reforms have increased the eligibility and access of more vulnerable female workers to maternity leave. There have also been increased initiatives to ensure a maternalist floor and in some countries to promote maternalist policies beyond the floor, often linked to breastfeeding. Where we see less movement, in both framing and in policy design, is towards more paternal co-responsibility in the care of children. Public discussions on the role of fathers in caregiving are still at initial stages, and few countries have seriously attempted to encourage fathers to become more involved through legislative incentives such as paternity or parental leave.

Overall, policy change regarding work and family since 2000 lies far behind the major structural changes the region has experienced. At the same time, there is an increasing recognition among political actors that work and family reconciliation needs public attention and state intervention, even as politicians may disagree about the best measures to do so. The biggest challenge in the years to come may well be fighting to broaden the fiscal space in the context of a region-wide economic downturn as well as to demonstrate the economic pay-off of investing in paternal and state co-responsibility in care.

NOTES

* This chapter is partly based on research conducted by the authors for the United Nations (available at http://www.unwomen.org/-/media/headquarters/attachments/sections/library/publications/2015/work%20family%20policy.pdf?la=en&vs=1639). Both authors are equal contributors.
1. The countries included in the definition of Latin America here are Argentina, Bolivia, Brazil, Costa Rica, Chile, Colombia, Cuba, the Dominican Republic, Ecuador, El Salvador, Guatemala, Honduras, Mexico, Nicaragua, Panama, Paraguay, Peru, Uruguay and Venezuela. These are all the Spanish-speaking countries of the Americas and Brazil.
2. Until recently almost all countries in the region legally discriminated against paid domestic workers, for example, in mandating longer legal work hours, making it especially difficult for this vulnerable group to attend to their own care responsibilities (Blofield, 2012).
3. One study of 400 low-income families in São Paulo found that half of non-resident fathers never contributed any child support, and less than 5 percent cared for their child once a week or more (Blofield and Madalozzo, 2017).
4. A third way in which policies reshape the interaction between paid and unpaid work involves regulatory public policies towards labor overall and towards care occupations in particular. See Blofield and Martínez Franzoni (2015a).
5. See Pribble (2013) for a compelling discussion of equity-enhancing social policies.
6. In some countries public sector and/or unionized workers – including state-level workers in federal countries – have made gains beyond the statutory minimums.
7. Leaves are funded in three different ways: fully by social insurance (Argentina, Bolivia, Brazil, Chile, Colombia, Cuba, El Salvador, Mexico, Panama, Paraguay, Peru, Uruguay, Venezuela); by employers and social security (Costa Rica, Dominican Republic, Ecuador, Guatemala, Honduras and Nicaragua) or by a government account set up for that purpose (Chile).

8. In the case of Brazil, since 1991 rural temporary workers have the right to maternity leave at minimum wage via the government, so this also increases coverage among women who may not be in the formal sector per se.
9. Employer-funded leaves can create problems for take-up rates, as seems to be the case in Chile (interviews with key social and political actors, July 2013), (Todaro and Yañez, 2004).
10. Part-time preschool can do much to foster social equity, if it reaches the poor and if it is of decent quality. From the point of view of work-family reconciliation, half-time care may be better than no care, although transportation to and from school and finding additional part-time care can in some cases be even more complicated than seeking full-time care in one location. Part-time preschool may also serve as a base from which to extend services full time. Indeed, there have been initiatives to extend preschool, as well as primary education, from half-time to full time, for example, in Brazil and Chile. Such reforms would likely have positive implications for work-family reconciliation, even if they tend to be framed in exclusively educational goals.
11. We were unable to verify the case of Venezuela.
12. In the long run, targeting the poor poses a serious threat to ensuring the quality of services, not to mention the fiscal priority of these services in times of economic austerity (Martínez Franzoni and Sánchez-Ancochea, 2014).
13. Even though in this chapter we do not explore institutional models in any detail, previous work such as the superb comparative study between Chile and Mexico (Staab and Gerhard, 2010) portrays rather different models, based on broad targeting and social assistance and social insurance, respectively. See also BID (2013).

REFERENCES

Aguirre, J. (ed.) (2012), *If You Build It, They Will Come: Evidence of the Impact of a Large Expansion of Childcare Centers on Attendance and Maternal Labor Supply*, Chile: Pontificia Universidad Catolica de Chile.
Berlinski, S. and N. Schady (eds) (2015), *Los primeros años: el bienestar infantil y el papel de las políticas públicas*, New York: BID.
Blofield, M. (2012), *Care Work and Class: Domestic Workers' Struggle for Equal Rights in Latin America*, University Park, PA: Pennsylvania State University Press.
Blofield, M. and R. Madalozzo (2017), 'Conciliando trabalho e família: Uma pesquisa para mensurar o hiato de gênero nas famílias de baixa renda em São Paulo', *Estudos Feministas* **25** (1), 215–39.
Blofield, M. and J. Martínez Franzoni (2014), 'Una década de cambios en las relaciones entre vida familiar y laboral en América Latina: Mayor corresponsabilidad estatal; incipiente corresponsabilidad paterna', *Revista CEPAL*, **114** (December), 107–26.
Blofield, M. and J. Martínez Franzoni (2015a), 'Maternalism, Co-responsibility and Social Equity: A Typology of Work-Family Policies', *Social Politics*, **22** (1), 38–59.
Blofield, M. and J. Martínez Franzoni (2015b), 'Are Governments Catching Up? Work-Family Policies and Inequality in Latin America', UN Women Discussion Paper No. 7, September.
CEPAL (2009), *Panorama Social*, Santiago: CEPAL.
CEPAL (2012), *Panorama Social*, Santiago: CEPAL.
Chioda, Laura (2011), *Work & Family: Latin America and Caribbean Women in Search of New Balance Conference Edition*, Washington, DC: World Bank.
Durán, M. de los Á. (2004), 'Cómo conciliar trabajo y vida familiar? Un desafío colosal', accessed November 30, 2015 at http://www.comfia.info/index.php?modo=leer&art=14814.
ECLAC (2009), *Social Panorama of Latin America*, Santiago: ECLAC.
ECLAC (2010), *Social Panorama of Latin America*, Santiago: ECLAC.
ECLAC (2012), *Social Panorama of Latin America*, Santiago: ECLAC.
Esping-Andersen, G. (1990), *The Three Worlds of Welfare Capitalism*, Cambridge: Polity Press.
Filgueira, F., L. Reygadas, J.P. Luna, and P. Alegre (2011), 'Shallow States, Deep Inequalities and the Limits of Conservative Modernization: The Politics and Policies of Incorporation in Latin America', in M. Blofield (ed.), *The Great Gap: Inequality and the Politics of Redistribution in Latin America*, College Park, PA: Pennsylvania State University Press, pp. 245–77.
Gerecke, M. (ed.) (2013), *A Policy Mix for Gender Equality? Lessons from High-income Countries*, Geneva: ILO.
Gobierno de la República de Cuba (2003), Act No. 234: De la maternidad de la trabajadora, August 13.
Hallman, K., A.R. Quisumbing, M.T. Ruel, and B. de la Briere (2005), 'Mothers' Work and Child Care: Evidence from the Slums of Guatemala City', *Economic Development and Cultural Change*, **53** (4), 855–86.

Hopenhayn, M., M.N. Rico, and J. Rodríguez (2011), 'Cuidado infantil y licencias parentales', *Desafíos* **12** (July), 1–12.
ILO (2010), *Panorama Laboral 2010, América Latina, Lima*, Geneva: International Labour Organization.
ILO (2012), *Labour Overview: Latin America and the Caribbean*, Geneva: International Labour Organization.
Koven, S. and S. Michel (eds) (1993), *Mothers of a New World: Maternalist Politics and the Origins of Welfare States*, New York: Routledge.
Martínez Franzoni, J. (2008), 'Welfare Regimes in Latin America: Capturing Constellations of Markets, Families and Policies', *Latin American Politics and Society*, **50** (2), 67–100.
Martínez Franzoni, J. and D. Sánchez-Ancochea (2014), 'The Double Challenge of Market and Social Incorporation: Progress and Bottlenecks in Latin America', *Development Policy Review*, **32** (3), 275–98.
Martínez Franzoni, J. and K. Voorend (2009), 'Sistemas de patriarcado y regímenes de bienestar en América Latina: Una cosa lleva a la otra?', Documento de Trabajo No. 37, Madrid: Fundación Carolina, Madrid.
Martínez Franzoni, J. and K. Voorend (2011), 'Are Coalitions Equally Important for Redistribution in Latin America? The Intervening Role of Welfare Regimes', in Merike Blofield (ed.), *The Great Gap: Inequality and the Politics of Redistribution in Latin America*, College. Park, PA: Pennsylvania State University Press, pp. 348–76.
Martínez Franzoni, J. and K. Voorend (2012), 'Blacks, Whites, or Grays? Conditional Transfers and Gender Equality in Latin America', *Social Politics*, **19** (3), 383–407.
Ministério da Previdência Social (2011), *Anuário Estatístico da Previdência Social*, Brasilia: Secretaria de Políticas de Previdência Social IBGE, PNAD.
Molyneux, M. (2007), 'Change and Continuity in Social Protection in Latin America: Mothers at the Service of the State?' Programme on Gender and Development, Paper No. 1, UNRISD, Geneva.
Orloff, A.S. (2009), 'Gendering the Comparative Analysis of Welfare States: An Unfinished Agenda', *Sociological Theory*, **27** (3), 317–43.
Pribble, J. (ed.) (2013), *Welfare and Party Politics in Latin America*, Cambridge: Cambridge University Press.
Provoste Fernández, P. (2012), *Protección social y redistribución del cuidado en América Latina y el Caribe: el ancho de las políticas*, Serie: Mujer y desarrollo No. 120, CEPAL.
Rede Brasil Atual (2013), 'São Paulo abre edital para creches, primeiro passo para acabar com troca de favores', accessed August 29, 2016 at http://www.redebrasilatual.com.br/educacao/2013/08/falta-de-edital-para-conven iamento-de-creches-levou-a-desigualdade-no-atendimento-7066.html.
Staab, S. and R. Gerhard (2010), *Childcare Service Expansion in Chile and Mexico: For Women or Children or Both?* UNRISD, Gender and Development Programme Paper No. 10, May.
Stampini, M. and L. Tornarolli (2012), 'The Growth of Conditional Cash Transfers in Latin America and the Caribbean: Did They Go Too Far?', Policy Brief 185, Inter-American Development Bank.
Todaro, R. and S. Yañez (ed.) (2004), *El trabajo se transforma: relaciones de producción y relaciones de género*, Santiago: Centro de Estudios de la Mujer.
UNDP and ILO (2009), *Work and Family: Towards New Forms of Reconciliation with Social Co-responsibility*, Santiago: United Nations Development Programme and International Labour Organization.

21. Family policy in India: contradictions, continuities and change
Rajni Palriwala and Neetha N.

INTRODUCTION

There is no explicit policy aimed at families with children in India, but assumptions regarding an *Indian* family permeate a state system that is active in formulating policy in diverse arenas. These assumptions, at times in consonance and at times in conflict with stated policy aims in these fields, shape related policy instruments and outcomes. There is, in other words, an implicit family policy in India grounded in a family model that is explicit in some aspects, such as composition, and both explicit and implicit in others, such as intra-familial relations, as will be elaborated through this chapter. This family model is deeply gendered and asserts an ideal of inter-generational relations in which constructions of culture, law, labour and the aftermath of colonial rule at the least provide axes of both continuity and change. Family policy in India is, thus, historically and socio-culturally embedded and fashioned also by shifts in the central direction and ideology of state policy. Of the vast spectrum that is relevant in tracing the dimensions of family policy in India, of particular importance are policy statements pertaining to women and children as separate categories that were conjoined, however, in the very existence of a single Ministry of Women and Child Development. In the case of women, there has been a change in the terms used in policy, not necessarily with much clarity as to their meanings or the shifts – from women's role and contribution to (national) development, to women's development and then to empowerment. With children, the shift has been from a sentimental construction of the nation's children and of children in need of protection, to the ideas of human resource development and children as investment. These changes have been operating simultaneously with a continuity in the idea that children are primarily the responsibility of the family and that intra-familial practices are altruistic,[1] especially with regard to children.

In the backdrop of international developments, neo-liberal economics and policies were instituted in India starting in the late 1980s. This was marked by a shift from a developmentalist state in which state responsibility, social justice and equality were central rhetorical and ideological pillars to one in which economic growth and the market became the guiding principles of state policies.[2] The effects may not have been dramatic in terms of the macroeconomic structure, but are evident in policy institutions and in social rights. Social security and family-based benefits are available as work-based rights in the organised/formal sector that employs just over 7 per cent of workers (Gandhi et al., 2013). Within this, however, it is mainly employees in the (shrinking) public sector that have these benefits, which are provided to a lesser extent in the private organised/formal sector. Even for public employees, pension provisions are reduced, though access to medical treatment and childcare leave provisions have been expanded.

There have also been contradictory developments in social policy beyond work-based rights. On the one hand, the already patchwork and residual welfare system has been further weakened; financial outlays in health and education programmes have been reduced and targeted programmes have replaced universal family benefits (as in food security instruments like the Public Distribution System or PDS).[3] On the other hand, there is an apparent abundance of policies, programmes and schemes, albeit constantly rearranged and renamed, as well as statistical manoeuvring in measurements of poverty that hide its extent. In public perception, shrinking social rights are not always visible. Due to international conventions, domestic electoral politics and social movements, there has been a number of initiatives, which have benefitted women as well as children. This includes an expansion in the Integrated Child Development Scheme (ICDS), which is the largest nutrition programme in the world and is directed at young children and mothers, and an employment guarantee programme,[4] which women in particular access. Despite this and perhaps because both the ICDS and the employment guarantee programmes are viewed as temporary welfare schemes rather than linked to universal citizenship rights and have not been given the required financial support, social and economic inequalities have not reduced. The declines in infant and maternal mortality rates are also little and very slow (Palriwala and Neetha, 2011).[5] The visible growth of a middle class and of educated, middle class women in new sectors of paid employment over the last two decades (central to images of India's growth story) has also obscured the weakening of social rights and the high levels of inequality and inequitable family life.

Overall, there is a continuing hegemony of gendered familialism in public policy affecting women and children, with the principle that the family is the first if not the only safety net. The construction of a simultaneously altruistic and patriarchal family is a continuing thread. In the following section, dimensions of the family in India relevant to an understanding of family policy are discussed briefly. This is taken further in the next two sections, which examine policies directed at mothers and possible parents. First, the official criteria for minimum wage calculations and orientation of programmes for women's employment are outlined. Next, the explicit model of family composition in population policy which is invoked in shaping all other policies that pertain to families with children is examined. Population policy is about restricting the number of children and thence about the children which families should not have. Policies specific to and directed at living children – children in and without families – are elaborated subsequently. The origins of various policies have shaped their particularities and led to continuities, despite shifts in changing domestic and international discourses on child rights. The last section returns to policies directed at parents as carers, specifically those that pertain to mothers, including maternity and childcare provisions. In each policy field a construction of family becomes apparent, suggesting elements of a family policy.

This analysis is based on a reading of official documents including policy statements, primary data on employment, sociological, anthropological, social work and historical studies on family, children, women's work and social policy, and draws substantially on our earlier work on the political and social economy of care in India (Palriwala and Neetha, 2009, 2011). Contradictions between ideas of family and intentions in policy statements and the divergence between them and programmes on the ground are evident. This not only reinforces socio-economic inequalities among families with young children, but acts to derogate children's rights, gender equality and the caring relationship.

OUTLINING THE FAMILY IN INDIA

If the concept of *family* is taken to mean structured inter-personal relations in the domestic and intimate spheres of life, including support and care of children, among the first concerns to be noted in mapping possible parameters of a family policy is the regional, ethnic and religious diversity in India, as did Shah (1989). This diversity continues to mean a plurality of laws, cultural ideals and practices in relation to marriage, descent, inheritance and residence, which in turn shape relations between fathers, mothers and young children. Patrilineal inheritance[6] and patrilocal residence were and are the most common practice, framing a family in which sons rather than daughters are the valued and counted children. Policy has tended to overlook diversity in familial living and assumptions that sons and men are the main earners and breadwinners have reinforced the patriarchal family ideal and practices, to the cost of other forms of family life. The little academic work on family and public policy linkages has tended to focus on the gendered differentiation of children with sons/men as heirs or workers and the linked gendered differences in rights to food, other consumption and in access, streams and outcomes of education[7] (see Agarwal, 2016). That public policy takes for granted women's and girl's responsibilities in everyday domestic work and care has received attention more recently. This has implications for labour policy in terms of maternity and care leave and for women's employment and thence for children in women-headed or nuclear family households.

It must be emphasised that in the Indian context, family policy cannot be understood or framed in terms of parents and young children alone (Shah, 1989). The ideal of the extended family, consisting of three or more generations related to each other through descent or marriage, is widely prevalent and affects not only adult inter-generational relations but also the care of young children. Adult children and parents have expectations of each other, in particular in ensuring the marriage of sons and daughters and care of ageing parents. Family-related state programmes and some voluntary organisations reaffirm these expectations. This is seen in social assistance to families in marrying off their daughters; it follows the view that dowry must be given at the marriage of daughters and that dowry makes them an economic burden on parents. This is particularly so among Hindus traditionally designated as upper or middle castes, Sikhs, Jains and Christians, but increasingly also those designated as lower caste and Muslims. Also marked is the expectation across region, class, caste and religion that sons (and not daughters) will live with their parents and support them in their old age.[8] This is reiterated through regulations and conflict regarding death benefits and pensions to state personnel as well as legal provisions by which ageing parents can demand financial support,[9] emphasising the fostering of parent-son ties.

The constant lamentation in public discourse that the extended family household is disintegrating is not supported by data. The decline in the number of married couples per household is slight and affects household living more than a radical change in intra-familial ties and exchanges of income and care (Palriwala and Neetha, 2011). It is based on a mythic construct of the past that obscures that much less than half of the population ever resided in extended households due to a range of factors – low life expectancy, lack of shared property, and social and economic conflict (Shah, 1998). Most importantly, the idea of extended family values is mobilised to argue for familial rather than state responsibility in the care of the young and old in families, downplaying the need for non-familial childcare or universal old age pensions. The lack of extended family living and support is perhaps most evident among those who most require extra-familial facilities – distress migrants, whose numbers have been increasing, and the labouring poor. These are families where all members need to work for a livelihood and none can be whole-time carers, who experience the greatest strain on familial incomes and resources. The care and development of children becomes fragile because familial carers cannot rely on their own resources or kinship networks (Palriwala and Neetha, 2011).

MINIMUM WAGES, WOMEN'S EMPLOYMENT AND FAMILY LIFE

Running through social policy is the assumption that women and in particular mothers are the unpaid carers of children (and the elderly), undoubtedly in keeping with social and cultural perceptions of family life and gender divisions in paid work. Policy frameworks, in turn, bolster these ideas and practice. State family policy and its contradictions are evident in the principles for calculations of minimum wages.

The Minimum Wages Act 1948 empowers the state to fix minimum wages for listed occupations/employment. A balance is sought between ensuring competitive market conditions and a *fair* family wage. The standard working class family is taken to consist of four consumption units – wife, two children and the earner – that is, a nuclear family with a male breadwinner. Requirements of food, clothing, housing and children's education are factored in and the earnings of women, children and adolescents are disregarded in arriving at the minimum rates. Such a calculation reflects a larger state orientation that women are subsidiary earners responsible for family care needs, but also conflicts with the idea of the extended family as a caring unit for children and the elderly.

Women's work participation[10] has long been low with only 21.1 per cent (2011–12) of women in employment. Subsidiary workers (who are not in full-time employment) account for about 22 per cent of women workers and self-employment for 56.2 per cent. The majority of female workers (over 62 per cent) are in agriculture with unpaid family helpers accounting for about 69 per cent of all self-employed. The agrarian crisis has meant the displacement of men from agriculture, but women too, who have also been displaced from industry. Growth in women's employment has been in sectors that can be combined with their family care work and are akin to it: in education (27 per cent) – particularly primary school teaching – or as domestic workers (from 6.7 to 11.7 per cent between 1999–2000 and 2011–12) (Neetha, 2014). The last of course suggests a shift in familial life as well as increasing inequalities not recognised in policy – families that can afford paid carers and those who work as carers, families that incorporate non-kin into their families and families that lose kin from care work.

Self-employment for women has been an important component of the poverty eradication and empowerment programmes since the early years of development planning in the country, but it acquired a new valency after the 1990s. It is the chosen route to counter women's declining employment as well as resolve the conflict between the stated aims of empowerment of women through income generation and education and the daily family responsibilities that are theirs. The 2016 draft national policy for women prioritises forms of paid employment for women that allow them to combine it with housework and notes that 'The availability/creation of part-time jobs and arrangement of flexi-hours in the organized sectors will be promoted' (GOI, 2016, p. 10). Given that this sector has been on the decline, it is home-based and part-time work that gives flexibility and timings of work hours, that hires cheap female labour and gives them some earnings, without undermining the institution of the *Indian* family and the gendered divisions of labour. Contradictions, however, still emerge – as with lifting the ban on night work for women in some provinces. The ban had been put in place with the reasoning that it was enabling family life and women's security, but now labour market requirements and a state rhetoric that espouses women's empowerment become the rationale to end it.

POPULATION POLICY IN INDIA

If there is one area of state action in which policy clearly addresses the family, it is in the emphasis and campaigns on population control. While planned parenthood has a long history in the Indian context, population size as the main obstacle to development and population control as the pre-eminent development policy gained ground from the 1970s (Rao, 2004). Three aspects of the population programme may be highlighted: the mechanisms to achieve targets; representations of the family; and the unintended devaluation of daughters. First, the population programme has employed a mix of incentives and coercive instruments (Basu, 1997; Rao, 2004; Tarlo, 2003), becoming in time essentially penal. Increasingly, parents with more than two children are deprived of rights. For women, this is a denial of maternity and care leave rights, aspects we discuss later, as well as benefits in natal and post-natal programmes in the case of a third child; in effect, a denial to the child of maternal care. The denial of rights has been extended to political rights. In various provinces, such as Madhya Pradesh, Rajasthan and Haryana, parents (of more than two children) have been disqualified from standing for elections to local bodies – the village council or an urban municipality. Thus, population targets are to be achieved through the derogation of citizenship rights to those with *too many* children rather than enabling the care and development of young children.

Second, as the programme became a central pillar of public policy, the representation of the family in posters on walls, leaflets and in the media consisted of a married, heterosexual couple and their two children, a son and daughter. The extended family was not part of this visualisation of family that was otherwise viewed as omnipresent across the country. Neither the social desire for an extended family nor aspects such as care for the aged by adult children that were part of other policy designs[11] were part of the population policy imaginary. The planned family – *we two, our two* being the slogan – was presented as the modern and the rational form of family, which would allow parents to educate their children and fulfil their responsibilities to them – whether of marriage or 'settling'[12] them in life. In time, there was an official recognition that the demographic transition still seemed distant and that people were limiting their family size by eliminating girls (John et al., 2008). The official representation of the ideal family in family planning campaigns shifted; the visuals used now popularised the idea of a family with one child – a daughter.

Third, and following from the above, while most provinces and districts have now entered the demographic transition, it has been accompanied by a dramatic decline in the juvenile sex ratio as parents plan families that include one or more sons, through sex selective abortions and neglect of female infants.[13] Programmes have been devised to revalue daughters, but their very framing has made the programmes ineffectual in countering the economic, social and cultural rationales (including old age care) to have and care for sons (John et al., 2008; Palriwala, 2016). Conditional cash transfers (CCTs)[14] for girl children (Sekher, 2012) are small in receivable sum and surrounded with bureaucratic procedures. Nor has economic and labour policy, as outlined above, done much to change the relative value of adult sons and daughters and thereby persuade parents to have only daughter(s). The next section picks up on the social and familial value of children and elaborates shifting approaches in policy directed at children.

CHILDREN AS A CATEGORY IN SOCIAL POLICY

The framing of public policy with respect to children has neither been static nor dramatically new, as seen in the last section. Running through social policies for children has been a vision of children as the nation's wealth, childhood and children as a welfare category. Most of these policies have been wide-ranging in the issues they encompass, emphasising and intertwining nutrition, education and health in particular, the predominant concerns in child and family policy, with childcare entering only in connection with these concerns. Some programmes are specifically focussed on children in poverty, on child labour, or on education. In all, there is an assumption that children are embedded in a parental family.

It is important to note that state programmes continue to be influenced and guided by past practices and discourses on children and childcare. The traumatic experiences of violence and separation at the time of Independence from British Rule and the partition of the sub-continent into India and Pakistan resulted in the displacement of large numbers of children and uncertain nationality of those born during this period (Butalia, 2000). Among the issues that came to the fore was the question of the relative responsibilities of state institutions and families that was partly resolved with an acknowledgement of the mother as the principal in decisions regarding a child's future (Balakrishnan, 2011). The state was to shoulder the responsibility of all children who were unwanted or left behind by mothers who had left for Pakistan, irrespective of the fathers' status. This did not undermine the patrilineal family in a public discourse in which the nation-state stepped in to protect women and their children and where most laws continued to acknowledge the father as the legal guardian. A sentimentalised nation was constructed as the family writ large and, while recognising and respecting the autonomy of the family, the nation-state was viewed as part of the family, especially so as to ensure the welfare of children (Balakrishnan, 2011).

The first five-year plan (1951–56)[15] identified health, nutrition and education as major welfare concerns with regard to young children. Programmes were implemented through a national agency – the Central Social Welfare Board (CSWB) set up in 1953 – that was to work through voluntary and community-based organisations. The state was to supplement the efforts of the family – read mothers – to care for children by encouraging efforts to train and educate 'ignorant' and poor mothers in nutrition and health in rural areas with some organised play activities for urban, primary school children. This was also in keeping with colonial and upper class constructions of civilising Indians through charity. From the second five-year plan (1956–61) and onwards, when economic development and industrial growth became policy principles, the idea of children as economic assets became central. With successive plans, the articulation of the need to invest in children for the future economic development of the country was strengthened. Yet, many public actors continued to argue for a training-linked welfare approach as outlined above and embodied in the CSWB and linked to voluntary organisations.

The 1974 National Policy for Children marks a changed framework in public policy for children, drawing on discussions that had started with the important but not widely known 1968 report of the Ganga Sharan Sinha[16] Committee that had been constituted by the Parliament. It put forth the view that children were also a human resource and direct state provision of services was necessary (Balakrishnan, 2011). The Integrated Child Development Scheme (ICDS) focussing on nutrition and health as well as the scheme for Assistance to Voluntary Organisations for Crèches for Children of Working/Ailing Mothers (see next section) were outcomes of this orientation in which welfare, social investment and direct state provision came together. The ICDS, the flagship nutrition welfare scheme of the central government, was to cover immunisation, health check-up and referral services, and health and nutrition education for expectant and nursing mothers in addition to supplementary nutrition for them and children below 6 years in age, with a few hours of day care for children aged 3–6 years. Initially rooted in a sectoral or vulnerable group approach, the ICDS was expanded into a universal and comprehensive programme in select regions and eventually spread to the entire country. The increase in the ICDS centres in the 2000s, despite cuts in social programmes more generally, was in large part due to social movement mobilisations and filing of court cases[17] that put pressure on the state. Strategies to address high infant, child and maternal mortality rates in line with the United Nations Convention on the Rights of the Child that India ratified in 1992 and the Millennium Development Goals were also factors.

For children older than 6 years, there was a loosely knit set of universal provisions, including family-based allocation of subsidised food through the Public Distribution System (PDS) and public education and health facilities. With poor amenities, the last, if available at all, were de facto for the poor; the middle and upper classes accessed private facilities. In the early 1990s, post-liberalisation, the PDS became a targeted programme (TPDS) for families officially classified as poor or very poor. The latest move, over the last five years, has been to make the various programmes for families with children into CCT schemes. Access to benefits has been linked to conditions such as school enrolment or institutional delivery. In effect, this can mean a denial of these rights since the facilities may be absent or avoided by the poor due to the costs of availing of them. Furthermore, in a scenario of constantly rising food prices the same cash sum may be insufficient to meet food requirements. Nor do cash transfer programmes take into account local specificities and the differential value accorded to family members: familial strategies can mean that the cash is spent on other family necessities, rather than the nutrition of young girls and women (Ghosh, 2011).

Social movement campaigns, particularly since the 2000s, on the right to food and of children to education, health and protection from abuse, not only pushed the state to reaffirm earlier commitments in policy documents, some programmes were expanded. The 2009 Right to Education Act (RTE) is an example in which state responsibility to ensure universal enrolment and retention of children in schools was concretised. The state had to provide free education to all children aged between 6 and 14 and parents were obliged to enrol their children in primary schools. Health (through nutrition and immunisation) and education remain the two most direct engagements of the state with children, often at one site as with the national Midday Meal Scheme[18] in government schools.

The 2013 National Policy for Children combines themes in the 1974 policy and in the 2003 National Charter for Children. Both in 1974 and in 2013, the premise is that children are national assets, are to figure as components of human resource development plans, and programmes are to enable them to become moral, motivated and 'robust citizens' (GOI, 2013a, p. 1). Equal opportunity for the growth of all children, differentiated on various social and economic lines, is also emphasised in both documents as is the preservation and strengthening of the family 'so that full potentialities of growth of children are realised within the normal family, neighbourhood and community environment' (GOI, 1974, p. 3). The underlying assumption is that the 'normal' family and neighbourhood is altruistic, caring and able, an assumption not always borne out in documented domestic violence and living conditions of the poor. Thus, the 2013 policy affirms the necessity 'to protect children from all forms of abuse, while strengthening the family, society and the Nation' (GOI, 2013a, p. 2) and to eliminate discriminatory conditions. It states that while 'all children have the right to grow in a family environment . . . families are to be supported by a strong social safety net in caring for and nurturing their children' (GOI, 2013a, p. 2). It reasserts the centrality of mothers/fathers/families and continues the earlier theme of educating 'parents and caregivers' (GOI, 2013a, p. 11). Simultaneously, it also emphasises the greater recognition of children as children in the 2003 National Charter, stating the 'inherent right to be a child and enjoy a healthy and happy childhood'[19] (GOI, 2013a, p. 2). In sum, the 2013 policy displays an adept incorporation of the current international policy language and a continuing commitment to health, nutrition and education needs of children.

Looking across the plethora of policy documents pertaining to children,[20] it can be argued that there have been no radical changes in the approach to or framework of policy pertaining to children; that the new has been added to the old and that programme changes have largely been an outcome of changes in the larger policy environment. The last advocates CCT schemes with conditions that are meant to persuade/teach parents to follow new practices with minimum cost to the state. As indicated earlier, there are implementation and conceptual problems with these schemes: they are oblivious to the deep entanglement of notions of children, wellbeing and family strategies in socio-cultural values and larger economic structures and possibilities, such that changes in the former are unlikely without change in the last. The 2013 document does not take cognisance of the macroeconomic context and thence of the contradiction between achieving its child welfare commitments and the effects of CCTs and cuts in social programmes that the overarching orientation of economic policy directs. In fact, in 2015, a dramatic financial cut (more than 50 per cent) in the ICDS allocation was made in the national budget, such that even the Minister of Women and Child Development expressed her unhappiness.[21]

These cuts further another contradiction or deliberate ambiguity in child and family policy, which pertains to crèches and day care, and early childhood education, exacerbating the already limited and patchy implementation of schemes for non-familial care of pre-school children. Initially, public responsibility for the daily care of children did not draw support among policy makers, except for orphans, destitute and disabled children. The strategy to expand the network of crèche and day care facilities run by communities and voluntary organisations gained advocates through a focus on early childhood education (Swaminathan, 1985). Shifts in this stance evolved until the 12th Plan (2012–17)[22] acknowledged day care as critical for children as children, as future national assets, for communities and for women's empowerment (GOI, 2013b). The largest number of state-sponsored crèches open to all children (aged 3–6 years) has emerged under the ICDS in centres known as *anganwadis*. As a result of concerted campaigns, the decision to convert *anganwadis* into *anganwadi*-cum-crèches-cum-pre-schools has been taken repeatedly. Yet, as per the data provided by the Ministry of Women and Child Development, only 11,500 (as against the 1.35 million operational) *anganwadis* had been converted into *anganwadi*-cum-crèches by 2014–15.[23]

The primary impetus for the ICDS and much of state policy pertaining to day care and pre-school facilities remains one of nutrition and health rather than childcare. Even as a nutrition and a pre-school programme, performance has been patchy, both aspects tending to do better in regions where childcare, pre-school and family welfare programmes have been a political issue (Drèze, 2006). With World Bank direction, there have been moves to shift the running of centres to voluntary organisations or village councils. In most provinces, the last continue to be dominated by the village elite, whereas many of the *anganwadi* workers and the children that are officially the priority are from families below the poverty line, Dalits and Adivasis.[24]

One more issue that must be addressed is that of child labour. The 1974 National Policy for Children highlighted it as a concern, but it was 12 years before the Child Labour (Prohibition and Regulation) Act (CLPR) (1986) was passed. The CLPR reflected two diverse views, incorporating a complete ban in 83 hazardous occupations and regulation in others. The 2016 amended bill furthers the earlier contradiction. A 1986 clause stated that 'no child under 14 years shall be permitted to be engaged in any hazardous occupation or be made to undertake heavy work'. Though the 2016 law extends this to a complete ban on child labour, it makes an exception of labour in *family enterprises* and outside school hours; and the list of hazardous industries is reduced to three for children over 14. The newly added family enterprise exception has been justified on the grounds of apprenticeship and poverty, overlooking the fact that family enterprises are embedded in highly exploitative services and sub-contracted/putting out production chains (Sinha, 2016). It also belies well-documented outcomes of the constraints of poverty and illiteracy on parents, combined with the lack of schools and poor infrastructural facilities. Families may be forced to place children in the least paying labour, sidelining ideas of childhood, parental hopes, and the special protection that children and their development require.

Apart from child-directed schemes and programmes, which encapsulate an implicit and explicit policy pertaining to parents with young children, childcare and family policy may be viewed from the perspective of maternity and childcare entitlements of women, the main familial carers. This is the focus of the next section.

MATERNITY AND CHILDCARE ENTITLEMENTS

Article 42 of the Indian Constitution mandates that 'The State shall make provision for securing just and humane conditions of work and for maternity relief.' In practice, labour laws are largely directed at the formal sector in which only a very small number of women workers are found (Abraham et al., 2014; Lingam and Kanchi, 2013). There are three different sets of rules for maternity and childcare entitlements that are applicable to different groups of women workers based on their employment status, with the earlier outlined sanctions pushing the two-child population policy cutting across all claims.

Workers in permanent public employment are the most privileged of all workers in terms of work-related benefits. Provisions for maternity leave at full pay for women employees were enhanced in 1997 from 90 days to 135 days and in 2006 to 180 days. The right of men to take 15 days leave immediately prior to the birth of a child to their wife or within six months of the birth has also been introduced and is widely taken. In addition to maternity leave, since 2006, woman employees in this sector are eligible for Childcare Leave (for minor children) at full pay for a maximum of 730 days (two years) per child over their entire service period, a provision that is fraught but being availed of.[25]

Women workers who are registered under the Employees State Insurance Act (ESI) 1948[26] and have been employed for 80 days in the last 12 months in industrial establishments that employ ten or more workers are eligible for 12 weeks of maternity leave at full pay. However, only those earning below a monthly wage of less than Rs. 21,000 are eligible,[27] which along with poor registration means relatively few women benefit.

The bulk of women workers – 95 per cent – are in the informal/unorganised sector and are covered by the Maternity Benefit Act 1961. The law covers women who have worked 80 days or more in any shop or industrial establishment and who are not covered under the ESI Act, entitling them to 12 weeks leave on part pay and some maternity expenses. However, employers in general do not record workers and women are therefore unable to gain from this entitlement. The history of the law has been large-scale non-implementation and violations, making for conscious and unintentional discouragement to new mothers to remain or join the workforce (Palriwala and Neetha, 2011). Given this experience, the recent amendment (2017) to the act providing for an enhancement of paid maternity leave to 26 weeks may not mean much for new mothers. On the other hand, there is an expansion of the general concept of the family in this amendment, as it entitles women adopting children as well as commissioning mothers (in surrogate parenting) to three months leave. Provision for maternity entitlement is also recognised under the Unorganised Workers Social Security Act, 2008, but the government has not yet implemented it (Sinha et al., 2016).

With roughly around three-quarters of women being *non-workers* and roughly half of both male and female workers being outside paid employment, employer-linked and employment-based entitlements are of limited value. The concern regarding maternal and infant mortality rates led to the introduction of various schemes. These include the National Maternity Benefit Scheme (NMBS) introduced in 1995 and the 2005 Janani Suraksha Yojna (JSY), which provide some ante-natal care and some costs of delivery. In 2010, the Indira Gandhi Matritava Sahayog Yojana (IGMSY) maternity benefit programme was launched on a pilot basis in 52 districts[28] across the country. All pregnant women aged 19 years and above and not entitled to paid maternity leave are eligible. CCT is the model for these schemes, with benefits limited to the first two live births and to women from households with incomes below the poverty line.[29] After revision in 2013, recipients may receive two instalments of Rs. 3000 each for the first two live births on timely registration, complete vaccination, attending counselling sessions and exclusive breastfeeding of the child. Studies indicate again both the inadequacy of the benefits and very poor coverage (Sinha, 2016).

For women with children, especially below 6 years of age, crèche and day care facilities are critical. There are provisions for crèches in the workplace under numerous sector-specific labour laws, covering factories, mines, plantations, construction workers, contract and migrant workers and, most recently, in the Mahatma Gandhi National Rural Employment Guarantee Scheme (MGNREGS). Information on the implementation of legally required crèche provisions and their functioning is very patchy (Swaminathan, n.d.), though activists (such as the FORCES network) focussed on the issue have undertaken documentation. The picture is generally dismal: non-functioning crèches, poor facilities, no arrangements for children under 3, crowding, lack of training and orientation of crèche workers and the absence of any form of professional monitoring, leading to a vicious cycle of deterrence and dissuasion in using the facilities and lack of demand (Gopal, 1983). Employers, even public sector companies, government offices and schemes such as the MGNREGS, avoid legal obligations to set up crèches, especially since women workers have little knowledge of their rights. However, intent on retaining their highly trained and well-paid women employees who may work long hours, a few public sector companies and some new private enterprises are providing crèche facilities at work or assisting their employees in making arrangements for children at home (through paid workers or shifts) (Datta, 2005; Hill, 2013). In most families with children, mothers have to opt for part-time work combined with childcare or choose between paid work and care of children/family time; some are able to draw on other female kin and/or paid workers to help with the last. There is a class and social differentiation in this – labourers, Dalits, Adivasis versus middle and upper class, professional women.

Non-workplace-based crèches/day care centres were started in the early 1950s by the CSWB (see above). The scheme of Assistance to Voluntary Organisations for Crèches for Children of Working/Ailing Mothers, begun in 1974, suggested that only where poverty forced mothers to work elsewhere or ill-health made them unable to care for children – in other words, in the case of the involuntary absence of mothers – would the state step in to care for children. As discussed earlier, the policy pronouncement of ensuring a family life for children has been concretised by steps that keep women as carers at home. Thus, day care was viewed as a response to family failures rather than a facility for all families. The National Crèche Fund was set up in 1993–94. In 2005–06, these schemes were integrated into a new programme titled Rajiv Gandhi National Crèche Scheme for Children of Working Mothers and (funding for) crèches were allocated to provinces on the basis of the proportion of the child population with uncovered districts/tribal areas given the highest priority. As with the ICDS, crèche services were to cover children in the age group of 0–6 years, providing supplementary nutrition, emergency medicines and contingencies.

CONCLUSION

Multiple layers of contradictions make family policy in India – in the imaginaries of the family, between these imaginaries and stated policy aims in diverse fields, particularly those related to population control, children's nutrition, education and health status, and motherhood, women's work and empowerment, and between instrumentalities in various policy programmes. Family policy is largely implicit and emerges through ever-present assumptions regarding the family that circulate in official and public discourse. The altruistic family and gendered familialism are hegemonic in the construction of who will care but also who may require care, including children, who are the focus in this book. While the idea of a *modern, planned* family has been tied to a nuclear unit in population and wage policies, there is a simultaneous espousal of the idea of a traditional, Indian family that will take care of children, the elderly and other vulnerable members. It is argued in this chapter that any analysis of programmes for families with children in India must take into account the socio-cultural constructions and practices of inter-generational and sexual divisions beyond a nuclear family unit.

Policy rhetoric regarding women's empowerment invokes economic independence, paid work and assistance in the care for children; yet, programmes are designed that keep women in low-paying, home-based work that will enable the continuity of gender divisions of labour in family life and care. The acknowledgement that children must have a childhood is undercut by the acceptance that children will work in family enterprises. That the *family* requires education in the ways of proper care of children is one plank, while another, by default and by principle, is that care can be left to this family. As discussed, programmes for families with children, such as nutrition, health and day care provisions in ICDS, are experiencing cuts in financial outlays, being converted from universal programmes to targeted ones such as the PDS, and from provision in kind such as food into CCT programmes as in the Right to Food. Such cuts and shifts do not take account of social inequalities, including of gender, the absence of infrastructure that families in need require or the inflationary trends in the economy. Despite this and albeit with differential outcomes, women and men aspire and strategise to make a better life for their children and their families, drawing on their own resources and whatever state institutions may put in place.

NOTES

1. Drawing on diverse ethnographies, anthropologists, such as Fortes (1969), argued that altruism or unselfish giving is the core of familial and kinship ties. While it has been extended in political theory to the idea of citizenship based on solidarity within an imagined community, feminists have argued that familial altruism is rooted in gendered inequalities.
2. The economic and political pressures under which this shift took place cannot be elaborated. This paragraph draws much from Palriwala and Neetha (2011).
3. Under the PDS or Public Distribution System, all residents who registered with the designated local government office were entitled to specific grains and 'basic needs' items that were sold at fixed prices through 'fair price' shops. This was the government's flagship anti-poverty programme, tacitly premised on a right to food. With liberalisation, the PDS was replaced by a targeted system – the TPDS – with differential pricing for those classified 'Below Poverty Line' and 'Above Poverty Line' and large sections were completely excluded from its ambit.
4. The MGNREGS guarantees 100 days of manual work, not necessarily continuously, at a minimum wage. The government is to initiate and/or organise work at sites within a 5 kilometre radius of where people live. In 2016, women made up 51 per cent of those working under the MGNREGS (PTI, 2016a).
5. The figures have worsened in recent years. In 2013, the infant mortality rate was 40 per 1000 live births and the maternal mortality rate was 167 per 100,000 live births (Niti Aayog, n.d.). The former rose to 41 in 2015–16 (NFHS-4, cited in PTI, 2017) and the latter to 174 in 2015 (World Bank study, cited in Kaul, 2017).
6. Pre-Independence Hindu law was the most exclusionary for women in inheritance rights, in which property was transferred in the male line to men. Laws have been changed and amended, most recently in 2006 for

Hindu property laws, but with marginal effect in women's inheritance and the cultural ideal of a patrilineal family (see Singh, 2013). The last is in particular undergirded by patrilocal residence, in which women move to the home of the husband and his patrilineal kin on marriage.

7. There is a noted difference in the enrolment of girls in government schools and non-technical education as against boys being placed in private schools (if families can afford it) and technical education (see John et al., 2008).
8. These hopes have stimulated the declining juvenile sex ratios in India (John et al., 2008), even though, as Vera-Sanso argues, 'recent social and economic policies are creating a situation where sons are less able and less willing to support their parents' (2007, p. 225). Also see Palriwala (1999) for a discussion on gender, kinship and family relations in India and Singh (2013).
9. Under S. 125 of the 1973 Criminal Procedure Code.
10. This follows the official definition of workers, which is based on the concept of gainful/productive employment. It not only indicates the problematic place of care work in family policy, but is also an indication of women's livelihood constraints.
11. This cannot be elaborated here. As Shah points out, this illustrates the 'fundamental contradiction' between the population policy and a policy for the aged that 'seeks to rely upon . . . the traditional family' (1989, p. 515).
12. Parents are expected to take all responsibility for education and facilitating sons in getting work and the means to a livelihood. Vera-Sanso (2007) sees a rise in the expectations and costs of the needs and rights of children across castes and classes in rural Tamil Nadu. This is a feature of public and social discourse across the country and a reason given to plan for smaller families.
13. The sex ratio at birth, based on the Civil Registration System is 887 girls to 1000 boys in 2014, falling from 909 in 2011 (cited in Bansal, 2016).
14. Conditions included birth registration, immunisation, school enrolment and delayed marriage of daughters; all except the first meant costs that could add up to be higher than the cash received.
15. National development has been formulated and carried out through five-year plans prepared by the Planning Commission of India. The Planning Commission was replaced by a new institution, Niti Aayog, in 2015, and the system of five-year plans came to an end with the 12th five-year plan in March 2017.
16. Ganga Sharan Sinha was a member of the upper house of parliament and part of the socialist wing of the ruling party.
17. By the Right to Food Campaign. See http://www.righttofoodcampaign.in/
18. Under this scheme, all children enrolled in lower and upper primary schools are provided a snack or a hot meal during the day at the school premises. See Palriwala and Neetha (2009).
19. This was possibly influenced by discussions that took place in the framing of the United Nations Convention on the Rights of the Child.
20. Other than those discussed, these include the ratification of the Convention on the Rights of the Child in 1992, the 2005 National Plan of Action (NPA) for Children, another exclusively for the Girl Child, and the 2007 11th Plan document on *Strategies for Children Under Six*, revised in 2011 for the 12th Plan.
21. See Yadav (2015).
22. See endnote 15.
23. The proportion of children aged 3–6 years who were in ICDS pre-school centres was 22.4 per cent in 2011 (calculated from figures taken from GOI, n.d.). This is prior to the 2015 budget cuts.
24. Dalit is a term used to name all castes who have suffered severe discrimination and deprivation as 'Untouchables' in the traditional Hindu hierarchy. Adivasi denotes categories of people who are distinguished by their so-called 'tribal characteristics' and by their spatial and cultural isolation from the bulk of the population. Both social groups are marked by poverty and social exclusion, though they can avail of specific and special provisions of positive discrimination.
25. For some, the childcare leave provision is seen to reinforce the stereotype of childcare as being women's responsibility alone. Others suggest that since it can be taken until the child is 18, women are 'merely resting at home' and it is misused and unnecessary. Some women workers find that they are denied the leave on various grounds, such as shortage of staff.
26. A range of industrial sectors is included. It is difficult to give an accurate estimate of the proportion of women workers covered, but it is roughly less than 3 per cent.
27. This may be placed against the estimated per capita income in 2015–16 of Rs. 77,435 (at 2011–12 prices) (PTI, 2016b).
28. Of a total of 640 districts in 2011.
29. Poverty line definitions are always controversial in India. At present the official benchmark is daily per capita expenditure of Rs. 27 and Rs. 33 in rural and urban areas, respectively. About 22 per cent of the population is below this cut-off point (Sangal, 2016).

REFERENCES

Abraham, A., D. Singh, and P. Pal (eds) (2014), *Critical Assessment of Labour Laws, Policies and Practices through a Gender Lens*, New Delhi: Ministry of Women and Child Development, Government of India.

Agarwal, B. (2016), '"The family" in public policy: fallacious assumptions and gender implications', in B. Agarwal (ed.), *Gender Challenges. Vol. 2: Property, Family, and the State*, Delhi: Oxford University Press, pp. 189–219.

Balakrishnan, V. (ed.) (2011), *Growing Up and Away – Narratives of Indian Childhoods: Memory, History, Identity*, Delhi: Oxford University Press.

Bansal, S. (2016), 'Sex ratio at birth on the decline', *The Hindu*, accessed 30 November 2016 at http://www.thehindu.com/todays-paper/Sex-ratio-at-birth-on-the-decline/article16728001.ece.

Basu, A.M. (1997), 'The "politicization" of fertility to achieve non-demographic objectives', *Population Studies*, **51** (1), 5–18.

Butalia, U. (ed.) (2000), *The Other Side of Violence: Voices from the Partition of India*, Delhi: Penguin.

Child Labour (Prohibition and Regulation) Act (1986), Ministry of Labour and Employment, Government of India, accessed 12 August 2017 at http://www.labour.nic.in/sites/default/files/act.pdf.

Child Labour (Prohibition and Regulation) Amendment Act (2016), Ministry of Labour and Employment, Government of India, accessed 12 August 2017 at http://www.labour.nic.in/sites/default/files/Notification_for_enforcementofchild.pdf.

Criminal Procedure Code, S.125 (1973), Ministry of Law and Justice, Government of India, accessed 12 August 2017 at http://lawmin.nic.in/ld/P-ACT/1974/The%20Code%20of%20Criminal%20Procedure,%201973.pdf.

Datta, V. (2005), 'Reaching the unreached: early childhood care and education intervention in India', in J. Patnaik (ed.), *Children in South Asia: A Critical Look at Issues, Policies and programmes*, Greenwich, CT: Information Age Publishing, pp. 81–111.

Drèze, J. (2006), 'Universalisation with quality: ICDS in a rights perspective', *Economic and Political Weekly*, **41** (34), 3706–15.

Employees State Insurance Act (ESI) (1948), Ministry of Labour and Employment, Government of India, accessed 12 August 2017 at http://www.labour.nic.in/sites/default/files/Act.pdf.

Fortes, M. (ed.) (1969), *Kinship and the Social Order*, Chicago, IL: Aldine.

Gandhi A., B.K. Sahoo, P. Saha, and S. Mehrotra (2013), 'Turnaround in India's employment story', *Economic and Political Weekly*, **48** (35), 87–96.

Ghosh, J. (2011), 'Cash transfers as the silver bullet for poverty reduction: a sceptical note', *Economic and Political Weekly*, **46** (21), 68–71.

Gopal, A.K. (1983), *Crèches in Plantations*, New Delhi: National Institute of Public Cooperation and Child Development.

GOI (Government of India) (1974), *National Policy for Children*. New Delhi: Department of Social Welfare.

GOI (Government of India) (2013a), *National Policy for Children 2013*, New Delhi: Ministry of Women and Child Development.

GOI (Government of India) (2013b), *Twelfth Five Year Plan (2012–2017): Social Sectors, Volume III*, New Delhi: Sage.

GOI (Government of India) (2016), *National Policy for Women: Articulating a Vision for Empowerment of Women* (Draft), New Delhi: Ministry of Women and Child Development.

GOI (Government of India) (n.d.), *Integrated Child Development Services Scheme (ICDS) Data Tables*, New Delhi: Ministry of Women and Child Development, accessed 11 August 2017 at http://icds-wcd.nic.in/icdsimg/ICDS-March%202011.pdf.

Hill, E. (2013), 'Extreme jobs and the household: work and care in the New India', in J. Elias and S. Gunawardana (eds), *The Global Political Economy of the Household in Asia*, Houndmills, Basingstoke: Palgrave Macmillan, pp. 194–210.

John, M.E., R. Kaur, R. Palriwala, S. Raju, and A. Sagar (2008), *Planning Families, Planning Gender: Adverse Sex Ratio in Select Districts of Madhya Pradesh, Himachal Pradesh, Rajasthan, Haryana, Punjab*, Bangalore: Books for Change.

Kaul, R. (2017), 'India's maternal mortality rate on a decline', *The Hindustan Times*, 27 May, accessed 11 August 2017 at http://www.hindustantimes.com/health/india-s-maternal-mortality-rate-on-a-decline/story-ZcnBG0kidtvPEkRnKNI0II.html.

Lingam, L. and A. Kanchi (2013), *Women's Work, Maternity and Public Policy in India*, New Delhi: Ministry of Labour and Employment, Government of India and the International Labour Organization.

Maternity Benefit Act (1961), Ministry of Labour and Employment, Government of India, accessed 12 August 2017 at http://www.labour.nic.in/sites/default/files/TheMaternityBenefitAct1961.pdf.

Minimum Wages Act (1948), Ministry of Labour and Employment, Government of India, accessed 12 August 2017 at http://www.labour.nic.in/sites/default/files/TheMinimumWagesAct1948_0.pdf.

Neetha, N. (2014), 'Crisis in female employment: analysis across social groups', *Economic and Political Weekly*, **49** (47), 50–59.

Niti Aayog (n.d.), *State Statistics – Infant Mortality Rate, Maternal Mortality Rate*, accessed 30 November 2016 at http://niti.gov.in/content/.

Palriwala, R. (1999), 'Beyond myths: the social and political dynamics of gender', in N. Kabeer and R. Subrahmanian (eds), *Institutions, Relations and Outcomes: A Framework and Case Studies for Gender-aware Planning*, New Delhi: Kali for Women, pp. 49–79.

Palriwala, R. (2016), 'Acts of omission and acts of commission: the adverse juvenile sex ratio and the Indian state', in T. Kaur (ed.), *Too Many Men, Too Few Women: Social Consequences of the Gender Imbalance in India and China*, Delhi: Orient Blackswan, pp. 279–301.

Palriwala, R. and N. Neetha (2009), *The Care Diamond: State Social Policy and the Market in India: Research Report 3*, Geneva: UNRISD, accessed 1 December 2016 at http://www.unrisd.org/80256B3C005BCCF9/(httpAuxPages)/4177D0C917369239C1257566002EA0C7/$file/IndiaRR3.pdf.

Palriwala, R. and N. Neetha (2011), 'Stratified familialism: the care regime in India through the lens of childcare', *Development and Change*, **42** (4), 1049–78.

PTI (2016a), 'Around 51% women participated in MGNREGA, maximum in last 3 years', *Daily News and Analysis*, 10 March, accessed 30 November 2016 at http://www.dnaindia.com/india/report-around-51-women-participated-in-mgnrega-maximum-in-last-3-years-2187797.

PTI (2016b), 'India's per capita income rises 7.4% to Rs 93,293', *The Economic Times*, 31 May, accessed 30 November 2016 at http://economictimes.indiatimes.com/articleshow/52524152.cms?utm_source=contentofinterest&utm_medium=text&utm_campaign=cppst.

PTI (2017), 'India sees improved sex ratio, decline in infant mortality rate: National Family Health Survey', *Huffington Post*, 1 March, accessed 11 August 2017 at http://www.huffingtonpost.in/2017/03/01/india-sees-improved-sex-ratio-decline-in-infant-mortality-rate_a_21864344/.

Rao, M. (ed.) (2004), *From Population Control to Reproductive Health: Malthusian Arithmetic*, New Delhi: Sage.

Right to Education Act (RTE) (2009), Ministry of Human Resources Development, Government of India, accessed 12 August 2017 at http://mhrd.gov.in/sites/upload_files/mhrd/files/upload_document/rte.pdf.

Right to Food Campaign (n.d.), accessed 11 August 2017 at http://www.righttofoodcampaign.in.

Sangal, P.P. (2016), 'Defining a poverty line for India', *Financial Express*, 22 May, accessed 2 December 2016 at http://www.financialexpress.com/opinion/defining-a-poverty-line-for-india/74725/.

Sekher, T.V. (2012), 'Ladlis and Lakshmis: financial incentive schemes for the girl child', *Review of Women's Studies: Economic and Political Weekly*, **47** (17), 58–65.

Shah, A.M. (1989), 'Parameters of family policy in India', *Economic and Political Weekly*, **XXIV** (10), 513–16.

Shah, A.M. (1998), *The Family in India: Critical Essays*, New Delhi: Orient Longman.

Singh, K. (2013), *Laws and Son Preference: A Reality Check*, New Delhi: UNFPA.

Sinha, S. (2016), 'The new law banning child labour is no ban at all', *Wire*, accessed 22 November 2016 at http://thewire.in/53128/unveiling-the-facade-of-the-child-labour-act/.

Sinha, D., S. Nehra, S. Matharu, J. Khanuja, and V. Leah Falcao (2016), 'Realising universal maternity entitlements: lessons from Indira Gandhi Matritva Sahyog Yojana', *Economic and Political Weekly*, **51** (34), 49–55.

Swaminathan, M. (1985), *Who Cares? A Study of Child Care Facilities for Low-income Women in India*, New Delhi: Centre for Women's Development Studies.

Swaminathan, M. (n.d.), 'Creches: at the workplace or residence? Not EITHER/OR but BOTH', Unpublished mimeo, private circulation.

Tarlo, E. (2003), *Unsettling Memories: Narratives of the Emergency in Delhi*, Berkeley, CA: University of California Press.

Vera-Sanso, P. (2007), 'Increasing consumption, decreasing support: a multi-generational study of family relations among South Indian Chakkliyars', *Contributions to Indian Sociology (n.s.)*, **41** (2), 225–48.

Yadav, A. (2015) '"Children are the worst affected": budget cuts are taking a toll on a crucial nutrition scheme', *Scroll*, 19 November, accessed 20 April 2017 at https://scroll.in/article/767475/children-are-worst-affected-budget-cuts-are-taking-a-toll-on-a-crucial-nutrition-scheme.

22. Family policy patterns in autocratic countries
*Dorian R. Woods and Rolf Frankenberger**

INTRODUCTION

While the literature on family policy in modern and western democracies is vast, there are few single or comparative studies of family policy in autocratic countries. This chapter therefore breaks new ground for comparative analysis. Autocracies are defined by the narrow concentration of governance and their coercive hold on power: extreme autocratic regimes are found in various geographical areas in Asia, Africa, Eastern Europe, Latin America and the Middle East. Autocratic countries include states such as Russia, China, Saudi Arabia, Cuba and Ethiopia. Until now, autocratic countries have had little attention from the family policy research community. As family policy has expanded globally, theoretical analysis has concentrated on western democracies, even though in some cases, autocracies have more generous family policy in eligibility and social expenditure than western democracies. It is surprising that autocratic countries are rarely used as country cases in family policy research or family policy regime typologies and very little is known about how policy instruments are applied or how policies have developed over time. Welfare state theories have emphasized causal factors in policy development such as politics, power and institutions: this makes the study of autocracies and their specific cases of governance and power dynamics especially relevant for investigating how politics, power and institutions affect policy. Family policy theorists have also concentrated on how policy affects gender equality and, yet, rarely is a step taken in order to analyse policy in countries with extremely unequal shares of power between men and women, social classes or ethnicities. An examination of family policy in states with widely disparate distributions of power could offer a multifaceted analysis of family policy, its development and instruments.

The close observation of autocracies and family policy is only at its initial stages, and this chapter is unique in analysing some patterns across autocracies. Our chapter asks the following questions: (1) What variations in family policy are there in autocratic countries – in particular, what patterns can be found in autocratic family leave policy? (2) How might such variations be explained? (3) How can such comparisons contribute to further family policy and gender analysis? Where feasible, we will make reference to autocratic countries in comparison to democratic ones. In particular, we examine how the characteristics of family leave policy in autocratic countries differ according to regime type in autocratic literature. We define family leave as paid or unpaid maternity, paternity and parental leave for the care of small children. The variations that we find in autocracies are distinctly grouped together and we propose that these variations should be explored with explanations of autocratic regime types and geographical locations. Culture and ideology is another factor that is worth exploring for family leave variation among autocraticies. We hypothesize that with an examination of family policy from the perspective of autocracies, new issues emerge that offer a new view to old theories but also to fundamental assumptions about the function of family policy, such as family policy's role in the legitimization of a state, its strong relationship to cultural heritages, and its explicit and implicit confirmation of societal ideals and ideology.

In the next section of this chapter we provide a literature review of approaches to examining autocratic regime types, family policy variation and family leave in autocracies. We present the theories outlined above as well as social policy analysis that has until now only concentrated, for example, on institutions, industrial development, social movements or political representation in democratically run governments. In the following section we outline our method, the data and our approach. We then proceed to compare demographics in autocracies, comparing economic activity of men and women as well as fertility and growth rates, which are central control variables for potential variations in family policies across countries and will be tested in the further analysis. The next section shows patterns of family leave policy, based on eligibility, length of leaves, generosity and differences for mothers and fathers. We then summarize the diversity of family policy across a number of autocracies, discuss patterns and approaches to family policy, analyse emerging gender issues and discuss explanations for such patterns. Heterogeneity in autocratic family policy is not surprising because, with absolute power, autocrats can change policies quite easily, but we argue in our conclusion that these patterns are not arbitrary, but depend on path-dependent trajectories as well as tradition and culture.

LITERATURE REVIEW

How does the literature define and characterize autocracies and can theoretical approaches applied to western democratic family policy variation also be applied to family policy patterns in autocracies? To answer the first question, autocracies have been defined generally as political systems 'in which the rulers are insufficiently, or not at all, subject to antecedent and enforceable rules of law – enforceable, that is, by other authorities who share in the government and who have sufficient power to compel the lawbreaking rulers to submit to the law' (Friedrich and Brzezinki, 1965, p. 5). There are three major data sets that rank autocratic institutions on a scale based on civil society, civil rights, political participation, representation and free elections. The Bertlesmann Foundation's Transformation Index (BTI) measures the quality of democracy and economic development in two-year cycles. The Freedom House index is another measure based on global freedom and the implementation of political rights and civil liberties. The last index, and the one we use for choosing our sample, is the annual Democracy Index published by the Economist Intelligence Unit. Democracies and autocracies are measured and compared to one another on a scale of full democracies, flawed democracies, hybrid regimes and autocratic regimes; at the extreme, there were 51 cases of autocracies in 2016.

In terms of measuring and explaining variation within autocracies, the literature seems to agree on general typologies. There is some cross-over between types, but, for the most part, mainstream literature on autocracies explain variance in terms of how autocratic governments institutionalize and legitimize their power (see Geddes, 1999, 2007; Hadenius and Teorell, 2007; Kailitz, 2013). Legitimization and justification of autocratic power are important factors in autocracies, according to the literature, because they do not otherwise receive social validation through free speech and fair elections. Following

Kailitz (2013), a typology of these regimes and their legitimization is as follows (see Table 22.1 for a full categorization):

- *Ideological autocracies* uphold legitimization of power through ideology, such as a (former) communist or religious ideological tradition. Examples of communist ideological autocracies are China, Cuba, Laos, North Korea and Vietnam.
- *Electoral autocracies* legitimize power through controlled elections. Examples include Ethiopia, Kazakhstan, Russia and Zimbabwe.
- *One-party autocracies* legitimize themselves as a single and major 'people's party', so electoral competition of political alternatives is discouraged and opposition is illegitimate. Examples are Chad and Uzbekistan.
- *Military regimes* legitimize their power through force as they decide on regulations and norms according to their own will without procedural justification. A current example is Mauritania.
- *Monarchies* legitimize themselves by drawing on the 'natural' right of the monarch to govern. Examples are Qatar, Saudi Arabia and the United Arab Emirates.
- *Personalist autocracies* are characterized by a lack of comprehensive institutions to legitimize a powerful individual who can change the political and societal rules arbitrarily. Examples include Eritrea and Sudan.

To answer the second question, we assume in this chapter that (family) policy plays an important role in legitimizing autocratic regimes, and we test whether specific family policy instruments will correspond to this autocratic typology. Because autocracies need to legitimize their power, we surmise with our first hypothesis that certain family policy patterns will emerge connected to legimization types. Analogous to the autocratic regime types are institutional constellations of autocratic power and our first hypothesis finds that institutionalism is a probable explanation for autocratic family policy variation. Because the availability of data on autocracies is limited and because we are examining 50 autocracies, an in-depth examination of historical institutionalism or path dependency is beyond the limits of this chapter. However, we explore family policy variation according to societal traditions and cultural settings, by testing a second hypothesis that regimes' family policy types are based on geographical location. (For more on cultural influences on family policy, see Pfau-Effinger, 2012.) The neo-Marxist approach is another theory that focuses directly on unions and collective actors as playing roles in promoting highly developed employment-related social policy. We find relatively little evidence in autocracies for strong union clout because civil society is weak in autocracies. However, indirectly related to union organization, communist ideology seems to be associated with well-developed family leave policy, which is another correlation we explore in the empirical evidence.

While early literature on families in autocracies has focused on the family's function merely as an oasis in a repressive political environment (see, e.g., Friedrich and Brzezinski, 1965), emerging research has concentrated on the family's role as welfare provider (see Baylouny, 2010, e.g., or Habtom and Ruys, 2007). Literature on cross-country analysis of gender issues and family policy in autocratic countries has mainly focused on the former Eastern Bloc countries, although there are some exceptional comparisons of gender issues in the Middle East (see Charrad, 2011; Moghadam, 2006). These studies are not explicitly focused on autocratic regimes as such. In the case of Eastern Bloc countries,

Table 22.1 Demographics

	Female labour force participation rate (2016)[a] (age 15–64)	Male labour force participation rate (2016)[a] (age 15–64)	Gender difference in labour force participation	Total fertility rate (2014)[b]	Population growth rate (2015)[c]	Infant mortality rate (2015)[d]	Regime subtype (Kailitz, 2013)
Autocracies							
Carribean							
Haiti	64.0%	72.4%	8.4%	3.0	1.17%	52.2	Electoral
Central Asia and Eastern Europe							
Azerbaijan	67.4%	72.8%	5.4%	2.0	0.96%	27.9	Electoral
Belarus	68.2%	76.6%	8.4%	1.6	−0.20%	3.4	Electoral
Kazakhstan	74.4%	82.6%	8.2%	2.7	1.14%	12.6	Electoral
Russia	68.6%	79.3%	10.7%	1.7	−0.04%	8.2	Electoral
Tajikistan	62.1%	80.4%	18.3%	3.5	1.71%	38.5	Electoral
Turkmenistan	50.2%	80.6%	30.4%	2.3	1.14%	43.7	One party
Uzbekistan	51.8%	79.7%	27.9%	2.2	0.93%	33.9	One party
Latin America							
Cuba	51.1%	79.1%	28.0%	1.6	−0.15%	4.0	Communist
Middle East and North Africa							
Afghanistan	19.9%	85.3%	65.4%	4.8	2.32%	66.3	Personalist
Algeria	18.5%	76.2%	57.7%	2.9	1.84%	21.9	Electoral
Bahrain	40.5%	86.6%	46.1%	2.1	2.41%	5.3	Monarchy
Egypt	24.9%	80.4%	55.5%	3.3	1.79%	20.3	One party
Iran	17.2%	76.4%	59.2%	1.7	1.20%	13.4	Ideocracy
Jordan	15.3%	67.8%	52.5%	3.4	0.83%	15.4	Monarchy
Kuwait	49.3%	85.6%	36.3%	2.1	1.62%	7.3	Monarchy
Libya	29.5%	81.8%	52.3%	2.5	2.23%	11.4	Personalist
Oman	31.6%	87.4%	55.8%	2.8	2.06%	9.9	Monarchy
Qatar	53.9%	94.5%	40.6%	2.0	3.07%	6.8	Monarchy
Saudi Arabia	21.1%	80.4%	59.3%	2.8	1.46%	12.5	Monarchy
Syria	13.1%	74.0%	60.9%	3.0	−0.16%	11.1	One party
United Arab Emirates	42.4%	92.0%	49.6%	1.8	2.58%	5.9	Monarchy
Yemen	27.1%	75.6%	48.5%	4.2	2.47%	33.8	Electoral
South and East Asia							
China	70.3%	84.3%	14.0%	1.6	0.45%	9.2	Communist
Laos	81.2%	79.3%	−1.9%	3.0	1.55%	50.7	Communist
North Korea	80.4%	89.6%	9.2%	2.0	0.53%	19.7	Communist
Vietnam	79.9%	86.9%	7.0%	2.0	0.97%	17.3	Communist
Sub-Saharan Africa							
Angola	61.0%	78.0%	17.0%	6.1	2.77%	96.0	Electoral
Burundi	85.7%	83.6%	−2.1%	6.0	3.27%	54.1	Electoral
Cameroon	72.1%	82.0%	9.9%	4.7	2.59%	57.1	Electoral
Central African Republic	72.1%	85.0%	12.9%	4.3	2.13%	91.5	Electoral
Chad	64.6%	79.3%	14.7%	6.2	1.89%	85.0	One party
Comoros	36.2%	79.8%	43.6%	4.5	1.77%	55.1	Electoral

Table 22.1 (continued)

	Female labour force participation rate (2016)[a] (age 15–64)	Male labour force participation rate (2016)[a] (age 15–64)	Gender difference in labour force participation	Total fertility rate (2014)[b]	Population growth rate (2015)[c]	Infant mortality rate (2015)[d]	Regime subtype (Kailitz, 2013)
Democratic Republic of the Congo	71.3%	71.9%	0.6%	6.0	2.45%	74.5	Electoral
Djibouti	38.9%	71.4%	32.5%	3.2	2.20%	54.2	Electoral
Equatorial Guinea	72.9%	93.8%	20.9%	4.8	2.51%	68.2	One party
Eritrea	80.3%	91.0%	10.7%	4.3	2.25%	34.1	Personalist
Ethiopia	79.9%	90.3%	10.4%	4.4	2.89%	41.4	Electoral
Gabon	42.5%	60.3%	17.8%	3.9	1.93%	36.1	One party
Gambia	72.8%	82.6%	9.8%	5.7	2.16%	47.9	One party
Guinea	82.3%	86.1%	3.8%	5.0	2.63%	61.0	One party
Guinea-Bissau	68.8%	79.2%	10.4%	4.8	1.91%	60.3	Electoral
Mauritania	30.2%	65.9%	35.7%	4.6	2.23%	65.1	Military
Niger	40.9%	90.6%	49.7%	7.6	3.25%	57.1	Electoral
Republic of the Congo	68.5%	73.7%	5.2%	4.9	2.00%	33.2	Electoral
Rwanda	88.4%	84.1%	–4.3%	3.9	2.56%	31.1	Electoral
Sudan	25.0%	73.2%	48.2%	4.4	1.72%	47.6	Electoral
Swaziland	42.8%	67.3%	24.5%	3.3	1.11%	44.5	Monarchy
Togo	82.7%	81.6%	–1.1%	4.6	2.69%	52.3	Electoral
Zimbabwe	78.8%	88.2%	9.4%	3.9	2.21%	46.6	Electoral

Source: Own compilation based on:
a. ILO (2016), 'Labour force participation rate by sex and age (%)', http://www.ilo.org/ilostat/
b. World Bank (2016), http://data.worldbank.org/indicator/SP.DYN.TFRT.IN?end=2014&start=1960_Total fertility rate represents the number of children that would be born to a woman if she were to live to the end of her childbearing years and bear children in accordance with age-specific fertility rates of the specified year.
c. Central Intelligency Agency *World Factbook* (2016), https://www.cia.gov/library/publications/the-world-factbook/rankorder/2002rank.html
d. World Bank (2016), http://data.worldbank.org/indicator/SP.DYN.IMRT.IN_Infant mortality rate is the number of infants who die before reaching 1 year of age per 1000 live births in a given year.

studies compare social policy development in autocracies with developing democracies indiscriminately. In one of these studies, Pascal and Manning (2000) follow the transition of former Soviet Bloc states' social policies and their gendered impact, finding that women struggle to cope and survive because the former support systems collapsed. While costs of balancing work and family were de-familialized in Soviet times, such resources have been falling away, and especially domestic violence and heavy domestic responsibilities are proving difficult for women. Other studies echo such sentiments (e.g., see Chapter 17 by Raţ and Szikra in this volume; Dugarova, 2016; Motiejunaite and Kravchenko, 2008; Robila, 2012). The context of these studies concentrate on breadwinner model types and the lack of de-familialization but they do not concentrate on autocratic political systems per se. This is unfortunate due to well-established theories of social policy development that, for example, point to the importance of politics and its role in creating and expanding policy.

From the literature, we know that comparative analysis of family policy in autocracies is rare (for an exception, see Woods and Frankenberger, 2016). Studies that look at family policy in countries that have autocratic regimes do not explicitly focus on autocratic regimes per se, or examine theories pertaining to autocracies. In the few cases that studies compare autocracies in relation to gender, they examine women's political representation, values and rights (see, e.g., the studies from Pickel, 2013 and Moghadam, 2006). An empirical comparison and grouping of autocratic family policy has not been attempted in the literature nor has family policy been an issue of empirical analysis for autocratic states. Such a gap in the literature has been the motivation for this chapter.

METHODOLOGY

One of the most difficult challenges of studying autocracies is the lack of reliable, available data and there is a scarce amount of comparative data on family policies. This chapter uses the ILO survey (2014), the World Policy Analysis Center (2016) and the Central Intelligence Agency (CIA) *World Factbook* (2016). We have narrowed our observation of family policy specifically to family leave policies because of the availability of the data set, the ease in which family leave policies can be compared, and because leave policies are a good case study of family policy for this study. The policy of leave schemes is closely related to women's labour force participation and gender equality, two issues that one would assume are not supported in particular autocratic regimes. These issues of equality are interesting for a variety of reasons: firstly, autocracies aim to segment societal inequality in order to preserve their elite power base. A broad and generous family leave policy seems to contradict this assumption. Secondly, this policy is emblematic of current discourse in family policy research in western democracies. A policy that is indicative of such discourse is most promising for closer observation of contributions this analysis might have for overall family policy research. Thirdly, family leave is for all purposes a straightforward policy for comparison: the instruments are similar in the sense that they all have equivalent time limitations and levels of reimbursements. This is not the case for allowances and benefits-in-kind which are subject to functional equaivalents and undefined boundaries between policy instruments and monetary amounts.

We examine three types of family leave policy: maternity, paternity and parental leave (see also Chapter 10 by Thévenon for an account of leave schemes). Complying with the ILO data set, we define maternity leave as protective leaves that are available to mothers right before or following the birth of a child. Paternity leave is available to fathers only, and immediately following the birth of the child. Parental leave is defined as leave that is available for parents on a longer term basis for the care of an infant or young child after the initial period (and expiry) of maternity or paternity leave (ILO, 2014, p. 164). The factors that we consider for comparing these types of leaves are wage replacement rates, length of leaves and eligibility. In addition to a comparison of absolute numbers, we also calculate a standardized measure for the generosity of leave regulations: we use the measure of Full Time Equivalents (FTE), as, for example, proposed by Gornick and Meyers (2003) and Ray et al. (2010) for the comparison of generosity in 21 high-income countries. FTE units are calculated as 'the wage replacement rate multiplied by the duration of leave' (Ray et al., 2010, p. 200). Sources of leave payments (state or company insurance plans) we discard for lack of space, but we note here that most leave schemes were state-provided, and it was generally the Middle East countries that funded leave schemes through companies. Interesting for us is an inter-country observation on gender, in terms of the ratio of a country's leave policy that is available for mothers and fathers.

In order to do justice to the high numbers of autocracies and to capture their variance, we include as many as possible in this chapter: 50 of 51 full autocracies designated by *The Economist*'s Democracy Index (The Economist, 2016, p. 2). The Ivory Coast was left out due to missing demographic and leave data. There is insufficient data on family leaves for Oman and Turkmenistan, so they are left out in some calculations. The high number of cases only allows for general comparisons with less specificities of cultures, economic and political stability or policy. Also, examining the historical developments of each autocracy is beyond the scope of this chapter. The qualitative clustering of autocracies is based on the variants of family leave length and generosity of wage replacements as well as in the differing eligibility in leave policy for mothers and fathers. It is complemented by a hierarchical cluster analysis using Ward-Clustering. In order to test our hypotheses we test for statistical covariations of autocratic clustering of maternity, paternity and parental leave with autocratic regime type, geographical location, male and female employment differences. In addition, we use multiple ANOVA in order to reveal significant variances between subtypes of autocracies and regional groups. We also consider communist ideology as specifically relevant for well-developed and gender-egalitarian family leave policy.

PATTERNS OF AUTOCRACIES: DEMOGRAPHICS

There is an extreme range of demographic characteristics in autocracies, in particular male and female labour force participation, fertility rates, infant mortality and population growth rates. These indicators are useful for our analysis because they provide background information on demographic issues that these countries are facing, and we find they are illustrative of the exceptional variety in core aspects of autocratic societal reproduction. Women's employment participation rates are also more varied in autocracies than in democracies and span from very little participation to even higher rates of participation than their male counterparts. These gendered aspects of family and labour market characteristics seem to also correlate to the heterogeneous family leave policy of autocracies. The magnitude of diversity in autocracies is apparent in our analysis of fertility, infant mortality and population growth rates (Table 22.1). For example, the lowest fertility rates in autocracies were 1.6 (China, Cuba, Belarus) to an extreme high value of 7.6 in Niger and Angola. The demographics of infant mortality rates also tended to diverge widely: Angola had a high rate of 96 deaths but Cuba had a low rate of four deaths per 1000. Another demographic indicator, the population growth rate, also shows variety: There are negative percentage growth rates in autocratic countries like Belarus (–0.20), Cuba (–0.15), Syria (–0.16) and Russia (–0.04), but also quite high growth rates in some of the Sub-Saharan African autocracies, such as Burundi (3.27) and Niger (3.25) or in the Middle East with Qatar (3.07).

296 *Handbook of family policy*

The economic need to support the family varies, and there is also extreme variation in female and male labour force participation rates in autocracies. Some autocracies have high rates of female labour market participation but ungenerous family leave policy, for example, in regions of Africa. Higher female labour force participation rates than men's could be found in Togo, Rwanda, Burundi and Laos. The high rates might be related to data accuracy or to counting the informal economy. However, the necessity of being active in the labour force does not seem to be related to requirements of benefit receipt. Another 19 autocracies have very similar male and female labour force participation rates, with minimally higher percentages of male labour force participation: Haiti, Ethiopia, Cameroon, Belarus, Vietnam, Russia, Guinea, China, Kazakhstan, Zimbabwe, Gambia, Democratic Republic of the Congo, Azerbaijan, Eritrea, Republic of the Congo, Guinea-Bissau, Central African Republic, Chad and North Korea. From a policy perspective, the need for family leave might be quite high in all of these countries, considering the high rates of female labour participation, but these rates are not related to benefits, as we will show in the next policy section. Congruent with little family leave policy are the low female participation rates in autocracies in the Middle East and North Africa: Algeria, Jordan, Niger, Egypt, Oman, Afghanistan, United Arab Emirates, Sudan, Libya, Yemen, Iran, Saudi Arabia and Syria. In addition, some Sub-Saharan African and Central Asian autocracies represent a middle range of male labour force participation rates – about 20 to 40 per cent more than women's, like Uzbekistan, Turkmenistan, Comoros, Djibouti, Mauritania, Niger, Sudan, Swaziland and Equatorial Guinea, where female participation rate is 72.9 and male participation rate is 93.8. The high rates of female labour force participation rates in Qatar might be due to the inclusion of domestic work in its formal employment data.

PATTERNS OF AUTOCRACIES: FAMILY LEAVE POLICY

Just as patterns of demography are extremely diverse in autocracies, so are the family leave policies. Table 22.2 shows autocratic regime type and family leave policy. Although standard maternity leave in autocracies is less varied from one another, it is more diverse than in democracies. Especially parental leave is strikingly disparate in autocracies. The length of leave, the eligibility for either mothers or fathers (or both) and the replacement rates for paid leave are our qualifier for further analysis of patterns. Leave lengths express the norms of how long the child should be cared for at home and when parents should return to the labour market. Leave eligibility for mothers and fathers illustrates both the extent of universalism and norms around gender roles. For example, if generosity in benefit is high and the leave is universal, than such a leave is more attractive for men to take up. Generosity calculated in Full Time Equivalent Units was less of a central issue for our analysis, although it corresponds with clustering of leave length and replacement rates. Generosity levels are nevertheless reported in the discussion, when autocratic regime types differ significantly. It should be noted, however, that the take-up of leaves from parents is often unknown and implementation of policies might vary widely.

Four groups of autocracies emerge after initial qualitative examination of their family leave policies. The first distinct group is comprised of eight electoral autocracies with a strong communist legacy. These countries have the longest maternity leaves, with an

Table 22.2 Family leave

	Maternity leave 2013		Paternity leave 2013		Parental leave 2013	
	Duration of maternity leave (in weeks)	Maternity leave cash benefits/wage replacement rate (% of previous earnings)	Duration of paternity leave (in national legislation)	Paternity leave cash benefits/wage replacement rate (% of previous earnings)	Duration of parental leave (in national legislation)	Parental leave cash benefits/wage replacement rate (% of previous earnings)
Autocracies						
Carribean						
Haiti	12	100% for six weeks	none	–	none	–
Central Asia and Eastern Europe						
Azerbaijan	18	100%	14 calendar days	unpaid	156 weeks (either parent or actual caregiver)	flat rate benefit
Belarus	18	100%	none	–	156 weeks (either parent or actual caregiver)	80% of the minimum subsistence wage
Kazakhstan	18	100%	5 days	unpaid	156 weeks (either parent)	unpaid
Russia	20	100% up to a ceiling	none	–	156 weeks, 76 paid (either parent or actual caregiver)	40% up to a ceiling
Tajikistan	20	100%	none	–	156 weeks, 78 paid (either parent or actual caregiver)	flat rate benefit
Turkmenistan	16	100%	–	–	–	–
Uzbekistan	18	100%	none	–	156 weeks (either parent or actual caregiver)	20% of minimum wage
Latin America						
Cuba	18	100%	none	–	39 weeks (either parent)	60%
Middle East and North Africa						
Afghanistan	13	100%	none	–	none	–
Algeria	14	100%	3 days	100%	none	-
Bahrain	9	100% 45 days	none	–	26 weeks (only mothers)	unpaid
Egypt	13	100%	none	–	104 weeks (only mothers)	unpaid

Table 22.2 (continued)

	Maternity leave 2013		Paternity leave 2013		Parental leave 2013	
	Duration of maternity leave (in weeks)	Maternity leave cash benefits/wage replacement rate (% of previous earnings)	Duration of paternity leave (in national legislation)	Paternity leave cash benefits/wage replacement rate (% of previous earnings)	Duration of parental leave (in national legislation)	Parental leave cash benefits/wage replacement rate (% of previous earnings)
Iran	13 (17)	66.7% for 12 weeks	none	–	none	–
Jordan	10	100%	none	–	52 weeks (only mothers)	unpaid
Kuwait	10	100%	none	–	17 weeks (mothers only)	unpaid
Libya	14	50% (100% for self-employed)	3 days	–	none	–
Oman	7	100%	–	–	–	–
Qatar	7	100%	none	–	none	–
Saudi Arabia	10	50–100%	1 day	100%	none	–
Syria	17	100%	6 days	unpaid	52 weeks (only mothers)	unpaid
United Arab Emirates	6	100%	none	–	none	–
Yemen	9	100%	none	–	none	–
South East Asia						
China	14	100%	none	–	none	–
Laos	13	100%	none	–	none	–
North Korea	13	100%	3 days	unpaid	52 weeks (either parent)	40%
Vietnam	26	100%	none	–	none	–
Sub-Saharan Africa						
Angola	13	100%	none	–	none	–
Burundi	12	100%	15 days	50%	none	–
Cameroon	14	100%	10 days	100%	none	–
Central African Republic	14	50%	10 days	100%	none	–

Country	weeks	pay	days	pay	up to 52 weeks (6 months renewable once, either parent)	unpaid
Chad	14	100%	10 days	100%		–
Comoros	14	100%	10 days	100%	none	–
Democratic Republic of the Congo	14	66,7%	2 days	100%	none	–
Djibouti	14	100%	3 days	100%	none	–
Equatorial Guinea	12	75%	none	–	none	–
Eritrea	9	paid (amount unidentified)	none	–	none	–
Ethiopia	13	100%	5 days	unpaid	none	–
Gabon	14	100%	10 days	100%	none	–
Gambia	12	100%	none	–	none	–
Guinea	14	100%	none	–	none	–
Guinea-Bissau	9	100%	none	–	none	–
Mauritania	14	100%	10 days	100%	none	–
Niger	14	100%	none	–	none	–
Republic of the Congo	15	100%	10 days	100%	none	–
Rwanda	12	100% 6 weeks	4 days	100%	none	–
Sudan	8	100%	none	–	none	–
Swaziland	12	100% 2 weeks	none	–	none	–
Togo	14	100%	10 days	100%	none	–
Zimbabwe	14	100%	none	–	none	–

Source: Own compilation based on ILO (2016).

average of 18.3 weeks: Russia and Tajikistan have 20 weeks; Uzbekistan, Kazakhstan, Belarus, Cuba and Azerbaijan have 18 weeks; and Turkmenistan has 16 weeks paid maternity leave. In terms of wage replacements, these communist ideological autocracies also tend to be the most generous with 100 per cent wage replacement for the complete maternity leave. Exceptions were Russia, which has a ceiling on wage replacements, and Kazakhstan which pays full wage levels up to only six weeks. Following maternity leave, Belarus, Russia, Kazakhstan, Azerbaijan, Uzbekistan and Tajikistan offer 156 weeks of consecutive parental leave (available to either of the parents) with 20–80 per cent of the last earnings for at least 52 weeks. Cuba covers 39 weeks of parental leave with 60 per cent coverage. Although Cuba is geographically far away from these former Eastern Bloc countries, it has enjoyed close ties to Russia and is mostly isolated from its geographical neighbours. Autocracies in the Eastern Bloc do not offer specific paternity leaves separate from parental leave, except for Azerbaijan with 14 days and Kazakhstan with five days of unpaid leave. This most generous leave corresponds with the relatively high rates of labour force participation of both genders and the little difference between men's and women's labour force participation. In terms of autocratic regimes, this first group is overwhelmingly dominated by electoral government systems. Only Turkmenistan and Uzbekistan have one party regimes.

A second group of four communist ideocracies, located in East and South Asia, has a slightly different type of generosity and eligibility for mothers and fathers in family leaves compared to the former Eastern Bloc communist autocracies and Cuba. This second group has relatively shorter maternity leaves and a glaringly different approach to paternity and parental leave. China, North Korea, Laos and Vietnam grant shorter maternity leave than the Central Asian countries, with no or little paternity leave. China offers 14 weeks maternity leave, Laos 13 weeks, North Korea 13 weeks, and Vietnam 26 weeks of maternity leave. Of the four countries, only North Korea offers paternity days (three unpaid) and parental leave (52 weeks at 40 per cent wage replacement for both parents). While the first group of Eastern Bloc autocracies has a generous parental leave for both mothers and fathers, this second Asian group is distinct in having hardly any parental leave. Similar to the first Eastern Bloc group, this second Asian group of countries contains some electoral autocracies and has communist heritage. On the other hand, there are Confucian cultural influences that set this second group apart from the first.

The Sub-Saharan African autocracies make up the largest group of autocracies with 23 countries, and contains mostly one party or electoral autocracies. These countries have a middle range of on average 12.8 weeks of maternity leave with little or no paternity leave and no parental leave (an exception being Chad with 52 weeks of unpaid leave for either parent). Payment during maternity leave is 100 per cent of wage replacement, with the exception of the Democratic Republic of Congo with 66.7 per cent, Guinea-Bissau with 75 per cent and the Central African Republic with 50 per cent. About half of the countries offer some paternity leave: Gabon, Comoros, Cameroon, Togo, the Republic of Congo, the Central African Republic and Chad offer ten days paternity leave at 100 per cent wage replacement. Mauritania offers five days, Rwanda four days, Djibouti three days, the Democratic Republic of Congo two days – all paid with full wage replacement; Burundi offers 15 days with 50 per cent paid paternity leave and Ethiopia offers five days unpaid. Electoral regimes dominate in over half of the countries but there are also quite a few one party regimes. The military, personalist and monarchist regimes are also represented in this group.

The fourth group of 14 autocracies come from the Middle East and North Africa and it is the last family leave model type. Of all the autocracies, these countries have the fewest weeks of maternity leave, although most weeks are paid with full wage replacement (the exception being Bahrain with 100 per cent for just 45 days, Iran with 66.7 per cent for 12 weeks, and Libya with between 50 and 100 per cent depending on self-employment). With an average of 11.5 weeks, the lengths range from a low of six weeks in the United Arab Emirates to a high of 17 weeks in Syria and Saudi Arabia, and in some cases, Iran. With four exceptions, all countries have no paternity leave (the exceptions being six unpaid days in Syria, one paid day in Saudi Arabia, three paid days in Algeria and three unpaid days in Libya). Parental leave is only available in five countries and these are all exclusively tagged for mothers (Jordan, Kuwait, Egypt, Afghanistan and Syria). These countries represent a variety of monarchy, electoral, military and personality autocratic regimes.

This qualitative clustering along the family policy provisions is strongly supported by statistical classification analyses. Hierarchical cluster analyses using Ward-Clustering with squared euclidean distance measures and z-transformed data on leave durations and replacement rates by and large reproduce the patterns of the qualitative clustering presented above. In particular, the cluster of countries with a (post-)communist legacy is vastly reproduced. It consists of Belarus, Russia, Cuba, North Korea, Tajikistan, Uzbekistan, Kazakhstan, Azerbaidjan and Vietnam, whereas China and Laos are grouped into another cluster with the Gulf monarchies and other states with short maternity and overall leaves and no paternity leave at all (Niger, Zimbabwe, China, Guinea, Haiti, Swaziland, Gambia, Angola, Laos, Afghanistan, Ethiopia, Syria, Egypt, Bahrain, Kuwait, Jordan, Qatar, United Arab Emirates, Guinea Bissau, Yemen and Sudan). The boundaries between Sub-Saharan and Middle East/North African countries are not that clear-cut in the cluster analysis as we qualitatively argue, but by and large Sub-Saharan African states also cluster statistically. A third cluster comprises Algeria, Djibouti, Rwanda, Mauritania, Togi, Cameroon, Comoros, Gabon, Republic of the Congo, Chad and Burundi. One smaller cluster comprises Iran, Libya, Equatorial Guinea, Democratic Republic of the Congo, Saudi Arabia and the Central African Republic. The four clusters for multiple ANOVA procedures reveal, as predicted by clustering, overtly significant variances of means.

EXPLAINING VARIATION

The four clusters mentioned above for multiple ANOVA procedures affirm overtly significant variances of means. We find autocratic regime type and region to be potential explanations for family leave variation in autocracies (Table 22.3), although there are some interesting relationships between family leave and demographics. Results for demographics show that difference in labour force participation between men and women is more closely related to family leave policies than other demographic characteristics: The higher the gender gap, the shorter the duration of maternity leave and paternity leave. Patterns in leave duration, generosity and availability are not closely related to employment rates. Whereas male and female employment covary significantly and negatively,

Table 22.3 Descriptives

Variable	N	Min.	Max.	Mean	Std. Dev.
Female labour force participation rate	50	13.1%	88.4%	54.7%	0.225991
Male labour force participation rate	50	60.3%	94.5%	80.5%	0.074272
Gender difference in labour force participation	50	−4.3%	65.4%	25.9%	0.210336
Total fertility rate (children per woman)	50	1.6	7.6	3.594	1.4703
Population growth rate	50	−0.20%	3.27%	1.78%	0.0088603
Infant mortality rate (per 1000)	50	3.4	96.0	37.132	24.7211
Duration of maternity leave (weeks)	50	6.0	26.0	13.420	3.6983
Duration of paid maternity leave (weeks)	50	2.0	26.0	12.900	4.3530
Average maternity leave wage replacement rate (% of previous earnings)	49	50%	100%	96%	12.5086
Full Time Equivalent Units (weeks) maternity leave	49	2.0	26	12.4	4.65
Duration of paternity leave (in national legislation, weeks)	49	0.000	2.143	.41983	0.632461
Average paternity leave wage replacement rate (% of previous earnings)	49	0.0	100.0	27.551	44.5594
Full Time Equivalent Units (weeks) paternity leave	49	0.0	1.43	0.29	0.54
Duration of parental leave (in national legislation)	48	0.0	156.0	27.708	53.2521
Duration of paid parental leave (weeks)	48	0.0	156.0	14.854	40.8688
Average parental leave wage replacement rate (in %)	48	0%	60%	4%	12.9746
Full Time Equivalent Units (weeks) parental leave	48	0.0	62.4	3.74	11.17

Source: Own calculations based on data from ILO (2014, 2016), The Economist (2016) and Kailitz (2013).

female employment is neither correlated with leave availability nor replacement rates. Instead, our calculations strongly indicate that longer family leave provision and higher generosity are related to lower fertility rates, population growth and infant motality.

Whereas the relationship between demographic and family leave variables are mostly insignificant, the differences in autocratic regime types can better account for variation. There is at least some significant differences between autocratic regime types. For example, monarchies differ significantly from other regime types, except from personalist regimes, by having the least generous regulations in maternity leave with shorter maternity leaves and shorter periods of pay, and the least FTE units (6.9). Monarchies also have significantly shorter paternity leaves than electoral autocracies. This reinforces the hypothesis that monarchies would rely on family policies that reinforce traditional family roles to legitimize themselves. Also, personalist regimes offer significantly less maternity wage replacement benefits than other regimes, thereby illustrating the short-term perspective of these regimes. As expected, communist ideocracies, have significantly higher wage replacement rates than all other subtypes, thereby reinforcing their legitimacy in line

Table 22.4 Analysis of variance – between groups combined for region and regime type*

Independent variable	Region			Regime type		
Dependent variable	Eta²	F	Sig.	Eta²	F	Sig.
Duration of maternity leave	0.488	8.372	0.000	0.366	5.085	0.001
Duration of paid maternity leave	0.45	7.207	0.000	0.389	5.594	0.000
Maternity leave replacement rates	0.055	0.501	0.774	0.135	1.34	0.266
Full Time Equivalent Units maternity leave	0.417	7.872	0.000	0.357	6.095	0.001
Duration of paternity leave	0.17	1.765	0.141	0.205	2.218	0.07
Paternity leave replacement rates	0.245	2.796	0.028	0.183	1.931	0.109
Full Time Equivalent Units paternity leave	0.290	4.497	0.004	0.125	1.565	0.200
Duration of parental leave	0.873	57.623	0.000	0.055	0.484	0.786
Duration of paid parental leave	0.714	21.018	0.000	0.041	0.358	0.874
Parental leave replacement rates	0.662	16.484	0.000	0.198	2.073	0.088
Full Time Equivalent Units parental leave	0.473	9.653	0.000	0.074	0.858	0.497

Note: * The Student-Newman-Keuls-Procedure has been calculated. Subsamples were only partly reproduced significantly, as significance in post hoc tests depends on the number of cases in subsample cells. Because these are below 5, effects might be distorted.

Source: Own calculations based on data from ILO (2014, 2016), The Economist (2016) and Kailitz (2013).

with equality-based provisions and communist ideology. Although autocracy types have different levels of paternity leave, these regimes do not significantly differ in benefits or duration. There are also no significant differences among the regimes in overall wage replacement and duration of paid parental leave.

Table 22.4 shows the main explanatory effects of regime type and region in comparison for all family leave provisions under research: there is a significance between autocratic clusters and their geographical location (Cramer's V: 0.572; p: 0.000). This suggests that cultural and traditional legacies are more important in shaping family policies than political regime types. If geographical location can be used as a proxy variable for culture and tradition, this would mean that, for example, Middle Eastern and North African traditional and paternalistic models of family and gender generate specific family policy, and women's roles, that are vastly reduced to home and child care, have a strong legacy in Middle Eastern family leave policies, granting the least generous maternity (9.6 FTE units on average) and parental (0 FTE units) leave provisions. The same seems to hold true to some extent for Sub-Saharan Africa (11 FTE units for maternity and 0 for parental leave) and Latin America/Carribean (12 and 11): these regions are slightly more generous, but also have traditional gender role models. One might expect similar results for Central and South East Asia, but countries in these regions are far more generous, at least, in terms of maternity and parental leave FTE units. This, we argue, can partly be explained by the influence of communist ideologies and their legacy in these autocratic regimes, if this ideology is also accounted for in Eastern Bloc countries' autocratic regime types (in addition to their designation as electoral or one party systems). In general, as regime type and regions are not statistically independent, with high significance of Cramer's V (0.60) and Contingency-Coefficient (0.768), there might be overlapping effects. For example, seven out of 14 regimes in the Middle East and North African region are monarchies, 15 out of 23 regimes in Sub-Saharan Africa are electoral autocracies, and 11 out of 11 regimes in Central Asia/Eastern Europe and South East Asia have a communist legacy. Further research is necessary in order to separate effects, even though the overall data problem remains. The overlapping communist and electoral or one party regime types for Eastern Bloc autocracies expose some difficulty in the autocratic regime typologies themselves. Autocratic regime types, nonetheless, have at least some explanatory power for the overall and paid duration of maternity leave and the duration of paternity leave. In all, regional belonging, however, can contribute most to explaining overall and paid duration of maternity leave, paternity leave wage replacement, parental leave duration and wage replacement.

CONCLUSION

There are some clear characteristics that emerge from a cross-comparison of autocracies, and distinct groups of autocracies can be discerned in regards to family leave policy. However, autocracies' family policies and demographics are not necessarily solely grouped by political structures (e.g., monarchies, one party systems, personalist autocracies and so on). Overall, we see a gamut of clustering from the most generous paid maternity and parental leaves for mothers and fathers in Central Asia/Eastern Europe and Cuba to minimal maternity in the Middle East/North Africa, with little or no paternity leave, and if parental leave is offered, then only for mothers. The South and East Asian autocracies cluster contiguous to Central Asian and Eastern Europe autocracies, and Sub-Saharan autocracies cluster closer to the Middle East/North Africa. These autocratic groupings are surprising as a whole because they are not necessarily linked to special patterns of legitimation we assumed to find in different types of autocratic regimes, although we found some overlaps. Instead, the autocratic groupings seem to be more related to world regions and culture. Former or current communist-influenced autocracies are highly generous with family leaves, but similarly influenced East and South Asian autocracies have distinctively less generous policy and more gender-specific policy, especially in terms of paternity and parental leave. Demographically, East and South Asian autocracies have, on average, a narrower gap in labour force participation among men and women than their Eastern Bloc neighbours. Even when autocracies have high levels of female labour force participation and high fertility rates, this does not necessarily translate into more generous leave policy, as we also see in Sub-Saharan African autocracies.

These family leave groupings seem to point to other explanations than just autocratic regimes or demographics: gender ideology and economics could be plausible alternative explanations. Family policy itself might be playing a legitimizing role, and we surmise that cultural (and regional) values and legitimacy are related. Repression and repressive capacity might serve autocrats well to remain in power for some time, but this is not a long-term means to secure it, as 'the use of force is costly and may not always be effective' (Gandhi and Przeworski, 2007, p. 1281). 'Legitimacy' can be instrumented to uphold and reinforce power, so certain types of family policy instruments can be used to legitimize specific autocracies. Scarce family leave policy in the Middle East might be a reflection of traditional family values dominant in these countries while more gender neutral family leaves in the former Eastern Bloc countries uphold the post-communist ideological heritage (i.e., in supporting full formal employment for men and women). And yet, the economic systems of the different regions of autocracies might play a vital role too. For example, the importance of informal economies in Asian and Sub-Saharan autocracies gives us pause to think about the waning significance of formal labour force participation, and ensuing (ir)relevance of family leave regulations for these workers. Also, many Middle East/North African countries' economies revolve around oil resources: having one economic revenue source impacts employment structures in a variety of ways, so that, for example, much of taxation is irrelevant and this could result in weak justification (and demand) for social and family policy.

Reconsidering family policy 'functions' is also intriguing for family policy analysis. So far, common analysis views the 'purpose' of family policy in terms of shaping personal decisions around family forms, directing behaviour and addressing problems of families, or mitigating family risk. More recent analysis views 'function' also in relation to work-life balance and the promotion of gender equality. And yet, with an examination of family policy from the perspective of autocracies, new issues emerge: family policy's role in the legitimization of a state, its strong relationship to cultural heritage, and confirmation of societal ideals and ideology. An examination of autocracies also highlights how the provision of family policy can be quite diverse for men and women across the globe. With autocratic countries, family policy analysis is confronted with what it means to have 'explicit' versus 'implicit' family policy. Indeed, when it comes to the 'function' of family policy, we are left to consider how structures and institutions play a role in organizing society, the ways in which family policy supports individual freedom, and how it dampens unrest, reduces government resistance and upholds elite control. Furthermore, this examination of autocracies shows the urgency of illuminating and understanding the actual use and take-up of family policy. Finally, this chapter generates further material for gender analysis and family policy development. More studies are clearly needed on the development of family policy as well as the impact of family policy on individuals and families. The striking differences but also patterns in family leave policy (and demographics) in autocracies can provide policy analysts with a more well-rounded investigation of family policy and policy development.

NOTE

* We would like to thank Marie Duboc for valuable comments and to Viktoria Kornhaas and Helen Schiff for research support.

REFERENCES

Baylouny, A.M. (2010), *Privatizing Welfare in the Middle East: Kin Mutual Aid Associations in Jordan and Lebanon*, Bloomington and Indianapolis, IN: Indiana University Press.
Charrad, M.M. (2011), 'Gender in the Middle East: Islam, states, agency', *Annual Review of Sociology*, **37**, 417–37.

Central Intelligence Agency (2016), *The World Factbook. Population Growth Rates in 2015*, accessed 15 December 2016 at https://www.cia.gov/library/publications/the-world-factbook/rankorder/2002rank.html.
Dugarova, E. (2016), 'The family in a new social contract. The case of Russia, Kazakhstan and Mongolia', Research paper for the United Nations Research Institute for Social Development, accessed 15 December 2016 at http://www.unrisd.org/unrisd/website/document.nsf/(httpPublications)/CEC5E5B16 F77613AC1257F61004ED67E?OpenDocument.
Economist, The (2016), 'Democracy Index 2015. Democracy at a standstill. A report from the Economist Intelligence Unit', accessed 15 December 2016 at http://country.eiu.com/article.aspx?articleid=1080324092.
Friedrich, C.J. and Z.K. Brzezinski (1965), *Totalitarian Dictatorship and Autocracy*, Cambridge, MA: Harvard University Press.
Gandhi, J. and A. Przeworski (2007), 'Authoritarian institutions and the survival of autocrats', *Comparative Political Studies*, **40** (11), 1279–301.
Geddes, B. (1999), 'What do we know about democratization after twenty years?', *Annual Review of Political Science*, **2**, 115–44.
Geddes, B. (2007), *Paradigms and Sand Castles: Theory Building and Research Design in Comparative Politics*, Ann Arbor, MI: University of Michigan Press.
Gornick, J.C. and M.K. Meyers (2003), 'Welfare regimes in relation to paid work and care', *Advance in Life Course Research*, **8**, 45–7.
Habtom, G.K. and P. Ruys (2007), 'Traditional risk-sharing arrangements and informal social insurance in Eritrea', *Health Policy*, **80**, 218–35.
Hadenius, A. and J. Teorell (2007), 'Pathways from authoritarianism', *Journal of Democracy*, **18** (1), 143–56.
ILO (2014), 'Maternity and paternity at work. Law and practice across the world', pdf file accessed 15 December 2016 at the website of the International Labour Organization, http://www.ilo.org/wcmsp5/groups/public/@dgreports/@dcomm/@publ/.../wcms_242615.pdf.
ILO (2016), 'Labour force participation rate by sex and age (%)', accessed 4 July 2018 at http:// http://www.ilo.org/ilostat/.
Kailitz, S. (2013), 'Classifying political regimes revisited: legitimation and durability', *Democratization*, **20** (1), 39–60.
Moghadam, V.M. (2006), 'Gender and social policy: family law and women's economic citizenship in the Middle East', in M. Karshenas and V.M. Moghadam (eds), *Social Policy in the Middle East*, Houndmills, Basingstoke: Palgrave Macmillan, pp. 221–53.
Motiejunaite, A. and Z. Kravchenko (2008), 'Family policy, employment and gender-role attitudes: a comparative analysis of Russia and Sweden', *Journal of European Social Policy*, **18** (1), 38–49.
Pascal, G. and N. Manning (2000), 'Gender and social policy: comparing welfare states in Central and Eastern Europe and the former Soviet Union', *Journal of European Social Policy*, **10** (3), 240–66.
Pfau-Effinger, B. (2012), 'Women's employment in the institutional and cultural context', *International Journal of Sociology and Social Policy*, **32** (9/10), 530–43.
Pickel, S. (2013), 'Demokratie, Anokratie, Autokratie und die Verwirklichung der Rechte von Frauen. Wechselbeziehungen zwischen Gender Empowerment und Regimepersistenz', in S. Kailitz and P. Köllner (eds), *Autokratien im Vergleich, PVS-Sonderheft 47*, Baden-Baden: Nomos, pp. 438–76.
Ray, R., J.C. Gornick, and J. Schmitt (2010), 'Who cares? Assessing generosity and gender equality in parental leave policy designs in 21 countries', *Journal of European Social Policy*, **10** (3), 196–216.
Robila, M. (2012), 'Family policies in Eastern Europe: a focus on parental leave', *Journal of Child Family Studies*, **21**, 32–41.
Woods, D.R. and R. Frankenberger (2016), 'Examining the autocracy-gender-family nexus', *femina politca*, **25** (1), 112–20.
World Bank (2016), 'Total fertility rates and infant mortality rates in 2014', accessed 15 December 2016 at http://data.worldbank.org/indicator/.
World Policy Analysis Center (2016), Adult Labor Database, McGill University, accessed 15 December 2016 at http://www.worldpolicycenter.org.

PART V

OUTCOMES OF FAMILY POLICIES

23. Children, poverty and public policy: a cross-national perspective
Janet C. Gornick and Emily Nell

INTRODUCTION

Child poverty raises near universal concern. While poverty is viewed as problematic throughout the life cycle – it afflicts children, working-age adults and the elderly – poverty among children is especially worrisome. Child poverty compels attention for several reasons: it is widely believed that children deserve protection from hardship; most children have little or no input into their economic circumstances; deprivation during childhood can have lifelong consequences; and some of the effects of child poverty have spillover effects, influencing schools and neighborhoods. Many argue that child poverty in rich countries is especially unacceptable, because it is rooted less in scarce national resources and more in the public and private institutions that distribute resources. Most countries tackle child poverty using a package of policy approaches; family policy is widely understood to be a powerful component. (For a detailed assessments of child benefit schemes, see Chapter 7 by Bradshaw in this volume.)

Over the last three decades, a large literature on child poverty has developed, much of it based on cross-national microdata produced by LIS (formerly, the Luxembourg Income Study), a data archive based in Luxembourg. Recently, other cross-national data have been used to study children's poverty. A growing body of research uses data from the European Union Statistics on Income and Living Conditions (EU-SILC) and/or from the Organisation for Economic Co-operation and Development's (OECD) Income Distribution Database.

Much of this literature has assessed individual- and household-level factors that shape children's chances of being poor *within* countries – including, especially, the structure of their families, and their parents' employment status and/or earnings. In addition, many studies have established that child poverty varies widely *across* countries, and that a substantial share of that cross-national variation is driven by diversity in national institutions, including both institutions that 'predistribute'[1] (e.g., labor market structures) as well as those that redistribute (e.g., tax and transfer policies). In general, the consensus in this literature is that the factors that increase the risk of poverty within countries are not the same as those that increase poverty rates across countries.[2]

In this chapter, using data from LIS, we take a fresh empirical look at cross-national variation in child poverty rates and patterns. We update prior findings, including our own, to 2010,[3] and we extend earlier analyses.

Although LIS has recently added datasets from several middle-income countries, the vast majority of the existing comparative literature on child poverty, based on the LIS data, has included only high-income country cases. One key extension is our inclusion – in the first part of our analysis – of several middle-income countries,[4] specifically a set of Latin American countries. Enlarging the set of countries to include these middle-income cases allows us to ask if patterns recognized earlier – such as the high poverty rates, in comparative perspective, among Anglophone and Southern European countries – are still evident when we consider a more diverse set of countries.

A second extension is that, within our policy analyses, we consider the poverty-reducing effect of total taxes and transfers (as is standard in the LIS literature) as well as the role of a subset of transfers targeted on families.

The chapter is organized as follows. In the subsequent section, we briefly review the literature on child poverty. In the following section, we describe the LIS microdata – our main data source – and summarize our empirical approach. In the subsequent section, we present our first results. Here, we consider cross-national variation in poverty rates based on disposable household income – a measure of post-tax-post-transfer income – among all persons, all children and young children. We assess poverty patterns using both a relative and an absolute poverty standard in order to account for variation in income levels both within and across countries. In this section, we include 24 high- and middle-income countries. We turn our attention in the following section to poverty outcomes based on (1) market income (income 'prior to' taxes and transfers); (2) income from the market *plus* 'family transfers'; and (3) total household income. This disaggregation gives us a window on the extent to which – and where – states use public policies to reduce market-generated poverty among children. In this section, we limit our analyses to 16 high-income countries. We excluded eight countries (in Southern Europe and Latin America) because it was not possible, in general, to reliably isolate the family transfers that are central to our study. To flesh out our analyses of poverty reduction based on microdata, we shift vantage points and take a brief look at the association between family benefits (both cash and tax breaks, using macro-data from the OECD) and child poverty reduction (due to redistribution, based on the LIS microdata). After assessing poverty and poverty reduction among all children, we consider two crucial risk factors that, within countries, shape children's likelihood of being poor. We consider associations among poverty, poverty reduction and family structure, and among poverty, poverty reduction and parents' engagement in paid work. In the final section, we present our conclusions.

A SYNTHESIS OF PAST RESEARCH

The issue of child poverty has attracted considerable attention among scholars using the LIS microdata. Over the last 30 years, nearly 100 LIS Working Papers have included child poverty outcomes; in many of these, child poverty is the central concern of the paper.[5] These studies are diverse with respect to conceptual approaches, poverty measures, countries included, years covered and substantive focus. Several focus on cross-national variation in within-country poverty determinants; many aim to identify and decompose the determinants of cross-national variation. (For a detailed review of this child poverty literature, see Gornick and Jäntti, 2012.)

Two especially comprehensive studies of child poverty, both using the LIS data, influenced the analyses reported in this chapter: a 2003 book (on poverty levels) by Rainwater and Smeeding and a 2008 journal article (on poverty trends) by Chen and Corak. In both of these studies, the core questions concern explanations for cross-country variation in child poverty outcomes.

Rainwater and Smeeding consolidated and expanded much of their earlier research on child poverty in their 2003 book *Poor Kids in a Rich Country: America's Children in Comparative Perspective*. The book is organized around several lines of inquiry, among them: cross-national variation in child poverty rates; the effects of population characteristics on poverty; and the role of different forms of income in alleviating child poverty in both one- and two-parent families. Rainwater and Smeeding assessed child poverty variation across 15 rich countries. A primary focus in their work is the role that household demography plays in explaining variability in child poverty rates, where demography includes household composition by gender, age and size, and the earning status of the head, spouse and other household adults. With their eye on explaining exceptionally high US child poverty rates, they concluded that demography is by no means destiny: the demographic composition of the United States contributes to its higher child poverty with respect to only half of their study countries and, in most of those cases, its contribution is modest.

Chen and Corak, in a 2008 *Demography* article, 'Child poverty and changes in child poverty', assessed trends during the 1990s in 12 high-income countries. They draw three lessons. First, demographic shifts played a relatively minor role in explaining child poverty trends throughout the 1990s (partly because these factors evolve slowly). Second, changes in employment and earnings mattered much more. Third, income transfer policy reforms aimed at raising labor supply have inconsistent effects on families' post-tax-and-transfer income. Social policy reforms interact in complex ways with other factors, such as the overall level of child poverty, the extent and functioning of the service and other sectors, and the overall hospitality of the labor market to low-skilled and other disadvantaged workers. Chen and Corak sum up with a cautionary note to policy-makers: 'there is no single road to lower child poverty rates. The conduct of social policy needs to be thought through in conjunction with the nature of labor markets' (Chen and Corak, 2008, p. 552). Thus, like Rainwater and Smeeding (2003), Chen and Corak find that, in explaining cross-national variation in child poverty, demographic variation matters modestly, while national labor market patterns and social policy factors both matter a great deal – and they matter via complex and interacting mechanisms.

Recent lines of work on child poverty are extending research based on income to integrate other types of outcomes, primarily indicators of material deprivation (which are, so far, not available in the LIS microdata). While the term 'material deprivation' varies across settings, overall it refers to households' or persons' inability to afford goods and activities that are typical in their society; this form of deprivation is independent of households'/persons' preferences with respect to these out-of-reach items. These 'beyond income' frameworks are consistent with current emphases within the European Union (the EU-SILC data include deprivation variables), the OECD and the United Nations, where the recently released Sustainable Development Goals stress multidimensional approaches to assessing wellbeing levels and trends. Bradshaw (2013) argues that deprivation measures are a more direct approach to measuring child poverty, compared with income-only studies. He recognizes, however, that the data and methodological challenges in this type of work are extensive and serious. Nevertheless, researchers in the field of child poverty can and should look forward to new and growing lines of work that stress multidimensional extensions to the more conventional income approach that we take in this chapter.

BRIEF REMARKS ABOUT THE EMPIRICAL WORK

Data

All of our results are based on harmonized *microdata* (that is, data available at the household and person level) contained in the LIS Database.[6] We start with 24 country datasets – all from LIS's Wave 8, which is centered on the year 2010. Our study countries include 19 high-income countries – five Anglophone countries (Australia, Canada, Ireland, United Kingdom, United States), four Continental European countries (France, Germany, Luxembourg, the Netherlands), three Eastern European countries (Estonia, Poland, Slovak Republic), four Nordic European countries (Denmark, Finland, Iceland, Norway), and three Southern European countries (Greece, Italy, Spain) – and five middle-income countries, all in Latin America (Brazil, Colombia, Panama, Peru, Uruguay).[7] (As noted, in the results section on poverty and redistribution in 16 high-income countries, we include only the Anglophone, Continental, Eastern European and Nordic countries.)

Variables and Empirical Approach

In our first analysis (Table 23.1, Figure 23.1), we calculate poverty rates based on *disposable household income* (DHI) – otherwise known as post-tax-post-transfer income. To enable us to compare poverty rates using both within- and across-country thresholds – an illuminating exercise when comparing countries with diverse standards of living – we use two different poverty lines. The first line, the 'relative' line, is drawn at 50 percent of median DHI. The 50 percent-of-median line is country-specific, meaning that 'relative' poverty refers to income relative to others in the same country. The second line, the 'absolute' line, is set at the level of the *official* US poverty line, which is then converted to international dollars, adjusted for purchasing power parities (PPPs). In cross-national research using absolute poverty lines, thresholds can be set at many different levels. In studies comparing absolute poverty across affluent countries, the US line (based on the price of food) is widely used.

To assess the role of state interventions in poverty reduction (Tables 23.2–4), we use multiple income definitions. First, we calculate poverty based on market income. We define *market income* (MI) as pre-tax-pre-transfer income – which includes income from labor, from selected sources of capital and from private transfers.

Second, to estimate the effects of family-related policies, we use a variable – 'family/children transfers' ('IATFAM', created by LIS and available in the LIS Database) – which includes (as available): (1) short-term work-related cash transfers from maternity, paternity or parental leave insurance schemes; (2) family-related cash transfers from public programs which are universal in structure; and (3) family-related cash transfers that are targeted on individuals or households in need.

Third, to estimate the effects of all taxes and transfers, we use DHI, again, which adjusts market income by subtracting direct taxes paid out (i.e., income taxes and social contributions) and by adding the value of all public transfers received. In Tables 23.2–4, we define *poverty reduction* using a simple accounting framework: it is the MI-based poverty rate minus the poverty rate after various state interventions are taken into account.

312   *Handbook of family policy*

Throughout our empirical work, we report person-level poverty rates, meaning the likelihood that persons (in the relevant group) live in a poor household. Income is always adjusted for family size, using the common 'square root' equivalence scale.

Throughout this chapter, we group countries into clusters, drawing on the well-known social science framework that classifies countries. These groupings are associated with both geography and overarching social policy designs. We make use of these clusters in our presentations – however imperfect they are – because they provide an organizing framework for assessing cross-national variation. They help us to identify empirical patterns across countries, and they bring into relief the importance of policy configurations for poverty reduction.

RESULTS: DISPOSABLE INCOME POVERTY IN 24 HIGH- AND MIDDLE-INCOME COUNTRIES

We begin with a general question: To what extent, and how, do overall poverty rates – that is, poverty rates among all persons – vary across these 24 countries? We ask that question, first, using the common approach in comparative research – that is, defining poverty in a relative framework, specifically with the poverty line set at 50 percent of each country's median. And, here, poverty rates are based on what households have 'at the end of the day', that is, household income after state-provided taxes and transfers have been taken into account.

Our results indicate that poverty varies dramatically across these 24 study countries – ranging from over 25 percent in Peru down to 6 percent in Iceland and Denmark (Table 23.1). We also see that patterns vary across clusters. The highest poverty rates are seen in the Latin American countries (cluster average, 21 percent), followed by the Southern European (14 percent) and Anglophone (13 percent) clusters. Lower poverty rates are seen, on average, in the Eastern European (9 percent), Continental European (8 percent) and Nordic European (7 percent) countries (Table 23.1, column A). Clearly, national contexts matter.

The results in Table 23.1 also indicate that poverty rates among children (those under age 18) and among young children (under age 6) follow similar patterns overall (columns B and C). Although poverty rates among children tend to be higher than among all persons, and (in more cases than not) even higher yet among the youngest children, in all three groups the country clusters line up in the same order, that is, with the highest poverty rates reported in the Latin American countries and the lowest in the Nordic countries. Cross-cluster poverty patterns are robust with respect to age.

Poverty Lines Matter: Poor Compared to Whom?

What about poverty with respect to a fixed real income poverty line, often called absolute poverty? Does the cross-national portrait of child poverty change when we consider not just poverty relative to one's own country, but poverty with respect to a common standard-of-living threshold that is applied to all 24 countries?

To explore this, we use US children as an illustrative case – in two ways. First, we use the official US poverty line to establish a threshold to be used across all 24 countries, and,

Table 23.1 Poverty rates: percentage of persons living in poor households (based on disposable household income) by age (relative poverty and absolute poverty, 2010)

	A	B	C	D	E	F
	Relative Poverty			Absolute Poverty (set at US line)		
	All Persons	All Children	Young Children	All Persons	All Children	Young Children
Anglophone						
Australia	14.1	14.4	15.5	6.0	7.1	7.5
Canada	12.6	14.4	16.4	6.6	6.9	8.0
Ireland	9.4	10.1	9.5	8.5	9.3	8.5
United Kingdom	10.1	9.2	10.9	9.0	8.1	9.5
United States	17.3	21.1	24.2	9.9	12.2	14.4
Average	*12.7*	*13.8*	*15.3*	*8.0*	*8.7*	*9.6*
Continental European						
France	9.2	11.5	12.4	7.4	8.9	8.92
Germany	9.4	9.9	11.2	6.4	6.9	9.0
Luxembourg	6.1	9.2	10.8	1.5	1.7	2.1
Netherlands	5.2	6.3	7.3	3.2	3.1	3.2
Average	*7.5*	*9.2*	*10.4*	*4.6*	*5.2*	*5.8*
Eastern European						
Estonia	11.9	13.0	9.8	43.0	37.5	32.1
Poland	9.6	12.0	11.0	41.0	47.3	44.1
Slovak Republic	8.0	12.7	13.2	23.2	30.2	34.6
Average	*9.0*	*12.1*	*10.7*	*31.1*	*34.4*	*32.9*
Nordic European						
Denmark	6.3	4.5	5.6	3.4	2.3	2.5
Finland	7.2	3.7	4.0	4.0	1.9	2.3
Iceland	6.1	7.3	10.5	3.3	3.4	4.9
Norway	7.6	5.1	6.2	3.8	1.7	1.9
Average	*6.8*	*5.2*	*6.6*	*3.6*	*2.3*	*2.9*
Southern European						
Greece	13.8	17.5	15.4	23.1	27.6	26.6
Italy	12.7	19.4	18.0	18.1	25.6	26.4
Spain	15.6	20.7	17.1	21.3	27.4	24.1
Average	*14.0*	*19.2*	*16.8*	*20.8*	*26.8*	*25.7*
Latin America						
Brazil (2011)	19.7	30.3	31.5	76.8	85.9	85.9
Colombia	20.0	25.0	25.6	87.7	92.5	91.9
Panama	23.2	31.3	32.4	71.7	81.7	81.4
Peru	25.5	30.7	30.7	81.7	87.2	86.8
Uruguay	15.2	24.0	25.6	65.9	76.7	76.5
Average	*20.7*	*28.3*	*29.2*	*76.8*	*84.8*	*84.5*

314 *Handbook of family policy*

second, we consider (below) how child poverty in the United States, specifically, stacks up in the two different comparative frameworks.

When we use the relative poverty framework, the child poverty rate in the United States, in this analysis, is 21 percent, the sixth highest among these 24 countries; child poverty is higher only in the five Latin American countries. When we shift to the absolute poverty framework, the story changes. The US rate falls to 12 percent, ranked 11th among these 24 countries; now child poverty is higher in all of the Eastern and Southern European countries as well as in the Latin American countries. These results should not surprise us, given that all of these countries are less affluent (GDP/capita is lower) than the United States. But what is surprising is that US absolute poverty remains high among a core group of rich comparator countries. US poverty, using the US line, exceeds that reported in all of the other Anglophone countries, as well as in all of the Continental and Nordic cases – and most of these comparator countries are less affluent than the United States. In cross-national terms, US child poverty stands out – and that is true for both relative poverty and absolute poverty.

This relative-versus-absolute poverty story is summarized in Figure 23.1 – with an emphasis on comparisons across these country clusters.[8] Two conclusions are apparent. First, poverty definitions matter. Comparative child poverty results differ sharply between the two analytic frameworks. These results highlight the importance of considering absolute poverty comparisons when studying countries with widely divergent standards of living.

Second, some clear patterns emerge: Latin American children are clearly the most likely to be poor, both relatively and absolutely. Nordic children (joined by children in the

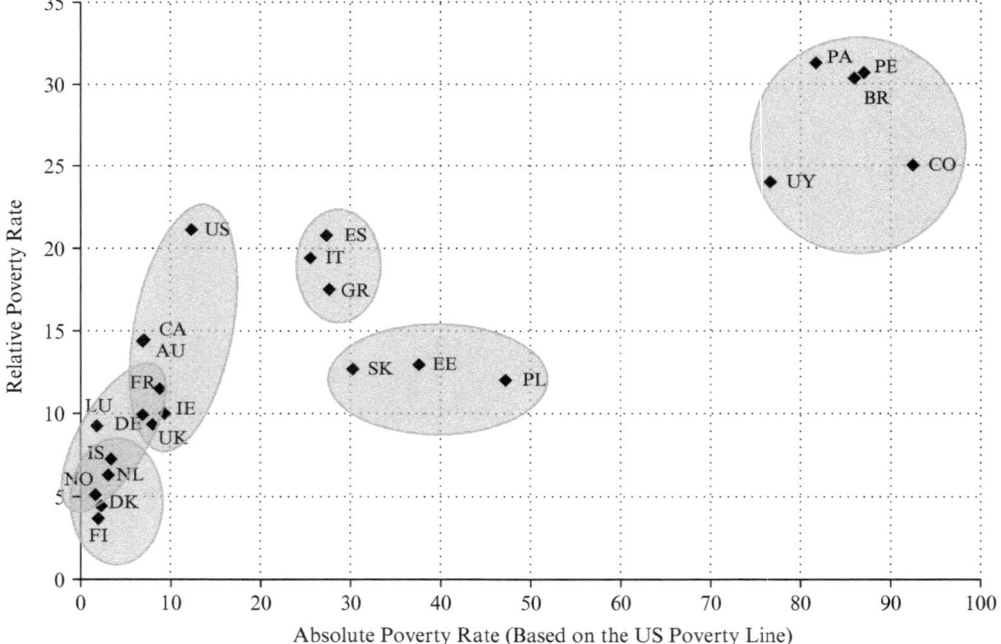

Figure 23.1   Relative and absolute child poverty rates, 2010

Netherlands) are the least likely to be poor, again, in both frameworks. Child poverty rates in the other clusters fall in between. Children in the Anglophone countries, on the whole, are about as likely to be relatively poor as are children in Southern and Eastern Europe, although they are notably less likely to live in absolute poverty.

RESULTS: POVERTY AND REDISTRIBUTION IN 16 HIGH-INCOME COUNTRIES

What role does the state play in reducing the risk of child poverty? In Table 23.2, we report the results of an analysis using a simple accounting framework to shed light on redistribution. We report poverty rates (at 50 percent of median DHI) based on market income (column A) and on market income *plus* family-related transfers (column B). We then present the extent of poverty reduction due to these family transfers (column C). Next we report child poverty rates based on disposable household income – which is income from the market and family transfers, plus other transfers, and net of taxes paid. Finally, we report the total poverty reduction – the difference between poverty rates based on market income and on disposable household income (column E).

Several results stand out.

First, family transfers – that is, transfers from maternity/paternity/parental leave schemes, and universal and means-tested transfers targeted on families – matter for children's poverty. In the Anglophone countries, they remove nearly 8 percentage points of market-generated poverty – reducing the average (country-level) poverty rate in this cluster from 32 to 24 percent. In the Continental and Eastern European countries, family transfers remove about 6 percentage points of poverty – and in the Nordic countries (where the market-driven poverty rate is the lowest), about 4 points.

Second, other transfers (e.g., unemployment, disability, survivors) – even net of taxes paid – reduce children's poverty further. Clearly, taxes and transfers (as a whole) serve to reduce children's poverty everywhere – on average, by 18 points in the Anglophone countries, and 11 to 13 points in the other clusters.

Third, the portion of total poverty reduction (from taxes and transfers) due to family transfers is substantial (column F) – but, overall, family transfers are not associated with the majority of poverty reduction. The amount of poverty reduction associated with family transfers ranges from over three-quarters in Estonia to about one-quarter in Denmark. On average, across these 16 countries, the average share of poverty reduction due to family transfers is 45 percent – or just less than half. It is crucial to note that these results must be taken as somewhat approximate. In the LIS data, it is not possible to render this variable ('IATFAM') identical in every country; in some cases, some components of these family-related income sources cannot be isolated as they are combined, in the microdata, with other income sources – sometimes wages, sometimes other transfers. Nevertheless, we conclude, the overall finding holds: *about half of all child poverty reduction, associated with tax/benefit systems, is due to these family transfers.*

One two-country comparison is especially illuminating. In the United Kingdom, the child poverty rate, based on market income, is 34 percent, slightly higher than in the United States, where it is 31 percent. But the magnitude of redistribution in the two

Table 23.2 Poverty rates: percentage of children living in poor households – market versus disposable income poverty (relative poverty at 50 percent median disposable household income, 2010)

	A	B	C	D	E	F
	Poverty Rate: Market Income	Poverty Rate: Market Income + Family Transfers	Poverty Reduction [Market – Market & Family]	Poverty Rate: Disposable Income	Poverty Reduction [Market – Disposable]	Share of Poverty Reduction due to Family Transfers
Anglophone						
Australia	28.1	19.5	8.6	14.4	13.7	0.63
Canada	26.1	20.2	5.9	14.4	11.7	0.50
Ireland	42.2	31.0	11.2	10.1	32.1	0.35
United Kingdom	33.7	24.8	8.9	9.2	24.5	0.36
United States	30.9	26.0	4.9	21.1	9.8	0.50
Average	32.2	24.3	7.9	13.8	18.4	0.47
Continental European						
France	29.8	21.5	8.3	11.5	18.3	0.45
Germany	21.4	16.2	5.2	9.9	11.5	0.45
Luxembourg	25.5	17.2	8.3	9.2	16.3	0.51
Netherlands	11.6	9.9	1.7	6.3	5.3	0.32
Average	22.1	16.2	5.9	9.2	12.8	0.43
Eastern European						
Estonia	22.2	15.2	7.0	13.0	9.2	0.76
Poland	27.1	22.7	4.4	12.0	15.1	0.29
Slovak Republic	22.3	15.5	6.8	12.7	9.6	0.71
Average	23.9	17.8	6.0	12.6	11.3	0.59
Nordic European						
Denmark	14.6	12.0	2.6	4.5	10.1	0.26
Finland	16.1	11.0	5.1	3.7	12.4	0.41
Iceland	17.1	13.6	3.5	7.3	9.8	0.36
Norway	16.6	13.4	3.3	5.1	11.5	0.28
Average	16.1	12.5	3.6	5.2	10.9	0.33
16-country average	24.1	18.1	6.0	10.3	13.8	0.45

countries is very different – with 25 percentage points of poverty 'removed' by taxes and transfers in the United Kingdom (over a third of that from family transfers), compared with 10 percentage points in the United States (half from family transfers). The result? Disposable income poverty – poverty after taxes and transfers – is much lower in the United Kingdom, 9 percent compared to 21 percent in the United States.

Family-related Transfers and Children's Poverty: The View from a Different Angle

Our findings from the LIS microdata suggest that about half of the reduction in child poverty due to taxes and transfers is associated with transfers targeted on families and/or children – where, again, we refer to paid leave schemes, universal allowance programs and social assistance targeted on families and/or children.

What is the evidence based on aggregate, country-level data on expenditures? The OECD provides data on country-level expenditures on family benefits (Social Expenditure Database, OECD, 2014). In Figure 23.2, on the horizontal axis, we present expenditures on family benefits (from the OECD) – including cash expenditures plus tax breaks towards families, and excluding spending on services. On the vertical axis, we present child poverty reduction due to taxes and transfers, as reported in the LIS microdata (Table 23.2, column E).

Figure 23.2 indicates that about half of the variation in child poverty reduction due to taxes and transfers (as indicated in the LIS microdata) is associated with variation in expenditures on family benefits. This provides confirmation of the finding drawn solely from the LIS microdata, that is, that about 45 percent of child poverty reduction, from taxes and transfers, comes in the form of family-related income supports. Clearly, family-related transfers matter for child poverty amelioration, and they matter a lot – but, overall, they are supplemented, in about equal measure, by other types of transfers.

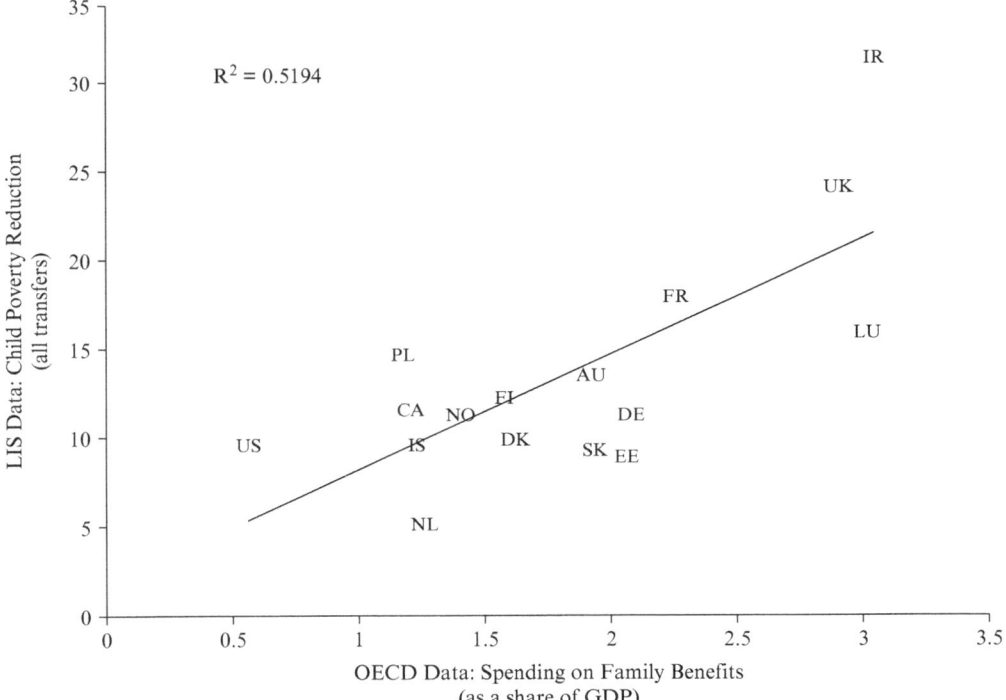

Figure 23.2 Family benefit expenditures and poverty reduction, 2010–11

Household Type Matters

The poverty literature has long stressed that children's economic wellbeing is shaped by their parents' partnership status. In particular, in many countries, the children of single mothers face an especially high risk of poverty. Is that the case in all of these countries?

We report poverty rates in Table 23.3 for children in two types of households: those in single-mother households and those in two-parent households. Several findings about child poverty and family structure are apparent.

We note first of all that child poverty rates (based on disposable household income) among children living with single mothers are strikingly high in many countries (column D). In the United States, remarkably, nearly half (46 percent) of all children in single-mother households are poor. In half of these 16 study countries, more than 30 percent of children in single-mother households are poor. In the best case scenarios – a mix of Nordic and Eastern European cases, and the United Kingdom – child poverty rates in these homes are in the range of 10–20 percent.

We also see that in all 16 countries, children living in single-mother-headed households are substantially more likely to be poor than are children in two-parent households – typically 3–4 times as likely (compare columns D and I).

In addition, we see that family-related transfers matter, and a lot – but so do other transfers. Notably, the share of poverty reduction attributed to family transfers is about a third for children with single parents (compare columns C and E) but nearly a half for children in two-parent families (compare columns H and J).

In both demographic groups, other transfers – not specifically targeted on families – are crucial for poverty amelioration for children. Across these 16 countries, taxes and transfers reduce market-income poverty among children in single-mother households by over 30 percentage points (column E), decreasing market-income poverty from a remarkably high 58 to 26 percent (on average). Among children in two-parent homes, market-income poverty is much less – about 18 percent (on average); taxes and transfers reduce that by about 10 percentage points (column J), to just over 7 percent (on average).

We also note again that national contexts matter. Among children with both single parents and two parents, both market-income and disposable income poverty tend to be highest in the Anglophone cluster and lowest in the Nordic group, although there are some exceptions.

Parents' Paid Work Matters

Finally, in most affluent countries, we assume that children in homes with no employed parents (or other adults) are at high risk of being poor, even after states intervene. Is that the case everywhere? We report poverty rates in Table 23.4 for children in two categories of households: those in which all adults in the household are employed and those in which no adults are employed.

Here we see some strong associations.

First, overall, among children living in households without employed adults, child poverty rates based on market income are – not surprisingly – sky high. On average, across these countries, market-income poverty is about 90 percent (column A). Family-related transfers reduce that, overall, by a few percentage points, but other transfers (combined

Table 23.3 Poverty rates: percentage of children living in poor households by family structure (relative poverty at 50 percent median disposable household income, 2010)

	A	B	C	D	E	F	G	H	I	J
	\multicolumn{5}{c	}{Single-mother Households}	\multicolumn{5}{c}{Two-parent Households}
	Poverty Rate: Market Income	Poverty Rate: Market Income + Family Transfers	Poverty Reduction [Market – Market & Family]	Poverty Rate: Disposable Income	Poverty Reduction [Market – Disposable]	Poverty Rate: Market Income	Poverty Rate: Market Income + Family Transfers	Poverty Reduction [Market – Market & Family]	Poverty Rate: Disposable Income	Poverty Reduction [Market – Disposable]
Anglophone										
Australia	72.3	49.9	22.4	36.0	36.2	18.2	12.5	5.8	9.6	8.7
Canada	60.1	49.8	10.4	38.2	22.0	20.6	15.2	5.3	10.5	10.1
Ireland	82.2	51.3	30.9	23.7	58.5	31.7	25.7	6.0	6.3	25.3
United Kingdom	75.5	59.1	16.4	14.1	61.4	21.9	14.9	7.1	7.6	14.3
United States	62.0	54.5	7.5	46.3	15.7	21.5	17.3	4.2	13.7	7.9
Average	*70.4*	*52.9*	*17.5*	*31.6*	*38.8*	*22.8*	*17.1*	*5.7*	*9.5*	*13.2*
Continental European										
France	60.4	51.6	8.7	29.5	30.9	24.3	16.0	8.3	8.2	16.1
Germany	66.6	58.3	8.3	39.8	26.8	12.6	7.9	4.7	4.2	8.4
Luxembourg	65.1	52.8	12.3	34.4	30.7	21.5	13.4	8.1	6.7	14.8
Netherlands	57.0	48.4	8.6	30.6	26.5	5.5	4.7	0.8	2.9	2.6
Average	*62.3*	*52.8*	*9.5*	*33.6*	*28.7*	*16.0*	*10.5*	*5.5*	*5.5*	*10.5*
Eastern European										
Estonia	44.9	37.1	7.9	30.4	14.5	17.2	10.7	6.6	9.4	7.8
Poland	51.5	46.1	5.4	18.3	33.2	23.5	19.1	4.4	11.1	12.4
Slovak Republic	37.6	34.6	2.9	16.7	20.9	19.9	13.5	6.4	11.8	8.1
Average	*44.7*	*39.3*	*5.4*	*21.8*	*22.9*	*20.2*	*14.4*	*5.8*	*10.8*	*9.4*

Table 23.3 (continued)

	A	B	C	D	E	F	G	H	I	J
	\multicolumn{5}{c}{Single-mother Households}		\multicolumn{4}{c}{Two-parent Households}	
	Poverty Rate: Market Income	Poverty Rate: Market Income + Family Transfers	Poverty Reduction [Market – Market & Family]	Poverty Rate: Disposable Income	Poverty Reduction [Market – Disposable]	Poverty Rate: Market Income	Poverty Rate: Market Income + Family Transfers	Poverty Reduction [Market – Market & Family]	Poverty Rate: Disposable Income	Poverty Reduction [Market – Disposable]
Nordic European										
Denmark	40.5	34.2	6.3	10.5	30.0	8.8	7.0	1.8	3.1	5.8
Finland	38.3	29.2	9.0	11.8	26.5	13.0	8.3	4.8	2.5	10.6
Iceland	55.0	46.8	8.1	24.3	30.6	9.1	6.4	2.7	3.4	5.7
Norway	53.5	45.2	8.3	16.8	36.7	10.5	8.0	2.5	3.1	7.5
Average	*46.8*	*38.9*	*7.9*	*15.9*	*31.0*	*10.4*	*7.4*	*3.0*	*3.0*	*7.4*
16-country average	*57.6*	*46.8*	*10.8*	*26.3*	*31.3*	*17.5*	*12.5*	*5.0*	*7.1*	*10.4*

Table 23.4 Poverty rates: percentage of children living in poor households by adults' labor market attachment (relative poverty at 50 percent median disposable household income, 2010)

	A	B	C	D	E	F	G	H	I	J
	\multicolumn{5}{c}{No Adults in the HH Employed}		\multicolumn{4}{c}{All Adults in the HH Employed}	
	Poverty Rate: Market Income	Poverty Rate: Market Income + Family Transfers	Poverty Reduction [Market – Market & Family]	Poverty Rate: Disposable Income	Poverty Reduction [Market – Disposable]	Poverty Rate: Market Income	Poverty Rate: Market Income + Family Transfers	Poverty Reduction [Market – Market & Family]	Poverty Rate: Disposable Income	Poverty Reduction [Market – Disposable]
Anglophone										
Australia	96.5	87.5	9.0	63.1	33.4	13.1	6.8	6.3	6.0	7.2
Canada	90.3	87.3	3.0	71.2	19.0	15.2	10.3	4.9	7.3	7.9
Ireland	96.7	90.4	6.3	30.1	66.6	14.0	3.2	10.8	1.8	12.2
United Kingdom	98.2	96.0	2.2	27.1	71.1	14.0	6.5	7.4	3.2	10.8
United States	85.6	82.5	3.1	70.0	15.6	16.2	11.8	4.4	9.5	6.7
Average	*93.4*	*88.7*	*4.7*	*52.3*	*41.1*	*14.5*	*7.7*	*6.8*	*5.5*	*9.0*
Continental European										
France	95.4	91.3	4.1	57.3	38.1	13.4	8.1	5.3	4.1	9.3
Germany	70.7	63.4	7.3	38.4	32.3	14.0	9.6	4.4	7.1	6.9
Luxembourg	92.7	92.5	0.3	41.4	51.3	15.1	7.7	7.3	6.3	8.7
Netherlands	90.9	90.8	0.1	39.3	51.6	4.8	3.6	1.1	3.6	1.2
Average	*87.4*	*84.5*	*3.0*	*44.1*	*43.3*	*11.8*	*7.3*	*4.5*	*5.3*	*6.5*
Eastern European										
Estonia	80.6	71.7	8.9	55.3	25.3	9.7	5.7	4.0	6.4	3.3
Poland	93.9	89.6	4.3	47.8	46.2	13.0	10.5	2.4	6.3	6.7
Slovak Republic	91.9	89.9	2.0	65.8	26.1	6.8	4.5	2.2	4.1	2.6
Average	*88.8*	*83.7*	*5.1*	*56.3*	*32.5*	*9.8*	*6.9*	*2.9*	*5.6*	*4.2*

Table 23.4 (continued)

	A	B	C	D	E	F	G	H	I	J
		No Adults in the HH Employed					All Adults in the HH Employed			
	Poverty Rate: Market Income	Poverty Rate: Market Income + Family Transfers	Poverty Reduction [Market – Market & Family]	Poverty Rate: Disposable Income	Poverty Reduction [Market – Disposable]	Poverty Rate: Market Income	Poverty Rate: Market Income + Family Transfers	Poverty Reduction [Market – Market & Family]	Poverty Rate: Disposable Income	Poverty Reduction [Market – Disposable]
Nordic European										
Denmark	91.4	82.7	8.7	22.3	69.1	3.4	2.4	1.0	2.0	1.5
Finland	87.3	80.4	6.9	21.3	66.0	4.3	2.4	1.9	1.3	3.0
Iceland	84.1	77.8	6.3	30.5	53.6	9.1	6.3	2.9	4.8	4.3
Norway	97.2	96.7	0.5	38.3	58.9	5.8	3.1	2.7	1.1	4.7
Average	*90.0*	*84.4*	*5.6*	*28.1*	*61.9*	*5.7*	*3.6*	*2.1*	*2.3*	*3.4*
16-country average	*90.2*	*85.6*	*4.6*	*44.9*	*45.3*	*10.7*	*6.4*	*4.3*	*4.7*	*6.1*

with taxes) reduce the poverty rate dramatically – cutting it in half (on average). Still, poverty rates among these no-employment families remain very high – at about 45 percent, on average (column E).

Second, the role of family transfers, while limited on average, varies sharply across these countries, accounting for a third of poverty reduction in Estonia, and about a quarter in Australia and Germany, but as little as 2–3 percent of total poverty reduction in Luxembourg, the Netherlands and Norway (compare columns C and E).

Third, living with employed adults is – not surprisingly – a strong protective factor for children everywhere. Market-income poverty, on average, is about 11 percent (column A). Family-related transfers reduce that to about 6 percent (column B) and other transfers and taxes lower it further, to about 5 percent, on average (column D).

Fourth, once again, county models seem to shape poverty outcomes. In the no-employment households, children's poverty (post-taxes-and-transfers) is highest in the Anglophone and Eastern European households and lower in the Continental European households; poverty in the Nordic countries is much lower. In the high-employment households, the pattern is similar, with markedly less child poverty in the Nordic cases.

CONCLUSION

It is clear that child poverty rates vary markedly across the countries studied here. The variation in child poverty takes many forms; it is evident vis-à-vis both market- and disposable income poverty, and within demographic and labor market status subgroups. Cross-national variation in children's risk of poverty is especially compelling when we consider absolute (or 'real-income') poverty. In relative poverty terms, child poverty rates vary from 4 percent in Finland to 31 percent in Panama, whereas in absolute terms, child poverty ranges from 2 percent in Luxembourg and Norway to over 90 percent in Colombia. Clearly, where children reside powerfully affects their likelihood of being poor.

We can also see, within the countries in our study, that children's likelihood of growing up free of income poverty is shaped by characteristics of their households. Overall, children whose parents are partnered and/or employed are substantially less at risk.

We note that states use a variety of instruments to alleviate market-driven poverty among families with children. One set of tools includes transfers targeted on families and/or children – that is, leave schemes, universal allowances and targeted family transfers. These are crucial for poverty reduction but they are not the 'whole story' anywhere. Based on both macro- and micro-level analyses, we conclude that – in general, across 16 affluent countries included in this part of our analyses – about half of poverty reduction attributed to tax/benefit systems comes in the form of these family transfers. Other, more generalized income supports are as crucial for reducing child poverty – and, in several countries, more so.

Finally, our results support a conclusion reached by many contributors to the cross-national literature on child poverty: keeping children's poverty, especially relative poverty, at comparatively low levels is potentially achievable through government interventions. But many countries fail to strenuously combat children's poverty. That failure cannot be explained by the absence of policy options; it is better explained by a lack of collective political will.

NOTES

1. Predistribution is a relatively recent term; it used to refer to institutions that shape market distributions.
2. For example, while being the child of a single mother raises the risk of poverty in nearly all countries, variation in the prevalence of single-mother households is weakly correlated with cross-national variation in child poverty.
3. This chapter draws on earlier works by the authors, including Gornick and Jäntti (2009, 2010, 2012) and Nell et al. (2016).
4. The World Bank classifies all the world's countries as 'high income', 'upper-middle income', 'lower-middle income' and 'low income'. All of the countries in this study are high income or upper-middle income. For convenience, we use the terms 'high income' and 'rich' interchangeably.
5. A large and diverse collection of comparative research papers on poverty is available on the LIS website. These papers, lodged in the LIS Working Paper series, are publicly accessible and available in full text. Over 300 papers address poverty, with about one-third including analyses of child poverty. See http://www.lisdatacenter.org/lis-wp-webapp/app/search-workingpapers.
6. See http://www.lisdatacenter.org for a detailed description of the Luxembourg Income Study (LIS) Database. The LIS Database contains approximately 300 datasets from nearly 50 countries. The data are available in repeated cross-sections (1980, 1985, 1990, 1995, 2000, 2004, 2007, 2010, 2013 and 2016); as of this writing, LIS is nearing completion of the 2013 wave and has started making available datasets from 2016.
7. In 23 countries, the data pertain to income received in 2010; in Brazil, the data correspond to income received in 2011.
8. In Figures 23.1 and 23.2, the abbreviations are as follows: Australia (AU), Brazil (BR), Canada (CA), Colombia (CO), Denmark (DK), Estonia (EE), Finland (FI), France (FR), Germany (DE), Greece (GR), Iceland (IS), Ireland (IR), Italy (IT), Luxembourg (LU), Netherlands (NL), Norway (NO), Panama (PA), Peru (PE), Poland (PL), Slovak Republic (SK), Spain (ES), United Kingdom (UK), United States (US), Uruguay (UY).

REFERENCES

Bradshaw, J. (2013), 'Child poverty and child well-being in comparative perspective', in P. Kennett (ed.), *A Handbook of Comparative Social Policy*, 2nd edn, Cheltenham, UK and Northampton, MA, USA: Edward Elgar Publishing, pp. 303–28.

Chen, W.-H. and M. Corak (2008), 'Child poverty and changes in child poverty', *Demography*, **45** (3), 537–53.

Gornick, J.C. and M. Jäntti (2009), 'Child poverty in upper-income countries: lessons from the Luxembourg Income Study', in S.B. Kamerman, S. Phipps, and A. Ben-Arieh (eds), *From Child Welfare to Child Wellbeing: An International Perspective on Knowledge in the Service of Making Policy*, New York: Springer, pp. 339–68.

Gornick, J.C. and M. Jäntti (2010), 'Women, poverty, and social policy regimes: a cross-national analysis', in P. Saunders and R. Sainsbury (eds), *Social Security, Poverty and Social Exclusion in Rich and Poorer Countries*, Antwerp: Intersentia, pp. 63–95.

Gornick, J.C. and M. Jäntti (2012), 'Child poverty in cross-national perspective: lessons from the Luxembourg Income Study', *Children and Youth Services Review*, **34**, 558–68.

Nell, E., M. Evans, and J.C. Gornick (2016), 'Child poverty in middle-income countries', LIS Working Paper No. 666, Luxembourg.

OECD (Organisation for Economic Co-operation and Development) (2014), Social Expenditure Database, Paris.

Rainwater, L. and T. Smeeding (2003), *Poor Kids in a Rich Country: America's Children in Comparative Perspective*, New York: Russell Sage Foundation.

24. Family policies and child well-being
Daniel Engster and Helena Olofsdotter Stensöta

INTRODUCTION

In recent decades, researchers have shown increasing interest in studying the relationship between welfare state policies and child well-being. This new body of research has grown out of the comparative political economy literature on welfare systems and patterns of inequality. Starting from a concern with socio-economic inequality (Esping-Andersen, 1990; Scruggs and Allan, 2006), researchers first investigated how different welfare systems relate to gender inequality (Lewis, 1992; Sainsbury, 1996) and inequality between generations (Lynch, 2006). More recently, researchers have turned their attention to the relationship between welfare policies and child well-being (Bäckman and Ferrarini, 2010; Engster and Stensöta, 2011; Martorano et al., 2014). Motivated in part by the United Nations adoption of the Convention of the Rights of the Child in 1990, which helped to put the well-being of children on the global agenda, researchers have begun to explore if and how welfare policies can support the well-being of children, usually defined as human beings under the age of 18 or 19 years old.

One fundamental question within this literature is how child well-being should be understood and measured. Ambitious data collection efforts by organizations such as the Organisation for Economic Co-operation and Development (OECD), United Nations International Children's Emergency Fund (UNICEF), World Health Organization (WHO) and others have substantially shaped this debate. Many of these data-collecting efforts have not only generated better data about children's lives but also broadened the definition of child well-being to include more dimensions. Growing numbers of scholars, for example, are incorporating children's subjective perspectives into their measures of children's overall well-being (Bradshaw and Richardson, 2009; OECD, 2009; UNICEF, 2007, 2013). The new attention to children's subjective perspectives corresponds with a general shift in research on children from a singular focus on children's 'well-becoming' toward a broader perspective that also encompasses children's present 'well-being' including a view of children as acting and reflective subjects (Ben-Arieh, 2005; Bradshaw et al., 2013; Kamerman et al., 2010). While this broader approach to children's well-being is not without its critics, most scholars now agree that child well-being is a multidimensional phenomenon. As Ben-Arieh and Frønes (2007, p. 249) express it, 'any attempts to grasp well-being in its entirety must use indicators on a variety of aspects of well-being'.

The purpose of this chapter is to review the literature on the relationship between welfare policies, family policies and child well-being, including both objective and subjective indicators. Because most research on the effectiveness of welfare and family policies has been conducted in Western countries, most of our discussion is also limited to this context. We conclude by noting some important gaps in the research and by raising some questions for future research.

CHILDREN'S WELL-BEING

Recent, large-scale comparative studies of child well-being generally agree about the central components of this concept (Bastos and Machado, 2009; Bradshaw and Richardson, 2009; Fernandes et al., 2012; Gordon and Nandy, 2012; Moore et al., 2008; OECD, 2009; UNICEF, 2013). UNICEF (2013) identifies five central domains of objective child well-being: material well-being, health and safety, education, behaviors and risks, and housing and environment. It further explores two dimensions of children's subjective well-being, or 'what children themselves have to say about their own lives' in regard to life satisfaction and the quality of their relationships. Other major studies of children's well-being, including Bradshaw and Richardson (2009) and the OECD (2009), identify similar objective and subjective domains of child well-being, although there are some minor differences between them.

Within the objective domains of child well-being, researchers further tend to agree on many of the best indicators. Under the health domain, for example, UNICEF (2013), Bradshaw and Richardson (2009) and the OECD (2009) all include infant mortality, low birth weight of newborns and the percentage of children who are immunized. Each of these three studies nonetheless also includes some indicators not included in the other studies, such as children who eat fruit daily (Bradshaw and Richardson, 2009), suicide rates among children aged 15–19 (OECD, 2009), and the mortality rate of children aged 1–19 from accidents and injuries (UNICEF, 2013). Thus, the exact definition of health, including which indicators should be used to measure it, remains open to interpretation.

Large-scale comparative scholarship on child well-being usually draws on the research of a number of organizations and studies. The Health Behavior in School-aged Children (HBSC) study provides data on children's life satisfaction, relationships, sexual habits, alcohol use, and other health-related attitudes and behaviors. The Program for International Student Assessment (PISA) assesses 15-year-olds' scholastic performance on mathematics, science and reading. The Trends in International Mathematics and Science Study (TIMSS) measures mathematics and science achievement at the fourth and eighth grades, and the Progress in International Reading Literacy Study (PIRLS) measures reading literacy among fourth graders.

Although most research on children's well-being has foused on wealthy Western countries, a number of scholars have also explored this concept in developing countries. David Gordon and his colleagues have developed an innovative approach ('the Bristol method') for measuring and comparing the extent and depth of child poverty across the world (Gordon et al., 2003), which has lately been expanded to include a large number of deprivation measurements (Gordon and Nandy, 2012). Camfield et al. (2009) argue for the benefits of using qualititative methods alongside quantitative ones to understand children's experience of well-being worldwide. Hoelscher et al. (2012) also discuss specific methods for monitoring child well-being in transition countries.

The domain of child well-being that remains most controversial among researchers is children's subjective well-being. Bradshaw and Richardson (2009) include a number of indicators of subjective well-being in their overall index of child well-being. UNICEF (2013) treats subjective well-being as an independent measure that ought not to be combined with objective measures in an overall index. According to the authors of the UNICEF report, the subjective domains of child well-being represent simply another way of measuring how children's lives are going, replicating in part the objective measures but focusing more on children's perceptions of how well their lives are going. The OECD, in turn, omits subjective indicators altogether from their child well-being index on the grounds that 'little is known about policy amenability of child measures of subjective wellbeing' (OECD, 2009, p. 4). On this last point, Bradshaw et al. (2013, pp. 22, 26) counter that subjective well-being corresponds at the macro level with objective measures such as material well-being, housing and environmental conditions (Bradshaw et al., 2013). This suggests that states can have some impact on children's subjective well-being by improving their material, housing and environmental conditions. In fact, state effectiveness in producing public goods and services correlates significantly with high levels of children's subjective well-being (Bradshaw et al., 2013, p. 26).[1]

Subjective measures can nevertheless be very contextually dependent. UNICEF (2007) uses 'family structure' as one indicator of children's subjective well-being – specifically, the percentage of children living in single parent families or in stepfamilies (Adamson et al., 2007). Sweden performs very poorly on this indicator, ranking 15th out of 21 countries. However, as Swedish divorce policies aim to preserve contact with both parents after a divorce, divorce is not necessarily an accurate indicator of the quality of children's relationships in this context.

Figure 24.1 shows where countries fall in regard to one important objective measure of child well-being – poverty – and one important subjective measure – life satisfaction.[2] Poverty is measued as the percentage of children living in households with less than 50 percent of the median income for a country. Life satisfaction shows an average of the percentage of young people aged 11, 13 and 15 with scores above the middle of the life satisfaction scale.

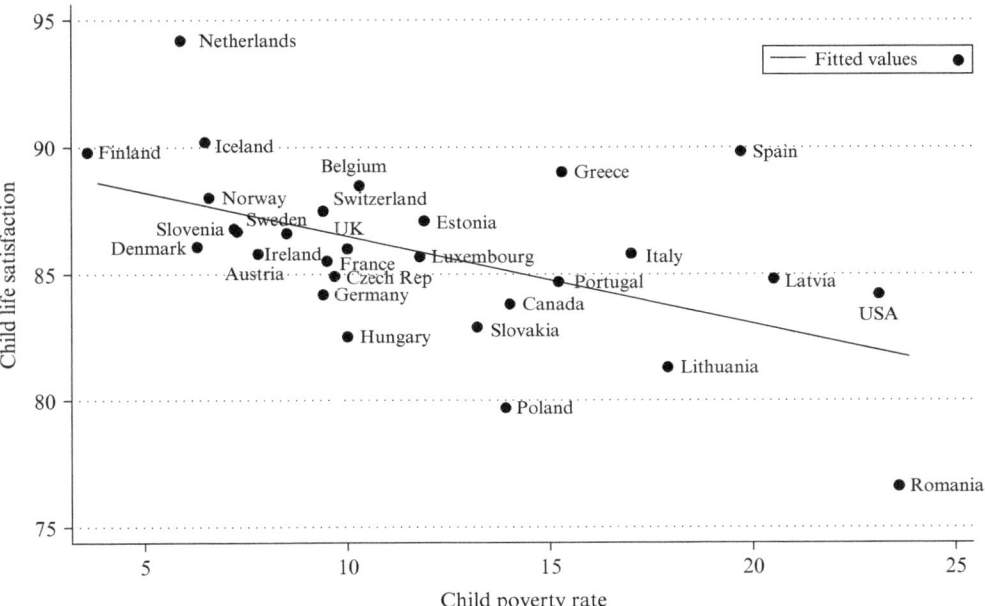

Figure 24.1 *Child poverty and life satisfaction*

Figure 24.1 shows a general correlation between low child poverty rates and high child life satisfaction, though there are some outliers such as Poland, Greece and Spain. The Netherlands, the Nordic countries and Slovenia achieve the lowest child poverty rates and highest child life satisfaction. Romania performs poorly on both measures.

Despite the advances that scholars have made in mapping out the major domains of child well-being, the field still has a couple of shortcomings. Most indices of child well-being omit important domains such as child physical and sexual abuse and neglect rates (see, however, OECD, 2011a, chapter 7). Child abuse and neglect not only negatively impact children's present well-being but also correlate with a number of long-term blights, including emotional problems, slower cognitive development, social maladjustment, elevated rates of substance abuse and school failure, poor mental and physical health, and increased incidence of criminal behavior (Reynolds et al., 2009). The omission of child abuse and neglect rates from most indices of child well-being is likely due to the lack of reliable cross-country data on this problem, but even so, given the huge impact abuse and neglect can have on children's lives, the absence of any measure of it does stand out. Most of the indicators of children's well-being also focus on children age 11 and above. Yet, child development experts generally stress the importance of the early years for children's long-term happiness and development (Conti and Heckman, 2014; Martinez et al., 2012). More attention to children's well-being during their early years would thus be welcome.

WELFARE AND FAMILY POLICIES AND CHILD WELL-BEING

This section reviews the types of policies that correlate with child well-being. In the comparative welfare state research, a distinction is often made between the provision of (a) cash and fiscal benefits and (b) services (Huber and Stephens, 2001). The distintion is not particularly useful when applied to family policies since some important family policies, such as job-protected paid parenting leaves, consist of a combination of cash transfers, entitlements and legal protections, and services such as early childhood education and care may be provided directly by the state or subsidized through cash transfers. Another point of critique is that the quality of services may vary, which the indicators do not capture.

General Welfare Policies

Previous research has shown that general social insurance policies such as unemployement insurance, sickness and disability benefits, and old age pensions are effective tools for reducing poverty and diminishing social-economic inequalities among the general population (Esping-Andersen, 1990; Korpi, 2000; UNICEF, 2007; see also Gornick and Meyers, 2003; Skinner et al., 2008). Because children are usually cared for by adults in private home settings, policies that reduce poverty and enhance health among the populace at large generally have positive effects on children's material well-being as well as the objective dimensions of their health. In fact, many general social insurance policies correlate positively with low child poverty and better health measures (Engster and Stensöta, 2011; Ferrarini, 2006; Gornick and Jäntti, 2009; Misra et al., 2007; see also Chapter 7 by Bradshaw and Chapter 23 by Gornick and Nell in this volume).

Researchers have also consistently found a strong relationship between greater public health insurance coverage and lower child mortality levels (Chung and Mutaner, 2006; Navarro, 2004). Education policies are, of course, also very important for children's development and subjective well-being, but discussion of the particular educational factors that positively and negatively affect child well-being is beyond the scope of this chapter. As noted above, state effectiveness in producing public goods and services further correlates significantly with higher levels of children's subjective well-being (Bradshaw et al., 2013, p. 26).

In a comparative country analysis, Kangas and Palme (2000) concluded that young people are particularly harmed by poverty, and highlighted some differences between countries. For example, household poverty is still largely an Anglo-American problem. Fritzell et al. (2012) note, however, that since the mid-1990s income inequality has also increased in the Nordic countries.

Economic recessions such as in 2008 can gravely impact the material well-being of children. In a recent analysis, Martorano et al. (2014) conclude that the Netherlands and the Scandinavian countries (excluding Denmark) did relatively better than the other countries while Romania and the United States performed well below average in response to the crisis.

Child Cash and Tax Benefits

Child cash and tax benefits may take a variety of forms: universal cash subsidies distributed to all parents with children, means-tested benefits distributed only to poorer parents, end-of-the-year tax breaks or credits, or some combination of these approaches. Numerous studies have found a significant correlation between more generous child cash and tax benefits and lower child poverty rates (Bäckman and Ferrarini, 2010; Bradshaw, 2014; Gornick and Jäntti, 2009; Misra et al., 2007; see also Chapter 7 by Bradshaw and Chapter 23 by Gornick and Nell in this volume). In most countries, child cash and tax benefits account for a larger percentage of the reduction of the pre-tax and transfer child poverty rate than any other welfare policy (Bradshaw, 2014). Their effectiveness further extends beyond wealthy Western countries. In a study of South Africa, Latin America and the Carribbean, Barrientos and DeJong (2006) concluded that child cash and tax benefits represent one of the surest policy tools for supplementing family incomes and lowering child poverty rates.

Aside from enhancing the material well-being of children, child cash and tax benefits have also been associated with other benefits such as lower child abuse and neglect rates which they presumably affect by lowering household stress (OECD, 2011a, pp. 254–5). Child cash and tax benefits can also contribute to children's higher educational attainment and achievement, particularly in combination with other family policies (Engster and Stensöta, 2011; Ravitch, 2013). Inasmuch as child cash and tax benefits contribute to lower child poverty rates, they would also seem to contribute at least indirectly to children's life satisfaction (see Figure 24.1).

While child tax benefits can significantly support children's material well-being, high marginal tax rates on second family incomes can have the opposite effect. By deterring women's employment, these policies generally have a negative effect on children's material well-being (Sainsbury, 1996).

Job-protected Paid Parenting Leave

Job-protected paid parenting leaves allow parents to take some time off from paid employment to care for their newborn children and return to their jobs at the end of the leave. Paid parental leaves are one important part of the dual-earrner gender model, which together with child care provision (Sainsbury, 1996) can have positive effects on child well-being by increasing household income (Engster and Stensöta, 2011; Halleröd et al., 2013; see also Chapter 10 by Thévenon in this volume). A number of studies have found a direct connection between generous job-protected paid parenting leaves and lower child poverty rates (Engster, 2012; Ferrarini, 2006; Misra et al., 2007). There is further research showing how gender equality policies such as parental leave and child care positively affect the level of employment among women and particularly mothers (Akgunduz and Plantenga, 2013; Ferrarini, 2006; Lewis, 1997; Sainsbury, 1996; Shim, 2013). By facilitating maternal employment, paid parenting leaves can substantially reduce child poverty levels as well as the risk of a family falling into poverty.

Researchers have also found a significant correlation between generous job-protected paid parenting leaves and lower infant (under 1 year old) and child (under 5 years old) mortality rates (Engster and Stensöta, 2011; Ruhm, 2000; Shim, 2013; Tanaka, 2005). In a study of 16 European countries over a 30-year period, Christopher Ruhm (2000) concluded that generosity in parental leave policies was positively associated with better child health outcomes – specifically lower infant and child mortality rates. Subsequent studies by Sakiko Tanaka (2005) and Joyce Shim (2013) have reached similar conclusions about the effectiveness of paid parenting leaves in reducing infant mortality but not unpaid leaves, probably because of low uptake.[3]

Public Funding for Early Educaton and Child Care

Like job-protected paid parenting leave policies, public funding for early education and child care is important for supporting a dual-earner family model, where women and men participate in paid work as well as share in the care of their children (see also Chapter 8 by Rostgaard in this volume). Many parents cannot afford to pay the high costs of quality child care without public subsidies (OECD, 2011a, pp. 143–4, 148–9). If child care is too costly, women, in particular, may stop working in paid employment in order to care directly for their children, increasing their risk of poverty. Public support for high-quality early education and child care can therefore facilitate higher levels of maternal employment and lower child poverty rates, particularly among single mother families (Engster, 2012; Lewis, 1997; Misra et al., 2007; OECD, 2011a, pp. 141–5). Some studies have also found a link between public child care services and lower child abuse and mortality rates among young children (Engster and Stensöta, 2011; Reynolds and Robertson, 2003).

Good-quality early education and child care also supports the development of children. In fact, probably the most important benefits of high-quality early education and child care are developmental – particularly for children from disadvantaged backgrounds. Studies in Sweden, Denmark, France, Germany, Norway, the United Kingdom and the United States have all concluded that quality early education and child care and pre-school programs improve children's reading, language and math skills, elementary, middle and high school performance, high school graduation rates, college attendance, labor force participation and adult wages (Esping-Andersen, 2009; Gambaro et al., 2014; Heckman and Masterov, 2007; Ruhm and Waldfogel, 2011). Cross-nationally, researchers have found that children who attended more than one year of some pre-primary early education and child care programs scored on average 54 points higher on the international PISA reading assessment – equivalent to more than one year of extra formal schooling (OECD, 2011b). Although disadvantaged children clearly enjoy the greatest benefits from early education and child care programs, more advantaged children can also benefit. Even holding constant for socio-economic backgrounds, students who attended more than one year of early education and child care scored on average 33 points higher (the equivalent of almost a year of extra formal schooling) on the PISA reading tests than those who had not (OECD, 2011b).

Subjective Dimensions of Child Well-being

Although Bradshaw et al. (2013) found that children's subjective well-being generally varies with objective dimensons of well-being, the link between social policies and children's subjective well-being is difficult to assess at the micro level as individual-level variation within countries is considerable. In an analysis of Swedish 15-year-olds over time, Nordlander and Stensöta (2014) found, for example, that subjective well-being on the individual level correlated not only with socio-economic background but also with gender, with the result that boys and girls of similar socio-economic backgrounds often assessed their well-being quite differently.

In general, subjective well-being depends to a considerable extent on establishing good realations between children and their parents, peers and other adults such as child care personnel. Children's access to social relationships and networks through early education and child care has been identified as important for enhancing their health and emotional wellbeing (Allan and Catts, 2012). There are a variety of ways that states can support this goal. For instance, the concept of child care *Kindergarten/Barnehage/Børnehave*, widespread in Germany and Scandinavia, focuses on establishing relationships within groups of children through common activities such as singing and playing together (Stensöta, 2004; see also Chapter 3 by Moss in this volume). Sylva et al. (2010) have shown that these pre-school practices can positively influence children's developmental outcomes. Research has also shown that parents, children and public employees can improve child well-being in pediatric primary care centers by working more closely together (Talmi and Fazio, 2012). Social work research supports this finding, demonstrating that counseling is much more effective for children when parents are integrated into the process (Corner and Haynes, 1991).

Another policy initiative for improving parenting quality is evidence-based behavioral parent training classes (Engster and Gonzales, 2012; see also Chapter 26 by Daly in this volume). Evidence-based behavioral parent training classes draw on current research about how different parenting practices affect children's behaviors and development in order to teach parents about positive child-rearing practices. Typical topics include teaching parents how to encourage their children's learning and cognitive development, the use of effective forms of discipline and so forth. Classes might also include information about child development, good nutrition, the benefits of breastfeeding and vaccinations, and the like. Although parent training classes have most frequently been used to help parents who have been reported to child protection services, there is no reason they might not be provided to the public at large. Several prominent parent training programs have achieved positive results with and received high evaluations from parents of diverse socio-economic and racial backgrounds in the United States as well as parents in Japan, Hong Kong, Germany, Switzerland, Norway, the United Kingdom, Australia and New Zealand (Sanders, 2008; Webster-Stratton, 2009). Meta-analyses of parent training programs have reported significant improvements in parent-child relations, due to improvements in parents' child-rearing skills, emotional adjustment, attitudes toward abuse, and actual abuse following the training (Kaminski et al., 2008; Lundahl et al., 2006).

CONCLUSIONS

Research on the relationship between family policies and children's well-being has come a long way in the last couple of decades. Extensive data collection has established a baseline of information about the status of children's well-being in a large number of countries. Because most of this data is comparative in nature, it can be used to highlight areas where particular countries are performing well or poorly. A substantial body of research has also emerged on the relationship between a number of social insurance and family policies, on the one hand, and several dimensions of child well-being, on the other hand. Much research nonetheless remains to be done.

Policies often come in 'bundles' and even if research now has more or less abandoned thinking in terms of welfare 'regimes', different sets of social welfare and family policies still often cluster together in ways that make it possible to identify different family policy regime types. Among these family policy regimes, those that most strongly support dual-earner families tend to achieve the best results for children on a number of measures (Engster and Stensöta, 2011). Even so, the very same combination of policies that is effective in one country might be less effective in other countries depending on the overall welfare state regime or background environment of social policy. Job-protected paid parenting leaves are only likely to increase women's employment, and thus reduce child poverty, for example, in countries where women can work in paid employment and there exist sufficient good-paying jobs. This observation becomes especially important as research on policies and child well-being expands to other parts of the world than the advanced industrialized countries. The problematic issue of whether policies can be 'exported' with good results seems more relevant today than ever (Martinez et al., 2012).

The relationship between policies and well-being for different population groups is also an evolving area of research. As discussed above, the recession of 2008 had consequences for the well-being of children and current and future societal changes such as new migration streams will surely impact the outcome of policies. Hence, there needs to be a recurrent assessment of whether children are 'lagging behind' the general population in well-being and particular attention needs to be paid to the well-being of different groups of children such as girls, immigrant children and others (Stensöta, 2016).

Researchers also still do not understand in detail the mechanisms by which particular policies work to enhance child well-being. A plausible connection exists between policies such as child cash and tax benefits and better housing and environmental conditions for children, for example, but whether or not the former directly contributes to the latter is not known. Indeed, improving the housing and environmental conditions of children can be complex. In order to achieve good housing for children, families not only need cash but also the availability of affordable and decent quality apartments and neighborhoods. Some intriguing questons also remain unanswered with regard to social policies and children's well-being, such as the long-term effects of gender equality on children's lives.

Research on the benefits of early education and child care on children could likewise be improved by developing better measures of quality child care, or on eligibility as Gauthier and Koops also point out in Chapter 2 in this volume. The quality of and eligibility for early education and child care is clearly important for achieving good outcomes for children, yet most cross-national research relies on fairly crude indicators of this variable (UNICEF, 2013, p. 21; see also Chapter 3 by Moss in this volume). Most research on early education and child care has also focused on children aged 3 and above (Gambaro et al., 2014, p. 7). How child care and early education affects children before age 3 has not been clearly established.

Finally, much work remains to be done on the effectiveness of family policies outside of rich industrialized countries. Most research on family policies and child outcomes has focused on Western Europe, North America, and Australia and New Zealand (Ben-Arieh et al., 2014, p. 12). Yet, many countries outside the industrialized West support at least some of the family policies discussed above. Given the limited research that does exist on these policies, there is some reason for believing that family policies can be universally effective in promoting child well-being (see also Chapter 26 by Daly in this volume). Conditional child cash transfer programs have proven very effective at reducing child poverty in South American countries (Barrientos and Dejong, 2006). A child support grant for poor children in South Africa has likewise been associated with improvements in children's physical and cognitive development (Bradshaw, 2014, pp. 2935–7; see also Chapter 19 by Knijn and Patel in this volume). The potential effectiveness of other family policies is nonetheless much less clear. Although most countries support job-protected paid parenting leaves, there exists very little research on their relation to child well-being in developing countries. Public child care support and parent training classes raise even thornier questions. Both might potentially contribute to child well-being in non-industrialized countries, but once again little research exists on this topic. Moreover, given the variability of child-rearing practices across the world, a great deal of adaptation would surely be necessary to apply these policies to different countries. Since social insurance and family policies have proven effective in enhancing child well-being in the industrialized Western world, there is nonetheless some reason to hope they can do the same in developing countries.

NOTES

1. Notably, however, higher levels of public expenditures on families were not found to correlate with higher levels of children's well-being.
2. Poverty data is taken from Martorano et al. (2014). Data on child life satisfaction is taken from Bradshaw et al. (2013).
3. Although the existence of job-protected paid parenting leaves has been consistently associated with better health outcomes for children, the extension of such leaves (from, say, six to twelve months) has been found to have few clear, beneficial effects on children's health (see, e.g., Baker and Milligan, 2008).

REFERENCES

Adamson, P., J. Bradshaw, P. Hoelscher, and D. Richardson (eds) (2007), *Child Poverty in Perspective: An Overview of Child Well-being in Rich Countries*, Research Report, Innocenti Report Card 7, Florence: UNICEF Office of Research.
Akgunduz, Y. and J. Plantenga (2013), 'Labor Market Effects of Parental Leave in Europe', *Cambridge Journal of Economics*, **37** (4), 845–62.
Allan, J. and R. Catts (eds) (2012), *Social Capital, Children and Young People: Implications for Practice, Policy and Research*, Bristol: Policy Press.
Bäckman, O. and T. Ferrarini (2010), 'Combatting Child Poverty? A Multilevel Assessment of Family Policy Institutions and Child Poverty in 21 Old and New Welfare States', *Journal of Social Policy*, **39** (2), 275–96.
Baker, M. and K. Milligan (2008), 'Maternal Employment, Breastfeeding, and Health: Evidence from Maternity Leave Mandates', *Journal of Health Economics*, **27**, 871–87.
Barrientos, A. and J. DeJong (2006), 'Reducing Child Poverty and Cash Transfers: A Sure Thing?', *Development Policy Review*, **24** (5), 537–52.
Bastos, A. and C. Machado (2009), 'Child Poverty: A Multidimensional Measurement', *Interntaional Journal of Social Economics*, **36** (3), 237–51.
Ben-Arieh, A. (2005), 'Where are the Children? Children's Role in Measuring and Monitoring their Well-being', *Social Indicators Research*, **74**, 573–96.
Ben-Arieh, A. and I. Frønes (2007), 'Indicators of Children's Well-being: What Should be Measured and Why?', *Social Indicators Research*, **84**, 249–50.
Ben-Arieh, A., F. Casas, I. Frønes, and J. Korbin (2014), 'Multifaceted Concept of Child Well-being', in A. Ben-Arieh, F. Casas, I. Frønes, and J. Korbin (eds), *Handbook of Child Well-being*, Dordrecht: Springer, pp. 1–27.
Bradshaw, J. (2014), 'Overview: Social Policies and Child Well-being', in A. Ben-Arieh, F. Casas, I. Frønes, and J. Korbin (eds), *Handbook of Child Well-being*, Dordrecht: Springer, pp. 2921–43.
Bradshaw, J. and D. Richardson (2009), 'An Index of Child Well-Being in Europe', *Child Indicators Research*, **2** (3), 319–51.
Bradshaw, J., B. Martorano, L. Natali, and C. de Neubourg (2013), 'Children's Subjective Well-being in Rich Countries', Working Paper 2013-03, UNICEF Office of Research, Florence.
Camfield, L., N. Streuli, and M. Woodhead (2009), 'What's the Use of "Well-being" in Contexts of Child Poverty? Approaches to Research, Monitoring and Children's Participation', *The International Journal of Childrens Rights*, **17** (1), 65–109.
Chung, H. and C. Muntaner (2006), 'Political and Welfare State Determinants of Infant and Child Health Indicators: An Analysis of Wealthy Countries', *Social Science and Medicine*, **63**, 829–42.
Conti, G. and J. Heckman (2014), 'Economics of Child Well-being', in A. Ben-Arieh, F. Casas, I. Frønes, and J. Korbin (eds), *Handbook of Child Well-being*, Dordrecht: Springer, pp. 363–402.
Corner, J. and N. Haynes (1991), 'Parent Involvement in Schools: An Ecological Approach', *The Elementary School Journal*, **91** (3), 271–7.
Engster, D. (2012), 'Child Poverty and Family Policies Across Eighteen Wealthy Western Democracies', *Journal of Children and Poverty*, **18** (2), 121–39.
Engster, D. and R. Gonzales (2012), 'Children and Justice: A Proposal for National Parent Training Classes', *Public Affairs Quarterly*, **26** (3), 221–41.
Engster, D. and H. Stensöta (2011), 'Do Family Policy Regimes Matter for Children's Well-being?', *Social Politics*, **18** (1), 82–124.
Esping-Andersen, G. (1990), *The Three Worlds of Welfare Capitalism*, Princeton, NJ: Princeton University Press.
Esping-Andersen, G. (2009), *Incomplete Revolution: Adapting Welfare States to Women's New Roles*, Cambridge: Polity Press.
Fernandes, L., A. Mendes, and A. Teixeira (2012), 'A Review Essay on the Measurement of Child Well-being', *Social Indicators Research*, **106** (2), 239–57.
Ferrarini, T. (ed.) (2006), *Families, States and Labour Markets: Institutions, Causes and Consequences of Family Policy in Post-war Welfare States*, Cheltenham, UK and Northampton, MA, USA: Edward Elgar Publishing.
Fritzell, J., O. Bäckman, and V. Ritakallio (2012), 'Income Inequality and Poverty: Do the Nordic Countries Still Constitute a Family of their Own?', in J. Kvist, J. Fritzell, B. Hvinden, and O. Kangas (eds), *Changing Social Equality: The Nordic Welfare Model in the 21st Century*, Bristol: Policy Press, pp. 165–85.
Gambaro, L., K. Stewart, and J. Waldfogel (2014), 'Introduction', in L. Gambaro, K. Stewart, and J. Waldfogel (eds), *An Equal Start? Providing Quality Early Education and Care for Disadvantaged Children*, Bristol: Policy Press, pp. 1–27.
Gordon, D. and S. Nandy (2012), 'Measuring Child Poverty and Deprivation', in A. Minujin and S. Nandy (eds), *Global Child Poverty and Well-being: Measurement, Concepts, Policy and Action*, Bristol: Policy Press, pp. 57–101.

Gordon, D., S. Nandy, C. Pantazis, S. Pemberton, and P. Townsend (eds) (2003), *Child Poverty in the Developing World*, Bristol: Policy Press.

Gornick, J. and M. Jäntti (2009), 'Child Poverty in Upper-income Countries: Lessons from the Luxembourg Income Study', in S. Kamerman, S. Phipps, and A. Ben-Arieh (eds), *From Child Welfare to Child Well-being: An International Perspective on Knowledge in the Service of Policy Making*, New York: Springer, pp. 339–70.

Gornick, J. and M. Meyers (2003), *Families that Work: Policies for Reconciling Parenthood and Employment*, New York: Russell Sage Foundation.

Halleröd, B., B. Rothstein, A. Daoud, and S. Nandy (2013), 'Bad Governance and Poor Children: A Comparative Analysis of Government Efficiency and Severe Child Deprivation in 68 Low- and Middle-income Countries', *World Development*, **48**, 19–31.

Heckman, J. and D. Masterov (2007), 'The Productivity Argument for Investing in Young Children', *Review of Agricultural Economics*, **29** (3), 446–93.

Hoelscher, P., D. Richardson, and J. Bradshaw (2012), 'A Snapshot of Child Well-being in Transition Countries: Exploring New Methods of Monitoring Child Well-being', in A. Minujin and S. Nandy (eds), *Global Child Poverty and Well-being: Measurement, Concepts, Policy and Action*, Bristol: Policy Press, pp. 179–206.

Huber, E. and J. Stephens (eds) (2001), *Developments and Crises of the Welfare State*, Chicago, IL: University of Chicago Press.

Kamerman, S., S. Phipps, and A. Ben-Arieh (2010) (eds), *From Child Welfare to Child Wellbeing*, New York: Springer.

Kaminski, J., L. Valle, J. Filene, and C. Boyles (2008), 'A Meta-analytic Review of Components Associated with Parent Training Program Effectiveness', *Journal of Abnormal Child Psychology*, **36**, 567–89.

Kangas, O. and J. Palme (2000), 'Does Social Policy Matter? Poverty Cycles in OECD Countries', *International Journal of Health Services*, **30** (2), 335–52.

Korpi, W. (2000), 'Faces of Inequality: Gender, Class, and Patterns of Inequalities in Different Types of Welfare States', *Social Politics*, **7** (2), 127–91.

Lewis, J. (1992), 'Gender and the Development of Welfare Regimes', *Journal of European Social Policy*, **2** (3), 159–73.

Lewis, J. (ed.) (1997), *Lone Mothers in European Welfare Regimes*. London: Jessica Kingsley Publishers.

Lundahl, B., J. Nimer, and B. Parsons (2006), 'Preventing Child Abuse: A Meta-analysis of Parent Training Programs', *Research on Social Work Practice*, **16** (3), 251–62.

Lynch, J. (2006), *Age in the Welfare State: The Origins of Social Spending on Pensioners, Workers, and Children*, Cambridge: Cambridge University Press.

Martinez, S., S. Naudeau, and V. Pereira (2012), *The Promise of Preschool in Africa: A Randomized Impact Evaluation of Early Childhood Development in Rural Mozambique*, Washington, DC: World Bank and Save the Children.

Martorano B., L. Natali, C. de Neubourg, and J. Bradshaw (2014), 'Child Well-being in Advanced Economies in the Late 2000s', *Social Indicators Research*, **118** (1), 247–83.

Misra, J., S. Moller, and M. Budig (2007), 'Work Family Policies and Poverty for Partnered and Single Women in Europe and North America', *Gender and Society*, **21** (6), 804–27.

Moore, K., C. Theokas, L. Lippman, M. Bloch, S. Vandivere, and W. O'Hare (2008), 'A Microdata Child Well-being Index: Conceptualization, Creation, and Findings', *Child Indicators Research*, **1**, 17–50.

Navarro, V. (ed.) (2004), *The Political and Social Contexts of Health*, Amityville, NY: Baywood Publishing.

Nordlander, E. and H. Stensöta Olofsdotter (2014), 'Grades – for Better or Worse? The Interplay of School Performance and Subjective Well Being Among Boys and Girls', *Child Indicators Research*, **7** (4), 861–79.

OECD (2009), *Doing Better for Children*, Paris: OECD Publishing.

OECD (2011a), *Doing Better for Families*, Paris: OECD Publishing.

OECD (2011b), *PISA in Focus: Does Participation in Pre-primary Education Translate into Better Learning Outcomes at School?* Paris: OECD Publishing.

Ravitch, D. (ed.) (2013), *Reign of Error: The Hoax of the Privatization Movement and the Danger to America's Public Schools*, New York: Alfred A. Knopf.

Reynolds, A. and D. Robertson (2003), 'School-based Intervention and Later Child Maltreatment in the Chicago Longitudinal Study', *Child Development*, **74** (1), 3–26.

Reynolds, A., L. Mathieson, and J. Topitzes (2009), 'Do Early Childhood Interventions Prevent Child Maltreatment? A Review of Research', *Child Maltreatment*, **14** (2), 182–206.

Ruhm, C. (2000), 'Parental Leave and Child Health', *Journal of Health Economics*, **19** (6), 931–60.

Ruhm, C. and J. Waldfogel (2011), 'Long-term Effects of Early Childhood Care and Education', IZA Discussion Paper Series, IZA DP No. 6149, Bonn.

Sainsbury, D. (1996), *Gendering Welfare States*, London: Sage.

Sanders, M. (2008), 'Triple P – Positive Parenting Program as a Public Health Approach to Strengthening Parenting', *Journal of Family Psychology*, **22** (3), 506–17.

Scruggs, L. and J. Allan (2006), 'Welfare-state Decommodification in 18 OECD Countries: A Replication and Revision', *Journal of European Social Policy*, **16** (1), 55–72.

Shim, J. (2013), 'Family Leave Policy and Child Health: Evidence from 19 OECD Countries from 1969–2010', Uunpublished dissertation, Graduate School of the Arts and Sciences, Columbia University.

Skinner, C., J. Bradshaw, and J. Davidson (2008), 'Child Support Policy: An International Perspective', Luxembourg Income Study Working Paper No. 478, Luxembourg.

Stensöta Olofsdotter, H. (2004), 'The Empathetic State. Childcare and Law Enforcement Policy 1950–2000' (Den empatiska staten. Daghemspolitik och polispolitik 1950–2000), Doctoral dissertation, Gothenburg Studies in Political Science No. 80. Livrena, p. 250.

Stensöta Olofsdotter Helena (2016), 'Is the Young Generation Lagging Behind?' QoG Working Paper Series, Quality Of Government Institute, Department of Political Science, University of Gothenburg. https://qog.pol.gu.se/Publications/workingpapers.

Sylva, K., E. Melhuish, P. Sammons, I. Siraj-Blatchford, and B. Taggart (eds) (2010), *Early Childhood Matters: Evidence from the Effective Pre-school and Primary Education Project*, New York: Routledge.

Talmi, A. and E. Fazio (2012), 'Commentary: Promoting Health and Well-being in Pediatric Primary Care Settings: Using Health and Behavior Codes at Routine Well-child Visits', *Journal of Pediatric Psychology*, **37** (5), 496–502.

Tanaka, S. (2005), 'Parental Leave and Child Health Across OECD Countries', *The Economic Journal*, **115** (February), 7–27.

UNICEF (2007), *Child Poverty in Perspective: An Overview of Child Well-being in Rich Countries*, Innocenti Report Card 7, Florence: UNICEF Office of Research.

UNICEF (2013), *Child Well-being in Rich Countries: A Comparative Overview*, Innocenti Report Card 11, Florence: UNICEF Office of Research.

Webster-Stratton, C. (2009), 'Affirming Diversity: Multi-cultural Collaborations to Deliver the Incredible Years Parent Programs', *International Journal of Child Health and Human Development*, **2** (1), 17–32.

25. Effects of work-family policies on parenthood and wellbeing
Caitlyn Collins and Jennifer Glass

INTRODUCTION

Becoming a parent makes adults happier and healthier – or does it? While popular cultural beliefs bolster this claim, a wealth of studies beginning in the 1970s find that overall mothers and fathers typically report lower levels of wellbeing than childless adults across industrialized countries. This finding emerged in the context of substantial economic and social changes in work and family life over the past four decades: an increase in women's labor force participation, a decline in men's earnings, and a rise in dual-earner and single parent families (Kohler et al., 2006; McLanahan and Adams, 1989). The finding that nonparents report greater happiness than parents presents a puzzle for researchers because decades of scholarship suggest the opposite: since Durkheim's (1897) classic study of suicide, research has found repeatedly that social roles and relationships such as parenting have positive benefits for adults' mental health (House et al., 1988; Mirowsky and Ross, 2003). This anomalous finding is a relevant and timely policy issue given its possible association with high rates of childlessness, stress and work-family conflict for adults, and poorer outcomes for children (Aassve et al., 2005; Gornick and Meyers, 2003; Mather, 2012).

Some scholars have employed theories of mental health and suggest that the emotional and financial costs of contemporary parenthood outweigh the emotional rewards of having children (Balbo et al., 2012; Begall and Mills, 2011; Evenson and Simon, 2005; Liefbroer, 2005; McLanahan and Adams, 1989; Nomaguchi and Milkie, 2003; Woo and Raley, 2005). Yet, the experience of contemporary parenthood varies widely from country to country depending on the sorts of resources and social supports offered to parents (Esping-Andersen, 1990; Kahneman et al., 2010; Savolainen et al., 2001). For example, Scandinavian countries offer extensive support and socialize the cost of childrearing across society, while some Mediterranean countries and the United States offer minimal support, compelling parents to find private solutions to meet their families' needs (Gornick and Meyers, 2003; see also Chapter 8 by Rostgaard and Chapter 10 by Thévenon in this volume). Parenthood can be particularly taxing and stressful in countries that offer little support to parents (Kahneman et al., 2010), and scholars have long suggested that increased institutional support such as readily available childcare would greatly improve mothers' and fathers' psychological wellbeing (Bird, 1997).

Although recent scholarship has begun examining cross-national variation in the relationship between parenthood and wellbeing (Kahneman et al., 2010; Ono and Lee, 2013; Savolainen et al., 2001), we still know little about why the parenthood gap in wellbeing is larger in some countries than in others. We suggest that the parenthood gap in wellbeing is associated with state-provided public policies supporting families, and that this is the most promising avenue for investigating country-level differences in parental status differences in happiness. In this chapter, we first review the literature on parental wellbeing in Organisation for Economic Co-operation and Development (OECD) countries. Second, we discuss the findings of studies that have considered whether, and to what extent, work–family policies lessen the time costs, financial costs and psychosocial stress associated with parenting. We provide several empirical examples from our research. We conclude by suggesting avenues for future research that help move the work–family policy agenda forward by understanding the relationship between macro-level contexts and micro-level emotional processes for parents in OECD countries.

PARENTAL WELLBEING IN ADVANCED INDUSTRIALIZED COUNTRIES

Across developed countries, considerable research has documented a significant negative association between parenthood and emotional wellbeing (Gilbert, 2007; Hansen, 2012; Kahneman et al., 2004; McLanahan and Adams, 1989; Nomaguchi and Milkie, 2003; Simon, 2008; Stanca, 2012; Umberson et al., 2010). This association has been found in all household types, for both mothers and fathers, and across a number of dimensions of emotional wellbeing – including depression, anxiety, generalized distress, life satisfaction, and the frequency of everyday positive and negative emotions like happiness and anger (Ross and Van Willigen, 1996; see Hansen, 2012; Nelson et al., 2013; Umberson et al., 2010 for recent reviews). Yet, the personal and household characteristics of parents also matter (Aassve et al., 2012; Umberson et al., 2010; Woo and Raley, 2005). Although married and cohabiting parents report less stress than single parents (Aassve et al., 2012; McLanahan, 1983; Simon, 1998; Woo and Raley, 2005), research shows consistently that across marital status types, parents residing with minor children – whose time, energy and financial demands are highest – show lower levels of wellbeing than adults who do not reside with children (Evenson and Simon, 2005).

What about older parents whose children have left home? Common reasoning suggests that empty-nest parents might be happier than childless adults since the emotional benefits of parenthood are thought to be greatest when children have grown up and become independent. However, research in the United States does not support this claim: empty-nest parents do not enjoy greater emotional wellbeing than childless adults (Bures et al., 2009; Evenson and Simon, 2005; Koropeckyj-Cox, 2002; Milkie et al., 2008; Pudrovska, 2009). In fact, Evenson and Simon (2005) found that there is no type of parent (including custodial, non-custodial, and step-parents of both minor and adult children) reporting significantly better mental health than nonparents in the United States.

Why is parenthood so often associated with lower levels of emotional wellbeing? Parenthood, like other major adult social roles, provides individuals with an important sense of meaning and identity, personal gratification and social connections to others, which improve mental health (Nomaguchi and Milkie, 2003; Umberson and Gove, 1989; Umberson et al., 2013). But the emotional rewards of parenthood could be overshadowed by the stress of raising children. Theories operationalizing how stress affects mental health (Pearlin, 1989) have the greatest potential to explain the parenthood gap in emotional wellbeing. Because children increase adults' exposure to a number of stressors, parenthood increases symptoms of anxiety, depression, distress and anger while decreasing positive emotions such as happiness.

Fawcett (1988) outlined three major types of burdens parents confront that undermine their emotional wellbeing: time costs, financial costs and psychosocial stress. First, parents who live with minor children experience substantial demands on their time and energy coupled with sleep deprivation (Avison et al., 2007; Nelson et al., 2013) and work-family conflict (Begall and Mills, 2011; Nomaguchi et al., 2005). The increased amount of time spent doing housework and caring for children decreases leisure time and time with one's spouse for married parents, which may decrease marital satisfaction (Claxton and Perry-Jenkins, 2008). In dual-earner households in which both parents work full time, parents experience high levels of time pressure, particularly in the United States (Mattingly and Sayer, 2006; Milkie et al., 2009; Nomaguchi, 2009).

Second, raising minor children at home is associated with increased financial strain (McCrate, 2005; Nelson et al., 2013; Warren and Tyagi, 2004). The added expense of having children can lead to economic hardship, which has negative repercussions for parents' psychological wellbeing (Mirowsky and Ross, 2003). For example, parents of young children in many countries have difficulties obtaining high-quality, affordable childcare (Bird, 1997; Kravdal, 1996; Ross and Mirowsky, 1988), while some parents of older children face the economic burden of financing children's higher education and independent living at the same time that they face their own retirement (Fingerman et al., 2012; Furstenberg et al., 2004; Warren and Tyagi, 2004). Low-income parents are exposed to additional sources of financial stress, such as the stress of living in unsafe neighborhoods with under-resourced schools, unreliable and inadequate daycare and healthcare for their children, and insufficient food (Edin and Kefalas, 2005; Heymann, 2000; Nomaguchi et al., 2005; Ross and Mirowsky, 1988).

Third, parents experience psychosocial stress from the daily ins and outs of parenting. Prolonged psychosocial stress is problematic because it can lead to poor performance, chronic fatigue, disinterest, dejection, lack of work motivation, memory and sleep disturbance, numbness, muscle pain, recurrent infections, and to chronic conditions like depression, diabetes and cardiovascular disease (Danielsson et al., 2012). Some research shows that women tend to experience greater stress and stronger negative shocks to wellbeing in the transition to parenthood (Nomaguchi and Milkie, 2003; Simon, 1992). Given that mothers still complete the majority of childrearing and housework in all industrialized countries, even when employed full time (Pettit and Hook, 2009), studies have explored whether wellbeing differs for mothers versus fathers in dual-earner households. The majority of studies show few differences (Evenson and Simon, 2005; Margolis and Myrskylä, 2011). While mothers report more work-family conflict (Gornick and Meyers, 2003) and less leisure time (Mattingly and Bianchi, 2003) than fathers do, fathers report more distress about the financial strains of parenting and the tension between breadwinning and spending time with children (Aumann et al., 2011; Simon, 1998).

Some aspects of parenting, like multitasking, are not experienced equally by mothers and fathers. Mothers spend on average ten hours more on multitasking per week than fathers, primarily on housework and childcare. These multitasking activities for mothers at home and in public lead to increased stress, negative emotions, work-family conflict and psychological distress (Offer and Schneider, 2011). At the same time, fathers' multitasking at home, which involves less housework and childcare, is not considered a negative experience. A survey of 909 working women in Texas found that childcare ranked 16th out of 19 possible pleasurable activities (Kahneman et al., 2004), behind watching television, preparing food, napping, housework, shopping and talking on the phone. These stressors, unsurprisingly, are more acute for single parents than for married and cohabiting parents (Aassve et al., 2012; Avison et al., 2007; McLanahan, 1983; Meadows et al., 2008; Simon, 1998), helping explain why single parents report the lowest levels of emotional wellbeing of all parents. Simon and Caputo (n.d.) find that although adults experience greater emotional wellbeing and less emotional distress at different stages of parenthood than others, they find no overall advantages of parenthood for adults' health and happiness.

The majority of scholarship to date has focused on the *proximate* sources of stressors that mediate the association between parenthood and emotional wellbeing, such as sleep deprivation and financial strain. Nelson and colleagues (2013) present a parent wellbeing model that maps the psychological mechanisms that mediate this relationship, outlining both why and how parents experience more or less wellbeing than nonparents. Their model identifies both positive mediating mechanisms (purpose/meaning in life; human needs; positive emotions; social roles) and negative ones (negative emotions; financial strain; sleep disturbance; strained partner relationships).

In this chapter, we extend this model by zooming out to highlight the *distal* sources of stress – like childcare and parental leave – that are rooted in the larger policy context in which adults raise children. Prior research suggests that these distal factors help mediate the relationship between parenthood and wellbeing. For example, Bird (1997) finds that children in the United States do not increase the psychological distress of parents in and of themselves: rather, children are associated with greater social and economic burdens, which increase parents' levels of distress. She argues that if parents were relieved of the economic hardship associated with having children by providing more material support to parents, they would not display significantly higher distress levels than nonparents.

Given that parenting is found to have both positive and negative effects on wellbeing, 'it should be possible to decrease the psychological costs of parenting by reducing the burdens or constraints that overshadow the more rewarding aspects of raising children' (Bird, 1997, p. 810). Research supports this claim: publicly provided benefits such as a statutory right to reduced working hours when children are young and cash allowances to parents are shown to reduce some of the stressors such as very long work hours and financial distress associated with raising children to adulthood in industrialized countries (Gornick and Meyers, 2003; Heymann et al., 2007; Ray et al., 2009). We therefore theorize parenting as a stressor buffered by institutional support (Glass et al., 2016), and argue that attention to the larger sociopolitical context – particularly different work-family policies – provides further insight into why the emotional effects of parenthood vary from country to country. We present a modified and expanded version of Nelson et al.'s model of proximate sources of stress (Figure 25.1) to highlight the distal policy supports that might improve parents' wellbeing. We are interested specifically in how work-family policies might affect the psychological mechanisms that mediate the relationship between parenthood and wellbeing. For example, how might paid parental leave and subsidized childcare impact the mediating relationship of financial strain and work-family conflict on the wellbeing of parents versus nonparents?

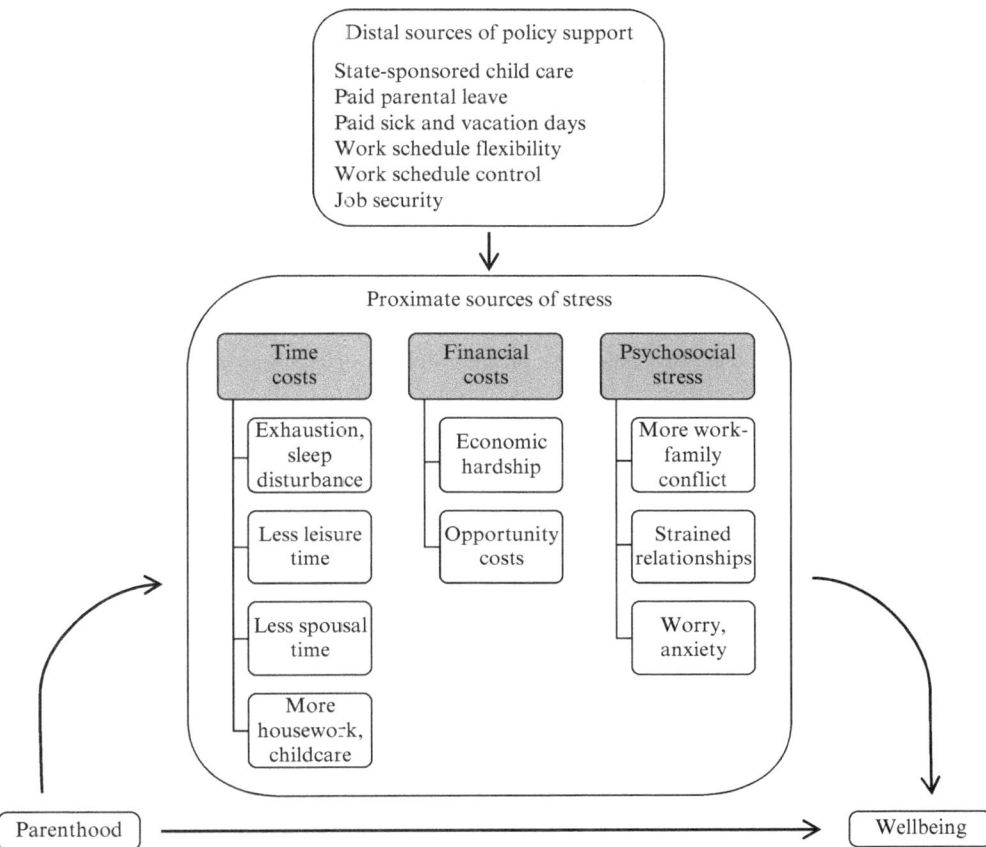

Figure 25.1 Distal supports and proximate stressors that mediate the relationship between parenthood and wellbeing

WORK-FAMILY POLICIES AND THE WELLBEING OF PARENTS VERSUS NONPARENTS

The welfare state regimes of advanced industrialized countries offer policy packages that vary widely in their levels of social support and resources to parents (Esping-Andersen, 1990; Kahneman et al., 2010; Savolainen et al., 2001). In the social-democratic regimes of Scandinavia, policies such as extensive childcare and workplace accommodations seek to reduce the direct financial costs and opportunity costs of parenthood, equalize the household division of labor, and ameliorate work-family conflict and overload (Gornick and Meyers, 2003; see also Chapter 15 by Eydal, Rostgaard and Hiilamo in this volume). Prior studies have identified these costs as the main sources of the parenthood deficit in emotional wellbeing across industrialized countries (Pollmann-Schult, 2014; Stanca, 2012). Within Europe, parents living in social-democratic countries tend to be happier than those living in countries with liberal or conservative welfare regimes (Aassve et al., 2012). In conservative welfare state regimes, such as Germany, policies have long tended to support a male breadwinner/female homemaker model of family life. On the other end of the spectrum, few policy supports are available for families with children in liberal welfare state regimes such as the United States and some Mediterranean countries. In these regimes, parents contend with the demands of childrearing using their own resources and social networks (Glass, 2000; Gornick and Meyers, 2003; Simon, 2008; see also Chapter 13 by Pfau-Effinger, Chapter 14 by Woods and Chapter 16 by Jurado Guerrero and Naldini in this volume).

In terms of wellbeing, women in the social-democratic welfare states seem to suffer the least as a result of childbearing, whereas women in conservative and Mediterranean states suffer significantly more. For liberal welfare regimes, the results are more mixed, and depend on the definition of wellbeing used (Aassve et al., 2005). The United States in particular is exceptional in its lack of policy provisions to offset the costs of childrearing and work–family conflict (Gornick and Meyers, 2003). Only one federal policy – the 1993 Family and Medical Leave Act – is designed to help people meet the dual demands of work and family. In a study of 22 OECD countries, the United States had the largest subjective wellbeing penalty for parenthood (Glass et al., 2016).

Although broad welfare state typologies are useful to help understand the relationship between parenthood and wellbeing cross-nationally, we suggest that an examination of *specific* public policies intended to reduce parental stressors better illuminates which policy contexts alleviate the gap in wellbeing between parents and nonparents in OECD countries. Next, we review findings on which policies help reduce the time costs, financial costs and psychosocial stress associated with parenthood.

Policies Ameliorating the Time Costs Associated with Parenthood

Vacation and sick day policies help parents preserve time away from work to care for and spend time with children (Gornick and Meyers, 2003), and have been shown to dramatically improve wellbeing among parents (Heymann et al., 2007; Hyde et al., 1995). Using data from 22 OECD countries, Glass and colleagues (2016) report a strong policy effect of vacation and sick days on parental happiness. Paid parental or maternity leave also enables parents of newborns to leave work temporarily to care for an infant. These policies together reversed the negative impact of parenthood on happiness (Glass et al., 2016).

Work schedule flexibility policies allow workers to organize their time in a way that makes the combination of employment and parenting feel more compatible (see Chapter 11 by den Dulk, Yerkes and Peper in this volume). Three types of work schedule discretion tend to be available for employees: the ability to change the starting and ending times of the workday; the ability to take time off during the workday to attend to personal matters; and the ability to refuse overtime work (Golden et al., 2013). In countries like Denmark and Sweden, strong work-time policies allow parents to temporarily reduce their working hours or set maximum weekly work hours, and in the UK, 'right-to-ask' laws support flexible work schedules (Hegewisch and Gornick, 2008). Golden and colleagues (2013) find a significant association between schedule flexibility and workers' reported happiness – particularly the opportunity to take time off during the workday, and to a lesser extent, to vary daily starting and quitting times. Lower stress levels are also reported among employees who control their work hours and schedules (Grzywacz et al., 2008). Others find that both parents and nonparents benefit from living in countries with a larger percentage of workplaces offering flexible schedules, with nonparents benefiting slightly more (Glass et al., 2016). They also find that work flexibility does not increase happiness more for parents than nonparents.

Policies Ameliorating the Financial Costs Associated with Parenthood

A large body of work suggests that parental wellbeing is strongly contingent on the financial costs borne by parents (Bird, 1997; Pollman-Schult, 2014). A comparative study of 94 countries finds that children's negative impact on parents' wellbeing is explained primarily by a large negative effect on household finances (Stanca, 2012). Although when approached globally, resident children are associated with decreased financial satisfaction for parents (Angeles, 2010), this is not the case in Nordic countries that have extensive work-family policy provisions (Hansen et al., 2009; Savolainen et al., 2001).

The cost and availability of childcare in particular has a strong influence on parents' wellbeing. Glass and colleagues (2016) find that policies lowering average childcare costs show the greatest potential to increase parental happiness. This is supported by Misra et al. (2007), who report that generous, high-quality childcare reduces financial strain and lowers poverty rates, particularly for single mother-headed families. In-depth interviews with middle-income working mothers in Sweden and the United States further support these findings: Swedish mothers did not report worrying about childcare costs, while American mothers reported enormous stress related to the high cost of daycare. American mothers spent significant time researching and securing care they could afford, and some were forced to quit work when they couldn't find affordable care (Collins, 2019). Without universal childcare, like Sweden has for children over 1 year old, no one daycare solution was reliable for American families – all were temporary arrangements that could shift unexpectedly. Daycare centers closed, babysitters started different jobs or moved, and relatives who helped out fell ill themselves. American mothers who had the most financial resources available to dedicate to childcare tended to be the happiest with the solutions they found. A wealth of research demonstrates that low-cost childcare improves parental wellbeing both by enhancing incomes and reducing stress (Ross and Mirowsky, 1988; Savolainen et al., 2001; Stanca, 2012).

Pollman-Schult (2014) reported that the financial costs of children negatively impact men's life satisfaction in particular, especially when the mother has left the labor force. This echoes the finding that the perceived financial costs associated with parenthood have a strong effect on men's entry into parenthood – negatively impacting countries' fertility rates (Liefbroer, 2005). Together, these findings suggest that both men's interest in starting a family and their life satisfaction after having children are deeply impacted by the financial aspects of parenthood (Pollman-Schult, 2014). More broadly, child benefits – which vary drastically from country to country – play an important role in ameliorating poverty for families (see Chapter 7 by Bradshaw in this volume).

Policies Ameliorating the Psychosocial Stress Associated with Parenthood

In countries that offer little policy support to parents, parenthood is particularly emotionally taxing and stressful (Kahneman et al., 2010). Insofar as work-family policies (i.e., parental leave, paid vacation and sick days, flexible work schedules, subsidized public childcare) give parents time to decompress, complete errands and household tasks, care for loved ones, and spend time both with and away from children, all of these policies help reduce parents' stress and worry (Collins, 2019; Glass et al., 2016; Gornick and Meyers, 2003). Interestingly, Glass and colleagues (2016) find that child allowances (cash benefits paid directly to families) show little impact on parental wellbeing, perhaps because the average cash benefit in most countries remains fairly low given the costs of raising children.

On the other hand, flexible work scheduling positively influences subjective wellbeing measures like work-life conflict, work stress and fatigue (Golden et al., 2013). Paid parental leave is positively associated with parental happiness (Glass et al., 2016). Research also suggests that the availability and length of maternity leave is related to women's mental health: women who take short leaves and have poor-quality marriages are most vulnerable to depression (Hyde et al., 1995). These paid childbearing leaves influence parental happiness likely because they strengthen later parent-child attachment and minimize the long-term employment costs of parenthood (Glass et al., 2016; Misra et al., 2011).

Childcare quality is also important for mothers' mental health and wellbeing. Qualitative research suggests that the availability of high-quality, affordable childcare substantially increases working mothers' sense of work-life balance and satisfaction in Sweden and Germany, while the absence of reliable childcare in the United States and Italy is a monumental source of stress for mothers who work outside the home (Collins, 2019). Gordon and colleagues (2011) report that mothers who choose their children's daycare facility based on perceptions of quality report lower depressive symptoms than those who choose for practical reasons such as cost, hours and location.

Overall, these findings suggest that policy differences between countries may help shape the balance of costs and rewards for parenthood (Glass et al., 2016; Hansen, 2012; Margolis and Myrskylä, 2011, 2015). Parents living in countries with the most generous work-family policies and greatest gender equality seem to derive the greatest emotional benefits from having children (Hansen, 2012). In fact, the inverse relationship between parenthood and happiness is completely eliminated in nations with the strongest policy packages – those with paid parental leave, paid sick and vacation leave, and work schedule flexibility (Glass et al., 2016). Because fertility tends to be low in countries where the costs of parenthood are particularly high (Hilgeman and Butts, 2009), work-family policies may be a mechanism by which governments can increase fertility by removing the disincentives to parenting, equalizing the cost of childrearing, and easing the combination of employment and parenthood (McDonald, 1997). Further, given the well-established relationship between parental and child wellbeing (Cummings et al., 2005), it is likely that work-family policies improve not only the wellbeing of parents but also their children (Glass et al., 2016). Policies like parental leave influence the stress of caregiving and the stability of a couple's relationship, household division of labor and children's relations to their parents (Almqvist and Duvander, 2014). Even more significantly, welfare state policies seem to improve the levels of happiness for countries' general populations, both parents and nonparents alike (Flavin et al., 2014; Glass et al., 2016).

Glass and colleagues (2016) constructed a Comprehensive Policy Index (CPI) for 22 OECD countries that combines work flexibility, paid vacation/sick leave and paid leave available to mothers and tested whether the nations that score higher on this index have a smaller gap in parental happiness. They find that the countries that offer the strongest family policies (i.e., those that score highly on the CPI) exhibit a net positive effect of

Effects of work-family policies on parenthood and wellbeing 345

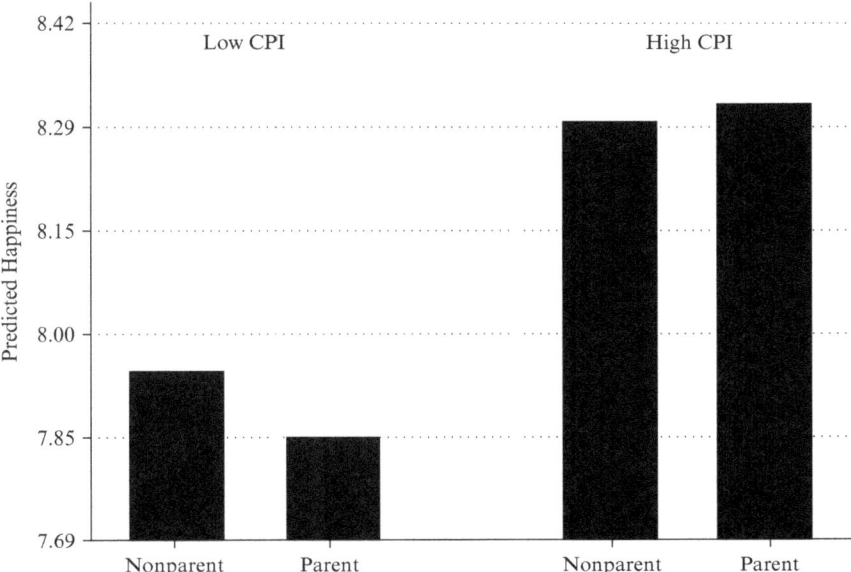

Note: All control variables at the individual and country level are held at their sample mean.

Source: European Social Survey and International Social Survey Programme, 2004–07 from Glass et al. (2016).

Figure 25.2 Estimated happiness (1–10 scale) for parents and nonparents with the Comprehensive Policy Index (CPI)

parenthood on happiness, while those that offer the weakest policies (i.e., those that score lower on the CPI) show a deficit in parental happiness compared to nonparents.

The extent of gender-specific responses to work-family policies has not been settled, but some studies suggest this possibility. The legacy of 'breadwinner-housewife' gender ideologies can be seen in men's responses to the financial demands of parenthood even as couples rely more heavily on women's earnings to meet those demands (Pedulla and Thébaud, 2015). Employed women, by contrast, seem more affected by the time pressures and multitasking associated with parenting children, which disproportionately fall to mothers (Offer and Schneider, 2011). This suggests that men might be more affected by income supports for parenting, while women may respond more to time and scheduling interventions.

CONCLUSIONS

We conclude by discussing the avenues that future research should explore to improve our understanding of how public policies impact parental wellbeing. The heuristic model by Nelson and colleagues (2013) includes only emotional/psychological wellbeing as an outcome, but objective measures such as financial debt, disease burden and cortisol (stress hormone) levels could also productively be used to measure the micro-level impacts of social policies. Future research should measure these objective aspects of wellbeing and uncover their role in producing both low second birth rates and low subjective wellbeing among parents. Better integration of health data with time-use studies across the European Union and English-speaking countries would also be helpful to see how policies change the daily patterning of activities and interactions in families of different household types. Scholars should especially focus on households disadvantaged by income, ethnicity or family structure (number of adults in the household) since these are the households most impacted by public policy or the lack thereof. We also need further research that investigates the role of partnership status (single, cohabiting, married), race and immigration status, age at parenthood and age of children, and social class on parents' response to social policies.

While policy makers seem to excessively focus on child wellbeing, the problem of low fertility ultimately stems from the effects of policies on *parents* because, although we want children to benefit from policies, policies affect the context in which adults make decisions about having children. We are missing the larger picture: why do parents decide (not) to have children, especially a second child after the first has arrived? Is the policy framework enough to still make parenthood desirable or is it just ameliorating the worst aspects of it? A research paradigm that focuses on the policy mix producing the highest level of Gross Domestic Happiness in families might ultimately resolve the problem of below replacement fertility faster than a focus on either cash transfers or fertility incentives. Currently, the costs of parenthood look so enormous in comparison to its mainly psychosocial benefits that many individuals simply opt out of reproduction. When the time and fiscal resource drain of raising children induces a free-rider problem in the reproduction of the next generation of workers and citizens, policy makers must attend to the fairness of the cost distribution among parents, employers and the state.

But this raises an important conundrum: that of how to increase policy support for parenting without harming those at other life stages. Some scholars (e.g., Ono and Lee, 2013) have suggested that social-democratic welfare states merely redistribute happiness among policy-targeted demographic groups in these countries. This suggests that the pro-family ideology of the social-democratic welfare states protects families from social risk and improves their wellbeing *at the cost of single persons*. However, Figure 25.2 suggests that the same policies that improve parental happiness also improve the happiness of nonparents, although to a lesser extent. Future research must determine the presence and extent of any redistribution of happiness between parents and nonparents, while simultaneously asking the thorny question of whether such redistribution is nevertheless in the best interests of children, families and the larger social good.

REFERENCES

Aassve, A., S. Mazzuco, and L. Mencarini (2005), 'Childbearing and well-being: a comparative analysis of European welfare regimes', *Journal of European Social Policy*, **15**, 283–99.
Aassve, A., A. Goisis, and M. Sironi (2012), 'Happiness and childbearing across Europe', *Social Indicators Research*, **108**, 65–86.
Almqvist, A. and A. Duvander (2014), 'Changes in gender equality? Swedish fathers' parental leave, division of childcare, and housework', *Journal of Family Studies*, **20** (1), 19–27.
Angeles, L. (2010), 'Children and life satisfaction', *Journal of Happiness Studies*, **11**, 523–38.

Aumann, K., E. Galinsky, and K. Matos (2011), 'The new male mystique', Families & Work Institute, accessed 23 September 2016 at http://familiesandwork.org/site/research/reports/newmalemystique.pdf.
Avison, W., J. Ali, and D. Walters (2007), 'Family structure, stress, and psychological distress: a demonstration of the impact of differential exposure', *Journal of Health and Social Behavior*, **62**, 911–26.
Balbo, N., F. Billari, and M. Mills (2012), 'Fertility in advanced societies: a review of research', *European Journal of Population*, **29**, 1–38.
Begall, K. and M. Mills (2011), 'The impact of perceived work control, job strain and work–family conflict on fertility intentions: a European comparison', *European Journal of Population*, **27** (4), 433–56.
Bird, C. (1997), 'Gender differences in the social and economic burdens of parenting and psychological distress', *Journal of Marriage and Family*, **59** (4), 809–23.
Bures, R., T. Korpeckyj-Cox, and M. Loree (2009), 'Childlessness, parenthood, and depressive symptoms among middle-aged and older adults', *Journal of Family Issues*, **30**, 670–87.
Claxton, A. and M. Perry-Jenkins (2008), 'No fun anymore: leisure and marital quality across the transition to parenthood', *Journal of Marriage and Family*, **70** (1), 28–43.
Collins, C. (2019), *Making Motherhood Work: How Women Manage Careers and Caregiving*, Princeton, NJ: Princeton University Press.
Cummings, E., P. Keller, and P. Davies (2005), 'Towards a family process model of maternal and paternal symptoms: exploring multiple relations with child and family functioning', *Journal of Child Psychology and Psychiatry*, **46**, 479–89.
Danielsson, M., I. Heimerson, U. Lundberg, A. Perski, C. Stefansson, and T. Akerstedt (2012), 'Psychosocial stress and health problems: health in Sweden. The National Public Health Report 2012. Chapter 6', *Scandinavian Journal of Public Health*, **40** (9), 121–34.
Durkheim, E. (1897), *Suicide: A Study in Sociology* (trans. J. Spaulding and G. Simpson, 1951), New York: Free Press.
Edin, K. and M. Kefalas (2005), *Promises I Can Keep: Why Poor Women Put Motherhood Before Marriage*, Berkeley, CA: University of California Press.
Esping-Andersen, G. (1990), *The Three Worlds of Welfare Capitalism*, Cambridge: Polity Press.
Evenson, R. and R. Simon (2005), 'Clarifying the relationship between parenthood and depression', *Journal of Health and Social Behavior*, **46**, 341–58.
Fawcett, J. (1988), 'The value of children and the transition to parenthood', *Marriage and Family Review*, **12**, 11–34.
Fingerman, K., Y. Cheng, K. Birditt, and S. Zarit (2012), 'Only as happy as the least happy child: multiple grown children's problems and successes and middle-aged parents' well-being', *Journals of Gerontology, Series B: Psychological Sciences and Social Sciences*, **67**, 184–93.
Flavin, P., A. Pacek, and B. Radcliff (2014), 'Assessing the impact of the size and scope of government on human well-being', *Social Forces*, **92**, 1241–58.
Furstenberg, F., S. Kennedy, V. McLoyd, R. Rumbaut, and R. Settersten, Jr. (2004), 'Growing up is harder to do', *Contexts*, **3**, 33–41.
Gilbert, D. (2007), *Stumbling on Happiness*, New York: Random House.
Glass, J. (2000), 'Toward a kinder, gentler workplace: envisioning the integration of family and work', *Contemporary Sociology*, **29**, 129–43.
Glass, J., R. Simon, and M. Andersson (2016), 'Parenthood and happiness: effects of work-family reconciliation policies in 22 OECD countries', *American Journal of Sociology*, **122** (3), 886–929.
Golden, L., J. Henly, and S. Lambert (2013), 'Work schedule flexibility: a contributor to happiness?', *Journal of Social Research & Policy*, **4** (2), 107–35.
Gordon, R., M. Usdansky, Z. Wang, and A. Gluzman (2011), 'Child care and mothers' mental health: is high-quality care associated with fewer depressive symptoms?', *Family Relations*, **60**, 446–60.
Gornick, J. and M. Meyers (2003), *Families That Work: Policies for Reconciling Parenthood and Employment*, New York: Russell Sage.
Grzywacz, J., D. Carlson, and S. Shulkin (2008), 'Schedule flexibility and stress: linking formal flexible arrangements and perceived flexibility to employee health', *Community, Work & Family*, **11** (2), 199–214.
Hansen, T. (2012), 'Parenthood and happiness: a review of folk theories versus empirical evidence', *Social Indicators Research*, **108**, 29–64.
Hansen, T., B. Slagsvold, and T. Moum (2009), 'Childlessness and psychological well-being in midlife and old age: an examination of parental status effects across a range of outcomes', *Social Indicators Research*, **94**, 343–62.
Hegewisch, A. and J. Gornick (2008), *Statutory Routes to Workplace Flexibility in Cross-national Perspective*, Washington, DC: Institute for Women's Policy Research (IWPR).
Heymann, J. (2000), *The Widening Gap: Why Americans' Working Families are in Jeopardy and What Can Be Done About It?* New York: Basic Books.

Heymann, J., A. Earle, and J. Hayeset (2007), *The Work, Family, and Equity Index: How Does the United States Measure Up?* Montreal: McGill University, Institute for Health and Social Policy.

Hilgeman, C. and C. Butts (2009), 'Women's employment and fertility: a welfare regime paradox', *Social Science Research*, **38** (1), 103–17.

House, J., K. Landis, and D. Umberson (1988), 'Social relationships and health', *Science*, **241**, 540–45.

Hyde, J., M. Klein, M. Essex, and R. Clark (1995), 'Maternity leave and women's mental health', *Psychology of Women Quarterly*, **19**, 257–85.

Kahneman, D., A. Krueger, D. Schkade, N. Schwarz, and A. Stone (2004), 'A survey method for characterizing daily life experience: The day reconstruction method', *Science*, **306**, 1776–80.

Kahneman, D., D. Schkade, C. Fischler, A. Krueger, and A. Krilla (2010), 'The structure of well-being in two cities: life satisfaction and experienced well-being in Columbus, Ohio and Rennes, France', in E. Diener, J.F. Helliwell, and D. Kahneman (eds), *International Differences in Well-being*, New York: Oxford University Press, pp. 16–33.

Kohler, H., F.C. Billari, and J. Ortega (2006), 'Low fertility in Europe: causes, implications and policy options', in F.R. Harris (ed.), *The Baby Bust: Who Will Do the Work? Who Will Pay the Taxes?* Lanham, MD: Rowman & Littlefield, pp. 48–109.

Koropeckyj-Cox, T. (2002), 'Beyond parental status: psychological well-being in middle and old age', *Journal of Marriage and Family*, **64**, 957–71.

Kravdal, Ø. (1996), 'How the local supply of day-care centers influences fertility in Norway: a parity-specific approach', *Population Research and Policy Review*, **15**, 201–18.

Liefbroer, A. (2005), 'The impact of perceived costs and rewards of childbearing on entry into parenthood: evidence from a panel study', *European Journal of Population*, **21**, 367–91.

Margolis, R. and M. Myrskylä (2011), 'A global perspective on happiness and fertility', *Population and Development Review*, **37**, 29–56.

Margolis, R. and M. Myrskylä (2015), 'Parental well-being surrounding first birth as a determinant of further parity progression', *Demography*, **52** (4), 1147–66.

Mather, M. (2012), 'Fact sheet: the decline in US fertility', World Population Data Sheet, Population Reference Bureau, accessed 26 September 2016 at http://www.prb.org/publications/datasheets/2012/world-population-data-sheet/fact-sheet-us-population.aspx.

Mattingly, M. and S. Bianchi (2003), 'Gender differences in the quantity and quality of free time: the U.S. experience', *Social Forces*, **81** (3), 999–1030.

Mattingly, M. and L. Sayer (2006), 'Under pressure: gender differences in the relationship between free time and feeling rushed', *Journal of Marriage and Family*, **68** (1), 205–21.

McCrate, E. (2005), 'Flexible hours, workplace authority, and compensating wage differentials in the U.S.', *Feminist Economics*, **11**, 11–39.

McDonald, P. (1997), 'Gender equity, social institutions, and the future of fertility', in *Women's Status and Family Dynamics*, Paris: UNESCO, pp. 13–33.

McLanahan, S. (1983), 'Family structure and stress: a longitudinal comparison of two-parent and female-headed families', *Journal of Marriage and Family*, **45**, 347–57.

McLanahan, S. and J. Adams (1989), 'The effects of children on adults' psychological well-being: 1957–1976', *Social Forces*, **68**, 124–46.

Meadows, S., S. McLanahan, and J. Brooks-Gunn (2008), 'Stability and change in family structure and maternal health trajectories', *American Sociological Review*, **73** (2), 314–34.

Milkie, M., A. Bierman, and S. Schieman (2008), 'How adult children influence older parents' mental health: integrating stress-process and life-course perspectives', *Social Psychology Quarterly*, **71**, 86–105.

Milkie, M., S. Raley, and S. Bianchi (2009), 'Taking on the second shift: time allocations and time pressures of U.S. parents with preschoolers', *Social Forces*, **88** (2), 487–517.

Mirowsky, J. and C. Ross (2003), *Social Causes of Psychological Distress*, New York: Aldine.

Misra, J., M. Budig, and S. Moller (2007), 'Reconciliation policies and the effects of motherhood on employment, earnings, and poverty', *Journal of Comparative Policy Analysis*, **9** (2), 135–55.

Misra, J., M. Budig, and I. Boeckman (2011), 'Work-family policies and the effects of children on women's employment hours and wages', *Community, Work & Family*, **14** (2), 139–57.

Nelson, S., K. Kushlev, and S. Lyubomirsky (2013), 'The pains and pleasures of parenting: when, why, and how is parenthood associated with more or less well-being?', *Psychological Bulletin*, **104**, 846–95.

Nomaguchi, K. (2009), 'Change in work-family conflict among employed parents between 1977 and 1997', *Journal of Marriage and Family*, **71** (1), 15–32.

Nomaguchi, K. and M. Milkie (2003), 'Costs and rewards of children: the effects of becoming a parent on adults' lives', *Journal of Marriage and Family*, **66**, 413–30.

Nomaguchi, K., M. Milkie, and S. Bianchi (2005), 'Time strains and psychological well-being: do dual earner mothers and fathers differ?', *Journal of Family Issues*, **26**, 756–92.

Offer, S. and B. Schneider (2011), 'Revisiting the gender gap in time-use patterns: multitasking and well-being among mothers and fathers in dual-earner families', *American Sociological Review*, **76** (6), 809–33.

Ono, H. and K. Lee (2013), 'Welfare states and the redistribution of happiness', *Social Forces*, **92**, 789–814.

Pearlin, L. (1989), 'The sociological study of stress', *Journal of Health and Social Behavior*, **30**, 241–56.

Pedulla, D. and S. Thébaud (2015), 'Can we finish the revolution? Gender, work-family ideals, and institutional constraint', *American Sociological Review*, **80** (1), 116–39.

Pettit, B. and J. Hook (2009), *Gendered Tradeoffs: Family, Social Policy, and Economic Inequality in Twenty-one Countries*, New York: Russell Sage Foundation.

Pollman-Schult, M. (2014), 'Parenthood and life satisfaction: why don't children make people happy?', *Journal of Marriage and Family*, **76**, 319–36.

Pudrovska, T. (2009), 'Parenthood, stress, and psychological well-being in late midlife and early old age', *International Journal of Aging and Human Development*, **68**, 127–47.

Ray, R., J. Gornick, and J. Schmitt (2009), 'Who cares? Assessing generosity and gender equality in parental leave policy designs in 21 countries', *Journal of European Social Policy*, **19**, 196–216.

Ross, C. and J. Mirowsky (1988), 'Childcare and emotional adjustment to wives' employment', *Journal of Health and Social Behavior*, **29** (2), 127–38.

Ross, C. and M. Van Willigen (1996), 'Gender, parenthood, and anger', *Journal of Marriage and Family*, **58**, 572–84.

Savolainen, J., E. Lahelma, K. Silventionen, A. Gauthier, and K. Silventoinen (2001), 'Parenthood and psychological well-being in Finland: does public policy make a difference?', *Journal of Comparative Family Studies*, **32**, 61–74.

Simon, R. (1992), 'Parental role strains, salience of parental identity and gender differences in psychological distress', *Journal of Health and Social Behavior*, **33** (1), 25–35.

Simon, R. (1998), 'Assessing sex differences in vulnerability among employed parents: the importance of marital status', *Journal of Health and Social Behavior*, **39**, 37–53.

Simon, R. (2008), 'The joys of parenthood, reconsidered', *Contexts*, **7**, 40–45.

Simon, R. and J. Caputo (n.d.), 'Parenthood in the United States: are there *any* benefits for the health and happiness of adults?', Unpublished manuscript, Wake Forest University and Max Planck Institute for Demographic Research.

Stanca, L. (2012), 'Suffer the little children: measuring the effects of parenthood on well-being worldwide', *Journal of Economic Behavior and Organization*, **81**, 742–50.

Umberson, D. and W. Gove (1989), 'Parenthood and psychological well-being: theory, measurement, and stage in the family life course', *Journal of Family Issues*, **10**, 440–62.

Umberson, D., T. Pudrovska, and C. Reczek (2010), 'Parenthood, childlessness, and well-being: a life course perspective', *Journal of Marriage and Family*, **72**, 612–29.

Umberson, D., K. Williams, and M. Thomeer (2013), 'Family status and mental health: recent advances and future directions', in C.S. Aneshensel and J.C. Phelan (eds), *Handbook of the Sociology of Mental Health* (second edn), Heidelberg: Springer, pp. 405–31.

Warren, E. and A. Tyagi (2004), *The Two-parent Trap: Why Middle-class Parents are Going Broke*, New York: Basic Books.

Woo, H. and R. Raley (2005), 'A small extension to "Costs and rewards of children: the effects of becoming a parent on adults' lives"', *Journal of Marriage and Family*, **67**, 216–21.

PART VI

FUTURE CHALLENGES FOR POLICY MAKING AND RESEARCH

26. Policies on family support and parenting support in a global perspective
Mary Daly

INTRODUCTION

Family-related concerns feature strongly in discourses about contemporary society. The stability and functioning of the family and the activity of child-rearing, along with factors relating to children's well-being and early development, usually dominate these debates. This is not empty rhetoric for there is evidence of a growth of both policy and provision oriented to family support and parenting support (see also Chapter 12, by Knijn, Martin and Ostner in this volume). While the two types of policy are not always defined in practice and there are overlaps between them, the former tends to be oriented to strengthening family functioning while the latter focuses more on parental practices around child-rearing. Relatively little is known about these developments in a global perspective and it is to this gap in knowledge that this piece orients itself. The chapter has two main aims: to identify key developments in regard to the forms and modalities of relevant policies and to assess the developments. The overall goal is to identify the evolving policy and uncover the extent to which concerns about the family and the role and practices of parents are mobilising policy agency in different parts of the world.

The chapter is based empirically on evidence gathered in 2014 as part of a UNICEF Office of Research project on family support and parenting support (Daly et al., 2015). Temporally, the analysis follows developments since 2000 or thereabouts. Four types of evidence were gathered and analysed as part of the research: a review of some 120 policy and other documents describing and outlining policy and provision; evidence gathered on 33 low- and middle-income countries by UNICEF country and regional offices; an expert consultation meeting on the subject organised by the UNICEF Office of Research in May 2014; and a detailed examination of the following nine country cases: Belarus, Chile, China, Croatia, England, Jamaica, Philippines, South Africa and Sweden. These countries were chosen so as to represent variation in: regional spread; social policy position on the family; policy modality and approach to family support and parenting support. As a selective set of case studies, the limitations should be noted especially in that the analysis may overstate the movement to family and parenting support globally and underestimate informal provision given that the latter may not show up in official policy or national coordination documents. The discussion and analysis that follow draw centrally from this evidence base and the overview report that was subsequently published (Daly et al., 2015).

DEVELOPMENTS OVERALL

Taking an overview of the global situation in this first section before we go into the detailed breakdown, the evidence suggests that family support and parenting support are active fields of policy across the range of settings considered in the research. This is not the case everywhere though – of the nine case study countries China and South Africa are notable for the relative underdevelopment of policy on both family support and parenting support. In both of these countries provisions for such support exist (offered especially by non-governmental organisations (NGOs) or through partnerships between the public authorities and NGOs) but in neither country are they an especially strong or widespread domain of public policy. The two Western European countries included among the case studies – England and Sweden – form the opposing end of the continuum with a very highly developed set of programmes and services oriented to both family and parenting support. Some of the provisions are long-standing in these two countries – for example, support to mothers of newborn and toddler children and social work for families – but others are relatively recent (such as the growth of parenting programmes and the adoption of a national policy on parenting support). But before we conclude that this is due to a regional or geographical pattern, we should note that Jamaica is another country where parenting support is highly developed. In fact, the country's family policy is mainly anchored in parenting support (Samms-Vaughan and Margaria, 2015). The policy focus on parenting support can be traced back to the early 1990s but since 2012 Jamaica has had a national parenting support policy which lays out a coordinated set of programmes and activities for work with parents of all children under 18 years. The Philippines is another interesting case in that it has had a Parent Effectiveness Service since 1978. Originally developed by the Social Welfare Project of the Department of Social Welfare and Development as support for families with young children at the barangay (village) level, it was reintroduced in 1991 as a component of early childhood education provision (Bruckauf, 2015a).

When one steps back from particular countries, some regional patterning is evident also. Looked at globally, Europe is the region where family support and parenting support are strongest whereas in other regions of the world – for example, South East Asia and sub-Saharan Africa – systematic, government-led support either for families or parenting is rare. Regions where policy seems to be developing strongly include Western Europe, the Central and Eastern European and Commonwealth of Independent States regions, Latin America and some parts of Africa and Asia.

It is rare for either family support or parenting support to have a unique policy space – in only a few national settings is this the case. More usually, family support and parenting support provisions extend into or emerge from a number of existing policy domains. Most widely, the following are the policy domains interlinking (to various degrees in different settings) with family support and parenting support:

- social/family services
- child protection
- early childhood education
- health
- education
- social protection programmes including cash transfers.

While these are the broad policy contexts, when we start to drill down deeper into the policy and provision in practice, it becomes important to differentiate between support that focuses on the family and that which targets parenting. Family support and parenting support are potentially quite different entities with the former oriented to the collective entity of family whereas the latter is more concerned with the practices of parents in how they rear their child(ren). Of the two the parenting-related measures are the narrower in terms of policy focus. They also tend to be the newer. Indeed, parenting is itself a relatively new term. While some professional uses of the term can be traced to the 1950s – and even earlier in Sweden with Gunnar and Alva Myrdal who advocated for parenting as an explicit policy aim – its popularisation into the everyday language of parenting manuals, parenting practice and so forth was generalised from the 1970s on (Faircloth et al., 2013; Lee, 2014; Smith, 2010). As a field of policy, parenting support is also relatively new whereas family support is more often a new term for support services that have existed for families for a long period, especially in the highly developed countries. Although they can of course overlap – most parenting-related policy, for example, assumes a family setting – it is best to treat them as distinct.

FORMS AND MODALITIES OF FAMILY SUPPORT

The evidence suggests that, where it exists, family support is being developed as an arm of family and child policy. It is being taken forward in two main forms:

- services to families with children – especially social, health and psychological services
- the establishment or reorientation of economic support to families and especially cash payments to incorporate a family psycho-social dimension.

Of the two, services have a stronger orientation to family functioning than cash benefits or economic support. As a service or set of services, family support is most recognisable as the equivalent of classic social casework services directed at families. Counselling or family development sessions are often a core element here and, depending on national infrastructure and the resources available, can take the form of a less intensive (and hence less resource costly) form of classic social work services for families. These services tend to be targeted rather than universal (although they may exist within a universalist orientation, especially in the high-income countries). The different family situations that are most frequently the focus of family support policies include: families in poverty and/or those in marginalised sectors of the population (such as migrants or ethnic minorities); those where the children have special needs (such as a disability of some kind); those where the children are considered to be subject to some kind of risk (such as violence, child neglect or abandonment); or situations where children are in need of kinship or other forms of non-parental care (e.g., due to neglect, orphanhood or HIV/AIDS).

Across countries the well-being of children appears to be the dominant motivation for family support services. The precipitating 'problem' varies regionally however. For example, in West and Southern Africa and South East Asia countering violence in child-rearing and abuse of children tends to dominate as precipitators of child welfare service interventions. In the Central and Eastern European and Commonwealth of Independent States countries, these risks also prevail but the momentum is also around reducing and preventing institutional care and increasing the numbers of children being reared in a stable family environment. The Belarussian and Croatian case studies underline that the measures are part of a paradigm shift towards elevating parental and family responsibility for child-rearing and downgrading the role of the state as a substitute for parents or family (Daly et al., 2015). In comparative perspective, family support tends to have a more preventative orientation in Europe but there, as elsewhere, the ideal of early child development as a policy exigency is also driving developments.

The second main form through which family support is being developed is cash payments to families for children. While these have long existed in the high-income countries, they are not only new in some settings but are being introduced or developed specifically for the purpose of improving child-rearing – it is for this reason that they should be understood as family support (Daly et al., 2015, p. 9). A quite widespread development – the United Nations (UN) has indicated that some 25 million households (equivalent to some 133 million people) in 18 countries of Latin America and the Caribbean receive conditional cash transfers (United Nations, 2012, p. 4) – conditional cash transfers could be characterised as a new generation of cash payments to families in that receipt of them carries conditions which are in turn pinned closely to bringing about a change in behaviour, especially in regard to child-rearing. In essence, to the extent that the new generation of cash benefits are being used explicitly to target and change aspects of familial functioning around child-rearing, they can be deemed a form of parenting support (Chopra, 2013). While it is arguable whether they should be considered as 'support' or a form of compulsion, they are typically intended as a double-pronged anti-poverty measure involving both income redistribution and the stimulation of human capital development by, for example, increasing the demand for school services and/or health services (European Commission, 2014). Notably, the programmes typically select women (usually the mother or the woman responsible for children in the household) as the primary recipient of the transfer. For some (e.g., Jenson, 2015) they are evidence of a new maternalism in social policy whereby social policies construct mothers as agents of child and family change. Conditional cash transfers have been the subject of both positive and negative research and commentary.[1]

There are a number of relatively novel aspects to conditional cash transfers. They are, for example, acting to blur a classic social policy differentiation between services and cash transfers. One sees this especially in programmes where casework and psycho-social support with and for families is a core part of the service constellation associated with the conditional cash transfer. One example is the kind of services offered as part of the conditional cash transfer programme *Chile Puente* (Chile Bridge). Set within the general social protection system (*Chile Solidario*), it is a form of personalised intervention targeted on particular families; to receive the cash transfer they must cooperate with a social worker as part of an agreed plan aimed at creating or restoring the family's capacities and basic functions (Bruckauf, 2015b). In fact, the family's participation and rights and obligations are formalised through a family contract signed for a period of 24 months. This sets out mutual responsibilities for the state and the family to work towards improving the family's conditions of living. A family counsellor ('support worker') assists the family in the following key areas: family life; personal identification; health and education; family dynamics; housing conditions; and employment/income. Work with the family can be quite intensive. A first phase involves 14 home visiting sessions which are thematically structured and delivered through discussion and a 'board game' with visual and other communication aids. This is followed by eight more sessions spread over a longer period (not exceeding two years). The goal is to effect a change in the family's dynamics through a custom-made plan of action. In effect, measures such as these seek to change a family's situation and the mental disposition of the parents through counselling and psycho-social support.

Of course developments within and across countries do not always align or pattern neatly. Countries also tend to follow a pattern that is specific or unique to them, which means that there are numerous specificities in how family support is understood and practised. For example, in China family support is mainly associated with intergenerational support within the family, especially regarding the provision of support and care to older relatives. The cross-national variations hinge quite closely on the meaning of family and the history and legitimacy of public policy on family-related issues. And yet while acknowledging national particularities, there are signs that supporting the ecological basis to families is a common underlying discourse and it seems to be accepted that what is needed is that families can uncover their own resources or be provided with support that helps them to integrate better into their 'community'. Hence, one sees the use of volunteers or community members engaged in offering family support in countries such as Belarus and the Philippines (although this may also be because of a lack of professionals).

FORMS AND MODALITIES OF PARENTING SUPPORT

Parenting support is also growing. The 'need' that it seeks to meet is to provide parents with information, education or training and practical support in regard to child-rearing. In comparison to family support, it is more of a niche policy, being the newer and smaller of the two domains. It is at its most developed in the high-income countries – suggesting that an existing infrastructure or platform of family-related provision provides a route or encouragement towards the development of policies focused around parenting. But from family policy to parenting policy is not an essential route or path of development, however, given cases like Jamaica where parenting education and support comprise the main plank of family policy.

Turning to look at the policy detail, variation is again widespread but parenting support seems to take two main forms as a service offer:

- health-related interventions for both parents and young children
- education and/or general support for parents.

As a health-related intervention, parenting support is mainly pursued through home visiting, usually for parents (mothers most typically) of infants and toddlers. This is the oldest form of parenting support in most countries – usually organised as part of maternal and child health services and delivered by nurses or para-professionals with some medical training (depending on the setting and context). The measures tend to be organised around two functions: health checks for and supervision of mother and baby, and informing and educating parents (usually mothers) about infant and child health and well-being.

This is the parenting support service that is most likely to be universal, in the high- and middle-income countries especially. But one sees some renewal of and change in this service in Western Europe. In England, for example, a Family Nurse Partnership service has been introduced with a specific focus on vulnerable mothers (especially those who are young and becoming mothers for the first time). A similar development has occurred in Germany with *Familienhebamme* (Ostner and Stolberg, 2015). These services often commence before birth, especially in the case of vulnerable mothers and families (although in Sweden they tend to be universal and also compulsory – conceived to improve general population health and well-being) and they continue for much of the child's first year.

This is a service that lends itself well to community and volunteer engagement. In some parts of South Africa, for example, community members are trained and supervised in the task of visiting expectant and new mothers regularly over a period of one year, to offer support through listening, guidance and information on a range of topics (Bray, 2015). These services are designed and run by the voluntary sector, often with financial support from private donors, then delivered through local government contracts to NGOs. According to Bray (2015), they are conceived as interventions that encompass knowledge of early childhood development, skills in affect-related care and early stimulation, and adherence to practices to protect child well-being (such as immunisation and regular health checks, monitoring children's care by others). While the service is directed at parents and their infants, delivery by local para-professionals (known as 'family and community motivators' or 'mentor mothers') is envisaged to bolster informal support mechanisms within the community.

The second main form of parenting support service is also oriented to informing and educating parents but it extends beyond health and new parenthood. At the core here are general educational programmes, one-to-one counselling, and coaching or peer mentoring in a community context designed either to improve parents' knowledge or 'upskill' them in parenting practices or techniques. This may be offered as part of early childhood education, school-parent liaison, family mediation as well as child protection and family welfare services. In some countries, for example, parents attend information, coaching and training sessions at the early education and care centres which their children are attending. In other countries, specific family service centres exist or have been set up (e.g., Belarus, Croatia, England, Jamaica, Philippines). In Jamaica, for example, these take the form of 'parents' places' – described more as a concept than a building, they are locations where parents can receive relevant information, attend courses or workshops, and receive referrals to other services (Samms-Vaughan and Margaria, 2015). In a less intensive form, parenting education may be made available through information sheets or booklets as well as websites, television campaigns and telephone helplines. Of these, information sheets and booklets are arguably the most widespread form of parenting support globally.

Parenting (education) programmes are an important form of parenting support across the countries covered by the UNICEF research (Daly et al., 2015). The number of programmes operating in a particular country may not be large or coverage may not be widespread but such programmes are very significant in that they contribute to a discourse about what is 'wrong' with parenting and how it can be fixed. In effect, they take forward a particular set of values and model of 'good parenting', based on a range of theories, mainly those of developmental psychologists (Lucas, 2011). They are particularly popular in the high-income countries from which they mainly originate.

Such parenting programmes are standardised, typically manual based, and delivered in packages of 8–12 sessions during which parents are taught about child development and offered the opportunity to reflect upon their own parenting beliefs and practices. While they usually have some in-built flexibility, they are essentially taking forward an orientation around parenting that is 'biased' towards the experience and predilections of elites in the richer countries. Another defining characteristic is that they typically have an assembled evidence base around operation or impact (although this is not necessarily evidence from the country where the programme is being applied).[2]

A somewhat different medium of parenting support intervention – and an alternative to the parenting programmes (especially in the middle- and low-income countries) – is also education based but takes the form of parental education measures through group work or home visits that seek to improve early stimulation of language and cognition and related abilities in children. These – like other constituent elements of parenting support – fall within the area of early education development. While these do not fall clearly under the heading of 'parenting support' or 'parenting programme' – and where they exist tend to be part of (early) education or childhood policy – they do contain parental support components which are often combined with interventions pertaining to health, nutrition and caregiver psycho-social well-being (Evans, 2006).

Parenting support is not exclusively about the provision of information, education or skills though. In some cases, the type of support provided approximates more to the core meaning of 'support', in the sense of peer support, or social support more broadly. Befriending and mobilising community support can be important modes of parenting support also. Enabling networks and networking among parents is both a goal and a modus operandi. In Sweden there is increased provision of centres or forums for parents to gather and build mutually supportive networks. The Parents' Places – local community-based information and service centres (including recreational services) – which exist widely in Jamaica are another example. There are similar developments in other countries also, and especially regions of the world which take a more communal approach to child-rearing. Networking and generating social support may also seek to counter the discrimination or stigma which faces certain families. To identify health and education as the two main orientations of parenting support does not mean that the relevant services are exclusively in the domain of health and/or education. Parenting support tends to cross service areas. And in this regard it is worth pointing out that it may also fall under the social policy (e.g., as in the conditional cash transfers).

ROOTS AND IMPLICATIONS

So where have these provisions come from and what type or types of family-related policy development do they represent?

They have not originated from any single source but represent a constellation of accepted practice in today's world. There are, however, a number of key developments that are pertinent to both explanation and critique.

Ideas about children and childhood have had centre stage in many of the developments identified as family and parenting support in this chapter. While there are different influences feeding into this, in my view the developments are mainly traceable in one way or another to the focus on children required by the wide acceptance of the UN Convention on the Rights of the Child and the 'space' it has opened up for policy innovation and intervention in a series of related fields. While children were to the foreground in the Convention, parents and families (as well as states parties) were formally recognised as having obligations to enable children's rights to be realised. The Convention, then, provided a 'space' for agency around the child, parenting and family policy. In particular, states were required to focus on how their obligations could be realised in policy and practice. But agency extends beyond states too.

A range of professional and academic actors – neuroscientists and psychologists to the fore among them – have become important actors in the field, in effect ratcheting up the stakes involved in child-rearing. With scientific researchers now claiming to be able to identify the deleterious effects of childhood disadvantage on subsequent progress through life, governments are urged to consider early childhood education and development as a core domain of public policy. There is not just a growing recognition but a sense of urgency about getting the conditions of early childhood – and especially early child development – right. A child-centred human investment agenda is prioritised in a number of the countries studied, something shared by both the high- and medium- to low-income nations. Countries as far apart as the Philippines and Sweden aspire to create the conditions for a healthy, productive next generation for example. The academic community has also played another role – in emphasising the possibility and importance of evidence-based policy, scholars have promoted particular interventions over others (and especially elevated manualised parenting programmes above other interventions because of their claimed success rate – see Knerr et al., 2013).

A further key set of actors are the international policy agencies and NGOs. They play a crucial role as policy entrepreneurs, especially in the medium- to low-income countries where they actively promote and directly engage in family and parenting support-oriented services. In particular, UNICEF and Save the Children are active in many of the countries studied for this research. In China, for example, Purposeful Parenting for Working Parents – a training component of a wider project conducted by the Centre for the Child's Rights and Corporate Social Responsibility – was pioneered by Save the Children, China as part of its global programme 'Strengthening Families'. It aims at reaching internal migrant workers whose children are left behind in home towns and villages. The training is made up of three key modules: parents' well-being; understanding your child; remote parenting (Save the Children, 2012). The latter is especially oriented to the parents of the more than 61 million children estimated to be 'left behind' by parental migration within China.

Together, these developments are at once generating and a part of an international discourse in the public and policy-making spheres which takes forward a greater acceptance of the state's role in intervening in family life, especially for the purpose of elevating parental responsibility and competence. The general backdrop is of increasing awareness of crises in children's lives. Research in Jamaica speaks of 'child shifting' whereby children are regularly moved among families and caretakers (Samms-Vaughan and Margaria, 2015); in China the many so-called 'left behind children' create a sense of urgency, whereas in sub-Saharan Africa, the pandemic of HIV/AIDS has profoundly affected children and this together with political unrest has led to a diversification of family forms and a major reduction in the numbers of caregivers available to children. The existence of high rates of violence against children in homes and communities, including corporal punishment, is also now increasingly seen as a problem by decision makers.

SIGNIFICANCE FOR SOCIAL AND FAMILY POLICY

This chapter confirms family support and parenting support as one of the growth areas in social policy and suggests that, viewed from a global perspective, family continues to be a powerful motivator of political agency and policy reform. The developments reviewed here also suggest that a concern with the quality and conduct of rather intimate elements of family life is at the core of a new momentum in social policy. For while family and parenting support have diverse roots, they rest fundamentally on a philosophy about the family and place emphasis on optimum familial functioning and parental child-rearing. This differs in key respects to the social investment approach – which is widely considered to be a leading philosophy underlying social and family policy growth at the present time (Morel et al., 2012; see also Chapter 9 by Lee and Baek in this volume). Where social investment argues for a growth in services oriented to the education and development of young children, and therefore spells a movement of children outside the home in key respects, family support and parenting support both represent a move back to the home. Family support – which this chapter has suggested needs to be differentiated from parenting support – in particular carries forward a strong familialist orientation, in several respects. First, in the high-income western countries especially, family support has developed as an alternative approach to initiatives targeting problems in individualised ways or in a manner that undermines the family as a collective unit of care and maintenance. It rests also on a particular understanding of the best way of harnessing family as a way of addressing such problems but also seeing the family as a problem (Pinkerton et al., 2004). The perspective has ecological, social integrationist roots. Relationships, interdependencies, support networks and local setting are the lingua franca of family support, and constitute the philosophical framework within which it understands and seeks to affect family life. With family isolation and lack of social support seen as a central concern, the perspective is especially oriented to integration of families into a range of social networks. In this respect, therefore, it highlights both informal support and social integration (Dunst, 1995). A further defining characteristic of family support is a focus on the strengths as against deficits of families and a recognition of families' capacity to define and respond to their own needs, provided they have the necessary support (Pinkerton et al., 2004). In key respects, then, the promotion of family support represents either a return to the family or continued support for the family as a collective institution.

In terms of what it portends about state policy, parenting support is similar in many respects. The fact that parenting support as a policy development represents a renewed interest on the part of the state and public discourse in how parents and caregivers approach and execute their role of child-rearing suggests neither a privatisation of parenting nor a disinvestment in family. Actually, in some ways it represents the opposite – greater intervention in processes heretofore considered 'private' (especially parenting of children beyond the toddler stage). However, parenting support has stronger individualistic tendencies than family support in that it locates the responsibility for parenting with parents rather than, for example, the state or the public authorities (Ramaekers and

Suissa, 2012). So while it confers resources on parents (especially information and skills), there is a sense in which such resourcing of parents spells a greater expectation of high performing parents who follow the guidelines and deliver the kind of child behaviour which is considered desirable.

CONCLUSION

This chapter has identified and explored a trend towards a growth of family policy and parenting support. The development centres on measures that seek to provide a range of resources (typically termed 'support') to improve familial functioning and increase parents' information, skills and competence for child-rearing. While the developments can be closely related in particular countries – and their exact form varies according to the family policy infrastructure that is in place (if any) – I have suggested here that for analytic purposes it is helpful to treat family support and parenting support as separate. This is for several reasons. First, as policies they differ in terms of their aims, orientations and underlying philosophies. Family support is oriented to the well-being and functioning of the collective unit of family (mainly understood as nuclear) and has an ecological understanding of family whereby it seeks to both improve the strengths of families and embed families in a range of 'support networks'. Parenting support is narrower in its remit in that it is primarily focused on parents and their way of child-rearing (as against family life more broadly) and seeks not just to offer resources to parents but also effect changes in how (some) parents rear their children.

A second reason why family and parenting support need to be differentiated is because they differ empirically in regard to where and how they are implemented in policy. Parenting support frequently sits alongside family support policy but it can also be a standalone policy in a setting where there is no developed family policy or indeed where family policy has tended to have a different focus. In some national settings the growth of family and/or parenting support involves the introduction of new policies and provisions; in others it involves a reorientation or reframing of existing policies. One has to distinguish between the high-income countries where policy is very well developed and where parenting support represents a specialisation of existing policy in a context of a well-developed policy architecture compared to the low- and middle-income regions of the world where family support and parenting support are expected to achieve a more generic set of outcomes and where they are much less specific in concrete policy terms.

What is new in these measures? These policies represent in some senses a dawning realisation that families need public 'support' – while of course the nature of that support varies and may be oriented to the control of individuals and families rather than the more neutral 'support'. From as far afield as the Commonwealth of Independent States to South Africa, the developments have roots in a desire to increase the family's care-giving resources. They can be part of a conservative discourse on 'the family' and they often go together with a wish to strengthen community and informal support systems (e.g., in Jamaica and South Africa). It is little surprise then that for some they are the latest incarnation of processes around controlling family and private life (Gillies, 2005), whereas for others they are a response to a genuine crisis of family and extant dysfunctional responses on the part of the state and other agents towards families (Pinkerton et al., 2004).

In essence, what I am suggesting here is that the measures have more than one type or level of significance and manifestation. First, there is a range of 'interested actors' involved (including professionals, academics, the international organisations, NGOs as well as the state). Second, from a social and family policy perspective, they portend a number of relevant developments and trends. They represent a blurring of the boundaries between cash transfers and services as modes of policy and in key respects are an alternative approach to that of social investment which is prominent nowadays. For this and other reasons, they pose an analytic challenge to the existing frameworks for studying family policy. These tend to focus mainly on cash transfers to the relative neglect of family-based services (with the possible excepton of childcare). If research is to take account of developments like family support and parenting support, we need to broaden our frameworks to include services along with cash transfers, to see the two as related, and to be mindful that family policy is a field where there is considerable diversity, policy change and policy innovation.

NOTES

1. See Milazzo (2009) for a broad-ranging regional overview of research results on conditional cash transfers.
2. There is a very large literature on parenting programmes, so much so that it is impossible to do justice to the literature. For good overviews see Evans (2006) and the papers collected at https://fyi.uwex.edu/whatworkswisconsin/ (accessed 10 July 2018).

REFERENCES

Bray, R. (2015), 'South Africa', in M. Daly, R. Bray, J. Byrne, Z. Bruckauf, A. Margaria, N. Pecnik, and M. Samms-Vaughan (eds), *Family and Parenting Support Policy and Provision in a Global Context*, Innocenti Insight, Florence: UNICEF Office of Research, pp. 91–7.

Bruckauf, Z. (2015a), 'The Philippines', in M. Daly, R. Bray, J. Byrne, Z. Bruckauf, A. Margaria, N. Pecnik, and M. Samms-Vaughan (eds), *Family and Parenting Support Policy and Provision in a Global Context*, Innocenti Insight, Florence: UNICEF Office of Research, pp. 84–90.

Bruckauf, Z. (2015b), 'Chile', in M. Daly, R. Bray, J. Byrne, Z. Bruckauf, A. Margaria, N. Pecnik, and M. Samms-Vaughan (eds), *Family and Parenting Support Policy and Provision in a Global Context*, Innocenti Insight, Florence: UNICEF Office of Research, pp. 48–54.

Chopra, D. (ed.) (2013), *A Feminist Political Economy Analysis of Public Policies Related to Care: A Thematic Review*, Evidence Report No. 9, Brighton: Institute of Development Studies.

Daly, M., R. Bray, J. Byrne, Z. Bruckauf, A. Margaria, N. Pecnik, and M. Samms-Vaughan (eds) (2015), *Family and Parenting Support Policy and Provision in a Global Context*, Innocenti Insight, Florence: UNICEF Office of Research.

Dunst, C. (ed.) (1995), *Key Characteristics and Features of Community-based Family Support Programs*, Chicago, IL: Family Support America.

European Commission (2014), *Study of Conditional Cash Transfers and their Impact on Children*, Final Report Volume 1, Brussels: European Commission.

Evans, J.L. (2006), 'Parenting programmes: an important ECD intervention strategy', Background paper prepared for the Education for All Global Monitoring Report 2007, http://unesdoc.unesco.org/images/0014/001474/147461e.pdf (accessed 10 July 2018).

Faircloth, C., D.M. Hoffman, and L.L. Layne (2013), 'Introduction', in C. Faircloth, D.M. Hoffman, and L.L. Layne (eds), *Parenting in Global Perspective: Negotiating Ideologies of Kinship, Self and Politics*, London: Routledge, pp. 1–19.

Gillies, V. (2005), 'Meeting parents' needs? Discourses of "support" and "inclusion" in family policy', *Critical Social Policy*, **25** (1), 70–90.

Jenson, J. (2015), 'The fading goal of gender equality: three policy directions that underpin the resilience of gendered socio-economic inequalities', *Social Politics*, **22** (4), 539–60.

Knerr, W., F. Gardner, and L. Cluver (2013), 'Improving positive parenting skills and reducing harsh and abusive parenting in low- and middle-income countries: a systematic review', *Prevention Science*, **14**, 352–63.

Lee, E. (2014), 'Introduction', in E. Lee, J. Bristow, C. Faircloth, and J. Macvarish (eds), *Parenting Culture Studies*, Houndmills, Basingstoke: Palgrave Macmillan, pp 1–22.

Lucas, P. (2011), 'Some reflections on the rhetoric of parenting programmes: evidence, theory, and social policy', *Journal of Family Therapy*, **33**, 181–98.

Milazzo, A. (ed.) (2009), *Conditional Cash Transfers: An Annotated Bibliography*, Washington, DC: World Bank.

Morel, N., J. Palme, and B. Palier (eds) (2012), *Towards a Social Investment Welfare State? Ideas, Policies and Challenges*, Bristol: Policy Press.

Ostner, I. and C. Stolberg (2015), 'Investing in children: monitoring parents', *Social Policy & Society*, **14** (4), 621–32.

Pinkerton, J., P. Dolan, and J. Canavan (eds) (2004), *Family Support in Ireland*, Dublin: Stationery Office.

Ramaekers, S. and J. Suissa (eds) (2012), *The Claims of Parenting: Reasons, Responsibility and Society*, Dordrecht: Springer.

Samms-Vaughan, M. and A. Margaria (2015), 'Jamaica', in M. Daly, R. Bray, J. Byrne, Z. Bruckauf, A. Margaria, N. Pecnik, and M. Samms-Vaughan (eds), *Family and Parenting Support Policy and Provision in a Global Context*, Innocenti Insight, Florence: UNICEF Office of Research, pp. 76–83.

Save the Children (2012), *Strengthening Families. Save the Children Programmes in Support of Child Care and Parenting Policies*, Stockholm: Save the Children Sweden.

Smith, R. (2010), 'Total parenting', *Educational Theory*, **60** (3), 357–69.

United Nations (2012), *Family-oriented Policies for Poverty Reduction, Work-Family Balance and Intergenerational Solidarity*, Washington, DC: United Nations.

27. Neglected families: developing family-supportive policies for 'natural' and (hu)man-made disasters
Lena Dominelli

INTRODUCTION

Family-supportive disaster intervention policies do not figure much in policies about disasters. This is a paradox because it is common knowledge in disaster discourses that the 'family', however defined to be culturally appropriate, provides the first community-based respondents when disaster strikes (FEMA, 2015). Family survivors and neighbours are also catalysts who keep response and recovery interventions going when officialdom would like to halt proceedings and they play vital roles in the remaining parts of the disaster cycle from prevention to reconstruction, initially struggling to survive and then moving beyond that to thrive and enhance future resilience (see also Chapter 28 by Björnberg in this volume).

In this chapter I contribute to filling this gap in the literature by considering the absence of family-friendly policies in disaster discourses (Masten and Obradovic, 2007) and argue for its remediation, utilizing my research in Sri Lanka around the 2004 Indian Ocean Tsunami,[1] in China around the 2008 Wenchuan Earthquake, the Philippines after Hurricane Haiyan in 2013, the Balkan floods in 2013, the UK's floods of 2013, and the 2015 Nepal earthquakes through my role as Chair of the IASSW (International Association of Schools of Social Work) Disaster Interventions Committee and research. These projects revealed that policy-makers presume availability of family resources for filling gaps that formal providers leave from evacuation onwards. Consequently, contingency planners anticipate family resources, linked to women's informal care as available when needed, despite ignoring their support through policy-making (Dominelli, 2013b). Additionally, research exposes the neglect of individual family members' differentiated experiences of disasters (Brown and Westaway, 2011; Coyne, 2013) which vary according to social divisions like gender, age, ability, sexual orientation, mental health and ethnicity. Thus, social policies formulated on a 'one size fits all' basis disadvantage women, children, older people, disabled people and others with specific needs, and require changing.

I conclude by identifying those features that would comprise family-supportive policies that develop family resilience and well-being before, during and after disasters, and incorporate the differentiated experiences of disasters of each family member. These will have to encompass different hazard conditions and all social divisions relevant to a given situation, and be locality specific and culturally relevant as well. 'One size fits all' responses are *in*appropriate. The IIPP research on Sri Lanka exposed differentiated experiences of disasters within communities:

> I was motivated to work with people of old age and who were poor. I worked with old people and poor communities. There were no professionals in the field. After we obtained the skills I felt how important it was to help these poor communities to grow and develop . . . [How social

workers] went about the work really impressed me. I wanted to learn more. I saw how the elderly [sic] changed. How receptive they were towards the work that was done with them. (Aid worker interview from IIPP)

DEFINING DISASTERS

A disaster arises when hazards, risks, exposure and vulnerabilities combine to produce human suffering beyond victim-survivors' capacity to cope. The formula expressing this is Risk equals Hazard x Exposure x Vulnerability (Kron, 2002). In emergency parlance, a disaster is a substantial event that:

- Causes severe destruction of property, injury and/or loss of life.
- Starts and ends at identifiable points.
- Impacts adversely on most of a population.
- Affects private daily routines, while formal responses occur in the collective 'public' domain, shared by many families, but experienced individually depending on gender, age, ability, ethnicity and other social divisions.
- Given its scale, requires external resources to enable individuals, families and communities to survive, thrive and enhance resilience following disaster.
- Is psychologically traumatic, causing distress in nearly everyone for a period (Dominelli, 2012; Luthar, 2006; Saylor, 1993; UNISDR, 2015).

Disasters are described as 'natural' if dependent on the physical forces of nature, for example, earthquakes, volcanoes and tropical storms; or, '(hu)man-made' when attributable to human activities or behaviour, for example, climate change, chemical explosions, armed conflicts and mass migrations caused by conflicts over territories, resources and ideological orientations as is occurring currently in Syria, Iraq and Afghanistan (Themne and Wallensteen, 2011). Both 'natural' and (hu)man-made disasters are increasing in frequency and intensity (UNISDR, 2015). Increasingly, these categories are considered permeable. Vitousek et al. (1997) argue that all disasters have a 'human' component. People have shaped the physical environment for so long that no place is exempt from their impact and this increases human vulnerability (Wisner et al., 2004). Melting ice-sheets, rising ocean levels, increased acidity in the ocean, increased frequency of flooding and loss of biodiversity are evidence of such effects (Holland et al., 2008). Climate change can intensify earthquakes and volcanic eruptions in the earth's dynamic ecosystem (Lamb and Davis, 2003; McGuire, 2012a, 2012b). These positions are contested by climate change deniers, challenging scientific reports (Giddens, 2009; IPCC, 2014). Social workers who have to address the consequences of disasters from evacuation to full recovery should become aware of these debates and their implications for practice (Dominelli, 2012). Disasters are considered as slow onset or rapid onset, depending on their temporality (Yule, 1993). Slow onset disasters may be years in the making, for example, climate change, farming practices that erode soil and over-use of water, thus contributing to drought. Rapid onset disasters are those that happen suddenly and are currently unpredictable, for example, earthquakes.

HOW DISASTERS AFFECT FAMILIES

The United Nations (UN) defines a family as 'the natural and fundamental group . . . entitled to protection by society and the State' (United Nations, 1948). Families, the basic unit of society (Wilson, 2013), are charged with socializing children, looking after dependent members and providing them with resources and support according to individual need (Stack, 1996). Families are constantly changing or evolving. Thus, the nuclear family of Victorian England is different from today's nuclear family. Families are considered malleable and there are many types of families encompassed by the term: nuclear family, extended family, lone-parent family, same-gender family, blended families, to name a few. Policy-makers idealize the family to assign responsibility for caring for vulnerable individuals, especially young children, disabled people, and older people, primarily to women (Noddings, 2002), usually with limited state support.

Moreover, guidance on what families should do in a disaster does not consider what resources and support women require to carry out these responsibilities before or after a disaster. Families are expected to be 'naturally resilient', that is, cope with whatever they have/get. My research on disasters (Dominelli, 2013a) revealed that women were: subjected to sexual and physical violence (including women relief workers); discriminated against in aid distribution; expected to sacrifice all for their families; and expected to behave according to existing, usually patriarchal, cultural norms. In Sri Lanka, cultural sensitivity for the Buddhist majority included building houses with a large and small kitchen for women to cook food in culturally appropriate ways – that is, to enable proper preparation of vegetarian foods. However, many housing providers neglected this cultural tradition in post-disaster reconstruction and did not consult Buddhist women who would have told them this was necessary to meet their housing needs.

Nahid Rezwana (2015), describing the lack of support for women following both the 2007 Cyclone Sidr and 2013 Cyclone Mahasen in Bangladesh, shows how social policies assume that despite cultural and resource barriers women encounter in helping themselves or their families, especially children and older relatives, they will cope and fulfil their duties, pre- and post-disaster. Despite women's lives being threatened by long hair and saris being caught in trees and debris flows because local tradition declares that women cannot alter these aspects of appearance and dress without drawing ridicule, they struggle to survive and care for their dependents against all odds. Consequently, women lose their lives in disproportionately higher numbers. One of the women in Rezwana's (2015, p. 95) study explains:

> A woman cannot run . . . A man can run and even take off their clothes . . . Women think, I have children, my honour and the honour of my husband . . . People may tease him [the husband] after disaster, 'your wife ran on the disaster day, taking off her clothes' . . . Whereas men take off their clothes and run for their live[s].

The type of disaster, its duration, intensity, amount of destruction, period of family displacement, whether internal (within or near a community's original location) or external (outside the area which can extend to another country) and cultural traditions can greatly influence family lives post-disaster. Psychosocial research suggests that the severity of the disaster experience can also be influenced by existing overall levels of adverse mental health conditions within a family (Dyb et al., 2011; Ebata and Borden, 1995). Other relevant factors that may exacerbate family vulnerability include:

- Parental incapacity.
- Substance misuse, especially alcohol and/or drugs by family members, particularly fathers and mothers.
- Increased conflict or violence against women, children and older people; and tensions around finances, roles, responsibilities, cultural expectations and aid distribution between members of one family and others in a particular community.
- Relocation of family members, especially children being sent to schools outside the local area and difficult for the family to visit daily.
- Income insecurity and job losses among main breadwinners.
- Parents becoming physically and emotionally unavailable when seeking to restore the family's pre-disaster status and situation.
- Presumed or actual death of and missing family members.
- Aggravation of minor injuries by inadequate medical care and medicines.
- Lack of children's social networks or opportunities to engage in normal routines and organized leisure and attend school (Ebata and Borden, 1995; Milazzo et al., 1995; Rezwana, 2015).

DIFFERENTIATED EXPERIENCES OF DISASTERS

Family vulnerabilities can be mitigated through advocacy and action prior to and after a disaster. Safe, well-sited, well-resourced, appropriately furnished and spacious evacuation centres that cater for differentiated family needs among children, disabled individuals, older people and women are essential in overcoming people's reluctance to use them (Rezwana, 2015). Having well-qualified medical personnel managing affordable, accessible, local medical facilities will increase family health resilience and strengthen family recovery processes before and after disasters (Walsh, 2006). Policy-makers' slow responses to differentiated experiences of disasters among the populace have created social policies incapable of addressing diverse needs. Identity traits have been ignored in disaster risk reduction strategies despite being highlighted for some time. Morrow and Enarson (1998) emphasized neglected gender in policy following Hurricane Mitch, but responses to date have been insufficient (Dominelli, 2013a, 2013b; Rezwana, 2015). Disabled people's needs in disasters have been considered more recently. The *Hyogo Framework for Disaster Risk Reduction (HFA), 2005–2015* (UNISDR, 2005) replaced by the post-2015 Framework (HFA2) discussed disability from March 2012 by stating that:

> Disability was recognized as an issue that has received far too little attention with the consequence of increasing exposure of the people with disabilities and missing the opportunity to draw on their unique capacities ... [and] identified as a priority for concerted action in the HFA2 with calls for their necessary participation in decision-making processes for disaster risk management.

Disabled people in different countries have conducted research into their own specific needs, identified how to end discrimination against them during disasters and demanded that policy-makers provide resources for disabled individuals and their families. They presented their endeavours at the 2015 Sendai World Conference on Disaster Risk Reduction, making that event inclusive of disabled people (UNISDR, 2009).

Children's specific needs have been defined primarily by adults asking family members and schools to protect them from harm. This includes protection from sex predators and people-trafficking rings; finding missing family members; and engaging schools in raising awareness of disasters and what children can or must do to protect themselves and alert their families (Nwe, 2005). Child protection rather than child agency has provided the major framework for such discussions, thus rarely involving children in deciding what would best meet their needs during disasters. Acknowledging children's agency is crucial in addressing their needs and involving them in post-disaster reconstruction. An aid worker in the ESRC project in Sri Lanka suggested:

> I would like to see more chances given to the children to work freely with children of their own age. It is also important to shorten the period that the children had to stay [in temporary accommodation] before they were [sic] able to go back to school, so that what the children missed was short[ened] and they would be able to catch up with their school work quickly. (Aid worker interviewed in IIPP)

The IIPP project also contained evidence that young people (children and teenagers) during the 2004 tsunami had complained that adults did not ask what they could do to assist in recovery and reconstruction initiatives, despite having many ideas to contribute to rebuilding processes. One young man illustrated the failure of authorities to channel young people's energies by taking his own action. With the support of his parents, he used a computer provided by aid donors to set up a business and provide villagers with email and computer services.

Identity attributes need recognition because these impact differently on people's experiences of disasters. Blaikie et al. (1994) and Dominelli (2012), among others, have identified population growth, over-urbanization including mega-cities, large slums in fragile ecosystems, and global economic pressures to exploit scarce material resources as stretching planet earth's capacity to provide for humanity's needs at the standards of living enjoyed by American families. Others have emphasized the extraction of fossil fuels through unproven technologies such as fracking (Climate Change Coalition, 2015), environmental degradation that impacts most adversely on poor people (Bullard, 2000), global environmental change and war (Gleditsch, 2012) as of concern to families. These global pressures are shaping and exacerbating local family vulnerabilities to natural disasters by eroding physical resilience and soil stability. These matters require urgent scientific attention, formal state regulation and social policies at local, national and international levels to ensure that personal, social and material vulnerabilities are not aggravated.

Consequently, further research into different factors that impact on physical and human – family and community – vulnerabilities to disasters, and the complex interplay between them, is necessary. Pelling and Uitto (2001, p. 55), talking about the complexity of issues that need investigation to enhance the resilience of families in small island states, argue that:

> Differentiating vulnerability between small islands to inform policy decision-making is difficult because of a lack of accessible data on key variables such as rural and urban service provision, the quality of housing infrastructure, detailed locations for human settlements, adherence to construction codes, insurance coverage, food security, disaster preparedness and emergency services.

International coordination and discussions are required for evidence-based action to be taken (OCHA, 2014). Such debates have to be consensual and include all nations as legitimate stakeholders. So far, climate change talks have failed to obtain an international legallybinding solution that reduces fossil fuel emissions despite early intervention costing less than intervening later (Stern, 2006). Such agreement must not sacrifice development for poor people in the Global South. They have contributed least to the problem, but carry the largest burden in terms of its effects (McGuire, 2012a, 2012b).

Despite these failings and known information gaps about the best ways forward, policy-makers have now acknowledged the differentiated experiences of disasters, and associated reconstruction processes afterwards, especially those linked to socio-economic and physical environmental development and sustainability within families and between nations. Article 1 of the UN General Assembly's 1986 Declaration on the Right to Development explicitly recognizes links between rights and development. It asserts that:

> The right to development is an inalienable human right by virtue of which every human person and all peoples are entitled to participate in, contribute to, and enjoy economic, social, cultural and political development, in which all human rights and fundamental freedoms can be fully realized.

This Declaration also called on each country to: 'take steps to eliminate obstacles to development resulting from failure to observe civil and political rights, as well as economic, social and cultural rights'. Action by all nations is needed to make resources available for green, sustainable development, take preventative action on greenhouse gas emissions (Dominelli, 2012) and promote family-friendly policies. Green socio-economic development was deliberated at the UNFCCC (United Nations Framework Convention for Climate Change) COP 21 (Conference of the Parties, 21st annual meeting) in Paris in December 2015. Social work has been represented in these deliberations since COP 16 in 2010 in Cancun, Mexico, through the International Association of Schools of Social Work (IASSW).

The post-2015 Agenda proposes to strengthen links between human rights and development goals, including rights-based approaches to poverty eradication to secure robust resilience. The *Sendai Framework on Disaster Risk Reduction, 2015–2030* also encompasses human rights and social justice. This was the first time these considerations had been included in formal disaster discourses.

FAMILIES RESPONDING TO DISASTERS

Families in disasters seek to maximize their chances of survival against incredible odds like having lost family members, friends, neighbours, homes, livelihoods, access to services including schools, medical facilities, water, sanitation, transportation, communication systems, all their resources including money, important documents, deeds to housing, banking facilities and access to humanitarian aid. These losses can have a deleterious impact on a family's capacity to build resilience immediately after the disaster and/or during long-term reconstruction. Women are particularly disadvantaged, often losing out in aid distribution through cultural barriers to their participation in post-disaster recovery and reconstruction (Dominelli, 2013a, b; Pittaway et al., 2007; Rezwana, 2015).

Men can lose much – livelihoods, family members, housing – and feel disempowered by the responsibilities associated with being the family's main breadwinner and protector. Some seek escape physically or psychologically by misusing drugs and alcohol or abusing their power through violence against family members, especially women and children, or fighting other men (Dominelli, 2014). One person in the ESRC project commented:

> [Camp life became more crowded] like communal living. So that did have an impact on . . . families. Alcoholism increased, drug addiction increased. More men became very lazy . . . Lazy because there was enough money coming in for them. They didn't have to go to work. The excuse was that they did not want to go to sea because of what they had seen – the tsunami and the people [drowning]. But the . . . real story was that they were getting enough money and they didn't want to tire themselves. (Teacher interviewed in IIPP)

Such behaviours indicate that existing difficulties between family members become intensified following a disaster. Supporting men through reconstruction initiatives, a concern usually neglected in emergency responses, constitutes an area of family-friendly policies requiring urgent attention (Dominelli, 2014).

Interestingly, current considerations are not only about individual families in disaster-prone areas of the Global South, preparing themselves for and responding to calamities. Families in the Global North, affected by flooding caused by increased moisture held in the air through climate change, are exposing policy failures. This includes the market's *in*capacity to support financial losses through insurance mechanisms when the risks are substantial. For example, substantial damage to property and land in southwestern England in the autumn of 2013, and northwestern England and southwestern Scotland in December 2015, have led victim-survivors to call for changes to actuarial assessments of flood risk in specific areas as the basis for insurance coverage. They demand that risks are pooled more widely to ensure that everyone can afford insurance. The British government has been working for several years with the Association of British Insurance to develop a national scheme that covers those living in flood-vulnerable remote areas. Their endeavours have led to the creation of the Flood Re Scheme that makes re-insurance for flood-affected households more affordable through government subsidy and came into force in April 2016 (delayed from summer 2015) (BBC, n.d.; FloodRe, n.d.). Current discourses are primarily about 'protecting the maximum number' in economically sustainable ways, and accepting that 'nature' causes these events. While this analysis of flooding causes is faulty, the Scheme instances social solidarity because risk is pooled nationally. However, some individuals not affected by flooding resent their inclusion in the Flood Re Scheme. Moreover, these discourses say little about the emotional impact of these losses on individual families, and how people find non-family resources to build resilience once the cameras have gone. Another consideration relates to employers' roles and responsibilities towards their employees' families so that paid responders can undertake emergency responses without worrying about their families' safety. Employer contributions to family well-being is coming under the spotlight in the Global North and seems crucial in improving performance of first responders and other professionals supporting victim-survivors (Landahl and Cox, 2009). This latter point indicates that these families are both victims of a disaster and survivors trying to cope and develop resilience when key members are unavailable to support them. Aid workers can be both victims and survivors who need resources and support, especially if their assistance is required for lengthy periods of time. Cronin et al. (2007) argued that supporting practitioners in developing and abiding by the tenets of self-care prevents burn-out and increases efficiency and effectiveness in helping others. Post-traumatic stress of various degrees applies to both victim-survivors and aid workers and can undermine resilience if their worries fester without assistance (Dyb et al., 2011).

Luthar (2006, p. 780) concludes that 'resilience rests, fundamentally, on relationships'. This may stress further families that have difficulty establishing good relationships or increasing their social capital and/or networks without additional support. Expectations that families tackle their own problems can exacerbate poor family relationships that preceded the disaster, for example, situations with existing income inequalities and/or violence. Goldstein and Brooks (2005, p. 23) argue that ecological transactional system approaches more adequately reflect 'individual differences in developmental pathways and contextual variation within families, communities, societies, cultures, and historical periods'. Policy-makers have to address variations in differentiated experiences of disasters to build robust resilience that goes beyond 'building back better' and embed these within families and communities.

FAMILY-FRIENDLY SUPPORT

Vulnerability within families varies according to age, gender, ability and ethnicity. The risks families face are further complicated by the type of disaster, its duration, degree of preparation, mitigation of risk and access to resources to assist evacuation, recovery and reconstruction. Many families remain unaware of key strategies for mitigating risks and caring for themselves, their families and neighbours following a disaster (Kellett et al., 2014). Many families do not know the science behind the risks they face, do not have access to early warning systems or do not receive training on resilience-building after previous disasters. Preparation and prevention form significant elements for families to consider when developing resilience under adverse circumstances. Suggestions for families preparing to act with greater resilience after a disaster occurs follow.

Families taking control of their situation to enhance their capacity to react before, during and after disasters, achieve greater resilience. Adults, usually the parents, take responsibility for the safety and well-being of those relying on their assistance. However, the entire family should be involved in decision-making to ensure that the specific needs of each member are met, to reach consensus for ways forward and to negotiate the following actions:

- Identify hazards in their environments (workplace, home, school) and consider which might lead to emergency situations/disasters.
- Consider how to mitigate the risks these hazards pose before disasters occur.
- Discuss as a family their possible reactions in an emergency, including their fears and hopes.
- Consider how each family member might find his or her abilities compromised in an emergency or disaster, especially their ability to cope and act independently if they have to find their own way to safety. Afterwards, discuss strategies for empowering each individual to safeguard their own safety and that of others, and how to access external resources.

- Develop the family's contact list including those outside the local area who may be easier to reach when local communications are inoperative or restricted; ensure each person has his or her own copy and knows what to do with it.
- Identify a place where the family can meet when safe to do so.
- Put together an emergency kit ('go bag') that includes extra batteries, first aid materials, at least 72-hours supply of food, water, special medications, battery-operated (solar-powered or wind-up) torch (flashlight) and radio, and personal supplies. For babies and toddlers, personal supplies include milk formula, diapers of the correct size, non-water-based soaps or hand and body washes; for nursing mothers they include ointments to protect the nipples and keep them clean; and for post-puberty, non-menopausal women and girls, sanitary towels. Ideally, each person should have their own kit, adapted to what they can safely carry. Copy important documents, for example, identity cards/passports, house deeds, and carry them in this kit.
- Consider how to protect family pets and animals before an emergency arises, including identifying a place of safety, who will take them there, when and how. Discuss scenario planning, participatory mapping of relevant sites and services, and possible options.
- Develop and agree a family evacuation plan that is flexible enough to respond to what actually happens during a disaster.
- Update family emergency preparedness and evacuation plans regularly. A number of websites that can assist in this task include those of the Red Cross, UN, Office for the Coordination of Humanitarian Affairs (OCHA), the European Union's ECHO and the American Federal Emergency Management Agency (FEMA), which were used to compile this list.

Individual families can help themselves, but need family-friendly policies and external resources to cope with and then thrive after a disaster. This may include support in resolving family-based problems that preceded the disaster, especially around domestic violence, substance misuse, resource inequalities and building their lives anew. Actions to realize human rights and social justice should be endorsed locally, nationally and internationally.

THE IMPLICATIONS OF FAMILY-FRIENDLY DISASTER RESPONSES FOR POLICY-MAKERS

Masten and Obradovic (2007, p. 18) claim that families have insufficient space in policy-making debates:

> The apparent lack of consideration and support at the family level in disaster planning is surprising given family responsibilities and the ease with which they can be reached through connections with schools, neighbourhoods, medical facilities, grocery stores, and other local settings.

Their statement suggests that policy-makers can access family members through various local spaces and obtain their views about specific policies that would help them during disaster interventions. They can also utilize formal means, including consultation documents, online surveys and disaster-specific referenda.

Policies should address the needs of all families including those of first responders and facilitate family-preparedness in the workplace and at home. Despite the variety of views about what to do and where responsibilities lie, first responders' energies should not be distracted by worrying about their own family's safety because attention was not given to their disaster awareness and risk reduction activities prior to a calamity occurring. Disaster prevention strategies, pre-disaster training and preparation, a family disaster plan that covers evacuation and whom and how to communicate with each other during a disaster play crucial roles in allaying fears and building confidence in individuals, families and communities. Policy-makers can support family-resilience building mechanisms and allocate the resources necessary to:

1. Fund community-based emergency and disaster risk reduction and awareness training that involve all family members in age-appropriate discussions at home, school and work.
2. Prepare all families for potential disasters by having first responders work with them to devise family emergency and evacuation plans as part of their preventative and preparedness strategy.
3. Build evacuation centres that are:
   - Located in easily accessible, safe places.
   - Well-provided with space and resources to meet the different needs of each family member, especially those occurring along gender, age, ethnicity and disability lines.
   - Situated near well-staffed, well-equipped, easily accessible medical care facilities.
   - Equipped to provide a normal routine for children, including schooling, age-appropriate toys, equipment and leisure activities.
   - Able to refer people to other services and provide the resources and transportation needed to get there.
   - Safe, pet-friendly places created nearby so that owners can see pets regularly without antagonizing other evacuation centre users.
4. Provide well-staffed mental health and psychosocial support services capable of meeting differentiated needs.
5. Monitor and evaluate evacuation centre performance after a disaster.
6. Plan and facilitate community reconstruction endeavours that involve local family members in deciding what their re-created community will look like, where it will be sited, and what facilities it will have. This should include enhanced community resilience, leisure amenities, risk mitigation, prevention and preparedness regarding future disasters, address socio-economic inequalities including poverty through improved livelihood and income generation schemes, better housing construction, transportation, communication, sanitation and water supplies.
7. Undertake research to improve future responses at all stages of the disaster intervention cycle (prevention, preparedness, immediate relief, recovery and reconstruction).
8. Endorse human rights, social justice and environmental justice through disaster intervention policies and practices.

POLICIES TO SUPPORT PRACTITIONERS ASSISTING FAMILIES IN DISASTER RESPONSES

Besides devising family-friendly policies that respond to differentiated needs among different family members, policy-makers should promulgate policies for practice and support practitioners for the essential work they do with individuals, families and communities before, during and after disasters. Such policies should assist practitioners in:

1. *Ethical Behaviour*. Acting ethically, ensuring no harm is caused by what is done or not done.
2. *Assessing Differentiated Needs*. Assessing needs thoroughly and taking account of each individual's differentiated requirements and experiences.
3. *Partnership*. Encouraging partnership working between practitioners and families.
4. *Resources*. Providing sufficient resources for practitioners to intervene effectively.
5. *Training*. Supporting practitioner training that equips them adequately for the stressful circumstances encountered when supporting other people and their own families who may also be disaster victim-survivors.
6. *Disaster Intervention*. Supporting practitioners' capacities to intervene at all stages of the disaster cycle – prevention, preparation and mitigation, immediate relief, recovery and reconstruction.
7. *Spatial Intervention*. Supporting practitioners' interventions at all levels: locally in micro-level practice: regionally and nationally through research that provides frameworks for intervention that can cover similarities and differences in experiences; and internationally through advocacy that addresses the universal aspects of policy and practice including human rights and social justice.
8. *Coproduction*. Engaging families and communities in coproducing strategies for practice and action plans.
9. *Emotionality*. Preparing practitioners and their families for the emotional demands of their work and providing psychosocial resources for this purpose.
10. *Interdisciplinarity*. Sustaining multidisciplinary and multi-professional approaches to practitioners' endeavours.
11. *Advocacy*. Supporting and responding to practitioners' advocacy efforts, particularly those aimed at learning from past experiences, enhancing resilience in future disasters, and passing social policies relevant to particular communities.
12. *Supportive supervision*. Financing team working and supervising practitioners to the highest standards.

Policy-makers, regulators and dispensers of resources, and governments have a considerable agenda of initiatives to mitigate disaster risk and promote sustainable development requiring urgent attention.

CONCLUSIONS

Family members and neighbours are among the first responders to disasters. The policy void currently left by the neglect of family-supportive policies for families to survive and thrive before, during and after disasters must be filled with family-friendly policies that strive to achieve precisely these goals. These policies should cater for different family types, differentiated individual experiences of disasters, and uphold human rights and social justice. Responding appropriately requires policy-makers to understand how family units operate and how their efforts may supplement those taken by the state, other helping organisations and commercial providers. Families have collective needs alongside specific individual member needs. This means that a 'one size fits all' approach to disasters is inappropriate and possibly dangerous, because it can exacerbate risks rather than reduce them. Families require additional resources and training to become disaster resilient. Social workers can play a crucial role in advocating for and lobbying policy-makers to ensure that the necessary changes are made to the political agenda for the delivery of family-friendly policies and resources for disaster interventions in practice.

NOTE

1. The Economic and Social Research Council (ESRC) funded the Internationalising Institutional and Professional Practices (IIPP) project.

REFERENCES

BBC (n.d.), 'Flood insurance scheme delay "disappointing", Somerset group says', accessed 10 July 2016 at http://www.bbc.co.uk/news/uk-england-somerset-33075944.
Blaikie, P., T. Cannon, I. Davis, and B. Wisner (eds) (1994), *At Risk: Natural Hazards, People's Vulnerability, and Disasters*, London: Routledge.
Brown, K. and E. Westaway (2011), 'Agency, capacity, and resilience to environmental change: lessons from human development, well-being, and disasters', *Annual Review of Environment and Resources*, **36**, 321–42.
Bullard, R., J. Ageyman, and B. Evans (2003), *Just Sustainability: Development in an Unequal World*, Cambridge, MA: MIT Press.
Climate Change Coalition (2015), *Fracking and Climate Change*, accessed 8 December 2015 at http://www.theclimatecoalition.org/fracking-and-climate-change.
Coyne, C.J. (ed.) (2013), *Doing Bad by Doing Good: Why Humanitarian Aid Fails*, Stanford, CA: Stanford University Press.
Cronin, M., D. Ryan, and D. Brier (2007), 'Support for Staff Working in Disasters', *International Social Work*, **50** (3), 370–82.
Dominelli, L. (ed.) (2012), *Green Social Work*, Cambridge: Polity Press.
Dominelli, L. (2013a), 'Gendering climate change: implications for debates, policies and practices', in M. Alston and K. Whittenbury (eds), *Research, Action and Policy: Addressing the Gendered Impacts of Climate Change*, London: Springer, pp. 77–94.
Dominelli, L. (2013b), 'Mind the gap: built infrastructures, sustainable caring relations and resilient communities in extreme weather events', *Australian Social Work*, **66** (2), 204–17.
Dominelli, L. (2014), 'The opportunities and challenges of social work interventions in disaster situations', *International Social Work*, **57** (4), 338–45.
Dyb, G., T. Jensen, and E. Nygaard (2011), 'Children's and parents' posttraumatic stress reactions after the 2004 tsunami', *Clinical Child Psychology and Psychiatry*, **16** (4), 621–34.
Ebata, T. and L. Borden (eds) (1995), *Children, Stress and Natural Disasters: A Guide for Teachers and School Activities for Children*, Champaign-Urbana, IL: University of Illinois.
FEMA (Federal Emergency Management Agency) (2015), *FEMA Strategic Plan*, Washington, DC: FEMA.
FloodRe (n.d.), accessed 15 July 2016 at http://www.floodre.co.uk.
Giddens, A. (2009), *The Politics of Climate Change*, Cambridge: Polity Press.
Gleditsch, P. (2012), 'Wither the weather? Climate change and conflict', *Journal of Peace Research*, **49** (1), 3–9.
Goldstein, S. and R. Brooks (eds) (2005), *Handbook of Resilience in Children*, New York: Springer.

Holland, P., A. Jenkins, and D. Holland (2008), 'The response of ice shelf basal melting to variations in ocean temperatures', *Journal of Climate*, **21** (11), 2558–72.
Intergovernmental Panel on Climate Change (IPCC) (2014), *Assessment Report on Climate Change: A Summary for Policymakers*, Geneva: UNFCCC, available at https://www.ipcc.ch/pdf/assessment-report/ar5/syr/AR5_SYR_FINAL_SPM.pdf Accessed on 21 August 2018.
Kellett, J., A. Caravani, and F. Pichon (eds) (2014), *Financing Disaster Risk Reduction: Towards a Coherent and Comprehensive Approach*, London: ODI.
Kron, W. (2002), 'Flood Risk = hazard x exposure x vulnerability', in J. Wu, T. Jiang, and L. King (eds), *Flood Risks and Land Use Conflicts in the Yangtze Catchment, China and at the Rhine River*, Cologne, Germany: GieBen, pp. 107–14.
Lamb, S. and P. Davis (2003), 'Cenozoic climate change as a possible cause for the rise of the Andes', *Nature*, **425** (October), 792–7.
Landahl, M. and C. Cox (2009), 'Beyond the plan: individual responder and family preparedness in the resilient organization', *Homeland Security Affairs*, **5** (4), 1–22.
Luthar, S.S. (2006), 'Resilience in development: a synthesis of research across five decades', *Developmental Psychopathology*, **3**, 739–95.
Masten, A.S. and J. Obradovic (2007), 'Disaster preparation and recovery: lessons from research on resilience in human development', *Ecology and Society*, **13** (1), 9–25.
McGuire, B. (2012a), 'Climate change shakes the earth', *Guardian*, 26 February, accessed 15 July 2016 at https://www.theguardian.com/environment/2012/feb/26/why-climate-change-shake-earth.
McGuire, B. (ed.) (2012b), *Waking the Giant: How a Changing Climate Triggers Earthquakes, Tsunamis and Volcanoes*, Oxford: Oxford University Press.
Milazzo, C., B. Flynn, and S. Friedman (eds) (1995), *Psychosocial Issues for Children and Families in Disasters: A Guide for the Primary Care Physician*, Rockville, MD: American Academy of Pediatrics Work Group on Disasters.
Morrow, B. and E. Enarson (eds) (1998), *The Gendered Terrain of Disaster: Through Women's Eyes*, Miami, FL: Florida International University.
Noddings, N. (ed.) (2002), *Starting at Home: Caring and Social Policy*, Berkeley, CA: University of California Press.
Nwe, Y.Y. (ed.) (2005), *Children and the Tsunami: A Year On*, Paris: UNICEF.
OCHA (Office for the Coordination of Humanitarian Affairs) (2014), *World Humanitarian Aid: Data and Trends 2013*, Geneva: OCHA.
Pelling, M. and J.I. Uitto (2001), 'Small island developing states: natural disaster vulnerability and global change', *Environmental Hazards*, **3**, 49–62.
Pittaway, E., L. Bartolomei, and S. Rees (2007), 'Gendered dimensions of the 2004 tsunami and a potential social work response in post-disaster situations', *International Social Work*, **50** (3), 307–19.
Rezwana, N. (ed.) (2015), 'Disasters and access to healthcare in the coastal region of Bangladesh: a gendered analysis', PhD thesis, Department of Geograhy, Durham University.
Saylor, D.F. (1993), 'Children and disasters: clinical and research issues', in D.F. Saylor (ed.), *Children and Disasters*, New York: Plenum Press, pp. 1–9.
Stack, C.B. (ed.) (1996), *All Our Kin*, New York: Basic Books.
Stern, N. (ed.) (2006), *Stern Review of the Economics of Climate Change*, Cambridge: Cambridge University Press.
Themne, L. and P. Wallensteen (2011), 'Armed conflict: 1946–2010', *Journal of Peace Research*, **48** (4), 525–36.
UNISDR (United Nations International Strategy for Disaster Reduction) (2005), *Hyogo Framework for Action on Disaster Risk Reduction (HFA), 2005–2015: Building the Resilience of Nations and Communities for Disaster*, Geneva: UNISDR.
UNISDR (United Nations International Strategy for Disaster Reduction) (2009), *UNISDR Terminology on Disaster Risk Reduction*, Geneva: UNISDR.
UNISDR (United Nations International Strategy for Disaster Reduction) (2015), *Sendai Framework for Disaster Risk Reduction, 2015–2030*, Geneva: UNISDR.
United Nations (1948), *Universal Declaration of Human Rights*, accessed 15 November 2015 at http://www.un.org/en/universal-declaration-human-rights/.
Vitousek, P., H. Mooney, J. Lubchenco, and J. Melillo (1997). 'Human domination of earth's ecosystem', *Science*, **277** (3), 494–9.
Walsh, F. (ed.) (2006), *Strengthening Family Resilience*, New York: Guilford Press.
Werner, E.E. (1995), 'Resilience in development', *Current Directions in Psychological Science*, **4**, 81–4.
Wilson, L. (2013), 'The family as a basic unit of society', accessed 8 December 2015 at http://drlwilson.com/ARTICLES/FAMILIES.htm.
Wisner, B., P. Blaikie, T. Cannon, and I. Davis (2004), *Risk: Natural Hazards*, London: Routledge.
Yule, W. (1993), 'Technology-related disasters', in D.F. Saylor (ed.), *Children and Disasters*, New York: Plenum Press, pp. 105–21.

28. Women's voices and human rights: perspectives on sustainable family lives
Ulla Björnberg

INTRODUCTION

Over several decades, women's movements have advocated for women's rights, highlighting that women are citizens with rights as individuals and have equal rights to economic participation, health protection and political rights. Women's movements around the world initiated a long period of knowledge accumulation on discrimination of women within various areas of societies.[1] With the growth of knowledge and information on women's living conditions, such as lack of education, lack of political influence, structural and interpersonal violence, neglect of maternal health and survival of children, poor reproductive health and lack of control of livelihoods, the need for political attention to improve the situation of women was claimed for. Within the United Nations (UN), organisations were established such as UN Women, which was given the role of collecting information and reports about women's living conditions, and the Convention on the Elimination of all Forms of Discrimination against Women (CEDAW). These activities have contributed to a process of global norm setting on women's rights which is still on the agenda for advocacy associations and activists around the globe.

It is recognised that violation of women's human rights impedes development goals. Women's rights have been put forward in global goal documents, such as the Millennium Development Goals adopted in 2000 and later transformed into the Sustainable Development Goals adopted in 2015 (United Nations, 2015a). All these documents have included goals for the improvement of women's human rights and living conditions as necessary conditions for social and economic development within countries. Their paid and unpaid contributions to the economies have repeatedly been underlined. In a wide sense, family policy can be understood as policy for protection of social reproduction. Families in all cultures and societies are considered to be the basic units for social reproduction. Female family members in most societies carry the main responsibility for those tasks that contribute to social reproduction and care of human resources. They give birth, raise children and provide livelihood, care and money. Thus, indirectly, family policy is connected to social development.[2] Women can in practice be regarded as heads of families although general assumptions in many cultures hold men to have that duty, supported by law, cultural and religious and gendered norms. Over the years, female advocacy groups and research have highlighted difficulties for women in making their own lives and those of their children in accordance with gender equality and human rights. Woman's challenges are related to a general predominance of male power rooted in patriarchal value systems that regard women as objects for male dominance. However, public and private awareness about the role of men in social reproduction as fathers and partners is increasing. For men, difficulties in adopting a more caring involvement in family, children and domestic work are linked to cultural norms that regard social reproductive work (caring, cooking, cleaning) in families as less valued than 'proper' paid work and not in accordance with masculine identities.

Women's ongoing fights to bring attention to their human rights are in many ways linked to family conditions. The negative aspect of these include forced marriage, neglect of maternal health, reproductive rights, right to livelihood and land ownership, violence and rape in family contexts, poverty and poor working conditions. Children's health and well-being are, especially in developing countries, dependent on women's situation. The problems have been well known for several decades, but despite international agreements improvements of the situation of women are slow.

In this chapter I focus on women's rights within family contexts using a global perspective. My perspective on the conditions of women's reproductive work is inspired by the capability approach developed by Nussbaum and Sen (1993) since it sheds light on the obstacles that women confront, based on structures, institutions and culture. It is important to illuminate discriminating practices on women just because they are women which prevent them from using their capabilities (Fredman, 2013). My aim is to argue for a feminist family policy. I will present some perspectives on conditions for family life against a background of changing living conditions for women, living in different family forms. Examples of these are changing ways of subsistence for women in a global economy, migration and social mobility. Economic conditions, cultural norms and values are challenges to the ways in which women can build and sustain the needs of family members and of themselves. I draw on evaluation reports from the CEDAW and other reports from the UN and the World Bank. I also draw on analysis of case studies on how conventions on women's human rights are implemented in national law (Hellum and Aasen, 2013a).

CHALLENGES FOR FAMILY POLICY

Changing Family Forms and Practices

Since the notion of 'the family' in contemporary societies is divergent and complex, the concept of family is better understood in terms of individual genders responsible for social reproduction. In sociological literature on contemporary families the diversity in family forms is theoretically and analytically approached with other definitions of 'family' such as 'family practices' (Morgan, 1996). The understanding of family within this perspective is not focussing on institutional aspects with defined roles for men, women and children but on practices within a network of family-like relationships. Furthermore, motherhood and fatherhood in academic debates as well as in family law and social policy are understood as individual relations to children which are to be regulated in laws for the well-being of children. The responsibilities for children are supposed to be shared regarding custody, maintenance and living arrangements, regardless if they live in the same household.

Globally, family structures have been in a process of change for several decades. Trends are similar but vary substantively between countries – from North to South, from rich to middle- and low-income countries. Europe, North America and parts of Asia have experienced the changes more intensely than other countries. Families take a diversity of forms such as transnational families, single parent, same sex families, cohabiting unions, divorce and separation leading to patchworked family relations. Changing family structures are characterised by a decrease in marriage rates and increased de-institutionalisation of family laws. Lifelong family unions tend to diminish and divorces and separations of unions increase. The destabilisation of union formations is followed by growth in lone parent families, which in individual cases might be followed by new union formations over the life span. More children live in households with siblings, half siblings and non-biological parents (mostly step-fathers). Parental responsibilities are individually regulated, such as custody regulations, maintenance obligations, visitation rights (Furstenberg, 2015). Fertility among women in Southern and Eastern Europe and advanced countries in Asia is sinking. Childlessness among women is growing in most parts of the world (Furstenberg, 2015). It is noteworthy that childlessness among both women and men is increasing in some countries, but lack of data for men does not give a full overview (Rostgaard and Möberg, 2015). Some of the reasons for sinking birth rates are linked to attitudes counteracting support for gender equality in families and in working life. The fertility decline in the literature is linked to both women and men entering parenthood later in life and for biological reasons they might not be able to have the number of children that they would like to have. The reasons behind the decision to postpone having children are the desire to have a stable life in terms of education that fits the labour market, the wish to have a stable position in the labour market, as well as the housing market, and the need to have a fairly regular income. The steep fertility decline in most Western and Asian countries is followed by a decreasing balance between older and younger generations since grown-up children remain longer in the parental homes, due to unemployment and lack of cheap housing. Parents continue to support their children financially and might end up with less money for their own retirement. Likewise, grown-up children will in many cases have to support their elderly parents.

The number of lone mother families is growing. It has been suggested that the increase in lone mother families is linked to growing socio-economic inequalities and poverty. For the United States, Furstenberg describes the pattern of a two-tier system, where men and women with insecure jobs, low education and low income don't marry but enter into unstable cohabitation unions. When children are born into these unions, the fathers have more complex paternal resources in terms of money and time. Women are left as lone mothers and enter a chain of insecure, low-paid jobs. At the other end, those adults with better jobs and higher income will accumulate resources for children and investment in more stable relationships (Furstenberg, 2014).

Transnational Family Practices

Migration, war and refuge contribute to many changes in the way family life is organised (see also Chapter 27 by Dominelli on family-supportive policies for disasters in this volume). Families split due to migration, refuge and labour mobility within and between countries and these are additional factors contributing to the rise in female-headed households. By the end of 2014, almost 60 million people had been forcibly displaced worldwide, the highest level recorded since the Second World War (United Nations, 2015b). Poverty, war and persecution are reasons for migration. Labour mobility is part of the interconnectedness between countries in the context of expanding international trade. Social services are commodities to be sold and purchased through the mobility of individuals worldwide, which triggers further mobility. Within the European Union (EU), free movement of persons between member states is part of a policy for economic growth. Thus, mobility and distance are common features of contemporary family life.

Increased scholarly attention has been directed at the phenomenon of transnational families (Baldassar and Merla, 2014; Anderson, 2000; Bryceson and Vuorela, 2002). Transnational families are not new kinds of family forms. However, they are constituted by many kinds of family practices. Men and women who migrate physically leave family members behind, but due to the expansion of communication techniques, relationships between kin are kept alive in various ways. But the problem is to what extent they are integrated into or excluded from national protective laws regarding labour, care, health, pregnancy and birth of children.

The notion of the care chain is an aspect of transnational family practices. Care chains are developing as a consequence of migrant labour within a care economy. Care chains have expanded within the politics of care where the purchase of care and domestic work is left to private solutions and where no other way of obtaining public services is available. It is about families in receiving countries that employ migrant labour for the care of children or the care of dependent family members and domestic work. Often the migrant worker leaves their own children in the care of someone in the sending country. This person is not necessarily a kin person, but could be a person who gets paid for the care work. Thus, care chains primarily also include circulation of care and involve women as both buyers and sellers of care.

'Circulation of care' is a phenomenon that explores how care within families is provided through various arrangements. Care circulation has been defined as care: 'Governed by "generalised asymmetrical reciprocity" within transnational kinship networks ... caregiving exchanges are embedded in the broader political economy of migration and transnationalism' (Baldassar and Merla, 2014, p. 8). They provide important substance for keeping families and a sense of responsibility and obligations within the kin network alive. Care of children and of older family members in the home country is arranged through support and care work that circulates in specific modes of exchange models that are negotiated within a kin network. Circulation of care is not 'hands on' but fills other care needs within families and kin. Sending remittances are important for provision of basic economic security. Care at a distance is rather emotional, giving moral support and guidance, giving advice, being present and giving support in everyday lives. Via Skype, exchanging messages and pictures over cell phones and other devices, or with the Internet, family relationships are upheld at a distance. However, circulation of care is not a sole family/kin business since the implementation of caregiving is dependent on the ways in which institutional settings and regulations frame the options and obstacles of mobile workers, migrants and refugees in the sending and receiving countries. The knowledge about circulation of care practices points at the need 'to encourage the development of national and transnational policies and services that facilitate family reunification and connectedness' (Baldassar and Merla, 2014, p. 22).

Circulation of care involves primarily women, but it also open for male caregivers, fathers and sons, to be included in care work. Women are mostly the main figure in a care circulation arrangement whereby they have the role of coordinator to overlook and follow the needs of the family members (Merla, 2014). Both care chains and circulation of care

are embedded within the expanding globalisation with mobility of capital and labour. In order to understand the conditions for families in contemporary societies, it is necessary to look closer into how they interrelate and provide implications for family policies that take into account women, children and men over the life course.

Reproductive Health

Reproductive health covers sexual education over the life span for everybody regardless of age and sexual identity, information on and access to contraceptives, maternal health and mortality, genital mutilation, and safe abortion (Wichterich, 2015). It is about women's and girls' rights to control the integrity of their bodies, on the one hand, and the obligations of states to implement the rights that they have guaranteed in ratification of human rights instruments, on the other (Aasen, 2013).

Goals that are of particular importance for women in connection with family policy are improvement of maternal health and reduction of maternal deaths. According to the World Health Organization (WHO), most maternal deaths are avoidable since preventative measures are well known. However, many women in developing countries do not have access to adequate health care services and skilled care during pregnancy as well as proper follow-up and support during and after childbirth.

Maternal deaths are caused by obstetric complication during pregnancy and childbirth. Unsafe abortions are included in the definition. Up to 30 per cent of maternal deaths are caused by unsafe abortions in some countries of Eastern Europe and Central Asia. Safety during and before unwanted pregnancy is vital. Access to family planning, sexual information and preventative means are examples of measures that could contribute to a reduction of poor reproductive health and deaths (WHO, 2015a).

Reduction in poor maternal health was prioritised within the Millenium Development Goals (MDGs) from 1990 to 2015. Many countries have managed to reduce the figures for maternal deaths. Globally, there was a decline of 45 per cent from 1990 to 2013. The maternal mortality rates in developing regions were 14 times higher than in developed regions. The United States, however, is an astonishing example within the developed countries as there was a steep rise during the period covered (WHO, 2015a).

Violence

Among the problems that women have to live with within the realm of family is violence, which is predominantly committed by close male partners within family circles. Estimates published by the WHO show that

> 1 in 3 women experience physical and/or sexual by an intimate partner or sexual violence by someone other than a partner in their lifetime. Violence against women and children is not just about individual physical injury but also have psychological consequences and it affects the sense of safety within the family. Women who experience partner violence are twice as likely to suffer from depression and 1.5 times more likely to have a sexually transmitted infection including HIV. They are also more likely to have unwanted pregnancies, unsafe abortions and when the violence occurs during pregnancy to suffer miscarriages, stillbirths, premature births and to have low birth weight babies. (WHO, 2015b)

It is also important to highlight that much violence is directed at girls and boys such as forced marriage, sexual abuse, corporal punishment, genital mutilation of girls, feticide, honour crimes, and child marriages where young girls have children with high risk of poor health and psychosocial suffering. These kinds of violence are family matters and should be regarded as targets for family policy.

In the international community much attention has lately been directed at physical and psychological violence against adult women including marital rape and forced marriage. Actions to reduce violence against women and children were included in the Sustainable Development Goals adopted in 2015. The WHO has declared: 'WHO strongly condemns violence against women and girls and supports partners' and countries' efforts towards the de-normalization of this type of violence' (WHO, 2015b). To be able to achieve this is to ensure gender equality and empowerment of women and girls. Impunity for perpetrators of sexual violence is another measure. Violence against children are violations of the convention of children's human rights.

Poverty

Due to poverty and environmental deterioration, families and individuals move from rural to urban areas. Women's poverty is directly related to the absence of economic opportunities and autonomy, lack of access to economic resources, including credit, land ownership and inheritance. Laws that regulate women's access to resources impede their opportunities for making a living. Households headed by women are among the poorest and, is for various reasons, the number of female-headed households increasing (see above). Women's exposure to poverty has profound consequences for women and children (see also Chapter 7 by Bradshaw on the role of child benefits in poverty eradication in this volume).

Reduction of extreme poverty has been high on the international agenda. Although the targets set within the MDGs of halving the proportion of people living in extreme poverty and hunger have almost been met, the world is still far from reaching the MDG of eradicating extreme poverty and hunger. In 2015, an estimated 825 million people were still living in extreme poverty and 800 million were still suffering from hunger. Eradicating poverty and hunger remains at the core of the post-2015 development agenda (UN Women, 2015).

Right to Property and Home Security

Laws that regulate women's access to resources in many different ways impede their opportunities for making a living. Closely linked to poverty is access to dwelling. Many women experience problems due to unequal regulations regarding ownership, inheritance and security in remaining in the home after being left alone with the children. There are several examples in the literature based on lived experiences about situations that illuminate the vulnerability of women and their families. The problems are linked to legal property rights, exposure to forced evictions and the rights to secure housing (Ikdahl, 2013). Several circumstances can put women in vulnerable situations such as the death of a husband and the legal consequences for women. Similar is the case of a divorce where the right to own property depends on the financial contributions of either spouse. As women generally have lower income or no income at all their contribution is lower, which leads to fewer rights in ownership. Parental deaths caused, for instance, by HIV/AIDS and Ebola contribute to orphanage, which can leave daughters' rights to inheritance of the home non-existent. In such cases, children as well as widowed mothers can be exposed to forced evictions. 'Women's property rights are contingent on their (temporary) membership of the family.' The notion of temporary membership 'hinges on notions that women are family members "in transit", where land is to remain in the family' (Ikdahl, 2013, p. 283).

Housing has been dealt with in several reports within human rights documents at the UN and the CEDAW. Following the threads from the 1990s shows the importance of collaboration between committees and conferences dealing with human rights, such as the International Covenant on Economic, Social and Cultural Rights (ICESCR) and the Committee on the Rights of the Child (CRC). The exposed situation of women is illustrated through co-analysis of different recommendations such as regulations of property rights and on analysis of equality between spouses. Secure housing and property rights are based on various laws and are especially evident where mobility of individuals and families within and between countries is high due to refuge, urbanisation, housing shortages and unequal distribution of dwellings in terms of renting and private ownership.

PRECARISATION OF LABOUR

Increasingly, at a world scale women are dependent on work for cash in the labour market or within the informal sector. Within the process of globalisation business investments and other global production systems have contributed to a feminisation of labour while focussing on low-paid jobs for women with low degrees of protection and social security (Sassen, 1998). Parallel to this development, informal job markets are expanding where social security and labour rights are even more absent. In general, more women are working, but often they are represented in temporary jobs, jobs with unhealthy working conditions, lack of social security and low pay, jobs that are undervalued and under-remunerated. The situation varies among countries but the trends are similar both in the wealthier western world and in developing countries. Many households are dependent on at least two earners. However, increased flexibilisation of work such as temporary jobs, jobs on demand and flexible work hours creates job markets where both women and men rely on multiple jobs for securing sufficient income for the household. Many countries have confronted the economic crisis and have had to implement austerity policies, which in most cases implies that public spending on social services is reduced. This development pushes women back into households and unpaid work or informal work.

The expanding labour markets are, however, insecure for women due to working conditions that are badly adapted to their responsibilities for children. One of the few reports that on a global scale have highlighted the harsh conditions for poor mothers to care for their children while working provides figures and analysis of mothers' and children's rights in connection to work and care (Heymann, 2006). For instance, working mothers in several cases are not allowed leave to take care of a sick child, lack of child care provision forces them to leave the child alone during work days, siblings (girls) are taken out of school to care for younger siblings. The report covers case studies from countries in various regions of the globe: Asia, Latin America, Russia, the United States. The author argues that it is a myth that extended families or women from the neighbourhoods are available for stable child care provision (Heymann, 2006).

Not surprisingly, precarious job situations and poor child care arrangements cause psychological stress for women and children. Women tend, in the main, to be more exposed to poor health. For instance, women working long hours and with low control of work tasks report more psychological stress than men. Lack of child care support and poorer working conditions, especially temporary and uncertain job contracts, play a significant role in poor health. Austerity policies have led to higher financial stress on the household, and concern about keeping on to jobs. This situation affects both men and women. In general, having a low educational level and/or being self-employed give the weakest opportunities for work-life balance (Hobson, 2014).

FAMILY POLICY AND WOMEN'S HUMAN RIGHTS

Women's human rights are anchored in a paradigm that regards social and economic development as linked to democracy, individuation and gender equality (Walby, 2009). Women's movements worldwide have for a long time argued for the elimination of discriminating social orders of family relationships that have detrimental effects on women and children. The continuous efforts by women's rights organisations and non-governmental organisations (NGOs) worldwide as well as activities of various committees within the UN have pushed nations towards an increased awareness of the implications of lack of attention to women's human rights and poor gender equality. In this chapter I have highlighted some of the most prominent problems that have been given international attention and prompted actions to reduce the problems. Women's rights are now on the agenda of international organisations such as the ICESCR, CEDAW, World Bank, WHO, UNICEF, international advocacy groups and NGOs. The CEDAW was established to follow up how those states that ratified the CEDAW Covenant have made progress in implementing its general recommendations. The CEDAW Committee has been engaged in monitoring improvements in 'constructive dialogues' with states about how women's situation in families and other areas can be improved through changes in laws, social and economic policies and practices.

Follow-up studies of the accomplishments of the CEDAW show that positive transformations of national laws and policies have been introduced in order to improve the situation of women. The CEDAW pays specific attention to women's disadvantaged position and demands for structural change. Also important is the focus of the Committee on 'substantive equality' and not only on formal statements on equal rights. The CEDAW's protocols and recommendations have frequently been used by advocacy and other civil rights organisations in requests for transformations of local laws. Case studies show that recommendations that are based on the involvement of women's organisations give social and political legitimacy to the reporting procedures of the states, although there are variations between states regarding space given to NGOs (Hellum and Aasen, 2013b).

However, there is frequent resistance towards changing regulations of family law and policy. For instance, many Islamic states have reservations to Article 2, stating that countries must eliminate discriminatory laws, policies and practices in the national legal framework, and Article 16, which establishes the right to equality in marriage and family relations. In comparison between regional reports, the EU has accomplished more progress in women's (or rather family) rights such as parental leave and access to reproductive health and maternal health. Within the EU more attention has been given to the rights of fathers to care leave, work regulations that acknowledge care needs within families, financial support to families through measures like tax credits or cash support.

Changing family forms and practices of family life are linked to the social effects of economic and political globalisation. The world is increasingly interconnected through international agreements regarding trade, investments in land for exploitation of natural resources such as water, minerals, air and of people as a labour force. National sovereignty and control over vital resources within a country is circumscribed by corporate interests for making a profit. Conditions connected with loans from international banks is another example of processes that are affecting living conditions, gender relations, families and children. Globalisation creates economic and political ties between countries and fosters the cultural transmission of values. But counter movements against increased inequalities and the negative effects of globalisation have fostered social unrest and idealist movements for the protection of nationalism within countries. The changing circumstances of women and of families have spurred fundamentalist ideas against gender equality and women's liberation with arguments for the maintenance of traditional family values or at least to restore these values. There are spokesmen for what they regard as natural family forms. Fundamentalist ideas are formed against reproductive rights such as abortions, sexual education, gender equality.

Neoliberal ideas about the positive role of markets in economic development argue for a reduction of state interference in the promotion of social development through public services and regulations. At the third Conference on Financing for Development in 2015, strong arguments were put forward that financing for development should be led by private capital in the future. The ideas have been opposed by civil society networks globally (Post-2015 Women's Coalition, 2015).

Criticism has also been raised regarding the global economic inequalities followed by global capital. A recent World Bank publication raised sharp criticism against how indicators and evaluations of developments and changes in countries are evaluated (Picciotto, 2015). The point of departure for the report is about the growth of social and economic inequalities within countries. With reference to the Credit Suisse Research Institute's *Global Wealth Report 2010*, 'The richest 0.5 percent hold well over a third of the world's wealth, while 68 per cent share only 4 percent.' Inequality between countries measured on an aggregate level has decreased, but inequalities within countries have increased. They argue that growth in social services, health promoting programmes and education for all are highly relevant for economic growth and prosperity (Credit Suisse Research Institute, 2010). Access to and the provision of public services like health, education and social security should not be regulated on the basis of the markets, but should be easily accessible for all citizens on an individual basis as a matter of social rights.

CONCLUSION

In this chapter I have argued that women's human rights should be a point of departure as well as a driver for family policy. Most of the problems that women have to cope with and which I have described in the chapter, such as poor maternal health, lack of reproductive health, poverty, violence against women and girls, are well known and have been the subjects of criticism for decades by women's movements. Respect for women's human rights is proclaimed to be important in agendas for social and economic development. In connection with the 20th anniversary of the Beijing platform (Bejing+20, 2015), national and regional reports have been submitted to UN Women about accomplishments and challenges for ameliorating the human rights of women. According to the country reports, much remains to be accomplished. Critical areas of insufficient progress include access to decent work and closing the gender pay gap; rebalancing of the care workload; ending violence against women; reducing maternal mortality and realizing sexual and reproductive health and rights (UNECE, 2015).

At individual levels, adaptations to transformations of societies through globalisation, urbanisation and poverty have resulted in lower fertility, increased incidence of divorces and separations of families. In particular, households headed by lone mothers have grown, and to some extent also lone father households. New migration patterns have resulted in family forms where information technology contributes to new transnational practices, such as circulation of care and care chains. These trends challenge the notions of what is to be accepted as families. The role of family policy is to contribute to sustainable families whatever form they take. Sustainable families give scope for all family members to make full use of their aspirations for a healthy life without constraints for achieving it. This means that family policy has to be mainstreamed into several policy areas, has to lean on implicit and explicit measures. Policies that aim to improve conditions for women, children and families will have to address legal norms governing housing, care, work outside the household for women. Policies also have to address fathers and husbands, as well as co-habiting partners and same sex family households. Destabilisation of family relations is spurred by the expansion of markets across the globe. New family practices across generations and kin relationships take varied forms. In the context of migration and refuge family policies will have to be regarded more as an international responsibility. The welfare of children and their upbringing call for measures that aim at sustaining family relations across boarders and across generations. Family policy makers should accept that wider kin relations are included in the care and support of children. Attention to children's human rights calls for measures to support family reunification. In refuge, families split and often women and children are left in vulnerable situations.

NOTES

1. A number of international women's conferences under the United Nations (Mexico City 1975, Copenhagen, 1980, Nairobi 1985 and Beijing 1995), the proclamation of the United Nations International Woman's year in 1975 and the United Nations Decade of Women (1976–85) gave rise to a tremendous growth in knowledge around the world on violation and non-recognition of the life situation of women across the globe. The Bejing Conference 1995 resulted in the Beijing Declaration and Platform for Action and was adopted by 189 member states meeting in China.
2. The CEDAW applies a holistic perspective on women's human rights through analysis of the ways in which structures and institutions exclude women from rights. The task of the CEDAW is to monitor implementations of rights into laws. Through analysis of texts in laws the CEDAW aims to 'engender socio-economic rights' through, for instance, its General Recommendations Optional Protocol and to contribute to discussions and concrete suggestions on the basis of reports from the countries that have accepted the Convention.

REFERENCES

Aasen, H.S. (2013), 'Maternal mortality and women's right to health', in A. Hellum and H.S. Aasen (eds), *Women's Human Rights: CEDAW in International, Regional and National Law*, Cambridge: Cambridge University Press, pp. 292–321.

Anderson, B. (ed.) (2000), *Doing the Dirty Work? The Global Politics of Domestic Labour*, London and New York: Zed Books.

Baldassar, L. and L. Merla (2014), 'Introduction. Transnational family caregiving through the lens of circulation', in L. Baldassar and L. Merla (eds), *Transnational Families, Migration and the Circulation of Care: Understanding Mobility and Absence in Family Life*, London: Routledge, pp. 25–44.

Beijing+20 (2015), Regional Review Meeting ECE.28.2014.3E.pdf, accessed 13 November 2015 at http://www.unece.org/genderwelcome-new/meetings-and-events/beijing-platform-for-action/inter-governmental-meeting/2014/beijing-20-regional-review-meeting/beijing-20-regional-review-meeting.html#/.

Bryceson, D. and U. Vuorela (eds) (2002), *The Transnational Family: New European Frontiers and Global Networks*, Oxford: Berg Publishers.

Credit Suisse Research Institute (2010), *Global Wealth Report 2010*, Credit Suisse Group AG, accessed 5 May 2017 at https://www.credit-suisse.com/ch/en/about-us/research/research-institute/publications.html.

Fredman, S. (2013), 'Actual added value of the CEDAW: socio-economic rights', in A. Hellum and H.S. Aasen (eds), *Women's Human Rights: CEDAW in International, Regional and National Law*, Cambridge: Cambridge University Press, pp. 228–30.

Furstenberg, F. (2014), 'Fifty years of family change: from consensus to complexity', *The Annals of the American Academy of Political and Social Science*, **654** (1), 2–30.

Furstenberg, F. (2015), 'Changing families around the world. The American family in a global context', Paper presented at the United Nations International Day of Families, Men in Charge? Gender Equality and Children's Rights in Contemporary Families, New York, 15 May.

Hellum, A. and H.S. Aasen (eds) (2013a), *Women's Human Rights: CEDAW in International, Regional and National Law*, Cambridge: Cambridge University Press.

Hellum, A. and H.S. Aasen (2013b), 'Conclusions', in A. Hellum and H.S. Aasen (eds), *Women's Human Rights: CEDAW in International, Regional and National Law*, Cambridge: Cambridge University Press, pp. 625–55.

Heymann, J. (ed.) (2006), *Forgotten Families: Ending the Growing Crisis Confronting Children and Working Parents in the Global Economy*, Oxford: Oxford University Press.

Hobson, B. (ed.) (2014), *Work Life Balance: The Agency & Capabilities Gap*, Oxford: Oxford University Press.

Ikdahl, I. (2013), 'Property and security: articulating women's rights to their homes', in A. Hellum and H.S. Aasen (eds), *Women's Human Rights: CEDAW in International, Regional and National Law*, Cambridge: Cambridge University Press, pp. 268–91.

Merla, L. (2014), 'A macro perspective on transnational families and care circulation: situating capacity, obligations and family commitments', in L. Baldassar and L. Merla (eds), *Transnational Families, Migration and the Circulation of Care: Understanding Mobility and Absence in Family Life*, London and New York: Routledge, pp. 115–33.

Morgan, D.H.J. (ed.) (1996), *Family Connections: An Introduction to Family Studies*, Cambridge: Policy Press.

Nussbaum, M. and A. Sen (eds) (1993), *The Quality of Life*, Oxford: Clarendon Press.

Picciotto, R. (2015), 'Bringing inequality back in from the cold: toward a progressive evaluation model', in R.C. Rist, F.P. Martin, and A.M. Fernandez (eds), *Poverty, Inequality and Evaluation: Changing Perspectives*, Washington, DC: World Bank Group.

Post-2015 Women's Coalition (2015), *Mission*, accessed 10 January 2016 at http://www.post2015women.com/mission/.

Rostgaard, T. and R.J. Möberg (2015), 'Fathering: the influence of ideational factors for male fertility behaviour', in G.B. Eydal and T. Rostgaard (eds), *Fatherhood in the Nordic Welfare States: Comparing Care Policies and Practice*, Bristol: Policy Press, pp. 30–31.

Sassen, S. (ed.) (1998), *Globalisation and its Discontents*, New York: Cambridge University Press.

United Nations Millennium Development Goals (2015a), *UN Development Report*, accessed 19 August 2015 at http://www.un.org/tsa/ffd.

United Nations (2015b), *The Millenium Development Goals Report 2015*, acessed 18 December at https://www.google.se/search?q=millennium+development+goals+report+2015&ie=utf-8&oe=utf-8&client=firefox-b&gfe_rd=cr&ei=rmwMWYf9AZSr8wevwIDACw.

UN Women (2015), *Progress of the World's Women 2015–2016: Transforming Economies Realizing Rights*, accessed April 2017 at http://www.unwomen.org/en/digital-library/publications/2015/4/progress-of-the-worlds-women-2015.

UNECE (2015), *Indicators for Gender Equality*, accessed 5 May 2015 at http://www.unece.org/index.php?id=38461.

Walby, S. (2009), *Globalization and Inequalities: Complexity and Contested Modernities*, London and Los Angeles, CA: Sage.
WHO (2015a), *Trends in Maternal Mortality: 1990 to 2013*, accessed 30 November 2015 at http://www.who.int/reproductivehealth/publications/monitoring/maternal-mortality-2013/en/.
WHO (2015b), *WHO Launches Toolkit to Help Countries Respond to Sexual Violence*, accessed 30 November 2015 at http://www.who.int/mediacentre/news/notes/2015/sexual-violence-elimination/en/.
Wichterich, C. (2015), 'Sexual and reproductive rights', accessed 30 November 2015 at http://www.gwi-boell.de/en/2015/07/23/sexual-and-reproductive-rights.

Index

Advisory Council on Governmental Policy 161
Africa, social security systems and social policies in 249
aid workers 369
ambitious data collection 325
analysis of variance 303
Angel Plan 119
An Outline of Foreign Social Insurance and Assistance Laws 12
ANOVA procedures 301
Anttonen, A. 183
Asian welfare state model 111
austerity 157
　policies 45, 383
Australia 84, 85, 111, 114
　parental leave benefits in 130
　trade unions 143
Austria
　attitudes indicating differences between 177, 178
　development of women's employment rates 174
　family policies in 168, 170–71, 174
　fundamental cultural transformation 175
　gender arrangements of 175
　gender culture of 175
　paid parental leave program 172–3
　welfare states of 168, 171, 173, 178
　women's caring role 171
autocracies
　defined 289, 290
　family leave policy of 295
　fertility rates in 295
　legitimization and justification of 290–91
　literature on families in 291
　measuring and explaining variation within 290
　observation of 289
　participation rates in 296
autocratic countries 289–90
　demographics 295–6
　explaining variation 301–4
　family leave policy 296–301
　literature review 290–94
　methodology 294–5
autocratic family policy 294

Back-to-Work scheme 240
Bahle, T. 210
Bailyn, L. 147
Bambra, C. 58
Beland, D. 97
Belarus 295, 296, 300, 355
Berg, P. 142
Bertlesmann Foundation's Transformation Index (BTI) 290
Bettio, F. 41
Beveridge, W. 85
'beyond income' frameworks 310
Bjornberg, U. 197
Black African households 250
Bologna agreement 157–8
Bradshaw, J. 55
'breadwinner-housewife' gender 345
breastfeeding 331
Brumit Kropf, M. 140–41
BTI *see* Bertlesmann Foundation's Transformation Index (BTI)
burden of reciprocity 45
Bureaus Jeugdzorg 159

Carbonnier, C. 41
care chains 379
caregiving 262
care of children 276
carers, child benefits 91–2
Care Work in Europe: Current Understandings and Future Directions 26
cash for care (CFC) 200–201
CCTs *see* conditional cash transfers (CCTs)
CEDAW Committee 383
Central and Eastern Europe 223
　child poverty 230–32
　familialism 224–6
　patterns of public expenditures 226–30
Central Social Welfare Board (CSWB) 279, 280, 284
Centre for the Child's Rights and Corporate Social Responsibility 358
CFC *see* cash for care (CFC)
changes in family policies 74
　CME/Social democratic welfare states 77–8
　encouraging female labor participation in CME/Conservative welfare states 76

family income protection, expansion in 77
  index scores 75
  LME/Liberal welfare states 77
Chau, R.C.M. 41
Child Allowance Law 119
child and family policy in Southern Europe 209
  childcare services, parental leave and reconciliation policies 211–14
  family benefits in comparative perspective 209–10
  family challenges and new policy drivers 215–17
  persistence of underdevelopment 214–15
  post-economic crisis scenario 217–18
childbearing 344
child benefits 84
  affordability 92
  child poverty 86–7
  fertility 89–91
  infrastructural problem 93
  Japan, in 90
  mothers or carers 91–2
  policy makers 92–3
  structure of package 90
  targeted social assistance or minimum income schemes 92–3
  UK case 85
childcare 96–8
  arrangements 383
  changing realities 97–9
  cost and availability of 343
  global agenda of 101
  institutional response of EU 99–101
  leave provisions 274
  in national policy making 101
    accessibility 103–6
    affordability 106
    organizational structure 102
    quality 106–7
    social expenditure 102–3
  quality 344
  services, quantity of 99
  subsidies 242
  theoretical framework 97
childcare provision 16
child/children
  abuse and neglect 328
  cash 329
  financial costs of 343
  health services 355
  labour 282
  as nature 28
  poverty and life satisfaction 327
  poverty risks 155
  rights, international discourses on 275
  shifting 358
  tax benefits 329
  well-being 351
childhood logic 27
childhood services in Latin America 265–6
Child Labour (Prohibition and Regulation) Act (CLPR) 282
child outcomes 18
child poverty 18, 86–7, 223, 249, 251, 308–9
  comprehensive studies of 309
  data 311
  disposable income poverty 312–15
  lines 312–15
  and redistribution 315–23
    family-related transfers and children's poverty 317
    household type matters 318
    parents' paid work matters 318, 323
  synthesis of research 309–10
  variables and empirical approach 311–12
  work on 310
child poverty rates 318, 327–8
  and patterns 308–9
  relative and absolute 314
child poverty reduction 317
child protection 161, 367
child-rearing 354
  cost of 344
  parental 359
  skills 331
  work interruptions for 261
child-related leave 124
Child Support Grant (CSG) 249–50, 252–3
  behavioural conditions 253
  design features of 254
  family structure of 254
  gender-neutral policy 253
  male breadwinner model 255
child well-being 325, 356
  comparative studies of well-being 326
  domain of 326–7
  family policies and 325–8
    child cash and tax benefits 329
    general welfare policies 328–9
    job-protected paid parenting leave 330
    public funding for early education and child care 330–31
    subjective dimensions of 331–2
  objective and subjective domains of 326
  objective measure of 327
  research on 326
  scholarship on 326
Chile Puente (Chile Bridge) 354

China
  family policies 245
  family support 355
  kindergartens 245
  maternity leave period 245
  Regulation for Kindergartens 245
  social security for individuals 244
circulation of care 379
citizenship education 157
Civil Union Act of 2006 257
climate change 368
CME/Conservative countries 76
CME/Conservative welfare states 69–70
  family policy encouraging female labor participation 76
CMEs *see* coordinated market economies (CMEs)
Collaborative Interactive Action Research (CIAR) 147
collective agreements 143
collective bargaining 142, 143
  work-family arrangements in 143
Committee on the Rights of the Child (CRC) 382
communist ideocracies 302
Comparative Family Policy Database 55
comparative study of changes in family policies
  CMEs *see* coordinated market economies (CMEs)
  LMEs and liberal welfare state regimes 68–9
  VoC 66–7
comparative study of child benefits
  CSB MIPI data 87
  net minimum wage, package and 88
  packages in rich countries 87–9
  pre and post transfer child poverty rates in 2013 89
comparative study of early childhood service culture
  Denmark, case of 25–7
  English language 32–3
  film 32
  language 32
  Reggio Emilia, case of 28–9
  research attention 31–2
  SOPHOS 32
  Sweden, case of 27–8
complementarity 42
composite indices 58
Comprehensive Policy Index (CPI) 344–5
conceptual issues in family policy 48
concerning proper behaviour 157
Conditional Cash Transfer programs 265

conditional cash transfers (CCTs) 279, 281
Confucian cultural heritage 236
Confucian cultural influences 300
Confucian value systems 41
consequences of family policy
contemporary family life, features of 379
contemporary parenthood 337
contextual realities 98
Convention on the Elimination of all Forms of Discrimination against Women (CEDAW) 376
coordinated market economies (CMEs) 67–8
  common problems in 69
  conservative welfare states, and 69–70
  female workers 69
  social democratic welfare states, and 70, 77–8
coproduction 373
core countries 14
co-responsibility
  executive policy effort on 268–9
  policies 262
CPI *see* Comprehensive Policy Index (CPI)
creative work-family management 147
criminal behavior 328
Critical Discourse Analysis 32
cross-national projects 39
crowding out 16, 41–2
CSG *see* Child Support Grant (CSG)
culture, defined 170
Cyclone Mahasen 365
Cyclone Sidr 365

Dahlberg 28
Daly, M. 38, 45
Da Roit, B. 41
Daycare centers 343
deal-types of countries 14
decommodification 40, 183
defamilialization 13–14, 40–41, 50, 183, 293
  Bambra's index 58
  private markets 41
degendering index 73
deinstitutionalization 156
delayed marriage 157
Democracy Index 290
democratic deficit 158
demographics 292–3, 295–6
  age structure and fertility 16
  leave variables 302
  transition 278–9
Denmark
  caring for small children 202
  CFC scheme in 201
  ECEC 200

father's quota 199
poverty level 205
descriptives 302
determinants of family policy
governmental expenditures 14
institutions role and gender ideology 16–17
methodological development 17
nonexpenditures-based indicators 14
theoretical explanations 16–17
work of Wennemo 16
DHI *see* disposable household income (DHI)
Disaster Interventions Committee 363
disasters
community vulnerabilities to 367
consequences of 364
description of 364
differentiated experiences of 363, 368
intervention 373
prevention strategies 372
discretionary spending 155
disorganized families 256
disposable household income (DHI) 311
do-democracy 161
domestic violence 293
draft national policy for women 277
'drivers' of policy change 156
dual-earner households 339
dual-earner support 58

Early Childhood Education and Care (ECEC) 51, 196, 209, 238, 262
early childhood service 24–5
culture 25, 31–3
schoolification 25
structure 25, 30–31
early comparative work
academic work 12–13
international and national organizations 12
East Asia 236
demographic profiles of 237
diverging approaches to 238
liberal market approach 238–40
regulated institutional approach 241–3
familistic root of 236–8
family policies in 238
Ebola 382
ECEC *see* Early Childhood Education and Care (ECEC); early childhood education and care (ECEC)
economic de-familisation *vs.* care-focused familisation 41
economic development 16
economic recessions 329
education 330
citizenship 157

parenting 355
public funding for early 330–31
quality of 253
elderly care 39–40
electoral autocracies 291, 302
eligibility criteria 267
Emilia, Reggio 29, 30
emotionality 373
emotional wellbeing
dimensions of 338
levels of 338
parenthood and 338
sources of parenthood deficit in 341
types of burdens 339
employees, work-family outcomes for 142
English language 32–3
equity-enhancing effects of policies 265
ESI Act, India 283
Esping-Andersen, G. 169, 183, 215–16
ESRC project in Sri Lanka 367, 369
ETUC *see* European Trade Union Confederation (ETUC)
EU Lisbon Strategy in 2000 99
European family policy models 209
European Trade Union Confederation (ETUC) 142
European Union (EU) 24
European Union (EU) Statistics on Income and Living Conditions (EU-SILC) 53
European Union Statistics on Income and Living Conditions (EU-SILC) 308
EU-SILC *see* European Union (EU) Statistics on Income and Living Conditions (EU-SILC)
EU Social Investment Package in 2013 96
evidence-based behavioral parent training 331
'exceptional' welfare state 184
expenditures
on family benefits 16
perspectives 50–51
extensive defamilialization 183

familialism 40
familialization 183
family
benefit systems 84–5
composition, explicit model of 275
defined 2–3
income protection index 73–4
and maternity leaves 72–3
Family and Medical Leave Act 341
family and state obligations
de-familialisation 40–41
in Europe (early 1990s) 36–40

familialisation 40–41
support and care 41–5
family and state support and care
   an assumption that grandparents will provide care 43
   care decisions 44
   childcare 42–3
   complementarity 42
   crowding out 41–2
   grandparent care 43
   neutral or mixed 43
   no assumption that grandparents will provide care 43
   policy environments 43–4
family-based benefits 274
family care and support
   family networks 45
   poverty 44
   wider family 44
family care leave 241
family/children transfers 311
family-friendly policies 371, 373
family leave 289, 296–301
   initial qualitative examination of 296
   types of 294
   variables 302
family life, forms and practices of 384
family models 6–7
family-nurse partnership 159
Family Nurse Partnership service 356
family obligations in Europe
   cash and care 37
   cash payments 39
   changes in practice 39
   family and employment 36
   family policy 37
   gender roles 39
   groupings of countries 38
   parenthood 38
   parenting support 38–9
   payments to family carers 39–40
   social change, and 37
   weakening of marriage 38
family planning 380
   campaigns, ideal family in 278
family policies 4–5, 325
   analysis 223
   Central and Eastern Europe *see* Central and Eastern Europe
   child-centred 49
   and child well-being 325–8
      child cash and tax benefits 329
      general welfare policies 328–9
      job-protected paid parenting leave 330
      public funding for early education and child care 330–31
      subjective dimensions of 331–2
   classifications 59–62
   comparative analysis of 293
   concepts of family 49
   cultural basis of 170
   databases 54–7
   defamilialism and familialism 60
   definition 2–3, 48–9
   distinct fields and scopes of 5–6
   early childhood education and care and parental leave policies 60–61
   in East Asia *see* East Asia
   expenditure data 55
   gender and care relations 50
   in India *see* India, family policy in
   initiatives 154
   institutional setting of 170
   intervention, kind of 49–50
   labour supply theory 60–61
   measured 50–53
   in Nordic countries *see* Nordic countries
   observation of 289
   OECD 54–5
      Family Database 61
   parent-centred 49
   path-breaking reform of 171–2
   patterns in autocratic countries *see* autocratic countries
   research 3–4, 289
      determinants, on 14–17
      early comparative work 11–13
      outcomes of 7–8
      outcomes, on 17–18
      studies on family policy regimes 13–14
   in South Africa *see* South Africa
   systems, national configurations of 154
   traditional concept of family 49
Family Policy Index 58
family policy indicators
   availability 53–4
   composite indices 58
   institutional factors, measuring 54
   league tables and scorecards 59
   reliability and validity 53
   time-variance 54
   typologies 58–9
family practices, definitions of 377
family-preparedness 372
family-related policy, types of 357
family-related state programmes 276
family-related transfers 317, 318
family relationships, social orders of 383
family solidarity 215

family structures 377–8
  changing 378
  cross-national indicators on 100
family support 351, 353
  developments overall 352–3
  forms and modalities of 353–7
  between high-, middle- and low-income regions 351, 353
  roots and implications 358–9
  significance for social and family policy 359–60
family-supportive disaster 363
family supportive supervisor behaviours (FSSB) 146
family survivors 363
family vulnerabilities 366
family welfare orientation 58
family well-being, employer contributions to 369
father-specific leave entitlements 131–4
female-headed households 378
female labour force participation 17, 70, 296
female work desirability 58
feminisation of labour 382
feminist social policy analyses 169
fertility 17
  among women 378
  child birth 89
  developing countries, in 91
  Japan 90
  middle-income and poorer countries 90–91
  rate in 2012 and percentage of GDP spent on family benefits and services 91
financial strain 339
Finch, J. 37
Finland 198
  CFC scheme in 200–201
  ECEC 200
  fathers' and mothers' employment 201
  father's quota 199
  payment rate 130
  poverty level 205
Finnish CFC system 201
firm-specific skills 69
flexibilisation 382
flexible labour market 157
Flood Re Scheme 369
forced marriage 376
fragile ecosystems 367
framework of welfare and production regime types
  capitalism frameworks 66–70
  country-level indicators 70–71
  family policy changes 74–8

policy goals 71
research approach, methods and data 70–74
France 215
  antisocial behaviour of young people in 160
  'child health', 'child protection' and 'cognitive stimulation' 162
  parenting support 158, 161
free powers of market 178
Froebel, Friedrich 97
Full Time Equivalents (FTE) 73, 294
Full Time Equivalent Units 296

GDP see gross domestic product (GDP)
GEEA see Gender Equality in Employment Act (GEEA)
gender culture 170
gendered familialism 275
gender equality 124
  perspectives 152
Gender Equality in Employment Act (GEEA) 243
gender gap 249
gender ideology 16–17, 140
gender inequality 249
gendering index 72–3
gender issues 291
gender-related risks 155
gender roles 72, 296, 303
general family support 58
generosity levels 296
Germany
  Act on Childcare Allowance and Parental Leave 172
  attitudes indicating differences between 177, 178
  development of women's employment rates 174
  family policies in 168, 170–71, 174
  family values 176
  fundamental cultural transformation 175
  gender arrangements of 175
  gender culture of 175
  male breadwinner model 128
  population 176
  welfare states of 168, 171, 173, 178
  women's caring role 171
  working time in 142
Glaser, K. 43
global economic order 157
global financial crisis 223
globalisation 384
  negative effects of 384
global knowledge economy 158

global production systems 382
good parenting 161, 356
Gornick, J. 51, 58, 60, 61
Great Recession of 2008 218
Greece
  female activity rates in 218
  unemployment in 217
Gregg, P. 92
gross domestic product (GDP) 236
  family income protection index 73

Haiyan (Hurricane) 363
Hammer, L.B. 146
Health Behavior in School-aged Children (HBSC) study 326
Heckman, J. 98
hierarchical cluster analyses 301
HIV/AIDS 358, 382
home care leave 129, 130
Hong Kong
  ECEC services in 240
  family support policies 239
  foreign domestic workers 240
  liberal market approaches 238
  Pre-primary Education Voucher 240
  white collar working mothers in 240
housewife model of family 176
housing shortages 382
human capital 114
  investment in 111
humanitarian aid 368
(hu)man-made disasters 364
human resources, social reproduction and care of 376
human vulnerability 364
Hungary 223
  child care services 225
  child poverty 225
  economic dependence in 230
  employment rate of mothers 229
  expenditures on family benefits 226
  family allowance 227–8
  family and population policies 224
  maternity leave 228
  poverty rates in 232
  relative poverty reduction of social transfers 231
  social policy regulations 224
  social spending on families and children in 224
Hurricane Haiyan 363
Hurricane Mitch 366

ICDS *see* Integrated Child Development Scheme (ICDS)

Iceland 198
  CFC scheme in 201
  father's quota 199
ideological autocracies 291
IIPP project 367
ILO Declaration of Philadelphia of 1944 12
ILO Maternity Protection Convention of 1919 12
impact of child benefits on net income 88
income transfer policy reforms 310
index construction
  degendering index 73
  family income protection 73–4
  family policy index scores 75
  gender equality 72
  work/family balance 71–2
India, family policy in 274–5
  children as category in social policy 279–82
  five-year plan 279–80
  maternity and childcare entitlements 282–4
  minimum wages, women's employment and family life 277–8
  outlining 276–7
  population policy 278–9
Indian Ocean Tsunami 363
Indira Gandhi Matritava Sahayog Yojana (IGMSY) maternity benefit programme 283
individualization 50
individualized human capital 158
infant mortality rates 275
informal care networks 261–2
informal job markets 382
Insofar 343–4
Integrated Child Development Scheme (ICDS) 275, 280
interdisciplinarity 373
intergenerational familial dependency 237
inter-generational relations 274
international agreements 16
International Covenant on Economic, Social and Cultural Rights (ICESCR) 382
international developments 274
international diffusion 16
international discourse 358
International Early Learning Study and Child Well-being (IELS) project 101
International Labour Organization (ILO) 12, 262
  Inquiry into the Cost of Social Security 12
  Recommendation Concerning National Floors of Social Protection 86
international policy agencies 358
International Social Survey Programme (ISSP) 176

international trade 379
intra-familial practices 274
ISSP *see* International Social Survey Programme (ISSP)
Italy 143, 216
   cultural hegemony on family definition and family issues 215
   family cash benefits in 210
   female voters in 217
   leave policies 214
   social policy for families 214

Jamaica 357
   child shifting 358
   national parenting support policy 351
   parenting education 355
Janani Suraksha Yojna (JSY) 283
Japan
   changes in family structures 112
   development of human resources 116
   family support policies 241
   ideal typology of 111
   leave system 120
   nature of social policies in 115
   paid maternity leave 242
   Parental Leave Law 120
   public social spending 236
   social investment policy 115, 118–20
   welfare state 118
Jensen, Jytte Juul 26, 27
job-protected paid parenting leave 330
juvenile delinquency 155

Kahn, A.J. 37, 182–3
Kahn, J. 58
Kamerman, S.B. 37, 58, 182–3
Kaufmann, F.X. 49
Keck, W. 40
Kelly, G. 45
Keynesianism 113
Kingdon, J.W. 153, 156, 158, 163
Korean type welfare state 111
Korpi, W. 55, 58, 59
Koslowski, A. 55
Kossek, N.L. 144
Kröger, T. 58
Kuronen, M. 39

labour markets 154–5, 382
   conditions 141
   outcomes 130
   requirements 278
labour mobility 378–9
labour supply theory 60–61
Latin America 261–2
   early childhood and education services in 266–70
   employment-based leaves 263–4
      maternity leaves 264–5
      paternity and parental leaves 265–6
   paid employment-related leaves for salaried workers 264
   parental leaves and care services 262–3
Law and Justice Party (PiS) 228
League of Nations 12
league tables and scorecards 59
leave eligibility 296
leave policies for parents 124
   cross-national differences in 125
   father-specific leave entitlements 131–4
   gender balance in 124
   leave days to care for a sick relative 130–31
   maternity leave entitlements 125–6
   parental leave and total period of paid leave 126–30
   public spending on leave 134–5
leaves, policy adoption on 264
Le Bihan, B. 39
left behind children 358
legal property rights 381
Leitner, S. 59–61
Lewis, J. 183
liberal approach 114–15
liberal family policy
   exploration of 184
   'minimalistic' characterization of 183
liberalization 117
liberal market approach 236, 238
liberal market economies (LMEs) 68
   liberal welfare state regimes, and 68–9
liberal models, family policy expansion 182, 183–4
   free markets and minimal social policy 182
   liberal family policy 182–6
   'targeting' and 'generosity' in family policies 186
   UK characteristics and developments 186–9
   US characteristics and developments 189–91
liberal welfare state regimes/LMEs 68–9
   expansion in family income protection 77
licensed childcare centres 242
LIS *see* Luxembourg Income Study (LIS)
Lisbon agenda 224
Lisbon Treaty 157
LIS microdata 308–9
LME/Liberal cluster 76, 77
Lorenz, Walter 32
low-income female workers 68–9
low-income parents 339
Lundberg, S. 92

Luxembourg Income Study (LIS) 53
Lyness, K.S. 140–41

macro-social phenomena 54
Mager, Karl 26
Mahasen (cyclone) 365
Mahatma Gandhi National Rural Employment Guarantee Scheme (MGNREGS) 283
Malaguzzi, Loris 29, 30
'male-breadwinner/female part-time carer' model 175
male caregivers 379–80
male dominance 376
  on organizations 141
mandatory spending 155
Mandel, H. 197
market defamilialization 184
market income (MI) 311
  poverty 323
Martin, C. 39
Mason, J. 37
material deprivation 310
maternal deaths 380
maternal employment 96
maternal mortality rates 275
Maternity Benefit Act 1961 283
maternity employment policy 16
maternity leaves 16, 72–3, 262–5, 294, 342
  entitlements 125–6
  expiry of 130
  public expenditure on 134–5
measurement approaches
  benefits, family 52
  expenditure perspective 50–51
  indicators 53–4
  internationally comparable expenditure data 51
  outcomes perspective 52–3
  social rights indicators 51–2
  social rights perspective 51
  standard indicators 52
  tax-benefit system 52
Meyers, M.K. 38, 51
MI see market income (MI)
military regimes 291
Millennium Development Goals 280, 376, 380
Minimum Wages Act 1948 277
Mitch (Hurricane) 366
modernization of welfare system 112–13
monarchies 291, 302
Moo-hyun, Roh 116
Morel, N. 41
mother
  child benefits 91–2
  family policy for 71

motherhood penalty 17
mothers' return to work after childbirth 17
Muller-Muralt, J. 173, 178
Multilinks Database 55
Mutual Help Child Care Centres 239
Myung-Bak, Lee 117

National Charter for Children 281
National Creche Fund 284
national family policy (NFP) 146, 250, 255
National Maternity Benefit Scheme (NMBS) 283
National Policy for Children 281, 282
national policy making, childcare in
  accessibility 103–6
  affordability 106
  organizational structure 102
  quality 106–7
  social expenditure 102–3
National Program to Combat Child Poverty 227
national sovereignty 384
natural-made disasters 364
neglected families 363–4
  disasters 364–6
    differentiated experiences of 366–8
    families responding to 368–70
    family-friendly support 370–71
    family-friendly disaster responses for policy-makers 371–2
    policies to support 373
neo-liberal economics 274
neoliberalism 114
neo-Marxist approach 291
Netherlands
  'child health', 'child protection' and 'cognitive stimulation' 162
  parenting support 158
  public family policies 145
  working time in 142
NFP see national family policy (NFP)
nonexpenditures-based indicators 14
non-governmental organisations (NGOs) 239, 351, 383
non-profit childcare centre 240
non-workplace-based creches 284
Nordenmark, M. 202
Nordic children 314–15
Nordic countries 195–6
  at-risk-of-poverty (AROP) 204
  care policies 198
  cash for care (CFC) 200–201
  childcare services for children 197
  child poverty in 196, 204–5
  contemporary family policies 196

definition of 195
dual earner/dual carer model 196
early childhood education and care services 199–200
ECEC services 200
employment 202
family benefit system 204
family cash benefits 203–4
gross domestic product (GDP) 197
importance of 195
from male breadwinner to dual earner/dual carer model 196–8
New Public Management 196–7
paid parental leave 198–9
purchasing power parity (PPP) 203
social expenditure on families 198
systems of family benefit packages 203
work and care 201–2
Nordic or Social Democratic welfare regime model 25
Nordic welfare model 195
components of 201
Nordic welfare states 173
North-western Europe, parenting support in 152–4
new problems and family policy framing 154–6
triggers of change for family policy turning points 156–8
North-western Europe, parenting support in drivers of change 158–62
Norway
CFC scheme in 200–201
father's quota 199

O'Connor 182–3
OECD countries *see* Organisation for Economic Co-operation and Development (OECD) countries
Old Age and Autonomy (OASIS) project 42
one-party autocracies 291
Open Method of Coordination (OMC) governance literature 99
Organisation for Economic Co-operation and Development (OECD) countries 24, 51, 66, 236
Family Database 54–5
family policies 54–5
institutional approach by 96–7
institutional response 99–101
overview of selection of family policy typologies based on 15–16
organizational culture 145
organizations 141

culture of 146
male-dominated 141
proportion of women in 141
Ostner, I. 183
outcome perspectives 52–3

paid domestic workers 262
paid leave
duration of 126
reserved for fathers 133
paid maternity leave 127, 128
paid parental leave 129, 342
paid parenting 330
parental child-rearing 359
parental deaths 382
parental happiness 344–5
parental leave 126–30, 265–6, 294
entitlements, use of 131
public expenditure on 134–5
'Parental Leave Act' in 1991 119
parental responsibilities 378
parental wellbeing 343
impact on 344
parenthood 157
costs and rewards for 344
deficit, sources of 341
emotional effects of 340
employment costs of 344
financial aspects of 343
and wellbeing 337–8
distal supports and proximate stressors 341
financial costs associated with 343
parental wellbeing in advanced industrialized countries 338–41
parents *vs.* nonparents 341–2
psychosocial stress associated with 343–5
time costs associated with 342–3
parenting 155, 353
aspects of 339
policy, changes in 152
privatisation of 359
programmes 356–7
public turn to 156
renewed focus on 154–5
'scientification' of 157
support intervention 357
parenting support 153, 357
defined 38–9
form of 356
in North-western Europe 152–4
drivers of change 158–62
new problems and family policy framing 154–6

triggers of change for family policy turning points 156–8
orientations of 357
parents' paid work matters 318, 323
parents' places 356
Parsonian family sociology approach 257
partial de-familialisation 40
participation society 161
paternal co-responsibility policies 263
paternity leave 263, 265–6, 294, 296
path dependency 33
  emphasizing 16
patrilineal inheritance 276
PCA *see* principal components analysis (PCA)
Pelikh, A. 43
persistence and change in family policies 168
  in conservative welfare states 170–71
    change in 171
    conservative 171
    paid parental leave 172–3
    promotion of the equal sharing of childcare 173–4
    public childcare for children under school age 171–2
  cross-national differences 168
  role of cultural differences 174–9
  role of women's employment 174
  state of research 169
  theoretical framework 169–70
personalist autocracies 291
Pfenning, A. 210
Philippines, The 355
physical violence 365, 381
PIACC *see* Programme for the International Assessment of Adult Competencies (PIACC)
Pierson, C. 155
PIRLS *see* Progress in International Reading Literacy Study (PIRLS)
PISA *see* Programme for International Student Assessment (PISA)
planned family 278
Poland
  child poverty 225, 230–31
  earnings-related paid leave 228
  effectiveness in child poverty 232
  employment rate of mothers 229
  expenditures on family benefits 226
  family policy 224–6
  implicit familialism 225
  maternity leave 228
  population policies 224
  relative poverty reduction of social transfers 231

risk of poverty 232
social policy regulations 224
social spending on families and children in 224
tax credits for families 226
policy adoption, comparative assessment of 267
policy change
  'drivers' of 156
  'triggers' of 156
policy design, gender and social equity implications of 262
policy entrepreneurs 153
policy reactions, combinations of 155–6
policy reality 98
policy-related international experts 154
political ideologies and power mobilization 16
poor families 45
population policy 275
Portugal
  family cash benefits in 210
  leave policies 214
'post-communist' welfare states 224
post-traumatic stress 370
poverty 44, 327, 378
  defining 312
  line 312–15
  measurements of 275
  prevention of 171
  rates 311–18
  and redistribution 315–23
    family-related transfers and children's poverty 317
    in high-income countries 311
    household type matters 318
    parents' paid work matters 318, 323
  reduction of 381
  risk of 318, 330
  women 381
poverty reduction 230, 311, 315–23
  family benefit expenditures and 317
PPP *see* purchasing power parity (PPP)
pre and post transfer child poverty rates in 2013 89
pregnancy 380
pre-school logic 27
pre-school teachers 27
pre-tax-pre-transfer income 311
principal components analysis (PCA) 61
private markets, de-familialisation 41
productive social policy approach 113
productive welfare 116
productivism 114
Programme for International Student Assessment (PISA) 24, 326

Programme for the International
    Assessment of Adult Competencies
    (PIACC) 24
Progress in International Reading Literacy
    Study (PIRLS) 24
property rights 382
psychological distress 339–40
psychological violence 381
Public Administrative Council 161
public discourse 279
Public Distribution System (PDS) 275,
    280
public funding for early education 330
public policy 276
    gendered familialism in 275
public spending on family 16
purchasing power parity (PPP) 311
    family income protection index 73
Purposeful Parenting for Working Parents
    358

Qatar, female labour force participation rates
    in 296
qualitative clustering 301
quality criteria 53–4

Rajiv Gandhi National Creche Scheme for
    Children of Working Mothers 284
Rathbone, E. 85
recipient-oriented childcare 117
redistributive social expenditure 111
re-familization 50
Regolamento delle scuole comunali dell'infamzia
    30
regulated institutional approach 236, 238
relative-*versus*-absolute poverty 314
re-producer of culture and knowledge 28
reproductive health 380
residual welfare system 275
rhetorical framing of childcare 97
rich child 29–30
Right to Education Act (RTE) 280–81
Roma ethnic minority 224
Romania 223
    earnings-related paid child care 229
    employment rate of mothers 229
    expenditures on family benefits 226
    family policy spending 227
    job-return bonuses in 229
    maternity leave 228
    optional familism 225
    relative poverty reduction of social transfers
        231
    risk of poverty 232
    social protection budget 228

Sabatinelli, S. 41
Sainsbury, D. 195
same sex families 378
same sex marriages 257
same-sex partnerships 49
Saraceno, C. 39, 40
schoolification 25
scientific child 28
scientific realities 98
SCIP *see* Social Citizenship Indicator Program
    (SCIP)
Second Order Phenomenological Observation
    Scheme (SOPHOS) 26, 32
secure housing 382
self-employment for women 277
self-reliance of families 255
semi-formalization 50
Semyonov, M. 197
Sendai World Conference on Disaster Risk
    Reduction (2015) 366
set-theoretic approaches 59
sex selective abortions 278–9
sexual violence 365
SHARE panel *see* Survey of Health, Ageing
    and Retirement in Europe (SHARE)
    panel
Siaroff, A. 58
Sidr (cyclone) 365
Simoni, R. 45
Singapore
    Baby Bonus Scheme 239
    Child Development Account 239
    ECEC services in 240
    family support policies 239
    financial incentives 239
    institutional approach 242
    liberal market approaches 238
    paid marriage leave for employees 239
single indicators 58
single mothers 50
single parents 49, 378
Sipila, J. 183
skilled labour 156
'skills begets skills' concept 98
Skinner, C. 38
skolledare 27
small-n problem 54
Social Citizenship Indicator Program (SCIP)
    51, 55
social democratic approach 114–15
social democratic welfare states 70, 77–8
social-economic inequalities 328
social equity 263, 265
social inequality 261
social insurance policies 328

social investment 111–12, 155, 156
　approaches 112, 114–15, 359
　approach in Western countries 112–14
　perspectives 114–16
　in South Korea and Japan 114–20
　welfare state 112
social legitimacy in society 140
social movement campaigns 280–81
social pedagogical family support 159
social pedagogy 26
social policy 113, 359
　designs 312
　reforms 310
Social Protection Strategic Framework 86
social protection system (*Chile Solidario*) 354
social reproduction 377
social rights perspective 51
social security 274, 382
　income-support benefits 215
Social Security Act 12
Social Security Programs throughout the World 12
social services 379
socio-economic change 170
socio-economic inequalities 275, 325, 378
South Africa 249–50, 356
　Black African and Coloured populations 251
　child support grant 252–5
　contexts and changing social dynamics 250–52
　deficiencies 257
　'disorganized' family 257
　female caregivers 253
　female-headed households 252
　gender-neutral eligibility criteria 254
　HIV and AIDS prevalence rates 251
　and household structures 252
　lone mother family 252
　national family policy 255–7
　population groups 250
　poverty reduction 253
　quality of education 253
　social assistance 252–3
　socio-economic and cultural processes 250
　unemployment of female beneficiaries 255
　universal child allowance 253
South African Social Security Agency (SASSA) 254
Southern Europe
　at-risk-of-poverty rate 217–18
　child and family policy in 209
　childcare services, parental leave and reconciliation policies 211–14
　child poverty rates 210
　demographic and social changes 215
　development of family benefits 214
　dual-earner families 211
　enrolment rates in formal childcare 211–12
　familialism 209
　family benefits in comparative perspective 209–10
　family challenges and new policy drivers 215–17
　family policies in 209
　formal childcare 212
　male and female unemployment rates 217
　maternity and paternity leaves 212
　maternity/initial leaves 213
　parental leave arrangements 212
　Parental Leave Equality Index (PLEI) 213
　part-time work 213
　persistence of underdevelopment 214–15
　post-economic crisis scenario 217–18
　poverty rates of children in 217–18
　public investment in childcare 212
　welfare states and family policies 211
South Korea
　changes in family structures 112
　childcare policies 118
　Equal Employment Act 242–3
　family policy 116, 118, 241
　ideal typology of 111
　institutional approach 242
　Labour Standard Act 242–3
　maternity and parental leave systems in 242
　nature of social policies in 115
　paid maternity leave 242
　social investment policy 115
Spain
　cultural hegemony on family definition and family issues 215
　family cash benefits in 210
　female activity rates in 218
　female voters 216
　marriage in 216
　paternity leave 218
　social policy for families 214
　unemployment in 217
spatial intervention 373
SPIN database 55
state co-responsibility policies 263
state-funded childcare facilities 117
step-families 49
Streeck, W. 155
stress
　distal sources of 340
　levels 342
　proximate sources of 340

stressors, proximate sources of 340
structural-functionalist model of societies 256
structure/culture divide
    early childhood service *see* early childhood service
    performative dimension 24
subcontract out filial piety 238
subjective well-being 326, 329, 331
Sub-Saharan African autocracies 300
subsidiary workers 277
substantial diversification 156
substantive equality 383
supported familialism 40
supportive supervision 373
Survey of Health, Ageing and Retirement in Europe (SHARE) panel 42
Sustainable Development Goals 376, 381
Sweden 353
    CFC scheme in 201
    ECEC 200
    father's quota 199
    trade unions 143
    working time in 142
Swedish parental leave reforms 134
Swedish population 113
Swedish pre-school curriculum 27–8
Swiss welfare state 171
Switzerland 168
    attitudes indicating differences between 177, 178
    development of women's employment rates 174
    employed women 174
    family policies in 170–71, 174
    gender culture of 175
    gender-neutral parental leave scheme 173
    paid maternity leave 173
    public provision of childcare 172
    welfare states of 168
    women's caring role 171

Taguchi, Lenz 28
Taiwan 243
    Affordable Childcare Centre Subsidy Programme 244
    Childcare Unemployment Allowance 244
    Community Childcare System Programme 243
    Early Childhood Education and Care Act 243–4
    family-based childcare for young infants in 244
    Grandparents Allowance 244
    Infant Care Subsidies Policy 244
    parents and grandparents in 245
    Universal Infant and Childcare System Plan 243–4
tax benefits 329
temporary jobs 382
The Economist's Democracy Index 295
The Hundred Languages of Childhood 29
Thelen, K. 155
Thévenon, O. 61
Tijdens, K. 143
TIMSS *see* Trends in International Mathematics and Science Study (TIMSS)
total period of paid leave 126–30
trade union membership 142
traditional Confucian values 237
transnational families 378
transnational family practices 379
travelling policy ideas 154
Trends in International Mathematics and Science Study (TIMSS) 24, 326
Trifiletti, R. 45
triggers 154
    of policy change 156
    specific configuration of 155
Tsunami (Indian Ocean) 363
Tyndik, A. 43
typologies of family policy regimes
    criticism from feminist scholars 13
    gender issues 13–14
    OECD countries, based on 15–16
    work of Lewis 13

UK
    characteristics and developments 186–9
    Childcare Tax Credit 187
    differences in family policy 182
    ECEC 187
    Employment Act and Social Security Act 187–8
    familialization 189
    family and family policy characteristics 185
    Family Credit and Income Support 186
    Family Credit program 186
    'generosity' of benefits 184
    Liberal/Conservative Coalition 188
    market defamilization 183
    Married Couple's Allowance (MCA) 187
    maternity and parental leave 187
    maternity rights 188
    National Childcare Strategy 187
    New Deal for Lone Parents program 186
    New Labour 'Third Way' agenda 186
    poverty rates 184
    public family policies 145

Statutory Maternity Allowance 188
Statutory Maternity Pay 188
Sure Start program 187
Troubled Families program 189
Union Reform and Employment Rights Act 1993 188
Welfare Reform and Pensions Act 1999 188
Working Tax Credit 188
UN Convention on the Rights of the Child 358
underdevelopment of family policy 215
UNICEF
   Office of Research project 351
   report 326–7
   research 356
United Nations (UN) 376
United Nations adoption of the Convention of the Rights of the Child 325
United Nations Convention on the Rights of the Child 280
United States 12
   Aid to Families with Dependent Children (AFDC) 189
   characteristics and developments 189–91
   differences in family policy 182
   Earned Income Tax Credit (EITC) 190
   ECEC 190, 191
   EITC 191
   family and family policy characteristics 185
   Family and Medical Leave Act (FMLA) 190
   Family Support Act 189
   'generosity' of benefits 184
   government 12
   insurance programs 191
   Job Opportunities and Basic Skills Program (JOBS) 189
   market defamilization 183
   Medicaid 189
   Omnibus Budget Reconciliation Act 190–91
   poverty line 311
   poverty rates 184
   Reaganomics 189
   Temporary Assistance for Needy Families (TANF) 191
   trade union behaviour 142
universal system of family allowances 210
Unorganised Workers Social Security Act 283
unpaid maternity 289
unpaid work 18
urbanisation 382
US-American policy developments 182

vaccinations 331
van Bochove, M. 41
variable-centred approach 48
variable-oriented approaches 48
varieties of capitalism (VoC) 66–7
   scholarship 67–8
Varieties of Capitalism (VoC) school 197
violence
   kinds of 381
   against women and children 380–81
VoC *see* varieties of capitalism (VoC)

wage-setting agreements 70
Walker, R. 45
Ward-Clustering 295, 301
welfare capitalism 114
welfare culture 170
welfare policies 325
welfare reforms 152
welfare state policies 325
wellbeing
   of children 353–4
   definition of 341
   parenthood gap in 337–8
   positive and negative effects on 340
Wells, K.J. 147
Wenchuan Earthquake 363
Wennemo, I. 85
White Paper on Families (WPF) 250, 256
WHO *see* World Health Organization (WHO)
wider family 44
women
   discrimination of 376
   draft national policy for 277
   employment 169
   fertility among 378
   labour market outcomes 17–18
   as objects for male dominance 376
   poverty 381
   property rights 382
women's voices and human rights 376–7
   challenges for family policy
      changing family forms and practices 377–8
      poverty 381
      property and home security 381–2
      reproductive health 380
      transnational family practices 378–80
      violence 380–81
   family policy and women's human rights 383–4
   precarisation of labour 382
   violation of 376
work-based rights 274
work-family arrangement 169–70
work/family balance index 71–2
work-family conflict 18, 339, 341

work-family interventions, effectiveness of 147
work-family policies 139, 146, 343–4
   adoption of 139–42
   effects of 147
   in European countries 216
   gender-specific responses to 345
   implementation of 144
   in Latin America *see* Latin America
   management of 144
      intervention research within the work-family field 147
      supervisory support 146–7
      supportive organizational culture 145
   managers' decision-making in 145–6
   role of 139
      trade unions and collective agreements 142–4
      supportive of 145
      training 140
      utilization of 145
      working hours and teleworking 139
work-family reconciliation policies 117
work-family situation, trade union influence on 143
work-life balance 383
work schedule
   discretion 342
   flexibility policies 342
World Bank, child benefits 92–3
World Health Organization (WHO) 380
WPF *see* White Paper on Families (WPF)

Yerkes, M.A. 143
Yu, S. 41